www.wadsworth.com

www.wadsworth.com is the World Wide Web site for Thomson Wadsworth and is your direct source to dozens of online resources.

At *www.wadsworth.com* you can find out about supplements, demonstration software, and student resources. You can also send email to many of our authors and preview new publications and exciting new technologies.

www.wadsworth.com
Changing the way the world learns®

Introduction to Social Welfare and Social Work

The U.S. in Global Perspective

Katherine van Wormer
University of Northern Iowa

THOMSON
BROOKS/COLE

Australia • Canada • Mexico • Singapore • Spain
United Kingdom • United States

Executive Editor: *Lisa Gebo*
Assistant Editor: *Alma Dea Michelena*
Editorial Assistant: *Sheila Walsh*
Technology Project Manager: *Barry Connolly*
Marketing Manager: *Caroline Concilla*
Marketing Communications Manager: *Tami Strang*
Signing Representative: *Jeffrey Krum*
Project Manager, Editorial Production: *Rita Jaramillo*
Art Director: *Vernon Boes*
Print Buyer: *Lisa Claudeanos*

Permissions Editor: *Sarah Harkrader*
Production Service/Compositor: *Mary Deeg, Buuji, Inc.*
Text Designer: *Jeanne Calabrese*
Copy Editor: *Linda Ireland, Buuji, Inc.*
Cover Designer: *Lisa Henry*
Cover Images: *Rupert van Wormer*
Interior Design Faces Graphic: *Robert Neubecker*
  c/o theispot.com
Cover and Text Printer: *Transcontinental Printing/ Louiseville*

Printed in Canada
1   2   3   4   5   6   7   09   08   07   06   05

For more information about our products,
contact us at:
Thomson Learning Academic Resource Center
1-800-423-0563
For permission to use material from this text or product, submit a request online at
http://www.thomsonrights.com.
Any additional questions about permissions can be submitted by email to thomsonrights@thomson.com.

Thomson Higher Education
10 Davis Drive
Belmont, CA 94002-3098
USA

Asia (Including India)
Thomson Learning
5 Shenton Way
#01-01 UIC Building
Singapore 068808

Australia/New Zealand
Thomson Learning Australia
102 Dodds Street
Southbank, Victoria 3006
Australia

Canada
Thomson Nelson
1120 Birchmount Road
Toronto, Ontario M1K 5G4
Canada

UK/Europe/Middle East/Africa
Thomson Learning
High Holborn House
50/51 Bedford Row
London WC1R 4LR
United Kingdom

Library of Congress Control Number: 2004110611

Student Edition: ISBN 0-534-64282-9

Instructor's Edition: ISBN 0-495-00817-6

To people of courage: conscientious objectors of the world, out-of-the-closet gays and lesbians, survivors of personal crime such as rape who take a public stand against this crime, murder victims' families who raise their voices against the death penalty, and above all, to the persons who see themselves not as citizens of a particular nation or commonwealth but, rather, as citizens of the world.

Brief Contents

Contents

Part 2 Social Work across the Life Cycle 259

Preface

The globalization of the world marketplace represents the most dramatic global structural change since the Industrial Revolution (Wilson & Whitmore, 2000). The change is not only structural; there are strong psychological ramifications as well. Nations are bound economically, politically, and even emotionally due to international commerce and mass communications. Associated with modernization and the encroachment of Western values, this very global interconnectedness is resented in some circles, most notably, those associated with extremism among a small minority of religious zealots. No one knew how strong that resentment was until that fateful day in September. It was no coincidence that the Twin Towers of the World Trade Center, symbols of the global market, were targeted. As the towers crumbled into rubble, the whole world watched; the missing and the dead represented many nationalities. Not only were innocent lives lost, but we in the United States also lost our innocence as we came face-to-face with the dual reality that many people hate us and that our taken-for-granted sense of security is no more. Security is gone because the attackers ("evildoers"), in many ways our creation, were not members of any one state but of a virtual state.

Communication is made possible universally by part of the resented modern technology—the Internet. Thanks to global satellites, we all watch the same news, see the same horrifying images. Thus a catastrophic event in one part of the world can ricochet throughout the world in short order. Space and time have become compressed. In the modern era, military threats—post-September 11—are no longer of state against state, but are transnational. Like the economy, environmental pollution, and diseases like AIDS, such threats are beyond the scope of any one nation to control. The call for a sustainable environment will have to be universal.

As we enter this global age, then—this age characterized by ethnic cleansing, suicide bombings, air strikes, the war on terrorism, suppression of civil liberties, and the decline of the welfare state to comply with the dictates of the free market economy—there is a need for new understandings, new approaches. Many problems that seem endemic to one state or one country can be understood only in an international context, as common problems with common solutions.

In recognition of this fact of global interconnectedness, the U.S. Council on Social Work Education (CSWE; 2001), which oversees all programs, today requires that students should be prepared to "recognize the global context of social work practice" (p. 6). Among the purposes of social work education, as spelled out in the document, are: to alleviate poverty, oppression, and other forms of social injustice; to promote breadth of knowledge and critical thinking; to prepare social workers to recognize the global context of social work practice; and to formulate and influence social policies and social services.

New to the accreditation standards is the change from the requirement to offer content on specific vulnerable populations such as racial, ethnic, and sexual minorities in favor of a more general approach. Section C under Foundation Curriculum Content states, "Programs integrate social and economic justice content grounded in an understanding of distributive justice, human and civil rights, and the global interconnections of oppression." The inclusion of course content on international issues in social welfare policy is also required.

The Canadian Association of Schools of Social Work (CASSW; 2000), similarly, ensures that students acquire "preparation in transferable analysis of the multiple and interesting bases of oppression, and related practice skill" (sec. 3.4.3) and, more specifically, "an understanding of oppression and healing of aboriginal peoples and, implications for social policy and social work practice" (sec. 5.10 L).

In my earlier book, *Social Welfare: A World View* (van Wormer, 1997), the major objective was to critically examine social welfare issues from an international perspective. The comparative approach was chosen as the best way to reveal the uniqueness of U.S. ideology regarding human needs and structural attempts to address those needs. In this book, as well, we will view the shaping of social welfare policy within the context of North American value dimensions and within the context of universal values as well.

Like my earlier work, this book, *Introduction to Social Welfare and Social Work: The U.S. in Global Perspective*, is designed to challenge, even provoke, readers into examining their preconceived notions concerning their country's treatment of the poor, the sick, and the elderly. The comparative approach helps reveal the uniqueness of U.S. ideology regarding human need and suffering. There is much to be learned from a study of alternative solutions to common problems.

This volume has been shaped to achieve two often mutually exclusive objectives. The first objective is to critically examine social welfare issues from an international perspective. It is imperative that students of social welfare recognize the bearing of cultural factors on a society's allocation of resources. International material challenges complacency and raises questions concerning the traditional policy responses of a given society.

The second objective of this book is to provide a useful and comprehensive study that covers in detail the fundamentals of the history and structure of the social welfare system in U.S. society. As a general textbook, the content is organized to follow course outlines for basic, introductory courses that examine social welfare programs, policies, and issues. *Introduction to Social Welfare and Social Work* also discusses specific populations that have suffered particular hardships within the broader society. These groups include women, African Americans, Native Americans, Latino/Latina Americans, gays and lesbians, persons with mental and physical illnesses, and the unemployed. The social, psychological, political, and economic dimensions of the United States' treatment of minority groups are highlighted. The cross-cultural perspective, additionally, provides a resource for both undergraduate and graduate foundation courses concerned with global problems and development.

Since 1997, when my earlier work entitled *Social Welfare: A World View* was published, the world has changed a lot. I did not anticipate the economic crisis in Japan that erupted in 1997, even though Japan was one of the nations—along with Canada, the U.K., Mexico, and Norway—that was singled out as a focal point for close attention in this book. A second major event that I perhaps could have foreseen, but did not, was the global battle over free trade, the explosion of protests all over the world culminating (but hardly ending) in the "Battle of Seattle" in December 1999. And then there has been the return to an unabashedly conservative and highly punitive era under a Republican-controlled government.

So I have written *Introduction to Social Welfare and Social Work: The U.S. in Global Perspective* as a new book for a new time. Compared to its predecessor, this volume is somewhat more directed to introduction to social work classes and policy classes, to provide an international lens through which students of social work can view their own country's social work and social policy practices. Although U.S. social welfare and social work are the focus of the discourse, parallels in social problems and their solutions have been drawn from throughout the world, most especially from our neighbor Canada. The link with Canada is especially appropriate today, as our sister organizations—the National Association of Social Workers (NASW) and the Canadian Association of Social Workers (CASW)—have agreed to seek a joint alliance "to catapult us as a committed leader into the international arena once again" (Mizrahi, 2002, p. 2).

Content and Structure

Due to the vastness of the subject matter and material available, the selection has necessarily been quite limited. Selections for boxed readings are based on interest, relevance to the chapter's subject matter, and didactic qualities. Readings in boxes on orphans in Romania, marketing of tobacco in Asia, and prostitution and slavery worldwide are chosen to parallel similar crises on the home "front." Most of the readings from across the world, however, are selected for the purpose of familiarizing readers with innovative practices that could be borrowed and used within the mainstream of American society. Such thought-provoking material from the worldwide press and autobiographical sketches are geared to personalize the more mundane presentation of the text itself.

Based on the knowledge provided in this textbook, students who complete a course in international social welfare (or a course in social policy with international content) should be able to: critically analyze how values play into social welfare offerings and social work practice; grasp how a society's social welfare system is dependent upon the financial and human resources available; grasp how the generosity of social service provision relates to the national ethos and paradigm shifts over time; learn of the structure of the provision of services; realize the social psychology of victim blaming; be familiar with the social work role in meeting the needs of individuals across the life cycle; view the social policy issues of the day within the context of the global corporate economy; and recognize the international similarities and differences in social work roles in the development and provision of social services. The emphasis is on those fields of practice in which social workers are most likely to be employed—fields such as child welfare, health and mental health, care of the elderly, and work with persons involved in the criminal justice system.

This textbook offers the following features:

■ An ecosystems/empowerment framework for viewing the personal dimension within the social environment

■ Composite portraits of alternative responses to social problems of global concern such as indigenous groups' handling of wrongs that have been committed and the harm reduction model for drug misuse in England

■ A critical analysis of social issues facing impoverished children and families in both industrialized and nonindustrialized nations

■ A presentation of social work values and the social work mission that is congruent with the principles of the United Nations (U.N.) Universal Declaration of Human Rights

■ Attention to the physical environment and the interrelationship between the environment and society, with emphasis on the need for a sustainable world

■ A focus on human rights, social justice, and restorative justice

■ A multifaceted survey of social welfare subsystems such as child welfare, health and mental health care, corrections, and services to the elderly (women's and ethnic minority issues are infused throughout the text)

■ Attention to oppressed populations including racial and ethnic minorities, indigenous populations, and gays and lesbians in various parts of the world

■ Dynamic excerpts from international and popular sources revealing the human side of social issues

■ Summary and Conclusion sections as well as Thought Questions at the end of each chapter to reinforce the emphasis on critical thinking

■ A comprehensive instructor's manual to accompany the book

Part I, "Social Welfare: Structure and Functions," includes six chapters. Chapter 1 introduces the student to the uniqueness of social work and the empowerment perspective. Critical thinking is defined in terms of cultural competence and global awareness. This chapter introduces the student to the social work mission and social work ethics within the context of social and economic globalization. Chapter 2 broadens the scope to a consideration of American values as the framework within which social welfare structure and policy evolved. The Scandinavian institutional approach to social welfare is contrasted with the American residual approach.

Chapter 3 takes a historical view of the emergence of social work as a profession within the backdrop of national paradigm shifts. Chapters 4 and 5 incorporate the approach recommended in CSWE's new *Educational Policy and Accreditation Standards* (2001) to prepare social work students to challenge economic and social oppression. Poverty, racial and ethnic discrimination, sectarianism, and oppression against women and children worldwide are among the topics addressed. Chapter 6 provides a human rights focus and introduces the student to the burgeoning concept of restorative justice, an innovation with revolutionary potential in meting out justice.

Part II, "Social Work across the Life Cycle" brings the reader into the professional domain. This section of the work consists of four chapters. Chapter 7 introduces subject matter pertaining to human behavior and the social environment and the bio-psycho-social-spiritual framework. Chapter 8 focuses on the child welfare setting and also schools future social workers as readers for social work policy and practice. This chapter explores family-centered practice for life crisis situations. Emphases include cultural awareness and restorative justice traditions such as family group conferencing and the strengths perspective. The subject of Chapter 9 is health and mental health care against economic constraints related to restraints from the global market. Chapter 10 provides an overview of aging care worldwide and end-of-life issues. The Epilogue "puts it all together," encapsulating basic themes of social work and of this book. Included in the appendices are the U.N. Universal Declaration of Human Rights, the National Association of Social Workers (NASW) and International Federation of Social Workers–International Association of Schools of Social Work (IFSW–IASSW) codes of ethics, a framework for formal anti-oppression policy analysis of U.S. governmental policies in historical and international perspective, and relevant Internet sites.

Acknowledgments

My thanks and appreciation to the University of Northern Iowa for the graduate college summer grant that allowed time and resources for me to write, write, write. Many individuals have contributed to the shaping of this book. First were the reviewers who encouraged me to pursue an international social welfare book and who offered invaluable suggestions: Najma M. Adam, Northeastern Illinois University; David Broad, University of Regina; John Graham, University of Calgary; Elizabeth Reichert, Southern Illinois University–Carbondale; Jim Stafford, University of Mississippi; Jade Stanley, Northeastern Illinois University; and Ted R. Watkins, Texas State University–San Marcos.

Next I want to express gratitude to Lucas Liddle, my work study student, and to Rosemary Rohde, my graduate research assistant, for their typing and library research, respectively. Rohde's contribution to the selection of content for the Instructor's Manual was substantial. Additionally, I'd like to thank my son, Rupert van Wormer, for his photographic contributions, the quality of which is here to be seen. Reverend Ramage, director of the Heatherbank

Museum of Glasgow, Scotland, deserves special mention for providing the historic "houseless asylum" drawing that highlights Chapter 3. Finally, a warm thanks to Lisa Gebo, executive editor of Brooks/Cole, for her nurturance and encouragement at every stage of production, and to Linda Ireland, copy editor, whose meticulous attention to detail, Iowa work ethic, and sense of humor are greatly appreciated.

References

Canadian Association of Schools of Social Work (CASSW). (2000). *Educational policy statements: Board of Accreditation manual.* Ottawa: Author.

Council on Social Work Education (CSWE). (2001). Educational policy and accreditation standards. Retrieved from http://www.cswe.org/accreditation

Mizrahi, T. (2002, February). From the president: Closer communication can unify us. *NASW News*, 2.

van Wormer, K. (1997). *Social welfare: A world view.* Belmont, CA: Wadsworth.

Wilson, M., & Whitmore, E. (2000). *Seeds of fire: Social development in an era of globalism.* Halifax: Fernwood.

About the Author

Katherine Stuart van Wormer, a native of New Orleans, is a professor of social work at the University of Northern Iowa, Cedar Falls. The author's international experience includes community service in working-class areas in Northern Ireland, where she taught English and actively participated in the Irish civil rights movement and campaign for nuclear disarmament. Ultimately becoming a social worker and alcoholism counselor in the United States, Dr. van Wormer was invited to Norway where she was the program director at Vangseter Treatment Center. More recently, she initiated a faculty exchange program between the University of Northern Iowa and the University of Hull, England, and presented papers on the global economy in Ireland and South Korea. A graduate of the University of North Carolina, the author holds a graduate degree in education from Queens University, Northern Ireland; a master's degree from Western Kentucky University; a PhD from the University of Georgia; and a master's degree in social work from the University of Tennessee, Nashville. Dr. van Wormer is the author of *Social Welfare: A World View* (Wadsworth, 1997); *Social Work with Lesbians, Gays, and Bisexuals: A Strengths Perspective*, coauthored with Joel Wells and Mary Boes (Allyn & Bacon, 2000); *Women and the Criminal Justice System*, coauthored with Clemens Bartollas (Allyn & Bacon, 2000); *Counseling Female Offenders and Victims: A Strengths-Restorative Justice Approach* (Springer, 2001); *Addiction Treatment: A Strengths Perspective*, coauthored with Diane Rae Davis (Brooks/Cole, 2003); and *Confronting Oppression, Restoring Justice: From Policy Analysis to Social Action* (Council on Social Work Education, 2004).

Personal Comment

Social work is where the action is. In the 1970s, it was sociology, and I became a sociologist. In the 1980s, it was social work, and I became a social worker. Today, it is still social work—as both workers in the field and anyone who is familiar with the books in the field (this one included) can attest.

Katherine van Wormer

About the Photographer

This book is enriched by the photographic talents of Rupert van Wormer, MSW, PhD candidate, Portland State. Rupert, the son of the author, practiced social work with homeless, mentally ill persons in Seattle from a harm reduction perspective. His keen interest in social justice and the environment, reflected in his pictures, goes back to his early teen years which were spent in Norway.

Social Welfare: Structure and Functions

Knowledge is power.

FRANCIS BACON, 1597

Social Work
and Social Welfare

Courtesy Head Start

You cannot talk about social work without talking about context, and social welfare provides the context within which social services are offered. You cannot talk about social welfare, likewise, without some sense of the role the global economy plays in shaping the health and quality of life in all its manifestations. The growing prosperity at one level of society is matched by rising insecurities and impoverishment at another level. This is where social work comes in.

A profession of many faces, social work touches the lives of millions of people with personal problems everyday. Many of these problems are rooted in flaws in the social structure; others stem from individual difficulties, perhaps related to disease or personal victimization. The profession of social work is dedicated to the maintenance and enhancement of the social functioning and health of individuals, families, and communities (Prigoff, 2000). Social workers:

- Help connect people to needed social services
- Provide counseling and psychotherapy to individuals and families facing some sort of crisis
- Organize to shape social legislation to help alleviate human misery

In this chapter, we explore social work in all its uniqueness and social welfare in its transcendent qualities. The basic concerns of social welfare—poverty, disability, disease, and care of the very young and the very old—have been the basic concerns of social work since its inception, and before that, of the faith-based charity work out of which the social work profession sprang.

Unlike the other chapters in this volume, Chapter 1 is largely theoretical: Its purpose is to lay the building blocks for the more factual material to follow. To this end, this chapter will:

- Define social work as a policy-based profession
- Make the case for an international understanding of social policy
- Address how social work relates to other disciplines and describe the basic fields of practice
- Introduce concepts relevant to professional practice—for example, the empowerment and strengths perspectives
- Introduce concepts relevant to social work theory—for example, the ecosystems perspective, the functionalist framework, and globalization
- Differentiate a worldview from a *world* view
- Discuss attributes of the social work imagination

The Uniqueness of Social Work

Because the field of social work is holistic and encompasses knowledge from a wide range of disciplines (psychology, sociology, and economics, among others), it is sometimes believed that there is no body of knowledge unique to social work at all. In fact, though, as a glance at a typical social work textbook indicates, social work can be distinguished from other professions in terms of its social activism and unabashed commitment to the most vulnerable members of the society. Historically, as Khinduka (2002) suggests, it is the dual responsibility toward individual betterment as well as social change that is a key characteristic of social work.

As professional helpers, social workers are everywhere where there are individuals, families, and communities in need. Social workers are the largest providers of mental health services in the country; they are also highly visible in child welfare offices, hospitals, women's shelters, correction establishments, and schools. Although as counselors and client advocates, their skills may overlap with the skills of other human service workers, what sets this profession apart is the expectation that social workers will work within the system to change the system. Khinduka provides an overview of the field as follows:

> While social workers for the most part work within the system and are supported by it, we also make demands that may look unrealistic or even outrageous at the time they are made. From opposition to child labor to advocacy for old age assistance, from fighting for better treatment of the mentally ill, the immigrants, the disabled and other unwelcome or stigmatized members of the community, to championing civil rights and women's rights, social workers have been in the vanguard of causes and movements that are often unpopular. (p. 10)

Compared to psychology, sociology, and counseling, social work—and this is what I tell my students—is where the action is. The titles of some leading recent books in the field of social work attest to the action focus: *Affecting Change: Social Workers in the Political Arena* (Haynes & Michelson, 2002); *The Empowerment Approach to Social Work Practice: Building the Beloved Community* (Lee, 2001); *The Policy-Based Profession: An Introduction to Social Welfare Policy Analysis for Social Workers* (Popple & Leighninger, 2004); and *Social Work Advocacy: A New Framework for Action* (Schneider & Lester, 2000).

According to the National Association of Social Workers (NASW; 1996), "The constellation of core values reflects what is unique to the social work profession" (p. 1). As spelled out in the NASW *Code of Ethics* (1996), the mission of social work is rooted in:

- Service
- Social justice
- Dignity and worth of person
- Importance of human relationships
- Integrity
- Competence (p. 1)

Social work, as Weick (1999) states, uniquely engages the social context. This fact is manifest most specifically in the *Code's* values of community service, social and economic justice, and human relationships.

The focus of the profession is the "person-in-the-environment." The person-in-the-environment conceptualization views the person and the environment not statically but in constant interaction. According to this conceptualization, the social worker, when engaged in individual counseling, must attend to environmental as well as personal factors.

As social work educators are aware, the social work curriculum is closely scrutinized by the national accrediting body, the Council on Social Work Education (CSWE), for its compliance with national directives for a relatively standardized curriculum. Major content areas to be covered are courses in human behavior in the social environment, policy, social work practice, community organization, research, and field placement. Material on oppression and injustice must be included in the course content at both the bachelor's (BSW) and master's (MSW) levels.

No other academic discipline contains such value-based criteria for accreditation or includes such a joint practice/policy emphasis. This stress on curricular interrelatedness and integration suggests that there are direct connections between the development of social work skills and knowledge for policy development.

In recognition of the many ways in which international developments and institutions impinge on U.S. social policy arrangements, CSWE (2003) included in its educational standards for accreditation a requirement for the inclusion of *international* content. The decision to "go global" also was informed by an awareness that, given the new technologies, the world is growing ever smaller, and common solutions can be found to common social problems if information is shared.

This emphasis on globalization of course content is not unique to the United States. In 2000, the International Association of Schools of Social Work (IASSW) undertook a world census of social work education programs. Results of the survey indicated that half of programs in Europe and South America hosted international students but that less than 25 percent of Asian and North American programs did (Barretta-Herman, 2003). Interestingly, analysis of the data on curriculum content revealed striking similarities in the courses offered throughout the five regions.

Social work programs should prepare students to understand and address local manifestations of our national actions. The implications for social workers are that through international organization they might be able somehow to influence national policies that affect other nations, often unfavorably. The potential for the more powerful countries to upset the physical, economic, social, or environmental security of residents in other countries creates an obligation for citizens to act to influence the policies of foreign countries as well as of their own, as Healy (2002) rightly argues.

See Box 1.1 to learn of social work's revitalized interest in playing a major role on the international stage through much more active involvement in the International Federation of Social Workers (IFSW), a formally recognized nongovernmental organization that reports to the United Nations (U.N.). The present task of the IFSW is to develop universal standards for social work education, ethical codes of conduct, and policy positions on issues of international persons (O'Neill, 2002). Because human rights are universal standards, the aim of which is to root out oppression and see that people's basic needs are met, a human rights focus for social work carries more power than the more elusive social

1.1 Profession Has Global Role: Social Work's International Stature Is Explored

Peter Slavin

Social workers can help "give globalization a human face." The answer to the question "Should the United States be the world's social worker?" is an unqualified *yes*. Social work organizations can and do influence what the United Nations (U.N.) does. Members are doing international social work in the United States as well as overseas. The National Association of Social Workers (NASW) needs to offer nonmilitary alternatives for dealing with terrorism. These were among the points that several dozen social work thinkers and activists made when they met at NASW's national office in Washington, DC, to consider what social work could and should be doing in the international arena.

Noting that "many social workers and social work educators are committed internationalists," NASW President Terry Mizrahi "called the meeting to start developing a strategy to make social work a visible and respected force" internationally. Leticia Diaz, the NASW staff member who organized the meeting, said that social workers are ahead of the organizations that represent them in understanding the importance of paying attention to international issues and finding ways to play viable roles internationally. "The practice is leading," stated Diaz, who pointed to Jamie Spector as an example. Spector, a social worker and NASW member, helped to develop the practice of social work in Bosnia during the war there. Howard University School of Social Work Dean Richard English noted that one of his colleagues, Professor Fariyal Ross-Sherriff, was in Pakistan organizing the repatriation of Afghan refugees.

Mizrahi said that recently, journalists—particularly columnist Tom Friedman of *The New York Times*—have been saying things about the United States like, "Who do you think we are—the social workers of the world?" She pointed out, however: Given that social workers value client and community self-determination and are skilled at mediating disputes, the United States could do a lot worse than adopt a social work approach to international relations.

Another goal expressed by Mizrahi is to strengthen the links between NASW and the Canadian Association of Social Workers (CASW) so that the North American region plays a bigger part in the International Federation of Social Workers (IFSW). Finally, she hopes to revitalize and connect the two NASW committees, the International Activities committee and the Peace and Social Justice committee, so that the association exercises more leadership internationally.

Globalization has been misunderstood as a strictly economic phenomenon, observed Professor M. C. "Terry" Hokenstad of the Mandle School of Applied Social Sciences at Case Western Reserve University in Cleveland. Hokenstad said globalization also has a social dimension, and social workers need to think about the equitable sharing of both its benefits and burdens so that the marginal sectors of society are not overlooked.

Hokenstad said the institutions that represent the social work profession internationally—the IFSW and the International Association of Schools of Social Work (IASSW)—are fragile because of limited finances and staffing. He called for strengthening both so they can be more effective in their work with the U.N., permitting them to advocate on such matters as development, refugees, health care, human rights, discrimination, children's rights, and peacekeeping.

Hokenstad, an IASSW representative to the U.N. advisory position, was one of 15 outside experts who formulated the U.N. plan on aging.

He said the two social work organizations have done some useful things at the U.N., but much more could be done. One possibility, he said, is to influence members of the U.S. Government Mission to the U.N.; another is to lobby to get social workers into jobs involving children, mental health, aging, and women's issues. Hokenstad noted that a senior official who works for U.N. Secretary General Kofi Annan directing social policy and development is a social worker from Australia, and other social workers have worked for the U.N. high commissioner for refugees.

IFSW ambassador Suzanne Dworak-Peck called on NASW to revitalize its leadership of IFSW, which represents half a million social workers in 77 countries. Dworak-Peck said that, in the past, NASW has made significant contributions to IFSW's work in areas ranging from human rights to ethics.

Those at the NASW meeting said there is a dormant network of internationally minded social workers waiting to be alerted. "People are desperate to know who others are, what they're doing, how to contact them," said Michael Cronin of New York City, IFSW representative at the U.N.

Social workers who want to work overseas are looking to network over the Internet to find opportunities, said Harriet L. Lancaster, chair of the International Activities Committee. Lancaster advised them to think about nontraditional jobs that call upon their training in social and community development and community organization. She said there are plenty of such jobs overseas, as well as jobs in this country with an international side, especially work with immigrants and refugees.

Marta Brenden of the Office of Refugee Resettlement (ORR) at the U.S. Department of Health and Human Services made the same point

graphically. Brenden told of a family of Iraqi refugees whose stern disciplining of a rebellious teenage daughter led to the sudden removal of six of their children by child protective services and charges of child abuse. Six months later, both of their adolescent daughters were still in foster care. In this situation, two cultures clashed over child-rearing practices, Brenden observed. Speaking generally about child welfare services and foreign-born families, she said, "Services set up to help these families were wounding them, adding to their difficulties."

Underneath these problems, Brenden said, lay the unwarranted assumptions that "refugee children settle themselves" and need no special assistance. The upshot of the Iraqi case was ORR help with holding a conference on the needs of refugee children and the funding of a new program to foster cooperation between private social service agencies and child welfare service agencies/services in abuse and neglect cases involving refugees.

Bernice Bennett, senior program officer of American International Health Alliances, discussed how social workers are used in multidisciplinary health partnerships in newly independent states in central and eastern Europe. Participants in the NASW meeting showed great interest in becoming involved in the partnerships.

Dean English observed that enrollment in courses about refugee migration at Howard and other social work schools has dropped to only a handful of students. "We've got a major job to do in convincing this profession that this is our domain, and we've got to reclaim it," he declared.

Source: *NASW News*, March 2002, pp. 1–2. Copyright © 2002, National Association of Social Workers, Inc., *NASW News*. Reprinted with permission of NASW Press. For a statement on the aims of IFSW, see http://www.ifsw.org/.

justice focus alone (NASW, 2003). We will explore the human rights configuration in some depth in Chapter 5.

Why an International Focus for the Text

Consider the following scenarios:

- A woman who has arranged for her child to be adopted tells the social worker that her abusive husband from Scotland is coming to claim the baby.
- A retired couple living on Social Security payments seeks advice on relocating to a retirement settlement in Mexico where they can afford the medicine they need.
- A social worker helps document the case of the trauma that would be caused to girls if they returned to Nigeria where they would risk genital mutilation.
- A military social worker relocates to a base in Germany to counsel American military families in which there is reported wife abuse.
- A Chinese American social worker working in a veterans administration unit finds that her presence triggers flashbacks in some Vietnam veterans.
- A lesbian couple meets with a social worker in hopes of adopting a child from a foreign country.
- A Mexican migrant worker who does not speak English requires inpatient treatment for alcoholism.
- An Arab American family is subjected to persecution, a fact made known to the school social worker when the child falls behind in schoolwork.

The common denominator in every case is the link between the United States and another country, and often the link is via the client. International and intercultural knowledge is necessary for social work practice in an ever-shrinking world. Child and family problems in the United States, too, increasingly resemble those on distant shores. Healy (1992) provides the following examples:

- Children toil long hours on the streets of Bombay, and a recent investigation uncovers thousands of labor law violations in New England.
- Babies with AIDS languish in New Haven, Connecticut; in Kampala, Uganda; and in Bucharest, Romania.
- Street children in Bogotá, Colombia, and homeless children in U.S. cities miss out on the education that could provide a chance for their future.
- Refugee children around the world and children in the United States are frequent victims and witnesses of violence.

For the kinds of real situations described in these vignettes, human service workers require a vast knowledge of the resources relevant to the resolution of social problems rooted in worldwide political economic realities. Connections must be made between the private violence of child abuse and the public violence of war, and between the individual's futile denial of drug addictions and the international denial of nuclear and military addiction and destruction of the environment (Mary & Morris, 1994).

To provide leadership on economic issues in order to influence legislation in the spheres of social work concern—health/mental health care, child welfare and protection, economic security, and so on—knowledge (as the opening quote to this chapter contends) is power. For a comprehensive understanding of economic forces that work against a caring social welfare state, an international perspective is essential. Knowledge that investment in human resources is apt to be seen as wasteful, according to market-oriented assumptions, for example, frames research in the direction not of humanitarian rationales, but frames it in the direction of cost-effective analysis. Then the argument, "Providing adequate child care to single mothers (or vocational training or health care) would be nice but we can't afford it" can be countered with proof that "We can't afford not to." To counter predictable arguments that proposed changes in social policies would never work, models can be found in other countries of those same policies that do work.

Introduction to Social Welfare and Social Work: The U.S. in Global Perspective has been written in the belief that a global perspective provides the most relevant and comprehensive framework within which to orient students to social welfare, the context within which social work is practiced. Following Healy (2002), this book is shaped in accordance with the belief that global perspectives are best infused within the curriculum instead of being offered as specialized course electives. Stand-alone international courses often do just that: they stand alone. Specifically, the advantages of the international format are as follows.

Promoting Interest

At first, it might seem strange to choose illustrations for social policy far removed from everyday life in North America. Yet the teaching/learning dyad is considerably enhanced by material that is emotionally compelling. Such examples, drawn from far and wide, jolt the imagination and prompt us to see parallels closer to home. Witness some recent media headlines and ponder the impact of each:

- SARS Illustrates How Shrinking World Means Growing Virus Peril (*Chicago Tribune*, 2003)
- Cambodia: Robinson Calls for End to Sex Slavery (*U.N. Wire*, 2002)
- Afghanistan: Women Still Not "Liberated" (Human Rights Watch, 2002)
- Eurasia and the [AIDS] Epidemic (Will, 2002)
- Norway Is Now First, U.S. Sixth in Human Development (United Nations Development Programme, 2001)
- Study: Earth's Resources Dwindling (*Los Angeles Times*, 2002)
- Report: AIDS to Orphan 25 Million (Sternberg, 2002)
- Why Do They Hate Us? (Ford, 2001)

Gaining Perspective

Persons who have lived in another country and been immersed in its folkways and language have a unique advantage in reviewing the social welfare system of either their home or host country. They can understand the host country's pattern and identify incongruities. They can quickly pinpoint the customs and values of both the country of origin and the adopted country. Most natives of a particular country do not enjoy this perspective; they do not see the forest for the trees. Nor do they know the variety of trees that may grow there.

A view beyond regional borders reveals problems and solutions in a broader light. Social work educator Linda Kreitzer (2002), for example, describes for us her cultural awakening as a teacher of social work at the University of Ghana:

> This experience continued my questioning of the teaching of western social work approaches in non-western countries but it also challenged my own assumption and Eurocentric thinking concerning western knowledge. I began to question and read about historical forces at work that seemed to encourage the hegemony of western knowledge over traditional cultural knowledge. This questioning has intensified since moving to Canada and listening to and learning from First Nations people concerning the historical forces that have affected their traditional livelihoods and ways of thinking and knowing. They too have been involved in the re-creation of indigenous ways of knowing and, in particular, in social work education. (p. 12)

Healy (2003), who has been actively involved in a 10-year exchange between the University of Connecticut and the University of West Indies in Jamaica, echoes these sentiments. Educators in the Caribbean are concerned that there is an overreliance on U.S. models and U.S. literature. Links between social work departments in the Caribbean and the United States and Canada allow for a great deal of cross-fertilization of ideas and practices. In Minnesota, Augsburg College has established an academic-field coordination work for study in Mexico by joining in consortium with other area colleges (Rodenborg, 2003, in private correspondence to the Baccalaureate Program Directors listserv of June 3). Joint syllabi have been written to meet the needs of the various schools.

Through globalized education, possibilities abound. Indeed, for students of social welfare, merely learning the facts pertaining to one's own national policies (e.g., legal stipulations and agency goals such as permanency planning) is less significant in the long run than learning to make connections between the facts to see how the parts belong to the whole. Policies come and go, but a holistic view can serve for all time. Recognition of commonalities and increased respect for differences help to dissipate fear and mistrust and ultimately promote world peace through improved international understanding (Elliott & Mayadas, 1999).

"Think globally, act locally," the saying of environmentalists, aptly sums up the viewpoint endorsed in these pages. In truth, one does not actually have to leave home to adopt a world view or global perspective. One can get beyond national parochialism through reading and listening and contemplating diverse ways of doing things or at least of viewing things. We all have a *worldview*—this word refers to our own regionalized view of the world and of our world. To adopt a *world view*, on the other hand, is to "see ourselves as others see us," to step back from time to time to recognize our own national uniquenesses—the capitalism, materialism, individual opportunity, whatever. A global perspective suggests an openness to new ideas and a willingness to work collaboratively toward the mutual benefit of all countries (Elliott & Mayadas, 1999). For creative, well-informed policymaking on the local or global level, a multicultural awareness is paramount. Central to such an awareness and appreciation of difference is an awareness that we are all as humans bound together by the common human condition, all seeking the same sort of earthly comforts and, at a higher level, the meaning of life.

Global interconnectedness is enhanced today by the revolutionary power of the Internet. Government can no longer shut off the news sources, even though countries such as China, South Africa, and Iraq continue to try to do so. Communication across cyberspace helps unmask lies and deceit in individual countries. When the U.S. president visits Europe or the Middle East, for example, one can compare European and Middle Eastern accounts and American accounts of the same visit to gain a multidimensional view and see how national overtures and communications are viewed from abroad.

Learning of Innovative Approaches

Common demographic, economic, and technological trends have confronted all the advanced industrialized societies with similar challenges (Kahn & Kamerman, 2002). Prime examples are the aging of the population while birth rates fall and the rising rates of labor force participation among women with young children. Such common problems may have different solutions based on cultural values. Americans can learn from Europeans, as Kahn and Kamerman indicate, as when they discover that many of them are entitled to paid and job-protected leaves following childbirth, one-month paid vacations from work, and subsidized child care. Two examples of nonmaterial technologies imported from other nations to the United States are the hospice movement from Britain and family group conferencing from the indigenous population of New Zealand. In substance abuse treatment, researchers, treatment providers, and a few police chiefs and mayors are looking into the harm reduction movement in the Netherlands for its crime-fighting possibilities. Going in the opposite direction, the passage of strict antismoking laws to protect people from the health ravages of secondhand smoke has spread from the United States to the far corners of the globe. At the macro level, feminist thought has revolutionized women's roles throughout the industrialized world and raised the consciousness of gender inequality practically everywhere.

Knowledge for International Work

Since social work degrees, especially at the master's level, are recognized internationally, Americans are sometimes recruited to work overseas. (At the time of this writing, widely publicized announcements have appeared in U.S. publications from the United Kingdom and Ireland.) For social work educators, opportunities for international teaching exchanges are becoming commonplace. Cultural competence and an attitude of thoughtful restraint concerning American accomplishments will go far in enhancing international collegial acceptance.

Social work practice on the home front likely will include work with immigrants and refugees. Each year, the United States takes in more than one million immigrants, including undocumented workers, according to news reports (London, 2000). Today, the U.S. population, in fact, has the largest proportion of foreign-born residents at anytime since World War I. Taking an international perspective, social workers can anticipate that newcomers will have close, intergenerational family ties and that many aspects of American society (e.g., dating customs; sales pitches, such as from "rent-to-own" furniture stores) will be unfamiliar to newcomers.

As the social work profession internationalizes and becomes increasingly active through nongovernmental organizations (NGOs), possibilities are opening up for the profession to be a significant player in influencing humane and human rights–oriented global policies (Healy, 2002). (Refer back to Box 1.1 to review the strategy to make social work visible once again on the world stage.) Social work's newfound impetus to help internationalize social values of social and international justice can draw on the human rights initiative as articulated by NASW's (2003) *Social Work Speaks* policy statement endorsing a human rights framework for social justice advocacy. "Social workers must," according to this statement, "become partners with the United Nations in advancing human development and human rights including economic human rights, and closing the economic gap" (p. 213). By tying particular injustice or circumstances to human rights, as Reichert (2003) similarly suggests, social workers can better advocate for clients and fulfill the primary mission of the profession.

Terms and Concepts

Social Welfare

Every society grapples with the question of how to distribute its wealth, power, and opportunities. The distributions may be relatively egalitarian, as in Scandinavia, or there may be huge disparities across the social class continuum. These differences may be modified by societal protections to insulate citizens from the throes of poverty.

The word *welfare* harks back to the Middle English word for well-being. In German the word used for social welfare is *wohlfahrt,* and in Norwegian it is *velferd.* The Spanish word is *bienestar,* and in French it is *bien-être,* which means, literally, well to be. All these meanings are highly positive. These words are related to the English word *benefit,* derived from Latin.

The Social Work Dictionary (Barker, 2003) gives the following definition of *social welfare:*

Social welfare:

1. A nation's system of programs, benefits, and services that help people meet those social, economic, educational, and health needs that are fundamental to the maintenance of society.
2. The state of collective well-being of a community or society. (p. 408)

Probably because of its association in the United States with the downtrodden of society, social welfare and welfare work have come to assume negative connotations. Persons "on welfare" are stigmatized by the wider society; the welfare system itself and its workers are stigmatized also. The fragmentation of issues encourages the ubiquitous complaint that our social welfare efforts are a "crazy quilt" of overlapping and conflicting programs that create waste (Marmor, Matow, & Harvey, 1990). Karger and Stoesz (2001) define social welfare policy as: "a subset of social policy [that] regulates the provision of benefit to people to meet basic life needs, such as employment, income, food, housing, health care, and relationships" (p. 3).

Welfare State

Much more confusing in its usage is the term *welfare state.* To writers such as Gould (1993), *welfare state* is a term that should be reserved for those countries that are committed to a policy of full employment and in which the state is responsible for the provision of comprehensive services, such as in northern Europe. Bryson's (1992) concern was that what was left of the *welfare state,* a term originating from Germany in the 1930s was quickly eroded in Germany and elsewhere by a counterreaction to leftist social policies. Since Bryson's book was published, Germany's economic pressures have led to a downward spiral. Bryson's definition of *welfare state* referred to the achievement of a minimum level of aid for citizens. The problem with this definition is in determining the meaning of minimum. *The Dictionary of Social Work* definition (Barker, 2003) of *welfare state* is less ambiguous:

> A nation or society that considers itself responsible for meeting the basic educational, health care, economic, and social security needs of its people. (p. 463)

This is the definition that will be used in this text. According to this definition, one could say that the capitalist countries of Japan and the United States have weak forms of the welfare state in contrast to Scandinavian countries.

Social Work

The profession most closely related to the provision of social welfare services is social work. *Social work* as defined by NASW is the professional activity of helping individuals, groups, and communities enhance or restore their capacity for social functioning and creating societal conditions favorable to this goal (Barker,

2003, p. 408). The term *social worker* is restricted to persons who are professionally trained in the skills and ethics of social work practice. Incorrect usage of the term sometimes occurs, as, for instance, when the mass media refer to any person who distributes food stamps as a social worker. A worker at a social welfare office may or may not be a member of the profession.

The definition of social work developed by both IFSW and IASSW in July 2001 is more inclusive and relevant to global concerns. The strong social justice and human rights focus is evident here as well:

> The social work profession promotes social change, problem solving in human relationships and the empowerment and liberation of people to enhance well-being. Utilising theories of human behaviour and social systems, social work intervenes at the points where people interact with their environments. Principles of human rights and social justice are fundamental to social work. (retrieved from http://www.iassw.soton.ac.uk)

How does social work differ from other helping professions? A major difference that I can see is that social work is an applied field similar to nursing and teaching; graduates can get licensed at the bachelor's or master's level for professional practice. *Psychologists* are generally expected to get a PhD in order to be licensed. They rely heavily on their psychological testing instruments in assessing their clients. *Marriage/family therapy* requires a master's degree for individuals to be qualified in their field. Graduate degrees in *counseling* are widely available, especially geared toward work in the public schools, although some states have licensing for mental health counselors. *Sociology* and *criminology* degrees prepare recipients for teaching or research at the doctorate level. *Psychiatrists* are physicians who rely primarily on their medical training for the treatment of mental disorders. Sometimes the term *social worker* is confused with *social welfare worker*. Social welfare workers who work at departments of human services may or may not have training in social work.

Note that all these occupations except for social work and, perhaps, counseling are specialized. And training is specialized in all those fields as well. Social workers are generally trained at both macro and micro levels. Also rather uniquely, as mentioned earlier, social work programs must be nationally accredited for one's degree to be accepted for licensing purposes; all programs must offer education in social welfare policy as well as skills-based courses.

Generalist Practice   Because of the versatility required of social workers, social work education provides for the inculcation of an eclectic knowledge base, diversified as opposed to specialized skills (except at the graduate level), and an emphasis on client empowerment. The CSWE (2003) *Handbook of Accreditation Standards* defines social work's broad-based approach as preparation for *generalist practice:* "Social workers are generalists, in the sense that they need to be prepared to work with a wide variety of social problems and with people at every stage of the life span." Moreover, as indicated in the CSWE (2003) handbook of standards and procedures, generalists must be prepared for practice with systems of all sizes—individuals, families, and communities. Like a general practitioner in medicine, the generalist social worker typically coordinates the efforts of specialists by facilitating communication among them (Barker, 2003, p. 176).

Most often, specialization occurs at the master's level, while the bachelor's level social worker typically performs case management, which involves coordination of services for clients. In fields such as substance abuse counseling and hospice work, however, a great deal of versatility is required for working with diverse populations, as is specialized knowledge in the addictions and medical arenas. Such knowledge is usually obtained on the job and not through undergraduate programming. Specialization at the graduate level is often in specialized fields such as health, mental health, administration, and child welfare.

Hospitals and mental health centers seek out licensed social workers, not only for their expertise, but because insurance companies increasingly reimburse only for members of this profession for activities related to counseling and therapy. Although many social workers engage in private practice, most are employed by a human service organization such as a school, correctional system, nursing home, or substance abuse treatment center (Morales & Sheafor, 2004). Before students choose to major in social work or any related field, they should consult relevant agencies concerning particular qualifications that are desired and particular courses that are recommended (e.g., addictions treatment or, increasingly, conversational Spanish).

More details on the social work profession, especially in regard to its growth and theoretical development, are provided in Chapter 3. Both Chapters 2 and 3 survey social work in an international context. Later chapters describe specialized practice in the criminal justice system, medical social work, child welfare, services for the homeless, and elder care.

Third World, Developing Country, Global South, and So On

In collaboration with the International Committee of the CSWE, a curriculum manual was produced by Healy (1992) for the purpose of providing teaching modules with international content for use by social work educators. This manual uses the term *developing country* to contrast the lower-income, less industrialized countries of the world with the more industrialized, higher-income countries labeled as *developed* countries. There are two major drawbacks to the use of these terms. First, the differentiation between developing and developed is pejorative. Second, the implication that economic growth necessarily breeds progress for the majority of people is faulty. Quite often progress exists only for the wealthy elite. In contrast to these notions, social development theory includes the meeting of common human needs (Healy, 1992). A newer term, *sustainable development,* refers to the achievement of social progress while preserving available resources for use by future generations.

The difficulty still persists in finding a term to adequately differentiate technologically advanced countries from others. After the 1960s, the terms *First*

World, Second World, and *Third World* gained currency. The origin of the terms is provided by Healy (2001):

> Describing the mostly Westernized industrialized nations; the Soviet Union and its satellite nations; and newly independent and nonaligned nations of Asia, Africa, and Latin America, respectively, these terms had relevance during the Cold War Era. The term Third World increasingly was known as a negative term, implying to some the idea of third rate or last in consideration; the actual derivation of the term is from a phrase describing the Third Estate in the French Revolution. (p. 14)

Other objections include the obsolescence of the Second World with the dissolution of the Soviet Union, and the fact that some countries that are considered Third World due to the level of poverty of the common people represent great accumulation of capital at higher echelons. Accordingly, the Third World concept will only be used in this book in quotes and selections from other sources.

Geographical labels such as *North* and *South,* as Healy (2001) suggests, can be confusing, probably due to the location of the advanced nations of Australia and New Zealand south of the equator. Ramanathan and Link (1999) offer the terms *Global South* and *Global North;* these terms clearly describe virtual geopolitical entities, and accordingly, I consider them appropriate delineations for today's global era. Additionally, this text also uses other neutral geographical terms (namely, *East* and *West*) and economically descriptive terms (e.g., *technologically advanced regions* and *the nonindustrialized world*) to highlight differences in standards of living. Where possible, specific regions of the world are named, for example, Latin America, sub-Saharan Africa, and Northern Europe.

Functionalism

Borrowed originally from biology, the functionalist perspective focused solely on the structure of an organism. However, the functionalist perspective in sociology provided for the viewing of social phenomena in terms of structure and function. Functionalist analysis asks the question, how is a given phenomenon functional for society? Or alternatively, how is it dysfunctional? A sociologist, for example, might analyze the functions and dysfunctions of deviant behavior. Related concepts are manifest and latent functions of a social phenomenon. *Manifest functions* are the obvious, stated reasons for an activity, while latent functions are the secondary, sometimes unintended, and often hidden motives behind its existence. Whereas Robert K. Merton (1949) in his classic definition of *latent functions* defined them as neither intended nor recognized, we will rely on the dictionary definition of *latent* as "lying hidden or underdeveloped within a person or thing, derivation is from the Latin verb, to be hidden" (*Webster's New World Dictionary,* 1991). See Table 1.1 for examples of manifest and latent functions.

Functional analysis is a useful technique utilized in sociology and anthropology to reveal the community value of a cultural trait or institution (such as religious rituals). Viewing a cultural norm (e.g., punishing those who shirk

Table 1.1 | Manifest and Latent Functions

Item or Activity	Manifest Functions	Latent Functions
Car	Transportation	Status
Higher education	Job preparation	Keeping people off job market
Military haircut	Neatness, cleanliness	Creating a new identity
Funeral	Burial of the dead	Grieving, funeral home business
Prisons	Protecting society	Getting revenge
War	Freedom, liberation	Economic interests, power
New Deal	Alleviate poverty	Preventing riots and Marxism
Welfare benefits	Provide for well-being	Controlling the poor

responsibility) in terms of manifest and latent functions and dysfunctions leads to new ways of thinking about social phenomena. This approach will be used as a means of explaining a number of concepts (e.g., social welfare and poverty) that are discussed in subsequent chapters of this book.

Regulating the Poor

Piven and Cloward (1993), following the functional analysis definition of Merton, viewed the social welfare system as a societal device for "regulating the poor" in the interest of capitalism. This is the latent function of social welfare. Creating consensus and encouraging social altruism—the rationales that figure so largely in traditional histories of social welfare—are the manifest functions of the social welfare system (Piven & Cloward, 1993). Chapter 4, which tackles the foundations of social welfare and poverty, will examine the "regulating the poor" thesis in greater depth. Of relevance to social values is the fact that the degree to which social control over the poor is exercised reflects the values of the dominant groups in society.

Social Needs and Power

Unlike the approach of the psychologist, the sociologist looks at needs subjectively and collectively. Needs are real if people perceive them to be real. Real or imagined, needs may stimulate innovation, social change, and the manufacturing of new products. The marketing of products creates a sense of need where, heretofore, there was none. Conversely, although living conditions may be quite low, there may be no perception of need. Mexican social workers, for instance, might see family strengths where visiting Americans might see only the lack of electricity and running water. At the same time, Mexican social workers will go beyond the giving of charity to individuals and also address the causes of social inequalities (Bibus, 1995).

Over the centuries, out of sheer ignorance, the root causes of problems have often been overlooked. For instance, in cities, sickness and death resulted from water contamination and personal filth. Today, similarly, the failure to recognize a need for birth control in some parts of the world is associated with mass misery and starvation. When a nation's rulers value military might over health and housing, the social welfare system is diminished accordingly. People in need are left to fend for themselves. Social values shift over time and are influenced by the vested interests in the society.

Whether or not cultural values differ according to social class is one of the enduring controversies within the fields of sociology and criminology. Sociologists generally agree that some American cultural values such as materialism and achieving status are universal, while other values such as delaying gratification and obeying social norms vary from class to class (Macionis, 2004). The middle classes are considered more scrupulous than are persons at either the upper or lower echelons. *Power* is a sociological concept of relevance to social welfare as a dimension of stratification as well as to social legislation and world dominance. In the tradition of Max Weber (1979/1922), power can be defined as the ability to get people to do what you want even against their will. Perhaps the key issue of interest to social welfare is who in the society has the power to get his or her perceived needs met and who does not. A related issue is who in society can meet these ends—achieving success—without violating the norms of society. For example, who can achieve wealth and status through conventional means and who must use illegitimate means to achieve the same ends?

Control of the media promotes power, and power promotes control of the media. No one has ever described this phenomenon better than George Orwell (1961/1948) in his haunting masterpiece *1984:* "Who controls the past controls the future; who controls the present controls the past" (p. 204). In that book, Orwell also introduced the notion of Thought Police and the personification of the world's scapegoat in the form of a man capable "of wrecking the structure of civilization" (p. 16).

From another angle, those with power ("the power elite") can shape a society according to the principles they value. In a real sense they control the flow of knowledge as well as the knowledge itself. For instance, corporations and companies advertising in the local newspaper may have an inhibiting effect on news reporting of various sorts because newspapers do not want to lose their funding. Information imparted in a political campaign, similarly, is apt to be influenced by the giant contributors to that campaign. The burgeoning political influence of conservative think tanks on the mass media is described in Chapter 3.

At the international level, inequitable distribution of wealth and military might are conditions that shape politics, economic alliances, and relationships. Abuse of this power is seen in industrialized countries, using sweatshop labor in developing countries to stock their own markets with material goods. In foreign policy, the abuse of political power, as defined in the late Senator Fulbright's (1966) *The Arrogance of Power,* is highly relevant in today's world where the defense industry has come to assume awesome powers.

Globalization

From the social work perspective, the gap between human problems and attention to their root causes is widening (Ife, 2000). The gap is widening due to the increasingly global nature of the forces that shape people's lives. Whether we are talking about employment pressures or reductions in government-sponsored protections, the globalization of the world's economy poses new threats to social workers (Rowe, Hanley, Moreno, & Mould, 2000). In terms of social movements, this globalization presents new opportunities as well.

So what is *globalization?* Is it an opportunity or a curse? When did we first hear the word? According to an article in *Newsweek* (Miller, 2002), the word *globalization* was rarely heard in the 1980s. A search of a major English news source found 158 stories using the word by 1991; this grew to 17,638 by 2000. In the early 1990s, the concept was associated with optimism and big thinking. It took on, according to the *Newsweek* article, "the aura of an elemental force. It came to mean whatever a person wanted it to mean, whether economic integration or the spread of wealth, Coca-Colonization or the spread of AIDS" (p. E6).

This critical view of corporate business practices echoes that of Marx and Engels (1963/1848), who provided remarkable insights in *The Communist Manifesto.* The following passage perhaps has more relevance today than when it was written:

> By exploitation of the world market, the bourgeoisie has given a cosmopolitan character to production and consumption in every land. To the despair of the reactionaries, it has deprived industry of its national foundation. Of the old-established national industries, some have already been destroyed and others are, day by day, undergoing destruction. They are dislodged by new industries, whose introduction is becoming a matter of life and death for all civilized nations: by industries which no longer depend upon the homeland for their raw materials, but draw these from the remotest spots; and by industries whose products are consumed, not only in the country of manufacture, but the wide world over. Instead of the old wants, satisfied by the products of native industry, new wants appear, wants which can only be satisfied by the products of distant lands and unfamiliar climes. . . . It forces all the nations, under pain of extinction, to adopt the capitalist method of production; it constrains them to accept what is called civilization, to become bourgeois themselves. In short, it creates a world after its own image. (p. 30)

Globalization is defined by Kahn and Kamerman (2002) as "the current buzzword used to describe the growing internationalization of the production of goods and services and the flow of capitalism" (p. 488). Globalization represents the movement over the past two decades from an economy in which national economies participated in a global market to a full-blown global economy in which the major corporations and banks transcend national boundaries. Sometimes the term *globalism* is used to refer to the ideological orientation underlying neoliberal policies advocating "free trade" in goods and services—to the inequitable effect of forces driven by markets and profit (Wilson &

Whitmore, 2000). This term is unambiguously used to denote negative consequences of globalization.

But globalization is social and educational as well as economic. Socially, globalization has been happening for centuries due to military conquest, trade, and missionary work. Advances in communication techniques mean that a wealth of information is available at our fingertips. Even in the radical magazine *Utne Reader,* Shuman (2002) touted the information revolution for its equalizing effect in giving small companies advantages they never had before in terms of the extraordinary capabilities of a tiny desktop computer.

The globalization of culture is an obvious aspect of globalization that is not entirely economic. This process is seen in the mass-produced, quasi-American cultural icons in the form of McDonalds, Levis, baseball, Coca-Cola, television shows, and, of course, the use of English words for things (Ife, 2000). As nations are bombarded with foreign images and music, there is concern that native performers will be ignored and indigenous traditions will be lost to the next generations.

Like cultural Westernization, the impact of the global economy is mixed. While the global market brings cheaper consumer goods and better jobs for skilled workers (e.g., for electronic engineers in Bangalore, India), economies with high wage costs lose jobs to economies with cheaper labor and fewer benefits, so "the race to the bottom" is inevitable. One result is a rising hostility to globalization and a mass movement against the multinational corporations for producing goods at Asian sweatshops or destroying the rain forest for the growth of cash crops for the world markets. In 1999, the "Battle of Seattle" made this opposition known to the world in protests against the World Trade Organization (WTO).

One of the most eloquent spokespersons of the anti-WTO movement, Arundhati Roy (2002), a renowned writer from India, offers this commentary. These remarks were written on the occasion of London's million-person march against the arms buildup against Iraq:

> In a country like India, the "structural adjustment" end of the corporate globalisation project is ripping through people's lives. "Development" projects, massive privatisation, and labour "reforms" are pushing people off their lands and out of their jobs, resulting in a kind of barbaric dispossession that has few parallels in history. Across the world as the "free market" brazenly protects Western markets and forces developing countries to lift their trade barriers, the poor are getting poorer and the rich richer. Civil unrest has begun to erupt in the global village. In countries like Argentina, Brazil, Mexico, Bolivia, and India the resistance movements against corporate globalisation are growing.
>
> To contain them, governments are tightening their control. Protesters are being labeled "terrorists" and then dealt with as such. But civil unrest does not only mean marches and demonstrations and protests against globalisation. Unfortunately, it also means a desperate downward spiral into crime and chaos and all kinds of despair and disillusionment which, as we know from history (and from what we see unspooling before our eyes), gradually becomes a fertile breeding ground for terrible things—cultural nationalism, religious bigotry, fascism and of course, terrorism.

All these march arm-in-arm with corporate globalization. (http://www
.guardian.co.uk)

All of us are heirs to opportunities, knowledge access, and possibilities scarce-
ly imaginable to our grandparents. At the same time, in the name of progress and
to spur the global market, rainforests have been leveled, the atmosphere polluted,
and people relocated by the millions. In our ever-shrinking universe, our global
village, national economies increasingly are interdependent. Decisions that affect
all of us are made on Wall Street, by the World Bank, and by transnational corporations. Across continents, aided by the tools of computer technology, the flow of
capital and ideas is happening at the speed of light. As international corporations
have grown into transnational corporations whose interests transcend the interests of any one state or enterprise, the national thrust to be commercially competitive becomes all-encompassing. Accordingly, the trends in one country—privatization, industrial automation, downsizing, focus on cost-efficiency—are the
trends in every country.

The "structural adjustment" to which Roy (2002) referred relates to the
mandatory austerity programs forced upon indebted governments by the international banks. The governments had been previously bankrupted, according to
Prigoff (1999), through the loans received for roads and utilities to benefit international trade and military weapons to maintain government control. These
industrializing nations were then seeking new loans to refinance due interest
payments. World Banks can best get cooperation for their harsh economic measures through working with dictatorships, as the measures are, of course, unpopular with the general populace. Prigoff summarizes the stringent banking
requirements for refinancing as follows: the elimination of restrictions on
imports and exports; privatization of national resources and public utilities;
cutbacks in health, education, housing, and spending; and the making of loan
repayments the top priority. As a result of these measures, the gap between rich
and poor is increasing exponentially, and the livelihoods of subsistence cultures
that have lived off the land have been destroyed.

The powerful forces of social, cultural, demographic, and political changes
associated with globalization have important implications for the social welfare
state and for social work practice. Under the impact of the growth of "free market" economies, existing social welfare institutions are precariously situated
between the retrenchment of entitlement programs and the concomitant
increase in demands for social services as poverty increases. Social workers thus
are compelled to do more with less. "How many professional social workers have
recognized that the same program for the downsizing of governments and redirection of national resources has been planned and provided on a global level by
officials of international banks and representatives of transnational corporations?" asks Prigoff (1999, p. 157).

Empowerment can be said to have occurred when individuals and organizations influence decision making through their representatives and/or act independently to effect social change. The first step in such organization globally is
the identification of commonalities. Torczyner (2000), accordingly, urges a uni-

versal human rights focus in advocacy for social and economic justice within the global economy. One of the ironies of history, Prigoff (1999) tells us, is that networks of grassroots women's groups and indigenous peoples have at their disposal the tools of electronic communications to use as tools of liberation. International social work is now fortified by such tools at the same time that it is energized by the dynamics of globalization.

In recognition of the current crisis facing the social work profession worldwide due to the cross-country dismantling of social services, the Canadian Association of Social Workers (CASW) produced a special journal issue of 2000 *Canadian Social Work,* which was republished as a special paperback edition. The articles in this edition, drawn from writers from across the world, collectively present the case that if we, as social workers, are to seek adequate solutions, we must engage in united action. Among the suggestions listed by Ife (2000) for social workers are these:

- Extending the practice of policy advocacy to international forums
- Making effective use of new technologies to link both workers and community groups globally
- Seeking social work roles and positions in international NGOs and U.N. agencies
- Incorporating a strong human rights analysis alongside more traditional social work, needs-based practice (pp. 62–63)

Culture and Cultural Competence

The concept of culture is central to anthropology. Culture is social heredity, or a way of thinking, feeling, and believing that sets one group apart from another. Culture is traditional knowledge that is passed down from one generation to the next (Podolefsky & Brown, 2001). The individual's behavior is controlled by his or her culture in many deep and pervasive ways. Even what we think of as personality is culturally determined. Culture can be considered the mold in which the individual figure is cast.

Because of the close relationship between personality and culture, members of one nation or tribe (or sex) appear homogeneous to outsiders. A group member absorbs the essential content of a culture by means of socialization.

Language shapes and is shaped by culture. In Mexico, for example, where there is a complete reliance on the family to provide care, a visiting American social worker had difficulty translating the sentence, "My mother-in-law is in a nursing home" into Spanish (Bibus, 1995). In Mexico, according to Bibus, the meaning of life is the family. In the United States, the meaning of life is work. These differences in values are reflected in the spoken vocabulary.

Anthropologists study other cultures; many believe this is the best means of understanding ourselves (de Roche, 1989). Our notions of love, freedom, justice, and the like are highly culturally bound. The principles and practices by which we live are not always self-evident. In working with persons from other cultural backgrounds, understanding the native culture or point of view is essential. This includes worldviews and value orientations.

Cultural competence is the social work term for the knowledge and skills that one needs for effective work with clients from diverse cultural backgrounds. Cultural competence entails more than familiarity with the cultural norms and values of a specific group; it involves an understanding of the uniqueness of one's own cultural beliefs and an openness to other customs, norms, and rituals.

Cultural competence entails recognition of society's prejudices—ethnocentrism, sexism, classism, heterosexism, and racism—and of our own possession of many of these traits. To fully appreciate cultural differences, self-awareness is a must. Social workers must recognize the influence of their own culture, family, and peers on how they think and act. Cultural competence requires continuous efforts to gain more knowledge about the client's culture—the norms, vocabulary, symbols, and strengths. The color-blind and gender-blind notions of many European American social workers are a denial of a person's whole being. Through accepting that significant differences do exist between people of different ethnic backgrounds, professionals are recognizing a person's wholeness and individuality. To tell a lesbian or gay person to "just stay in the closet and you'll be all right" or "don't ask, don't tell" is to deny that person an important part of him- or herself. To tell an African American "we're all the same under the skin" is to deny the importance of race in the society. Multicultural social welfare education exposes people to divergent thinking as they are forced to examine formerly taken-for-granted assumptions.

Cultural competence becomes more and more critical to effective social work practice as global interdependency increases. Professional developments in other countries are becoming especially relevant to those in the United States as social problems become universal. Much as nations of the Global South have looked to nations of the Global North for models of social work education, truly reciprocal exchanges are becoming the focus today to prepare graduates for the increasingly global nature of social work practice—for example, with clients of diverse national, ethnic, religious, social, and cultural backgrounds and with persons from other countries. Otherwise, instead of cultural sensitivity, ethnocentrism would prevail.

Ecosystems Theory

The view of culture as an integrated whole borrows a concept from the biological sciences in which the organs of the body complement each other in remarkable ways to comprise a functioning system. Like an organism, culture has form and pattern. There is a degree of order and a system that is greater than the sum of its parts. To the anthropologist, the related patterns of the environment, the resources available for exploration within it, the organization of people to utilize the resources, their beliefs about what they do and the relationships between the larger group and themselves are all part of the system out of which individuals structure their behaviors (Esber, 1989).

Once a sense of culture and its values is acquired, the social scientist can analyze the values in a systematic fashion. Is there internal consistency between ascribed values and practices? Which values are conducive to smooth functioning of the society and which are obstacles to smooth functioning? (Berger, McBreen, & Rifkin, 1996). In Northern Ireland, for instance, the dominant cultural values and beliefs favor school segregation for Catholics and Protestants. How is this arrangement conducive to harmony? How might it lead to conflict? What changes might one predict? In many of the countries of Eastern Asia, traditional values are being examined as well.

Ethnocentrism

According to Podolefsky and Brown (2001), the paradox of culture is that as we humans learn to accept our own cultural beliefs and values, we unconsciously learn to reject those of other people. Sumner (1940/1906) called the outlook that one's group is superior to other groups *ethnocentrism,* and defined it as "that view of things in which one's own group is the center of everything and all others are scaled and related with reference to it" (p. 13). Immigration provides an example of potential conflict as disparate value systems exist side by side. Boundaries between groups can become increasingly thick and exclusionary. Neighborhoods are affected by an influx of immigrants; the workplace is affected also as newcomers flock to accept jobs that locals would find undesirable.

Such a complex set of potential problems must be addressed by the social welfare system; a holistic, nonethnocentric approach to the delivery of services is essential. Awareness of one's own culture's peculiarities is the first place to start. We must learn about our own culture, according to Nakanishi and Rittner (1992), before we can learn about other cultures. The reverse is true also; we must have an appreciation for other cultures and their values before we can come to appreciate or even grasp our own. We are like the introspective hero of *Absalom, Absalom!* (Faulkner, 1936, p. 174) who must leave the South before he can answer questions regarding the South such as, "What's it like there? What do they do there?"

Margaret Mead, in her autobiography *Blackberry Winter* (1972), provides this approach to unraveling the intricacies of a new culture. The goal is to "understand a myriad of acts, words, glances, and silences as they are integrated into a pattern one had no way of working out as yet, and finally, to 'get' the structure of the whole culture" (p. 275).

Interactionism

The discipline of social psychology falls midway between psychology and sociology in terms of the size of the population being studied. Social psychology studies the individual interacting with the group, and the group as internalized within the individual. In other words, as C. H. Cooley (1983/1909) eloquently stated, "Self and society are twin born." Interactionism, reciprocity, internalization of norms—these are fundamental concepts of social psychology that have clear relevance for social work. Like social psychology, social work views individuals in constant interaction with other individuals and with the environment.

As the theoretical frameworks for later chapters of this book concern issues such as special populations and oppression, and crime and punishment, we will draw upon two classics from social psychology—Gordon Allport's *The Nature of Prejudice* (1981/1954) and Erving Goffman's *Asylums* (1961). Allport's discussion of the theory of displaced aggression—the redirecting of anger from one source onto a vulnerable person or group—is highly informative. Unemployed persons may scapegoat other oppressed groups, for example. Goffman's analysis of punishment rituals is equally compelling. An individual who, through whatever cruel circumstance, comes to acquire a role—the role of prisoner, say—may internalize that role to the point of undergoing observable behavior change. *Labeling theory* from sociology is a related concept. The individual receives a label from society (e.g., juvenile delinquent) and then, through a self-fulfilling prophecy, becomes the image of that label. This process involves the development of a distinctive self-identity, which is quite often a negative one.

Interactionism is a major concept used in family counseling. In the language of systems theory, the basic principle of interactionism is that cause and effect are intertwined. Members of alcoholic families, for example, become aware of how pain and substance misuse fuel each other until the two become almost one and the same (van Wormer & Davis, 2003). In the language of ordinary conversation, we talk of a "vicious cycle." The saying "What goes around, comes around" is another way of saying the same thing.

Prejudice

Prejudice, which we can define as a preconceived and unjustified negative attitude, is a widely studied phenomenon. Before turning to the social psychology of prejudice, let us consider the cultural dimensions. Prejudice against others who are different is largely learned through others' comments, attitudes, and possibly a negative experience with members of the disfavored group. A history of war, territorial disputes, persecutions, and economic exploitation exacerbates prejudice in the exploiters who must justify their group's deeds. Those who are exploited, quite naturally, will be prejudiced as well. Once ethnic or racial hatred is entrenched, the tendency is for it to escalate. As people become defined as enemies, their misdeeds are remembered and dwelled upon. Thus, in the former Yugoslavia, as in Azerbajan and in Northern Ireland, William Faulkner's (1951) description of the postbellum South is hauntingly apt: "the past is never dead; it's not even past" (p. 92).

The classic sociological question is: What are the functions of prejudice? Prejudice solidifies the group and encourages internal bonding. By scapegoating an outgroup, the powers-that-be in a society are protected. For example, during periods of economic depression in the South, the poor whites targeted blacks. In the United States today, with the working class effectively divided along racial

lines, the power elites can rule without opposition. Each of these functions listed can be construed, of course, as dysfunctions. Chapter 4 on societal oppression
chronicles some of the pain associated with oppression related to prejudice.

The social psychology of prejudice is both complex and intriguing.
Bogardus's social distance scale devised in 1928, and used by generations of college students across the years, provides a measure of acceptance of various designated groups. The particular groups selected vary by geographical location
and concerns of the day. This familiar technique asks respondents to indicate to
which extent, on the following scale, they would admit members of various ethnic, religious, and racial groups: (1) to live in my country; (2) to employment in
my occupation; (3) to my neighborhood; (4) to my club as personal friends; and
(5) to close kinship or marriage.

Generally, the closer the contact, the greater the reluctance to accept persons
who are different from ourselves. In his definitive study entitled *The Nature of
Prejudice,* Allport (1981/1954) was struck by the generalization of outgroup
prejudice, or the tendency for an individual to be intolerant of all forms of diversity. Prejudice is basically a trait of personality, claims Allport, one that is correlated with hostility and fear. Social psychologists, in fact, are inclined to regard
such generalized prejudice as a symptom of a particular type of personality.

Empirical support for the existence of a personality dimension in prejudice
was provided during the 1940s by a team of researchers who carried out an in-
depth investigation into the dynamics of anti-Semitism (Levine, 2002). The
study was inspired by events that had occurred in Nazi Germany. Adorno,
Frankel-Brunswick, Levinson, and Sanford (1950) devised an F-scale to measure
fascist or authoritarian tendencies. Among items included in this scale are the
following:

■ Obedience and respect for authority are the most important virtues children should learn.
■ There is hardly anything lower than a person who does not feel great love,
  gratitude, and respect for his or her parents.
■ Sexual offenders ought to be publicly whipped or worse.
■ The businessperson and the manufacturer are much more important to
  society than the artist and the professor.

Findings were that scores on the F-scale correlated quite strongly with scores on
scales of anti-Semitism, general ethnocentrism, and political conservatism (also
dogmatic communism as revealed in a later study). To explain the development
of authoritarianism, Adorno and his associates looked at early child-rearing
practices. Employing arbitrary and harsh methods of discipline, authoritarian
parents may produce children whose feelings of frustration are repressed. This
hostility may be displaced and directed instead toward powerless groups in
society.

A recently published study in the American Psychological Association's
Psychological Bulletin utilized advanced statistical methods to detect personality
patterns in politically conservative persons (Jost, Kruglanski, Glaser, & Sulloway,
2003). Data gathered were culled through 50 years of research literature and

involved an unprecedented 22,818 cases. The material originated from 12 countries and included political speeches and interviews, opinions rendered by judges, and experimental field data. The findings, which were widely reported in international news reports and on the Internet, linked the following common psychological factors to political conservatism:

- Fear and aggression
- Dogmatism and intolerance of ambiguity
- Avoidance of uncertainty
- Need for cognitive closure and structure
- Resistance to change
- Endorsement of inequality
- View of reality in terms of black and white—no shades of gray
- Terror management—shunning or punishing outsiders

In a follow-up interview about their findings, a member of the research team, Jack Glaser (interviewed by Maclay, 2003), conjectured that in times of crisis, right-wing populism may have more consistent appeal than left-wing populism. George W. Bush, Ronald Reagan, Hitler, Mussolini, and talk-show host Rush Limbaugh were mentioned as examples of right-wing conservatism because they preached a return to an idealized past and condoned inequality in some form.

Intolerance of ambiguity is a trait that deserves more research; for example, how does anger and a seeking after retribution enter into the picture? In any case, the linking of political ideology to personality dynamics helps to explain why so often facts from government intelligence and other reliable sources are discounted in favor of more simplistic truths. These findings help explain further why relatively new ideas such as gay marriage or the creation of a world court are apt be so strongly resisted in far right-wing quarters. The Josh et al. (2003) study is reminiscent of Adorno et al.'s (1950) work in its attribution of political ideology to personality characteristics. I prefer Adorno's use of the term *authoritarianism* instead of *conservatism* because many of the Russian communist party leaders evidenced the same personal traits. (For more on the psychological dimension of human behavior, see Chapter 7.)

Not only personality dynamics but also collective forces play a key role in promoting prejudice. Years ago, when experimental research on human subjects could be done much more freely (without permission from academic research boards), social psychologists studied the role of intergroup competition for scarce resources in promoting collective hatred. Experiments with 12-year-old summer campers revealed that conditions of extreme competition produced conflict and hostility between rival groups. When a situation was set up, however, where all opposing teams united to achieve superordinate goals, feelings of harmony and trust prevailed (Sherif & Sherif, 1966). The findings of such small-group experiments are relevant to situations experienced on the larger scale, such as keen competition with outsiders over well-paying jobs.

How can ethnic and racial prejudice be prevented or offset? The basic remedies range from societal to individual efforts. Although *media campaigns* against racial and ethnic hatred have had limited success, the inclusion of members of diverse groups in advertisements reinforces the notion of an integrated society. *Legal remedies* such as outlawing hate crimes and segregation practices can change attitudes, as citizens who are forced to comply with the laws may, in complying, conform their attitudes to be consistent with their behavior. *Group therapy* with individuals from varied backgrounds can enhance communication and the recognition of the universality of problems and feelings. *Individual therapy* can be of value in teaching empathy skills and in focusing on underlying problems that perhaps indirectly are related to intolerance. Finally, *exposure to films and books* depicting the lives of persons who have had to overcome prejudice may go a long way toward breaking our sense of dissimilarity with members of particular populations. The more we come to identify with others, the more we realize how much we have in common.

Blaming the Victim

A concept derived from psychologists of the social psychological school, *victim blaming* refers to a fundamental tendency in American culture (Ryan, 1976; Zastrow, 2004). This tendency occurs when the downtrodden or underdogs of society are held responsible for creating their own distress. Because of the reciprocity involved, the victim tends to internalize the blame attached to his or her condition (the self-talk is "I have failed"), and the negativity may become a self-fulfilling prophecy (the self-talk becomes "I will never amount to anything").

In an article astutely titled "All the World Loathes a Loser," Lerner (1971) indicates our vulnerability to the suffering of other people. We are only vulnerable, however, to the suffering of a hero. Condemning the victim (of crime, disease, or an abusive relationship) is a response we create privately without awareness so as to maintain our sense of justice in the world. The seemingly natural tendency is to believe that the unfortunate victim somehow merited his or her fate.

Pervasive in the American psyche, the phenomenon of blaming the victim is a generic process applied to almost every social problem in the United States (Ryan, 1976). As a traditional ideology related to the work ethic, intellectual, scientific, and religious forces have all historically fed the mythology. As noted by Dolgoff and Feldstein (1999), the growth of industrialism, the development of the Protestant work ethic, and Social Darwinism each have contributed to blaming the victim. In Chapter 3, we discuss these historical currents. Internal (genetic) differences among individuals have been paraded out as the rationale for social inequality (Herrnstein & Murray, 1994). New support has been lent to the old suspicion that social welfare programs cause more problems than they solve.

A unique phenomenon of the blaming-the-poor rhetoric of the past decade is the success in enlisting the lower-middle classes in the service of the higher-level interests in targeting the poor as society's scapegoats. "Welfare reform," for example, was a characteristically punitive ploy that received widespread support. Chapter 4 considers the blaming-the-victim ideology in terms of the social implications relating to poverty.

What is the opposite of victim blaming? Is it tolerance? Or support? In the helping professions, the opposite of blaming is *empathy*. Empathy is the ability to identify with another person and, through a leap of the imagination, to momentarily view the world through the other's eyes. A Sioux prayer reveals the difficulty in acquiring this virtue: "Oh Great Spirit, keep me from judging a man until I've walked a mile in his moccasins." And in the words of a Kentucky gospel hymn I once heard in Bowling Green, "Do not accuse, condemn, or abuse, till you've walked in my shoes."

These theoretical concepts of social psychology—interaction, prejudice, and victim blaming—offer explanatory knowledge that helps us understand and predict human behavior. Seemingly bizarre aspects of human behavior are often normal reactions to abnormal situations. Such explanatory knowledge guides the practitioner in addressing several "why" questions: Why is a rape victim often blamed for her or his own victimization? Why do prison populations rise and fall with the national mood? Why are gays and lesbians subject to attack especially by rowdy groups of young males?

Empathy is one of the most important traits in helping people; empathy is often imparted more through body language and feeling than words. More than empathy is required, however, as many victims tend to blame themselves and lose faith in their ability to find a way out of a seemingly hopeless situation; without help and encouragement, they lose hope. This is where the empowerment approach comes in.

Empowerment

Zoya Taylor (1999), in seeking a framework for social work that would be relevant and meaningful internationally, singles out two fundamental values—preventing harm and promoting social justice—and one moral principle—dedication to empowerment—on which social workers universally should agree. Empowerment, according to Taylor, encompasses both a state of mind, as in feeling empowered, and a capability to exert control over events. The notion of empowerment, when linked with supporting efforts to fight injustice and oppression, can be viewed as transcending individualistic Western values and as applicable cross-culturally.

Empowerment practice is aimed at assisting people who experience systematic forms of discrimination, harassment, and oppression (Robbins, Chatterjee, & Canda, 1999). *Empowerment,* according to GlenMaye (1997), describes the transformation from individual and collective powerlessness to personal, political, and cultural power. Of special relevance to victimization is the gaining of a sense of personal power—assuming responsibility for recovery and change, which may entail helping others.

Empowerment entails an emphasis on the development and nourishing of strengths and positive attributes (Kirst-Ashman, 2003). The empowerment and strengths perspectives are the dominant social work treatment models today. Although often indistinguishable, the empowerment framework is more political and apt to be used in a context of work with disadvantaged populations, sometimes at the macro level. The strengths perspective, in contrast, tends to be used in direct practice with individual clients.

As its name indicates, the strengths approach builds on clients' strengths and resources. Saleebey (2002) calls this a "versatile practice approach, relying heavily on ingenuity and creativity, the courage and common sense of both clients and their social workers" (p. 1). From a strengths perspective, social workers strive to help clients tap into their personal resources and those of their family and community.

The counseling relationship can serve as a powerful tool in helping clients find an alternative course toward fulfillment and beginning to change self-destructive thoughts and behavior. Efforts to build or enhance personal power in people who feel powerless is a basic component of the strengths perspective.

For work in the addictions field, which has traditionally focused on breaking denial and on harsh confrontation, the trend is increasingly geared toward a more positive, empowering, ethnic-sensitive approach (van Wormer & Davis, 2003). Meeting the client where the client is: This is the contemporary focus of substance abuse treatment.

Our Social Work Imagination

A mark of greatness, as Katherine Kendall (1989) suggested, is a breadth of vision. In her portrait of three extraordinary social work leaders of the 1930s—Alice Salomon of Germany, Eileen Younghusband of the United Kingdom, and Edith Abbott of the United States—Kendall explained their deep commitment to international concerns. Every social work graduate at the University of Chicago in Edith Abbott's day, for example, was exposed to a view of the field and the profession that encompassed history and comparative study. Salomon and Younghusband worked with the League of Nations and the U.N. In their international vision and flexibility, these female pioneers personify what I mean by *social work imagination*. As Kendall concluded, "In embracing the necessity to join social reform with individual help, they long ago settled the question of whether social work should be equally concerned with therapeutic action and social action" (p. 30).

To paraphrase Kendall: Good social work is not therapy *or* social action; it is both/and. Both/and as opposed to either/or thinking is the kind of thinking associated with creative thought and also with feminist therapy. (Either/or thinking or black-and-white thinking in addictions treatment is equated with rigidity and a tendency to relapse.)

Because no two clients are alike and no communities are alike, social work is complex, and the key elements are unpredictable. Social work is both an art and a science. (Keep in mind that art and science are intertwined, nondichotomous components in creation; there is art in empirical truths and science in artistic creations.) Sometimes, as Ann Weick (1999) suggests, social work knowledge, because it is intuitive, is dismissed as soft, fanciful, and without substance. As Weick describes the helping process:

> Good practice requires tolerance for mess—for holding many conflicting views together at one time and committing oneself to a process whose outcome is unpredictable. The ability to act effectively in this zone of uncertainty requires special skills. Social work has no instruments or remedies characteristic of other helping professions such as nursing. (p. 331)

I remember hearing in graduate school that English majors trained in social work make the best therapists due to their ability to empathize with characters in literature. They probably also possess powers of imagination and tolerance for ambiguity. Goldstein (1999) corroborates the connection between literacy and human understandings. We need to go beyond reason alone, he suggests, to use our own greater curiosity and imagination: "The circumstances we are trying to understand are always in flux and change, full of the kinds of mystery and enigmas that are the essence of great literature" (p. 386).

Like the poet, the therapist must use the medium of language, being forever cognizant of the underlying meanings of words and labels. Saving a life may entail helping the client to view his or her life through a different lens—to find meaning in an existence seemingly shattered by alcohol, violence, or physical or mental illness.

Because the family is a system composed of members in constant and dynamic interaction with each other and because each family has developed a pattern, a rhythm that is more than the sum of its parts, family therapy can tax one's creative energies to the maximum. Taibbi (1992) magnificently captures the essence of couples counseling:

> I am there to help them work their mediums. Like the conductor of an operatic orchestra, I am down in the pit, ready to signal an entrance, ready to augment and support their own voices so that their drama can go forward; like a stage manager, I stand ready to hand them whatever props they may need. I am less concerned with their marriage and more concerned with how they can express their visions. (pp. 42–43)

Social workers often need to be intermediaries between people and their worlds, at times serving as cultural bridges, able to deal in multiple worlds of understanding (Witkin & Harrison, 2001). We learn to listen for the "method in the madness" of personal narratives, to recognize the political ramifications of personal despair, and to work with troubled persons as collaborators in a mutual quest for truth.

Our social work imagination, a term comparable to C. Wright Mills's (1959) concept of the sociological imagination, refers to that combination of empathy, suspension of disbelief, insight, and resourcefulness that makes for exceptional social work practice (van Wormer, 1997). The pronoun *our* is used to provide a more personal touch, a shared enterprise. Social workers need to be intermediaries, to open up the world to another, even as they gain a new or altered perspective from the same source. The energy of mutual discovery feeds on itself, recharges itself. Social work imagination makes it possible to perceive the congruities in the incongruities, to discern the false dualism between the private and the public, to experience the beauty of social work against the bureaucratic assaults, and to see the past in the present and in the present, vestiges of what has gone before. Such artistry is the foundation for a narrative approach to working with people and their ordeals of living (Goldstein, 1999).

Attend one of the regional, national, or international social work conferences. The wealth of ideas exchanged and the political fervor to challenge injustices makes a sharp contrast to some of the dreary empiricism that dominates the conferences of our sister professions that I have attended, and which, if we are not careful, will seep into our own.

In June 1998, the theme of the Canadian National Social Work Conference was "Social Work—Our Roots, Our Future." The Native or Aboriginal contribution to this event (e.g., The Tree of Creation workshop on prisoner treatment) echoed themes on cultural interconnectedness provided by the powerful keynote addresses at the start of each day. At the CSWE conference in February 2003, international and multiethnic perspectives were pervasive. New that year were Asian American and Latino symposia. David Gil's invitational presentation, "Preventing Violence in a Structurally Violent Society: Mission Impossible," brought a standing ovation from a large crowd. By the following year, the global focus had been elevated from a topic for individual presentations to the overarching conference theme, "Social Work in a Global Society."

There are many ways of knowing and, of course, many kinds of knowers, as Ann Hartman (1990) wisely suggested. There are, according to Hartman, researchers, practitioners, and clients:

> Some seekers of truth may take a path that demands distance and objectivity, whereas others rely on deeply personal and empathetic knowing. . . . Some truth seekers strive to predict, whereas others turn to the past for an enhanced understanding of the present. (p. 4)

Successful practice depends on solid *theory.* Without a solid theoretical base, the social worker is unable to critically evaluate his or her client's circumstances and, thus, is unable to comprehend human behavior as being, in part, a product of structural arrangements and power disparities in the family at the micro level and/or pressures and power disparities in the wider social realm. The key question for the social worker to ask at either the family or societal level is: Who benefits? For example, in discrimination against gays and lesbians in the military, the "Who benefits?" question should help us be aware of any vested interests by individuals or social institutions in punishing nonnormative gender behavior. In finding the answers, we are brought face-to-face with intransigent forces in the power structure. Such questioning is at the heart of critical thinking and critical consciousness.

Critical Thinking

Critical thinking can be defined as the ability to put phenomena (problematic and triumphant) in perspective. We need to be able to see parts of the whole—practitioners urge clients to partialize problems or to break them down to manageable parts—and the whole in the parts, or the context. Critical thinking takes us beyond the surface to grasp what is "really going on"; in other words, it helps us to not take the "facts" we read or hear about at face value. Kirst-Ashman (2003) delineated two dimensions that are integral to critical thinking: (1) the questioning of beliefs, statements, and assumptions and the seeking of relevant information concerning the veracity of the claims; and (2) formulating an informed opinion or conclusion based on the evidence.

Most relevant to the subject of social welfare is the ability to discern the underlying, latent purpose (e.g., in the social policy of so-called welfare reform). Critical thinking can help people identify propaganda in the way new government spending policies (e.g., for military buildup or changes in the tax laws) are presented to the public and carried in the mass media. A comparison of national and international accounts will often reveal alternative perspectives on the same piece of information.

The ability to view contemporary social policy in historical and cultural context (see Chapter 3) and to analyze national policy from a global perspective are key aspects of critical analysis. Above all, inasmuch as viewing the world from the perspective of our own cultural beliefs is as inevitable as is thinking in the language we have learned to speak, we need to recognize our own tendency toward ethnocentrism. As social work—particularly Western, English-speaking social work—moves to offer examples of a professional ethos to the rest of the world (and to consider modifications in this ethos based on input from abroad), social workers must be reflective in posture and hospitable to new ideas (Martinez-Brawley, 1999).

See Box 1.2 by social work educator Elisabeth Reichert, who describes how her academic department's study abroad course broadens students' horizons.

Critical consciousness involves an understanding of the encompassing social-structural context of human problems. This term has its roots in the form of collective field activities developed in Latin America under the leadership of Paulo Freire. Having lost confidence in the capacity of their official leaders to bring development to their countries, grassroots organizations formed to work among the poorest and most needy groups of society. Chilean social work education was revolutionized as a result of the pedagogical instruction of Freire, an exiled Brazilian educator living in Chile. From 1965 to 1973, when a military dictatorship intervened to suppress the program and persecute the social workers who were organizing the countryside, a real participatory democracy characterized social work education. Today, throughout Latin America, schools of social work are training their students in this collectivist form of organization. This development has given Latin America social work its own identity that supplements the elements it shares with social work elsewhere (Healy, 2001). Freire's conceptualization of emancipatory pedagogy is still valid today:

> The critically transitive consciousness is characterized by depth in the interpenetration of problems; by the substitution of causal principles for magical explanations; by the testing of one's findings and by openness to revision; by the attempt to avoid distortion when perceiving problems and to avoid preconceived notions when analyzing them; by refusing to transfer responsibility; by rejecting passive positions; by soundness of argumentation; by the practice of dialogue rather than

1.2 Study Abroad—A Unique Learning Experience

Elisabeth Reichert

Since 1996, the School of Social Work at Southern Illinois University at Carbondale has offered a study abroad course in Austria, Germany, and Switzerland. The course usually occurs during the last two weeks of May each year. Twenty students from all parts of the United States participated in the May 2002 course.

Participants in the course visit social service agencies in the three European countries and learn how those countries address social problems. Field visits include a visit to a heroin and methadone distribution center in Switzerland, a country in which drug policies differ significantly from those in the United States. Other field visits involve the study of human rights, health care, and child welfare.

Purpose of Study Abroad

The primary rationale for a study abroad course in social work is to provide students with the opportunity to obtain knowledge about social welfare policies and practices in other cultures not easily obtainable in the classroom. In addition, by directly experiencing social work in other cultures, students can gain insight into universal values held by counterparts.

As the past president of the International Association of Schools of Social Work (IASSW) stated, "Internationalization of social work education is not utopian ideology, but a useful approach to widening and sharing knowledge toward improving the course and experiential offerings of teachers and programs. The concentration of the world into reachable and comparable units makes the sharing more urgent, [even] while [we must continue] recognizing and acknowledging the individual, regional, and cultural differences that remain" (Beless, 1996, p. 2). Issues of concern to social workers are becoming increasingly international in scope. For instance, child abuse and neglect, inadequate health care, and unemployment are issues that confront social workers all over the world. Learning how other countries address these issues can provide valuable information in confronting the same or similar problems at home.

Despite an emphasis on cross-cultural educational exchanges, the social work profession in the United States offers few opportunities for students to study social work in other countries. A likely result of a limited exposure to other cultures is a failure to appreciate or understand what others can offer and a tendency to focus primarily on the familiar.

To free the study of social work from its narrow perspective, development of cross-cultural exchanges is essential. Learning about different policies and practices can help social workers gain insight into different cultures, as well as their own culture. Many countries experience similar social problems, but address these problems in diverse ways.

Although a social work educator may successfully convey aspects of international content to students in a classroom, certain policies and practices may be more effectively taught in the actual setting where the policy or practice occurs. A direct experience in the locale of foreign policies and practices can add context and significance to the learning process that might otherwise be missed. Taking students to the actual site of different policies and practices complements the classroom experience.

Benefits of Study Abroad

A well-structured study abroad course can promote creative thinking and foster intercultural collaboration in education, research, and practice. At a minimum, it can provide knowledge about policies and practices in other countries that would be difficult to obtain in the traditional classroom environment at home. Through this type of educational exchange, students can develop connections to social workers and student counterparts in other countries.

Student Reactions to Course Experiences

Based on the experience of participants in the Southern Illinois University at Carbondale School of Social Work course, reactions to practices and policies of other countries can vary dramatically.

For example, each year students visit a comprehensive drug treatment center in Switzerland where social workers dispense methadone and heroin to people with addictions who meet strict criteria. In conjunction with this visit, students learn about the Swiss policy of publicly dispensing hypodermic needles to prevent the spread of AIDS and other diseases. People with addictions can also purchase needles from machines. Public bathrooms and other areas have receptacles available for hygienic disposal of the needles.

Participants in the course have often stated that, before the course, they had little or no knowledge about Swiss drug practices and policies. There is no true legalization of drugs in Switzerland, as is commonly represented in the United States. Only those with hard-core addictions are eligible for the Swiss program of distributing heroin or methadone. Otherwise, possession of those and other drugs generally is illegal. By actually visiting a Swiss drug center, participants in the course have learned firsthand the truth about Swiss policies and practices.

In response to the field visit to the Swiss drug center, student reactions have varied. One student said, "I personally have never had any contact with a heavy drug user, let alone a whole bunch of them coming to a van to pick up their needles for the day. This was very overwhelming to me, and I know that it sounds as if I am very sheltered, but it is just one thing I have never had to deal with." Some students have expressed approval of the Swiss approach to heroin addiction, while others have been adamantly opposed to any legalization of heroin. The key point, though, is that, for the first time, participants were able to actually see firsthand how legalization of drugs functions in Switzerland, something that was a truly foreign concept to the participants before they took the course.

In general, students have had positive experiences in the course. One student noted, "Before I came to Europe . . . I didn't realize that social workers worked together on issues. I just thought that the United States did their thing and other countries did theirs." Other students have said that it makes sense for countries to learn from each other, to sometimes look at social work from a different perspective, and that "we should all study how other countries help their people and learn from it." All students have noted the importance of field visits and interacting with social workers from the host countries. One student said that "you can read or hear about different things forever, but until you have experienced them, you cannot truly understand."

Most participants in the course have agreed that the course has broadened their perspective about social work in the United States and other countries. Students have commented favorably about the more extensive government intervention in the host countries than in the United States regarding social issues. Some have felt "we could do more for our people in terms of government support." The vast majority of students have stated that exposure to Austrian, German, and Swiss social work policies opened their eyes to the existence of different policies. "This course definitely led me to think differently about social work issues such as health care, drugs, and orphans," one student said after the course.

However, a few students have adopted a more nationalistic sentiment toward social work: "I feel that social work in the United States is ahead of other countries; we really have an edge on other countries because of the way we are educated." This comment appears to indicate that, at least for one student, exposure to other ways of social work practice can reinforce an ethnocentric perception of social work education.

On the whole, though, over the several years in which the university course has occurred, participant responses have clearly indicated benefits from experiencing different concepts of policy and practice. Students have emphasized that they felt they obtained knowledge that could not have been adequately conveyed through classroom teaching in their home country. This exposure to a unique cultural and learning experience provides the foundation of all study abroad programs.

REFERENCE

Beless, D. (1996). Learning from our international colleagues. *CSWE Social Work Education Reporter*, 44(3), 2.

Source: E. Reichert, "The Role of a Study Abroad Course in Undergraduate Social Work Education," *Journal of Baccalaureate Social Work*, 4(1), 61–71. Reprinted by permission of Elisabeth Reichert.

polemics; by receptivity to the new for reasons beyond mere novelty and by the good sense not to reject the old just because it is old—by accepting what is valid in both the old and new. (p. 17)

Feminist educator bell hooks (1994) articulated Freierian premises in terms of "teaching/learning to transgress" and identified critical thinking as "the primary element allowing the possibility of change" (p. 202). Within social work, similarly, feminist therapy stresses worker-client collaboration at every stage of the therapy process and the linking of political and personal issues (see Bricker-Jenkins & Lockett, 1995; van Wormer, 2001). A related aspect of critical thinking is cultural competence (described earlier in this chapter), an indispensable ingredient for working in a multiculturally diverse and complex environment.

Summary and Conclusion

The purpose of this introductory chapter has been to provide the vocabulary and theoretical context for viewing social welfare internationally and multidimensionally. Central to our understanding of the American welfare state is a familiarity with some of the basic concepts from social psychology (e.g., the nature of prejudice and victim blaming), sociology (functionalism and power), economics (globalization and the market economy), and anthropology (ecosystems theory and cultural competence). These concepts are just a part of the vast knowledge base relevant to grasping the psychological, political, and social dimensions of social welfare. Social work, the ultimate applied social science, embraces an interdisciplinary knowledge base under the rubric of ecosystems theory. Drawing upon the terminology of the ecosystems perspective, the American welfare state can be viewed both within the context of a seeming jumble of contradictory goals and also against the backdrop of a more or less cohesive set of enduring cultural values.

Consistent with social work's focus on the person-in-the-environment, the focus of this book is on the *country-in-the-world*. The country is the United States, the topic is the social welfare system, and the framework is a holistic or ecosystems approach.

The reality of global interdependence extends to everyday social work practice. The increasing numbers of undocumented immigrants, refugees, and cross-cultural child welfare cases reflect the growing diversity of the U.S. population. In this chapter, the case has been made that to provide competent service, persons in the helping professions need familiarity with the values and customs of diversified populations. At the policy-making level, knowledge of other countries' social welfare innovations can contribute to the resolution of domestic problems. While comparative study of other Western welfare systems introduces the student to sophisticated social welfare options, a recognition of a commonality of social problems between the United States and countries in the eastern and southern hemispheres is crucial to the amelioration of mutual concerns. The ubiquity of organized crime, terrorism, drug abuse, and disease epidemics graphically illustrates the interdependence of nations. Other problems such as high infant mortality, homelessness, and street crime represent the shared failure of nations to meet the needs of all their citizens. In short, for creative, well-informed policy making on the local or global level, a multicultural worldview is paramount.

That globalization, or the dictates of the global market, is an ever-present force shaping each nation's social policies is a major theme of this chapter, one that will surface again and again throughout the pages of this book as we explore political and human rights issues across the life span. Problems connected to the global economy constitute opportunities for social transformation through united social action. This is where the influence of international social work may come into play. It may seem ambitious and even unrealistic of NASW leaders to seek to make an impact on world policy. And yet, if we listen to the words of our leaders and recognize the significant role that IFSW (an official NGO that reports to the U.N.) plays, we can only wonder what has taken the U.S. social work profession so long to follow this course. As the headline in *NASW News* (Slavin, 2002) proclaims, "The Profession Has [a] Global Role" to play. (Also see Box 1.1.) The answer to the question "Should the United States be the world's social worker?" (p. 4) is in the affirmative as well.

By the same token, the world has a role to play in U.S. social policy. There is much to be learned from social welfare policies and programs in other societies. Consistent with the goals of critical thinking, learning about social welfare policies in other lands and of policies related to human rights can help us all comprehend connections between the structure of economic and political systems and their social outcomes. Outcomes, of course, often show a sizable gap between rhetoric and reality.

Highlighted in this chapter was the uniqueness of social work, a profession with a mission. Social work is unique among the helping professions in its policy focus and unique among policy-making bodies in its counseling function. Guiding social work, in theory if not always in practice, is the empowerment framework. The general expectation is that social workers will draw on a strengths approach as both a model and a method.

In this age of predictability, accountability, and number-crunching, sometimes there is little room for the kind of growth that comes from nurturance and the give-and-take of unplanned dialogue. Effective social work practice requires the best use of what I call our social work imagination to help people find a will and a way to go on in the face of awesome difficulty. For the strengths-based therapist, the method is first listening—listening to the client's story, not passively and uncreatively, but with full attention to the rhythms and patterns—and then, when the time is right, observing and sharing until, through mutual discovery, events can be seen in terms of some kind of whole. The challenge is to find themes of hope and courage and, in so naming them, to reinforce them.

The empowerment perspective is not intended to be applied solely to individual coping strategies. Not only is the personal also political, but economic and social hardships must be understood to take place within the context of global causality as well. Consistent with the person-in-the-environment and empowerment-in-the-person conceptualization, the focus is on multifaceted intervention. In the generalist tradition of social work, social workers learn to intervene at any point—at the individual, family, neighborhood, or societal levels. Both as citizens and as professionals, social workers look toward social policy; change efforts directed here have the most potential for improving social services and challenging injustice. This takes us into the realm of social values, the topic to which we now turn in Chapter 2.

Thought Questions

1. How does the opening quote "Knowledge is power" relate to the subject matter of globalization?
2. Discuss three ways in which social work is a unique profession.
3. What is the mission of social work? How does this relate to ethical values in general?
4. "The world is growing ever smaller." Discuss.
5. Review Box 1.1. How can social workers help give globalization a human face?
6. Is globalization strictly an economic phenomenon? Discuss positive aspects of international interconnectedness.
7. Discuss ways in which the average social worker encounters global problems in everyday work.
8. Review the definition of *welfare state*. To what extent does the United States qualify as a welfare state?
9. Compare the terms *developing country* and *sustainable development*. What is the effect of globalization on the latter?
10. Discuss contemporary military buildup in terms of manifest and latent functions.
11. Describe the notion of regulating the poor.
12. What does Orwell's *1984* have to say about our government today?
13. "Marx and Engels' analysis of the world trade performances has more relevance today than in 1848." Discuss.
14. How can color-blind and gender-blind notions be a denial of realities?
15. Give some examples of the concepts of *ethnocentrism* and *blaming the victim*.
16. Explain how the "authoritarian personality" relates to prejudice. Refer to child-rearing techniques.
17. Describe some ways that ethnic and racial prejudice can be prevented.
18. Discuss the qualities of a social work imagination.
19. From the perspective of critical thinking, what kinds of questions might one ask about a given social policy?
20. What is the personal/political configuration?

References

Adorno, T., Frankel-Brunswick, E., Levinson, D., & Sanford, N. (1950). *The authoritarian personality.* New York: Harper & Brothers.

Allport, G. (1981/1954). *The nature of prejudice.* Reading, MA: Addison-Wesley.

Bacon, F. (1597). Religious meditations, of heresies. *The Quotations Page.* Retrieved from http://www.quotationspage.com

Barker, R. (2003). *The social work dictionary* (5th ed.). Washington, DC: NASW Press.

Barretta-Herman, A. (2003). IASSW begins analyzing world census data. *Social Work Education Reporter, 51*(2), 21.

Berger, R., McBreen, J., & Rifkin, M. (1996). *Human behavior: A perspective for the helping professions* (4th ed.) Boston: Addison-Wesley.

Bibus, A. (1995). Reflections on social work from Cuernavaca, Mexico. *International Social Work, 38*(3), 243–252.

Bricker-Jenkins, M., & Lockett, P. (1995). Women: Direct practice. In R. L. Edwards (Ed.), *Encyclopedia of social work* (19th ed., pp. 2529–2539). Washington, DC: NASW Press.

Bryson, L. (1992). *Welfare and the state: Who benefits?* New York: St. Martin's Press.

Chicago Tribune. (2003, May 5). SARS illustrates how shrinking world means growing virus peril. Reprinted in *Waterloo-Cedar Falls Courier,* p. A1.

Cooley, C. (1983/1909). *Social organization: A study of the larger mind.* New Brunswick, NJ: Transaction.

Council on Social Work Education (CSWE). (2003). *Handbook of accreditation standards and procedures* (5th ed.). Alexandria, VA: Author.

de Roche, C. (1989). Empathy and the anthropological imagination. *Practicing Anthropology, 11*(3), 6–7.

Dolgoff, R., & Feldstein, D. (1999). *Understanding social welfare* (5th ed.). Boston: Allyn & Bacon.

Elliott, D., & Mayadas, N. (1999). Infusing global perspectives into social work practice. In C. Ramanthan & R. Link (Eds.), *All our futures: Principles and resources for social work practice in a global era* (pp. 52–59). Belmont, CA: Wadsworth.

Esber, G. (1989). Anthropological contributions for social work education. *Practicing Anthropology, 11*(3), 4, 11.

Faulkner, W. (1936). *Absalom, Absalom!* New York: Random House.

Faulkner, W. (1951). *Requiem for a nun.* New York: Random House.

Ford, P. (2001, September 27). Why do they hate us? *Christian Science Monitor.*

Freire, P. (1973). *Education for critical consciousness.* New York: Seabury Press.

Fulbright, W. (1966). *The arrogance of power.* New York: Vintage.

GlenMaye, L. (1997). Empowerment of women. In L. M. Gutiérrez, R. J. Parsons, & E. O. Cox (Eds.), *Empowerment in social work practice* (pp. 29–51). Belmont, CA: Brooks/Cole.

Goffman, E. (1961). *Asylums.* Garden City, NY: Anchor.

Goldstein, H. (1999, July–August). The limits and art of understanding in social work practice. *Journal of Contemporary Human Services, 80*(4), 385–395.

Gould, A. (1993). *Capitalist welfare systems: A comparison of Japan, Britain, and Sweden.* New York: Longman.

Hartman, A. (1990). Many ways of knowing. *Social Work, 35*(1), 3–4.

Haynes, K. S., & Mickelson, J. S. (2002). *Affecting change: Social workers in the political arena* (5th ed.). Boston: Allyn & Bacon.

Healy, L. (1992). *Introducing international development content in the social work curriculum.* Washington, DC: NASW Press.

Healy, L. (2001). *International social work: Professional action in an interdependent world.* New York: Oxford.

Healy, L. (2002, February 15). Internationalizing social work curriculum in the twenty-first century. *Electronic Journal of Social Work, 1*(1), 1–15.

Healy, L. (2003). Regional interests sustain NACASSW and partners. *Social Work Education Reporter, 51*(2), 17–18.

Herrnstein, R., & Murray, C. (1994). *The bell curve.* New York: Free Press.

hooks, b. (1994). *Teaching to transgress: Education as the practice of freedom.* New York: Routledge.

Human Rights Watch. (2002, December 17). Afghanistan: Women still not "liberated." Retrieved from http://www.hrw.org/press/2002/12/herat1217.htm

Ife, J. (2000). Localized needs and a globalized economy. In W. Rowe (Ed.), *Social work and globalization* (pp. 50–64). Ottawa: Canadian Association of Social Workers.

Jost, J. T., Kruglanski, A. W., Glaser, J., & Sulloway, F. J. (2003). Political conservatism as motivated social cognition. *Psychological Bulletin, 129*(3), 339–376.

Kahn, A., & Kamerman, M. (2002). International aspects of social policy. In J. Midgely, M. Tracey, & M. Livermore (Eds.), *The handbook of social policy* (pp. 479–491). Thousand Oaks, CA: Sage.

Karger, H., & Stoesz, D. (2001). *American social welfare policy: A pluralist approach* (4th ed.). Boston: Allyn & Bacon.

Kendall, K. (1989). Women at the helm: Three extraordinary leaders. *Affilia, 4*(1), 23–32.

Khinduka, S. (2002, September 19). Installation address. St. Louis: George Warren Brown School of Social Work.

Kirst-Ashman, K. K. (2003). *Introduction to social work and social welfare: Critical thinking perspectives.* Pacific Grove, CA: Brooks/Cole.

Kreitzer, L. (2002, June). Globalization and indigenization: Power issues in social knowledge. Unpublished thesis proposal: University of Calgary.

Lee, J. (2001). *The empowerment approach to social work practice: Building the beloved community.* New York: Columbia University Press.

Lerner, M. (1971). All the world loathes a loser. *Psychology Today, 5*(1), 54–56, 66.

Levine, A. J. (2002). The politics of the authoritarian personality. *World and I, 17*(12), 270–278.

London, R. R. (2000, June 26). Knocking on Europe's door. *Time.* Retrieved from http://www.time.com

Los Angeles Times. (2002, June 25). Study: Earth's resources dwindling. Reprinted in *Waterloo-Cedar Falls Courier,* p. A2.

Macionis, J. (2004). *Society: The basics* (7th ed.). Upper Saddle River, NJ: Prentice-Hall.

Marmor, T., Matow, J., & Harvey, P. (1990). *America's misunderstood welfare state: Persistent myths, enduring realities.* New York: Basic Books.

Martinez-Brawley, E. (1999). Social work, postmodernism and higher education. *International Social Work, 42*(3), 333–346.

Marx, K., & Engels, F. (1963/1848). *The communist manifesto.* New York: Russell & Russell.

Mary, N., & Morris, T. (1994). The future and social work: A global perspective. *Journal of Multicultural Social Work, 3*(4), 80–101.

Mead, M. (1972). *Blackberry winter: My earlier years.* New York: William Morrow.

Merton, R. (1949). *Social theory and social structure.* Glencoe, IL: Free Press.

Miller, K. (2002, December 16). Is it globaloney? *Newsweek,* E4–E8.

Mills, C. W. (1959). *The sociological imagination.* New York: Oxford University Press.

Morales, A., & Sheafor, B. (2004). *Social work: A profession of many faces* (10th ed.). Boston: Allyn & Bacon.

Nakanishi, M., & Rittner, B. (1992). The inclusionary cultural model. *Journal of Social Work Education, 28*(1): 27–35.

National Association of Social Workers (NASW). (1996). *Code of ethics.* Washington, DC: NASW Press.

National Association of Social Workers (NASW). (2003). International policy on human rights. In NASW, *Social work speaks: NASW policy statements 2003–2006* (pp. 209–217). Washington, DC: NASW Press.

O'Neill, J. (2002, September). Profession boosts its international profile. *NASW News,* p. 4.

Orwell, G. (1961/1948). *1984.* New York: Harcourt, Brace, Jovanovich.

Piven, F., & Cloward, R. (1993). *Regulating the poor: The functions of public welfare.* New York: Vintage Books.

Podolefsky, A., & Brown, P. (2001). Introduction. In A. Podolefsky & P. Brown (Eds.), *Applying cul-tural anthropology: An introductory reader* (5th ed.). New York: McGraw-Hill.

Popple, P. R., & Leighninger, L. (2004). *The policy-based profession: An introduction to social welfare policy analysis for social workers* (3rd ed.). Boston: Allyn & Bacon.

Prigoff, A. (1999). Global social and economic justice issues. In C. Ramanathan & R. Link (Eds.), *All our futures: Principles and resources for social work practice in a global era* (pp. 156–173). Pacific Grove, CA: Brooks/Cole.

Prigoff, A. (2000). *Economics for social workers.* Belmont, CA: Wadsworth.

Ramanathan, C. S., & Link, R. (1999). *All our futures: Principles and resources for social work practice in a global era.* Pacific Grove, CA: Brooks/Cole.

Reichert, E. (2003). *Social work and human rights: A foundation for policy and practice.* New York: Columbia University Press.

Robbins, S., Chatterjee, P., & Canda, E. (1999). Ideology, scientific theory, and social work practice. *Families in Society, 80*(4), 374–384.

Rowe, W., Hanley, J., Moreno, E., & Mould, J. (2000). Voices of social work practice: International reflections on the effects of globalization. In B. Rowe (Ed.), *Social work and globalization* (pp. 65–87). Ottawa: Canadian Association of Social Workers.

Roy, A. (2002, September 2). Not again. *The Guardian.* Retrieved from http://www.guardian .co.uk

Ryan, W. (1976). *Blaming the victim.* New York: Random House.

Saleebey, D. (2002). Introduction: Power in the people. In D. Saleebey (Ed.), *The strengths perspective in social work practice* (3rd ed., pp. 1–22). Boston: Allyn & Bacon.

Schneider, R., & Lester, L. (2000). *Social work advocacy: A new framework for action.* Belmont, CA: Wadsworth.

Sherif, M., & Sherif, C. (1966). *Groups in harmony and tension.* New York: Octagon Books.

Shuman, M. (2002, July–August). The end of globalization. *Utne Reader,* 51–53.

Slavin, P. (2002, March). Profession has global role: Social work's international stature is explored. *NASW News, 47*(3), 1–2.

Sternberg, S. (2002, July 11). Report: AIDS to orphan 25 million. *USA Today,* p. 5A.

Sumner, W. (1940/1906). *Folkways.* Boston: Ginn & Co.

Taibbi, R. (1992, October). Creativity: Working the medium. *Family Therapy Networker,* 42–43.

Taylor, Z. (1999). Values, theories and methods in social work education: A culturally transferable core? *International Social Work, 42*(3), 309–318.

Torczyner, J. (2000). Globalization, inequality and peace building: What social work can do. In B. Rowe (Ed.), *Social work and globalization* (pp. 123–146). Ottawa: Canadian Association of Social Workers.

United Nations Development Programme. (2001, July 10). Norway is now first, U.S. sixth in human development. In *Human Development Report 2001.* New York: United Nations.

U.N. Wire. (2002, August 21). Cambodia: Robinson calls for end to sex slavery. New York: United Nations Foundation.

van Wormer, K. (1997). *Social welfare: A world view.* Belmont, CA: Wadsworth.

van Wormer, K. (2001). *Counseling female offenders and victims: A strengths-restorative approach.* New York: Springer.

van Wormer, K., & Davis, D. R. (2003). *Addiction treatment: A strengths perspective.* Pacific Grove, CA: Brooks/Cole.

Weber, M. (1979/1922). *Economy and society.* Berkeley: University of California Press.

Webster's New World Dictionary of the English Language (3rd ed.). (1991). New York: Simon & Schuster.

Weick, A. (1999). Guilty knowledge. (Knowledge building). *Families in Society, 80*(4), 327–339.

Will, G. (2002, November 11). Eurasia and the epidemic. *Newsweek,* 80.

Wilson, G., & Whitmore, E. (2000). *Seeds of fire: Social development in an era of globalism.* New York: Apex Press.

Witkin, S., & Harrison, W. (2001, October). Whose evidence and for what purpose? *Social Work, 46*(4), 293–296.

Zastrow, C. (2004). *Introduction to social work and social welfare: Empowering people.* Belmont, CA: Brooks/Cole.

A four leaf clover is a break in pattern, a slight dissonance, which can only be seen against an awareness of the orderly configuration in the grass. . . . Often a dissonance, the interruption in one pattern you have learned to expect, is key to a larger pattern.

MARY CATHERINE BATESON, 1984, PP. 202–204

American Social Values and International Social Work

© Rupert van Wormer

Before reviewing the unique history of social work as a profession, which is the task of Chapter 3, a historical and sociological overview of the *context* in which social work has evolved is in order. This focus on context is crucial for both practice and policy considerations. Social work practice exists in a certain time and space; as thoughtful commentators have indicated, it can be neither acultural nor ahistorical (Kreitzer, 2002; Payne, 1997).

In the policy arena, likewise, a clear understanding of the cultural ethos is crucial to effecting social change. Such an understanding can help us to identify stumbling blocks that might impede such change, as well as possibilities that might be exploited in boosting progressive initiatives.

To speak of cultural ethos is to speak of cultural values. Key questions to consider in our professional endeavors, following C. W. Mills (1959), are: What values do people cherish? To what extent are these values supported by the growing trends of our era? And to what extent are these values threatened (e.g., by rapid technological or cultural change)? In the latter situation, as Mills informs us, public issues may develop into personal troubles. When this happens on a large scale, personal troubles may become social problems. How society responds to such problems is a product of the social values.

The primary purpose of this chapter is to delineate the major, agreed-upon American values and to view each value in an international context. Values are viewed not as discrete phenomena but as elements along a continuum, for example, individualism versus collectivism, punitiveness versus compassion. A basic assumption of this formulation is that all societies subscribe to relatively the same values (e.g., materialism), but to different degrees. It is a question of priority. This brings us to the second major purpose of this discussion, which is to reveal how priorities may vary across ethnic and cultural lines. Some Native American tribes may prioritize personal responsibilities over punctuality, for example. The work ethic is clearly prioritized in some Asian countries, such as South Korea and Japan, over family recreation or relaxation.

A third purpose of this chapter is to describe American social work values, which both reflect and contradict mainstream belief systems. The emphasis will be on the relationship between cultural ethos and the social welfare system. Throughout our discussion, we will be cognizant of both consistencies and dilemmas in each value dimension and of how difficult consensus is to achieve in pluralistic societies such as the United States. The final section of the chapter briefly describes cultural clash on the strategically located island of Guam and international developments in social work education from various selected regions of the world—Chile, the Caribbean, South Korea, Cuba, and Canada. Looming through all these case examples is the lesson that to be culturally relevant and meaningful, social work must adapt professional modalities to the norms of a given region. That the Global North has much to learn from practices of the Global South is a further lesson accruing to these histories.

Societal Values and Social Policy

In confronting what Bruce Jansson (2001) termed, in his book with a title of the same name, "the reluctant welfare state," our first task is to come to terms with our ideological heritage. The basis of this heritage is found in a people's social values. Values are defined by anthropologists Podolefsky and Brown (1994) as "the ideals of a culture that are concerned with appropriate goals and behavior" (p. 284). Contradictions come into play in the gap that often exists between the ideal and the real, for example, the ideal of racial equality versus the reality of institutional racism.

Social psychologists, as we saw in Chapter 1, posit that through interaction with significant others, we come to see ourselves as others see us: Through internalizing these perceptions, we come to take on the social values of these others. This is the process of socialization. Social psychologists have studied social value orientations in small groups (Baron & Graziano, 1991). Personal values of cooperation, altruism, competitiveness, and individualism are revealed in problem-solving laboratory situations. Cooperators are more inclined to make prosocial, mutually beneficial choices than are individualists or competitors. Generalizing from the microcosm to society, it can be seen that socialization of norms of helpfulness and cooperation is congruent with the dominant value orientations that support the welfare of the group or community. In making prosocial, mutually beneficial choices, cooperators and altruists demonstrate values that are congruent with the guiding principles of the social welfare state.

In this chapter and throughout this book, when we speak of social welfare, we are talking also of social justice. The link between social welfare and social justice is that they both have to do with the distribution of resources. Social justice, as we saw in Chapter 1, is the preeminent social work value. In contemporary social work, the term *social justice* has come to mean the right of citizens of the welfare state to have their needs met and to be treated fairly (Barusch, 2002; Graham, Swift, & Delaney, 2000; Lee, 2001). Along these lines, Healy (2001) writes of social justice as distributive justice or principles relating to how scarce resources are allocated, whether the allocation is based on merit or equality. (Chapter 6 expands upon this definition to encompass a human rights framework.)

How is the wealth in a given country distributed? Which should be given greater weight—equality or freedom? How much poverty and misery is one state or nation willing to tolerate? Why are there such vast sociopolitical differences in the provision of services around the world? The answers can be sought in the predominant social values of a people, or the national ethos. The means of ensuring the welfare of a people, in fact, may be determined as much by the national mood—the values and beliefs of the day and the place—as by the economic circumstances. In the final analysis, it is not the level of a nation's wealth but the sharing of resources that reveals the society's social consciousness. The value positions of the majority (elites) in society invariably, according to Gil (1998), influence the development of policy and constrain the range of changes of the status quo. Social values and social policies are in constant interaction, with social values shaping political legislation while legislation promotes and reinforces the values of society. Consider, for example, how once segregation was ended in the Deep South, the acceptance of the principle of racial integration became the norm, especially strong among the younger generations.

We cannot leave the subject of the interplay between values and policy without recognizing the role of the media in the equation. Media presentations, especially widely watched television broadcasts, both reflect and promote values. The power of the media to shape public opinion was explored by Krugman (2003) in a *New York Times* opinion piece, "Behind the Great Divide." The great divide at issue was the difference in views toward what was then the pending war against Iraq. Krugman compared U.S. television news headlines that proclaimed "Antiwar Rallies Delight Iraq" with a very different, much more positive, portrayal of the huge rallies that took place throughout the world. This difference in reporting, as Krugman speculated, may relate to different perceptions internationally regarding the role of the media. The American perception may be that the job of the media is to prepare the public for a coming war. The European media, apparently having a different agenda, are far more critical of U.S. foreign policy. Accordingly, opinion polls, even in Britain, show that citizens ranked the United States as the world's most dangerous nation. "Why America Scares the World" was a *Newsweek* cover story, published immediately before the bombs started falling on Iraq (Zakaria, 2003). What scares Europeans and others, as Zakaria argues, is how America uses its power—militarily and economically—to dominate the world. A recent Associated Press (2004) opinion poll found that a majority of people living in the two countries bordering the United States and five major European countries surveyed said they thought the Iraq war has fueled terrorism. In contrast, only a third of the Americans felt this way.

Certainly, differing mass media portrayals can be expected to reflect and promote social welfare policies as well. Here, again, there is a great divide between American attitudes and the much more liberal European attitudes concerning the role of the government in providing social benefits. There are, of course, historical/cultural distinctions as well.

The welfare state evolved as a historically purposive phenomenon that differed considerably among individual nations in accordance with predominant religious and cultural strains. Building on de Tocqueville's (1951/1835) and sociologist Robin Williams's (1979) widely cited array of crucial American values (work ethic, equality, individualism, democracy, etc.), I have delineated nine value dimensions of most direct relevance to the U.S. social welfare system. These value dimensions are:

1. Work versus leisure
2. Equal opportunity versus equality
3. Mobility versus stability
4. Competition versus cooperation
5. Individualism versus collectivism
6. Independence versus interconnectedness

7. Materialism versus spirituality
8. Nuclear family versus extended family
9. Moralism versus compassion

If you view this set of value dimensions as two columns, the items in the left-hand column are closely interrelated; they represent the essence of American values and, with the possible exception of moralism, the basic qualities of modernization. In any case, the above set of continua serves as a framework for the following discussion of American cultural attributes. The language "this versus that," following Erikson's (1963) famous model of challenges across the life span (trust versus mistrust, etc.), is meant to indicate not a dichotomy but a continuum of attributes and characteristics found in human society. Keep that fact in mind as you study the various cultural characteristics; in reality, there are no pure forms of such phenomena, but only degrees of one thing or another.

Work versus Leisure

The right to work—implying the right to be provided with a job—and the right to leisure are embodied in the United Nations (U.N.) Declaration on Human Rights (refer to Chapter 6). Neither is recognized in the U.S. Constitution as a given.

Work, in the sense of the work ethic, is one of the oldest and most enduring (if not endearing) of the American cultural attributes. The notion of the work ethic encompasses the traits that the typical employer desires: punctuality, efficiency, and productivity. Workers deficient in these qualities will be eliminated. This impulse has its roots in the religious beliefs of the early colonists, the Puritans, beliefs later bolstered in the secular sayings of Benjamin Franklin.

The value placed on hard work is closely tied to moralism. Few ideas, as Wagner (1994) indicates, dominate Western political and social discourse as much as the idealized work ethic—"the view that all who are able-bodied and of working age have a moral obligation to work and that they are slothful or pathological if they do not" (p. 718). Without launching into a historical thesis, I will briefly set forth the principles described so brilliantly by the German sociologist Max Weber (1958/1905) in his classic, *The Protestant Ethic and the Spirit of Capitalism.* Weber compared work productivity levels in Protestant and Catholic regions of Germany, and elsewhere, as evidence for his theory correlating Protestantism and capitalism. Protestantism emphasized the autonomy of the individual and repudiated dependence on the Church, priesthood, and ritual, according to Weber. The qualities of self-discipline, hard work, and communal service were viewed as likely signs of salvation. Martin Luther's belief in work as a "calling" gave Protestantism a singularly practical bent. John Calvin, who was Luther's counterpart in France and later Switzerland, provided the first great systematic formulation of the Reformation faith. Taking Luther's argument one step further, Calvin introduced the notion of predestination into the Protestant vocabulary. Predestination is the doctrine of God's election or choice of souls to salvation or damnation. The interpretation of predestination, carried by way of England and Scotland (through the preaching of John Knox) to America, was that those predestined to salvation could be identified in this life through the evidence of their wealth. Although one's fate was sealed, in a sense, Calvinist philosophy posited that indications of this fate could be detected on earth. Using this line of reasoning, the wealthy could justify not only their wealth but also their exploitation of workers to accumulate it (Day, 2002). The belief system also legitimated forcing people to work for their own good. Max Weber (1958/1905) described Calvinism as that which was not leisure and enjoyment but activity that served to increase the glory of God. Waste of time thus was perceived as a deadly sin. And condemnation of the sinner was justified.

With its emphasis on individual achievement, frugality, and opportunity, the creed of Calvinism has very much affected the American character, even long after the direct religious connection has been lost. In this vein, the 18th-century inventor and atheist Benjamin Franklin espoused the principles of the Protestant work ethic in his often quoted sayings, for example, "early to bed, early to rise makes a man healthy, wealthy, and wise"; "the early bird catches the worm"; "time is money"; and "a penny saved is a penny earned."

In locating the roots of the American work ethic, we need to take into account geographical as well as ideological factors. As settlers arrived on the bountiful American landscape, there was no limit to the possibilities for work that needed to be done. So the work ethic was continually rewarded at every turn; in the American colonies, unemployment was unknown. Just how intransigent was the religioeconomic ideology is seen in its ability to outlast its religious roots and to influence welfare policy to this very day.

"Why Americans Work So Hard" was the title of an article in *Business Week* (Koretz, 2001). Observers, according to the article, have long remarked on the sharp disparity between American and European work habits. According to international economic sources, Americans average just under 2,000 hours of work per employed person annually compared to just over 1,500 in Germany. The workweeks in the United States are longer and the vacations considerably shorter. The explanation cited in the article is that the large pay disparities in the United States lure workers to work harder for a chance of advancement. My argument is that the very system encouraging wage differentials and rewards for long hours of work is part of the cultural pattern.

Indeed, a focal point of American culture is work and preparation for work. Through one's occupation or profession, an individual gains status and a sense of self-importance. Equality of incomes from work is seen as undesirable because of the feared deleterious effects on work incentives and because of the detraction from social esteem which high pay engenders. The work ethic is a highly valued attribute in the United States; leisure time for workers is among the least in the industrialized world. Since 1996, when welfare reform was introduced under the Clinton administration, millions of adults and their children (from 5.1 million to 2.2 million) have been removed from the welfare rolls. "Many in Congress," according to a *Business Week* report, are playing "who can be more pro-work than the other guy" (Bernstein & Starr, 2002).

Before I visited Korea, I generally agreed with the literature claiming that the American work ethic is the strongest in the world. Then I learned of a land so competitive that children rarely play; they are tutored during most waking hours until their education culminates in rigorous university entrance exams. In late adolescence, students return home from crash courses at midnight (I saw them riding the buses) only to be awakened, according to my Korean hosts, for school in the wee hours of the next morning. Consistent with the Korean work focus is the situation in a neighboring country, Japan. An English teacher (Butler, 2003) from Texas who lives in Yamogota, Japan, observes:

> It's fair to say that Japanese people are unbelievably busy. Working ten hours a day, and often coming in on days off, they rarely take a vacation of more than three or four days. A straight week is a hedonistic luxury. Students have less than a month for summer vacation, and even then they have all kinds of assignments to do. (p. 65)

My experience of the Norwegian work ethic was that Norwegians are industrious people but that much of their work is done during off hours—building cabins in the woods, training and grooming their dogs, and washing the windows. Many jobs are only six hours per day; little work is done at Easter, Christmas, and in July. The right to leisure is a fiercely guarded right.

In France, too, leisure is one of the top values, as indicated in surveys. Bréchon (2000) summarizes survey data of a random sample of almost 2,000 French citizens. French surveys reveal the most important aspects of life are prioritized as follows:

Family	Leisure
Work	Religion
Friends and acquaintances	Politics

The emphasis that emerged from the national survey reported by Bréchon is that French people want to balance their professional lives with other activities, particularly leisure activities.

Although American workers may not see leisure time as a right, a lot of people are beginning to wonder if the "rat race" is worth it. In an article in the *Christian Science Monitor,* entitled "Long Workdays Draw Backlash" (McLaughlin, 1998), we read of workers on strike at U.S. West and Northwest Airlines; a major issue was forced overtime. As the interests of global competition take precedence over the worker, manufacturing plants are moving into a pattern of alternating day/night 12-hour shifts. Workers get a 3-day weekend every other week. The impact on their family life, health, and safety is enormous. In her thought-provoking column, Molly Ivins (2001) describes the stress of even the usual 8-hour shift in a factory as grueling. The addition of 4 extra hours can be downright inhumane and dangerous in factories with already high personal injury rates. We will cover more specifics of the "blue-collar" working world in Chapter 4.

Equal Opportunity versus Equality

Closely related to the work ethic is the belief system that says "America is the land of opportunity." Opportunity means the opportunity to fail as well as to achieve success. Equality is used here in the European sense of equalizing social benefits and living standards "from the cradle to the grave." Opportunity is the counterpart not of equality but of inequality in the sense that when taxes are low, economic incentives for business are favorable, and when income disparities are high, the climate is ripe for some to "be more equal than others."

The American system of mass education that is relatively accessible and affordable is consistent with the belief in equal opportunity. When we talk about people's beliefs that success is achieved through hard work, we tap into the value system that fuels "the American Dream" (Draut, 2002). Draut, a nationally recognized expert on political polls, laments the inherent conflict in American values: the belief that you can get ahead with hard work and that people must take responsibility for their own economic well-being. Consistent with the North American opportunity ethos are minority-targeted early education programs, job training, and higher educational, "opportunity-enhancing programs to help disadvantaged individuals compete on an equal footing with more privileged youth."

Wilson (1996), in the book *When Work Disappears,* makes an interesting point. Compensating programs receive public support in the United States because they reinforce the belief that the allocation of jobs and economic rewards should be based on individual effort. Such opportunity-enhancing programs (unlike quotas or preferential initiatives) are "less likely to be perceived as challenging the values of individualism and the work ethic" (p. 204). Such government-sponsored overtures, in themselves, provide substance to the widely held belief that the road to upward mobility is open to those who "play by the rules."

There is undeniably much truth to the "rags-to-riches" ideology. With ambition, luck, education, and a support system, refugees and other immigrants often do achieve their dreams. Through my mother's refugee work in Bowling Green, Kentucky, I have had the privilege of following the success stories of families who arrived from the former Soviet Union and Bosnia with almost nothing and without even the ability to speak English. Today they are doctors, accountants, an aircraft maintenance engineer, a beautician, paralegal assistant, restaurant owner, musician, and one, sad to say, thief. The United States and Canada are two nations in the world with relatively open and supportive immigration policies. The United States prides itself on being a "nation of immigrants," and Canada similarly exults in its multicultural mosaic patterns of appreciation of differences. This is not to say that the treatment of immigrants does not leave much to be desired (see Chapter 4), only that opportunity for asylum seekers and those in special occupational categories is better in the less-crowded countries with strong traditions of resettlement. (Europe's policy is geared toward temporary asylum rather than assimilation of refugees.)

An important distinction needs to be made between values of equality of opportunity (the North American value orientation) and equality of living standards (the Nordic model). (See Nelson & Shavitt, 2002.) Often the impetus toward equality means differential treatment of unlike people to equalize the result. Consider this news story from Finland, as reported on the radio broadcast All Things Considered ("Speeding in Finland," 2002). "Like other

Scandinavian countries," according to the broadcast, "Finland imposes fines based on income." So it happened that a wealthy man (his income along with his wealth calculated along with the fine on the police officer's computer) was fined $103,000 for driving over the speed limit! The purpose of this approach? To ensure that the penalty will hurt as much whether you are rich or poor.

Societies that pride themselves on egalitarianism take an *institutional* approach to social welfare provision. At the opposite end of the continuum is the *residual* or "safety-net" approach characteristic of what we have in the United States. These terms were originally coined by Wilensky and Lebeaux (1958) as ideal-typical constructs to contrast the narrow role the government plays in providing social services in some societies with an approach geared toward the needs of the people.

In the residually oriented society, of which the United States and Japan are prime examples, a stigma is attached to receiving welfare aid. The causes of welfare clients' difficulties are often seen as rooted in their own malfunctioning—the persons themselves are blamed for problems perceived as stemming from their own inadequacies (Zastrow, 1999). Only when unemployment becomes extremely high overall (such as in the Great Depression) do we begin to reduce the stigma and move from a residual position to an institutional one. Under conditions of mass economic crisis, then, the system rather than the individual receives the blame.

In social welfare, residual thinking leads to the kind of programs in which eligibility is based on desperate need—proving the breakdown of the other systems that should be working. In order to investigate eligibility, officials must be thoroughly familiar with the circumstances of their clients' lives, thereby ensuring that only the deserving poor receive assistance. Programs are deemed successful in terms of reducing rather than expanding the numbers who receive help: Getting the able-bodied off welfare and on the work rolls is the rallying cry. Aid, such as it is, is only provided on a short-term basis for individuals in crisis situations. The values that underpin residual thinking are capitalism, independence, and belief in opportunity.

"Safety-Net Programs Are Set for Cuts amid Slowdown": So read a headline in *USA Today* (Weisman, 2001). One of the central points of welfare reform, according to politicians interviewed in the article, was to "sever the link between the economy and benefits and promote self sufficiency" (p. 12a). But given the faltering economy, some Democrats cited in the article were worried that cuts in federal spending to help former welfare recipients get jobs would leave many families destitute.

An *institutional* or social insurance approach to public welfare would provide a very different scenario with regard to aid. The institutional approach is preventive rather than curative, universal rather than particularist. Social welfare, according to this perspective, is a necessary and desirable part of the social structure. To provide economic security as an alternative to the historic patterns of inadequate, piecemeal relief is the basic purpose of the welfare state. Why allow people to fall into destitution at all when you can offset poverty at its source? An individual's difficulties, according to this conceptualization, are attributed to causes beyond his or her control.

Means-tested programs, such as the Temporary Assistance to Needy Dependent Children (TANF), are criticized for their stigmatizing and punitive implications (Midgley, 2000). Midgley contrasts this program with the British National Health Service, which provides a range of tax-funded medical and health services to all citizens without regard for their ability to pay. In the United States, Social Security and public education are two of the nation's few universal social programs. Both of these programs are regarded as rights for the many rather than privileges for the few. As a result, they are willingly funded. Poor people's programs, in contrast, can be abolished in the next political campaign. David Wagner (2000) contrasts the U.S. system of "charity, therapy, and correction" (p. 178) with the model of most European nations that provide all their citizens with basic health care, subsidized child care, extensive paid vacations, and automatic pensions.

The metaphor of the safety net, associated with the residual approach is, in fact, a better descriptive term for the institutional mode of social welfare. To grasp the meaning of the metaphor, imagine the trapeze artist losing his or her balance and falling down hundreds of feet to be saved by the safety net below. This metaphor is relevant to U.S. welfare, in the sense that the individual is allowed to fall. Yet, in contrast to the trapeze artist who can recover to perform again, the American worker who contracts a disease may never be able to start afresh, even following a full recovery. The job may be gone; the house may be sold; and the health insurance may have expired. There is the element of shame, besides. Although there is some distress in a failed acrobatic, perhaps, there is no deep humiliation at such a mishap. As the artist rebounds, the audience claps in admiration or, at least, support. In the case of an individual requiring society's safety net, however, help may not be forthcoming; the criteria for receiving aid may not be met. If there is help, the recipient does not receive a round of applause from onlookers. The universalist social welfare state, in contrast, does provide a real safety net to the troubled citizen.

Under the economic pressures of globalization, there is a tendency of convergence in regard to social welfare provisions. Drawing on European income data, Fritzell (2001) determined that in the United Kingdom, income inequality has increased; this gap between the rich and the poor is evidenced in mounting rates of child poverty. In the Scandinavian countries, however, despite a rise in levels of unemployment, income inequality remains relatively low. So much is equality a Nordic and particularly a Norwegian value, as Fritzell indicates, that even against the pressures of the global economy, associated as it is with higher unemployment, the Nordic countries still manage to maintain a high level of equality in the distribution of income.

In summary, one could say that the residually based society offers avenues of success to "those who can" and will, while providing for only a minimum of protection for persons not in a position to seize the opportunity to achieve success.

Mobility versus Stability

A value related to work is the desire to "get ahead," to move upward and onward. A significant proportion of Americans are geographically mobile as well, moving their households every five years. Children often attend school in several school systems before they graduate. The American ideology promotes a belief in progress: Workers are expected to climb the corporate ladder and to be willing to relocate if necessary for career advancement; persons receiving government aid are expected to get training and to quickly gain their independence. Because the United States was once a land of unparalleled resources and opportunity, people who are downwardly mobile or who remain at the bottom are often held responsible for their lowly status.

I am using the term *mobility* here to describe more than social and geographical mobility—to get at the kind of restlessness that often has been said to typify the American character. Thus, from the most widely quoted commentator on early American society, Alexis de Tocqueville (1951/1835), we learn:

> America is a land of wonders, in which everything is in constant motion and
> every change seems an improvement. The idea of novelty there is indissolubly
> connected with the idea of amelioration. (p. 18)

Thom Hartmann's (1997) hypothesis of genetic traits carried over from hunter and farmer societies gives some credence to the notion that societies which evolved out of an agricultural tradition tend to be more stationary and less adventure-seeking than societies (or tribes) of hunters. Farmers, according to Hartmann, are cautious, not easily bored, and patient. Hunters are more impulsive and multifocused on the environment. Descendants of hunters as schoolchildren find it hard to concentrate and are easily distracted, highly energetic, and restless. They are liable to be diagnosed as having ADD (attention deficit disorder). In fact, Hartmann's book is entitled *Attention Deficit Disorder: A Different Perception.* So-called ADD children and adults are inclined to excel in many ways beyond the classroom, especially in sales and other competitive fields. ADD is prevalent in America but rare in Japan. As Hartmann notes, the ancestors of the Japanese people lived in a purely agricultural society for at least 6,000 years.

Europeans view Americans and Australians as "brash and risk-taking," Hartmann further suggests. Consider the types of people who would have fled the "old world" to take a dangerous journey across the Atlantic. These adventurers, presumably, would have carried with them the genetic material that might have caused their descendants to crave mobility over a more routine lifestyle, and competition over cooperation.

Competition versus Cooperation

One need not search far in the American popular press for evidence of competition. (Just glance through the advertisements.) Typically there are stories in any given week celebrating personal and team victories in events ranging from sports to spelling bees, the win-or-lose outcomes of courtroom battles, television reality shows that feature survival exploits or intense dating competitions, and intense pressure among youth to gain entrance into certain elite colleges. In other words, competition is everywhere in a society that prides itself on being the world's superpower.

Perhaps this value should be labeled personal achievement instead of competition. The fact is that competition may be the means rather than the end to the kind of high personal achievement that is so valued in American society. To win, nevertheless, Americans from childhood are taught to compete. Writing on the U.S. system of education, Ediger (2000) likens the emphasis on pupil competition as a spur to learning the beliefs of the marketplace economy. "The free enterprise system in education," as Ediger notes, "has always stated that the United States became great due to competition in the market place where goods and services are bought and sold" (p. 14). Proposals for a voucher system of schooling, for example, pit charter schools against regular public schools in attracting students. Many services in these new schools are privatized to reduce costs. Free technological equipment may be provided along with programs containing advertising, which students then watch in class.

Mass-testing programs compare individual children, schools, and whole school systems on the basis of standardized measures of achievement. Ediger compares this approach with one of cooperation. Advocates of cooperation favor helping students individually to proceed at their own pace to learn what they need to learn and want to learn.

The best way to discover a nation's values is to move into the country; learn the language; work in an indigenous, nonacademic setting; use the local services; and, above all else, send your children to the local schools. In Norway, I did all these things. Although I was more interested in seeing the fjords than in studying values, it was the striking uniqueness of Scandinavian culture that had the most lasting impact on me. The theme of the Norwegian and Scandinavian cultural ethos can be summed up in one word, *egalitarianism*.

On the competition-to-cooperation continuum, the Norwegians are far down to the cooperation end. The value of cooperation (*samarbeid*, literally "to work together") is instilled in the family in early childhood and reinforced throughout school life; it permeates every aspect of culture. The school antibullying programs originated in Norway; in fact, in my experience as a parent, bullying in Norway's schools is exceedingly rare. One brief story will suffice to illustrate the point: My 12-year-old son returned from his first day of school seemingly amazed. "Mom, a boy fell down on the playground," he said. "He was crying and crying; the other children went over to him and comforted him." This comment was, of course, as much a comment on the American playground as it was on the Norwegian one.

Nelson and Shavitt (2002) provide the kind of empirical verification of cross-cultural differences concerning individual achievement that is a rare find in the literature. The comparison is between American and Danish students. Danes, as the authors indicate, share a similar language and culture with Swedes and Norwegians; all three groups look down on conspicuous success and bragging. Denmark and Norway additionally share a ubiquitous, unwritten social modesty code; this code is reflected in interpersonal norms as well as in benevolent social welfare policies toward the least fortunate in society. Nelson and Shavitt term this "horizontal" as opposed to "vertical" values. The social structure in the United States, in contrast, is vertically oriented, a phenomenon, as the authors note, that is likely a reflection of the frontier spirit of exploration in combination with the Protestant work ethic. The American notion of equality is actually equal opportunity. This notion is reflected in the tax system and resource allocation, as these authors further suggest.

In their research findings based on in-depth interviews with a small sample of Americans and Danes, Nelson and Shavitt found that while a majority of Americans mentioned achievement in relation to happiness, none of the Danes did. The Danes' first priority was family and the second was work. Single American men almost unanimously mentioned work goals alone. These findings from the interviews were confirmed in the second portion of this study, which compared answers to 60 items related to achievement. Questionnaires were administered to 82 communications students in Denmark and to 152 comparable students in the United States. Results confirmed that Danes scored much higher on values related to protecting the environment, social justice, equality, and peace than did their U.S. counterparts. Americans were oriented toward success, ambition, and gaining influence. Perhaps the most telling part of this article is found in the beer slogans that introduce it:

> *Probably* the best beer in town.
> —Carlsberg Beer advertising slogan

> Best-selling Beer in America
> —U.S. beer slogan (p. 439)

Individualism versus Collectivism

Nelson and Shavitt (2002) perceive Scandinavian culture as individualistic compared with a collectivist mentality, such as that found in Turkey, but not when compared to Anglo-Saxon culture such as that of North America. Scandinavian culture seems capable of a solidarity that is phenomenal. American people, on the other hand, are especially noted for their individualism, mainly to do with competition and self-reliance. At the same time, within homogeneous contexts, such as in high school and the military, conformity to group norms is the standard. In social psychological experiments, Americans generally emerge as conformists to a fault. Even in experiments supposedly inflicting pain, average Americans have been shown to obey to the bitter end, simply because the experimenter commanded them to. Blass (2002), writing in *Psychology Today* believes such findings hold over time and cross-culturally.

Interestingly, in an experimental situation designed by Milgram (1977), Norwegians far outscored the French on the conformity dimension. The study placed subjects in a situation in which they were presented with obvious judgmental fallacies concerning the length of sound tones. The Norwegians conformed to group consensus overwhelmingly and accepted criticism impassively. French subjects, on the other hand, tended to hold their ground; in response to criticism, they made retaliatory responses. Americans, although not included in that experiment, would probably, judging by comparable studies, take a position somewhere in the middle. In my sojourn in Norway, I was struck by the group solidarity, the sense of "we-ness" time and again. It did not surprise me to read in a recent news report that the Norwegian court decided it is punishable to prevent a spouse from being integrated into Norwegian society (Norwegian Radio Broadcasting [NRK], 2004). The case involved a middle-aged immigrant who had been brought to Norway by her Algerian husband, and who was forced to dress in traditional clothing and not allowed to speak with other classmates at the end of class. (The child welfare department had ordered the woman to take a language course in Norwegian.) Although the prosecutor asked for a sentence of one and a half years, the court doubled the sentence to three years, a long sentence by Norwegian standards.

Japanese society is generally understood to be highly consensual. According to an article in *The Economist*, "The fondness for group activity means most Japanese travel in groups, a habit that is said to date back centuries to the days when they flocked from temple to temple to hear Buddhist teachers" ("Consensus and Contraction," 2002, p. 8). In Japan, the article continues, foreigners are tolerated more than welcomed and often held responsible for the rising crime rate. In the absence of sizable minority populations, Japan is culturally homogeneous and devoid of much social disruption; it is a largely egalitarian society, the unifying principle of which is termed *wa*.

United States society is hardly harmonious to the same extent. Although Americans tend to conform to their peers (and to noxious work rules, for example, submitting to urinalysis and even lie-detector tests for employment), they are noted for "rugged individualism." According to anthropologist Alvin Wolfe (2002), the American cultural creed extols the virtues of self-reliance and rugged individualism. The belief that each person shapes his or her own destiny, the denial of structural causes of poverty, the blaming of victims, and the acclaim of the wealthy as heroes are all a part of this cultural ethos. This ethos is embodied in American tradition.

In the 1830s, the French social philosopher Alexis de Tocqueville (1951/1835) characterized the people on this continent as individualists. The risk to the American character, said de Tocqueville, was that in the future, isolation might prevail. Still, today, the primary value dimension that sums up the cultural climate in the United States is this trait of individualism, this sense of "I" rather than "we." The focus on self at the personal level is matched on the political level by unilateral foreign policy.

On this side of the Atlantic, welfare programs are geared to specific individuals or groups who are functioning poorly. (In Europe, the focus is more on the population as a whole.) In the United States, social welfare programs that focus on changing the internal person, rather than the external system, have been favored. This is not to say that a collective spirit has not prevailed at various key periods in U.S. history. Kaplan and Kaplan (1993) provided careful documentation to show that public opinion in the post–World War I era favored strong government intervention; surveys of that time revealed that a substantial portion of the population thought in collectivist terms. Wolfe (2002), likewise, contrasted the collective spirit of progressive periods in U.S. history with the social climate surrounding the welfare reform movement of today. Again, for a short period in the mid-1960s, the national fervor was for social and economic equity. (Chapter 3 will expound on this argument further.)

From a global perspective, American individualism comes across as rather extreme, even offensive. Sikeena Karmali (2003), who was born in Africa to Indian parents but who was educated in Canada, described the East/West divide. As she observed:

> The self is the orienting principle of the West, perhaps even of modernity as a whole. All things—community, the nation, religion, spirituality, even God—are subordinated to the individual, which is the highest form of good. If we take a cursory glance at contemporary Western media, we find that the self is the supreme subject of conversation—my mind, my body, my home, my fashion, my spirit. There seems to be an earnest endeavor—in talk shows like *Oprah* and sitcoms like *Friends,* in the proliferation of lifestyle coaches, personal trainers, nutritionists, and shrinks—to perfect the individual.
>
> The East, with its heavy hand of tradition, functions through consensus. Loyalties and duties are ascribed by birth. Community, and not self, is the orienting principle. (p. 93)

Karmali's hope is that East and West will come together as soulmates and that she herself, as a product of both worlds, somehow will be able to "integrate these values where they are needed" (p. 93).

Hirayama and Hirayama (1999) draw a sharp contrast between the American emphasis on fostering a competitive spirit in the child, encouraging self-sufficiency from an early age, and the Japanese cultivation of a sense of group identity and solidarity. Unlike in American society, however, social structure in Japan is hierarchical.

Collectivist ideology accords prime importance to collective forms of association in which people share resources and decision making (Midgley, 2000). As a European manifestation, collectivists believe that the state is jointly owned by its citizens and that the state is the most effective agent for meeting social needs. Among indigenous populations such as certain African tribes, collectivism takes the form of traditional ways of knowing and a sense of intrinsic unity between individuals and communities (Kreitzer, 2002).

Wright (2001) described value themes carried from Africa that are still in evidence among African Americans today. Among the values singled out by Wright are: oneness with nature and spirituality, mutual aid aimed at survival of the group, a present orientation and spiral concept of time, and intergenerational bonding.

Independence versus Interconnectedness

Independence is closely related to individualism in the same way that interconnectedness is related to collectivism. Within the family as well as society, Americans strive to be fiercely independent. The word *codependency,* which signifies a too-close emotional dependence, accordingly, has taken on extremely negative connotations. Parents train their children to be independent and to one day leave the "nest." The myth of independence suggests that each individual is singularly in control of his or her own destiny, according to Tropman (1989). As people age, they fight to hang on to their independence as long as possible. The value of independence has important implications for social welfare. Prolonged dependence on government help is actively discouraged, and many Americans refuse to accept benefits because of personal pride. "The Lord helps those who help themselves" is a commonly heard refrain.

At the international level, the United States has a strong propensity to lead or to "go it alone" but rarely to collaborate in international decision making. This propensity also figures in the governmental refusal to sign international accords on behalf of human rights or conventions banning chemical and biological weapons or land mines. In comparison with the United States, the nations of Europe, for example, appear to be far more interdependent in their dealings with each other. If we agree with Midgley (2000) that globalization can serve to provide sustainable development and enhance people's welfare, then we need to advocate for a perspective more in keeping with the demands of this global age.

The sense of interconnectedness is a staple of traditional indigenous culture. The First Nations peoples in North America rely on the metaphor of the Medicine Wheel, which exemplifies the wholeness of all life. The Medicine Wheel teaches about the cycle of life, a cycle that encompasses infancy through old age, the seasons, and four directions of human growth—the emotional, mental, physical, and spiritual. This is not a linear system; all the parts are interconnected. American Indian teachings are traditionally presented as narratives and shared within a talking circle. Don Coyhis (2000), the director of White Bison, a substance abuse treatment center, incorporates the wisdom of the Medicine Wheel in his treatment programming. In Indian country, the heart of the sobriety movement, as explained by Coyhis, revolves around a return to cultural values and folkways. Among these values are: a strong emphasis on *being* not doing and cooperation over competition; a group emphasis; working only to meet one's needs; nonmaterialism; right-brain orientation; and living in harmony with nature. The theme of these values is social interconnectedness. This is one of the many insights offered by Coyhis:

> The elders have shared with us the Native understanding that all things are related and connected. There is a level in the unseen world where we are all connected to one another. . . . For example, one of the teachings of the Medicine Wheel says that the Honor of One is the Honor of All. And if that is true, then the Pain of One is the Pain of All. (pp. 90–91)

Materialism versus Spirituality

America is hated in many parts of the world for its perceived embrace of godless and value-free materialism and for its imposition of the same on the rest of the world (Church, 2002). In fact, materialism should not, strictly speaking, be considered a *value,* because the term is laden with undesirable connotations. But the United States is clearly a capitalist nation, and status is accorded to those with high earning power or, in upper-upper-class settings, to those who have access to inherited wealth. Americans may be accused on occasion of flaunting their wealth. The number of toys that many American children have would be considered, in some circles, obscene. And at the macro level, American capitalism is a cause of both resentment and emulation in every part of the globe. De Tocqueville (1951/1835) perhaps missed the point to some extent when he said: "The love of wealth is therefore to be traced, as either a principle or accessory motive, at the bottom of all that Americans do; this gives to all their passions a sort of family likeness" (Book III, p. 17). The reason I say that de Tocqueville may have missed the point is because so much of the individual materialism is only surface-deep, symbolic perhaps of a longing for something else, something that was missing earlier in life.

Throughout her writings, bell hooks captures the essence of the search for meaning that sadly has caused so many to worship at the throne of money. In *Salvation: Black People and Love,* bell hooks (2001) describes how the focus on material gain has affected the black family: "Like the culture as a whole, masses of Black people now look to material success as the sole measure of value and meaning in life. . . . Gaining access to material privilege will never satisfy needs of the spirit. Those hungers persist and haunt us" (p. 15).

In an article entitled "Through New Eyes," Ron Marks (2003), the dean of the Tulane University School of Social Work, describes how a group of American social work students adapted to the special rhythm of a Tibetan community in India. He writes:

> Whether witnessing a cremation or interacting with a person with leprosy, we discovered a spiritual richness among the Tibetan refugee community in Dharamsala, despite the material poverty. We, in turn, learned to measure modernity in a more humble way. (pp. 36–37)

Otherworldly, Americans are not. From the traditional Native perspective, Don Coyhis (2000) defines mainstream culture as geared toward the "seen world." "In our cultures," he says, "we have Give-Away ceremonies or Potlatches where you give away what is valuable to you. This emphasizes the nonmaterial side of things" (p. 96). "In Indian country," as he further suggests, "status is related to a person's character" (p. 100).

The United States as a nation has a strong religious character. In a recent *U.S. News & World Report*/PBS poll, nearly two-thirds of Americans said that religion is very important in their lives, and close to half stated that they attend worship services at least once a week (Sheler, 2002). Evangelical Christianity has made a strong comeback in recent years, and there has been much talk in the

Bush administration of plans for funding faith-based initiatives for social services. The national thrust toward religiosity is confirmed in a recent worldwide survey undertaken by the PEW Research Center (2002) that found that among wealthy nations, the United States is the only one in which a majority of the people say that religion plays an important role in their lives. Included among the wealthy nations were Britain, Canada, Italy, Germany, France, Korea, and Japan.

Organized religion is often much more visible in the United States than is spirituality. Spirituality, as defined by Canda and Furman (1999), "relates to a universal and fundamental aspect of what it is to be human—to search for a sense of meaning, purpose, and moral frameworks for relating with self, others, and the ultimate reality" (p. 37). (See Chapter 7 for a discussion of social work's rekindled focus on spirituality.)

Nuclear Family versus Extended Family

Try to conjure up an image of *the extended family.* Probably your image is on the order of *My Big Fat Greek Wedding,* with dozens of cousins talking all at once; the African American three-generation household; or a mass gathering at the traditional Irish wake. For the child growing up in such a commonwealth of relatives, what a life! Think of the nuclear family, in contrast, and images of small, isolated family groupings in large empty spaces flood the mind. "The Incredible Shrinking Family" is the title of a chapter in Robert Reich's (2000) *The Future of Success.* Although Reich's concern is the impact of the new working arrangements in the postindustrial society, the result is fewer children and longer working hours for both partners. Geographical mobility to "where the jobs are" leaves the older generation and aunts and uncles behind. In terms of economic support, the vulnerable members of the family, such as the elderly and the disabled, are more likely to be supported through social welfare provisions than by their kinfolk.

Throughout the nonindustrialized world, kinship arrangements are very different. Marriage may be viewed as a union between families rather than individuals. Residences may be shared intergenerationally. In India, for example, the social institution that is key to Hindu life is the joint family (Nimmagadda & Cowger, 1999). Social workers providing counseling to troubled family members, such as those in an alcoholic family, often find, according to Nimmagadda and Cowger, that acceptance of one's fate and fierce loyalty by wife to husband may prevent the alcoholic from changing but also may provide a strong support system. Although trained in Western models of individualism, social workers routinely adapt these foreign models to the norms of the local culture. For a compelling description of a Bedouin-Arab social worker's role as conflict mediator in a complicated marital situation, see Al-Krenawi and Graham (2001). The emphasis in the intervention was, consistent with Arab cultural norms, on the good of the family, rather than the good of the individual.

Elizabeth Kenny (in private correspondence, June 2002) compared concepts of time in Mexico and the United States and the impact of the time dimension on family life:

The Mexican mother of a friend of mine has told me that Americans greatly value time. She pointed out that this especially affects family values. Whereas in Mexico, the family has a long dinner together every night no matter what, here in the U.S. everyone is rushing to the next event. In Mexico, each person is more a member of a family than an individual.

Daly, Jennings, Beckett, and Leashore (1996) recommend that social workers be cognizant of African American cultural perspectives and approach these from a nondeficit model. Evidence indicates, for example, that African American women coping with domestic violence are apt to be particularly sensitive to the influence of family and support systems. It has been found, as Daly et al. indicate, that social supports from the extended family, in fact, serve to decrease spouse assaults in African American homes. Increasingly, social workers trained in a strengths perspective look to the wider family as a major resource and recognize the importance of honoring all different kinds of family forms, for example, those that are blended with children from previous marriages, nonkin families, and same-sex parented families. Kinship care is the traditional, informal arrangement preferred over adoption by the Association of Black Social Workers for children in need of care (Suppes & Wells, 2003). Child welfare workers increasingly rely on kinship care arrangements in cases of parental absence or neglect.

Moralism versus Compassion

Just as work has a strong impact on family roles and patterns of adaptation, so too does that strange bedfellow, the cause at once of so much good and so much grief, known to students of culture as *moralism*. Were I to describe the essence of the American character in one word, then this would be it: *moralism*. In a sense, moralism transcends the other values such as work. Commentator Forrest Church (2002), author of *The American Creed: A Spiritual and Patriotic Primer*, aptly captures the spirit of American history in the following statement: "We demonstrate our greatness not by force of might or by virtue of our unquestioned economic dominance but through rigorous moral endeavor, ever striving to remake ourselves in our own image" (p. 21).

In international affairs, moralism sometimes gets played out as righteousness. So argue Barnett, Weathersby, and Aram (1995) in an unlikely source—the *Business Forum*. American executives have inherited cultural values that hinder them from meeting the demands of the global marketplace. Attitudes that are a legacy of the Puritan Fathers—the good versus evil, simplistic view of the world coupled with the belief that Americans are a "chosen people"—create barriers in the business world, according to the authors. They urge that a sense of global community and a systems perspective need to replace this simplicity in worldview.

A carryover from Puritanism, moralism is indeed one of the singular features of American society. Tropman (1989) defined moralism as the tendency to be judgmental about affairs and events. So pervasive is this notion to Americans that poverty becomes a moral issue, and money becomes the focus of moral judgment, according to Tropman. Time and again, the issues of responsibility and fault have been major concerns in addressing social problems. These themes generate one of the central social welfare conflicts—punishment versus compassion.

So entrenched is moralism in American discourse that, as an article from the conservative British magazine *The Economist* ("Living with a Superpower, 2003") argues, domestic issues, even technical matters such as stem-cell research and gun control, become moral questions. There also may be a link between moralism and militarism, as the article speculates. Data to support the contention of the article that Americans and Europeans view the world differently comes from the PEW Research Center's (2002) international poll on national attitudes in 44 countries.

Punitiveness is the negative side of moralism. Punitiveness, as Grimsrud and Zehr (2002) suggest, is an issue having to do with the values by which human beings shape their lives. The paradigm of retributive justice that dominates Western criminal justice is a recipe for alienation. Over the past decade, we have seen the construction of new jails and prisons expand exponentially; the war on drugs and the war on welfare have accompanied the prison growth. Fortunately, as Grimsrud and Zehr further indicate, present-day alternatives to retributive criminal justice are emerging that reflect the general thrust of "biblical" justice. These initiatives, which are at the compassionate end of the continuum and include victim-offender reconciliation programs and healing circles, are discussed in Chapter 6.

Before turning from our overview of American values to examine how these social values are translated into social policy, one rather (unintended) humorous illustration from a serious Norwegian news story on drugs and prostitution can serve to illustrate international differences. The practice of locking up Russian prostitutes who had been flocking into Norway was the subject of a news article by Barth-Heyerdahl (1999). One such Russian woman was quoted by police as thanking the police, stating that she felt she had stayed at a hotel for 14 days and was pleased that she had been given 1,000 kroner to take back to Russia. The kroner represented the pay she received for simply staying at the jail; this was the equivalent of one month's pay to an ordinary worker or one year's pay for a pensioner in Russia.

Guam: A Case Study in Culture Clash

Throughout the history of the world, conquering nations have come to dominate smaller, weaker nations, especially those with desirable resources or occupying strategic geographical locations. Social work educators from the University of Guam write in Box 2.1 of the small Pacific island of Guam, today an American territory with a unique cultural history. The Chamorro, an indigenous people believed to be of Mayo-Polynesian descent, are the preservers of the ancient Guam culture, a culture that was historically matrilineal and

2.1 U.S. Military and U.S. Welfare: Partners in (De)Colonizing Micronesian Islands

Gerhard J. Schwab and Vivian L. Dames

Guam is a Micronesian island with 212 square miles in land area that is located in the Western Pacific approximately 6,000 miles or 13 jet hours from the U.S. west coast, 15 time zones from Washington, DC, and within 5 jet hours of Manila, Hong Kong, and Tokyo. Guam has a multicultural and international community. The 2000 Census enumerated a population of 154,000 consisting of 37 percent indigenous Chamorros, 26 percent Pilipinos, 7 percent Whites, and 30 percent other Asians and Pacific Islanders. The Chamorro people of Guam still live under colonial rule of the United States.

The region of Micronesia, which means "little islands," is comparable in area to the continental United States and represents a great diversity of languages, cultures, topography, political status, and approaches to socioeconomic development.

One thing the peoples in Micronesia have in common is their histories of adaptation and resistance to colonization by different foreign powers, their first-hand experience with militarization and war, their continuing strategic importance to the United States, and their dependency on "American welfare." Guam has the longest colonial history of any Pacific island. It was a Spanish colony for 300 years until the United States wrested it away in 1898 as a spoil of the Spanish American War. Guam and its people remained a ward of the U.S. Navy for half a century, except for the period 1941–1944 when the island was occupied by Japanese forces. When U.S. military forces reoccupied the island, the movement for U.S citizenship, begun in the early 1900s, was renewed.

In 1950, the U.S. Congress designated Guam as an unincorporated territory and conferred U.S. citizenship on its inhabitants. However, the project of decolonization for Guam remains unfinished. The ambiguity of Guam's political status, the unfulfilled promise of self-determination for the Chamorro people, and the uncertainty about Guam's political future continue to have profound ramifications in many aspects of everyday life and for all social institutions, including education and social welfare. For instance, U.S. citizens in Guam cannot vote in U.S. presidential elections and are not eligible for certain federal welfare programs (e.g., Supplemental Security Income).

Guam remains the most militarized of all the islands. However, beginning in the 1970s, Guam developed a significant tourism industry, mostly visitors from Japan, as an alternative economic base. After a boom during the 1980s, this industry began to decline. In 1990, 15 percent of the population in Guam was living below the U.S. poverty line. In 2000, this had increased to almost 25 percent of the population. Although indigenous Chamorros make up the greatest number of these individuals, Micronesians migrating from the other islands are disproportionately overrepresented among those living in poverty.

The other islands of Micronesia came under U.S. control in a different way. After World War II, the United Nations (U.N.) established a Trusteeship Council to oversee the promise of self-determination for 11 trusteeships worldwide, including the islands of this region (except Guam) that had been under the control of Japan. Of these trusteeships, only

Micronesia was designated by the U.N. as a strategic trust, called the Trust Territory of the Pacific Islands (TTPI). The United States was assigned to be its administering authority, and it was placed under the U.N. Security Council. Political status negotiations, begun in the 1970s, resulted in the eventual termination of the TTPI, the creation of four new political entities, and the beginning of a new chapter in U.S. federal relations with these insular areas. The Republic of Palau to the west; the states of Yap, Chuuk, Pohnpei, and Kosrae, which constitute the Federated States of Micronesia (FSM) in the middle; and the Republic of the Marshall Islands (RMI) to the east, each negotiated to become a freely associated state with the United States. The Compacts of Free Association are treaties in the form of joint congressional executive agreements. The agreements recognize the sovereignty of the islands and their right to complete control over domestic matters. The freely associated states accept federal funding in exchange for exclusive access of the United States to these nation's lands, airspace, and waterways for military purposes. By 1975, the islands north of Guam split off to become the Commonwealth of the Northern Mariana Islands (CNMI), with formal U.S. citizenship conferred in 1986.

In a recent meeting sponsored by the North Pacific Justice and Development Commission of the Pacific Catholic Bishops Conference, community organizers from all Micronesian islands regions met to discuss current social problems in the area. They summarized the three major social problems as:

1. *Social breakdown of extended familial systems.* Throughout Micronesia, extended familial systems have undergone dramatic changes: Ownership and trusteeship arrangements of land have changed; production, distribution, and consumption patterns of food have changed; new resource systems have become available to families. Associated with these changes are the emergence of smaller families and an increasing degree of uncertainty about and breakup of traditional roles and responsibilities among family members. Hence, more and more, families are no longer able to provide the stability, orientation, and support to their members in order to prevent social ills such as domestic violence, substance abuse, suicide, and other social problems.

2. *Lack of good governance.* The introduction of modern government structures in the context of traditional authority structures poses great challenges to all island communities in Micronesia. The individual citizens often lack the personal knowledge and skills to fully understand, access, and participate in the newly introduced bureaucratic government structures. Additionally, there is a lack of organizational and institutional means to monitor and ensure the proper administration and distribution of public resources. Elected officials, in return, often use this almost complete absence of control to advance their personal and financial gains rather than the common good of the community that elected them into public office.

3. *Self-determination of the Chamorro people.* After long periods of colonial rule and wartime occupations, the peoples of Micronesia were finally afforded the inalienable right of political self-determination. However, this fundamental collective right is still denied to the indigenous Chamorro people of the unincorporated U.S. Territory of Guam.

Source: Reprinted with permission of Gerhard Schwab and Vivian Dames, Social Work Program, University of Guam.

matriarchal. During the Spanish occupation, the culture was preserved by the women—women whose influence was ignored by the Spaniards. Today, accordingly, many of the traditions remain—the belief that the land and its produce belong to everyone, a powerful concern for mutuality rather than individualism, spirituality rather than material values, and reverence for elders (Government of Guam, 2004). A strong military presence, however, as revealed in the reading in Box 2.1, threatens to overwhelm the native cultural ethos.

The Shaping of U.S. Social Policy

Robert Barker (2003) provides the following definition in *The Social Work Dictionary:*

> Social policy: the activities and principles of a society that guide the way it intervenes in and regulates the relationships between individuals, groups, communities, and social institutions. These principles and activities are the result of the society's values and customs and largely determine the distribution of resources and the level of well-being of its people. Thus, social policy includes plans and programs in education, health care, crime and corrections, economic security, and social welfare made by governments, voluntary organizations, and the people in general. It also includes social perspectives that result in society's rewards and constraints. (p. 405)

A variety of historical, cultural, and political forces shape social welfare policy. In my delineation of American value constructs, the work ethic emerged as one of the most enduring themes in social welfare history. Relevant to this ethic, programs that require work or are work-related (unemployment benefits and Social Security) have more political clout than programs that are not work-related (aid to families in need). The most vigorously challenged programs involve aid to able-bodied people.

Because mobility and competitiveness are basic tenets in U.S. society, workers are expected to be willing to compete with fellow workers and even relocate to "get ahead." Pay raises based on merit rather than seniority reinforce the sense of competition. Those unwilling to be mobile and competitive are not highly regarded.

The emphasis on personal achievement and independence encourages citizens to strive for success. Those who fall behind may be regarded as losers and treated accordingly. Proposals designed to equalize the distribution of wealth predictably make little headway in a competitive social structure. In the United States, lack of compassion for the poor is compounded by the ethos of moralism. Because poor people are stigmatized and even blamed for their circumstances, there is no strong working-class political movement, no labor party with a platform of social benefits.

As the tides of political change come and go, and as the public mood shifts, so do the social policies. Once ingrained, they tend to reinforce the social values

Portland, Oregon, peace protest, April 2003. Residents, including social workers, protested the war against Iraq. Consistent with the social work peace mission, NASW publicly opposed the war.

that shaped them in the first place. The cycle is complete with values shaping policies, and policies, values. One could make the case, for example, that the value of equality of opportunity led to racial integration while the policy of integration greatly furthered the belief in equality. The value-policy configuration is further affected by economic forces. Values such as a religious belief that hard work is good for the soul can promote economic investment and growth; economic growth, in turn, can reinforce the Protestant work ethic. At the same time, the religious value of compassion can influence a willingness to donate to charity to help others who have fallen on hard times.

We can see how economic policies and social values intersect in the example of means-tested welfare benefits. Such programs, associated with the poor and minorities, generate more opposition than support. As Piven and Cloward (1993) correctly noted, the effects of the stigmatization are far-reaching—dampening support for other welfare state programs. Citizens resent paying taxes for services for which they themselves receive no benefit. Accordingly, fragmented initiatives that reach only narrowly defined groups, such as affirmative programming, are apt to be phased out over time.

Social Work Values and American Values

As a profession that emerged out of a socioreligious ethos with the goal of help- ing society's vulnerable people, social work has promoted values that generally reflect a more compassionate stance than those of many other professional groups. A commitment to human welfare, social justice, and individual dignity is an enduring characteristic of the social work profession. A further commit- ment to the tradition of social and political activism has characterized the field since the days when the founders worked for women's suffrage, children's and minorities' rights, and universal peace.

Let us take a closer look at the core social work values and then see to what extent they are compatible or in conflict with mainstream American values. As spelled out by the NASW *Code of Ethics* (1996), the six core values are: service, social justice, dignity and worth of the person, importance of human relation- ships, integrity, and competence. At a glance, these core values seem to corre- spond rather well to the fundamental American values singled out in this chap- ter. Service relates to the work ethic, as do integrity and competence. Dignity and worth of the person corresponds to individualism and equal opportunity. The importance of human relationships is an attribute most closely related to the nuclear family or any family. Moralism, a force for placing moral and ethical considerations ahead of personal interests, is a shared value of mainstream America and the social work mission. The form that the moralism takes, how- ever, ranges from the highly punitive at one end to highly compassionate at the other.

"The primary mission of the social work profession," as spelled out in NASW's (1996) *Code of Ethics,* "is to enhance human well-being and help meet the needs and empowerment of people who are vulnerable, oppressed, and liv- ing in poverty. . . . Social workers promote social justice and social change with and on behalf of clients" (p. 1).

So referring back to our list of American value dimensions, the contradic- tions between social work's altruism and the American creed become more apparent. Competition as opposed to cooperation, materialism versus spiritual- ity—the contradictions abound. Popple and Leighninger (2004) see such value conflicts exemplified in the societal reluctance to provide adequate care for poor, especially nonworking families. The objective of discouraging adult dependency is addressed, according to these authors, by the values of individualism and work.

In its ideal incarnation, the welfare state is most congruent with social work values, beliefs, and principles: social insurance such as social security programs, universal as opposed to residualist benefits, and a collectivist orientation. Among the core values of social work, the most prominent and perhaps least well understood is the value of social justice. In the toolkit distributed by NASW (2003a) for March, which is National Social Work Month, "preserving rights, strengthening voices" was the year's theme. Beneath the practicality of social work, according to the toolkit, "lies a strong value system that can be summarized in two words: social justice" (p. 25). *Social justice* is defined as the view that everyone deserves equal economic, political, and social rights and opportunities. Social justice and peace are interconnected, according to this document, inasmuch as where there are gross inequalities of money and power, "whether between workers and managers, nations and nations, or men and women," there can be no peace (p. 25).

NASW, in a statement issued by the president, strongly opposed preemptive military action against Iraq (Mizrahi, 2002). This position is consistent with policy positions that the social work profession has taken over the years on a number of issues, included among them poverty, the death penalty, use of violence against children, and human rights (see NASW, 2003b, *Social Work Speaks)*. The ethical principle that underlies the taking of such positions is embodied in the *Code of Ethics* requirement that social workers challenge social injustice. The integrity principle that reminds social workers that they should do what is right for their clients and for the society as a whole provides further justification for the profession's willingness to take a public stand on the issues of the day.

The core social work values and broad ethical principles that serve as guidelines for the social work profession are codified in NASW's (1996) *Code of Ethics*. The values set forth in this *Code* (e.g., respect for human dignity, the importance of client self-determination) are embodied in the design of our social work curriculum as well (Robbins, Chatterjee, & Canda, 1999). The *Code* is reprinted in full in Appendix B. Pay special attention to Section 6, Social Workers' Ethical Responsibilities to the Broader Society. This section, which enjoins social workers to promote the general welfare of society "from local to global levels" (section 6.01), is the most germane to the focus of this text. The International Ethics of Social Work Principles and Standards is available at http://www.ifsw.org. At this Web site, moreover, one can find links to the codes of ethics of member states of the International Federation of Social Workers (IFSW). A scanning of the codes from the United States, Britain, Scandinavian countries, and Australia reveals that the codes from Denmark and Britain contain the strongest statements on human rights. Characteristically, the Norwegian code expresses concern for children, and Sweden places adherence to human rights ahead of local laws.

Included in the British code of ethics is the new IFSW international definition of social work. This definition was adopted at the IFSW General Meeting in Montréal, Canada, in July 2000:

> The social work profession promotes social change, problem solving in human relationships and the empowerment and liberation of people to enhance well-being. Utilising theories of human behaviour and social systems, social work intervenes at the points where people interact with their environments. Principles of human rights and social justice are fundamental to social work.
> (http://www.ifsw.org)

 Of key significance in this definition is the inclusion of terms like *empowerment, liberation of people,* and *human rights.* These values represent, as Zoya Taylor (1999) indicates, fundamental humanitarian values of social work, values that are culturally universal. Social work's dedication to the moral principle of empowerment, as Taylor further notes, can function as a unifying concept to transcend the individualistic values found in Western textbooks. For Payne (1997), too, empowerment practice is not limited to enablement of individuals but can be directed toward oppressed communities and social systems in need of structural reform. Taylor goes further. "We need," she asserts, "a morality based on social consciousness and collective responsibility as against individualism" (p. 312).

Let us now consider how cultural values are played out when aspects of social work practice and social work education are transplanted from one nation to the next. In the following international descriptions, note the ubiquity of far-right policies associated with the global market.

Chile

The credit for the birth of the social work profession not only in Chile but in the whole of South America goes to Alejandro del Rio, a doctor and leader in the field of public health, and his friend and advisor, René Sand, a renowned Belgian physician (Kendall, 2000). In 1925, at the invitation of Sand, del Rio visited the newly founded school of social work at Brussels and upon his return to Chile, with government help, set up a comparable two-year course at Santiago. Initially, as Janet Finn (2002) informs us, European influences predominated. However, by the 1940s, with the establishment of a Chilean–United States exchange, American texts were translated into Spanish, and a U.S. model of professional social work came to dominate. Social work in Argentina followed the same pattern (Healy, 2001).

All this was to change in the 1960s in conjunction with radical social forces that swept through Latin America, as well as the rest of the world, at this time. In Chile, the urban poor, workers, students, and teachers came together "to claim voice, space, and political power" (Finn, 2002, p. 454). Having lost faith in the capacity of their official leaders to bring development to their countries, grassroots organizations formed to work among the poorest and most needy groups of this society. Imported models of social work were discarded. Under the pedagogical leadership of Paulo Freire (see Chapter 1), Chilean social work education was revolutionized. Freire's influence on social work theory extended far beyond Chile's borders.

Chilean social work thrived under the socialist Allende government. All this was to come to an untimely end, however, when a CIA-backed military coup launched 17 years of dictatorial rule. Concomitant with the dismantling of the progressive Chilean welfare state, social work faculty and students were among those who were detained and who "disappeared." Others suffered as well through elimination of the pension system and the workers' compensation fund, which was initiated to lower the cost of labor (Borzutzky, 2002). (This transformation of the administration of social security funds to the private sector was to be widely touted in the United States as a model program.)

Today, although no longer under the control of a brutal military regime, Chile is a society, according to Borutzky, ridden with social and economic inequalities and with a weakened sense of solidarity. Structural adjustment requirements of the international banking system have had a negative impact on the social welfare system of Chile, as on all debtor nations of the global economy. The term *structural adjustment* refers to the set of adjustments or so-called reforms that are required by international banks as a condition for future loans and for refinancing on payments due on existing loans. Under Chile's market economy, such adjustments have placed particularly heavy burdens on women (Finn, 2002).

Despite the economic retrogression in Chile, the legacy of Friere's collectivist work that started among the peasants and clergy lives on. His teachings have inspired educators and organizers throughout the world, educators such as bell hooks (1994) who argues so eloquently that learning is teaching and teaching is learning, and activists such as Mary Bricker-Jenkins of the welfare rights movement. Friere's message that social work must be understood in the context of social structure and of the importance of linking theory and action through praxis shaped the mission of the Social Welfare Action Alliance (SWAA; Reisch & Andrews, 2001).

The Caribbean

At a special presentation on critical issues in Caribbean social work at the Council on Social Work Education (CSWE) Annual Program Meeting led by Lynne Healy (2003), an interesting discussion ensued during the question-answer stage. The issue had to do with offenders from Jamaica and other Caribbean countries who were deported after serving time in the United States for drug violations. Because the ex-convicts had been criminalized in prison as a result of America's war on drugs, their return has resulted in gang violence and organized crime. One country even tried to refuse to accept them back until the United States put pressure on the government. Jamaica was advised to place these unwelcome ex-convicts in special prisons. The tragedy, as pointed out by the discussants, was that migrants who had gotten caught up in mostly minor violations, then had become hardened and far more antisocial after a stint in a U.S. prison. The implications for their social workers involved helping family members deal with family violence and other related problems. The situation shows how a policy based on values in one part of the world can have unanticipated consequences somewhere else.

The negative impact of structural adjustment programs on social welfare systems of debtor nations is again clearly evidenced in the case of Jamaica. Under structural adjustment incentives, cutbacks in public services in health, education, housing, and public assistance are mandated to make loan repayment the priority (Prigoff, 1999). In Jamaica, the impact of structural adjustment mandates on social welfare, and therefore on the burgeoning profession of social work, was especially pronounced. Between the late 1970s and 1980s, the percentage of public expenditure on debt payments rose from 17.7 percent to about 40 percent while the percentage on education dropped significantly, as did spending on all the social services including health care (Healy, 2001). Wardle (2002) concurs: In 1973, Jamaica was one of the most prosperous states in the Caribbean, but by 1990, it was bankrupt. Formal control over economic policy has shifted from Jamaica to Washington and the International Monetary Fund (IMF).

"How can we protect the values of social work given the new global realities?" This was one of the questions asked by social work educators at the CSWE session on Caribbean social work issues. Despite setbacks and government cutbacks, however, the image conveyed of social work education, especially in the area of creative group work with troubled children, was of vibrant programming. Worthy of special mention is the Model of Violence Prevention developed at the University of West Indies. This program has worked with traumatized children, children who have witnessed serious violence, to help them express their feelings and develop a sense of trust and safety.

South Korea

Globalization has brought much prosperity to the countries of East Asia, especially to China where labor is cheap and the workers industrious, but also to Korea and Japan due to their high-quality exports. At the end of the Korean War, Korea was poorer than India; by the 1990s it had joined the Organization for Economic Cooperation and Development (OECD), the club of the advanced industrialized nations. Stiglitz (2002) credits the Korean government with the active steps taken to ensure that the rising tide of growth did, in fact, lift most boats. In the resulting economic environment, business flourished. The bubble did burst in 1997, however, a fact that Stiglitz attributes in part to stringent IMF policies, such as the suggestion that Korea borrow money from foreign bankers. This act increased its vulnerability to world markets and to further pressure from the IMF. Fortunately, in recent years the economy has rebounded.

Kyungbae Chung (2002) attributes the Korean philosophical belief in a balanced social order to the traditional worldview of Taoism. Balanced order can be achieved, as Chung explains, only when the needs of humanity and nature are in order. In the wake of the 1997 financial crisis, Korea has improved its social safety net to aid crisis recovery and help people return to the job market. Chung presented his paper at the international conference held at Seoul National University on issues in social welfare.

Speaking at the same conference, Sung Ja Song (2002) traced the roots of Korean social work to the aftermath of the Korean War in the 1950s. Early programs were for refugees and people in need of public relief. Following the mass unemployment that occurred in 1997, social workers and members of nongovernmental organizations have played a key role in distributing aid to people. Today, amazingly, as Song indicates, there are 62 social welfare departments in two-year colleges, 103 departments in four-year colleges, and 82 graduate programs. Each year 9,000 social workers graduate.

In his presentation, Song was highly critical of the importation of individualistic models from the West that are not suitable for the more family-centered Korean society. In Korea, in contrast to individualized societies such as the United States and Scandinavia, personal interdependency is encouraged. Accordingly, the treatment focus is not just the children but the whole family. In Song's words:

> Korean families are more family relationship–centered systems, have male dominance values, and the families of parents-in-law have more influence in the family decision-making process. These are the aspects which one cannot find in the western literature. Therefore, we need critical thinking about the traits of Korean families and attention to differences in cultures. (p. 11)

During the formalized critique that followed the presentation of this paper, discussants acknowledged trends related to the global market—the drastic decline in the birthrate, increasing reports of violence, changing roles for women, and increasing need for care of the aged. To meet the changing needs of society, according to discussants, social work needs to adopt macro-level approaches to problems, not base interventions on so-called problem families.

| Cuba |

For the following information, my gratitude is to David Strug and Walter Teague (2002) who traveled to Cuba in search of lessons we can learn from Cuban social work education. The Cuban situation in reintroducing social work in a communist nation is unique. Other nations, such as China and the countries of the former Soviet Union, for example, did away with social work training in the belief, evidently, that the profession was unnecessary under a Marxist government. Originally, in the turmoil of their revolution, Cuba closed its school of social work; the school had been founded at the University of Havana in 1943. In 1971, however, training was provided to students at technical training institutes to perform social casework in Cuba's clinics and hospitals.

In the 1990s, concomitant with Cuba's increased participation in the global economy, as Strug and Teague (2002) indicate, growing social and economic crises occurred. Income disparity worsened due to the influx of foreign capital from abroad and tourism. In 2000, to meet the need to provide professional training for young people, the Cuban government opened three schools of social work, which were unique in their idea for these youths to help other youths, and in their integration of social work practice skills with political sociology. The focus is on providing training for government service to conduct nationwide public health and educational programs. Social workers live and work in needy communities; employment following the training is guaranteed. We can learn important lessons from Cuba's success in providing this large-scale training for government-guaranteed employment in community organization work.

| Canada |

In the 2003 film *Bowling for Columbine,* which won the Academy Award for the year's best documentary, Michael Moore devoted the last segment to Canada and the way Canadians live. The theme was the high U.S. homicide rate and America's fascination with guns. Although Moore's facts were somewhat misleading—he implied that Canadians have as many handguns as Americans do—the interviews with Canadian youths and politicians revealed a country where the people were happy with their social welfare system, not paranoid about crime, and sufficiently trusting of their neighbors to leave their homes unlocked.

NASW has started looking northward as well. For the first time in history, there is now a formal joint relationship between NASW and CASW (Canadian Association of Social Workers). One of the purposes of the alliance is to strengthen the collaboration to act jointly on IFSW issues; these two nations are member countries of the North American region of IFSW (Stoesen, 2003). According to Terry Mizrahi, cited in the article by Stoesen, "We looked at issues of poverty as human rights issues, how to improve child welfare systems, developing standards for international social work practice and dealing with racial, ethnic and cultural diversity" (p. 6). Mizrahi singled out Canadian models of practice, the Canadian health care system, and entitlements as areas about which we have a lot to learn from Canada.

The impact of the global market on Canada is twofold—pressures of NAFTA (North American Free Trade Agreement) and from the wider corporate-controlled economy. NAFTA is often referred to simply as the Free Trade Agreement. In their book *Canadian Social Policy,* Graham, Swift, and Delaney (2000) argue that, at least in part because of NAFTA, Canadian politicians have started looking south of the 49th parallel for political precedents. Although social welfare cutbacks have not been as severe as those in the United States and the United Kingdom, retrenchment and workfare are, as Graham et al. suggest, policies that are bandied about. The Free Trade Agreement was formalized between the United States and Canada in 1994. Between 1971 and 1996, the gap between Canada's richest and poorest deepened considerably. Child poverty has increased especially among the Native population. Universal family allowances were abolished in 1993; resources are now targeted to low-income families only.

Canadian authors and social work educators Wilson and Whitmore (2000) turn our attention to Mexico where the people, as they argue, have not experienced the "win-win-win" predictions of NAFTA advocates in which each partner country would benefit from the trade of its specialized products. The winners in all three countries have been the transnational corporations. For Canada, the effect has been a declining standard of living and a weakening of the social safety net. Wilson and Whitmore's recommendation is for popular organizations (e.g., IFSW) that also think and work transnationally to counter the corporate interconnectedness.

"Profession Has Global Role" was the headline of a *NASW News* article (Slavin, 2002). The dilemma facing Canadian social work, according to the article, is how to provide professionalized services when requirements for the vision of services are being downgraded. The issue is privatization, one of standards of the global market cost-saving policies. Traditionally, in Canada, social services were provided directly by the government. In today's competitive market economy, performance is quantified, caseloads have risen, and agencies are expected to do more with less. Services are subcontracted out to private firms that save money by hiring unqualified human services workers. The results, according to the article, are particularly damaging to Aboriginal peoples and recent immigrants.

Under the pressure of the global economy, will Canadian social services come to resemble those of their southern neighbor? This question was posed on the Canadian Social Work Discussion List (Listserv correspondence, November 7, 2001, at CSOCwork@pdomain.uwindsor.CA). Listserv member Jim Poushinsky responded to the query as follows:

> [The Canadian] necessity of co-operation has become institutionalized in our social programs such as wealth transfer payments between have and have-not provinces, medicare (universal health care), unemployment insurance, and welfare. So philosophically, I think Canadians are by necessity team players who understand the need to work together, whereas individual Americans can to a much greater extent survive by "making it on their own."

Poushinsky goes on to contemplate the possibility of a reversal in Canadian sensitivities:

> Now as we watch our dollar dropping to 62 cents relative to the U.S. dollar, as we contemplate our national resource base being wiped out with the disappearance of fishing stocks, the U.S. tariffs shutting down our softwood lumber exports and threatening our grain, and third world industries undercutting our mining and manufacturing businesses, I believe we are about to rediscover our co-operative roots. (p. 1)

Summary and Conclusion

The world over, common societal needs generate similar institutional responses, and national ideologies shape the level of care provided. Despite surface similarities, however, there are vast international differences in the magnitude of the problems encountered and in the nature and pattern of services developed to deal with them. The idea that social welfare is a guarantee of well-being for all citizens is more firmly rooted in some countries (e.g., in the northern parts of western Europe) than in others. Countries that value independence, autonomy, and minimal governmental interference, like the United States, are likely to be resistant to sweeping welfare legislation. Countries with strong labor and socialist parties, on the other hand, are more apt to be amenable to the social service provisions.

The study of social welfare systems, therefore, must attend to values within which this system derives. A society that provides universal cradle-to-grave protections to all citizens is apt to include in its numbers many who lack the drive to "get ahead." A society, conversely, whose values center on equal opportunity to achieve or fail (but without any cushion to protect those who fail), a society that allows for a huge income and wealth differential among its citizens, is apt to include in its numbers many who live in the throes of poverty.

The purpose of this chapter was to examine U.S. social values from an objective viewpoint (to the extent that is possible) to help us "see ourselves as others see us." Filtered from the literature of international social work and anthropology, nine value dimensions emerged with relevance to social welfare. These are: work versus leisure; equal opportunity versus equality; mobility versus stability; competition versus cooperation; individualism versus collectivism; independence versus interconnectedness; materialism versus spirituality; nuclear family versus extended family; and moralism versus compassion. Comparative analysis showed that except for the family construct that is associated with modern industrialization (where family size is shrinking), the attributes on the left-hand side of the continua (work, equal opportunity, etc.) are characteristically American, while those on the right-hand side are representative of advanced welfare states such as those found in the Nordic countries. Moralism is a trait that in American politics and policy making transcends all the others (except perhaps for materialism and the nuclear family arrangement).

The final sections of this chapter viewed how the values and social policy are intertwined and how social work and American values are not always compatible, and sometimes are even contradictory. With examples drawn from Chile (whose grassroots efforts have inspired social work the world over), South Korea (representative of a highly vigorous East Asian model), Jamaica (illustrative of a modernizing region),

Cuba (illustrative of a communist nation that is introducing some elements of capitalism), and Canada (representing a progressive nation of the Global North), we have seen how globalization has affected the profession of social work. Revealed in these international portraits too is the global interconnectedness among nations' social values. This international thrust is reminiscent of the international contacts between the profession's founding mothers in Europe and the United States in the late 19th century. Today our global interdependence is being strengthened by common forces, common concerns: The problems facing social workers go beyond national boundaries. By the same token, whether their method is psychotherapy or community action, and whether they work in Singapore, Ireland, Canada, or the United States, social workers are united by common professional values; such values emphasize altruism and goodwill and transcend the cultural nuances of a particular region.

Internationally oriented social workers very often have ideas, given their familiarity with social programs in other forms in other places, that can be useful, even inspiring, in influencing public policy on the home front. Enhancing social and economic development for all the people is often a major concern. The starting point for policy shaping and policy making is an understanding of cultural ethos; timing is everything in introducing policy initiatives and reform. The next chapter extends this cultural understanding into the historical arena, the focal point of which is the growth and development of social work. Because this profession is the one most closely bound to social welfare, the history of social welfare, in effect, becomes the history of social work.

Thought Questions

1. How does the metaphor of finding four-leaf clovers relate to understanding a culture?

2. Explain the meaning of the title of Jansson's book, *The Reluctant Welfare State*.

3. According to social scientists, how do people come to acquire social values?

4. Discuss how the media both reflect and promote social values. What is the role of the media in wartime?

5. Which of the values listed in the nine value dimensions, in your opinion, best encapsulates the "American way of life"?

6. Trace the historical roots of the work ethic. What was Max Weber's theory? Relate to the teachings of Calvinism and Benjamin Franklin.

7. Today we are a secular nation: To what extent do you think the Protestant work ethic applies or does not apply at this time?

8. Discuss the value put on work in several different countries.

9. Differentiate equal opportunity from equality.

10. Discuss welfare reform as a residually based program.

11. "To destroy a social welfare program, make it means-tested." Discuss this claim.

12. Argue that mobility is a key characteristic of U.S. society.

13. Describe a society in which the social climate is cooperation-based rather than competition-based. What is *samarbeid*?

14. Define individualism. What does the Milgram study demonstrate?

15. Contrast the concept of the Indian Medicine Wheel with the mainstream U.S. focus on independence.

16. How is individualism a fact of life, even a corrupting force, worldwide?

17. "The Incredible Shrinking Family": Discuss this concept.

18. Relate the force of moralism to punitiveness in American society.

19. Discuss the shift in social policy initiatives as they parallel the shift in society's values.

20. What is unique about social work values and how do they contrast with mainstream values?

References

Al-Krenawi, A., & Graham, J. R. (2001). The cultural mediator: Bridging the gap between a non-western community and professional social work practice. *British Journal of Social Work, 31*, 665–685.

Associated Press. (2004, March 4). World thinks Iraq war fuels terrorism. *Waterloo-Cedar Falls Courier*, p. A1.

Barker, R. (2003). *The social work dictionary* (5th ed.). Washington, DC: NASW Press.

Barnett, J., Weathersby, R., & Aram, J. (1995). American cultural values: Shedding cowboy ways for global thinking. *Business Forum, 20*(1–2), 9–14.

Baron, R., & Graziano, W. (1991). *Social psychology*. Fort Worth, TX: Holt, Rinehart & Winston.

Barth-Heyerdahl, Ø. (1999). Politiet kvier seg for å fengsle russere. *Aftenposten*. Retrieved from http://www.aftenposten.no

Barusch, A. S. (2002). *Foundations of social policy: Social justice, public programs, and the social profession*. Itasca, IL: F. E. Peacock.

Bateson, M. (1984). *With a daughter's eye: A memoir of Margaret Mead and Gregory Bateson*. New York: Pocket Books.

Bernstein, A., & Starr, A. (2002, June 4). Welfare reform, round 2. *Business Week*, 60–62.

Blass, T. (2002, March–April). The man who shocked the world. *Psychology Today, 35*(2), 68–74.

Borzutzky, S. (2002). Chile's fully funded system. An analysis of its impact on the state and the society. Paper presented at the International Conference on Social Welfare. Seoul, Korea. Seoul National University, October 11–12.

Bréchon, P. (2000, Autumn). Values of the French: A quantitative approach. *Isuma, 1*(2). Retrieved from http://www.isuma.net

Butler, L. (2003, January–February). "Living on Tokyo time." *Utne Reader, 65.*

Canda, E. R., & Furman, L. D. (1999). *Spiritual diversity in social work practice: The heart of helping.* New York: Free Press.

Chung, K. (2002). Generative balanced model of welfare. Paper presented at the International Conference on Social Welfare, Seoul National University, Seoul, Korea, October 11–12.

Church, F. (2002, September 11). The American creed. *The Nation,* 19–22.

Consensus and contraction. (2002, April 20). *The Economist* (Supplement), 8–10.

Coyhis, D. (2000). Substance abuse and cultural issues in Indian country. In J. Krestam (Ed.), *Bridges to recovery: Addiction, family therapy, and multicultural treatment* (pp. 79–114). New York: Free Press.

Daly, A., Jennings, J., Beckett, J., & Leashore, B. (1996). Effective coping strategies of African Americans. In P. Ewalt, E. Freeman, S. Kirk, & D. Poole, *Multicultural issues in social work* (pp. 189–203). Washington, DC: NASW Press.

Day, P. (2002). *A new history of social welfare* (4th ed.). Boston: Allyn & Bacon.

de Tocqueville, A. (1951/1835). *Democracy in America* (P. Bradley, Trans.). New York: Alfred A. Knopf.

Draut, T. (2002, March 14). The conflicted American: Public opinion on poverty, income inequality, and public policy. Paper presented at the Annual Conference of the Neighborhood Funders Group, San Francisco, CA.

Ediger, M. (March 2000). Competition versus cooperation and pupil achievement. *College Student Journal, 34,* 14–21.

Erikson, E. (1963). *Childhood and society.* New York: Norton.

Finn, J. L. (2002). Raíces: Gender-conscious community building in Santiago, Chile. *Affilia, 17*(4), 448–470.

Fritzell, J. (2001). Still different? Income distribution in the Nordic countries in a European comparison. In M. Kautto, J. Fritzell, B. Hvinden, J. Kvist, & H. Uustalo (Eds.), *Nordic welfare states in the European context* (pp. 18–41). London: Routledge.

Gil, D. (1998). *Confronting injustice and oppression: Concepts and strategies for social workers.* New York: Columbia University Press.

Government of Guam. (2004). The culture of Guam. Government Web site. Retrieved March 20, 2004 from http://ns.gov.gu/culture

Graham, J., Swift, K., & Delaney, R. (2000). *Canadian social policy: An introduction.* Scarborough, Ontario: Allyn & Bacon Canada.

Grimsrud, T., & Zehr, H. (2002). Rethinking God, justice and treatment of offenders. In T. O'Connor (Ed.), *Religion, the community, and the rehabilitation of criminal offenders* (pp. 259–285). New York: Haworth.

Hartmann, T. (1997). *Attention deficit disorder: A different perception.* Grass Valley, CA: Under Wood Books.

Healy, L. (2001). *International social work: Professional action in an interdependent world.* New York: Oxford University Press.

Healy, L. (2003). Social work values, ethics and standards: International perspectives. Special presentation at the Council on Social Work Education 49th Annual Program Meeting. Atlanta, GA, February 27–March 2.

Hirayama, H., & Hirayama, K. (1999). Cross-cultural application of empowerment practice: A comparison between American and Japanese groups. In W. Shera & L. Wells (Eds.), *Empowerment practice in social work: Developing richer conceptual foundations* (pp. 246–258). Toronto: Canadian Scholars' Press.

hooks, b. (1994). *Teaching to transgress: Education is the practice of freedom.* New York: Routledge.

hooks, b. (2001). *Salvation: Black people and love.* New York: Harper Collins.

International Federation of Social Workers (IFSW). (2000). Social work, definition. Retrieved from http://www.ifsw.org

Ivins, M. (2001, August 2). People aren't made for working 24/7. *Des Moines Register,* p. 7A.

Jansson, B. (2001). *The reluctant welfare state.* Belmont, CA: Wadsworth.

Kaplan, C., & Kaplan, L. (1993). Public opinion and the "economic bill of rights." *Journal of Progressive Human Services* 4(1), 43–58.

Karmali, S. (2003, January–February). Unraveling the East-West myth. *Utne Reader,* 92–93.

Kendall, K. (2000). *Social work education: Its origins in Europe.* Alexandria, VA: Council on Social Work Education.

Koretz, G. (2001, June 11). Why Americans work so hard. *Business Week*, 34.

Kreitzer, L. (2002, June). *Globalization and indigenization: Power issues in social work knowledge.* Unpublished thesis, University of Calgary, Canada.

Krugman, P. (2003, February 18). Behind the great divide. *New York Times*. Retrieved from http://www.truthout.org/docs

Lee, J. (2001). *The empowerment approach to social work practice.* New York: Columbia University Press.

Living with a superpower. (2003, January 2). *Economist*. Retrieved from http://www.economist.com

Marks, R. (2003, Spring). Through new eyes. *Tulanian*, 28–37.

McLaughlin, A. (1998, August 28). "Long workdays draw backlash." *Christian Science Monitor*, 11.

Midgley, J. (2000). The institutional approach to social policy. In J. Midgley, M. B. Tracey, & M. Livermore (Eds.), *The handbook of social policy* (pp. 365–376). Thousand Oaks, CA: Sage.

Milgram, S. (1977). *The individual in a social world: Essays and experiments.* Reading, MA: Addison-Wesley.

Mills, C. W. (1959). *The sociological imagination.* New York: Oxford University Press.

Mizrahi, T. (2002, October 7). Letter addressed to President George W. Bush concerning NASW opposition against going to war against Iraq. Retrieved from http://www.socialworkers.org

National Association of Social Workers (NASW). (1996). *Code of ethics.* Washington, DC: NASW Press.

National Association of Social Workers (NASW). (2003a). Preserving rights, strengthening voices. *NASW social work month toolkit.* Washington, DC: NASW Press.

National Association of Social Workers (NASW). (2003b). *Social work speaks* (6th ed.). Washington, DC: NASW Press.

Nelson, M. R., & Shavitt, S. (2002, September). Horizontal and vertical individualism and achievement values. *Journal of Cross-Cultural Psychology, 33*(5), 439–458.

Nimmagadda, J., & Cowger, C. D. (1999). Cross-cultural practice: Social worker ingenuity in the indigenization of practice knowledge. *International Social Work, 42*(3), 261–276.

Norwegian Radio Broadcasting (NRK). (2004, February 2). Dømt for å nekte integrering. NRK.no. Retrieved from http://nrk.no/redskap/utskriftsvennlig

Payne, M. (1997). *Modern social work theory* (2nd ed.). Chicago: Lyceum.

PEW Research Center. (2002, December 19). Among wealthy nations, U.S. stands alone in its embrace of religion. Retrieved from http://people-press.org

Piven, F., & Cloward, R. (1993). *Regulating the poor: The functions of public welfare* (updated ed.). New York: Vintage.

Podolefsky, A., & Brown, P. (Eds.). (1994). *Applied cultural anthropology* (2nd ed., Introduction). Mountain View, CA: Mayfield.

Popple, P., & Leighninger, L. (2004). *The policy-based profession: An introduction to social welfare policy analysis for social workers.* Boston: Allyn & Bacon.

Prigoff, A. (1999). Global social and economic justice issues. In C. Ramanathan & R. J. Link (Eds.), *All our futures: Principles and resources for social work practice in a global era* (pp. 157–173). Belmont, CA: Wadsworth.

Reich, R. (2000). *The future of success: Working and living in the new economy.* New York: Vintage.

Reisch, M., & Andrews, J. (2001). *The road not taken: A history of radical social work in the United States.* Philadelphia: Brunner-Routledge.

Robbins, S. P., Chatterjee, P., & Canda, E. R. (1999). Ideology, scientific theory, and social work practice. *Families in Society, 80*(4), 374–384.

Sheler, J. L. (2002). Faith in America. *U.S. News & World Report*, 38–49.

Slavin, P. (2002, March). Profession has global role: Social work's international stature is explained. *NASW News, 1*, 2.

Song, S. J. (2002, October 11–12). Changes in family and social work practice in Korea. Paper presented at the International Conference on Social Welfare, Seoul National University, Seoul, Korea.

Speeding in Finland. (2002, February 12). All things considered. National Public Radio.

Stiglitz, J. (2002). *Globalizing and its discontents.* New York: W. W. Norton.

Stoesen, L. (2003, January). NASW, Canadians bolster relationship. *NASW News*, 6.

Strug, D., & Teague, W. (2002, September 2). New directions in Cuban social work education: What can we learn? *Social Work Today*, 8–11.

Suppes, M. A., & Wells, C. C. (2003). *The social work experience: An introduction to social work and social welfare* (4th ed.). Boston: McGraw-Hill.

Taylor, Z. (1999). Values, theories and methods in social work education: A culturally transferable core? *International Social Work, 42*(3), 309–318.

Tropman, J. (1989). *American values and social welfare: Cultural contradictions in the welfare state.* Englewood Cliffs, NJ: Prentice-Hall.

Wagner, D. (1994, November). Beyond the pathologizing of nonwork: Alternative activities in a street community. *Social Work, 39,* 718–727.

Wagner, D. (2000). *What's love got to do with it?* New York: New Press.

Wardle, H. (2002). Marsby and friends: Informality, deformalisation and West Indian Island Experience. *Social Identities, 8*(20), 255–271.

Weber, M. (1958/1905). *The Protestant ethic and the spirit of capitalism.* New York: Scribner & Sons.

Weisman, J. (2001, April 16). Safety-net programs are set for cuts amid slowdown. *USA Today,* 12A.

Wilensky, H., & Lebeaux, C. (1958). *Industrial society and social welfare.* New York: Free Press.

Williams, R. (1979). Change and stability in values and values systems: A sociological perspective. In M. Rokeach (Ed.), *Understanding human values: Individual and societal.* New York: Free Press.

Wilson, M., & Whitmore, E. (2000). *Social development in the age of globalism.* Nova Scotia, Canada: Fernwood.

Wilson, W. J. (1996). *When work disappears: The world of the new urban poor.* New York: Vintage Books.

Wolfe, A. W. (2002). Welfare reform—Self-sufficiency or what? In A. Podolefsky & P. J. Brown (Eds.), *Applying cultural anthropology: An introductory reader* (pp. 282–285). Mountain View, CA: Mayfield.

Wright, E. M. (2001). Substance abuse in African American communities. In S. L. A. Straussner (Ed.), *Ethnocultural factors in substance abuse treatment* (pp. 31–51). New York: Guilford.

Zakaria, F. (2003, March 24). Why America scares the world: And what to do about it. *Newsweek,* 18–33.

Zastrow, C. (1999). *Introduction to social work and social welfare* (7th ed.). Belmont, CA: Wadsworth.

*An awareness of history should make us appreciate
the long sweep of development as a never-ending process.*

KATHERINE KENDALL, **2000**, P. **108**

*Tomorrow night is nothing but one long sleepless wrestle
with yesterday's omissions and regrets.*

WILLIAM FAULKNER, **1948**, P. **431**

Emergence of Social Work

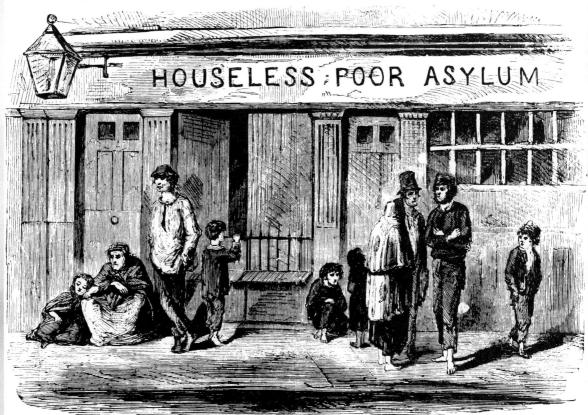

1846. People wait to gain entry to a poorhouse in Scotland. Reprinted with permission of Heatherbank Museum of Social Work, Glasgow, Scotland.

Learning isolated bits of information may help prepare a person for a game such as Trivial Pursuit, but true understanding grows by studying the interconnectedness of things. To appreciate such interconnectedness, we need to journey backward and forward in time. Only in this way can we see how the rhythms and patterns in one period become repeated in a somewhat different form in a later period. Historically, social welfare has progressed in a circular rather than a linear fashion; its evolution can be conceived in terms of rotating ideologies.

The story of social work begins with the history of social welfare, and the history of social welfare goes back at least to the Middle Ages. We will lay the groundwork, then, for our story of the emergence of social work in reviewing selected milestones in early social welfare history that had a bearing on the evolution of social work—the technological discoveries, paradigm shifts related to the new technologies, and religious upheavals. The major portion of this chapter chronicles the history of social work in terms of prime movers, whether influential people or events.

Before presenting the case for an international focus in social work as an imperative for the 21st century, I describe social work as an empowering profession in today's world. As a profession whose roots are planted in the informal and formal responses to human misery in England and North America, and as a profession that was both shaped by historical movements and helped to fashion them, social work has managed to survive by blending with the times. Franklin (1990) revealed how social work has responded to the ideological ethos of the times by offering interventions—community action (during progressive times) and individual casework (in conservative periods)—that were compatible with the popular currents of the day. In our consideration of these trends, we have to remember that there was much overlap between the interventions, until one or the other won out, and that countervailing forces were always present simultaneously. Shining through all the periods were vestiges of empowerment. (So it is today, as the leaders of the social work profession relentlessly and forthrightly confront the conservative onslaught on the social welfare state.) This remains no less true now than formerly, and no less true in other parts of the world than in the West.

In examining the practice of social work cross-culturally in this chapter, two key themes emerge: The first is that social work as a profession somehow has managed to maintain a shared value base across time and space, even during the most palpable shifts in ideological temperament. The second, and this one seemingly contradicts the first, is that social work necessarily must reflect the cultural ethos of which it is a part.

Milestones in Early Social Welfare History

The history of social welfare beginning in Europe and continuing in America over the last several hundred years is a tale of neglect and cruelty; of paternalism (or maternalism) and compassion; of integrity and deceit; of arrogant social control punctuated by racism, sexism, and classism; of new ideas superimposed on old ideas; and finally, of old ideas superimposed on the new. Looming over the whole scene is the age-old dilemma of how to balance the care for the weak and deprived against the need for strong work incentives. A society too soft may breed laziness and malingering, one too harsh may breed death and isolation. Over the centuries, nation-states have leaned one way or another and espoused varying doctrines based on ideas such as survival of the fittest, requiring people to work in order to eat, and taxing the rich to provide for the poor.

A perusal of Table 3.1 reveals the key roles of foreign conquest, modern technologies, and political ideology on the system of public welfare. The road from 1066 when the Normans (French speakers of Scandinavian descent) under William the Conqueror brought feudalism to the British Isles to the enclosures that sent the serfs scurrying across the land to the cities to the Protestant Reformation to the Industrial Revolution and, finally, to union organizing and social reform, can be viewed in terms of one long progression toward modern capitalism. Except for the religioeconomic changes associated with the Protestant revolution, and the Black Death of 1348, the other turning points were accompanied by technological advances such as the ox-drawn cart and the invention of the steam engine.

Most prominent among all the events shown in Table 3.1, in terms of U.S. social welfare history, was the Protestant Reformation of 1517. The religious event had repercussions that extended far beyond the realm of the church into the realms of capitalism, social welfare, work, education, and the British settlements of the "New World."

The Protestant Reformation

After he was excommunicated for posting his 95 theses on the door of a Catholic church in Wittenburg (opposing the use of indulgences and other corrupt church practices), Martin Luther founded what later would turn out to be Protestantism. By challenging the notion of papal authority, encouraging church members to read and study the scriptures in their own language, and replacing rituals with sermons, the Protestant church increased the involvement of parishioners in their own religious lives (Jansson, 2005). While Luther's memorable act of defiance weakened the Holy Roman Empire politically and fostered the development of the nation-state, the course of social welfare history was forever changed as well. At the heart of the change was Luther's introduction of the notion of vocation as a calling to do God's work in all things— whether as a member of the clergy or as a teacher, farmer, or laborer (Day, 2003). This notion of a calling ultimately revolutionized the social system in that it gave a meaning to work which went beyond work itself. As Dolgoff, Feldstein, and Skolnick (2003) indicate, Luther's teachings improved the morale of laborers, giving them a sense of duty in an honest day's toil. All of this, however, would not have been of such ultimate significance for American society had Henry VIII of England borne a healthy son. Desperate to have a male heir through remarriage and forbidden by the Pope to divorce, the monarch wrested

Table 3.1 | Milestones in the Development of British Social Welfare

Date	Event
1066	Norman Conquest; feudalism, introduction of French words into English, and unification of the country under law.
1348	The Bubonic plague (The Black Death) kills one third of the population of Europe; religious minorities and poor women are scapegoated.
1350	Statute of Laborers passed to restrict workers from traveling or organizing to take advantage of the labor shortage resulting from the plague.
1517	Martin Luther posts 95 theses on door of a Catholic Church.
1533	Henry VIII breaks away from Rome and converts himself, and therefore the nation, to Protestantism.
1536	John Calvin systematizes Protestant thought; his notion of predestination is to have an indelible effect in Britain and the New World.
1601	Poor Law provides for local poor relief allocations and transfers responsibility for welfare aid from the church to the government.
1750–1850	Industrial Revolution reinvents the meaning of work.
1769	Steam engine invented and hastened migration to the cities.
1776	Adam Smith publishes *The Wealth of Nations,* which provides a rationale for the cruelties of unfettered capitalism.
1800	London's population reaches one million.
1834	The New Poor Law embodies the principle of survival of the fittest into law with the purpose of making public aid less attractive.
1838	Dickens's *Oliver Twist* gives human misery in the Industrial Age a human face.
1845–1855	Irish potato famine kills nearly one million while even more emigrate.
1848	Marx and Engel's *Communist Manifesto* published; it puts a new face on the notions of capitalism and class struggle.
1859	Darwin's *Origins of Species* published; it shows the advantages to various species of survival of the fittest.
1869	Charity Organization Society (COS) established; this development is to help professionalize charity work.
1881	Germ theory of disease is generally accepted.
1884	Toynbee Hall, the first settlement house, established in London.
1904	Establishment of the first British schools of social work.
1911	National Insurances Act passed, inspired by Bismarck's lead; the Act provided unemployment insurance and became a model for other nations.
1942	Beveridge Report recommends an integrated social security system for Britain.
1946	National Health Service established.

control of the English branch of the Catholic Church. England accordingly became Protestant.

The stress on literacy in Protestantism, on reading the Bible in one's own language, had quite an impact on the impetus for education (Jansson, 2005). An unintended consequence was the split of Protestantism into various denominations and sects related to interpretations of Christ's teaching. The Puritans and Quakers were among the dissenters from the established Church of England who were eventually to set sail for what is now America. Dissident Catholic groups followed. To summarize: One defiant act of a disenchanted priest in 16th-century Germany had a monumental impact on U.S. history and, likewise, on the world. (Refer back to Chapter 2 to read about the Protestant work ethic.)

Elizabethan Poor Law

Another date listed in Table 3.1 with special significance for social work history is 1601. With the end of the Catholic Church charities and in the wake of enclosures, population growth, and urbanization, government overseers of the poor administered laws providing for public relief. Local parishes and counties were now required to provide work for the poor and houses of correction for criminals and idlers. For the first time, care for the poor was a secular, not a church, function.

The Elizabethan Poor Law was to remain the major codification of laws for dealing with poor and disadvantaged people for more than 200 years (Barker, 2003). It also was destined to become the basis for dealing with poor people in Colonial America. The principal provisions of the Elizabethan Poor Law are listed by Johnson (1995) and Trattner (1999) as follows:

1. Administration of poor relief at the local level
2. Relative responsibility, which was the doctrine that parents were responsible for the support of their children and grandchildren, and grown children for their dependent parents and grandparents
3. The taxing of people in each parish to pay for their own poor
4. The classification of the destitute into three categories: the able-bodied or "sturdy beggars," the impotent poor who could be cared for at the poorhouse ("indoor relief") or be given "outdoor relief" or aid in their homes such as food or fuel, and dependent children who could be given apprenticeships or trained for domestic service

Conditions at the workhouse were intended to ensure that no one with any conceivable alternative would seek public aid (Piven & Cloward, 1993). Compassion and punitiveness were thus skillfully linked in one composite piece of legislation. Separating the poor into "deserving" and "undeserving" made poverty for some a blameworthy condition. This significant development still has an impact on us centuries later throughout the Anglo-Saxon world (Johnson, 1995).

Consistent with their structuralist conception of welfare as a means to regulate the poor, Piven and Cloward (1993) argue that Western relief systems arose not out of concern for the general good but as a desperate response to mass disturbances that threatened the status quo. When the emergence of the wool industry put a premium on available land, and when the impact on the dispossessed farmers threatened political unrest, the provisions for relief were expanded.

The New Poor Law of 1834

The New Poor Law was an attempt to reform the prior Elizabethan Poor Law in Britain. The underlying emphasis of the new law was on self-reliance. Its vision was deterrence; its methods were repressive; and its purpose was to cure the perceived evil of pauperism (Kendall, 2000). The new, harsh moral view of poverty reflected in this law allowed the destitute to be admitted to the workhouse and to receive the in-kind, as opposed to cash, form of relief only. Public assistance was not considered a right, nor was government seen as responsible for the unemployed. Most memorable, perhaps, the principle of *less eligibility* was established. According to this principle, people who were given aid had to get less than the lowest-paid worker (Barker, 2003). The aim of this poor law, in short, was not to end poverty but to force relief applicants to accept any type of labor available. The reader will not be hard put to see that many of the attitudes of the mid-19th century, incorporated into the New Poor Law, remain with us today.

As always, even in the mid-19th century, there were mitigating factors at work. The brutal working conditions in the new industrial age that demanded serious reform were both immortalized and dramatically exposed in the collective works of Charles Dickens. Dickens's popular novels, serialized in journal form and read across all of England, produced an outcry that helped generate an awakening of sorts, a new humanitarianism.

Then there was the influence of Karl Marx. Marx (1818–1883), who was preeminently a theorist of capitalist society, set the stage for revolution and bloodshed when he and Engels collaborated to write the *Communist Manifesto* (1963/1848). Exiled from Europe after the Revolutions of 1848, Marx and Engels moved to London. The economic and political philosophy introduced by these writers views the history of society as the history of class struggle. From the Marxist perspective, the relationship between capitalists and workers derives from the control the capitalist has over the means of production and the product. The labor and socialist movements adapted many of their principles from Marxism.

Political organizations such as the Fabian Society, an English Socialist group, were influential in instituting practical reforms such as working hours legislation, housing projects, and mass education. Charity organizations and settlement houses sprang up out of the same impetus toward reform. In the United States, less influenced by a socialist and labor party voice than Britain, the welfare system was modeled on the English poor laws and the ideologies that undergirded them. The enforcement of such laws was unmitigated by sufficiently potent counter impulses (see Jannson, 2005; Piven & Cloward, 1993; Trattner, 1999).

Colonial America

Just after the passage of the Elizabethan Poor Law in 1601, settlements began to be established by colonists in North America. As dissenters from the Church of England, Puritans were inspired by Calvinist theology (belief in predestination) and favored a strict religious creed.

In an analysis of early town records in 17th-century Massachusetts and Connecticut, Dolgoff et al. (2003) reveal how the "deserving" poor were maintained and supported by the townships. Vagrant and idle persons, on the other hand, were warned to leave town. Vagrants and those who harbored them were subject to prosecution. The Poor Law mentality was alive and well in the so-called New World; provisions were followed scrupulously because they were widely familiar to England's emigrants, and because they helped maintain order in the new land. Concepts of the worthy and unworthy poor, the favoring of indoor (such as in a workhouse) over outdoor relief, and the principle of less eligibility (the poor must be supported below the level of the lowest-paid worker) were implanted early in the Atlantic coast colonies. Because of the absence of unemployment, the work ethic made even more sense here than in the home country. And then, there was the religious factor: The ethos of the Protestant ethic was suffused throughout the whole social system.

European Christians, as Jansson (2005) indicates, long held the belief that their duty was to try to convert the indigenous population to Christianity. The heathens who did not convert could be exploited in various ways. The Americas, of course, were densely populated with indigenous tribes. As the emigrants from Europe grew more and more plentiful, the greed to have access to all forested and other unfarmed land became all-consuming. Native Americans were pushed into signing various treaties under threat of coercion, while intoxicated, or in exchange for gifts including guns (Jansson, 2005). The Native peoples, we must keep in mind, had a different concept of land than did the white settlers. Consistent with their sense of spiritual interconnectedness and reverence for nature, the concept of private ownership of land, water, and plant life was completely alien (Gesino, 2001). The end result of the clash of cultures and interests was that the U.S. government broke the treaties, and the Indians were relocated further and further west (Kirst-Ashman, 2003). Relevant key events in U.S. history with a bearing on social welfare are highlighted in Table 3.2.

In summary, following Jansson (2005), the major social and cultural factors that shaped American social welfare policies in the Colonial era were: an emphasis on individualism and limited government, the lack of a large class of landless people, a weak central government, and the subjugation of persons of color. For themselves, the leaders of the new country elevated the concept of liberty over that of equality.

Table 3.2 | Milestones in the Development of American Social Welfare

Date	Event
1776	Declaration of Independence.
1788	Constitution ratified by the states.
1791	Bill of Rights ratified.
1838–1839	Forced march of the Cherokees.
1848	Mexican government forced to cede Texas and California.
1852	First compulsory education law passed in Massachusetts.
1854	President Pierce vetoes bill inspired by Dorothea Dix to provide aid for the mentally ill. Most states built public mental hospitals, nevertheless.
1860	Over 27,000 miles of railroad track built.
1861–1865	Civil War; more than 600,000 Americans killed.
1865	Thirteenth Amendment to the Constitution, abolishing slavery.
1865–1872	Freedmen's Bureau provides relief for newly freed slaves.
1865–1900	Rapid industrialization.
1877	First Charity Organization Society (COS) in the United States.
1880–1914	Twenty-one million immigrants arrive.
1881	Practice of medicine revolutionized through germ theory of disease.
1889	Hull House opened, Chicago.
1898	First American school for social workers established; later becomes Columbia University School of Social Work.
1899	First juvenile court in Chicago.
1918	Compulsory education laws established in all states.
1919–1933	Prohibition leads to much corruption.
1920	Nineteenth Amendment grants suffrage to women.
1929	Great Depression begins with crash of stock market.
1931	Jane Addams is awarded the Nobel Peace Prize.

Informal and Semi-Formal Helping

Most of the help for the poor has come from its own—the poor helping the poor with limited resources. Mutual aid among African Americans was based on a cultural heritage that stressed strong extended family ties and the tradition of adopting nonrelatives into the family network. Individual interests were not placed above the group; cooperation and sense of community prevailed. Before the Civil War, there were half a million free persons of African descent in the United States (and four million slaves); half of the freed slaves were in the South (Day, 2003). A great deal of charity work was done by these free blacks; they had

1933	New Deal proclaimed by Franklin Roosevelt.
1935	U.S. Social Security Act; Aid to Families with Dependent Children (AFDC); Alcoholics Anonymous founded.
1945	World War II ends; United Nations (U.N.) established.
1948	Universal Declaration of Human Rights ratified by nations of U.N.
1952	The Council on Social Work Education (CSWE) is founded to accredit schools of social work.
1955	The National Association of Social Workers (NASW) is created through a merger of existing organizations.
1956	The International Federation of Social Workers (IFSW) is established as an international social work organization.
1964	Great Society programs; food stamp program; Civil Rights Act.
1965	Medicare and Medicaid are added to the Social Security Act.
1969	Stonewall Inn riot initiates gay rights movement.
1972	Supplemental Security Income program enacted as a social insurance program for workers who had paid into the system.
1975	Passage of the Education for All Handicapped Children Act, now known as Individuals with Disabilities Education Act, provides for appropriate, often mainstreamed education for children with disabilities.
1978	Passage of the Indian Child Welfare Act to prevent the removal of Native American children from the Native American community.
1990	The Americans with Disabilities Act protects disabled persons from employment discrimination. The U.N. Convention on the Rights of the Child takes effect.
1996	President Clinton signs into law the Personal Responsibility and Work Opportunity Reconciliation Act "to end welfare as we know it."
2001	September 11 becomes a day etched in the world's memory as the airplane bombings of New York's Twin Towers lead to a war on terrorism and much additional loss of life in Afghanistan and Iraq.
2003	Medicare drug bill is signed into law by President George W. Bush, providing some coverage for prescription medication and a windfall for pharmaceutical companies and private health care organizations.

churches, relief associations, and societies for mutual aid. Among the slaves, obligations to kin and a general altruistic behavior promoted the collective survival of a people in a cruel and racist society. Today, a whole reexamination of slavery and the slave society that existed has been bolstered by the placing online of interviews with former slaves that were undertaken as a part of the Federal Writers' Project in the 1930s. These audio recordings of former slaves, excerpts of which were aired on Public Radio International, are riveting in their language and personal revelations of another time (Minzesheimer, 1998).

Farmers of all races and ethnicity historically have maintained their common welfare through offering collective aid in times of need—crop failures, barn burnings, illness. Men have generally been responsible for the heavy labor while women have bonded together for childbirth, child care, cooking, and other nurturant activities. Such a sense of communalism is preserved to some extent in rural areas and maintains its pure form among the Amish today.

Since the early colonial period, much help has been provided by the churches. Good works were viewed as an obligation owed to God and as more rewarding to the giver than to the receiver. In the North, as private fortunes accumulated, individuals and private groups supplemented public relief activities or assisted families whom they knew. In the South, private efforts of a large-scale variety were even more sustained (Trattner, 1999). There, according to Trattner, Calvinist principles of hard work were less pressing, while the spirit of *noblesse oblige* and chivalry was engendered in a class of people who were trying to maintain a social system not unlike that of feudalism.

In the United States, in contrast to many European nations, the separation of church and state had a significant bearing on the manner in which aid to the indigent populace was distributed. The flourishing of numerous sects in America led to a near-competitive atmosphere for helping the poor and, hopefully, winning converts. Nearly all forms of relief emanated from church groups: Protestants established orphanages, reform schools, mental hospitals, new kinds of prisons (an area of recognized Quaker activity), and institutions for the handicapped. The Quakers, in particular, spent an enormous amount of time, effort, and money aiding the needy (Trattner, 1999). Their work in rescuing slaves and abetting their escape is well known. The Catholic Church gave special attention to the needs of African and Native Americans, and especially to needy children (Day, 2003). Formed in the 18th century in New Orleans, the Ursuline Sisters ran a private home for mothers and children left homeless, initially from wars with the Indians. This home became America's first residential institution for orphaned children (Barker, 2003).

Formal Aid

Whereas outdoor relief was more common in the South, poorhouses in the North existed as a carryover from the early poor laws. By 1832, practically all of New York's counties had poorhouses run by political appointees whose pay was drawn from the inmates' work. The deserving and undeserving poor alike were confined in places where the rates for malnutrition and disease were quite high. The death rate for children was astronomical. After 1875, laws removed children from these work "dungeons of death" and placed them elsewhere.

When Sunday School teacher Dorothea Dix volunteered to teach at an insane asylum in 1841, she was set to embark on one of the most memorable crusades of the century—an effort to end the barbaric treatment of the indigent mentally ill. To Dix, the only way to rectify the problem lay in federal intervention. Building a network of support from the clergy, press, and politicians, Dix ultimately got a bill to allocate funds and land for the construction of mental hospitals passed by both houses of Congress. President Pierce's veto of the bill was based on the argument that the states, not the federal government, should provide charity. This single act set a precedent for the next 75 years that the federal government refrain from providing social welfare services. However, as Dolgoff et al. (2003) indicate, federal aid and land were given readily for the building of railroads and to reward soldiers for their service.

Like other major catastrophes, the Civil War created conditions that demanded immediate public aid. Singularly, affirming federal responsibility over states' rights, the Civil War laid the groundwork for the United States to ultimately become a welfare state (Day, 2003). First, even before the war was over, the social welfare needs of the soldiers and their families demanded attention. Whether in regard to medical care, housing, or financial support, the needs of the veterans were considered apart from the needs of the civilian population, and the veterans' needs were addressed without stigma or vacillation. In fact, from the time of the Revolutionary War, veterans were recipients of aid, universally, in recognition of their personal service and sacrifice. Generous grants to federal lands, pensions, and other types of aid were bestowed upon them.

Although the nation had abolished slavery forever, little thought was given for the welfare of the former slaves or of the society in which they would live. Thousands of ex-slaves took to the roads, wandering aimlessly from county to county. It is safe to say that more families were broken up by the first year of freedom than by any year of slavery (Nevins & Commager, 1981). Thousands of newly freed men and women died of disease and starvation or were victims of violence. The vast majority became sharecroppers who worked on white people's farms. Meanwhile, in the North, sweeping industrial activity resumed.

Though reluctant to assume a welfare role, the federal government in 1865, during Reconstruction, established the Freedmen's Bureau as part of the War Department. The purpose of this first federal welfare agency was to provide temporary relief, education, and health care for the newly freed slaves. One of the interesting functions of the Bureau was the work it did in reuniting families separated by slavery and the war, solemnizing prior slave unions, and arranging for the adoption of orphans. Despite the fact that it was seriously underfunded and ended its work abruptly, the Freedmen's Bureau established an important precedent in its offering of emergency, comprehensive relief during a serious social upheaval. Foreshadowing the New Deal of the 1930s and the war on poverty of the 1960s, the history surrounding the Freedmen's Bureau provides backing for Piven and Cloward's (1993) basic premise that "relief arrangements are initiated or expanded during outbreaks of civil disorder produced by mass unemployment, and are then abolished or contracted when political stability is restored" (p. XV).

Europe: A Contrast

While the Protestant ethic still prevailed in "the land of pilgrims' pride" and the British reform movement got underway in earnest, over in Europe, the birthplace of Protestantism, the first general social insurance scheme was introduced. Chancellor Otto von Bismarck's sickness insurance law provided to employees, in defined types of industry, medical care and cash benefits during a period of sickness. These benefits were to be financed through contributions by both employers and employees. In 1884, accident insurance was made compulsory. Several years later, workers' pensions were introduced. Austria followed suit, as did Sweden, and the Netherlands in 1901. In contrast, in Britain and the United States, where the threat of revolution was less potent, self-help was provided through friendly societies and savings banks (*Encyclopaedia Britannica,* 1998).

Bryson (1992) offers an interesting contrast between England and Sweden in terms of treatment of the landless poor. Whereas England engaged in a brutal process of forcing the rural poor off the land, Sweden (where industrialization arrived later) transferred land to peasant ownership. These historical differences between the two countries, notes Bryson, remain fundamental to understanding the more positive attitudes of Swedish people to government and the welfare state to the present day.

Industrial Growth in the United States

Within the span of one person's lifetime, industrialization, which came later than in Britain and was first apparent in the North, literally transformed the American landscape. Energy production soared to such an extent that the nation went from being primarily agricultural in 1859 to primarily producing manufactured goods 50 years later. The vast increases in both the population and the physical size of the cities presented the country with a set of problems reminiscent of England in earlier days. The streets of American cities were overcrowded, filthy, and rampant with disease (tuberculosis was common) and crime. Factory conditions were abominable; 18-hour days were not unheard of, women worked night shifts, and industrial accidents were frequent.

Two countertrends responded to the dehumanizing social conditions of the day: social Darwinism and Christian charity. *The Origin of Species,* written by Charles Darwin (1859), discussed the evolution of plants and animals. A happy union of laissez-faire economics and the doctrine of survival of the fittest, social Darwinism became the prevailing philosophy of the era (Trattner, 1999). As the wounds of the Civil War began to heal and wealth became almost an end in itself, the poor were once again blamed for their condition of poverty.

A severe economic depression of the 1870s threw large numbers of people out of work, and rioting and disorder ensued. Unions, which were just beginning to organize, were blamed by many for the economic crisis of the nation. Churches and private citizens set up soup kitchens and distributed fuel and clothing to the poor. Charity organization societies and settlement houses were established to provide formal but voluntary services to the poor.

Paradigm Shifts

Social work in Europe and the United States began in the 1890s in response to problems caused by industrialization and its corollary, urbanization. An outgrowth of the charities and corrections movements, social work practice has been greatly influenced by the development of the social welfare system.

Whereas technological advances have often outpaced our ethical and political understanding of how to cope with them, social workers and their antecedents have been key mediators between societal forces and the people they serve. Social workers, in other words, have helped those caught in the grip of rapid social change adjust to new circumstances. As society's "great humanizers," social workers alternately have been accused of overidentifying with the poor and of "being co-opted" by the system. This apparent dualism, between individual and society and between inner and outer directedness, in fact, is as old as social policy and, of course, far older than its professional link, social work. This dualism has haunted the profession since well before it even could be considered a profession.

Thomas Kuhn (1962) introduced the world of science to the notion of *paradigm shift.* A paradigm shift is a dramatic change in worldview by society often representing a revolutionary break with past ways of viewing reality. Such shifts in thinking generally take place as a result of some sort of crisis, whether due to scientific discoveries or economic/military forces. Relevant to social welfare history, our concern is where society places the blame for personal impoverishment—on the individual or on the society. We can term this the social/self dualism. Causal attribution has important treatment and public policy implications.

We can characterize America's social welfare history, accordingly, as one long series of pendulum swings between two opposite poles, with the focus of individual attribution at one end and the focus of social reform at the other. Although both of these currents have run simultaneously throughout the last century, one side or the other typically has tended to dominate at any one time. One generation's certainty has become the next generation's foolishness and blindness, to use Ehrenreich's (1985) apt phraseology. Or to continue with the metaphor, we might say that gravity invariably pulls the pendulum downward toward the other direction.

A social reform emphasis characterized the Progressive Era before World War I, and the 1930s, and 1960s. Social work leaders rose to prominence in each era: The foremother of social work, Jane Addams, is associated with the urban reform movement of the Progressive Era; social worker Harry Hopkins helped initiate the New Deal and the creation of the modern welfare state; and the idealistic war on poverty offered a bonanza in jobs for community action workers, and social work education expanded enormously during this period.

And then there were those in-between years when individualism triumphed. The private interest of the hedonistic 1920s, the political hysteria and anti-idealism of the 1950s, the attack-the-underdog mentality of the Reagan era, and the war on welfare first launched under the Clinton administration were all manifestations of ideological shifts away from the social activism of the previous age.

Franklin (1990) offers a cyclical framework to the emergence of three social work methods of practice—social casework, group work, and community organization. The origin of each method is linked, curiously, to the prevailing ideology of a specific political cycle in U.S. history, as Franklin's framework suggests. We could almost say, taking a literal meaning of the term, that each dominant practice modality was "politically correct" in its day. Whether society's focus was more on personal troubles, on public issues, or somewhere in between, the priorities of social work and the methods of treatment have followed. In this chapter, we will view the paradigm shifts as social work has oscillated between opposite ends of the political pendulum in response to the ideological and socioeconomic influences of the times.

The Origins of Social Work

Social work as we know it today was derived from a merger of the Charity Organization Societies (COSs) and the settlement house establishments (Haynes & White, 1999). Whereas the professional side of social work has its roots in COS altruism, the social justice strain is grounded in the settlement house tradition. Both movements were based largely on English models and tradition. Patronage, piety, poor laws, and philanthropy: These are the four Ps singled out by Specht and Courtney (1994) in their incisive book *Unfaithful Angels: How Social Work Has Abandoned Its Mission.* The four Ps are different arrangements for dealing with social problems that developed after the breakup of feudal society but which preceded the modern period. *Patronage,* an ancient custom still extant today, entails an independent system for boosting some members of the population (often minorities) into prominence. Political patronage for a particular ethnic group (e.g., the Irish immigrants in Boston) and social worker advocacy on behalf of the poor are two obvious examples. *Piety,* a term used to refer to the religious aspect of serving needy people, is another historically derived aspect of social work. Throughout history, thousands of church organizations have provided such help. The values of the *poor laws* are reflected in the middle-class morality that regulates the poor and their receipt of government aid. Programs for the poor are both means-tested and mean-spirited, and most are deliberately made unattractive (Specht & Courtney). *Private philanthropies* frequently served as a desirable alternative to public relief. "Alms for the poor" in its present form is represented in help provided by the private/voluntary sector; this includes support ranging from United Way agencies to the faith-based initiatives touted by the George W. Bush administration.

Charities and Corrections Movement

Claiming that individual failure was the reason for poverty was the underlying rationale of the Charity Organization Society (COS), which was founded in London in 1869. The Victorian reformers saw lack of character as the reason for poverty, not starvation wages, slum housing, lack of education, or poor health care (Kendall, 2000). Gradually, in Britain, it took the influence of the Fabian socialists to prove the fallacy of the belief that the poor were responsible for their own condition, as Kendall points out. This shift in the British focus was later reflected in the form that social work education took in the United

Kingdom, with its emphasis on the social sciences. In contrast, social casework was to become the hallmark of U.S. social work education. The social casework–based COS quickly moved to virtually every large city in the country, beginning with Buffalo, New York. In Canada, too, the COS legacy, the reform-the-person approach, was a guiding educational principle (Mullaly, 1997).

The decades from 1877 to World War I were a time of deep economic, social, and political crisis. Consistent with the ethos of the age, a scientific solution was directed to both the protection of the poor from starvation and a validation of the work incentive. Ehrenreich (1985) refers to three organizing principles of the operation of the COS: the use of business methods in controlling the flow of allocations, the perpetual focus on the moral status of the clients (were they deserving of aid?), and the key role of the friendly visitor or caring helper and mentor. As these often upper-class charity workers grew immersed in the world of the poor, a curious but predictable thing happened to them—they began to recoil at the paternalism and victim blaming inherent in the social system and to see poverty as a cause as well as a result of certain forms of social behavior (Franklin, 1990; Trattner, 1999).

Mary Richmond, later renowned for establishing the principles of social work education, began her career with the COS of Baltimore in 1888. Unlike other founders of the profession, Richmond was not a member of the privileged classes; she was entirely self-educated, in fact. Although she did not intend it, Richmond's individualistic casework focus helped prepare the profession for its later embrace of psychiatry, psychoanalysis, and psychotherapy (Specht & Courtney, 1994). Nevertheless, Richmond's keen attention to the individual as a part of a social unit and her advocacy of understanding the person in the situation is surprisingly consistent with modern multifocused formulations. Richmond's ideas were set forth in *Social Diagnosis* (1917), the first major textbook to be used by practicing social workers. The psychosocial conceptualization of human behavior introduced in this work might have come to fruition in the years that followed with the usual revision and reformulation of new theoretical paradigms had it not been for the influence of something even more magnificent—the voluminous works on the unconscious by Sigmund Freud.

In the meantime, as the COS began to develop a relevant knowledge base and to formalize social casework techniques of social service and delivery, the way was paved for the emergence of a new profession. Emphasizing personal attention and individual work with clients, this well-formulated model gained preeminence in conjunction with social work's transition from a voluntary to a paid enterprise. The inevitable tendency of scientific charity, with its emphasis on the objective and factual, was to make the use of volunteer visitors, untrained and part-time, increasingly difficult to justify (Trattner, 1999).

The credit for being the world's first professional social worker goes to Octavia Hill, an English pioneer in housing management who worked to improve the lives of the tenants even as she managed the property. Inspired by Christian socialism, Hill's work in helping the poorest of the poor reorganize their lives has been sadly neglected in the chronicles of social work. Fortunately, Katherine Kendall (2000) has perused her writings and other historical material of 19th-century England to make her contribution now a part of the historical record.

The first salaried social worker was a trained COS worker, Mary Stewart, who was hired in 1894 to interview patients at the Royal Free Hospital in London (Kendall, 2000). Her major role was to determine whether or not patients qualified for free treatment at the clinic (Amundsen, 1994). By the turn of the century, the organized charities were establishing formal training as the first step in professionalization. Volunteers were now being placed under the authority of social workers who shaped policy and covered the field. The professional charity workers, not the volunteers, began to be acknowledged authorities on the needs of disadvantaged and/or deviant people (Day, 2003). As mentioned earlier, social work derived from two movements, each with a very different ideological base. Whereas the individualistic casework method came to prominence later, when the emphasis on personality superseded the social action thrust, the community-oriented focus never has been entirely absent from a profession bent on "helping people help themselves." Nor is it entirely absent today.

The Settlement House Movement

An outgrowth of the deplorable urban conditions of the time and also modeled on English innovations, the settlement house movement began in the 1880s. After visiting Toynbee Hall, a house for the poor in the worst part of London in 1889, Jane Addams returned to Chicago to found with her associate, Ellen Gates Starr, the American equivalent of Toynbee Hall at Hull House. Eventually, Hull House was to become the most famous settlement in the world. Secular from the beginning, settlement houses in the United States had social change, rather than spiritual goals, as their focus. The individual religious motivation of the founders and volunteers, however, is not to be underestimated.

Settlements sprang up in most large cities over the next 15 years, their number reaching 300 at their peak in 1915. Set up in immigrant neighborhoods, upper- and middle-class people themselves—unmarried women, college students, teachers, and doctors—moved into slums as residents. The belief that poverty perhaps could be eliminated was a theme of the liberal Progressive Era.

There was, in fact, a strong undercurrent of thinking during the decades before World War I that was to offer a source of inspiration to the settlement house workers. The principal sources of such inspiration for early social workers included the secular and religious utopian philosophies of the 19th century, early feminist thinkers like Elizabeth Cady Stanton, radical trade unionism, the Social Gospel Movement, and the Socialist and Communist parties (Reisch & Andrews, 2001).

The years from 1900 to 1930 are characterized as the time of progressivism. In contrast to their friendly visitor counterparts, settlement house workers regarded themselves as social reformers rather than charity workers. With their goal to bridge the gap between the classes and their emphasis on prevention rather than treatment, these workers lived side by side with their urban neighbors and worked together with them to improve social conditions. In actively participating in the life of the neighborhood and of their poor and immigrant clients (in the United States), these upper- and upper-middle-class young men and women (mainly women) sought to raise the cultural, moral, and intellectual level of the community. The settlements provided a day nursery for working mothers, health clinics, and classes in English, dance, drama, art, and sewing.

Gradually, consistent with their intimate knowledge of their charges, the settlement workers became politicized and pursued social reform through legislation and social policy change. We must recognize, too, as we learn from Reisch and Andrews (2001), that many of the first generation of social workers like Florence Kelley or Ellen Gates Starr were radicals before they became social workers. These reformers helped bring about changes in child labor laws, in women's labor laws, and in the institutional care of the disabled and the "feebleminded" (Johnson & Schwartz, 1997). The establishment of child welfare services and juvenile courts, likewise, had its inception here. Rather than looking down upon the poor or seeking to impose their way of life upon them, settlement workers placed their focus on reforming society. Out of this heritage came one of social work's primary methods of intervention, a self-help model of community organization (Mullaly, 1997). As Jane Addams stated in her autobiography (1910):

> We early found ourselves spending many hours in efforts to secure support for deserted women, insurance for bewildered widows, damages for injured operators, furniture from the clutches of the installment store. The settlement . . . constantly acts between various institutions of the city and the people for whose benefit these institutions were erected. (p. 167)

To view an amazing collection of historical documents and images, visit the Hull House Web site at http://www.uic.edu/jaddams/hull/urbanexp/. Less well known to Americans but no less interesting is the Heatherbank Museum of Social Work in Glasgow, Scotland, the only museum totally dedicated to social work and welfare in Europe (information at http://www.lib.gcal.ac.uk/ heatherbank).

A question not addressed in the autobiography is, how did the settlement movement respond to the needs of black people who were just beginning to migrate into the northern cities during the Progressive Era? Trattner contrasts attitudes of the COS workers who stressed the individual moral causes of poverty and were largely indifferent to the problems of the destitute blacks, with settlement house workers who advocated the unpopular cause of equality for all Americans. Long before it was in vogue to do so, at least some settlement house workers helped foster black pride and Afro-American culture, according to Trattner. To their credit, settlement leaders actively participated in the creation of the National Association for the Advancement of Colored People (NAACP) and the National Urban League. Yet, consistent with the social climate of the day, while they opposed racism, these leaders did not advocate integration (Philpott, 1978). Realists as well as idealists, these women, such as Jane

Addams and Mary McDowell, knew that neighborhood prejudices militated against the mixing of blacks and whites in settlement house.

After 1900, according to Philpott, the settlements for "colored people" never had the capacity to provide black Chicago with adequate, much less equal, service. On the other hand, the nation's settlement houses were largely segregated, with many in the South created and staffed by African American women and reserved for blacks only. In Chicago, argues Trattner, the Frederick Douglass Center had workshops and clubrooms for boys, and held classes in manual training for boys and domestic service for girls to prepare black youths for the only jobs open to them in that day. Philpott (1978), however, is less charitable concerning the true purpose of the segregated settlement houses. His documentation, drawn from historical records of the day, suggests that the Douglass Center's true purpose was not to help the poor blacks but to attract the black elite and to insulate them from the less educated blacks who were pouring into "the black belt" in large numbers. The Emmanuel Settlement, founded and directed by Fannie Emmanuel, a dedicated African American, operated under a different philosophy. Fostering neighborhood pride, this center was a place where a person could get relief, both in the monetary and emotional sense of the word. With little or no financial support from whites, however, the settlement closed in less than five years. To learn the history of the little-known settlement schools where black and white women together delivered services to the community, see Spratt (1997).

Portrait of Jane Addams

By the turn of the last century, as Specht and Courtney (1994) indicate, Jane Addams was the most famous woman in America. By the culmination of her career in 1931, she was awarded the Nobel Prize for her efforts for peace during World War I. But who was Jane Addams really?

Although recounting some facts from her early life, Addams's autobiography, *Twenty Years at Hull House,* reveals very little personal detail about the author. The qualities that do shine forth are an abiding concern for the underdog, optimism, perseverance, and feisty leadership. Her fondness for her father, a devout Quaker to whom the book is dedicated, clearly set the stage for Addams's unpopular pacifism during World War I—a position that branded her a subversive and radical for the rest of her life. Jane Addams was to be given the dubious honor of first being made a life member of the Daughters of the American Revolution and then subsequently being expelled. Just as she had been universally acclaimed prior to the war, Addams experienced a fall from grace unparalleled among public figures in U.S. history (Reisch & Andrews, 2001).

Works on Quaker history include Jane Addams and others associated with the settlement movement as Quakers by upbringing. As described in *The Story of Quaker Women in America* (Bacon, 1986, p. 147): "Jane Addams herself was the daughter of self-styled Hicksite John Addams, whom she adored. Although never a member of a Quaker meeting, she maintained close ties with Quakers

Jane Addams, seen here on the right, showed the courage of her convictions in protesting all wars. Reproduced by permission.

throughout her life." Addams, in fact, was sent as a representative of the Society of Friends to distribute aid following the human wreckage of World War I.

Feminist and lesbian sources, too, proudly claim Addams as one of their own. Faderman (1991) includes Addams among those whose love for women was at least in part a search for allies to help wage the battle against women's social impoverishment. Changing the lives of the poor, these women themselves were changed by their confrontation with the cruel realities from which they otherwise would have been sheltered. Ellen Starr, the close friend with whom Addams cofounded the Hull House, was Addams's first serious attachment according to Faderman. Her devoted companion throughout most of her life, however, was Mary Rozet Smith. Most historians and social work scholars nevertheless have preferred to present Addams as one who never knew love. In any case, the pairing off of unmarried women into so-called "Boston marriages" did not raise comment in her day, as it did not have sexual connotations.

Professionalization

Less interesting, perhaps, but of more significance to the development of the social work profession was the training furnished to the friendly visitors and resident workers of the COS and settlement houses—respectively, the two precursors of social work. At first, the training consisted mainly of apprenticeship. Then, in addition to teaching on the job, agencies began to use more formal training that consisted of lectures, reading, and discussion (Johnson & Schwartz, 1997). Participation at the annual National Conference of Charities and Corrections drew together all those concerned with social welfare issues. Although their reform efforts were major, and considered radical by the standards of the day (e.g., they rallied for a 40-hour workweek), the charities and corrections people were ruled by a fierce Victorian morality.

Social work education began in rudimentary form in the training provided by Octavia Hill to the women who wanted to help impoverished people manage their lives and finances. "It all began," notes Katherine Kendall (2000) "with Octavia Hill a pioneer in housing management, when she embarked in the late 1870s on the training of her 'fellow workers,' as she called them, in the principles necessary for helping impoverished tenants to help themselves" (p. v). This training occurred not in New York but in London and later expanded in 1890 into a more formally organized program of courses under the auspices of the Women's University Settlement in London.

Earlier, toward the end of the 19th century, Mary Richmond presented a paper titled "The Need for Training Schools in Applied Philanthropy." The impact of this presentation was considerable because it paved the way for the founding of formal social work education. In 1898, a professional summer course was sponsored by the Charity Organization Society of New York. This led, in 1904, to a one-year graduate program of what was to become the first American School of Social Work at Columbia University. Parallel developments took place in Germany as well. But the credit for establishing the first clearly defined school of social work goes to a group of social reformers in the Netherlands (Hokenstad & Kendall, 1995). According to documentation provided by Lorenz (1994) and Kendall (2000), the first school of social work was founded in Amsterdam in 1896, and owed its existence to philanthropy and the international settlement movement.

A basic principle known in the sociology of professional development is that every occupation striving to gain recognition as a profession is in search of a solid, theoretical foundation. In the period before World War I, social work's knowledge base was derived largely from sociology, a social science geared toward the understanding of poverty and the need for community-based social care. Drawing on scientific surveys, sociology showed that persistent poverty in society was not primarily the result of personal failings but of systematic structural inequality. Yet, in the United States, social work practice still remained focused on individuals, generating a search for theories that primarily explained interpersonal processes.

The term *social work* was used for the first time, according to Lorenz (1994), in Germany (*Sozial Arbeit*) and in the American settlement movement.

The use of the term attests to the social nature of the profession and is consistent with the occupation's historical origins. In his historic address to the National Conference of Charities and Correction in 1915, Abraham Flexner, MD, uttered a stinging rebuke to the social work occupation, much to the disappointment of his audience. Social work, he declared, unlike law and medicine, could not claim to be a profession. The field lacked a systematic body of knowledge and theory, and autonomy as social workers did not exist—they merely assisted the real professionals as auxiliary staff. Although this historic commentary could have been regarded as a male attacking a female-dominated profession using criteria of the male model of achievement, the listeners buckled under. They would acquire professional status somehow. The social workers were determined to get the recognition due them.

The Freudian Influence and Growth of Casework

The lifeline thrown to a fledgling profession came in the form of psychoanalytic theory, the teachings of which began to be disseminated among U.S. social work educators after Freud's historic visit to Clark University in 1912. However, according to Lorenz (1994), the wholesale adoption of these theories from another discipline in the United States and Britain still would have failed to satisfy the criteria set forth by Flexner. Ultimately (but not before still another major paradigm shift during the Great Depression), the significance of the adoption of the Freudian paradigm was that it paved the way for social workers to reinvent themselves in the form of psychotherapists.

The liberal political climate disappeared almost overnight when, under the presidency of Woodrow Wilson, the United States entered World War I. This was when settlement house leaders fell out of favor with the public sentiment because of their active opposition to the military buildup and ensuing aggression. Other factors also reinforced the reactionary drift of the country. The victory of bolshevism in Russia, which culminated in the Red Scare of 1919–1920, put a taint on all community-type collective activity. As public suspicion and distrust grew, the settlement houses suffered considerably (Trattner, 1999). Financial support was withdrawn, and people began to look elsewhere to solve social problems. Social reform became now equated with radicalism, and radicalism was considered dangerous.

As the war ended, women also lost much of the independence they had acquired. Identifying women as the weaker sex, Freudian theory provided a rationale to justify a return to the status quo at a time when women, having had a taste of power, might otherwise have been inclined to want to keep it (women were given the right to vote but very little else).

Then there was the matter of racism. As the middle classes and socially mobile immigrants moved out of the central city into the suburbs, new people moved in—Puerto Ricans, Mexicans, and African Americans replaced the Europeans of an earlier day. Less public sympathy was generated toward these darker-skinned residents; assimilation was less of an option for them and their children than for their predecessors, in any case.

With the settlement house philosophy demoted in the public eye, Mary Richmond was catapulted to leadership within the profession. In 1922 she "clarified" the social casework method to bring it more in line with the personality focus, which was rapidly gaining currency. The psychosocial view of human behavior was replaced by a more narrow perspective, but one which was as exciting as it was revolutionary. In her autobiography, Bertha Reynolds (1963) uniquely captures the thrill of her own education into the mysteries of the human mind and beyond:

> We learned about the working of the subconscious, and many things in everyday life became clear to us. We saw fears displaced from childhood, jealousy displaced from other persons, hostility disguised as solicitude, desire as fear, and wish as certainty. We watched each others' slips of the tongue with glee and lived in a world where nothing was quite as it seemed and was frequently the opposite. We learned that the normal could best be understood through study of the abnormal, just because, in states of disease, inhibitions are lost and the workings of the mental mechanism can be seen, as are the works of a clock when its back is removed. No wonder we felt that we had been fooled by appearances all our lives and that we now had the key to wisdom in human relations. (pp. 58–59)

The Great Depression and Social Work

But alas, no sooner had the discovery of the unconscious rewritten our understanding of human behavior than a national economic calamity struck. A fascination with probing the unconscious gave way to more immediate concerns.

When the Great Depression hit, following the stock market crash of 1929, the unemployment rate reached, by 1933, a high of 24 percent. President Herbert Hoover's response was to rely on the voluntary social welfare sector. Demonstrations, strikes, and riots occurred nationwide as the financial panic worsened. Images recalled by Olsen (1994) represent the decade: apple sellers, the bread line, the migrant-worker, and the man with his sign stating, "I will work for food." When Franklin Roosevelt assumed the presidency in 1933, the banking system was threatened with collapse; millions of transients roamed the nation, and one of every four farms was foreclosed. The magnitude of mass suffering, in short, was intense; everyone was affected one way or another by the crisis. In the climate of social upheaval that was fast approaching, the time was right for a startling departure from prior welfare traditions. As Roosevelt promised in his campaign speeches, he worked to regularize production, provide federal public works and unemployment insurance, and to get the federal government to assume responsibility for relief. Much of what he accomplished was done in a dazzling 100 days.

As a part of a wave of New Deal legislation, the Civilian Conservation Corps provided jobs immediately in the national forest. The Public Works Administration, in contrast, was slower to get started but had more impact when it did so. Social worker Harry Hopkins of Iowa was appointed to head the Emergency Relief Act program and, after that, the Works Progress Administration. Francis Perkins, also a social worker, was appointed to serve as Secretary of Labor. Perkins thus became the nation's first female Cabinet official and helped draft much of the New Deal legislation in the 1930s and 1940s. Her most notable achievement, according to Segal and Brzuzy (1998), was her influence in the development of the landmark Social Security Act (Brownell, 1998). Much of the inspiration for the programs instituted under this act came from progressive European developments; Perkins, in fact, traveled to Europe to study European provisions as a model for the United States.

To all needy, unemployed persons and their dependents, massive relief grants were provided under the auspices of the Federal Emergency Relief Administration. In order to preserve people's self-respect, the president called for a public works program to provide a job for every able-bodied unemployed person; wages were to be below those paid by private employers but higher than relief payments. Piven and Cloward (1993) assess the overall significance:

> Work relief is remembered mainly for these accomplishments—for the dams and roads and schools and hospitals and other public facilities built by so many men in so short a time. . . . By once more enmeshing people in the work role, the cornerstone of social control in any society, it went far toward moderating civil disorder. (p. 97)

Roosevelt's reform of the economic system established safeguards to curb exploitation of workers while obtaining the benefits of regulation of prices, wages, and production for businesses and the nation. Business leaders had to agree to refrain from using child labor, to allow workers to join unions, and to honor specified minimum working conditions (Jansson, 2005).

The greatest legacy, by far, from the wave of measures known collectively as the New Deal was the Social Security Act of 1935. Designed to alleviate financial dependency through two lines of defense—contributory social assurance and public assistance—the Social Security Act included: a national old-age insurance system; federal grants to states for maternal and child welfare services, aid to dependent children, medical care, and rehabilitation for the handicapped; and a federal-state unemployment system. Opposition from the American Medical Association prevented the adoption of a national health plan (Barusch, 2002). Health insurance for the elderly (Medicare) and for the very poor (Medicaid) were added to the Social Security Act in 1965.

The lack of provision for the unemployed, able-bodied worker was a significant deficiency in the Social Security Act. Yet, despite its shortcomings, the legislation contained in the Social Security Act in 1935 provided the framework for the United State's social welfare system and was a demonstration of the federal responsibility for meeting the urgent needs of the nation's citizens. Above all, the solution for social problems was sought, at this historic time, in the system or in the social and economic conditions of the day, not in the individuals themselves. What transformed the 1930s, recalls Olsen (1994), was when the president of the United States became part of our struggle: "How simply and directly he spoke to us from the beginning; relief, recovery, reform" (p. 27).

While the United States moved swiftly to offset social unrest under the leadership of a determined President Roosevelt, north of the border in Canada men were herded, military style, into boot camps reminiscent of poorhouses (Guest, 1988). By the end of the decade, however, Canadians also realized that it was the economy at fault, not the individuals. World War II solved the unemployment problem (in the United States), but Canadians demanded full economic and social security, and therefore a comprehensive welfare program was launched. A universal system of family allowances and old-age benefits were included in the program. Universal health care, however, had to wait until later.

The Great Depression had a radicalizing effect on the nation's conscience and on the social work profession as well. During a time of disillusionment and despair with the capitalist system, caseworkers grew critical of the narrow Freudian focus. The growing prevalence of poverty made it difficult to lay the blame on individual weakness. Due to the massive programming introduced "to get America moving again," the demand for social workers, especially trained social workers, increased exponentially. Under social legislation enacted under the New Deal, the administrators and planners drew heavily upon the knowledge, assistance, and heritage of social workers; and the profession assumed an unprecedented importance in American life (Trattner, 1999). So, as always, the focus of social work shifted in tandem with the exigencies and ideologies of the day, and caseworkers moved away from one-on-one counseling and probing of the mind, to client advocacy and intervention geared toward resource linkage (Macht & Ashford, 1990).

As new public welfare workers faced taxing working conditions, huge caseloads, crowded workplaces, and little job security, they looked toward social work unions and other activist groups for help (Popple & Leighninger, 2005). Despite the heightened awareness of the effectiveness of collective action during a period of social change, American social workers were torn between their image of professionalism and the desire to better working conditions through collective bargaining. In the Depression era, according to Popple and Leighninger, mainstream social work chose to resolve the dilemma by endorsing the roles of "expert witness" and "consultant" to policy workers, rather than assuming a more adversarial stance. This resolution of a potentially volatile issue has never been seriously challenged. European social workers, in contrast, perceived no inherent conflict between unionization and professionalism. In many countries, in fact, the professional organization is the union.

On both the North American and European continents, the pendulum, which so recently had swung toward social action and government relief efforts, now had predictably gravitated toward the other direction. A growing national backlash against New Deal reforms and union strikes, along with the escalation of war in Europe and Asia, contributed not only to hostility against the labor movement in the early 1940s, but also to social work's renewed interest in the individual treatment aspects of the field (Popple & Leighninger, 2005). So social work was back to shaping the individual to fit the system instead of adjusting the system to help the individual, back to wrestling with private troubles over public issues. After World War II, group work became professionalized, borrowing a reconceptualization of Freudian thought to relate the basic principles (transference, defense mechanisms such as regression and repression, and so on) to the dynamics of group interaction. Then, as professional training was required, this form of social work practice "came of age."

An Overview of Women's Leadership in the Profession, 1910–1955

Unique among the social sciences and most of the professions, the field of social work was created and given its shape and character by women. In the words of Kendall (1989):

> There were men in the field—even some good men—but women ran the show. Many if not most, of the great deans of schools of social work in that period were women. Private agencies were run by women, even when they were headed by men. . . . (p. 23)

The field of social work, as we have seen, emerged out of the work of charity organization societies and the engagement of the settlement movement in immigrant and working-class neighborhoods. Of the top best-selling and most influential books in social work, six of eight were written by women (Chambers, 1986). While men outnumbered women in executive positions, according to Chambers, women dominated in supervisory roles.

The women's influence in Europe was especially strong. Lorenz (1994) recounts the history. As women were regarded by society as the natural and traditional embodiment of charity, most schools of social work founded by churches had a clearly defined mission for women within the organizations. Middle-class women entered social work as a means of carving out personally rewarding and socially acceptable occupations for themselves. The energetic pioneer of German social work, Alice Salomon, who had a PhD in economics and was closely linked to the American settlement movement, was convinced that only women could create a culture of caring that would raise welfare services above a preoccupation with material concerns. To preserve women's preeminence in the field, Salomon reserved the schools of social work exclusively for women. Furthermore the schools effectively resisted being accorded university status to resist absorption by male-dominated institutions. Although by far the largest number of women's schools of social work existed in Germany, a practice that continued until after the Second World War, other European countries also had separate social work schools for women. In Austria, France, Hungary, Italy, Norway, Portugal, Romania, and Switzerland, these women's schools represented the only social work training institutions. The underlying theme of the early female social work schools, according to Lorenz (1994), was the commonly heard motto, "the personal is political." For the pioneers of social work education, the transfer of female nurturing qualities into professional attributes was a means of transforming society to being maternalistic rather than paternalistic or bureaucratic.

Examining the events that led to an eventual male "takeover" of the profession in the United States, Jan Andrews (1990) argues that women not only led the profession in its early years but also continued to shape the course of social work until as late as 1955. Seeking an explanation of the shift toward male dominance in leadership positions in the field, Andrews conducted an extensive search through the social work archives. The four basic explanations gleaned from the literature are as follows: the decline of feminism after 1920 when women had won the right to vote; the decline in the settlement house community living experience, which had provided a home and sense of mission for single women; reinforcement of women's family roles (under the influence of psychoanalytical thought); and the effects of major cataclysmic events such as the Great Depression and World War II, which favored male over female wage earners and elevated war veterans to positions of prominence.

Perhaps for a combination of all these reasons, the unique partnership of "strong women and gentle men," which shaped the profession of social work during the formative periods, began to fragment when men emerged largely in command of agencies, graduate school education, public policy, and welfare administration (Chambers, 1986). The rapid and vast expansion of welfare bureaucracies and the emphasis on public accountability, cost-effectiveness, and the like tended to favor having men in management positions and women in hands-on positions.

European Influence

Rarely in the American literature is the European influence on the U.S. social work profession mentioned. The reader of American textbooks, therefore, is apt to be unfamiliar with the international sweep of knowledge or with the historical precedence of ideas. Yet knowledge, like the economy, reflects the global interconnectedness of human phenomena; ideas and methodologies are enriched cross-culturally.

A notable exception to the ethnocentric histories that characterize the social work literature is Kendall's (2000) *Social Work Education: Its Origins in Europe*. Born in 1910, Kendall is keenly aware of the tendency to overlook the voices of the past in recording history. Kendall's work, informed by years of international social work and, in recent years, of research at the Washington, DC, Library of Congress (where she was provided with her own study room), offers a comprehensive picture of the origins of social work that, hopefully, will broaden our perspective in the years to come.

Another major contributor to the history of social work is German social work educator (currently university lecturer in Cork, Ireland) Walter Lorenz. In his evaluation of the profession's unwitting service as pawns of the Nazi state, surely the grimmest episode in social work history, Lorenz (1994) reveals the repercussions on both sides of the Atlantic. Because of a climate of patriotism, tyranny, and lack of organized resistance to an immoral regime, social work ended up complying with the fascist, exclusionary policies of the Nazi period. In turn, the inevitable siege against the profession took the form of direct threats to its members and particularly to its educators. The large proportion of social workers who were Jewish or who had Jewish connections were forced to surrender their positions and flee the country. Many others were attacked and persecuted for their social democratic leanings. Through this enforced wave of emigration, American social work was considerably enriched. The work of Gisela Konopka, a political prisoner who escaped Germany and fled to the United States, and then returned to postwar Germany to play a key role in developing West German social work in a humanistic direction, provided a theoretical grounding for group work practice that enhanced its prestige and professional image. Under skilled leadership, as Konopka demonstrated, the group could become a powerful mechanism for interpersonal growth and development; the therapeutic possibilities of the group process were unlimited. Konopka is considered the mother of social group work in Germany. For a biography of Konopka's fascinating life, read Andrews (2002).

German and Scandinavian social work benefited from cross-fertilization as Konopka and many other visiting experts forged the link between European and American traditions. In Europe, as Lorenz indicates, social work had an important part to play in rebuilding societies devastated by war. Through imparting self-help skills and replacing fascist authoritarianism (and countering the communist variety) with egalitarian practices, American social work methods had high priority within foreign-aid programs of the United States and the United Nations. The availability of American social work literature translated into several European languages enhanced the assimilation of American methods in social work education on the wider European horizon. The spirit of progress was infectious, and yet we must recognize, as Lorenz argues, that the massive program of "re-education" provided to postwar Europe represented, in an ideological sense, a retreat from the social and worldly mission of social work.

The famous Beveridge Report set up the British social welfare system as we know it today, with its National Health Service and the attempt to end poverty through enhanced social policies. The Marsh report in Canada echoed the British report. Both were blueprints for comprehensive and largely universal welfare states; it was a shift from residual to institutionally based ideology (Graham, Swift, & Delaney, 2000). A universal Family Allowances program came into being in 1944; regardless of family income, *all* Canadian mothers of children under the age of 16 received a monthly allowance. In 1951, the Old Age Security Program was converted from a selective to a universal program as well; everyone over age 70 became qualified to receive a pension. Universal health care was not achieved until 1966.

Professional Vulnerability and the McCarthy Era

Social work, as we have seen throughout this chapter, cannot be understood apart from the dynamics of the larger society. To know the temper of the age is to know social work. As Bertha Reynolds (1963) observed from personal bitter experience, "Adaptation to the climate of community opinion was, of course, as old as social work itself" (p. 261). Between the reality and the ideal, and the politics and values, the tension at times can be overpowering. Inasmuch as social workers tend to work for the state, either directly or indirectly (through funding), they have to answer to the state. Therefore, their helping roles, at times, may be circumscribed. Under Hitler, as we have seen, social work's vulnerability to political misuses was especially pronounced. Social work assessments, in fact, were used to separate out the unworthy and nonproductive elements from society; this use of professionals trained in scientific methods helped justify the ultimate annihilation of large segments of the population. Social workers, in effect, were rendered accomplices to murder. First the state came for their clients. Welfare workers failed to protest; and in the end, the state came for them—the workers.

Social work's vulnerability to serving the interests of the state was evident in the extreme in Nazi Germany. In Khomeini's Iran, similarly, social workers and students of social work found it impossible to uphold their professional values under the severe duress of a reactionary social revolution (Healy, 2001; van Wormer, 1997). Under repressive regimes in Chile and South Africa, the vendetta against social workers has included political imprisonment. Although the magnitude of comparable events in the United States pales beside the horrors inflicted elsewhere, the ethical dilemma—how to maintain one's personal and professional integrity in an unfree society—is the same. We are talking here of that ultraconservative and almost paranoid period during the late 1940s and early 1950s when free speech was stymied under the banner of anticommunism, and the social work profession was effectively quashed.

The emphasis on security in a repressive and war-ready society perpetuated a climate of suspicion of all behavior outside of the mainstream. This hysterical climate was personified by Senator Joseph McCarthy who stood in the national limelight to ferret out communists and "fellow travelers." In the melee that followed, thousands of teachers, social workers, journalists, and government workers lost their jobs for supporting unions or other liberal causes. The age—the 1950s—has since been characterized as the McCarthy era.

In the United States and Canada (where anticommunist campaigns were somewhat less public and extensive than in the United States), homosexuality became viewed as a national, social, and sexual danger. In right-wing conservative (and even liberal) discourse, gays and lesbians were associated with communism and spying for the U.S.S.R. (Union of Soviet Socialist Republics) due to their supposed targeting for blackmail (Kinsman, 1994). Homosexual vulnerability to compromise with Soviet agents was taken for granted even in the absence of evidence to back it up. Mass firing and transfers were carried out in the U.S. military and among the Canadian police, national defense units, and civil servants. The criminalization of homosexual behavior made the task in both countries much easier than it would have been otherwise.

In the southern United States, the uncertainty and budding paranoia on the part of the power structure pertained to the issue of integration. Change was in the air, and many southern whites feared that their society would be turned upside down as "separate but equal" was ruled to be unequal. Many white southerners claimed that states rights were the real issue, and they suddenly became concerned with the issue of voter literacy. White and black integrationists were branded as "red" (i.e., communist), since the emergent movement for civil rights was labeled as communist-inspired, an accusation that stuck well into the next decade.

Through the political darkness and enforced silence of the McCarthy era, women were also suppressed. Freudian teachings about proper roles for women, which had been played down during the duration of the war when women were needed for industrial work, now resurfaced to send white women home and African American women back to their menial labor. Ambitious women "did not know their place" and were considered not to be appropriately feminine. Female social workers, likewise, had to step aside for the sake of men, who now became the majority of those who held doctorates in social work. Tracked into dead-end casework positions, women watched while men were groomed for agency administration and policy leadership (Brandwein, 1995).

Mass persecutions, witch hunts, fallout shelters, air raids, the mandate for conformity in word, deed, and dress styles—all attributes of the 1950s—raise the difficult question of why these phenomena occurred at this time. Macht and Ashford (1990) provide a partial explanation: Despite the sense of prosperity and optimism, the 1950s also included a sense of insecurity. An ever-present possibility of war and an economic system undergoing major changes involving stepped-up specialization and routinization of work contributed to a generalized sense of uncertainty. The buildup of the defense industry, labeled by President Eisenhower as "the military-industrial complex," was another probable factor in the growth of a repressive mentality. Then the propaganda machine, launched to perpetuate the war industry in the absence of a major war, helped stimulate a national hysteria. Whatever the reasons for the climate of intolerance that shook the nation in the 1950s, the important point is that everywhere critics of the government and of "the American way of life" were branded as public enemies and were socially and professionally ostracized.

Even during this time of severe repression, there were internal challenges urging the social work profession to take a stand. These challenges, however, fell on deaf ears until the emergence of a completely new political experience in the turbulent 1960s (Franklin, 1990). In *Security Risk* (1986), Fisher, a progressive social worker, recalls how, labeled a risk to national security, he was discharged as a result of the Truman loyalty program, the purpose of which was to weed out radicals and dissenters from politically sensitive positions. In those times, in light of the political nature of their profession, social workers found themselves especially vulnerable. Refusing to stand together, they were "bumped off" one by one for signing petitions for peace, attending radical meetings, or merely for being so accused. Although most social workers suffered from the fallout of the climate of fear, the profession did little or nothing to protect them (Schreiber, 1995). The social work literature of the day does not mention the kinds of pressures people in public service were under. So while group work was evolving into group psychotherapy, social workers were playing it safe politically, and sadly, a mood of quiescence prevailed. Many good people were sacrificed and had their high profiles suppressed, never to be regained.

Bertha Reynolds

The flight from social reform and service to the poor could not proceed without uneasy words of warning from at least some quarters (Trattner, 1999). In any historic period in any country, there are always people who stray from the common mentality or, as in the words of Thomas Gray's *Elegy*, "far from the madding crowd." Bertha Reynolds (1963) was one of those people. Written from the perspective of her later years, Reynolds's autobiography recounts the closing of the prison gates around social work during the public hysteria that accompanied the Cold War period.

The impact on social work, according to Reynolds, was immediate and profound. While schooled in psychiatric social work and a major contributor to this approach, Reynolds was conscious of the impact of economic and social conditions on her clients; politically, she was an acknowledged Marxist and a union organizer. Her writing records in extraordinary detail events of the political scene when prominent radical figures, such as herself, found themselves jobless, shunned, and uninvited to professional meetings and conferences (Ehrenreich, 1985; Reisch & Andrews, 2001). Reynolds's memoir, *An Uncharted Journey*, provides an excellent resource for grasping the essence of a bygone era, a time that is often forgotten but of no small consequence. Events at the 1940 social workers' national conference are described by Reynolds (1963) as follows:

> Our whole profession was jolted out of any complacency it may have had by the news from California that relief allowances had been cut to starvation levels and denied entirely unless clients would accept labor at starvation wages; that trained social workers in public assistance who protested were replaced by untrained political henchmen; that social workers even suspected of being members of the CIO union were being fired. (p. 263)

At the convention Reynolds, true to character, delivered a speech that addressed the issues of client rights and their rapid deterioration. In the years ahead, in fact, conditions were only to get much worse. The growth of the social work profession was significantly affected by the demolition of social work unions, whose existence was a legacy of the leftist rank-and-file movement of the 1930s. While the discredited social work profession requested government help for their needy clients who were reduced to paupery, the mass media focused on accounts of clients who refused to work and on others who received special coddling from the welfare office. The attacks on public assistance in the press prepared the way for new stern "economic" measures against the sick, aged, and children in New York and elsewhere. Thus the intolerance in one area of life (e.g., of the poor) was matched by intolerance in another area (of the sick and the aged). The political repression of group workers whose work focused on the least-advantaged segment of the population is described in detail by Reisch and Andrews (2001). In the government's urgency to restrict care of the nation's most vulnerable citizens, the parallels between this period and the early 21st century are as striking as the differences.

In 1950, the national government moved against persons with ties to the Communist Party or to any organization from a long list of "Communist-front organizations." The Soviet Union was seen as a serious menace to the Western world, and fear, according to Reynolds, reached into every corner of American life. So great was the fear generated, in fact, that schools of social work were under extreme pressure to not even discuss McCarthyism or its impact. Thus, as Reynolds noted, even at a university—whose mission it is to educate in an atmosphere of freedom of thought—all academic freedom was stifled.

Social Work in the Awakening of the 1960s

From his leadership in the Montgomery bus boycott of the late 1950s, Martin Luther King's oratory powers, self-sacrifice, and Gandhi-like willingness to die for a cause galvanized the nation. The mass movement for the rights of African Americans that culminated in the historic passage of the Civil Rights Act of 1964 set the stage for political mobilization of a host of oppressed groups. Wills (1994) poignantly captures the mood of the era:

> The sixties split the skies. Only the Civil and two world wars so neatly clove our history into a Before and After. And the sixties were more divisive than World War II, which drew people together for the war effort. The sixties drove people apart—husbands from wives, children from parents, students from teachers, citizens from their government. Authority was strengthened by World War II. It was challenged by the sixties. (p. 40)

Central to an understanding of the ethos of the age (an ethos that was not even apparent until the decade was over) is a recognition of the transformation of young people that occurred through the hope and optimism generated by the civil rights movement. As a result of mass mobilization, public martyrdom, and a sympathetic press, justice prevailed. People said, "We shall overcome," and in truth, they did overcome. This brilliantly successful movement set the pattern for others to demand their and others' rights: Mexican farm laborers under the charismatic leadership of Cesar Chavez; women; gays and lesbians; Native Americans; and the elderly. Catholics in Northern Ireland, similarly, sang civil rights songs and held sit-ins and mass rallies to protest discrimination against Roman Catholics. In the United States and Europe, mobilized protests against the war in Vietnam helped bring that conflict to a close even in the absence of military victory.

After he helped push the Civil Rights Act through Congress, perhaps sensing the mood of the nation, President Lyndon Johnson declared a war on poverty, and a major expansion of social welfare programs followed. The optimism of the era is captured in the term *the Great Society*, which refers to the war on poverty and what it represented. The phrase sounds grandiose today; then it did not. Under the umbrella of the Office of Economic Opportunity, many programs were introduced, including: Volunteers in Service to America (VISTA); Upward Bound, a program to help poor and ghetto children enter college; Operation Head Start to prepare lower-income children for school; Legal Services; and the

Job Corps. Part of the impetus for these programs sprang out of massive urban riots in poor black communities during the mid-1960s.

Franklin (1990), as mentioned at the beginning of the chapter, linked three distinct methods of social work practice—casework, group work, and community organization—to the socioeconomic and political forces in American society. With the advent of the sixties, the neo-Freudian formulations and emphasis on human development gave way to community organization and direct action strategies. There was a great deal of criticism of social casework, some from outside the profession. Most notably Saul Alinsky (1971) urged against helping people adjust to the system in favor of radically changing the system.

Strongly influenced by the civil rights movement and the Great Society program in 1964, the social work profession began to shift its focus from casework to social policy. The new goals of the eradication of poverty and racism fired up a new generation of social workers. The shift in the profession's emphasis became apparent in the editorial content of social work's leading journals. This progressivism, in fact, is still evident today as editors of the mainstream journals continue to focus on the crises in social welfare, human rights issues, and the need for social and political action. The social work code of ethics (see Appendix B) reflects an expanded interest in social policy and in the ramifications of such policy for the poor and vulnerable populations.

The New Conservatism

In the final analysis, who can say why the pendulum swings the way it does throughout history? Piven and Cloward (1993) offer at least a partial answer: We should never underestimate, they note, the power of well-organized social action by the masses or the threat of such action in compelling the administration to embark on a change of course. Fear of a major challenge to the established order, indeed, may be a key motivating factor in gaining concessions for workers and others in need. Conversely, mass apathy and lack of organization by the working and lower class can be their undoing.

Whatever the reasons, for the first time since the 1920s, under the leadership of newly elected President Ronald Reagan, the radical right boldly attempted to reform American society. In the absence of viable opposition, laissez-faire capitalism resumed its hold on the nation. This ideology cast high taxes, regulation, and welfare assistance to the poor as the major impediments to economic growth and prosperity (West, 1994). The decade brought us a tax cut, particularly for the highest-income group, large cuts in domestic spending, and the largest peacetime military buildup in American history. This paradigm shift, which edged up slowly on the nation, was reinforced in externally funded academic writings and in the corporate-controlled mass media. The idea that government programs (such as Aid to Families with Dependent Children [AFDC] and food stamps) represented a giant drain on tax dollars went virtually unchallenged by political leaders. In the political rhetoric of the time, only those governmental programs and services that were intended to help the poor and the powerless were seen as a problem.

In 1988, drawing on negative stereotypes of poor women, advocates of welfare reform justified the need for a mandatory work program designed to channel welfare recipients into the low-wage labor market (Rose, 1990). The Family Support Act transformed AFDC from an income-maintenance program to what Rose calls a punitive government work program. Various invasive and expensive programs have been conceived to monitor the morality of welfare clients with the underlying premise that aid is for the deserving poor only, and that aid can be used to control behavior.

The mood of the mid-1990s was captured tellingly by Piven (1995):

> For the poor it's back to the workhouse and the orphanage. The press tends to credit Newt Gingrich (speaker of the House) with this Nineteenth Century scenario, embodied in the House Republican's Contract with America. But Gingrich certainly didn't invent the assault on welfare. He only had to modify a script written and rehearsed by the Clinton Administration, and then by Congress, where some twenty welfare "reform" bills were introduced over the past year.... Democrats and Republicans alike have hit upon welfare bashing as a way to appease an anxious and increasingly angry electorate. (pp. 22–23)

When President Clinton gave his first inaugural address, the wave of joy and optimism at the prospect of a Democratic administration was palpable. The mood was eloquently captured in the words of the inaugural poet, Maya Angelou (1993), who shared them on this proud occasion:

> Lift up your eyes upon
> This day breaking for you
> Give birth again
> To the dream.* (verse 10)

But, alas, with a conservative mood sweeping the nation and an eventual Republican-controlled Congress, the promise of change (e.g., the open acceptance of gays and lesbians in the military; health care reform) did not occur. "Aside from his peccadilloes," note Karger and Stoesz (2002), "Clinton will be remembered as a centrist president, one who behaved more like a moderate Republican than a liberal Democrat" (p. xv). This brings us to the 1996 Personal Responsibility and Work Opportunity Reconciliation Act, popularly known as "welfare reform." With the passage of this act, at the end of President Clinton's first term, the 60-year entitlement to family assistance essentially was over.

A newspaper clipping I saved from The New York Times (Pear, 1996), in a front-page headline entitled "Millions Affected," illustrates the significance of the president's act:

> It is expected to save $55 billion over six years as it dismantles a welfare program created by Democrats in the New Deal....
>
> With today's action, Mr. Clinton fortifies his credentials as a "new Democrat" and strengthens his position going into this fall's Presidential election. But he disappointed many Democratic party loyalists, and civil rights advocates, labor union leaders, and religious organizations. (p. 1A)

---

*From On the Pulse of the Morning by Maya Angelou, Copyright © 1993 by Maya Angelou. Used by permission of Random House, Inc.

The bill that Clinton signed effectively supplanted the AFDC program with Temporary Assistance to Needy Families (TANF). As the name implies, TANF was time-limited: two years for welfare recipients to enter the workforce; five years as a lifetime limit to receive the temporary help. Funding is to the states in the form of block grants; these grants replace food stamps, child care, and school meals. The states can continue such programs if they so desire, but in light of shrinking state budgets, continuation of such programming is not likely. These changes represent a strong retrenchment from federal responsibility for social welfare. This shift in responsibility in the provision of welfare aid from the federal government to the states is referred to as *devolution*. As a result of devolution, there is a great variation among TANF programs in the various states (Segal, Gerdes, & Steiner, 2004).

Historian Michael Katz (2001) fills us in on the often overlooked role of the governors of the states, foremost among them, Tommy Thompson of Wisconsin, in leading the campaign to devolve public assistance to the states. A new consensus among conservative governors rested on a dislike of welfare, hostility to its recipients, and faith in mandatory work as the key to reform. In seizing the initiative, as Katz points out, state governments precipitated a historic transformation of American welfare.

As of 2003, large numbers of welfare recipients had been moved off the rolls. The economic boom of the previous few years had led to the creation of sufficient low-wage jobs in the service industry to make leaving welfare possible. Major obstacles to future success of the program are: the rise in unemployment; lack of access to health care benefits for many of the working poor (such access was provided to AFDC recipients); the fact that many of the poor people live in ghettos or rural areas where job opportunities are few; the fact that the minimum wage is not a living wage; and the lack of affordable child care.

So what is the meaning for the social work profession of this "slide to the bottom"? Rosa Perez-Koenig (2001) considers this very dilemma of how to work for social justice in an increasingly unjust society. Her words are provocative:

> Rather than "working" the system harder on behalf of their client's immediate needs, social workers must now seek to work *against* a system that is intent upon denial of moral responsibility for responding to those needs. Toward that end, social work practitioners are encouraged to embrace an "empowerment" approach to their relationship with clients. (p. 10)

I concur with the empowerment approach as the optimal framework for addressing the needs of our clients: empower our clients; empower ourselves. But what happens to social workers, asked Hartman (1989)—and this was in the "good old days"—who cherish Bertha Reynolds's ideals as they attempt to serve clients in conservative America? The means available to help clients, increasingly, are limited. The near obsessive emphasis on accountability for every dollar spent and cost-effectiveness translates into mounds of paperwork and fundraising efforts by progressively harried staff. Most social workers, observes Hartman, remain in stressful positions and make the most of it. Others move into areas of greater political influence; still others leave the profession altogether. Many social workers, perhaps reluctantly, flee to private practice.

As they explored the issue in *Unfaithful Angels: How Social Work Has Abandoned its Mission*, Specht and Courtney (1994) were far less empathic toward members of the profession who established careers in psychotherapy:

> In increasing numbers, social workers are flocking to psychotherapeutic pastures, hanging out their shingles to advertise themselves as psychotherapists just as quickly as licensing laws will permit. For the most part, professional associations of social workers and schools of social work are active participants in the great transformation of social work from a professional corps concerned with helping people deal with their social problems to a major platoon in the psychotherapeutic armies. (p. 8)

Well-written and refreshingly iconoclastic, *Unfaithful Angels* is a highly useful resource for viewing today's variety of social work practitioners in a historical context. Specht and Courtney correctly take the psychotherapeutic field to task for having fallen captive in many instances to popular therapies such as "codependency work," excessive individualism, and the like. They also take the social work field to task for bestowing professionalism, prestige, and respect singularly to clinicians. Still, as one who has engaged in clinical work in private treatment settings and yet has opposed privatization in the United States and abroad, and as one who fled the empiricism of sociology and arrived upon the social work scene late, I wish to make the negative case. Social work is alive and well, and so is its mission. Such is the major argument of this chapter.

Has Social Work Abandoned Its Mission?

Unlike related fields in the social and behavioral sciences and counseling education, social work is highly self-critical, culturally aware, and therefore, introspective. Every accredited social work program stresses policy as well as counseling issues. The fact that academics of the caliber of the late Harry Specht and his associate Mark Courtney have chastised the field for its parochialism, paradoxically, may actually be one of the many encouraging developments in social work today. Specht and Courtney's (1994) book offers a kind of soul-searching that is the attribute of a truly altruistic profession. Other positives in this enduring field are: the outpouring of politically relevant articles, editorials, and policy statements in *Social Work* and *NASW News*, the leading professional journals in the field promoting social justice and peace; the continuing idealism of social work students; the strident, multicultural, and policy emphasis including progressive mandates by the Council on Social Work Education (CSWE) requiring all social work education programs to profess an ethical commitment to social justice; the strong feminist influence in social work and social work education; the new impetus for global and environmental awareness; and the dominant framework that informs practice on both the micro and macro level.

To bolster my arguments against the Specht and Courtney (1994) thesis, I will draw on the focus of the literature of the profession, studies of our social work students, professional mandates for multicultural social work education, radical feminism, and outreach to the global community. This final section of the chapter draws on the concept of the social work imagination as first presented in Chapter 1.

Our social work imagination, the psychic and creative energies generated by people we now call social workers, has existed in some form or another for the better part of a century. The term *social work imagination* is defined here as a drawing on one's inner resources to help advance the cause of social welfare at the macro level and to help individuals cope at the micro level. Such imagination challenges all our creative resources to discover, in collaboration with the client, what countless others may have overlooked—some obvious solution to a problem, perhaps, or some new way around a difficulty.

In discovering principles that were later to become the standards of the burgeoning profession of social work, the founding mothers were clearly individuals of vision and courage. The original twin missions of social work, according to Simon (1994), were those of relieving the misery of the most desperate among us and of building a more just and human order. These intertwined missions, as Simon further suggests, continue to command the allegiance of members of the empowerment tradition. The National Association of Social Workers (NASW; 1996) echoed these sentiments in the Preamble to the social work *Code of Ethics*: "The primary mission of the social work profession is to enhance human well-being and help meet the basic human needs of all people, with particular attention to the needs and empowerment of people who are vulnerable, oppressed, and living in poverty" (p. 1).

The challenge to social work today, as previously, is the callousness and intransigence of the political right. Nevertheless, the spirit of the foremothers of social work lives among us now, critical and irrepressible.

Professional Writings and Policies

The National Association of Social Workers (NASW) is a politically viable and dynamic organization with a membership of over 150,000 (keep in mind that only approximately one-fourth of social workers are official members). With membership, subscriptions to *Social Work*, *NASW News*, and a chapter newsletter are automatic. The NASW lobbies extensively for improved social welfare programs as well as for its own professional representations in health care, mental health treatment, and so on. As an academic discipline, the political involvement sets social work apart from other related areas of specialization. Graduates of nationally accredited programs are able to benefit from having a credential that is regarded as professional (applied), rather than as strictly academic—or a degree that qualifies the recipient for a specific job.

Headlines from *NASW News* reports from 2001–2003 concern such issues as: pressing governors on child welfare; lobbying for mental health parity; curtailing the ill effects of welfare reform; and writing an update on the prevention of bullying. These headlines say a lot about social work's continued social action on behalf of the poor and oppressed.

Among journals in the field devoted specifically to human rights and poverty issues are: *Affilia: Journal of Women and Social Work, Journal of Gay/Lesbian Social Services, Multicultural Social Work,* and *Journal of Progressive Social Work.* Each year during March, Social Work Month, NASW distributes booklets to its members containing the annual theme. As stated in the NASW (2003) "Preserving Rights, Strengthening Voices":

> This year, Social Work Month specifically recognizes social workers and their dedication to children's rights, civil rights, disability rights, lesbian and gay rights, crime victim's rights, labor rights, women's rights, human rights, among many other movements. The profession began, and continues to lead, many efforts that enhance human well-being. (p. 11)

In honor of this event, NASW director Elizabeth Clark (2003), in her monthly column, proclaimed:

> As each of you celebrates Social Work Month, you should take great pride in our activist legacy, our steadfastness and the importance of what we do every day. (p. 3)

Does this sound like a profession that has lost its soul?

The Idealism of Social Work Students

What brings students to major in social work? Why do people choose social work as a career today? Has their motivation shifted over the years? Csikai and Rozensky (1997) designed a survey to address this very issue. In a convenience sample of 78 bachelor's of social work (BSW) students and 72 master's of social work (MSW) students, results indicated high levels of idealism for all students, with a somewhat more professional focus among older and male students. Similarly, in a survey of over 700 Midwestern undergraduate social work majors, Hanson and McCullagh (1995) addressed these questions. The purpose of the study, conducted over a 10-year period, was to determine if monetary rewards and prestige surpass altruistic motivations as reasons for pursuing social work as a career. Although men scored slightly higher than women on the self-interest factor, for both genders, service to others emerged as an overriding reason for choosing the social work major. This was a motivation, moreover, that did not change significantly over the course of the study. The predominant reason for entry into social work was to make a contribution to society.

Limb and Organista (2003), who have provided the most comprehensive study to date, used secondary analysis of a statewide California sample of nearly 7,000 entering MSW students. Findings indicated that these students were less attracted to private practice relative to other areas and that students of color, especially American Indians, were the most motivated to work primarily with persons in poverty. Overall, a slight majority chose societal change over individual adaptation when asked which social work change strategy they most favored.

In contradiction to Specht and Courtney's (1994) claim that the social work mission has shifted from work with the disadvantaged to a focus on preparing students for lucrative private practice careers, a survey of the NASW membership shows that although a majority now work for private organizations, including religious ones, only 20 percent work exclusively in private practice (O'Neill, 2003). Half the social workers in the survey indicated mental health as their primary practice area, while another 16 percent indicated child welfare/family was their major practice area. Social workers with two to four years experience earned $35,600 in 2002. (Keep in mind that this survey was of NASW members, most of whom have master's degrees.) In my opinion, a major advantage of licensing laws for MSW practitioners is the opportunity to be self-employed and to provide counseling for individuals in need of psychotherapy. Sliding-fee scales make such counseling more affordable than treatment by other mental health professionals. Another interesting fact about social workers is the high representation of minorities (about one-third) who receive social work degrees and the high percentage of women (84 percent of those receiving master's degrees) (CSWE, 1999).

Theoretical trends in social work education and the literature provide further testimony to the vitality of the field. Keep this in mind as you read the following sections of this chapter, which cover multicultural education, feminist theory, the empowerment perspective, and renewed global awareness.

Multicultural Social Work Education

Due to the importance of accreditation to university social work programs (graduates must have degrees from accredited programs to be considered professional social workers), the Council on Social Work Education (CSWE) fulfills a vital, if at times intimidating, function. On the other hand, a negative aspect is the often rigid standardization of the social work curriculum (see Markward, 1999).

People of color and other diverse groups constitute a large proportion of the clients social workers serve. In recognition of the need for multicultural competence, the CSWE mandate is for social work course curriculum to include content on populations at risk—such as ethnic minorities, women, and those of diverse sexual orientations—ideally infused throughout the entire curriculum. The emphasis of the *Educational Policy and Accreditation Standards* (2002), as stated in Standard 4.2, is that programs "provide content related to implementing strategies to combat discrimination, oppression, and economic deprivation and to promote social and economic justice." (See http://www.cswe.org to read the requirements in their entirety.) The significance is that mere cultural competence is not enough; educators, as role models, must publicly stand up against injustice and oppression.

Malcolm Payne (1997) offers a thoughtful cautionary note concerning the risk of subordinating alternative cultures to Western interpretations or of denying real philosophical differences in cultural views. His recommendation is for an antiracist and antioppressive stance that offers a more comprehensive way of understanding issues relating to power imbalances (and I would add, scapegoating of the poor and minorities). Racially integrated accrediting teams monitor the programs to ensure that course syllabi and textbooks are geared toward human diversity. The popularity of books such as *Social Work Practice and People of Color* (Lum, 2004), *Empowering Women of Color* (Gutiérrez & Lewis, 1999), *Cultural Competence Practice* (Fong, Furoto, & Furoto, 2001), and *Multicultural Social Work in Canada* (Al-Krenawi & Graham, 2003) portend well for the future of the profession. The importance of the recruitment and retention of minority and female faculty and students is emphasized.

Although the United States may not lead the world in its social welfare policies, in the area of antidiscrimination legislation, it has paved the way. Paralleling national legislation, North American social work has moved from a reactive to a proactive stance. In social work education in most of Europe, in contrast, a multicultural, pluralistic approach is espoused. The aim has been to be gender-blind and color-blind rather than proactive. According to Lorenz (1994), this tolerance perspective does not address racism and discrimination as realities. Belatedly, the United Kingdom took a decisive lead when the accrediting body directed social work educators to teach not only the skills for ethnically sensitive practice, but the skills for challenging institutional and personal racism as well. Since the publication of Lorenz's text, unfortunately, this process of infusion of multicultural content has suffered a setback stemming from reactionary government legislation, in conjunction with a staunch media attack (Penketh, 2000).

America's CSWE requires that five areas be covered in all social work training institutions: human behavior and the social environment, social work practice skills, research, social policy, and the field practicum. Additionally, CSWE also requires that course content include attention to social justice, ethics and values, diverse populations, and populations at risk. The combination of macro- and micro-level offerings reinforces the person-in-the-environment conceptualization of the profession. Thus, while social workers engage in community organization work, they may draw upon the basic counseling and interviewing skills in community activism and negotiation. Similarly, social work clinicians ideally will be aware of the external policy issues impinging on their clients' lives and of the importance of political advocacy on behalf of the disadvantaged and vulnerable.

Ethnic-sensitive practice raises social workers' awareness of racism in a wider society, and of how social conditions related to powerlessness are integral to the experiences of persons of color. To be effective, social workers must be aware of their own prejudices and fears before they can help their clients achieve self-awareness. By identifying and building upon existing strengths, the worker empowers the client to get involved in mutual aid groups for social support as a first step in the change process (Gutiérrez, 1991; Gutiérrez & Lewis, 1999). The Canadian professional social work associations likewise are pursuing initiatives to promulgate multiculturalism through cross-cultural immersion activities (Al-Krenawi & Graham, 2003). The CASSW (Canadian Association of Schools of Social Work), like its U.S. counterpart, requires educational content to prepare students for antioppression practice. At Carleton University in Ottawa, Canada (as described on its Web site), for example, students are prepared to address personal and social problems from a structural perspective: The emphasis is on changing the social structure. The CASSW (2000) requires schools of social work to disseminate antioppression training (see http://www.carleton.ca/ssw).

The Feminist Influence

Just as the African and gay/lesbian lobbies within social work have been well organized and effective in shaping CSWE and NASW policies, feminism also has been a major influence in the field. Feminist social work, the aim of which is to remove oppression due to sexism, has its roots in the women's movement of the 1970s. Yet, as we know from the history of social work, strong women have shaped the profession from the start. The antifemale bias of psychodynamic theory that has been widely noted (Payne, 1997) can be viewed as a bit of an anomaly within social work history. In any case, when the psychoanalytical therapies were dominant in the 1920s and again in 1950s, the special needs of women clients and therapists took a backseat to protecting men from women who might otherwise undermine them. The dramatic decrease in female authorship of policy and planning publications was a tangible indicator of women's declining role in policy leadership during this period (Brandwein, 1995).

Thanks to the grassroots feminist movement that reemerged in the 1970s, awareness of women's needs and issues became paramount once again. Women's problems were depathologized and then politicized. Founded as a field of strong women (most of whom remained unmarried by choice) and supportive men who stood alongside them, social work stands uniquely among the professions in being woman-centered. The fact that writers of the feminist school today decry the underrepresentation of females in top administrative positions shows that the feminist voice in social work is alive and well (Dominelli, 2002; Payne, 1997; Reisch & Andrews, 2001).

In its concern for social justice and commitment to initiating change as a collaborative effort, social work shares a number of features with feminism (Dominelli, 2002). Parallels between feminist thought and social work are found in their mutual belief that: the personal is political and vice versa; the problems lie in the structures of society rather than in the fault of the disadvantaged; the perpetuation of poverty in women is systemic; and violence inflicted against women and children is an instrument of power (Andrews & Parnell, 1994). Both perspectives—feminism and social work—seek to bridge the gap between the personal and the political through the process of empowerment (Dominelli, 2002). Both perspectives challenge all forms of institutionalized oppression. The generalist model in social work, the predominant approach which incorporates ecosystems concepts and directs interventions at all levels of the system (the individual, the family, the community, and society), also guides feminist practice. This multidimensional formulation belies the presumed dichotomy between psychotherapy and community organization and neatly bridges the gap between them.

Although the majority of social workers may not have the kind of ideological commitment to call themselves feminist therapists and to employ a systematic feminist methodology in their work, many therapists have come to question the highly normative views of the family that earlier were *de rigueur* in family therapy. A proliferation of workshops, papers, and conference sessions have focused on women's issues, and gender sensitivity has given credence to the female voice and experience (Hartman, 1995). In light of developments since the mid-1980s, Mary Valentich (1996) fully expects that feminist perspectives will become more influential for all social work practitioners and their clients. Gender-specific counseling with female offenders has recently made tangible inroads within the criminal justice system (van Wormer, 2001).

Social work practice with women has developed in the last two decades from a concern about sexism and women's issues to an emerging model of practice grounded in feminist theory, scholarship, and action (Bricker-Jenkins & Lockett, 1995). So, far from arguing that social work today has abandoned its mission, one could much more accurately conclude that social work, on the contrary, has expanded its horizons, moving into new directions without losing sight of the old. Whether social work will be able to maintain its historic position as advocates for the poor and marginalized depends on the force of the present-day right-wing backlash against all victims of society in conjunction with the economic dictates of managed care. In a society driven by high economic competition, a barrage of criticism against the entire social work field and a reduction in client benefits can be anticipated.

An Empowerment Perspective

Related to feminist social work—and in fact, an outgrowth of the feminist movement—is the empowerment framework. Simon's (1994) landmark study, *The Empowerment Tradition in American Social Work*, traces the origins of empowering practice. Since the 1890s, as Simon informs us, "empowerment practitioners, in each era using different language to characterize their work, have viewed clients as persons, families, groups, and communities with multiple capacities and possibilities, no matter how disadvantaged, incapacitated, denigrated, or self-destructive they may be or may have been" (p. 1).

Within the social work practice literature, a focus on client strengths has received increasing attention in recent years. Unlike related fields such as psychology or counseling, moreover, the term *strengths perspective* or *strengths approach* has become standard rhetoric in social work practice, as seen in Chapter 1. The strengths perspective, as Saleebey (2002) notes, assumes that power resides in people and their communities and that we should do our best to promote power by refusing to label clients, and trusting them to make the appropriate decisions.

The strengths perspective has been applied to a wide variety of client situations: work with the mentally ill, child welfare clients, homeless women in emergency rooms, the elderly, and African American families. The concept of strength is also part and parcel of the growing literature on empowerment, feminist therapy, narrative therapy, the client/person-centered approach, and the ethnic-sensitive model. Pertaining to groups and communities as well as to individuals, the strengths perspective can help reveal the light in the darkness and provide hope in the most dismal of circumstances. As informed by strengths theory, the therapeutic goal is to help people discover their areas of strength so that they can build on them in an ever-spiraling movement toward health and control. Effective social work practice is both an art and a science; the linking thread between them is the creativity, persistence, and breadth of vision we can call our social work imagination.

Two popular textbooks, *Generalist Social Work Practice: An Empowering Approach* (Miley, O'Melia, & DuBois, 2005) and *The Empowerment Approach to Social Work Practice* (Lee, 2001), incorporate the principle of strengths into every phase of the helping process. Yet, although the literature consistently articulates the importance of a stress on clients' strengths and competencies, we must all be cognizant of the reality of standard clinical practice built on a treatment problem/deficit orientation, a reality shaped by agency accountability and the dictates of managed care. Third-party payment schemes mandate a diagnosis based on relatively serious disturbances in a person's functioning (e.g., organic depression or suicide attempts) and short-term therapy to correct the presenting problem. Furthermore, the legal and political mandates of many agencies (the elements of social control embodied in both the institution and ethos of the agency) may strike a further blow to the possibility of partnership and collaboration between client and helper (Saleebey, 2002). In the United States, as in every nation, pressures from the global market economy affect social welfare policies in terms of retrenchment in treatment offerings. The decline in social standards in combination with budget cuts for "talking forms of treatment" and reductions in resources available present major obstacles to strengths-based practice.

The Impetus for Global Awareness

In their history of radical social work, Reisch and Andrews (2001) contemplate the impact of radical thought on social welfare in "its emphasis on peace and international cooperation—whether expressed through the ideas of socialist internationalism, universal sisterhood, multicultural solidarity, or the fraternity of labor" (p. 233). Militarism and global interdependence are incompatible, as are spending on the military-industrial complex and a well-financed social welfare system.

"We need to launch a new initiative that links our international peace and social justice and cultural competency agendas, and builds closer alliances with schools of social work and social work organizations in the U.S., Canada and beyond." This commentary was offered by NASW president Terry Mizrahi (2001, p. 2) in response to the September 11 airplane strikes on the Twin Towers. As we saw in Chapter 1, the social work profession is today returning to its roots in recognition that it has a global role to play.

The social work profession the world over is concerned with the devastating effects of poverty, hunger, illness, homelessness, inequality, injustice, and violence. The globalization of the economy and society affects social work practice in every nation. Just as the nations of the Global North have dominated free market economics and the diffusion of technologies, social work practice knowledge has pursued a similar course with knowledge flowing in one direction—from north to south. From the global perspective, a fact that has so often been overlooked is that social workers in industrialized nations, where there increasingly are problems of poverty and homelessness, have much to learn from social workers in regions which have been facing myriad human and social ills for some time. Much has already been learned from other countries, such as from the grassroots organizing in Latin America, as we will see in the following chapter on economic and social oppression.

To enhance this exchange of information and knowledge and to help students acquire an international perspective on their own work, an unprecedented number of departments and schools of social work have established international exchanges. Typically, in such exchanges, students and faculty take or teach courses on foreign campuses. Often, as at Augsberg College and the University of Northern Iowa, students do their field placements abroad or welcome the exchange students to their campuses. In one unique arrangement, the University of Connecticut has introduced a Web-based course to include participation of Jamaica and Trinidad. Monmouth University offers an international and community development concentration in their master's program. "Think globally, act globally" is the theme of their program.

At the meeting of the International Commission of CSWE (February 27, 2003), the results were presented of a survey of U.S. social programs concerning their international activities. Brief results of the survey of a subset of 87 responses indicated that 85 percent offered some international program activity and that about a third had international field opportunities. Journal resources widely available for social workers and researchers wishing to learn from other lands include: *Social Development Issues, European Journal of Social Work, The Journal of Multicultural Social Work, International Social Work, IFSW News,* and *The Journal of Social Work and Societal Policy.*

Impact of the Global Market Economy on Social Work

In recent years, the perspective of social work has broadened to challenge widely held assumptions of industrial society, assumptions equating unsustainable economic growth with progress. The sustainable development model—a central theme of such books as *The Handbook of Social Policy*, edited by Midgley, Tracy, and Livermore (2000); *Social Work and Globalization*, edited by Rowe (2000); *The Global Environmental Crisis: Implications for Social Welfare and Social Work*, edited by Hoff and McNutt (1994); and *Social Welfare: A World View* (van Wormer, 1997)—integrates environmental concerns and ecological principles. What is needed now, argue Hoff and McNutt, is nothing less than a complete rethinking of our relationship to the natural world. An understanding of the interplay between poverty and environmental degradation is central to the social development model. The imminent threat of global environmental collapse compels the social work profession to adopt a truly comprehensive ecological framework—to take a proactive stance toward the depletion of resources and to promote policies toward sustainable social development.

American social workers are just at the crossroads of assuming a worldwide and environmental focus, and of grasping the fact that social problems are becoming more interconnected and nations more interdependent in a global economy. Rosemary Sarri (1997) urges the infusion of international content in social work education for exposure to comparative options and innovations for addressing economic and social issues.

Summary and Conclusion

The history of social welfare is as old as humankind. To understand the universality of social welfare, we have ventured in this chapter across time, geography, and religion. Contemporary social welfare can trace its roots, in part at least, back to the mutual aid of an agrarian community, the medieval church, and the paternalism associated with feudalism. We have seen, in every era, the inherent connections among religions, social values, economics, and technology. In understanding how the social welfare system grew and changed, it is important to note not only the milestones (such as the codification of laws), but also the upheavals—the kinds of unpredictable cataclysmic events that throw the whole social system out of balance. The impact on one part of the system—the mass desolation wrought by war or plague—evokes compensatory change in other parts of the system as well. The path from migration to urbanization and then to stratification has perhaps been more circular than linear. The one thing we can say with certainty is that when massive and threatening social movements of the poor have arisen, social institutions have quashed them. One such major social institution is, of course, social welfare.

As we have seen in this chapter, paralleling the growth of a complex class and gender stratification associated with wage labor, social welfare emerged from communal aid into a formalized system of social control. We have seen how the poor (beggars, transients, and disabled)

came to be provided with help according to a standardized set of criteria.

To summarize the themes of this chapter: The history of social work is a proud history, the story of strong women and gentle men in many ways ahead of their time who worked for social reform or to help individuals in distress. There were, of course, some low moments—conformity under Hitler's Germany and under McCarthyism in the United States, and the dominance of psychoanalytical theory in the 1920s and 1950s.

The history of the development of the social work profession and of its educational institutions reveals that its evolution has often been stymied by the ideological rhythms of the wider society. Historically, the ideology has alternated between two seemingly opposing foci—one, the personal, and the other, the political. Franklin (1990) has revealed how social work reflected the ideological influence of the times in its interventions—community action, social casework, group therapy—that were compatible with the popular currents. We have to remember that there was much overlap between the interventions, until one or the other won out, and that countervailing forces were always present simultaneously.

Whereas the Charity Organization Societies founded prior to the 1890s generally are regarded as having been individualistic in focus, with the emphasis mainly on determining individual eligibility to receive charity, the settlement house movement tends to be presented as the prototype of community organization in motion—as an organization not only for social reform, but also for cultural education. World War I had a dampening effect on progressive thought, as did Flexner's stunning and somewhat insensitive rebuke of social work for its failure to qualify as a genuine profession. These dual influences, in conjunction with growing anti-immigrant and racist sentiment in the United States, created a situation ripe for a wholehearted endorsement of the psychoanalytical approach. With its relatively coherent theory of personality, psychoanalysis provided a rationale for diagnosis and treatment that had been lacking.

When the Great Depression hit, social workers thrived under the New Deal as society set out to rebuild itself. Canada experienced a comparable shift from attention to personal attributes (or lack thereof) to putting the "social" back in social work.

Going from action to counteraction or counterreaction, a new war fever built up, and a conservative mood followed. In the aftermath of World War II, group work based on psychodynamic principles was introduced as a new trend, the teaching of which rapidly spread to Europe. Minimal attention was paid to social concerns until the 1960s, another period of rejuvenation for the community approach.

At the present time, the radical right once again is a major force to reckon with, an international ideology associated with forces in the global market economy. Privatization is a related worldwide trend affecting social work conditions of employment, unionization, and the availability of mental health services. Conditions ripe for mass unemployment related to technological advances are countered by a media-generated outcry to force public welfare recipients to go to work. While some nations, such as those in Scandinavia, continue to look to the government for solutions to social ills, in other parts of the world the increasing chasm between rich and poor and the conservative onslaught on the social welfare state have created difficulties for the social work profession. A deliberate targeted attack on Britain's social workers has been especially forthright.

As Europe opens its borders—France and England are now physically joined for the first time—the exchange of faculty and students is bringing a cross-fertilization of ideas and approaches in its wake. The social work profession in the United States, Canada, and Britain has established leadership in feminist therapy, with Britain making progress in antidiscrimination policies, which are now being adopted internationally.

Social workers share a global mission. The social ills confronting the profession—inflation, national indebtedness, the influx of political and economic refugees, underemployment, homelessness, the AIDS pandemic—differ in degree but not in kind. Every country's economy today is affected by a global market and intense competition to market products. In the past, models of practice have been superimposed into various educational structures by representatives from the Euro-American world: Visiting instructors were British or American; the textbooks were in English and emphasized individualized models; and therefore, the transfer of knowledge was largely unilateral.

But as British social work educator Robert Harris (1990) reminds us, the development of an understanding for local customs and policy is something that is absorbed as much as learned; it is a part of a context of learning and living that is simply unique in different places. Knowledge imparted from the outside, in this context, develops a life of its own. Frameworks employed that do not fit are discarded and modified or exchanged for those that do. In Africa, Latin America, and Asia, the forms of social work have been molded to the contours of the landscape. Meanwhile, social work educators in the West are seeking new forms of intervention. The days of unilateral exchange of knowledge from West to East or North to South may be over.

Thought Questions

1. How did Martin Luther's split with his church's practices come to have such an impact in England?

2. Relate Luther's teachings to the work ethic.

3. List the principal provisions of the Elizabethan Poor Law. How did it come about? What is the historical significance?

4. Compare the New Poor Law with its predecessor. What is the principle of less eligibility? Is that principle still with us today?

5. What were some of the major social and cultural factors that shaped American social welfare in the colonial era?

6. Describe the culture brought by the early European settlers to the so-called New World.

7. How were the "deserving" and the "nondeserving poor" treated in colonial America?

8. Describe the form that mutual aid took among African Americans in the South.

9. What was the role of the churches in providing informal care?

10. What contributions did the Freedman's Bureau make to social welfare?

11. Recount how industrialization transformed the American landscape.

12. Discuss the evolution of social work in light of political shifts of the pendulum. Can the personal and the political be truly separated?

13. During which period was a community action emphasis apparent? When did individualism triumph?

14. Trace the history of the Charity Organization Society (COS). Compare the philosophy and work of the COS with those of the settlement house workers.

15. Trace the history of the settlement house movement. Compare this development with the COS movement.

16. How did the settlement house leaders respond to the needs of African Americans? What was the contribution of the Emanuel Settlement?

17. Give the personal history of Jane Addams. How did she fall out of public favor?

18. Discuss the growth of formal training for social workers. How did the new profession get a name?

19. What are Mary Richmond's contributions to social work? How was the interpretation of her theoretical formulation reshaped by psychoanalytical thought?

20. What was the impact of Flexner's stinging rebuke to social work in 1915? How did the profession strive to remedy the situation?

21. Describe the excitement generated by the new Freudian view of human behavior.

22. Describe the economic and social situation that existed in 1933 when Franklin Roosevelt assumed the presidency.

23. What were the highlights of the New Deal legislation? What is the significance of the Social Security Act of 1935? What were the deficiencies?

24. How did the Great Depression change things? How did the New Deal affect social workers?

25. Discuss the backlash against the New Deal reforms that followed World War II.

26. Recall the pioneering work of Gisela Konopka. How did she combine theory with method in a unique way?

27. Discuss the role of the anticommunist hysteria. How did homosexuality enter the picture? What happened to social work?

28. What were some factors in the rise of McCarthyism? Relate to the life of Bertha Reynolds. What was the view of persons receiving social welfare benefits? Discuss parallels between the 1950s and today.

29. Discuss the impact of the civil rights movement on social work.

30. Describe the climate of social change that took place in the mid- and late 1960s. What was the Great Society, and what were the results?

31. Discuss the changes in attitudes and policies toward social welfare as a result of the new conservatism.
32. What is the basic thesis of *Unfaithful Angels: How Social Work Has Abandoned Its Mission?* Argue in favor of or against the position taken by Specht and Courtney.
33. Describe the National Association of Social Workers (NASW) and its political viability. Describe the make-up of the profession and students' attitudes.
34. Differentiate the European tolerance position from the North American antidiscrimination stand.
35. What is ethnic-sensitive practice?
36. Discuss the parallels between feminist thought and social work.
37. Define the strengths perspective and how it is applied in social work practice.
38. How is the profession's growing international commitment evidenced?

References

Addams, J. (1910). *Twenty years at Hull House.* Norwood MA: Norwood Press.

Alinsky, S. (1971). *Rules for radicals: A practical primer for realistic radicals.* New York: Random House.

Al-Krenawi, A., & Graham, J. R. (Eds.). (2003). *Multicultural social work in Canada: Working with diverse ethno-racial communities.* Oxford, England: Oxford University Press.

Amundsen, R. (1994). Da sosionomyrket ble til (When social work began). *Sosionomen, 9,* 26–30.

Andrews, J. (1990). Female social workers in the second generation. *Affilia, 5*(2), 46–59.

Andrews, J. (2002, Fall). Reflections on writing a biography of a living hero: Gisela Konopka. *Reflections,* 11–22.

Andrews, J., & Parnell, S. (1994, April 29). *A training model to integrate feminist principles into education.* Paper presented at the Biennial Midwest Social Work Education Conference, St. Paul, MN.

Angelou, M. (1993, January 20). *On the pulse of the morning.* Poem read to the nation at President Clinton's Inauguration Ceremony.

Bacon, M. (1986). *The story of Quaker women in America.* San Francisco: Harper & Row.

Barker, R. (2003). *The social work dictionary* (5th ed.). Washington, DC: NASW Press.

Barusch, A. S. (2002). *Foundations of social policy: Social justice, public programs, and the social work profession.* Itasca, IL: F. E. Peacock.

Brandwein, R. (1995). Women in social policy. *In Encyclopedia of social work* (19th ed., pp. 2552–2560). Washington, DC: NASW Press.

Bricker-Jenkins, M., & Lockett, P. (1995). Women: Direct practice. *In Encyclopedia of social work* (19th ed., pp. 2529–2539). Washington, DC: NASW Press.

Brieland, D. (1990). The Hull-House tradition and the contemporary social worker: Was Jane Addams really a social worker? *Social Work, 35*(2), 134–138.

Brownell, P. (1998). Women, welfare, work and domestic violence. In A. Roberts (Ed.), *Battered women and their families* (2nd ed., pp. 291–309). New York: Springer.

Bryson, L. (1992). *Welfare and the state: Who benefits?* New York: St. Martin's Press.

Canadian Association of Schools of Social Work (CASSW). (2000). *Education policy statement: Board of accreditation manual.* Retrieved from http://www.cassw-access.ca

Chambers, C. (1986). Women in the creation of the profession of social work. *Social Service Review, 60*(1), 1–26.

Clark, E. (2003, March). Choosing the words we live by. *NASW News,* 3.

Council on Social Work Education (CSWE). (1999). *Statistics on social work education in the United States, 1998.* Alexandria, VA: Author.

Council on Social Work Education (CSWE). (2002). *Handbook of accreditation: Standards and procedures* (5th ed.). Alexandria, VA: Author.

Council on Social Work Education (CSWE). (2003, February 27). Meeting of the international commission of CSWE, Atlanta, GA.

Csikai, E. L., & Rozensky, C. (1997). *Journal of Social Work Education, 33*(3), 529–538.

Darwin, C. (1859). *The origin of species.* London: Murray.

Day, P. (2003). *A new history of social welfare* (4th ed.). Boston: Allyn & Bacon.

Dolgoff, R., Feldstein, D., & Skolnik, L. (2003). *Understanding social welfare* (6th ed.). New York: Longman.

Dominelli, L. (2002). *Feminist social work theory and practice.* Hampshire, England: Palgrave.

Dominelli, L. (2003). *Anti-oppressive social work theory and practice.* Hampshire, UK: Palgrave.

Ehrenreich, J. (1985). *The altruistic imagination: A history of social work and social policy in the U.S.* Ithaca, NY: Cornell University Press.

Encyclopaedia Britannica. (1998). Social welfare. In *The new encyclopaedia Britannica* (Vol. 27, pp. 372–392). Chicago: University of Chicago Press.

Faderman, L. (1991). *Odd girls and twilight lovers: A history of lesbian life in twentieth-century America.* New York: Columbia University Press.

Faulkner, W. (1994/1948). *Intruder in the dust.* New York: Library of America.

Federico, R. (1990). *Social welfare in today's world.* New York: McGraw-Hill.

Fisher, J. (1986). *Security risk.* Sarasota, FL: Piney Branch Press.

Fong, R., Furoto, S., & Furoto, S. (Eds.). (2001). Cultural competence practice: *Skills interventions and evaluations.* Boston: Allyn & Bacon.

Franklin, D. (1990). The cycles of social work practice: Social action vs. individual interest. *Journal of Progressive Human Services, 1*(2), 59–80.

Freire, P. (1973). *Education for critical consciousness.* New York: Seabury Press.

Gesino, J. P. (2001). Native Americans: Oppression and social work practice. In G. Appleby, E. Colon, & J. Hamilton (Eds.), *Diversity, oppression, and social functioning: Person-in-environment assessment and intervention* (pp. 109–130). Boston: Allyn & Bacon.

Graham, J. R., Swift, K. J., & Delaney, R. (2000). *Canadian social policy: An introduction.* Scarborough, Ontario: Prentice-Hall.

Guest, D. (1988). Social security. In *Canadian Encyclopedia* (Vol. 3, pp. 2032–2034). Edmonton, CA: Hurtig Publications.

Gutiérrez, L. (1991). *Empowering women of color: A feminist model.* In Bricker-Jenkins, M., Hooyman, N., & Gottlieb, N. (Eds.), *Feminist social work practice in clinical settings* (pp. 119–211). Newbury Park: Sage.

Gutiérrez, L., & Lewis, E. (1999). *Empowering women of color.* New York: Columbia University Press.

Hanson, J., & McCullagh, J. (1995). Career choice factors for BSW students: A 10-year perspective. *Journal of Social Work Education 31*(1), 28–37.

Harris, R. (1990). Beyond rhetoric: A challenge for international social work. *International Social Work, 33*, 203–212.

Hartman, A. (1989). Still between client and community. *Social Work 34*(4), 387–388.

Hartman, A. (1995). Family therapy. In *Encyclopedia of social work* (19th ed., pp. 983–990). Washington, DC: NASW Press.

Haynes, D., & White, B. (1999). Will the "real" social work please stand up? A call to stand for professional unity. *Social Work, 44*(4), 385–391.

Healy, L. (2001). *International social work: Professional action in an interdependent world.* New York: Oxford University Press.

Hoff, M., & McNutt, J. (Eds.). (1994). *The global environmental crisis: Implications for social welfare and social work.* Aldershot, England: Avebury.

Hokenstad, M., & Kendall, K. (1995). International social work education. In *Encyclopedia of social work* (19th ed., pp. 1511–1520). Washington, DC: NASW Press.

Jansson, B. (2005). *The reluctant welfare state* (5th ed.). Belmont, CA: Wadsworth.

Johnson, H. W. (1995). Historical development. In H. Johnson, et al., *The social services: An introduction* (pp. 3–10). Itasca, IL: F. E. Peacock.

Johnson, L., & Schwartz, L. (1997). *Social welfare: A response to human need* (4th ed.). Boston: Allyn & Bacon.

Karger, H. J., & Stoesz, D. (2002). *American social welfare policy: A pluralist approach* (4th ed.). Boston: Allyn & Bacon.

Katz, M. B. (2001). *The price of citizenship: Redefining the American welfare state.* New York: Henry Holt.

Kendall, K. (1989). Women at the helm: Three extraordinary leaders. *Affilia, 4*(1), 23–32.

Kendall, K. (2000). *Social work education: Its origins in Europe.* Alexandria, VA: Council on Social Work Education.

Kinsman, G. (1994). Heterosexual hegemony. *Canadian Dimension, 26*(3), 21–23.

Kirst-Ashman, K. (2003). *Introduction to social work and social welfare: Critical thinking perspectives.* Pacific Grove, CA: Brooks/Cole.

Kuhn, T. (1962). *The structure of scientific revolutions.* Chicago: University of Chicago Press.

Lee, J. (2001). *The empowerment approach to social work and practice: Building the beloved community* (2nd ed.). New York: Columbia University Press.

Limb, G., & Organista, K. (2003). Comparisons between Caucasian students, students of color, and American Indian students on their views on social work's traditional vision. *Journal of Social Work Education, 39*(1), 91–109.

Lorenz, W. (1994). *Social work in a changing Europe.* London: Routledge.

Lum, D. (2004). *Social work practice and people of color: A process-stage approach* (5th ed.). Belmont, CA: Brooks/Cole.

Macht, M., & Ashford, J. (1990). *Introduction to social work and social welfare* (2nd ed.). New York: Macmillan.

Markward, M. (1999). Point/counterpoint: Do accreditation requirements deter curriculum innovation? *Journal of Social Work Education, 35*(2), 183–186.

Marx, K., & Engels, F. (1963/1848). *Communist manifesto.* New York: Russell & Russell.

Midgley, J., Tracy, M., & Livermore, M. (2000). *The handbook of social policy.* Thousand Oaks, CA: Sage.

Miley, K. K., O'Melia, M., & DuBois, B. (2005). *Generalist social work practice: An empowering approach* (5th ed.). Boston: Allyn & Bacon.

Minzesheimer, B. (1998). Heeding slavery's voices. *USA Today,* p. D1.

Mizrahi, T. (2001, November). International issues come home. *NASW News,* 2.

Mullaly, B. (1997). *Structural social work: Ideology, theory, and practice* (2nd ed.). Toronto: Oxford University Press.

National Association of Social Workers (NASW). (1996). *Code of ethics.* Washington, DC: NASW Press.

National Association of Social Workers (NASW). (2003). *Social work month toolkit: Preserving rights, strengthening voices.* Washington, DC: NASW Press.

Nevins, A., & Commager, S. (1981). *A pocket history of the United States* (7th ed.). New York: Simon & Schuster.

Olsen, T. (1994, January 3). The thirties: A vision of fear and hope. *Newsweek,* 26–27.

O'Neill, J. (2003, February). Private sector employs most members. *NASW News,* 8.

Payne, M. (1997). *Modern social work theory* (2nd ed.). Chicago: Lyceum Books.

Pear, R. (1996, August 1). Millions affected: After hearing president, more in party back measure in house. *New York Times,* p. 1A.

Penketh, L. (2000). *Tackling institutional racism: Anti-racist policies and social work education and training.* Portland, OR: International Specialized Book Services.

Perez-Koenig, R. (2001). Actualizing social justice within the client/social worker relationship. In R. Perez-Koenig & B. Rock (Eds.), *Social work in the era of devolution: Toward a just practice* (pp. 3–16). New York: Fordham.

Philpott, T. (1978). *The slum and the ghetto: Neighborhood deterioration and the middle-class reform.* New York: Oxford University Press.

Piven, F. (1995). Poorhouse politics. *The Progressive, 59*(2), 22–24.

Piven, F., & Cloward, R. A. (1993). *Regulating the poor: The function of public welfare* (updated ed.). New York: Vintage.

Popple, P., & Leighninger, L. (2005). *Social work, social welfare, and American society* (6th ed.). Boston: Allyn & Bacon.

Prigoff, A. (1999). Global social and economic justice issues. In C. Ramanathan & R. J. Link (Eds.), *All our futures: Principles and resources for social work practice in a global era* (pp. 157–173). Belmont, CA: Wadsworth.

Reisch, M., & Andrews, J. (2001). *The road not taken: A history of radical social work in the United States.* Philadelphia, PA: Brunner-Routledge.

Reynolds, B. (1963). *An uncharted journey.* New York: Citadel Press.

Richmond, M. (1917). *Social diagnosis.* New York: Russell Sage Foundation.

Rose, N. (1990). From WPA to workfare: It's time for a truly progressive government work program. *Journal of Progressive Human Services, 2,* 17–42.

Rowe, W. (Ed.). (2000). *Social work and globalization.* Ottawa: Canadian Association of Social Workers.

Saleebey, D. (2002). Introduction: Power in the people. In D. Saleebey (Ed.), *The strengths perspective in social work practice* (pp. 1–22). Boston: Allyn & Bacon.

Sarri, R. (1997). International social work at the millenium. In M. Reisch & E. Gambrill (Eds.), *Social work in the 21st century*. Thousand Oaks, CA: Pine Forge Press.

Schreiber, M. (1995). Labeling a social worker a national security risk: A memoir. *Social Work, 40*(5), 656–660.

Segal, E., & Brzuzy, S. (1998). *Social welfare policy, programs, and practice.* Itasca, IL: F. E. Peacock.

Segal, E. A., Gerdes, K. E., & Steiner, S. (2004). *Social work: An introduction to the profession.* Belmont, CA: Brooks/Cole.

Simon, B. L. (1994). *The empowerment tradition in American social work: A history.* New York: Columbia University Press.

Slavin, L. (2002, March). Profession strained in Canada. *NASW News*, 15.

Specht, H., & Courtney, M. (1994). *Unfaithful angels: How social work has abandoned its mission.* New York: Free Press.

Spratt, M. (1997). Beyond Hull House: New interpretations of the settlement movement in America. *Journal of Urban History, 23*(6), 770–777.

Stiglitz, J. E. (2002). *Globalization and its discontents.* New York: W. W. Norton.

Stoesen, L. (2003, January). NASW, Canadians bolster relationship. *NASW News*, 6.

Trattner, W. (1999). *From poor law to welfare state: A history of social welfare in America* (6th ed.). New York: Free Press.

Valentich, M. (1996). *Feminist theory and social work practice.* In F. Turner (Ed.), *Social work treatment: Interlocking theoretical approaches* (pp. 282–338). New York: Free Press.

van Wormer, K. (1997). *Social welfare: A world view.* Belmont, CA: Wadsworth.

van Wormer, K. (2001). *Counseling female offenders and victims: A strengths-restorative approach.* New York: Springer.

West, C. (1994, January 3). The '80s market culture run amok. *Newsweek*, 48–49.

Wills, G. (1994, January 3). The sixties: Tornado of wrath. *Newsweek*, 26–27.

Wilson, M. G., & Whitmore, E. (2000). *Seeds of fire: Social development in an era of globalism.* Halifax, Canada: Fernwood.

Every gun that is fired, every warship that is launched, every rocket fired, signifies, in the final sense, a theft from those who hunger and are not fed, those who are cold and are not clothed. The world in arms is not spending money alone. It is spending the sweat of its laborers, the genius of its scientists, the hopes of its children.

DWIGHT D. EISENHOWER, **1953**

Economic Oppression

© Rupert van Wormer

People in poverty are not necessarily oppressed—the poverty may be shared throughout the society—and people who are oppressed are not necessarily poor. Yet economic oppression is inextricably linked with social oppression, as oppression involves domination over coveted resources. People who are socially oppressed are often poor; persons in poverty are very much inclined to be the objects of discrimination in their everyday lives.

According to U.S. Census data for 2000, one in six children lives in poverty today. Approximately 12.7 percent of all families live below the official poverty rate (Central Intelligence Agency [CIA], 2002). Many of the working poor are in this group. Whereas 30 years ago, full-time work at the minimum wage lifted a family out of poverty, today it does not. A recent study from the Department of Housing and Urban Development determined that Chicago area workers earning the federal minimum wage would have to have the equivalent of three and a half jobs to afford a typical two-bedroom apartment (Sichelman, 2003). Even in more affordable cities, a large percentage of residents cannot afford to pay fair market rent. To make up for the low wages and to compensate for a weakened safety net, more people are working at two jobs and/or longer hours at their primary job.

And yet, the nature and extent of poverty in the United States, shameful though it is compared to the countries of northern Europe, pales beside the nature and extent of poverty worldwide. In the poorest nations of the world—for example, countries in sub-Saharan Africa, Haiti, and Bangladesh—life expectancy is 25 years less than in the wealthiest nations (Watkins, 2001). Poverty in these regions is endemic; every day people struggle just to survive.

From the richest and most generous social welfare states to the most impoverished nations, globalization affects us all. Constraints of the marketplace and dominance by the rich nations over the poor create a situation of economic oppression on a massive scale. All politics, in this sense, is global; the most productive nations can be expected to seek markets for their products and trade arrangements that work to their advantage. As the powerful nations set the rules through their big banks, one expects a climate conducive to increasing privatization and the accumulation of vast sums of capital in the hands of the few.

According to the capitalist growth/trickle-down theory, all nations are seen as developing along a predictable continuum of progress from the traditional societies composed of isolated tribes to modern economies (Wilson & Whitmore, 2000). The stated expectation is that rapid increases in economic growth will "trickle down" to the masses, that international economic competition will benefit "developing" and "developed" nations alike. In truth, the reality is quite the opposite: The source of much oppression can be found in the economic development model itself—and in the neoliberal agenda, which is really a neoconservative agenda, as Wilson and Whitmore suggested.

Thus the stage is set for oppression both among nations and within nations. That economic oppression cannot be separated from racial and ethnic oppression is a basic assumption of this book; this chapter is devoted to the economics of oppression, and Chapter 5 can correctly be viewed as an extension of the same discussion, especially the sections on classism, racism, and sexism. This chapter begins with an overview of the problem of poverty and its causes and consequences on a world scale. The impact of the world banks and free trade agreements is among the topics discussed. The reality of poverty in the United States is described against the backdrop of economic inequalities. The second and final portion of this chapter views the impact of global competition and the new technologies on the world of work and the worker. This discussion of economic and social oppression concludes with some thoughts on how some of the most unsavory aspects of globalism can be ameliorated. (Note: The term *globalism* is used in this chapter, as well as the rest of this book, to denote the economic aspects of globalization.)

The Nature of Oppression

Oppression takes many forms. It can occur when one race or group of people exploits and suppresses another race or group; it can affect whole families and classes of people who are economically disadvantaged or exploited by the system; and it can occur within the family, taking the form of gender violence as well as child abuse and neglect. Membership in a disempowered group has personal as well as political ramifications. As defined in *The Social Work Dictionary* (Barker, 2003), *oppression* is:

> The social act of placing severe restrictions on an individual, group, or institution. Typically, a government or political organization in power places restrictions formally or covertly on oppressed groups so that they may be exploited and less able to compete with other social groups. The oppressed individual or group is devalued, exploited, and deprived of privileges by the individual or group who has more power. (p. 307)

Some of the key words used in this definition—*power, exploited, deprived, privileges*—are key variables related to oppression that will crop up again and again on the following pages of this book. Oppression, loosely speaking, can be defined as inhumane or degrading treatment of a group or individual based on some defining characteristic. The word *oppress* comes from the Latin *opprimere*, which means to press on or press against (Dalrymple & Burke, 1995).

Economically, oppression may involve *exploitation.* This may consist of harnessing the poor and foreign to do the dirty work of society or, at the macro level, of using poor nations as cheap sources of labor. *Marginalization* is a second component of economic oppression. Marginalization occurs when certain classes of persons are denied full participation in the fruits of citizenship. When I lived in Northern Ireland, for example, Catholics, herded into gerrymandered districts, had limited voting and therefore political power (hence the slogan of the Irish civil rights movement: "One man, one vote").

Structural violence refers to the various forms of harassment, ridicule, and intimidation to which oppressed groups are subjected (Gil, 1998). Structural or societal violence may be used by dominant social classes, as Gil suggests, to defend the established way of life against challenge from dominated and exploited classes. Poverty, as we learned from Gandhi, is a form of violence in itself—"the worst form of violence" (cited in Ramanathan & Link, 1999). There is much overlap between the categories of poverty and violence. Imagine a two-headed arrow between them. The sale of land mines by U.S. companies to warring nations, for example, can be considered both violence and exploitation of the worst sort. The term *violence* can be conceived here in both a physical and structural sense.

As we move to a deeper examination of poverty, that scourge in this technologically advanced age, keep in mind the three aspects of oppression—exploitation, marginalization, and structural violence. First, we will take a look at poverty on a global scale, then at poverty in the world's richest country—the United States.

Poverty Worldwide

Poverty kills. In its wake, it brings hunger, disease, high infant mortality, homelessness, and even war. The weight of poverty falls most heavily on vulnerable groups in every society—women, the elderly, minority groups, and children. In poor households on the Indian subcontinent, for example, men and boys usually get more sustenance than do women and girls, while the elderly get less to eat than the young (Dasgupta, 1995). Amid the wealth of new economic opportunities today, 1.2 billion people still live on less than $1.00 a day (United Nations Development Programme [UNDP], 2002). The richest one percent of the world's people, according to the same report, receive as much income each year as the poorest 57 percent. Although the poorest of the poor tend to come from rural areas of Asia and Africa, there are also pockets of poverty in the industrialized world.

In rich countries, most discussion of poverty centers on a person's situation in comparison to the situations of others in the society—the lack of adequate housing, access to quality education and good jobs, and so on. *Relative poverty* is based on such comparisons (Barusch, 2002); it is defined by the general standard of living in various societies and by what is culturally defined as deprivation. Thus by the standards of most inhabitants of India, the Mexican villager would be "well off." The Mexican, in turn, would perceive migrant work in the United States as an opportunity to "get ahead" (Macionis, 2004). In the United States, the official government poverty level is based on the cash income for individuals to satisfy minimum living needs according to comparative expectations. The poverty level for a family of four is currently $9 an hour (Shulman, 2003).

In contrast, *absolute poverty*, which readily can be identified in a global context, involves a deprivation of resources that is life-threatening. Arguably, there is a degree of absolute poverty even in a rich nation such as the United States where inadequate nutrition, health care, and heating are unfortunate realities. Yet, as Macionis reminds us, such immediately life-threatening poverty in a modernized nation strikes only a small proportion of the population. By contrast, over one billion inhabitants in the nonindustrialized world are unable to satisfy such basic needs as adequate nutrition, access to safe and sufficient water, clean air to breathe, proper sanitation, and health care including vaccines and family planning. In the decade between 1990 and 2000, East Asia and the Pacific regions reduced their nations' poverty considerably due to a quadrupling of the gross domestic product (GDP), or the total value of all goods and services produced in one year. Sub-Saharan Africa, however, ended the century 5 percent poorer (UNDP, 2002). But many poor nations (54 of them) are worse off now than they were 10 years ago, according to the annual U.N. Human Development Report (Gavlak, 2003). Life expectancy has gone down, in part because of the spread of HIV-AIDS.

Global Hunger

Close to 75 percent of the world's population live in poor nations of the world, with most of the poor in the Southern hemisphere. Overdependence on the exportation of cash crops to other nations in exchange for hard currencies has added considerably to the food shortage problems of some developing nations such as Ethiopia, India, and China (Estes, 1992). The extent of world hunger is staggering. The number of people who die every few days of hunger and starvation, according to Estes, is equivalent to the number who were killed instantly in the bombing of Hiroshima. Simply put, poverty has a global face; people are dying every minute of the day from lack of basic nutrition.

In a frightening passage from her book, *Don't Be Afraid Gringo*—a powerful diatribe against the United States—Alvarado (1987) of Honduras speaks from the heart:

> Look at my granddaughter. She's a year old and has diarrhea right now. My daughter took her to the doctor, but the medicine they gave her only made the child sicker. Now they say she has second-degree malnutrition, and that we have to feed her healthier food—eggs and milk and things like that. But where are we supposed to get the money for these foods? (p. 24)

This is just one example of the many vicious cycles facing the poor. As Stiglitz (2003) indicated, "Many are caught in a series of vicious spirals: lack of food leads to ill health which limits their earning ability, leading to still poorer health" (p. 83).

Macionis (2004) provides a graphic portrait of the face of poverty in Madras, India, one of the largest cities in a country that contains one of three of the total number of the world's hungry. In his powerful description, Macionis juxtaposes the Western visitor's response of horror with the traditional coping strategies of the survivors: Arriving in Madras, the visitor immediately recoils from the smell of human sewage and contaminated water that is unsafe to drink. Madras, like other cities of India, teems with millions of homeless people; people work, talk, bathe, and sleep in the streets. As Macionis suggests, however, the deadly cruelty of poverty in India is eased by the strength of families, the religious tradition of *dharma* (the Hindu concept of duty and destiny), and a sense of purpose to life. The absence of danger, illegal drug activity, and anger are striking to the outsider. Banerjee (1997), similarly, found hidden strengths in her research in the slums of Calcutta, strengths related to personal integrity in the midst of abject poverty. Compared to North Americans, East Indians have an altogether different experience of poverty, as of life itself. Yet the suffering resonates.

In the Western hemisphere, squalor reigns supreme in the small, deforested nation of Haiti. An article in the *New York Times* by Gonzalez (2002) reveals the interconnectedness of malnutrition, lack of sanitation, and disease:

> The poor cram themselves into the dingy cells and even inside the old sentry towers that look out over the surrounding shanties where 2,000 more souls live without water, schools, or electricity. Some are so desperate they eat pancake-like disks of bouillon flavored clay.... Pigs waded through streams of human waste and poked their snouts into mountains of garbage in a drainage canal. Young women dropped plastic buckets into a sewer and hauled out a gray water.... Children commonly died from malaria or diarrhea, while tuberculosis and AIDS killed their parents. (p. 1A)

In 1994, the United States led an invasion of Haiti to restore the democratically elected president to power. When the new government proved to be as corrupt as the previous one, the United States blocked all foreign governmental aid (Gonzalez, 2002). As in other situations of economic boycott, the ordinary people pay the price. "There are mighty historical and economic forces that keep the poor down; and there are human beings who help out in this grim business, many of them unwittingly." So wrote Michael Harrington (1962) in his classic, *The Other America*. For facts on hunger in America, see the section on food stamps in Chapter 5.

Explanations for the Existence of Poverty

International forces shape the economic structures of all nations. These forces are sociological, economic, situational, and cultural. From the international literature, I have filtered out the following explanations of poverty that are germane to an understanding of its persistence: poverty as functional for the power elites; poverty due to global competition for markets; overpopulation; war and preparation for war; and inadequate social welfare provisions. We will look at each one separately.

Function-of-Poverty Explanation

To discover the functionalist explanation for the existence of poverty, we have to go back to Gans (1995). Keep in mind that, as Gans noted, what is functional for affluent groups in the society is not necessarily functional for the society as a whole. Gans's arguments are that poverty is endemic in society in its capacity to:

- Ensure that society's "dirty work" is done
- Subsidize through low wages many activities of the affluent
- Create jobs for a number of occupations and professions (e.g., correctional officers, the police, and Salvation Army ministers) that serve the poor

- Provide buyers for goods (e.g., day-old bread) that no one else wants
- Maintain the legitimacy of dominant norms by identifying the poor as deviants
- Allow helpers to feel noble and altruistic
- Provide vicarious pleasure for the affluent in the supposed wild sexual doings of the lower classes
- Guarantee the status of those in higher classes
- Further the upward mobility of the nonpoor through restricting channels of mobility for the poor
- Help to keep the aristocracy busy in caring for and teaching the poor
- Make high culture possible by providing labor to create monuments of civilization
- Provide "low" culture, which is frequently enjoyed by the rich
- Act as a source for arousing conservative opposition (e.g., against "welfare chiselers")
- Provide foot soldiers for wars and land for urban renewal
- By not voting, keep the interests of the poor from "cramping the style" of others

A useful exercise is to take this list and apply it on the global level. What functions do poor nations serve for rich ones? Are they sources of cheap labor? Do they suffer from a "brain drain" because educated elites are moving to more prosperous lands? Are they places for corporations to dump banned or defective products? Can these countries be controlled politically through the dispensing of financial aid?

The *dysfunctions* from the point of view of poor people and poor countries are, of course, more obvious than the functions. The dysfunctions of poverty for the poor are seen in intense suffering, economic dependency, and high death rates. The dysfunctions for the dominant groups are more subtle: They are manifest in deep divisions between the haves and the have-nots, violence that is an outgrowth of harbored resentment, environmental despolation, and the spread of disease, including epidemics.

Poverty and Global Competition for Markets

Survival in a highly competitive global economy affects the modern social welfare state of the industrialized world. To compete in what Reich (2002) terms "the new economy," corporations and government are compelled to become more efficient. To aid corporations, government often frees up investment capital through curbing corporate tax rates. The loss of tax revenue encouraged by corporate growth exacerbates the staggering levels of governmental debt and leads to an eventual deterioration in public services (Karger & Stoesz, 2002). These policies practically ensure a host of social problems and a downsizing in social welfare programs to rectify them. For the corporations themselves, the pressures of international competition can lead to economic restructuring, which in turn promotes rapidly changing technology and a reduced need for workers. The greater the accumulated capital by industry, the greater the investment in technology to manufacture the products. Meanwhile, the lack of stable employment in a community is associated with mounting social problems.

Trade imbalances stemming from a combination of declining exports and increasing imports have had an especially devastating impact on nations with already high levels of foreign indebtedness. Overdependence on food imports has threatened local agricultural efforts and reduced the level of self-sufficiency still further. The poorest countries whose inhabitants are on the brink of starvation end up exporting their own scarce food grains as cash crops to generate the foreign exchange required to pay their foreign debts. As agribusiness has gained control of considerable arable land, both meaningful work and economic self-sufficiency have been destroyed. Multinationals, moreover, push the sale of nonessential, even harmful items such as soft drinks, fast food, tobacco, alcohol, white bread, and infant formula. The latter product has become downright lethal for infants in the absence of pure water and sanitary cooking equipment. In any case, the creation of markets for unhealthy, even addictive products is wreaking havoc in parts of the world where such products have come to represent Western fashions and lifestyle (Schlosser, 2002). Money spent on such artificially created desires is money taken away from the family's food, clothing, and shelter.

Overpopulation

The highest population growth rates are being registered in the world's poorest countries, giving support to the notion that poverty fuels population growth (Hartmann, 2002). Meanwhile, growth in many of the industrialized nations is expected to decline. Falling fertility rates in countries ranging from Japan to Korea to Germany to the countries of the former Soviet Union have had serious implications for the economies of those nations. In Western Europe, Ireland and France have the highest fertility rates at about 1.9 to 2 children per woman of childbearing age; in Spain and Italy, the figure has collapsed to 1.2 ("The French Family," 2003). As Europe's working population shrinks, properly managed immigration is a must to ensure that future needs of the European labor market are met, according to an EU report from Brussels ("Zero Immigration 'Not an Option,'" 2003). The United States stands virtually alone among industrialized nations in that its population (thanks to immigration) is expected to almost double over the next 50 years. One anomaly contained in the *2002 World Population Data Sheet* report (Hartmann, 2002) is the influence of the AIDS pandemic on projections for growth in southern African countries such as Zimbabwe, Botswana, and South Africa, an effect that is expected to distort the impact of high fertility rates in these regions.

Literacy for women is highly correlated with low birth rates. In the nation of India, for example, in southern states such as Kerala, where the literacy rate for girls and women is quite high (estimates range from 85 to 100 percent) despite a relatively high poverty rate, birth rates have fallen in contrast with most of the rest of India, where family planning efforts have been less effective (Parthasarathy, 2002).

The connection between poverty and overpopulation is apparent in the pressure that conditions of poverty put on families to produce more offspring to have additional hands to carry out the work—fetching water, planting, chopping wood, and so on. The connection between poverty and overpopulation is apparent, too, in the scarcity of resources and the territorial disputes that ensue when the population exceeds maximum limits. Internal battles and even warfare often result as migrating populations seek new territory and as nations compete with nations for control over arable land, fresh water, and oil. Drought and food shortages in 1998 helped fuel the war in Congo, for example, when Rwanda sent refugees from its overcrowded nation into Congo for food (Squitieri, 1998). Competition over resources is a phenomenon that is related to greed as well as need. We need only consider the history of conquest and internal fighting in the Middle East.

War as a Cause of Poverty

While economic rivalry of one sort or another can be considered a key factor in war, war and the preparation for war can have dire economic consequences. Drawing on international data from the United Nations, North Atlantic Trade organization, and the U.S. government, Sivard (1993) documents the ravages of warfare and the international trade in weapons. Where massive supplies of arms have been shipped into countries in desperate need of economic aid, both the death toll and the flood of refugees have increased. Prolonged fighting across the globe has destroyed crops and devastated agricultural areas, turning countries into ecological wastelands. In Somalia, for example, torn by tribal warfare in the early 1990s, famine claimed as many as 1,000 victims a day.

Warfare is predominantly a male activity. The economic costs of war and the preparation of war often fall more heavily on girls and women as they become less valued than boys and men. This inequity is reflected in infanticide and in reduced health care and nutrition for females. In some regions, and especially in South Asia, men and boys eat first. Girls in impoverished nations are more than four times as likely to be malnourished as boys (United Nations, 1995).

War is self-perpetuating. As groups take up warfare in response to warlike neighbors, the fighting spreads geographically in a diseaselike manner (Ehrenreich, 2003). Losses suffered in earlier conflict sow the seeds for new wars of reconquest and retaliation. In our time, as Ehrenreich suggests, the costs of war, and of war-readiness, are probably larger than at any time in history due to pressures to keep up with the extremely expensive, ever-changing technology of killing. North Korea offers what Ehrenreich terms "a particularly ghoulish example, where starvation coexists with nuclear weapons development" (p. 15). In the spring of 2003, in preparation for the invasion of Iraq, the U.S. Congress appropriated $75 billion as a down payment on the cost of war—with $1.7 billion already committed to reconstruction (Delahunt, 2003). This amount rose to another $87 billion by legislation that passed in 2003. The war on terrorism has pushed the war against poverty that afflicts billions of people off the international agenda (Agence France Presse, 2003). Without massive help, as social work educator Terry Hokenstad (interviewed by DeAngelis, 2003) tells us:

> A lot of people are going to need very basic goods and services like food, shelter and medicine, and they're going to need to create viable livelihoods . . . without these local structures . . . Iraq could suffer a similar fate to the one Afghanistan currently faces. In that country, there's only one viable national business: a poppy-growing trade used to produce heroin. (p. 3)

Poverty Stemming from Inadequate Social Welfare Provisions

When a nation's tax revenues are concentrated on military deployment, this means that money and other resources are not available to boost the quality of the welfare state. Social welfare provisions are unavailable for disabled, unemployed, and other vulnerable people in the society to shield them from the throes of cruel circumstances. Whether care is formal or informal, the availability of help in times of severe crisis is essential to ensure survival of a population. The lack of such aid compounds the social problems related to poverty.

Structural adjustments or requirements imposed upon debtor nations by the world banks have necessitated cost cutting in domestic spending to pay off the debts. Indebtedness to foreign powers prevails as well; such debt usually is connected to foreign aid for military expenditures. Cutbacks in health care and other social services are reflected in maternal and infant mortality rates and the spread of disease. We will now consider the dynamics of globalization in greater depth.

Poverty and Globalization

Globalization today is not working for many of the world's poor (Stiglitz, 2003), nor for the environment or for the stability of the global economy. The transition from communism to a market economy has been so badly managed in some countries, as Stiglitz (winner of the Nobel Prize in economics and author of the national bestseller *Globalization and Its Discontents*) pointed out, that poverty has soared as incomes have plummeted. The problem is not with global interdependence; the problem, as Stiglitz indicated, is with some of the rules of the game—rules set up by the IMF (International Monetary Fund), World Bank, and the WTO (World Trade Organization). Global trade is highly regulated through these organizations, with the powerful holding sway and the playing field being far from level (UNDP, 2002). Argentina's liberalization program, for example, received praise as an economic model for other countries, yet today the Argentine economy is in a state of total collapse, as the country's indebtedness to international banks has exceeded the nation's ability to meet payments (Petras & Veltmeyer, 2002). Few companies have had the scale and

Homeless man, Waterloo, Iowa. The safety net function of the U.S. welfare state has grown steadily weaker, while the ranks of unemployed have grown as well.

financing to compete with the top U.S. and European multinationals on an open market. Free trade, in fact, is not so much free as restrictive for producers in the poor countries; trade barriers deliberately inhibit certain imports that especially hurt farmers from poor regions of the world. Industrialized nations have held onto their trade barriers in such areas as agriculture, while demanding that less influential nations lower their tariffs. At a much publicized meeting of the WTO members in Cancun, Mexico, talks collapsed due to the rift between the need of rich countries for farm subsidies and the need of poor countries for an end to the dumping of cheap goods on their markets (Nicholson, 2003).

World Banks and Monetary Policies

The cornerstone for international trade agreements was laid after World War II with the establishment of two international agencies to be accountable to member nations and to address the needs of the post–World War II world. The IMF was established to encourage expansionary policies in nations in need of financial assistance for economic development and to oversee monetary policies (Karger & Stoesz, 2002). In its original conceptualization, as Stiglitz indicated, the IMF's focus was primarily to preserve economic stability (Stiglitz, 2003). A public institution, the IMF reports to ministries of finance and world banking institutions. The United States essentially holds veto power. In the 1980s, as Stiglitz recalls, the mission of IMF underwent a complete turnabout consistent with the right-wing capitalist ideology of the day. This ideology, which still dominates international finance today, "reflects a paradigm that degrades the natural environment and converts living human beings into disposable commodities" (Prigoff, 1999, p. 166).

In contrast to the IMF, the establishment of the World Bank was specifically for the purpose of providing credits and long-term loans to the poorest nations (Healy, 2001). In recent years, under pressure from women's groups, it has embarked on some progressive policies geared to helping poor women in poor countries obtain loans for microenterprise creation. Stiglitz, who served as senior vice president of the World Bank until 2000, has seen a change occur at the World Bank; he has seen the bank working more *with* rather than *against* governments in promoting exports and new enterprises. In this regard, the worldwide antiglobalization protest movement has not been without an impact.

Much of the focus of the antiglobalization demonstrations has been on the WTO. Founded in 1995, the WTO was created to accelerate the emergence of global markets and to produce the equivalent of a global constitution to ensure a healthy business climate for international commerce. The Geneva-based WTO is described in an article in *Time* as "both traffic cop and top court of the global economy" (Hornblower, 1999, p. 40). In his preface to *Seeds of Fire* (Wilson & Whitmore, 2000), John Foster comments on the results:

> Instead of sustainability, it [the global economic constitution] overrode environmental regulation. Instead of health it prescribed genetically modified foods and overpriced pharmaceuticals. Instead of transparency and democracy, it represented secrecy and corporate privilege. Instead of human rights, protection for owners of "intellectual property" and investors. (p. 10)

Fueled by policies of the IMF, industrializing countries have been forced to cut spending, privatize, lower taxes, reduce labor rights, and eliminate subsidies for basic food items (Torczyner, 2000). Privatization, as Torczyner contends, "is a principal vehicle through which universal programs are dismantled and responsibility for social protection devolves from the state to the private market" (p. 129). In parts of Latin America where governments are often corrupt, privatization (e.g., of public utilities) may promote greater efficiency. Results have been uneven, however. Privatization, according to an article in the *Economist,* has become deeply unpopular; privatization of a water firm in Bolivia in 2000, as well as of an electricity generator in Peru, was scrapped after riots ("Wanted: A New Regional Agenda for Economic Growth," 2003). Collectively these policies have made nations and regions more attractive to foreign investment. Corporations, in order to remain competitive, have moved across the globe in search of ever-cheaper labor and increased tax incentives from governments. Wilson and Whitmore (2000) referred to these competitive times in a chapter heading as "the age of 'disposable humanity.'"

In the age of the global economy, the gap between rich and poor nations has widened considerably. Already by the 1990s, more than 80 percent of the world's income was concentrated in the richest 20 percent of the world's nations (Sivard, 1993). While in 1980, median income in the richest 10 percent of countries was 77 times greater than in the poorest 10 percent, by 1999 that income gap had grown to 122 times (Economic Policy Institute, 2001). Only in South East Asia and the Pacific have the nations expanded their economies over the last decade (UNDP, 2002). The largest increase in people suffering from hunger and disease has been in southern Africa, where a combination of natural and human-created disasters has created mass starvation and environmental deterioration. Sub-Saharan Africa and Eastern Europe are the only regions in the world where life expectancy has declined since 1990. In six sub-Saharan countries, more than 20 percent of the children are malnourished (UNDP, 2002). Modern technologies introduced from abroad increase the national debt and benefit the top echelons at the expense of the others.

Within nations, likewise, the gap between rich and poor has been getting larger. Although exact data from cross-country and within-country comparisons are hard to come by, a review of the available evidence on inequality by UNDP indicates that worldwide, within-country income inequality has been increasing over the past 30 years. In Mexico, the poorest 40 percent receive less than 10 percent of the gross national product (GNP), and in Brazil the poor receive only 7 percent. In South Africa, 5 percent of the population, mostly whites, own 88 percent of all private property. Within poor countries, existing wealth is diverted to the rich, leaving the majority of the population in absolute poverty (Healy & Whitaker, 1992).

In 2002, there were twelve billionaires in Mexico and seven in Brazil. The billionaires' money came from a Wal-Mart venture and from banking in Mexico and banking and telecom interests in Brazil (*Chronicle* Staff, 2002).

Free Trade Agreements in North America

The same new political, neoliberal (meaning neoconservative) ideologies that guide the global market across continents guide the capitalistic fervor closer to home (for residents of North America). Just as in Latin America and Africa, world banks have become the principal movers of social policy under the North American Free Trade Agreement (NAFTA); the erosion of the people's social and economic interests is a given. In the United States, Canada, and Mexico, thousands of manufacturing jobs have been lost and labor protection legislation repealed. The impact of the replacement of full-time, highly paid manufacturing jobs with part-time, temporary labor coupled with a reduction in social welfare benefits has been especially evident in Canada, while in both Mexico and Canada, small home-grown businesses have folded in competition from major corporations such as Wal-Mart that sell high-quality, low-priced goods imported from Asia. According to a *Wall Street Journal* news report, Wal-Mart stores today account for more than half of all Mexican supermarket sales

(Millman, 2004). Meanwhile, grain imports from north of the border have driven Mexican farmers into deep crisis (Valente, 2001).

In 1995, when NAFTA was in the final process of ratification between the United States and Canada, I attended an international social work conference at the University of Calgary. A volatile exchange between right-wing politicians and social workers ensued. While the visiting politicians lauded the economic blessings that would arise, the largely Canadian audience mourned the anticipated loss of well-paying jobs, the weakening of labor unions, the loss of support for arts and culture, and the loss of social benefits.

Now, in the 21st century, we can survey the results, preliminary though they are. Canadian author Naomi Klein (2002), best known for her iconoclastic book *No Logo,* provides documentation that, in many ways, the corporations' profit strategies are backfiring, creating a core of activists from Toronto to Buenos Aires who no longer feel they have a stake in the system. In an interview that was conducted by Slaughter (2002), Klein offered a more personal view:

> Capitalism works like a drug addict. The drug is growth and the need for constant expansion. Neo-liberalism is the syringe of the moment. . . . (p. 35)
>
> You could say that I was a child of the welfare state, in a sense. Both my parents worked in state institutions they believed in. Both of the institutions my parents worked for (the National Film Board and public health medicine) have been basically dismantled. Everything innovative about Canada's health care system has been axed due to cost-cutting, and it's rapidly becoming a two-tiered system. (p. 37)

In Canada, the promised growth in jobs in high-technology sectors has not materialized. In the name of making Canada more competitive, worker benefits have declined while worker productivity has increased through new labor-saving technology, speedups, and more overtime work (Wilson & Whitmore, 2000). Productivity, similarly, is up south of the Canadian border as well while total employment rates have fallen for the same reason (Pinkerton, 2003).

There is much talk of job loss to Mexico, and of Mexico as the winner of the free trade agreements. When NAFTA was extended south of the border, Mexican trade surplus was expected to rise. In fact, according to Wilson and Whitmore (2000), austerity measures imposed by the big banks have resulted in a net loss for Mexican industries and a dependency on foreign transnationals for markets and technology. Meanwhile, the flood of cheap imports from Asia by way of the United States has sounded the death knell for small, independent businesses.

As for the promise of new and better jobs with trade liberalization, working conditions at the *maquiladoras* (export processing plants) have become notorious for human rights violations against the poorly paid, mostly young female employees who toil through 12-hour workdays in these plants and live in shantytowns near the U.S. border (Diebel, 2001). According to a report conducted by the Mexican Institute of Labor Studies and Investigation, the only types of investment that have grown since 1994 are the stock market and the maquiladora industry. "NAFTA Forces Mexican Farmers to Work in U.S." (Knight Ridder Newspapers, 2003) beams one headline. Mexico's corn farmers have had to abandon their families and family businesses because of plummeting prices caused by an influx of subsidized American corn, according to the article. Many such farmers are flocking north of the border so as to be able to send home money to family members who remain behind.

The student-led antisweatshop movement has raised the consciousness of many persons in the Global North about the worker conditions in the sewing industry, such as the Korean-owned factories in El Salvador. These plants, in fact, are moving away to seek even lower environmental health standards than those found in Tijuana or Juarez, and higher standards in skills and efficiency such as they have found in China (Diebel, 2001). The rest of Latin America is watching; the election of anti–free trade agreement candidates in Brazil and Ecuador reflect broad-based opposition to NAFTA expansion. Still, as expected, the government of Chile signed a free trade agreement with the United States, the first such accord with a South American country. Critics in Santiago expressed concerns that only a small percentage of businesses would benefit and small farmers would be hurt ("U.S. Signs Free Trade Pact with Chile," 2003).

Under NAFTA investment provisions, foreign investors are allowed to sue governments for domestic environmental regulations that are detrimental to business. Mexico, for example, was forced to pay the U.S.-based Metalcad corporation $16.7 million because local elected authorities forbade the building of a toxic waste dump in an environmentally sensitive location (Gallagher, 2002).

Empire Theory

Increasingly in the left-wing press and European sources, the term *empire* is heard with reference to U.S. ventures, both economic and military. Three recent hot-selling books, *Empire* by Ferguson (2003), *American Empire: The Realities and Consequences of U.S. Diplomacy* by Bacevich (2002), and *Empire* by Hardt and Negri (2000), discuss this radical shift in the political order that has transformed the concept of the nation-state. *Empire* implies an expansion of borders, a commonwealth of peoples or nations under a single government.

Consider the recent speech by renowned Indian novelist and environmental activist Arundhati Roy (2003):

> What can I offer you tonight? Some uncomfortable thoughts about money, war, empire, racism, and democracy.... Some of you will think it bad manners for a person like me, officially entered in the Big Book of Modern Nations as an "Indian citizen," to come here and criticize the American government.... But when a country ceases to be merely a country and becomes an empire, then the scale of operations changes dramatically. So may I clarify that tonight I speak as a subject of the American Empire? (p. 1 of 12)

In her speech, Roy chronicles America's history in financing and arming the Ba'ath regime in Iraq, then overthrowing both the Taliban government in Afghanistan and the Saddam regime in Iraq. America's media empire, controlled by a tiny coterie of people, according to Roy, has made the war against Iraq palatable to the American people through careful stage management. In conjunction with the war on Iraq and the so-called reconstruction, American defense contractors that contributed to the Republican campaign have been awarded multi-million-dollar reconstruction contracts.

Empire theory—a term I am introducing in this book to denote the conceptualization of global capitalism as an entity that transcends national borders, an entity bigger than any one country—harks back to Marx and Engels' (1963/1848) *The Communist Manifesto.* The blurb for the book *Empire,* in fact, likens that book to *The Communist Manifesto.* In the following passage from the *Manifesto,* Marx and Engels offer an understanding of the self-perpetuating forces of the world market that probably has more relevance now than it did when it was written:

> By exploitation of the world market, the bourgeoisie has given a cosmopolitan character to production and consumption in every land. To the despair of the reactionaries, it has deprived industry of its national foundation. Of the old-established national industries, some have already been destroyed and others are day by day undergoing destruction. They are dislodged by new industries, whose introduction is becoming a matter of life and death for all civilized nations: by industries which no longer depend upon the homeland for their raw materials, but draw these from the remotest spots; and by industries whose products are consumed, not only in the country of manufacture, but the wide world over. Instead of the old wants, satisfied by the products of native industry, new wants appear, wants which can only be satisfied by the products of distant lands and unfamiliar climes. . . . It forces all the nations, under pain of extinction, to adopt the capitalist method of production; it constrains them to accept what is called civilization, to become bourgeois themselves. In short, it creates a world after its own image. (p. 30)

The notion of empire clearly goes beyond the geographical and economic realm into the realm of ideology. Writing on the global economy, Luttwak (1999) effectively captures the essence of the neoliberal belief system. Americans, he contends, are natural-born missionaries, unburdened by doubt or prevarication. Their enthusiasm for a certain idea (e.g., fad diets or antidrug legislation) is boundless. With regard to free market capitalism, the formula to which fashionable economists and corporate CEOs (chief executive officers) subscribe is that what is good for business is good for all: Privatization plus deregulation plus globalization = capitalism = prosperity. This formula for economic success is embedded in a distinctive legal system and in Calvinistic values that allow for the sharp inequalities that global competition entails.

Let us now consider the implications of economic globalization for poverty in the United States.

Impact in the United States

At the other end of the equation from Mexico and Canada is the country with presumably the most to gain from global trade—the United States. To gauge the impact, let us turn to relevant facts from the U.S. Bureau of Labor Statistics (2003). From that source we learn that rural factories across the nation cut 4.6 percent of their payrolls in 2002, and about 140 plants closed;

nearly 500,000 jobs were lost in February and March of 2002 alone. In fact, as a recent Federal Reserve report indicates, the operating capacity at the nation's factories is the lowest since 1983. In articles such as one entitled "Globalization Squeezes Rural Factories" by David Pitt (2003), we read of factory closings in places like Galesburg, Illinois, and Amana, Iowa. Such closings in rural America, which leave the areas destitute, are casualties of the competition with cheap labor in other parts of the world.

A total of 181,000 jobs were lost in 2002 after a 1.4 million drop in 2001 (Hagenbaugh, 2003). It was the first back-to-back annual job decline since the 1950s. The gain is to U.S. manufacturers—to the major, transnational corporations. The loss is to the U.S. worker and to the government in lost tax revenues, both from the overseas businesses and from workers who lose their source of income. And the trend is not in manufacturing alone (which workers eventually will lose to automation anyway), but also in the highest-paying service industries. Information technology is leading the offshore exodus (Gongloff, 2003). Today, India, China, Ireland, Israel, and the Philippines all are experiencing a boom in exporting computer-based services. The relocation of factories or movement of operations through cyberspace represents a boon to such regions where the cost of living is low and the imported jobs allow for a higher standard of living than that which could be obtained otherwise. Already by 2000, as former U.S. Labor secretary Robert Reich (2000) predicted, some 50,000 Indians were entering and retrieving Internet data, handling customer calls, and doing online accounting. Today, hundreds of thousands of Indian and Chinese technicians, programmers, and software engineers are working for U.S. and British companies from their own computers in Asia. Indian radiologists now analyze CT (computed tomography) scans and chest x-rays for American patients; they do their work not far away from where accountants are processing U.S. tax returns (Schwartz, 2003). Alarmed by the loss of white-collar jobs to foreigners and the increasing unemployment of well-educated workers, American lawmakers are trying to limit the numbers of such jobs that can be exported ("A New Battle Over Offshore Outsourcing," 2003).

"There may be dreary times in Silicon Valley but in Bangalore, India . . ." begins an article on high-tech research in a recent issue of *BusinessWeek* (Kripalani, 2002, p. 52). The construction boom in research and development labs all over Bangalore represents a new wave of investment that is making this region a hub of global research activity. Already some 25,000 engineers work in these labs. The attraction to computer firms such as Texas Instruments of India is the high standard of engineering education, command of the English language, global experience of Indian-educated engineers, and an average annual wage of $12,000 for a PhD. Another key advantage of reliance on labor on the other side of the globe is the time difference. Work orders sent at the end of the day in the United States are received in the morning in India, and then returned for the start of the following day in the United States. A similar state of affairs occurs in Ireland where the educational level is high, English fluency outstanding, and the time difference a major advantage.

America's loss is China's gain as well. Chinese factories are flooding the world with cheap goods, everything from television sets and DVD players to bicycles and clothes. Whereas in Mexico, businesses complain of high taxes, inefficiency, a weak infrastructure, and a shortage of highly skilled workers, China is superior in every category (Malkin, 2002). The Chinese economy, according to an article in *BusinessWeek,* is expanding by an enviable 8 percent (Clifford, 2002). The fear for the U.S. economy is deflation as prices fall (deflation is associated with a reduction in investment due to fear of loss) and a forced collapse of the price of competing American products. In Japan, the world's second largest economy, deflation is playing havoc with the economy, so the overpriced real estate market has collapsed and consumer spending has taken a nosedive (Grimond, 2002). Because Japanese banks and insurers hold massive amounts of U.S. securities and their companies have numerous branches in the United States, Japan's financial crisis can have global repercussions. The rising star, by almost any measure—growth in the GDP, employment, fiscally healthy companies (e.g., Samsung and Hyundai), or banking—is Korea. According to a recent article in *BusinessWeek,* today's Korea has emerged from being a rigid, isolated society "to one that is plugged-in, dynamic, and increasingly high-tech" (Bremner, 2002, p. 54).

In summary, world economics today is highly complex. For the United States, Canada, and Mexico, the free trade agreements are far from the win-win-win situation that the true believers in unfettered capitalism predicted. The outsourcing trend with manufacturing jobs to Asia is well underway, while the white-collar job migration is just starting to crystallize. Workers in North America can expect to experience repercussions that parallel the revolutionary shifts in the global market.

European Union

Both economically and militarily, competition to U.S. hegemony is represented in the integration of European nations through the rapidly expanding European Union (EU). The process of European integration began shortly after the Second World War with two primary objectives: the economic reconstruction of war-ravaged Europe and the creation of a unified region promoting peace ("History of the European Union," 2003). As of 2004, EU membership includes the 15 original countries from western Europe plus 10 new states, mostly Eastern Europe countries including Poland and Hungary. The EU's parliament endorsed the bloc's expansion. The assembly pledged that the expanded EU would speak with a common voice in world politics and continue to fight crime and protect human rights (Brand, 2003). In the EU, worker protection has been provided through improved labor standards legislation (Broad, 2000). In contrast to NAFTA, funds are transferred from wealthier to less-advanced nations to reduce disparities among members (Valente, 2001). Two major accomplishments are the use of a common currency (the Euro) in many of the countries and a Court of Justice to interpret community law, protect citizens' human rights, and settle disputes between states.

A major advantage of EU membership is that workers can move freely among the countries; agreements are currently being reached to recognize professional credentials cross-nationally. Students can attend universities throughout the region as well. Perhaps the most promising dimension of the EU is its attention to social problems, especially those that transcend national boundaries. In anticipation of workers' displacement through global competition, for example, the Commission of the European Union has taken a stand in favor of shortening the workweek for everyone. (NAFTA would do well to emulate this position.)

On the negative side, the leveling of standards mandated in the agreement is resulting in serious "modifications" in welfare programs in Denmark, Finland, and Sweden. Although these modifications will likely improve provisions in the countries with the least-developed social welfare systems, states with generous benefits are required to reduce them (Healy, 2001). Farmers cannot be subsidized as they have been, as their produce has to compete with food grown much more cheaply in southern Europe, and women stand to lose many of their special benefits. Accordingly, much political controversy has ensued throughout Scandinavia over some of the consequences of Europeanization to these welfare states, a situation that is referred to within the EU as the "North/South divide." In Sweden, where opposition to EU membership has always been strong, especially among women, membership has been generally regarded as partly responsible for the erosion of the Swedish welfare state (Gould, 2001). To date, as of 2003, Norway and Iceland have resisted joining to preserve their high standards of social welfare.

In September 1995, I attended a social work conference of agency practice teachers for field placement at the University of Warwich, England. The impact of the EU in terms of stepped-up competition and stress on productivity and cost-effectiveness was strongly evidenced in the presentations and the small-group discussions that followed. "What are some of the paradoxes in your social work practice?" asked one speaker. The audience provided the following responses (most speakers were quite emotional):

- Training people for jobs that are disappearing
- Raising of quality standards, yet no time to do all the work
- Lack of resources and lack of time to meet the new demands and increased workloads
- Extensive documentation
- Diminishing role of professional social work under the shift to case management
- Quality assurance becoming quantity assurance
- Deskilling of jobs

Since that meeting, the impact of managerialism and market forces on British social work has only grown more pronounced (see Dominelli, 2002). Although the terminology used at the convention was distinctly British and unique to social work, the themes that emerged are universal to the workplace in the global era, which is the subject to which we now turn.

Work in the Global Era

Perhaps the most conspicuous impact of globalization poverty has been through labor market developments (Mishra, 2002). In the United States, as elsewhere, as Mishra indicates, between 1973 and 1999, while the GDP grew at an annual rate of 2.8 percent, real average wages of production and nonsupervisory workers declined over the same period. "Where Did My Raise Go?" (Kadlec, 2003) was the cover story of an issue of *Time* magazine in 2003. Shrinking paychecks, along with eroding health and pension benefits, is the new reality for many Americans, according to the article. One job title defying the trend is CEO: CEOs in the United States now earn 300 times the pay of the average worker, up from 56 times in 1989. The top 100 CEOs earn more than $35 million annually apiece. No other industrialized nation has such a discrepancy: Norway has the lowest pay differential—big business executives are paid 17 times the average worker ("Lave Lønnsforskjeller i Norge," 2003). Pension guarantees and other benefits for CEOs have been increasing as well.

Perhaps both the cost-cutting at lower levels and pay raises at the highest levels are symptomatic of the global imperatives. The spread of technology and skills, of Internet communication and cheap shipping, means that today more U.S. firms must compete against foreign rivals that are more formidable than ever before (Kadlec, 2003).

Downsizing, outsourcing, wage flexibility, cost-efficiency, accountability, productivity: these are just a few of the buzz words causing workers in many parts of the world to cringe. Commentators have studied the impact of Wal-Mart, the $244-billion-a-year retailer, to highlight its ruthless tactics in wiping out its rivals and threatening the economies of small towns by driving all the small companies out of business. Wal-Mart has excited attention of another kind, however. According to *The New York Times* (Hays, 2003), this retailer has become a best-selling topic for the Harvard Business School, which sells Wal-Mart case studies to business schools around the world. Wal-Mart has become the company to watch and the company to emulate. Its policies—everything from its fight against unions to its provision of partner benefits to gays and lesbians—are highly influential and receive close scrutiny by economists. Wal-Mart's use of new technologies is closely scrutinized by economists as well.

Every major period of technological development affects the structure and organization of society. In a book entitled *The End of Work,* but which perhaps more aptly should be called *The End of the Worker,* economist Rifkin (1996) captured the new economic ethos. Wave after wave of technological innovation affects not only manufacturing sectors (where robots are replacing people) but the service sector as well (where computers, automated teller machines, and voice-recognition technologies are eliminating the need for human contact). But just as important as technology itself are the *control* and the *use* of the technology—in short, the degree of regulation of industry or the government's role in ameliorating or not ameliorating the consequences of the structural changes for the benefit of people. The social protections are as important as the technology itself.

The social welfare of a people is intricately linked to the way they earn their living, the availability and conditions of their employment, and the sexual division or nondivision of labor. In most modern or modernizing societies, an individual's sense of self-worth is affected by the work that the individual does and the significance attributed to that line of work. Work is essential to human dignity, a fact set out so meaningfully in the 1948 U.N. Declaration on Human Rights. Article 23 is composed of four parts, providing the rights: to free choice of employment; to just and favorable conditions; to equal pay for equal work; and to sufficient remuneration to ensure an existence worthy of human dignity (see Appendix A). Article 23, however, is in the second covenant of the Universal Declaration—the part that, unfortunately, was not signed by the United States because the rights granted go beyond those of the U.S. Constitution.

If unchecked, structural shifts in the economy can have devastating consequences for workers and their families. As self-sufficient national economies risk being overtaken by fierce competition driven by cheap and temporary labor, many workers have now grown expendable, and work security and incentives have disappeared. It used to be "the carrot and the stick." Now it is simply "the stick." Consider the following headlines from a variety of news sources:

> "Job Survivors Shoulder More Work" *USA Today* (Armour, 2001)
> "Deaths of Hispanic Workers Soar 53%," *USA Today* (Hopkins, 2002)
> "Where Did Everyone Go? Firms Are Laying Off Workers Even as Business Revives," *Time* (Cullen, 2002)
> "Even the Supervisor Is Expendable," *BusinessWeek* (Little, 2001)
> "Giant Sucking Sound Rises in the East," *Utne* (Utne, 2003a)
> "Japanese Corporations Bully Workers into Quitting," *Waterloo-Cedar Falls Courier* ("Japanese Corporations," 1999)

The list could go on and on. What we learn from such sources is that competition among companies is reflected in competition among workers. We learn that poultry processors and nursing home aides epitomize the harshness of much of the new low-wage work where workers suffer soaring injury rates and yet frequently lack health benefits. In many high-growth industries, work is faster than ever before and, therefore, the personal stress is greater also. Moreover, the once solid foundation for millions of middle-class families—the corporate career—is sinking rapidly.

As workers become increasingly expendable, their sense of security vanishes. The by-products of pressure on the job—family violence, employee violence, substance abuse, divorce, and stress-related illness—are on the rise in the United States and elsewhere. Writing in *The Two-Income Trap*, Warren and Tyagi (2003) provide some chilling statistics. For example, two-income families make 75 percent more in inflation-adjusted dollars today than 30 years ago, but have less money to spend, and bankruptcies and health insurance costs are at record highs. In Iowa, which is known for its strong work ethic, to make ends meet, many workers are taking two jobs and relying on methamphetamines to stay alert. Accordingly, meth addiction rates have soared; treatment centers and prisons are barely able to cope with the end result.

In a chapter entitled "The Obsolescence of Loyalty" in his book on work, *The Future of Success,* Reich (2000) notes that not only is company loyalty to workers a relic of the past, but so also is any sense of responsibility to the hometown. The focus of businesses in what Reich terms "the new economy" is singularly on earnings, on maximizing the value of investors' shares, and not on making contributions to the arts in the hometown community. Today's corporate headquarters can be anywhere near international airports; suppliers and partners are nowhere in particular, and they continually change as the market changes. Commercial relationships are fleeting. It is hard to talk of social responsibility by organizations in this situation, according to Reich: "[I]n this emerging cyber-landscape it will be odd to speak of institutional loyalty because there will be fewer clear boundaries around any institution" (p. 84).

Today's workers who once considered themselves to be removed from employment practices in other places (e.g., Mexico or China) are being made painfully aware of the extent to which their lives are interconnected with the lives (or livelihoods) of workers throughout the world. The corporations, no longer clearly identifiable as American or Japanese or Swedish, are *transnational* enterprises. The operations flow with increasing ease back and forth across borders, gyrating in response to worldwide economic forces.

The focus of Reich's book is not poverty per se, but rather the opportunities and risks of the new labor market and the winners and losers in the world of business. His analysis does reveal, however, that job security, even in Japan where jobs were once guaranteed for life, will soon be replaced as harsh competitive "realities" of intense global competition dictate the treatment that workers receive.

For a closer look at the world of work from the vantage point of the lowest-paid worker, we turn to two sources, both of them bestsellers—*The McDonaldization of Society* and *Fast Food Nation.* Interchangeable workers, homogenization of products, standardized work routines, and technologies that take care of most of the "brain" work (e.g., making change)—these are among the characteristics of the fast-food restaurant singled out by sociologist George Ritzer (2000) in his popular (especially in Britain) *The McDonaldization of Society.* The process by which the principles of the fast-food restaurant "are coming to dominate more and more sections of American society as well as of the rest of the world" (p. 1) is epitomized in the global McDonald's chain, according to Ritzer. Not only characteristic of the restaurant business, the process is also affecting education, travel, organized leisure-time activities, politics, the family, and, of course, work itself. Significantly, the term *Mc* has come to symbolize mass-produced services, as in *Mc*Dentists, *Mc*Papers, and *Mc*Day Care. The McDonald's model has succeeded because where time is at a premium in a work-crazed society, it offers the consumer efficiency, predictability, and food for little money. For the worker, however, the setting is often dehumanizing; the average fast-food worker lasts only three months. Workers take no pride in their work or creations; they only pride themselves on the speed with which the work is performed. The pseudofriendliness with customers can be taxing in its own way.

Speed and efficiency have come to a head in a singularly bizarre way—the installing of high-tech, computerized hiring systems to screen job applications. In *The End of Work*, Rifkin (1996) describes the process in detail: An optical scanner stores images of a résumé in a computer database. In less than three seconds, the résumé can be scanned to generate the appropriate acknowledgment letter. Applications are then processed by the computers and relegated to the appropriate job category. Personal-sounding replies are sent to each hopeful applicant.

Most of the gains in efficiency, as Ritzer observes in *The McDonaldization of Society*, are on the side of those who are pushing rationalization upon us. Is it more efficient, for instance, to pump your own gas or to use exact change on a bus? Are prerecorded voices on the telephone responsive to our needs? Borrowing from Max Weber, Ritzer shows how, with greater and greater bureaucratization, the rational has become *irrational*. In agreement with Rifkin's major thesis in *The End of Work*, Ritzer predicts that the most likely response to complaints about dehumanization of the worker will be simply to eliminate more and more of the humans. One area where people, at least air force pilots, will be happy to surrender their role to machines involves dangerous bombing missions. During the attack on Iraq, we heard in the TV news of "unmanned aerial vehicles" and pilotless drones. These killing machines are increasing in efficiency and taking much of the danger out of dropping bombs. In Silicon Valley and practically everywhere else, the new technologies are helping employees do more work in less time; for this reason, productivity is up, and yet firms are getting leaner in terms of job opportunities (Stone, 2003).

Fast Food Nation: The Dark Side of the All-American Meal by Schlosser (2002) takes us into the world of the modern food industry, a world that is founded on the premise of cheap food, cheap labor. The actual cost to life is reflected in the increase of food-borne disease, near-global obesity, loss of the family farm, animal abuse, and chopped-off fingers. If you want to enjoy fast food (on any given day, one-fourth of the adult population visits a fast-food restaurant), do not read this book. Learning of the chemicals that are added to food to make it taste like what it is (e.g., hamburger flavor), not to mention the chemicals fed to the animals for abnormally fast growth, will make your appetite for this food wane. Our interest here, however, is in the work angle. Meatpacking is now the most dangerous job in the United States, and farming and cattle-raising are now corporate enterprises. Notes Schlosser:

> The industrialization of cattle-raising and meatpacking over the past two decades has completely altered how beef is produced—and the towns that produce it. Responding to the demands of the fast food and supermarket chains, the meatpacking giants have cut costs by cutting wages. They have turned one of the nation's best-paying manufacturing jobs into one of the lowest-paying, created a migrant industrial workforce of poor immigrants, tolerated high injury rates, and spawned rural ghettos in the American heartland. (p. 149)

IBP (Iowa Beef Packers), which is now owned by Tyson Foods, has been inundated with lawsuits related to unsafe working conditions (workers typically are forced to make one knife cut of beef every two or three seconds), pressure not to report injuries, scandals related to the recruitment of undocumented workers, and the fondling of female employees. In addition, the relentless pressure of trying to keep up with the line has encouraged widespread methamphetamine use among meatpackers.

To avoid lawsuits and for economic reasons, much of the most dangerous manufacturing work is being relocated abroad where safety standards are lax. According to recent research from the International Labour Organization (ILO), two million workers die each year through work-related accidents and diseases (Takala, 2002). The biggest killer in the workplace is cancer related to work with hazardous materials such as asbestos and radiation. Agriculture, logging, fishing, and mining are the most hazardous industries.

Agriculture

The nature of work is undergoing transformation not only in the industrial arena but also in agriculture, where a high-technology revolution is well underway. Family farms have been replaced by corporate operations that stretch for thousands of acres (Schlosser, 2002). Widespread use of chemical pesticides, fungicides, herbicides, and advanced harvesting equipment associated with this type of land usage promotes high productivity with little land and few farm laborers. Worldwide subsidies and IMF inducements promote the planting of high-yield monoculture crops requiring advanced harvesting equipment, often for international export. Like ranching, farming is not just an occupation but a whole way of life—an expression of the values of independence, hard work ("sun up to sun down"), community bonding, and intergenerational pride in land ownership. So the economic crisis facing the family farmers and ranchers is a threat to more than their livelihood. The suicide rate among ranchers and farmers in the United States is now about three times higher than the national average (Schlosser, 2002). The farm income crisis has decimated rural communities in the United States and Canada. A Canadian study from the *Agribusiness Examiner* likens agricultural restructuring by transnational companies to the free market programs imposed on highly indebted nations in Latin America as a condition for receiving further loans. The emphasis in both cases is on increased foreign investment and production for export (Qualman, 2002).

In Costa Rica, agricultural intensification has occurred rapidly in one generation. Cultivation of tobacco, a highly profitable crop, makes possible the purchase of modern consumer goods. Through the use of dangerous chemicals, several other crops can be produced on one plot of land. The temptation to risk damage to the ecosystem for short-term gains and to go into debt to invest in expensive equipment to maximize production can lead to ecological and financial disasters in the long run.

The massive displacement and dislocation of farm labor over the past century has deprived millions of people of their chosen livelihood. Through mechanical, biological, and chemical innovations, productivity has risen considerably. Fewer and bigger farms have been the end result. Today in Iowa, a hands-free combine that sells for tens of thousands of dollars allows for precision farming that increases yields significantly (Wilde, 2004). It is expected that before long, a robot tractor will plow the fields by remote control. On a global basis, unsustainable land use has led to desertification, deforestation, and environmental contamination. China, the rice capital of the world, is facing an agricultural upheaval according to a report in *The Wall Street Journal* (Kahn, 1995). Eclipsing a 5,000-year history of peasant agriculture, modernization is claiming the land. Grain output, consequently, cannot keep pace with the soaring demand as arable land is sacrificed for industry and meat production. Heavy importation of wheat will be necessary to feed a nation that contains one-fifth of the world population on only one-fifteenth of its arable land.

While all of the Central American countries have been devoting substantial effort to industrialization, agriculture has been an important part of their attempts to finance this process. Export agriculture in combination with cheap food policies is an essential part of the Southern Hemisphere's linkage with the world market. In Mexico, the elimination of tariffs on U.S. produce threatens to wipe out the livelihood of millions of Mexican farmers. Mexican farmers average just 13 acres, a legacy of land reform introduced after the Mexican Revolution. In an article entitled "Farmers Are Getting Plowed Under," Smith (2002) predicts a huge fight with Mexico over the lifting of tariffs on rice, potatoes, pork, and chicken. Farmers and pork producers recently marched hundreds of squealing pigs through one of Mexico's small towns in protest.

The goal of the export agriculture as directed by the world banks is to enhance foreign exchange on the global market. The consequent change in land use patterns due to this thrust has been dramatic. Poor and indigenous people have been displaced. The increased concentration of land ownership in the hands of a few in Mexico has led to violent uprising and much political unrest among the Chiapas Indians. Throughout Latin America, in fact, much of the land is now devoted to pasture for cattle, an export commodity that employs relatively little labor. And peasant agriculturalists have become an underemployed urban poor struggling to survive as shoeshine boys, servants, and street vendors.

Worker Stress in the Industrialized Society

"Stress Pushes Rural Iowans to Brink" was a headline in *The Des Moines Register* (Fitzgerald, 2003). Even though crop yields were excellent, "economic pressures are pushing farmers to the brink emotionally and financially and stymieing the next generation of farmers," according to the article (p. A1). Evidence is in the form of the number of calls to Iowa Concern, a hot line established during the 1980s farm crisis, which has now set a record with 951 rural residents seeking legal, financial, and mental health advice. The stress that farmers feel with the world changing so rapidly around them is symptomatic of what is happening to workers everywhere.

There are two kinds of stress related to the pressures of competition in the global economy. The first is job stress itself; the second relates to the insecurity of work in an era of rapid change when the worker may become "redundant," to use the British term.

High levels of stress in the workplace emerged from a survey of Canadian workers as a key factor in work-related stress. Government, health, and education employees evidenced the highest levels of discontent; about half stated that they lacked the resources to do their job well (Laver, 1999). In Britain, according to a survey of 600 workers regarding work stress, one in five respondents said the incredibly long work days were triggering "desk rage" or displaced aggression against fellow workers (Milne, 1999). A comparable U.S. poll reported by Kimbrell (1999) showed that 88 percent of workers said their jobs required them to work longer hours and 68 percent complained of having to work at greater speeds. The increase in jobs serving consumers at the expense of high-paying manufacturing jobs often produces a sense of powerlessness and meaninglessness in the worker, as Kimbrell contends.

Many of the service jobs (e.g., at Wendy's) announce on their billboards that they are hiring "smiling faces." HyVee of Iowa, a grocery chain, has as its advertising slogan "a smile in every aisle." In a lawsuit from California, 13 workers filed grievance against Safeway's smile-and-make-eye-contact orders, complaining that such a policy makes them vulnerable to being propositioned by shoppers who mistake the company's imposed friendliness for flirting.

Job-related stress is exacerbated in a tight job market. When Barbara Ehrenreich (2001) applied for low-wage jobs as a part of her research for the exposé *Nickel and Dimed,* she was shocked at the intrusiveness of the application process. Pre-employment personality tests included questions such as: "Do you suffer from moods of self-pity?" and "Do you consider yourself a loner?" For jobs ranging from store clerk to Wal-Mart greeters, as Ehrenreich discovered, the applicant must submit to invasive drug screenings.

Forced overtime is a growing source of dissatisfaction. As more workers are laid off, the remaining workers are working harder than ever to take up the slack. Because of the high cost to companies for health care insurance and other benefits, it is cheaper to pay overtime to the regular staff than to hire more staff. "Long Workdays Draw Backlash" read a headline in the *Christian Science Monitor* (McLaughlin, 1998). "In a nation where workers average enough extra hours to equal about three more weeks of work per year than they did just ten years ago," writes McLaughlin, "some economists are predicting a period of adjustment on the issue of overtime." Much recent labor strife (e.g., airline pilots strikes) is related to the desire of workers to spend more time with their families or simply to rest from the pressure at work.

The consequences of overwork are reflected in headlines such as this: "Amphetamine Use Rises in Workplace: Tests Show 17% Spike in '02" (Jones, 2003). The consequences of overwork are also reflected in a drop in the amount of sleep by adult Americans. While the average workweek has climbed to 46 hours per week, the average weeknight's sleep has decreased to 6.7 hours for persons aged 18–54. This fact comes from the National Sleep Foundation (2003). Today many factory jobs are moving to 12-hour, 4-day-a-week shifts. The number of hours truck drivers can drive successively on the road has been increased to 11 consecutive hours, with a 10-hour break required between shifts (Keogh, 2003).

New rules were proposed and passed by the U.S. Congress to give employers more "flexibility" in awarding overtime pay for most workers who exceed 40-hour workweeks, and yet Americans already work 350 hours (or 9 workweeks) more per year than the typical European (Ivins, 2003, 2004). According to an article in *BusinessWeek,* even the hard-working Japanese have reduced their yearly total of hours worked by 191 hours. Italians get over 40 vacation days per year, the French about 36, Germans and Brazilians over 30, and British, Canadians, and Japanese 20-plus, while in the United States, the average length of vacation is a paltry 12 days (Brady, 2002). Another interesting statistic is the average workweek. A global study by a New York–based market research firm found, not surprisingly, that Koreans average 55.1 hours per week, while workers in the United States and China tied at 42.4 hours. (The U.S. average has risen to 46 hours since this survey was done.) The shortest workweek of countries studied was found in France, Italy, Britain, and Canada at just over 40 hours. (France recently cut their workweek to 35 hours to tackle unemployment.) Hardest working next to the Koreans were Turks, Argentines, Vietnamese, and Tawainese—all over 53 hours ("Koreans Put in Most Time on the Job, Survey Shows," 2003). Such long work hours take a toll psychologically, are correlated with heart attacks and other illnesses, and even hinder productivity in the long run, as Brady (2002) has indicated.

Jobs that do not provide opportunities to learn and grow, that are mere drudgery in other words, can lead to a sense of alienation. *Alienation* is defined as the condition in industrial society in which the individual's sense of self and significant aspects of the person's physical and social environments are experienced as estranged and out of personal control. Because of global pressures, the reality in manufacturing today is to structure the work around the machines rather than the people who run them. Every hour a factory is idle is costly and is an economic drain on the company's bottom line. Writing in *The Wall Street Journal,* Aeppel (2001) describes the case of a would-be preacher forced to work on alternate Sundays at Goodyear Tire and Rubber Company, which has moved to 12-hour shifts; days off vary each week. The toll on the workers, especially on single parents with children, is enormous.

Impact on the Family

The impact on the family of the mounting work pressures is of sufficient magnitude as to be of concern to all those in the helping professions including the clergy. Workers at low income levels often find that one job is not enough; some take on a second or even a third job. University students typically attend the university full-time while holding down a full-time job at the expense of the educational experience.

Grueling work schedules coupled with increasing job insecurity are taking a toll on working-class families. When there is a shortage of money, tensions mount, and conflict often develops among individual members. Depressed wages, a frenetic pace set at the workplace, the rapid rise in temporary work, decreased long-term employment, the growing disparity between the haves and have-nots, and the dramatic shrinking of the middle class are placing unprecedented stress on the American workforce (Rifkin, 1996). As jobs have been eliminated, the survivors are now doing the tasks of two or three people.

Unable to maintain a home, pay for higher education for their children, save for retirement, or maintain their purchasing power, the working poor endure a major crisis at every turn—for example, when a car breaks down or personal illness occurs. People often blame themselves for problems that are structural in nature.

As hard as Americans work, the Japanese dedicate themselves to their work with a sense of obligation that is difficult for the Westerner to understand. The boundaries between work and after-hours recreation (often at a karaoke bar) are not clearly drawn. Overwork leading to death is common enough in Japan to have been given a name—*karoshi*, which means dropping dead at one's desk (Mucha, 2000).

Work-related family crisis is occurring not only in North America and East Asia but universally. In Mexico City, small children are sometimes literally tied to their beds while the parents work. This lack of child care is a worldwide phenomenon, according to a report on world trends released by the Population Council in New York (Knight-Ridder, 1995). Increasingly, according to this report, mothers are raising children alone and also working outside the home; fathers are absent because they have migrated for work and/or formed new families; and children are at high risk of being poor and left to fend for themselves. In terms of workload, women everywhere are found to work many more hours than men when nonpaid work is counted.

At the opposite end of the work continuum among industrialized nations is the attitude toward work in Scandinavia. A guide to business customs in Sweden describes business meetings as formal and goal-oriented. At the same time, the business person is advised to:

> Arrange the timing of meetings thoughtfully. Offices are often deserted on Friday afternoons, particularly in the summer, and the whole country seems to close down from July to August and during the winter school half-term holiday. Try to fix meetings for early morning. Late afternoon is equally unpopular due to thoughts of going home, as are the few days before a public holiday such as Easter, when executives want to clear their desks. (Hutchings & Hatchwell, 2002, p. 328)

My experience working at a Norwegian alcoholism treatment center was comparable. Norwegians work hard while at work, but their leisure time is highly valued. Social workers were expected to work about six hours a day. Workers thought nothing of taking the day off for a dental appointment, and a year's (paid) leave for pregnancy was provided. Sick leave for emotional problems related to work stress could last a year as well. Employers, therefore, are well advised to treat the workers well. We had a lot of stress attached to work in alcoholism treatment, so most of the staff took sick leave at some point. The pay they received was comparable to what they had earned while working. Sweden, under pressure from the EU, because of the excessive number of sick days workers were taking, has placed some restrictions on such absences. My impression of Scandinavians was that much of their industriousness was directed toward activities outside of work—toward building cabins in the mountains or teaching their children (toddlers) to ski, for example. Family ties were close, and family life was enhanced through such shared activities, most of which were out of doors and not limited to any season.

Unemployment

From the societal point of view, full employment serves to provide stability of the citizenry, a healthy tax base, and a sense of community among those who have a stake in its survival. Even in a poor, working-class neighborhood, law-abiding role models are available to help socialize the young. Close family ties can be sustained when the adult members can find gratifying work.

The social functions of a phenomenon often can be understood more in its absence than in its presence. So it is with employment, especially fulfilling employment. The psychological toll from loss of a job can be enormous, especially in a society such as the United States where a person's status in society is determined by the person's occupational role and achievement in that role. Little allowance is made for failure even given the realities of today's work world.

People who follow the ups and downs of the stock market often notice that as a company's stock market values go up, the numbers of workers laid off goes up as well. Such companies are investing in advanced technology, sometimes even raiding employees' retirement funds to do so. All nations in the global economy desire a certain level of unemployed workers to keep the wages down. On Wall Street, in fact, as announcements are made of low unemployment, the stock market typically suffers a decline for this reason. Murray Dobbin (1998) spells out this phenomenon for Canada. For 15 years, Dobbin says, governments have been transforming the Canadian economy and society, gearing up for competition in the global economy—an economy, it was assumed, that would always continue to grow. Now, according to Dobbin, Canadian governments have savaged the domestic economy; they have implemented a policy of permanent recession—deliberately high unemployment aimed at lowering labor costs.

There is nothing new historically in company downsizing and worker displacement due to technological advance. In earlier stages of automation, for example, machines took much of the drudgery out of work; but then workers who were laid off from automated factory work moved into related manufacturing work or white-collar jobs. Before, when one door was closed, another one opened. Decline in one area of employment was more than offset by opportunities elsewhere. If there is something unique about the latter-day technological revolution, it is the absence of hope and the absence of belief in the future. For generations, Americans have considered a brighter future to be their birthright, and upward mobility for their children a must. In light of the changing realities in the workplace and in the absence of a cultural shift in sync with the new realities, no longer will parents be able to pin their hopes on the next generation to accomplish what they could not. Workers in a highly competitive society cannot count on the generosity of government assistance to help them out with financial aid or innovative worker training programs. In disagreement with Reich (2000), who sees the solution in terms of job retraining, my question, following Rifkin (1996, 2004), is: retraining for what? If highly skilled computer experts in Silicon Valley are losing their jobs, perhaps we had better move beyond platitudes and locate the real culprit in continued job loss.

A special report in *BusinessWeek* (2004) provided some answers that social scientists and laypersons would do well to consider. According to that report, outsourcing is not the problem that politicians and the media claim it to be, based on the following:

> The real culprit in this jobless recovery is productivity, not offshoring. Unlike most previous business cycles, productivity has continued to grow at a fast pace right through the downturn and into recovery. One percentage point of productivity growth can eliminate up to 1.3 million jobs a year. . . . Companies are using information technology to cut costs—and that means less labor is needed. Of the 2.7 million jobs lost over the past three years, only 300,000 have been from outsourcing, according to Forrester Research Inc. (p. 37)

Their analysis explains why the economic boom is not being reflected in the predicted job growth; their analysis gives credence to Rifkin's earlier predictions about workerless companies as well.

A second culprit in the jobless recovery is the cost of health benefits. As reported in a recent article in *The New York Times* (Porter, 2004), the relentless rise in the cost of employee health insurance has become a significant factor in the employment slump. In the second quarter, the cost of health benefits rose at a 12-month rate of 8.1 percent, which was more than three times the inflation rate. Accordingly, businesses are holding back from hiring people despite economic growth. The hiring slump is especially pronounced in the high-wage, high-benefits sectors like manufacturing, according to the report.

These economic insights tell us that productivity and economic growth should continue worldwide and that the challenge is not to move jobs from one country to the home base, but to take advantage of the labor-saving technologies to free up time for the people to perform more meaningful, community-building functions (e.g., providing care for the frail elderly). And could we not find a way to share the enormous wealth accruing to the soaring productivity?

In the meantime, worker anxiety seems destined to remain high. According to the ILO, the number of unemployed worldwide has grown by 20 million to 186 million (ILO, 2004). In the United States, the number of unemployed persons has hovered around 6 percent: This is the official rate based on the number of people looking for work. People who have become discouraged and stopped looking for work are not counted (Herbert, 2003). Speaking before the national gathering of social work educators, Rifkin (2004) estimated the actual unemployment rate at 9 to 11 percent. Keep in mind the statistical impact of high incarceration rates for young men coupled with the unprecedented graduate school enrollments associated with the lack of changing employment needs—facts that keep the unemployment rates lower than would otherwise be the case.

In Iowa about 4,500 manufacturing jobs have disappeared as employers have lost business due to imported products or sought lower production costs outside the United States (Ryberg, 2003). The mere threat of relocation has broken the backs of the labor movement and created a situation of anxiety and distrust for both worker and management. Farmers meanwhile have suffered the consequences of severe indebtedness due to the purchase of expensive farm equipment when the ability to repay the loans depends on such unpredictable factors as the weather or the price of beef or corn. The consolidations of companies that buy and resell what farmers produce have introduced an additional dimension of uncertainty into the business of farming.

Two determinants of social well-being strongly affected by globalism are: the labor market (i.e., the availability of well-paid employment), and social policies that help to insulate people from vicissitudes in the labor market (Mishra, 2002). In most places, the world's people are suffering from lack of both social supports—lack of job security and lack of social protection from job loss.

Researchers find a strong association between unemployment and emotional problems. During a recession, mental hospital admissions increase, as do suicides, divorce rates, and incidences of child abuse (Zastrow, 2004). Even children of the unemployed suffer from mental health problems, as well as rejection by peers, developmental delays, and increased depression (Allen-Meares, 1995). Joblessness, poverty, reluctance to marry, and family breakup are all highly intercorrelated. These long-term effects help explain why African Americans marry at much lower rates than other groups in the United States (Coontz & Fobre, 2003). Substance abuse and job loss are reciprocally related. Zastrow (2004) listed suicide, emotional problems, insomnia, psychosomatic illness, social isolation, and marital unhappiness among the consequences of long-term unemployment.

Widespread unemployment can be devastating not only for the individual but also for the society. The consequences are reflected in early teenage pregnancy, homelessness, crime statistics, and even mass civil disorder, inasmuch as persons outside of the work economy are divorced from the ordinary social structure. On the financial side, widespread unemployment also leads to diminished tax revenues. This, in turn, is associated with reduced government services. Those in the workforce who pay taxes are resentful of others who do not; they are apt to support punitive policies to force nontaxpayers to take low-wage jobs.

In an article poignantly entitled "The Unpeople," and seemingly ahead of its time, British journalist Jeremy Seabrook (1991) contemplated the impact of successive waves of unemployment, first from unionized industrial labor, and then from expulsions from the "caring" professions under Thatcher conservatism. He writes:

Socialism is off the global agenda. The market reigns supreme. The West has won. There is no longer any need for dissent. Hence the time has come for silencing, for marginalizing, side-lining. We have become unpersons, by means of the most genteel and delicate of violent suppressions; by being deprived of a livelihood. . . .

Everywhere, people are being evicted from livelihoods, displaced from their habitats by the same processes that are depriving us also of security and continuity. Indigenous peoples, tribal and forest people are being ousted for the sake of the resource-base. . . .

The children of rice-farmers in Thailand must migrate to Bangkok and Phuket to supply the demand for sex workers, fuelled in large measure by the demands of western tourists. Subsistence farmers in India and the Philippines are being forced from their lands by the urgent need of their governments to service mountainous debts. . . .

The displaced fishing communities of Kerala and Penang are subject to the same forces as those that make families homeless in New York or Hackney; the people under the bridges of London or Paris with their fires and bottles of drink are the sisters and brothers of those under the motorways of Sao Paulo and Mexico City.

Indeed, as the logic of the global marketplace extends further, people in Bombay and Seoul will be competing for work with the people of Birmingham or Naples, or even Moscow. (pp. 15–16)

Seabrook's predictions sadly have turned out to be "right on target." What he did not anticipate, however, is the strong countermovement, the public consciousness that has sprung up. Let us look at some of the strategies that are being used to confront trends that may not be so inevitable after all.

Strategies to End Poverty in the United States

Some government measures to reduce poverty are commendable. Federal tax policy, as Karger and Stoesz (2002) concede, has shifted from actually exacerbating poverty to alleviating it. Elimination of income tax on very low incomes is a measure that is palatable to the American people in its reinforcement of the work ethic. The earned income tax credit, which was introduced in 1979, has been expanded in recent years. The increasing popularity of tax credits, particularly those aimed at low-income families, suggests that policy change efforts could well be directed here. According to Dolgoff and Feldstein (2002), incentives for families receiving TANF (Temporary Assistance for Needy Families) to work are enhanced because a program subsidizing *earned* income is not stigmatized. The working poor in a moralistic society are considered among the deserving poor. Moreover, this program brings a large benefit to children in the families of the working poor, though benefits are not increased beyond two children: This is one aspect of the program that is criticized. Other drawbacks are that recipients receive payments in one lump sum, many parents are unaware of the program, poor workers without children get only minimal benefits, and there are no provisions for destitute persons who cannot find work.

In a list of recommendations for shaping legislation relevant to the TANF block grants to the states, the National Association of Social Workers (NASW) focused on three areas:

1. Reducing the number of families living in poverty
2. Improving assistance to recipients with multiple barriers to self-sufficiency
3. Enhancing the capacity of the welfare system infrastructure (O'Neill, 2003, pp. 1, 10)

A significant additional recommendation is that education and training count toward state work participation rates. Also included under work activities should be treatment for mental disorders and substance abuse, which impede people's success in living a full life, taking care of their children, and so forth.

Workers' Rights Mobilization

Raising the minimum wage level is the most obvious way to lift workers out of poverty. More than 60 U.S. cities, counties, and public agencies have boosted minimum wages for their workers (but not all workers) by several dollars so that these workers get a living wage ("Study Shows 'Living Wage' Helping to Reduce Poverty," 2002). The real way to eliminate the "welfare problem," as Seccombe (1999) informs us, is to restructure or enhance jobs in the lowest tiers of the labor market, which—even with its faults—is a logical refuge in times of trouble.

Devoted to the principle that people who work full-time should not live in poverty, the living wage movement is a grassroots effort that is directed at the local level where business groups are less all-powerful than they are in Congress. At several college campuses, students have successfully protested on behalf of campus cleaning crews and other low-wage workers, demanding that their pay be sufficient to support a small family.

Strategies to provide high-quality and affordable child care for workers are crucial as well. So argues Robert Reich (2000). Other effective strategies are paid parental leaves, tax deductions for child care and elder care, and flexible work times. Minnesota, forever a progressive state, has achieved some success in providing generous transitional help for persons on the welfare rolls to get them into sustainable jobs (Stodghill, 2000). Looking to Scandinavia in this context, we find that Sweden, along with Norway, is the prototype of the child-caring society. Most Swedish children spend the first year or two at home with their parents because parental leave covers most of the lost income (Arenander, 2001). Municipalities are required to provide preschool to all children aged one to five. Elementary schools offer child enrichment programs and light meals after school (Arenander). Although some aspects of Sweden's welfare state are being carefully scrutinized due to global competition and EU requirements, there is still a minimum of five weeks' vacation for all full-time workers (Utne, 2003b). It is hard to imagine any better way to prevent job burnout than allowing a period of rest and family life. Besides, a reduction in the work year would offer more employment possibilities for others.

If the provision of health care were the responsibility of the state rather than employers, the workweek could be shortened. Without the added expense of health benefits, employers would be free to employ more workers instead of pushing the present workforce into overtime. The end result is that then there would be more jobs to pass around. Japan, facing unaccustomed threats of unemployment, is looking into job sharing as a plausible solution (Dawson, 2001).

Keep in mind Rifkin's (1996) points about the technological revolution that is only barely underway in an ever more automated global economy—the workerless factories, and the association between high productivity, rising stocks, and a drastically reduced workforce. Then consider the federal mandate to reduce the welfare rolls even while the availability of well-paying jobs is shrinking. Why have fewer workers doing more work at this time? Why are people silent in the face of these assaults? In fact, as Piven (2000) informs us:

> It's not as quiet as it seems. Below the radar screen of press and politicians, scores of grassroots groups are waging fights at the local and state level to expose the realities of welfare reform and the low-wage labor market. . . . As the new policies began to bite, protests emerged—over the irrationality of yanking poor women out of college to sweep the streets in abusive workfare programs or of cutting paltry cash grants to punish families for breaking any of the new and mindless rules that welfare departments are generating. Grassroots organizations are not just waging a low-intensity war of resistance. They are also promoting model policies that might lay the groundwork for a new national legislative agenda, including expanded health insurance, childcare subsidies, public jobs programs, and living wage ordinances. . . .
>
> The Maine Association of Independent Neighborhoods and its partners won the Parents as Scholars program, which allows college attendance to count as work while "stopping the clock" for women in school. Such initiatives have also succeeded elsewhere. (p. 4)

The Kensington Welfare Rights Union

A multifaceted movement seems to be emerging to challenge the corporate-reactionary alliance that has dominated the United States for the past two decades. The poor pay the heaviest price for that domination, and so should be in the lead of any movement that dislodges it. In fact, there is such a movement today, a grassroots organization of poor and homeless families. The Kensington Welfare Rights Union (KWRU) has been actively building a mass movement to end poverty since 1991. Social workers involved in the movement see themselves not as advocates but as allies, seeking collaboration in all dimensions of the necessary work in organizing to end economic oppression. One of the highlights of KWRU was the "New Freedom Bus Ride" that crossed the country. At each stop along the route, local groups joined members of the radical social work organization SWAA (Social Welfare Action Alliance) for rallies and teach-ins to focus on ways the United States was in violation of the U.N. Declaration of Human Rights (Lee, 2001). Today, KWRU is one of over 50 groups that have come together in a network called the Poor People's Economic Human Rights Campaign. A prime mover in this organization, Mary Bricker-Jenkins (2002), describes the mission and one extraordinary victory of KWRU in Pennsylvania:

We are working to fulfill an often-ignored dream of Martin Luther King—that the poor of America would unite across racial and ethnic lines to become an "unsettling force" that would challenge and change a system that would not feed and clothe and house its people. (p. 8)

After obtaining the support of Lawrence Curry, member of the Pennsylvania House of Representatives, the elements of an alliance were in place. Two MSW (master's of social work) students who did their field placement with KWRU drafted the Curry Resolution, which called for a study of ways to integrate human rights principles into the laws and policies of the state. Pennsylvania NASW lobbyists joined the lobbying effort. The Curry Resolution passed, and the legislature must now hold hearings on economic human rights in the state. New leadership is now emerging in several communities. "By the time we finish this campaign," notes Bricker-Jenkins (2002), "scores of social workers, people living in poverty, and others will have come together as allies to make poverty and economic vulnerability visible in the state" (p. 9). (For information about the campaign, see http://www.kwru.org.)

Influencing public policy, learning strategies, and so forth can begin with grassroots action. Intellectually it can begin with policy analysis, a formal exercise to raise consciousness about the issues and factors involved in instituting policy. See the Outline for Anti-Oppressive Policy Analysis in Appendix D, which provides a framework for viewing U.S. policy in international and historical perspective. (To learn about lobbying initiatives at the state level, consult http://www.statepolicy.org, which is operated by the Influencing State Policy Association.)

In a related event, the Immigrant Workers Freedom Ride, launched in September 2003, departed from 10 cities with stopovers in 103 cities to raise awareness about the plight of immigrant workers in America and to protest anti-immigrant laws (Bustos, 2003). The involvement of social workers and students of social work in such mass organizing efforts is consistent with the educational policy of the Council on Social Work Education (CSWE; 2003), which stipulates that one of the purposes of social work education is "preparing social workers to alleviate poverty, oppression, and other forms of social injustice" and "to recognize the global context of social work practice" (p. 32).

From a global perspective, Midgley's (1995) advocacy for an empowerment approach for social change should be heeded. Empowerment is what the welfare rights movement centered in Philadelphia is all about. Such an approach attributes women's subjugation not only to patriarchy but to imperialism and neocolonialism. To achieve control over their lives, women must mobilize through coalition building, much aided today by electronic communication and organizations such as the United Nations Development Fund for Women (UNIFEM; 2000), a U.N. effort to advance gender issues within regional trade treaties and to strengthen women's economic capacity as entrepreneurs and producers. Such global networking for the dismantling of corporate rule and the construction of an alternative global reality is now well underway (Prigoff,

1998). Until recently, women's needs have been almost entirely overlooked by international development agencies, but today the women themselves are providing important leadership in this movement.

Summary and Conclusion

The dysfunctions of poverty at home and abroad are represented in disease, malnourishment, the daily struggle to survive, chronic indebtedness, and personal resentment. Whether within nations or between nations, disparities in wealth are associated with greed, resentment, and war. Wars, in turn, lead to mass migrations of people. Across the world refugees from conflict migrate from the poor countries into the wealthier ones, joining the already large number of immigrants who have crossed borders for economic reasons. A major loss to the poor countries is the brain drain of doctors and scientists who were educated at their governments' expense but whose talents will be utilized elsewhere.

We talked in this chapter of the dysfunctions of poverty. A major dysfunction in regard to mass poverty is engendered in the system of rationalization that arises to justify it and perpetuate it. Just as we dehumanize the enemy during wartime in order to reduce any qualms in battle and guilt feelings later, so we dehumanize the poor and homeless in order to justify our handling of them. In dehumanizing the poor, we are dehumanizing ourselves. We are blaming the victims for even being victims in the first place. Blame of another is psychologically easier to handle than guilt.

Only by helping people to understand and confront their personal troubles of economic and social hardship within the context of global causality can we hope to find appropriate solutions. Such has been the aim of this chapter in a nutshell—to pinpoint the correlates of poverty in areas as diverse (but interconnected) as: war; pressures from the global markets to raise capital at the expense of welfare programs and reduced funding to the states; retrenchment of government support for social services; privatization; the "race to the bottom" associated with one-sided free trade agreements; the elimination of factory jobs by new technologies; and, in the immediate present, weakening of labor unions due to industry's ability to relocate. The revolution in industry that got underway at the turn of this new century is replicated in agriculture through the mass production of cash crops. The revolution is not necessarily bad; the new technology can be regarded as a godsend, freeing people to use their talents and develop social capital in the local community instead of industrial products. But in this global age, we need to promote cultural values to correspond to the new realities—to promote areas such as education, health care, recreation, and social work where the work possibilities are infinite. We also need to spread the dividends from the booming global economy around more evenly.

Hovering over the whole issue of work are these questions: What is the meaning of work in our lives and our family lives? How can society adapt to a rapidly changing work milieu? And what happens to people who have lost their livelihood? The loss is in human potential. This is an appropriate stopping point as we prepare to embark on an exploration of phenomena that are both the cause and effect of economic restructuring and oppression: the "isms," for example, classism, racism, and sexism.

Thought Questions

1. Discuss the significance of the quote from President Eisenhower that begins this chapter.
2. What does globalization mean? Distinguish between *globalization* and the *global market,* or what Wilson and Whitmore called *globalism.*
3. "Literacy for women is highly correlated with low birth rates." Discuss.
4. Discuss the connection between overpopulation and poverty.
5. Relate war to poverty. Is the relationship reciprocal?
6. Can an argument be made that structural adjustments on the macro level are replicated in welfare reform at the local level?
7. "The IMF, World Bank, and WTO are some of the most powerful organizations in the world." Argue for or against this statement.
8. Discuss the growing gap between the rich and the poor in terms of the reasons for this gap.
9. Account for the protests worldwide against the WTO.
10. How has NAFTA benefited or not benefited Mexico? Why did some Canadian social work educators oppose the free trade agreement?
11. What is empire theory? With reference to foreign policy, can America be considered an empire? Discuss the quote from *The Communist Manifesto* on the power of world markets.
12. How is China an economic threat to Mexico?
13. How is membership in the EU a move forward for some countries and a move backward for others?
14. List three major changes in the nature of work in the global era. What is the human toll of over- and underemployment?
15. What is the significance of the title *The McDonaldization of Society?*
16. Describe working conditions at IPB/Tyson Foods.
17. What are some strategies for alleviating poverty? What can we learn from more worker-friendly countries?
18. Discuss roles for social workers in regional movements for poor people's rights. Why rely on an international document such as the Universal Declaration?

References

Aeppel, T. (2001, July 24). Long shifts, odd schedules disrupt life off the job; safety, health are issues. *Circadian in the News.* Retrieved from http://www.circadian.com/publications/wsj.html

AFL-CIO. (2003). A real minimum wage raise or . . . ? Retrieved from http://www.aflcio.org/issuespolitics/minimumwage

Agence France Presse. (2003, December 2). War on terror drains funds from poverty fight. *Truthout Forum.* Retrieved from http://www.truthout.org

Allen-Meares, P. (1995). Children: Mental health. In NASW, *Encyclopedia of Social Work* (pp. 460–465). Washington, DC: NASW Press.

Alvarado, E. (1987). *Don't be afraid Gringo.* New York: Harper & Row.

Arenander, I. (2001, April 29). Sweden sounds like Eden for working parents. *Women's News.* Retrieved from http://www.womensnews.org

Armour, S. (2001, June 1). Job survivors shoulder more work. *USA Today,* p. B1.

Bacevich, A. (2002). *American empire: The realities and consequences of U.S. diplomacy.* Cambridge, MA: Harvard University Press.

Banerjee, M. (1997, Summer). Strengths despite constraints: Memoirs of research in a slum in Calcutta. *Reflections,* 36–45.

Barker, R. (2003). *The social work dictionary* (5th ed.). Washington, DC: NASW Press.

Bartlett, D., & Steele, J. (2003, February 3). The really unfair tax. *Time,* 47.

Barusch, A. (2002). *Foundations of social policy: Social justice, public programs, and the social work profession.* Itasca, IL: Peacock.

Billingsley, A., & Morrison-Rodriguez, B. (1998). The black family in the 21st century and the church as an action system: A macro perspective. In L. See (Ed.), *Human behavior in the social environment from an African perspective* (pp. 31–47). New York: Haworth Press.

Brady, D. (2002, August 26). Rethinking the rat race. *BusinessWeek,* 142–143.

Brand, C. (2003, April 9). EU approves expansion for new members. *The Cincinnati Post.* Retrieved from http://www.cincinnati.com

Bremner, B. (2002, June 10). Cool Korea: How it roared back from disaster and became a model for Asia. *BusinessWeek,* 56–58.

Bricker-Jenkins, M. (2002, Fall). Organizing to end poverty: A story of strategy and tactics. *BCR Reports, 13*(20), 8–9.

Broad, D. (2000). *Hollow work, hollow society? Globalization and the casual labour problem.* Halifax: Fernwood.

BusinessWeek. (2004, March, 22). Where are the jobs? *BusinessWeek,* 36–37.

Bustos, S. (2003). Demonstrators roll on immigrant freedom ride. *USA Today.* Retrieved from http://www.usatoday.com

Central Intelligence Agency (CIA). (2002). *World factbook.* Washington, DC: Brasseys.

Chronicle Staff. (2002, March 11). Fewer billionaires. *Latin Business Chronicle.* Retrieved from http://www.latinbusinesschronicle.com

Clifford, M. (2002, December 2). How low can prices go? China's cheap exports worry the West. *BusinessWeek,* 80–91.

Coontz, S., & Fobre, N. (2003, April 26–28). Marriage, poverty, and public policy. Retrieved from http://www.prospect.org

Cooper, J., & Madigan, K. (2002, December 23). Why cutting unemployment will be one tough job. *BusinessWeek,* 25–26.

Council on Social Work Education (CSWE). (2003). *Handbook of accreditation standards and procedures* (5th ed.). Alexandria, VA: Author.

Cullen, L. (2002, November 18). Where did everyone go? *Time,* 64–66.

Dalrymple, L., & Burke, B. (1995). *Anti-oppressive practice: Social care and the law.* Buckingham, England: Open University Press.

Dasgupta, P. (1995, February). Population, poverty, and the local environment. *Scientific American, 272,* 40–45.

Dawson, C. (2001, December 24). Japan: Work-sharing will prolong the pain. *BusinessWeek,* 48.

DeAngelis, T. (2003, May 12). Social work contributions can assist Iraq's independence. National Association of Social Workers. Retrieved from http://www.socialworkers.org

Delahunt, W. (2003, May 7). Bush offers aid to Iraq, nothing for America. *The Patriot Ledger.* Retrieved from http://ledger.southofboston.com

Diebel, L. (2001, April 11). Report: NAFTA largely a failure for workers. *The Toronto Star.* Retrieved from http://www.commondreams.org

Dobbin, M. (1998, November). Exploding the tax-cut myths. *The CCPA Monitor.* Canadian Centre for Policy Alternatives.

Dolgoff, R., & Feldstein, D. (2002). *Understanding social welfare* (6th ed.). Boston: Allyn & Bacon.

Dominelli, L. (2002). *Anti-oppressive social work theory and practice.* New York: Palgrave MacMillan.

Economic Policy Institute. (2001, September 26). Letter addressed to Congress by the president of the Economic Policy Institute, Jeff Faux. Retrieved from http://www.citizen.org

Ehrenreich, B. (2001). *Nickel and dimed: On not getting by in America.* New York: Metropolitan Books.

Ehrenreich, B. (2003, April). The roots of war. *The Progressive,* 14–15.

Eisenhower, D. (1953, April 16). Speech delivered before the America Society of Newspaper Editors, Washington, DC.

Estes, R. (1992). World hunger and nutrition. In R. Estes (Ed.), *Internationalizing social welfare education: A guide to resources for a new century* (pp. 168–175). Philadelphia: School of Social Work.

Ferguson, N. (2003). *Empire.* New York: Basic Books.

Firestone, D. (2003, June 1). 2nd study finds gaps in tax cuts. *The New York Times.* Retrieved from http://www.truthout.org

Fitzgerald, A. (2003, January 19). Stress pushes rural Iowans to the brink. *Des Moines Register,* p. A1.

Francis, D. (2003, January 27). Upward mobility in real decline, studies charge. *Christian Science Monitor,* 21.

The French family: Keep it up. (2003, May 3). *The Economist,* 53.

Gallagher, K. (2002, May 1). Economic progress, environmental setback. Interhemispheric Resource Center. Retrieved from http://www.globalpolicy .org

Gans, H. (1995). *The war against the poor.* New York: Basic Books.

Gavlak, D. (2003, July 8). Poor nations not better off decade later, says UN report. *Voice of America.* Retrieved from http://www.voanews.com

Gil, D. (1998). *Confronting injustice and oppression: Concepts and strategies for social workers.* New York: Columbia University Press.

Gongloff, M. (2003, March 13). U.S. jobs jumping ship. *CNN/Money.* Retrieved from http://www .cnnmoney.com

Gonzalez, D. (2002, July 30). 8 years after invasion, Haiti squalor worsens. *New York Times,* p. A1.

Gould, A. (2001). *Developments in Swedish social policy: Resisting Dionysus.* New York: Palgrave.

Grimond, J. (2002, April 20). What ails Japan? *The Economist,* 3–4 (Supplement).

Hagenbaugh, B. (2003, January 13). Productivity up as wage growth slows. *USA Today,* p. B1.

Hardt, M., & Negri, A. (2000). *Empire.* Cambridge, MA: Harvard University Press.

Harrington, M. (1962). *The other America: Poverty in the United States.* Baltimore, MD: Penguin.

Hartmann, S. (2002). Population: 99 percent of growth seen occurring in developing world. *UN Wire.* Retrieved from http://www.unwire.org

Hays, C. C. (2003, July, 27). The Wal-Mart way becomes topic A in business schools. *New York Times,* p. BU10.

Healy, L. (2001). *International social work.* New York: Oxford University Press.

Healy, L., & Whittaker, W. (1992). Global poverty, hunger, and development: Basic issues and impact on family child well-being. In L. Healy (Ed.), *Introducing international development content in the social work curriculum.* Washington, DC: NASW Press.

The Hellenic EU presidency. (2003, March 30). Website of the Greek presidency. Retrieved from http://www.eu2003.gr

Herbert, B. (2003, April 18). Starting over. *Des Moines Register,* p. D1.

History of the European Union. (2003, March 30). European Union. Retrieved from http://www .eu2003.gr

hooks, b. (1993). *Sisters of the yam: Black women and self-recovery.* Boston: South End Press.

Hopkins, J. (2002, March 25). Deaths of Hispanic workers soar 53%. *USA Today,* p. B1.

Hornblower, M. (1999, November 29). The battle in Seattle. *Time,* 40–44.

Hutchings, J., & Hatchwell, E. (Eds.). (2002). *Insight guide: Sweden.* Masapath, NY: Langenscheidt.

International Labour Organization (ILO). (2004, January). Global employment trends. ILO. Retrieved from http://www.ilo.org

Ivins, M. (2003, April 24). Workplace flexibility. *Alternet.org.* Retrieved from http://www .alternet.org

Ivins, M. (2004, August 27). Under the radar: The Bush administration redefines workers' rights to overtime pay. *Memphis Flyer.* Retrieved from http://www.memphisflyer.com

Japanese corporations bully workers into quitting. (1999, July 25). *Waterloo–Cedar Falls Courier,* p. A3. Reprinted from *Los Angeles Times.*

Jones, D. (2003, May 27). Amphetamine use rises in workplace. *USA Today,* p. B1.

Kadlec, D. (2003, May 26). Where did my raise go? *Time,* 44–54.

Kahn, J. (1995, March 10). China's industrial surge squeezes grain farms. *Wall Street Journal,* p. A1.

Karger, H., & Stoesz, D. (2002). *American social welfare policy: A pluralist approach* (4th ed.). Boston: Allyn & Bacon.

Keogh, B. (2003, April 24). New rules allow truckers to drive more hours. *Chicago Tribune.* Retrieved from http://www.centredaily.com

Kimbrell, A. (1999, January–February). Breaking the job lock. *Utne Reader,* 47–49.

King, M. (1996, November 12). Suicide watch. *The Advocate,* 41–44.

Klein, N. (2002). *No logo: No space, no choice, no jobs.* New York: Picador.

Knight-Ridder Newspapers. (1995, May 30). Report: Families breaking up, many women overburdened. *Waterloo–Cedar Falls Courier*, p. A3.

Knight-Ridder Newspapers. (2003, November 16). NAFTA forces Mexican farmers to work in U.S. *Waterloo–Cedar Falls Courier*, p. C3.

Koreans put in most time on the job, survey shows. (2003, May 27). *Muzi News.* Online at http://www.muzi.com

Kripalani, M. (2002, November 2). Calling Bangalore: Multinationals are making it a hub for high-tech research. *BusinessWeek,* 52–53.

Lave Lønnsforskjeller i Norge. (2003, May 8). NRK (Norwegian government broadcasting service). Retrieved from http://www.nrk.no

Laver, R. (1999, May 31). The best and worst jobs. *Maclean's Online.* Retrieved from http://www.macleans.ca

Lee, J. (2001). The empowerment approach to social work practice: Building the beloved community (2nd ed.). New York: Columbia University Press.

Little, D. (2001, July 23). Even the supervisor is expendable. *BusinessWeek,* 78.

Luttwak, E. (1999). *Turbo-capitalism: Winners and losers in the global economy.* New York: HarperCollins.

Macionis, J. (2004). *Society: The basics* (7th ed.). Upper Saddle, NJ: Prentice-Hall.

Malkin, E. (2002, November 5). Manufacturing jobs are exiting Mexico. *New York Times,* p. W1.

Marx, K., & Engels, F. (1963/1848). *The communist manifesto.* New York: Russell & Russell.

McLaughlin, A. (1998, August 28). Long workdays draw backlash. *Christian Science Monitor,* p. B6.

Midgley, J. (1995). *Social development: The development perspective in social welfare.* London: Sage.

Millman, J. (2004, March 31). Mexico's ports go global. *Wall Street Journal,* p. A13.

Milne, S. (1999, September 2). Rising stress brings "desk rage" at work. *Guardian Unlimited.* Retrieved from http://www.guardianunlimited.co.uk

Mishra, R. (2002). Globalization and poverty in the Americas. *New Global Development, 18*(1–2), 37–49.

Mucha, B. (2000, June). Work to live, live to work? The changing faces of corporate Japan. Keizai

Koho Center Fellowships. Retrieved from http://kkefellowships.ness.org

National Sleep Foundation. (2003). Sleep in America poll. Retrieved from http://www.sleepfoundation.org

A new battle over offshore outsourcing. (2003, June 6). *BusinessWeek.* Retrieved from http://www.businessweek.com

Newman, N. (2002, July 25). A war on immigrants to fight the war of terrorism?: Lessons from the failed war on drugs. Retrieved from http://www.commondreams.org

Nicholson, P. (2003, September 15). Viewpoint: Blame game over WTO failure. BBC News. Retrieved from http://newsvote.bbc.co.uk

O'Neill, J. (2003, June). Services in Spanish unavailable to many. *NASW News, 48*(6), 4.

Parthasarathy, A. (2002, February 4). Kerala all set for leap in IT literacy. *The Hindu.* Retrieved from http://www.hinduonnet.com

Petras, J., & Veltmeyer, H. (2002, Fall). Argentina: Between disintegration and revolution. *Covert Action Quarterly, 74,* 27–34.

Pinkerton, J. (2003, September 14). Those U.S. factory jobs are gone for good. *Waterloo–Cedar Falls Courier,* p. B5.

Pitt, D. (2003, May 16). Globalization squeezes rural factories. *Wichita Eagle.* Retrieved from http://www.kansas.com

Piven, F. (2000, May 8). Welfare movement rises. *The Nation.* Retrieved from http://www.commondreams.org

Porter, E. (2004, August 19). Cost of benefits cited as factor in slump in jobs. *New York Times,* pp. A1, C2.

Poverty line is far below families' basic needs, new study reveals. (2002, September 6). Retrieved from http://www.aflcio.org

Prigoff, A. (1998). Economic development policies: Institutional forms of violence against women. In E. Fernandez, K. Heyex, L. Hughes, & M. Wilkinson (Eds.), *Women participating in global change* (pp. 85–90). Proceedings of the International Association of School of Social Work, Women's Symposium Publication Committee, Hong Kong.

Prigoff, A. (1999). Global social and economic justice issues. In C. S. Ramanathan & R. J. Link (Eds.), *All our futures: Principles and resources for social work practice in a global era* (pp. 156–173). Belmont, CA: Wadsworth.

Qualman, D. (2002, December 2). Canadian study shows "structural adjustment" of agricultural policies reap devastating effects for farmers. *Agribusiness Examiner.* Retrieved from http://www.macleans.ca

Ramanathan, C., & Link, R. (1999). *All our futures: Principles and resources for social work practice in a global era.* Belmont, CA: Brooks/Cole.

Reich, R. (2000). *The future of success: Working and living in the new economy.* New York: Vintage Books.

Reich, R. (2002). The treadmill of the new economy. Interview with Robert Reich. *The American Prospect.* Retrieved from http://www.prospect.org

Rifkin, J. (1996). *The end of work: The decline of the global labor force and the dawn of the post-market era.* Los Angeles: J. P. Tarcher.

Rifkin, J. (2004, February 28). Plenary address: The new economy. Presented at the Council on Social Work Education, Annual Program Meeting, Anaheim, CA.

Ritzer, G. (2000). *The McDonaldization of society* (3rd ed.). Thousand Oaks, CA: Pine Forge Press.

Roy, A. (2003, May 18). Instant-mix imperial democracy (buy one, get one free). Speech at the Riverside Church, New York City. Retrieved from http://www.commondreams.org

Ryberg, W. (2003, January 5). Starting over. *Des Moines Register,* p. D1.

Schlosser, E. (2002). *Fast food nation.* New York: Houghton-Mifflin.

Schwartz, N. (2003, June 9). The job market. *Fortune.* Retrieved from http://www.fortune.com

Schwartz-Nobel, L. (2003). *Growing up empty.* New York: HarperCollins.

Seabrook, J. (1991, June 28). The unpeople. *New Statesman and Society,* 15–16.

Seccombe, K. (1999). *"So you think I drive a Cadillac?" Welfare recipients' perspectives on the system and its reform.* Needham Heights, MA: Allyn & Bacon.

Shulman, B. (2003). *The betrayal of work.* New York: New Press.

Sichelman, L. (2003, October 17). Affordable rentals out of reach for most. *Newsday.* Retrieved from http://www.newsday.com

Sivard, R. (1993). *World military and social expenditures.* Washington, DC: World Priorities.

Sklar, H. (2001, August 29). Minimum wage—It just doesn't add up. Retrieved from http://www.commondreams.org

Slaughter, J. (2002, October). Naomi Klein. *The Progressive,* 33–37.

Smith, G. (2002, November 18). Farms are getting plowed under. *BusinessWeek,* 53.

Squitieri, T. (1998, December 31). From a "new world order" to "age of chaos." *USA Today,* p. A12.

Statistics Canada. (2003). 1990s a good decade for the rich. CBC News. Retrieved from http://www.cbc.ca

Stiglitz, J. (2003). *Globalization and its discontents.* New York: W. W. Norton.

Stodghill, R. (2000, June 12). Off the dole: Minnesota's welfare reform proves a winner. *Time,* 65.

Stone, B. (2003, August 11). Men at overwork. *Newsweek,* 36–39.

Study shows "living wage" helping to reduce poverty. (2002, March 14). *Waterloo–Cedar Falls Courier,* p. A2.

Takala, J. (2002, May 24). Work related fatalities reach 2 million annually. International Labour Organization. Retrieved from http://www.ilo.org

Torczyner, J. (2000). Globalization, inequality and peace building: What social work can do. In W. Rowe (Ed.), *Social work and globalization.* Montreal: International Association of Schools of Social Work.

United Nations. (1995). *The world's women 1995: Trends and statistics.* New York: United Nations.

United Nations Development Fund for Women (UNIFEM). (2000). *Progress of the world's women 2000.* New York: United Nations.

United Nations Development Programme (UNDP). (2002). Human development report. Retrieved from http://www.undp.org

U.S. Bureau of Labor Statistics. (2003). Usual weekly earnings summary. U.S. Bureau of Labor Statistics. Retrieved from http://www.bls.gov/news

U.S. signs free trade pact with Chile. (2003, June 9). *New Zealand Herald.* Retrieved from http://www.nzherald.co.nz

Utne, L. (2003a, March–April). Giant sucking sound rises in the East. *Utne,* 22.

Utne, L. (2003b, May–June). Life is a smorgasbord. *Utne,* 64–65.

Valente, M. (2001, July). How Mexico has fared: The lessons of NAFTA. *World Press Review,* 21–22.

Verschelden, C. (1993). Social work values and pacifism: Opposition to war as a professional responsibility. *Social Work, 38*(6), 765–769.

Wanted: A new regional agenda for economic growth.
(2003, April 26). *The Economist*, 27–29.

Warren, E., & Tyagi, A. W. (2003). *The two-income
trap: Why middle-class mothers and fathers are
going broke.* New York: Basic Books.

Watkins, K. (2001, May 16). More hot air won't bring
world's poor in from the cold. *International Herald
Tribune*, 8.

Wetzstein, C. (2002, September 25). Recession
decreases income, increases poverty rates.
Washington Times. Retrieved from http://www
.washtimes.com

Whitlock, K. (2001). *In a time of broken bones.*
Philadelphia: American Friends Service
Committee.

Wiesel, E. (1982). *Night.* New York: Bantam Books.

Wilde, M. (2004, July 11). Hitting pay dirt.
Waterloo–Cedar Falls Courier, p. C1.

Wilson, M., & Whitmore, E. (2000). *Seeds of fire:
Social development in an era of globalism.* Halifax,
Nova Scotia, Canada: Fernwood.

Young, I. (1990). *Justice and the politics of difference.*
Princeton, NJ: Princeton University Press.

Zastrow, C. (2004). *Introduction to social work and
social welfare: Empowering people* (8th ed.).
Belmont, CA: Wadsworth.

Zero immigration "not an option." (2003, June 3).
BBC News. Retrieved from http://www.bbc.co.uk

What happens to a dream deferred?
Does it dry up
Like a raisin in the sun?

LANGSTON HUGHES, 1967, P. 14*

Social Oppression

© Rupert van Wormer

Oppression is a term, as Iris Young (1990) argues, that is favored by social activists, a central term of political discourse. It would not ordinarily be used in mainstream writing or speech and is inconsistent with the ideology of opportunity that dominates U.S. politics. In traditional usage, the word *oppressive* might be used to describe conditions in a meatpacking factory or life in an authoritarian country ruled by a dictator or very hot summer weather. I use the term *social oppression* in the title of this chapter to refer to the personal forces that keep people from achieving their potential.

In each form of social oppression—racial, ethnic, religious, sexual—there is a dominant group that receives the unearned advantage or privilege, and a targeted group that is denied the advantage (Ayvazian, 2001). Such inequalities are kept in place inasmuch as the powers-that-be are able to maintain their position through ideology or force. From Ayvazian's perspective, ideology is the propagation of doctrines that legitimizes inequality. Violence or the threat of violence also may come into play in suppressing rebellion.

Think back to the Deep South under segregation: The ideology of paternalism was highly effective in alleviating the guilt of a caste of people who prided themselves on taking care of members of an "inferior race." According to the ideology of the day, "colored" people needed to be taken care of; servants were sort of like family members emotionally, while financially they were more or less in bondage (see Dollard [1988/1957] *Class and Caste in a Southern Town*).

Mullaly (1998), citing Foucault (1977), brings our attention to the more usual and subtle forms of oppression. His suggestion is that we go beyond viewing oppression as the inherent or even conscious acts of one group against another and consider the institutionally based forms that flow from the social structure itself. Oppression is ingrained, according to Mullaly, in our systems of education, criminal justice, the delivery of health and social services, and the like. Dominelli (2002), similarly, talks of the tyranny of the workplace as one of the structural elements of power that is located in the institutional and cultural domains. Because oppressive dynamics are embedded in ordinary social activities, they do not consciously have to be thought about by either oppressor or the oppressed, and are easily denied by most.

This chapter continues from where the previous chapter on economic oppression left off by exploring the age-old "isms" in society—classism, racism, sexism, heterosexism, and sectarianism. In reality, these isms all overlap to varying degrees, as particular individuals occupy more than one category at once. Moreover, the effects of membership in dual or multiple categories are more synergistic than additive. A woman who is poor and uneducated, for example, might suffer from sexism far more than might her middle- or upper-class counterpart. So keep these facts in mind as you contemplate the dynamics of classism, racism, sexism, and so on. In actuality, there are no clear-cut divisions between and among these categories; these phenomena are discussed separately here for the sake of simplification.

One more item to keep in mind as you read about each of these "isms" concerns the interesting but often overlooked fact of causation. These phenomena (e.g., classism and racism) are inclined to be self-sustaining and cyclical. Here is how this works: Society discriminates because of prejudice, and then when the disadvantaged group fails to achieve what others achieve, the members of that group are called ignorant or lazy. A related truth from social psychology is our tendency to externalize—when we exploit or otherwise mistreat individuals or groups, we come to blame these people for their disadvantaged state. Class, racial, and gender divisions are thereby reinforced.

Classism, the first topic of this chapter, extends our discussion of economic oppression in the previous chapter into the realm of interpersonal dynamics. *Classism* is probably the most fundamental and neglected "ism" in the social work and political literature (so much so that the spell-check program in my Word software does not even recognize the term).

Classism

Class, or one's socioeconomic status in the community, is a key determinant of one's life chances—of one's access to health care, educational opportunities, and marital/partner prospects. Renowned educator bell hooks (2000) addressed this issue as follows:

> Class matters. Race and gender can be used as screens to deflect attention away from the harsh realities class politics exposes. Clearly, just when we should all be paying attention to class, using race and gender to understand and explain its new dimensions, society, even our government, says let's talk meaningfully about ending racism without talking about class. (p. 313)

Classism refers to the social exclusion of people on the basis of social stratification; it is oppression of people thought to be socially inferior—whether on the basis of poor living standards or lack of education or grammatical speech. Classism occurs at all levels of society. Its existence is singularly pronounced in the higher echelons by the attitudes of upper-uppers toward the class just beneath them, the "nouveau riche" who are thought to lack taste and refinement. The "nouveau riche," in turn, resent the upper-uppers who mostly inherited their wealth and did not earn it on their own merit. But the kind of classism that we are concerned with in this book is more closely related to deprivation than snobbery, the deprivation of the lower classes (including the working class) as a result of the structure of the social, political, and economic institutions of society. We can call this *institutional classism,* a term which I am introducing in this book and which parallels institutional racism.

Institutional classism refers to the sort of routine practices built into the system that, unintentionally or not, restrict people's life chances on the basis of their socioeconomic status. Examples might be a school's scheduling of parent-teacher conferences at times when working-class parents cannot attend, a social agency's refusal to have a sliding fee for therapy services, and paying workers below a living wage but then expecting them to maintain a certain standard of living. The dominant group reinforces its position, as Mullaly (1998) suggests, by measuring other groups according to the dominant norms.

Any number of novels and autobiographies—most famously, *The Grapes of Wrath*, *Angela's Ashes*, and *Bastard Out of Carolina*—have depicted the cruelties in life at the bottom. (In the books named, each book's hero also demonstrates tremendous resilience in overcoming the conditions of oppression.) What we can learn from such works is the extent to which socioeconomic exploitation is realized through the structural relationship between the haves and the have-nots. Classism extends beyond the mere distribution of material resources into the area of social status.

Today, given the procorporation, antiunion free market conditions, stratification by class is becoming ever more pronounced. Under free market conditions, the rich grow richer and the poor, poorer. Equalization of wealth and privilege is not a priority of transnational corporations or of the political structures that they, to a large degree, control. Whether between countries or individuals, socioeconomic inequality generates more inequality as the comfortable come to disavow the needy. Economist James Galbraith (1998) explains this phenomenon: "[Inequality] increases the psychological distance separating these groups, making it easier to imagine that defects of character or differences of culture, rather than an unpleasant turn in the larger schemes of economic history, lie behind the separation" (p. 24).

Most people in the United States identify with the middle class and are as oblivious to class privilege as they are to the notion of class itself. Class identity, as Mantsios (2001) suggests, has been stripped from popular culture. Yet, if we turn to research, we learn that the class position of one's family, rather than hard work or even intelligence, is probably the single most significant determinant of future success (Rothenberg, 2001). The differences start before birth and relate to matters of maternal health and nutrition, prenatal care, and infant mortality. The quality of child care and school education, for example, closely parallels one's position in the social strata. Since 45 percent of school funding comes from local sources such as property taxes, the per-pupil spending in poor school districts is far below that in prosperous suburbs (Pinkerton, 2003). (Curiously, the right to education is not included as a basic right in the U.S. Constitution.)

The educational backgrounds of African Americans may be weak due to the low quality of many public schools in predominantly minority neighborhoods, which makes it harder for them to obtain professional training and to compete for jobs on any level. The decline in high-paying, blue-collar jobs has decreased the opportunities through which parents without much education themselves have been able to earn enough to help their children go to college. More and more, African Americans are laid off from manufacturing jobs, overrepresented in the service industries, and underrepresented in the professions. The clamping-down on affirmative action programs leaves African Americans and Latinos especially vulnerable to shifts in the economic winds (Zastrow, 2004). As quickly as African Americans moved ahead in the 1990s, they have now fallen backward. The African American unemployment rate in 2003 stood at 11.1 percent, higher than that for Hispanics (8.2 percent) and double the rate for whites (5.5 percent), according to an article from the *Chicago Tribune* ("Black Jobless Rate Climbs," 2003).

Traditionally, the United States has prided itself on being a land of high social mobility, a land of opportunity where hard workers can achieve "the American dream." This fact is brought stunningly to life in the 1950s award-winning portrait of African American family life in Chicago, *A Raisin in the Sun* (Hansberry, 1994/1958). In this book, Mama remembers: "Big Walter used to say . . . 'Seem like God didn't see fit to give the black man nothing but dreams—but he did give us children to make them dreams seem worthwhile'" (pp. 45–46). Mama is a maid and her son a chauffeur, but her daughter plans to be a doctor and, as the son says to a white racist in the play's dramatic climax, "We are proud of her." This play was written before the civil rights act was passed. A great deal of social mobility has taken place since that time. We should not become complacent, however. Sobering new research, based on statistical analysis of earnings across several generations, indicates that, on average, fully 60 percent of the income gap in one generation persists into the next generation (Francis, 2003). Children of poor families, sadly, tend to be poor as well.

And what does poverty really mean? Poverty, even in a society of plenty, is not merely the absence of wealth; it means people having to live on diets consisting of beans, macaroni and cheese, stale bread, and even dog and cat food. It means lack of security against criminals—high susceptibility to victimization by shooting, robbery, rape, and/or assault. Privation is associated with the urgent social ills of homelessness, substance abuse, and infectious diseases such as tuberculosis and AIDS. New neuroscience studies have even produced some evidence showing that a healthy and mentally stimulating environment early in life has a measurable impact on IQ scores (*Chicago Tribune*, 2003). Being poor is not just one aspect of a person's or family's life; in short, it is a whole way of living. Each deprivation and disability becomes all the more intense because it exists within a web of deprivations and disabilities (Harrington, 1962).

Perhaps the harshest and most unmitigated poverty in the United States is to be found in the agricultural fields. In a news article entitled "Harvest of Shame," Sallah (1994) equated life in the squalor of run-down migrant camps in Belle Glade, Florida, with life in "Third World" countries. The downtown area of this community is a jungle of dilapidated rooming houses, most of them with communal toilets, exposed wiring, and broken windows. Crack cocaine and "hustling" (prostitution) are a way of life. The death rate from AIDS is four and a half times the national average in this community.

As we discuss issues related to class and classism, namely, the distribution of wealth in U.S. society and the war on the poor in the form of welfare retrenchment, a point worth bearing in mind is that, in the United States, unlike in most European countries, there is a denial of class identity; there is no working-class newspaper and no labor party to represent the interests of the working class.

Distribution of Wealth

In conjunction with grasping the unique American values discussed in Chapter 2—the Puritan-based Protestant work ethic and the tendency to blame society's unfortunates—an understanding of the disparities in the distribution of wealth starts with the political system, with the way candidates are elected in a two-party system. In the 2000 election, corporations gave $1.2 billion in political contributions; this was 14 times that of the labor unions (United Nations Development Programme [UNDP], 2002). India, similarly, relies on extensive corporate funding of political parties; most European countries, however, place severe limits on such funding. True campaign finance reform, in which the government would pay for TV and press coverage rather than the candidate's private resources, would do much to democratize the process. Such finance reform would free politicians from the influence of powerful interest groups such as the gun industry, military-industrial complex, pharmaceutical companies, and for-profit hospitals, to name only a few.

Study Box 5.1 and Box 5.2 carefully to grasp the end result of the U.S. election process as revealed in government and taxpayers' expenditures.

Paralleling the gap between rich and poor countries is the gap between rich and poor people within rich countries. The United States now ranks sixth after Norway, Sweden, Canada, Belgium, and Australia for its standard of living on the United Nations (U.N.) Human Development Index (UNDP, 2002). Japan was in ninth place. In the United States, disparities among ethnic, gender, and economic groups are stark. According to Statistics Canada (2003), in recent years, Canada's richest people got richer while low-income families saw little or no improvement in their finances.

In the $330 billion tax cut plan passed by the U.S. Congress in 2003, taxes on stock dividends were reduced to benefit the wealthy. Proponents of the plan correctly complained that this was a double tax; the benefit is disproportionately to the main stockholders. Another double tax that has barely been mentioned, however, and of which few of us are even aware, relates to the thousands of dollars that workers pay in Social Security taxes and Medicare tax each year. This money is never seen, and yet it is taxed as personal income—in effect, becoming a tax upon a tax (see Bartlett & Steele, 2003).

In Chapter 4, we learned the extent to which the world's wealth is concentrated in the coffers of the most highly industrialized nations. Among the advanced nations, the United States leads in the proportion of income going to the wealthiest fifth (who receive 56 percent of all U.S. income; Boshara, 2003). Some countries in Latin America, such as Brazil, have far greater disparities. Still, measures of income alone are not the best way to gauge the gap between the rich and the poor. Individuals do work for income, after all, but wealth is inherited as a birthright. So we need to look at overall wealth rather than income. What we find is that the top 20 percent of the population owns 83 percent of the nation's wealth; even worse, the top one percent who earns about 17 percent of the national income, owns 38 percent of the national wealth. The bottom 40 percent owns less than one percent of the nation's wealth (Boshara, 2003).

5.1 Where Your Income Tax Money Really Goes

Total Federal Funds (outlays): $1,926 Billion

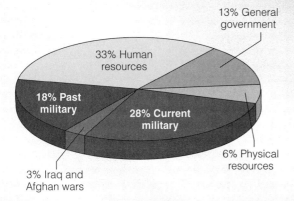

13% General government

33% Human resources

18% Past military

28% Current military

6% Physical resources

3% Iraq and Afghan wars

Source: War Resisters League, 2003, 2004. Retrieved from http://www.warresisters.org/piechart.htm. Reprinted with permission of the War Resisters League.

Current Military, $536B: Military Personnel $109B, Operation and Maintenance $164B, Procurement $67B, Research and Development $66B Construction $6B, Family Housing $4B, Retired Pay $44B, DoE Nuclear Weapons $17B, 50% NASA $8B, International Security $8B, 50% Homeland Security $16B, Ex. Off. Pres. $10B, Misc. $6B

Iraq and Afghan Wars, $50B: *Though the cost of the Iraq and Afghanistan wars is not included in the president's budget, it is included here because the administration will request supplemental funding after the Nov. 2004 election.*

Past Military, $349B: Veterans' Benefits $69B; Interest on National Debt (80% estimated to be created by military spending) $280B

Human Resources, $633B: Education, Health/Human Services, HUD, Food/Nutrition programs, Labor Department, Soc. Sec. Admin.

General Government, $244B: Legislative, Justice Dept., State Dept., International Affairs, Treasury, Gov't Personnel, 20% interest on national debt, 50% of NASA, 25% Homeland Security

Physical Resources, $114B: Agriculture, Commerce, Energy, Interior Dept., Transportation, Environmental Protection, Army Corps Engineers, NSF, FCC, 25% Homeland Security

How These Figures Were Determined

The War Resisters League creates this leaflet each year after the president releases a proposed budget. The figures here are from a line-by-line analysis of projected figures in the "Analytical Perspectives" book of the *Budget of the United States Government, Fiscal Year 2005*. The percentages are federal funds, which do not include trust funds such as Social Security that are raised and spent separately from income taxes. What you pay (or do not pay) by April 15, 2004, goes only to the federal funds portion of the budget. The government practice of combining trust and federal funds (the so-called unified budget) began in the 1960s during the Vietnam War. The government presentation makes the human needs portion of the budget seem larger and the military portion smaller.

"Current military" spending adds together money allocated for the Department of Defense ($431 billion) plus the military portion from other parts of the budget. Spending on nuclear weapons (without their delivery systems) amounts to about one percent of the total budget. "Past military" represents veterans' benefits plus 80 percent of the interest on the debt. Analysts differ on how much of the debt stems from the military; other groups estimate 50 to 60 percent. We use 80 percent because we believe if there had been no military spending, most (if not all) of the national debt would have been eliminated. The govern-

(continued)

5.1 *continued*

ment willingly borrows for war, but finds nothing extra for crises in human needs.

We have split the money in the new Homeland Security Department between Current Military, General Government, and Physical Resources. The military portion includes the Coast Guard (which WRL has always included in military), a small amount in Homeland Security that is coded military in the federal budget, and half of "Border and Transportation Security"; the other half we have placed according to the coding in General Government. The category "Emergency Preparedness and Response" (the work of the former FEMA) is within Physical Resources. While some may see legitimate measures within this budget to prevent terrorist attacks, we also believe that the mission of this department involves a militarization of U.S. society and a system of widespread arrests designed to enhance fear and mistrust and nibble away at civil liberties. We also believe that if Homeland Security represents "defense" of the United States, then it is all the more clear that the current Department of Defense should be returned to its original name, War Department.

The Government Deception

This pie chart represents how the government views the budget. This is a distortion of how our income tax dollars are spent because it includes Trust Funds (e.g., Social Security), and the expenses of past mili-

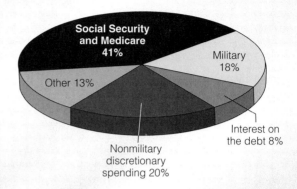

Source: *Budget of the United States FY2005*, Feb. 2, 2004, Table S-12.

tary spending are not distinguished from nonmilitary spending. For a more accurate representation of how your federal income tax dollar is really spent, see the large chart at the beginning of this article.

Sources for this information and more: http://www .costofwar.com; Center for Strategic and Budgetary Assessments, http://www.csbaonline.org; Council for a Livable World, http://www.clw.org; Pew Research, http://people-press.org; http://www.unknownnews.net/casualties.html; Center for Defense Information, http://www.cdi.org; Center for Budget and Policy Priorities, http://www.cbpp.org; National Priorities Project, http://www.natprior.org; World Policy Institute, http://www.worldpolicy.org/projects/arms; and http://www .abc.net.au/news/newsitems/s947282.htm.

Class polarization is the term used by Phyllis Day (2003) for this disparity between the poor and the wealthy as a result of the increasing economic gap. According to Day, this is one of the most crucial problems facing the American institution of social welfare at the present time. While more of the middle classes are moving into a lower standard of living through unemployment, lower wages, and a rise in the number of single-parent families, people with wealth are consolidating their holdings.

Because of the indirect but very significant impact of the global economy on all of us, including social work clients, Day suggests that an internationalist perspective is vital. The poor are growing poorer the world over for many of the same reasons that more people are becoming poor in the United States. Curiously, even in the United Kingdom, after six years under a Labour govern-

5.2 **Which Path to a Safer World?**

Tools for Peace	Cost	Tools for War
11 blankets for refugees	$100	11 hand grenades
3-day training for 160 youth in peace building	$4,000	1 rocket launcher
Enroll 2 children in Head Start	$14,000	1 cluster bomb
2 home health aides for disabled elderly	$40,000	1 hellfire missile
Associate degree training for 29 RNs	$145,600	1 bunker-buster guided bomb
Rent subsidies for 1,000 families	$586,000	1,000 M-16 rifles
Annual salary/benefits for 15 RNs	$763,000	1 minute of war on Iraq
Improve, repair, modernize 20 schools	$46 million	1 hour of war on Iraq
WIC program nutrition for 200,000 families	$130 million	7 unmanned predator drones
Eradicate polio worldwide	$275 million	3 tests of missile defense system
Best vaccinations for 10 million children worldwide	$350 million	6 trident II missiles
Child care for 68,000 needy children	$413 million	Amphibious Warfare Landing Ship Program
7,000 units of affordable housing	$494 million	1 year military aid to Colombia
Prevent cuts to education programs (FY 2003)	$1.1 billion	1 day of war in Iraq
Minimum support to save Amtrak train service	$1.2 billion	2 months U.S. war force in Afghanistan
Annual salary/benefits for 38,000 elementary teachers	$2.1 billion	1 stealth bomber
Double federal funding for mass transit	$12 billion	1 year cost of war in Afghanistan (2001/2002)
Health care coverage for 7 million children	$16 billion	1 year of nuclear weapons program
Save 11 million lives worldwide fighting infectious diseases	$38 billion	1 month U.S. current military spending

The costs of war-making are staggering, especially while cities and states face huge budget deficits. The administration has hidden its real priorities by not putting the costs of the war on terrorism and the war on Iraq in its budget. Stay informed about the real budget and other means to enhance security by seeking information from the groups that follow.

Partial source list: Center for Defense Information, http://www.cdi.org; Federation of American Scientists, http://www.fas.org; Center for Budget and Policy Priorities, http://www.cbpp.org; National Priorities Project, http://www.natprior.org; World Policy Institute, http://www.worldpolicy.org/projects/arms; Children's Defense Fund, http://www.childrensdefense.org; UNICEF, http://www.unicef.org; *The New York Times* (11/12/01, 3/18/02, 10/13/02, 12/05/02); World Health Organization, http://www.who.int; National Center for Education Statistics, http://nces.ed.gov; and Mennonite Central Committee, http://www.mcc.org/us/colombia/dollars.html.

ment, the gap between the rich and the poor is at its largest in over a decade. Part of the reason rests with forces in the global economy, but another factor may be that what once was a tax on high incomes of 60 percent was later substantially reduced under the Conservatives (Waugh, 2003). Other countries such as the United States have made similar adjustments to award high-income earners so they can keep a higher percentage of their income. We now explore in more detail the economic inequality in the United States.

The Poverty Line

Every year around Labor Day, the U.S. Census Bureau releases its income, poverty, and health insurance figures. Figures for 2003 show that for the third straight year, the number of people living below the poverty line or lacking health insurance rose. Overall, the median household income remained stagnant while the national poverty rate rose to 12.5 percent from 12.1 percent in 2002 (Connolly & Witte, 2004). The official poverty line is $18,810 for a family of four, and $9,393 for an individual. On average, a family of four needs more than $33,000 to afford food, housing, child care, health insurance, transportation, and utilities (AFL-CIO, 2002).

Let us examine how the formula for calculating poverty levels is arrived at. The poverty line is calculated on a 40-year-old formula that was derived from a federal worker who estimated the cost of a basket of food, multiplied by three, and added estimates of what rent, transportation, and other necessities cost (Piven, 2000). In the formulation, no heed is taken to regional cost variations, out-of-pocket medical expenditures that vary dramatically between age groups, or income other than a standard paycheck (Weisman, 2003). A recent analysis by a private forecasting company found that tying poverty rates to housing values would have a dramatic impact in terms of regional poverty estimates: Massachusetts would leap to near the top of the list, and Arkansas, where the median house price is under $100,000, would drop from one of the poorest states to the midpoint (Weisman, 2003). Other calculations would be affected as well by a reformulation; for example, because of their higher medical costs, more seniors would be considered below the poverty level than children. Eligibility for emergency housing assistance would be expanded in cities such as Boston where housing is extremely expensive. Formulas for allocation of Medicaid funds would change as well if regional differences were taken into account.

War against the Poor

There have always been efforts, according to Piven (2000), to attack welfare recipients and welfare, usually on the same grounds: that welfare causes poverty, laziness, and sexual immorality. These arguments were made in England in the 1830s; for a time they subsided, but from the 1980s on, these arguments have resurfaced. The mass media, especially television broadcasts, as Piven observes, have ignored the plight of the poor, as have politicians: The poor, in their belief that the political system has turned against them, have mostly given up their right to vote.

The war against the poor is reflected in the lack of a living wage, which in the past made "being on welfare" in many states more remunerative than full-time work, and in the retrenchment in social welfare benefits. The blaming-the-poor ethos has focused attention on the supposed shortcomings of the poor and on the importance of getting adults, even mothers of young children, into the workforce. This focus has diverted attention from the structural problems related to corporate domination of the economy.

The minimum wage in 2003 was $5.15, with efforts in Congress to boost it to $6.65 over the next 18 months. The federal minimum wage was enacted in 1938 to put a firm floor under workers and their families, strengthen the depressed economy by increasing consumer power, create new jobs to meet rising demand, and stop a "race to the bottom" as employers moved to cheaper labor states (Sklar, 2001). As it stands, the inflation-adjusted value of the minimum wage is 24 percent lower today than it was in 1979, according to a report from the AFL-CIO (2003).

How do people live on 40-hour-a-week, minimum-wage jobs when rents take up most of their paychecks, not to mention other expenses such as car repairs and emergency room visits? The best way to find out about others' lives is often to become a participant-observer, and this is just what Barbara Ehrenreich (2001) did. She recorded her findings in a book entitled *Nickel and Dimed* that was much talked about the year it was released. For three months, in preparation for writing this book, Ehrenreich left behind everything but her car to work at low-wage jobs across the United States. Without revealing her identity, she waited tables, cleaned motel rooms, and worked at Wal-Mart. Her goal was to survive on her earnings as she learned what it was like to join the ranks of the working poor. Only the second goal was achieved. Even without small children to support and with earnings above the minimum wage, Ehrenreich failed to make ends meet. The result was exhaustion and anger—anger over the need to have two jobs just to get by, and anger over working conditions in which workers are banned from talking to each other, denied bathroom privileges, kept on their feet for hours at a time, and forced to allow management to search their purses at will and to order urine tests for drugs.

The fatigue caused by poverty, argues Ehrenreich (2001), may explain why there is so little social unrest among low-wage workers—their passivity and resignation, and their lack of interest in unionization. Rental prices soar, but wages fail to rise. Homelessness is often one paycheck away. In fact, many workers are homeless.

As the economy takes a nosedive, people lose their jobs and homes. Some move in with relatives, but others, especially persons with mental disorders, are apt to end up on the streets. The war against the poor is perhaps at its most ferocious in the crackdown directed at the nation's estimated one to three million homeless (numbers are uncertain). Many cities are passing tough laws against panhandling, loitering, and sleeping in public places. San Francisco, for example (where an estimated 19,000 are homeless each night), voted to reduce their benefits by 85 percent (Stein, 2003). In a sample of 49 cities, the National Law Center on Homelessness and Poverty found a 22 percent increase in the past three years in prohibitions on loitering (Ritter, 2002). Requests for emergency shelter are up an average 19 percent according to a survey undertaken by the U.S. Conference of Mayors (Ritter, 2002). More than ever before, mothers with children are ending up on the streets. Policies to end homelessness through providing permanent housing for persons and families in need have received less attention than policies for getting the homeless out of view from the general public (Stein, 2003). Citizens are demanding that the streets be cleared, yet federal funds for the kind of massive relief effort that is needed are lacking. Ratnesar (1999) offers the following explanation for the national indifference: Democrats have revised their image as the party of the dispossessed by acceding to welfare reform, cutting aid to the homeless, and courting middle-class votes.

Food Stamp Reductions

With poverty on the rise and compassion for the poor at a low ebb, the richest nation in the world forces millions of its citizens to rely on private charity for handouts. With the minimum wage so far below a living wage, food has become the expendable item in the low-wage workers' budget. Lieberman (2003), in her article entitled "Hungry in America," conceives of hunger as a lens through which the assault on public programs in the United States can be viewed. Food programs for the elderly have suffered a steep decline in federal appropriations (e.g., the once generously funded Meals on Wheels program). For all poor families, and especially for single adults, the food stamp program fails to meet the need; privately operated food providers now serve at least 23 million people a year and turn many more away.

The current Food Stamp Act was passed in 1964; eligibility depends on family size and income. Until 1977, there were purchase requirements, but these were dropped as many poor people could not afford to buy the stamps. Today, there are stringent work requirements for the able-bodied recipients between 16 and 60 years old.

Growing up Empty by Schwartz-Nobel (2003) is a nonfiction narrative that takes us into the world of the hungry in the land of plenty. Stories presented in this book introduce us to military families virtually abandoned by the government, forced to apply for food stamps and to food banks at the end of the month when the food stamps ran out. Other narratives were provided by people who had lost their jobs and by women and children who were escaping situations of family violence.

Today there are over 33 million Americans who are hungry or live on the edge of hunger, according to the latest U.S. Department of Agriculture and U.S. Census Bureau surveys (Food Research and Action Center, 2003). This represents an increase of 2 million from 1999. Women and children make up 75 percent of that population. That the widespread hunger and food insecurity in America is driven by gaps in federal nutrition programs and low family incomes is a key finding of the report by the Food Research and Action Center. Schwartz-Nobel (2003) blames the increase in part on the federal budget cuts including $27 billion in food stamps.

The plight of the working poor who earn too much money to qualify for food stamps, medical care, and other forms of medical assistance is discussed in *Growing up Empty* as well. Some of the workers with the worst and lowest-wage jobs are former recipients of welfare aid, mothers with small children removed from welfare rolls because they have exceeded the new time limit of five years. Because some are physically or emotionally incapable of holding a job even if they could get one, they are apt to join the ranks of the hungry and malnourished.

Welfare Reform

As you read about the hardships imposed upon the poor by many aspects of welfare reform, consider the parallels between the U.S. reform effort and the IMF's structural adjustment programs in terms of their impacts in forcing governments to restrict the resources that go to impoverished communities and in balancing budget deficits "on the backs" of the poor. This insight was provided by social work educators from the University of the West Indies, Mona, and Jamaica as cited by Link (2002).

Temporary Aid to Needy Families (TANF) is predicated on the belief that recipients should be moved off public welfare and into private employment as quickly as possible (Karger & Stoesz, 2002). TANF is a part of the Personal Responsibility and Work Opportunity Reconciliation Act that was passed by the Clinton administration in 1996. Permitting the states to exempt on 20 percent of their welfare population, the law exempts from lifetime and work requirements the disabled, older adults, and those who care for a developmentally disabled family member (Fiske, 2002). Two basic philosophical beliefs underpinned this legislation. First was the impetus to get tough with people who did not work full-time or who had children while receiving family assistance. Second was the desire to transfer responsibility for public assistance from the federal government to the states—this is called *devolution*. As Schram (2002) correctly suggests, this maneuver can lead states to compete in a "race to the bottom" in trying to reduce their attractiveness to nontaxpayers. The punitive thrust was certainly evident in the welfare-to-work initiatives. In terms of social justice, the abolition of the notion of welfare aid as a rational entitlement for persons in need was a revolutionary step, a repudiation of the very concept of the social welfare state.

In the first few years after the welfare-to-work legislation was passed, politicians and journalists alike pointed to the following accomplishments: breaking the cycle of dependency for mothers who received welfare, and slashing the nation's welfare rolls in half (Cohn, 2000). Case after case of success stories of former welfare mothers who got the training they needed for a successful career filled the press and air waves. A rising economic tide around the turn of the present century eased the transition for single mothers with limited skills into the job market. But what would happen to these people in a recession? That was a question pondered by only a few researchers such as Abramovitz (2002), Bernstein and Greenberg (2001), and Danziger (1999).

Another question that loomed in the background was what would happen to persons who were generally unemployable in some way, such as those with emotional or substance abuse problems? What happens to children in families where the parents lack the skills or discipline for work?

By 2002, the results were coming in—some positive, some negative. The positive results were largely related to the fact that in the late 1990s, the United States had the lowest unemployment rate in 30 years. In the year 2000, the over-all poverty rate fell: Low wage workers nationally saw their wages rise in conjunction with the booming economy (Abramovitz, 2002). Among the positives of welfare reform, Link (2002) noted the giving of people a sense of change in policy that needed overhauling and the giving of administrators the opportunity for greater flexibility at the local level. Bernstein (2002) reported a finding with an unexpected twist: The share of the nation's children living in single-parent households declined in the late 1990s. This positive result was soon turned on its head, however, as researchers at the Urban Institute discovered through a closer analysis that, due to the loss of benefits and the irregular hours of low-wage jobs, children increasingly were being moved into the homes of relatives, friends, and foster families (Bernstein, 2002). The change in living arrangements was most pronounced in African American families, consistent with their tradition of kinship care.

We should also approach with caution the assumption that, because the social welfare caseloads have been reduced, workers are earning enough to support their families. Indeed, as the robust economy and job growth of the 1990s gave way at the turn of the new century, mass media headlines like the following from mainstream sources have been typical: "More, Not Less 'Extremely Poor': A Wider Measure of Welfare Reform" (Heller, 2002, *Business Week*); "Welfare Numbers Hold Steady, Despite Limits" (Santiago, 2002, *Des Moines Register*); "Welfare Reform Has a Darker Side" (Eby, 2002, *Waterloo–Cedar Falls Courier*). As presented in these articles, the facts are these:

- According to analysis from the Urban Institute, the numbers of persons termed "extremely poor" rose from 1996 to 1998 (Heller, 2002).
- Data from Iowa reveal that while many families were bumped off the welfare rolls, many others who left for jobs have been laid off due to the economic downturn (Santiago, 2002).
- An extensive Iowa study showed that during the first years of reform over-all earnings increased, but not for persons entering the system later; marriage rates were reduced by 8 percent; spouse abuse increased; for recipients required to take jobs, more children were placed in foster homes; and children's success at school declined (Eby, 2002).

The majority of single mothers forced into the workforce have serious problems paying for adequate child care, obtaining medical care for themselves and their children, and arranging for transportation. We can conclude from the data on the effects of welfare reform that TANF has focused on reducing welfare payments, rather than reducing poverty and promoting the well-being of low-income families.

Why is the work of nurturing small children in the home not regarded as work? This is the question asked by Rosemary Link (2002) as she places America's rigid welfare reform policies in international perspective. In countries such as Scandinavia and Italy, the emphasis is on child allowance, family services, day-care provision, and the overall well-being of the child. The social charter of the European Union recognizes the value of work in the home, especially that of child care.

One major shortcoming of welfare reform singled out by Link (2002) clearly relates to classism. This is the fact that the states have cut support for four-year education in favor of two-year education and other job-training programs. This effect is especially evident in departments of social work education, which earlier had prided themselves on helping welfare recipients move into professional careers. Relevant to classism also is the contrast Link draws between society's admiration of middle- and upper-class parents who choose to stay home with their children in the early years to give them a good start in life and the condemnation of poor mothers with far fewer resources who make the same choice.

Ehrenreich (2002) broadens the scope of the analysis to place welfare reform within the context of a wave of class warfare. This warfare, she explains, started decades ago when business leaders began to view their somewhat demanding workforce as underproductive and not globally competitive. Various forms of surveillance were inflicted upon workers to the extent that the low-wage workplace became a virtual dictatorship. At the same time, the lack of a safety net in society for nonworking persons contributed to job competition and worker compliance. As Ehrenreich concludes:

> To the extent that welfare served as a shield, however inadequate, against the worst forms of workplace exploitation, welfare was and remains a class issue. Racism and misogyny helped blind many to this fact six years ago, when welfare reform was passed, but we cannot let that happen again. (p. 15)

Welfare for the Rich

Tax policy helps eradicate poverty by providing funding for social welfare, including educational programming and social services. Recent changes in the tax code allow a tax credit for low-income people, an important development in providing relief to the working poor. But the bulk of government assistance is meted out not to the economically disadvantaged—to women, children, and the elderly, or even to the middle classes whose real wage earnings have declined steadily over the past decade—but to the richest 10 percent of the U.S. population. There is a kind of welfare for the wealthy and for large corporations (e.g., tax relief for mismanaged savings and loans institutions) that is not available to the poor (Dolgoff & Feldstein, 2002). In fact, the share of the national wealth going to the richest segment of the population continues to rise.

Consider the recent tax cut of $330 billion. A furor developed soon after its passage as analysis from the Urban-Brookings Tax Policy Center (Firestone, 2003) revealed that about one-third of households, mostly those that are low-income, would not benefit from the law. Single parents with children who pay no taxes will get nothing. Most of the benefits go to those in the highest income brackets. Major stockholders stand to gain considerably from the new tax laws, as do people in the highest income tax bracket. Tax rates on stock dividends have been reduced to 15 percent. The highest income tax rate is now reduced from 38.6 percent to 35 percent (Welch, 2003).

Laws are made by members of Congress. Because of limited restrictions in the United States on media efforts and campaign finance, elected officials typically represent the interests of big spenders. Without a U.S. labor party, as mentioned previously, the interests of the working class are apt to be overlooked. And without a parliamentary system, which allows for representation of multiple parties with a variety of interests, no labor party (or Green party) is apt to gain many votes or to be a viable force in shaping legislation.

In 1964, incomes over $200,000 were taxed at the rate of 70 percent; this rate was lowered to 50 percent in 1981. In 2001, the top taxable rate was 38.6 percent (Tax Policy Center, 2002). In 2003, under George W. Bush's tax cut plan this upper limit was reduced to 35 percent as stated above. This bending of the tax code in response to lobbying, as Karger and Stoesz (2002) indicate, is a long-standing practice often associated with corporate influence. Corporations are the beneficiaries of huge tax breaks and subsidies at state, local, and federal levels that come at the expense of public services and the individual taxpayer (Reich, 2000). Subsidies to massive agribusiness operations and the defense industry are examples of gigantic public relief programs (Huff, 1992). Subsidies for the rich and the superrich are seen in caps on Social Security contributions, which are only paid up to a certain level of income; tax deductions for home mortgages; and a lower rate of taxation on investments than on salaries. Another fact to keep in mind is that, unlike the income taxes that are deducted from paychecks in advance, the government only gets to use this money at the end of the year when taxes are paid. Self-employed persons and business owners have a wide number of deductions at their disposal. Purchases of expensive pieces of artwork for the office, for example, are often made as a tax-dodging scheme. (Remember the priceless paintings that were lost in the collapse of the World Trade Center.) Billionaire investor Warren Buffett (Associated Press, 2004) recently made headlines with an appraisal he provided in his company's annual report, "If class warfare is being waged in America, my class is clearly winning" (p. A2).

Still these tax loopholes of self-employed persons are nothing compared to the kind of tax maneuvers available to major companies. Most of these maneuvers, as noted in a special report in *Business Week,* "The Rise of the Wall Street Tax Machine" (France, 2003), are shrouded in secrecy. Because of this culture of secrecy, it is, by definition impossible to estimate how big the tax shelter for business actually is. One estimate provided in a recent Harvard University study cited in an article by Byrnes and Lavelle (2003) is that for the year 1998, U.S. companies avoided paying tax on nearly $300 billion. "Enron is not just one bad apple," a tax expert is quoted as saying in the article (p. 85). But most ways of ripping off the public through tax avoidance are perfectly legal and derive from tax laws that enable companies to generate huge capital losses on paper to offset big capital gains. (The real estate business works the same way with extensive deductions for depreciation.) As only one example, companies can take advantage of immense stock-option deductions when employees invest in the business. Another strategy is the shifting of income and assets (and pharmaceutical patents) overseas to other countries such as Bermuda (Byrnes & Lavelle, 2003).

How do the major corporations get away with such practices? One answer is in the enormous resources invested in the form of tax lawyers, strategists, and lobbyists. Microsoft lobbyists, for example, when rebuffed by the IRS, have taken issues to Congress to get lawmakers to rewrite the tax law. The success of such strategies is revealed in the drop in corporate tax contributions from 4 percent of the GDP in 1965 to 2.5 percent in 2000 to 1.5 percent in 2002 (Byrnes & Lavelle, 2003). Over the years, the tax burden has shifted increasingly to individuals.

Another answer to the success of corporate practices was provided in less complicated times by John Galbraith (1992) and Michael Harrington (1962). According to Galbraith, such practices are successful because of public commitment to laissez-faire government policies combined with strategies designed to convince voters that in rewarding the rich, we are benefiting society. Dismissal of the underclass as architects of their own unhappy fate is the final component in promoting this ideology. In his classic work on poverty, *The Other America,* Harrington (1962) observed:

> As long as the illusion persists that the poor are merrily freeloading on the public dole, so long will the other America continue unthreatened. The truth, it must be understood, is the exact opposite. The poor get less out of the welfare state than any group in America.
>
> History and ideology, in short, have caused us to take one attitude toward public or private welfare services for the affluent, another attitude toward subsidy for the upper-middle classes, and still another attitude toward public welfare services for the poor. (p. 172)

Racism

Racism and classism, as mentioned earlier, are closely intertwined. In this section, my goal is to examine the economic factor in racism—to show how racial antagonisms have been used by powerful interest groups to maintain support for their self-serving policies. (An example of the success of this strategy is evidenced in rural Kentucky where poor farmers vote Republican in clear violation of any personal interests.)

Racism can be defined as a form of racial oppression based on the color of one's skin or other distinctive or imagined physical features. Racial oppression, like sexual oppression, is reflected in both individual and institutional acts, decisions, and policies that neglect, overlook, or subjugate the individual or the group (Appleby, Colon, & Hamilton, 2001).

That racism is a worldwide phenomenon was evidenced in the U.N. Conference against Racial Discrimination, Xenophobia, and Related Intolerance held in 2001 in Durban, South Africa. This conference addressed issues of race hatred against minority groups ranging from the Roma (Gypsies) of Europe, to the slaves in Sudan, to the Dalits ("untouchables") of India, to the indigenous peoples of Australia. When the Palestinians threatened to highjack the discussions, however, the United States and Israel pulled

out. There was much criticism at the time of the American refusal to participate (Hanson, 2001).

No one with any self-respect, and certainly no politician seeking a following, would claim to be a racist. It is not difficult, however, to practice racism
under the guise of something else—for example, welfare reform, promoting
equal opportunity, and the like. When welfare assistance began to be seen as
income support for unmarried mothers, a large portion of whom were black,
the program no longer seemed like insurance. It began to look like a handout to
the undeserving poor (Reich, 2000).

Welfare Racism: Playing the Race Card against America's Poor—this title says
it all (Neubeck & Cazenave, 2001). The thesis expressed here is that the racial
exclusions, disparities, and hurdles to success are not unintended consequences
of the way the welfare system is set up. Instead these difficulties are a manifestation of racism, conscious and unconscious, of the kind of racist attitudes held
by members of powerful interest groups (and the powerless persons who do
their bidding). Such people see the world in terms of us and them; they do not
identify their interests with the poor.

Welfare reform was billed to the public as a workfare scheme, a way to help
single mothers become self-sufficient. From there it was an easy step to establish time limits for the mothers still receiving aid. Racism entered the picture in
that large numbers of the children whose mothers have been forced off the welfare rolls are children of color (and so perceived by the public). The attack
against welfare, as Tice and Perkins (2002) suggest, is preeminently a racial
attack. "The same racial agenda," as they further contend, "is behind both welfare cutbacks and [attacks on] affirmative action, often coded in language of 'no
special rights,' as if people of color were currently equal and asking for privileged treatment" (p. 314). Seccombe (1999), who conducted extensive interviews with welfare recipients for her book *So You Think I Drive a Cadillac?*, concurs. The racist view that welfare is a program primarily for the African
American community has been acknowledged by interviewees of both races to
be a widely held attitude by the general public.

Statistics reveal the results of welfare reform for African American families:
In 2001, there were as many African American children living in extreme poverty (8.4 percent) as during the recession of 1992. One in five African American
children lived below the official poverty level in that year. These figures from
the Children's Defense Fund, based on U.S. Census survey data, go a long way
toward explaining the surge in the number of families who had to double up
with other families in living quarters or live in homeless shelters in that year
(Watson, 2003). And in their tri-annual national survey of consumer finances,
the Federal Reserve found that from 1998 to 2001, the median net worth of
families of color fell 4.5 percent to a mere $17,100 while white families' median
net worth rose 17 percent to $120,900 (Leander-Wright, 2003). Net worth was
measured in terms of assets, income, and debts.

Although unemployment among African Americans fell to record lows
during the economic boom of 2000, it was a case of "last hired, first fired" once
the economy slowed (Hager, 2001). A study for the National Urban League

showed that the African American unemployment rate tends to be double the overall rate. Researchers pinpoint, as causes, a lack of technical skills, a shortage of jobs in inner-city areas, inner-city crime, high arrest rates, and the legacy of slavery (Billingsley & Morrison-Rodriguez, 1998; Schiele, 1998).

Nevertheless, to overemphasize historical abuse and community problems as the cause of poverty may be to fail to acknowledge the very real structural influences stemming from intense global competition and technological change. The economic downturn has been especially hard on workers without a college degree—the segment of the population that is disproportionately composed of African Americans (Armour, 2002a). The loss of well-paid manufacturing jobs for black males has had a ripple effect on the stability of the black family. Writing in *Sisters of the Yam,* bell hooks (1993) contemplated the reality of society's oppression:

> Black people are indeed wounded by forces of domination. Irrespective of our access to material privilege we are all wounded by white supremacy, racism, sexism, and a capitalist economic system that dooms us collectively to an underclass position. Such wounds do not manifest themselves only in material ways, they affect our psychological well-being. . . . (p. 11)

European American cultural oppression in which "the other" is vilified has led to internalized racism and placed many African American youths at risk of self-destructive behavior (Schiele, 1998). The lack of hope that they have today for future success in pursuing "the American dream" is related at least in part to the exportation to foreign countries of the kind of jobs that would have made the reality of stable employment possible. Resentment and alienation are the predictable consequences.

Gil (1998) masterfully establishes a global link between racial oppression within nations such as the United States and United Kingdom and colonialism and exploitation of other societies that are deemed racially and/or culturally inferior. In one long but succinct sentence, Gil presents the essence of global racism:

> In spite of important objective and subjective differences, the experiences of Native American peoples, coercively imported slaves from Africa, Hispanic, and Asian legal and undocumented immigrants and migrant workers, and Jews and other ethnic groups fleeing poverty, persecution, and pogroms in Europe, reflect the practices and dynamics of economic, social, and psychological domination and exploitation imposed by many societies upon "strangers," ever since the development of agriculture. (p. 27)

Sexism and the Feminization of Poverty

The human rights aspect of sexual oppression is one of the subjects of Chapter 6 to follow. Here we will emphasize the economic and occupational realities of female oppression. The fact that, of families in the United States headed by single women, 37.1 percent are below the poverty line has led some scholars to coin the term *feminization of poverty.* The combined effects of the dual labor market, occupational segregation, and sex and race discrimination have resulted in a median income for full-time working women of $29,544 compared to a figure for males of $38,961 (U.S. Census Bureau, 2000b). The class-action sex discrimination lawsuit against Wal-Mart Stores (involving 1.6 million women) has revealed a picture of rampant sexism and sexual harassment as well as consistent blocking of female employees from management positions (Armour, 2004).

Women's earnings relative to men's have increased over the past two decades, but this fact is a reflection, not of a rise in women's income, so much as a decline in men's income during this period. Men still earn substantially higher wages than women, even when they are working in traditionally "female" occupations such as nursing and social work. Recent data from the U.S. Census Bureau reflect a job market that has failed to match otherwise strong economic growth, and women's income has declined even more than men's. Women made 76 cents for every dollar earned by men; this was a decline from 77 cents in 2002 (Connolly & Witte, 2004). The rising jobless rate is harder on women than on men in many ways, given their low-wage and part-time, often interrupted work (Curphey, 2003). Women's unemployment reached 9 percent in 2003. Keep in mind that women are more likely than men to leave their jobs due to family illness, sexual harassment, or domestic violence.

The causes of female poverty are complex. The high divorce rate coupled with the infrequency of mothers receiving child support from fathers forces many women to find jobs immediately or go on welfare. Low-paying service jobs—such as waiting tables in fast-food restaurants and motel housekeeping work—drive many women to welfare dependency as a means to escape from such daily drudgery, lack of essential work benefits, and child care concerns. Programs designed to compensate for the absence of a male breadwinner in the family are means-tested and highly punitive. When men are absent, women's prescribed role as family caretaker is ignored and devalued by the system—a fact that reinforces women's marginality in society and ensures that women and their children will have high representation among the destitute. Until the importance of nurturing and shaping young lives through domestic caretaking is regarded as primary work, the feminization of poverty will continue. The federal and state program reductions in job training, education, and child care implemented by the Reagan, Bush, Clinton, and George W. Bush administrations have had a major impact on already poor women and children.

In *Nickel and Dimed,* as we have seen, Ehrenreich (2001) set out to see for herself what life at the margins of low-wage jobs is like. She discovered that even for women without children, affordable housing was hard to get. Her coworkers often lived in their cars or shared crowded apartments with relatives.

Collectively, the accumulation of social services cutbacks has served to legitimize the negative attitudes held by many Americans toward the poor. Also, as long as working- and middle-class mothers with children are joining the labor market (to help ends meet), the sentiment is that other women should not have another option.

At the end of the life span, as we will see in Chapter 10, women pay again for their abbreviated, low-paid work careers. Qualifying far less frequently than men for adequate pension plans, most elderly women must rely on Social Security as their sole source of income. Accordingly, 14 percent of elderly females compared to 8.4 percent of elderly males are in poverty (Kijakazi & Primus, 2000). Were Social Security privatized, women who have less than men to invest in a private account would be the losers. Widows and divorced women would receive no protection (Davis, 1999).

How are women doing worldwide? According to a report from the World Health Organization (2000), 70 percent of the world's people living in poverty are female. The United Nations (2003), in a report entitled "The World's Women 2000," provided the following statistics:

- In many countries of the developed regions, more than half of mothers with children under age three are employed.
- Women now comprise an increasing share of the world's labor force—at least one third in all regions except northern Africa and western Asia.
- Self-employment and part-time and home-based work have expanded opportunities for women's participation in the labor force but are characterized by lack of security, lack of benefits, and low income.
- The informal sector is a larger source of employment for women than for men.
- More women than before are in the labor force throughout their reproductive years even though obstacles to combining family responsibilities with employment persist.
- Women, especially younger women, experience more unemployment than men and for longer periods of time than men.
- Women remain at the lower end of a segregated labor market and continue to be concentrated in a few occupations, to hold positions of little or no authority, and to receive less pay than men. (http://www.unstats.un.org)

Gender equality in education has not been achieved, with the least progress having been made in southern Africa, according to the U.N. Human Development Report (UNDP, 2002). In the U.N. report, a gender empowerment measure is used to compare countries. The Scandinavian countries, not surprisingly, earn the top rankings for female empowerment. Some poorer countries such as the Bahamas and Trinidad are ahead of some richer countries such as Italy and Japan in creating opportunities for women.

For women, the impact of globalization has generated opportunities for some, especially persons with higher levels of education and access to capital. But for many poor women, globalization has intensified existing inequalities and even loss of livelihoods and labor rights (United Nations Development Fund for Women [UNIFEM], 2000).

The often touted success stories of women who get to work for transnational corporations are refuted by international human rights organizations. As the executive director of MADRE, a women's human rights organization, Stromberg (2001) stated in response to such claims:

> In our experience with recently opened markets, women are virtual prisoners in many factories, subject to physical violence including sexual assault, strip searches,

attacks on union organizers, and forced consumption of amphetamines to increase output. Women work longer hours than their male counterparts, are paid half the wages, and suffer from serious work-related health problems, including lung damage, memory loss and numbness from exposure to toxic materials. And they are forced to live in overcrowded slums that lack basic municipal services and are rife with contaminated water, rats, insects, and industrial pollutants. (p. 2 of 3)

In their recent book, *Global Woman: Nannies, Maids, and Sex Workers in the New Economy,* Ehrenreich and Hochschild (2003) put a human face on the trials and hardships of women who migrate, often thousands of miles, to work in the new economy. The theme linking many of the stories in this collection is the impossible choice many of these impoverished women face: They can stay in their own countries and fight for survival or leave their children behind and provide for their support through work in a prosperous nation. Some of these women end up nurturing children of women in wealthy nations who themselves are working too many hours to provide that care. But these are the more mundane stories. We also read in *Global Woman* of rural girls sold into sexual slavery in Thailand and destined to get AIDS. And we read of the exploitation of foreign domestic workers in the United States who are not legally allowed to change employers. In such situations of abuse, women have nowhere to go.

Heterosexism

Related to sexism and to the rigid codes of gender conformity is the societal oppression of gays, lesbians, and bisexuals. This form of discrimination, although not inevitable, is worldwide. Cultural attitudes play a significant role in all matters related to sex and sexuality. Discrimination against persons perceived as sexually deviant can be horrendous.

As defined by Barker (2003), *heterosexism* is "the belief that gay men and lesbians are deviant, abnormal or inferior to heterosexual people, usually manifested as bias against gay men and lesbians. The term *homophobia* is similar but implies a stronger feeling involving feelings of fear, anger, and disgust" (p. 195). Homophobia derives from anxiety concerning the perceived threat of homosexuality (van Wormer, Wells, & Boes, 2000).

Gays and lesbians are one group that can be attacked generically even as they are standing in front of those doing the attacking, simply because their presence is so often not realized. This is a part of heterosexism—the tendency to assume that the people one knows and works with are heterosexual. Yet gays and lesbians make up at least 5 percent of the population ("Gays Comprise 5 Percent of Electorate in 2002, New Poll Finds," 2002). Sex education in school, accordingly, needs to pertain to homosexual as well as heterosexual practices, though it rarely does.

Homophobia goes beyond heterosexism; it entails a heightened attention to the doings of gays and lesbians and often the scapegoating of persons of different sexual orientation. Of all the forms of oppression, the oppression of gender nonconformity is perhaps the most virulent. Unlike most victims of acts of prejudice and discrimination, sexual minorities are taunted on the basis of behavioral characteristics and inclinations that are thought to be freely chosen. Homophobia involves an element of teaching persons so disposed to nonconformity a lesson, often a very public lesson. Parents of gender nonconforming children, perhaps, put the pressure on their kids the worst of all. Unlike members of other minority groups, moreover, the very groups they might use for support—their families, their church—may be the first to turn against them. The psychological toll of being attacked on all fronts can be enormous.

Sometimes oppressed groups turn society's hatred within—onto themselves. In their research on the relationship between suicide risk and sexual orientation, Remafedi, French, Story, Resnick, and Blum (1998) found evidence of a strong association between suicide risk and bisexuality or homosexuality in young males. A Canadian study conducted through the University of Calgary's center for the study of suicide interviewed young adult men who answered questions on portable computers (King, 1996). The results were startling: Gay and bisexual subjects were found to have 14 times the rate of attempted suicide as heterosexuals. The sample size for celibate males, interestingly, was extremely small. The Canadian study is unique in that it is based on a cross section of young males, not on a sample of persons already known to be gay. (See Chapter 8, Box 8.1, to learn of social work roles in advocating for gay and lesbian youth.)

Lesbians suffer a double whammy from homophobia because of its link with sexism. A woman who steps outside the rules of patriarchy and threatens its authority expects to be hated and feared by men and heterosexual women who seek social change but fear the lesbian label (Pharr, 2001). The effect on the women's movement—as women are divided from women by the male power structure—has been devastating. The passage of the equal rights amendment was defeated in several states because of its linkage by opponents with same-sex marriage. This same issue helped decide the 2004 election.

Employment discrimination against gays and lesbians is commonplace; except in some cities that have passed antidiscrimination ordinances, such discrimination is perfectly legal. In Iowa, for example, an employee can be fired on the grounds of being homosexual. Dismissal in the U.S. military occurs under the "don't ask, don't tell" policy when gays and lesbians let their sexual orientation be known. Today, some branches of the military seem bent on engaging in a witch-hunt to weed out gays and lesbians (Reasons & Hughson, 2002). In contrast to U.S. policy, the United Kingdom, Australia, and Canada have integrated their military forces with little fanfare.

Hate crimes against gays and lesbians, especially by young males, are commonplace. Two of the most famous examples are the torture and murder of Matthew Shepard, a University of Wyoming student, in 1999 and the more recent baseball bat slaying of a 41-year-old gay man in Vancouver, Canada. Despite the large numbers of hate crimes inflicted upon gays and lesbians (1,393 assaults that resulted in injury or death were reported to the FBI in 2001), hate crime legislation includes sexual orientation as a protected class in only 21 states (Reasons & Hughson, 2002).

The denial of marital rights to same-sex partners is one of the deprivations of gays and lesbians with the gravest social and economic consequences. These consequences involve the denial of a range of rights and benefits, including income tax deductions, family health benefits (with most companies), the right to have a say in medical emergencies, and child custody and visitation rights. The rejection of gays and lesbians by major social institutions deprives a sizeable segment of the population of the help and support they need. Alienation from the traditional church's teachings, lack of awareness of counseling services, the living of a lifestyle that is taboo in most circles, and abuse inflicted by peers and family members all combine to close the avenues to much-needed social support. The human rights aspect of denial of the benefits of marriage and civil disobedience in this regard is discussed in Chapter 6. The result of such deprivation of legal protection is a loss not only to gays and lesbians but also to the society generally, which is deprived of gay and lesbian talents and contributions (van Wormer, 2004).

Many excellent self-awareness exercises have been developed to help people explore their own sexuality. They may want to contemplate the continuum of sexual orientation to see where they rank between 100 percent heterosexual and 100 percent homosexual. The famous Heterosexual Questionnaire devised by Rochlin (2000) that begins "What do you think caused your heterosexuality?" is very effective in getting heterosexuals to discover how it feels to be put on the defensive about one's sexual attraction.

Earlier we discussed estrangement from the church as a possible outcome for those who come out as gay or lesbian. It is paradoxical that religion, a source of strength to so many, can also be a force of destruction when an individual's very being is condemned. We turn now to a discussion of oppression that is built on traditional, doctrinal beliefs in the form of religion.

Sectarianism

The Oxford Modern English Dictionary (1996) defines *sectarian* as "bigoted or narrow-minded in following the doctrines of one's sect; a bigot." My definition of *sectarianism* is that it is a form of political oppression in the name of religion. When I lived in Northern Ireland, for example, I was told that the differences between Protestant and Catholic were not about religion but about politics. I was also told the conflict was a question of class. Only one woman wanted to talk about the religious aspect. She said the religious differences in Northern Ireland made more sense than the racial differences in America because they pertain to "things of the mind." As in most situations, it was not a case of either/or but of both/and: Politics and religion were combined.

Similarly, with Islamism, politics that include beliefs about gender roles are both fused and confused with the religious message. Here, and I underscore this point, I am referring not to Islam proper but to the fundamentalist branch of Islam, the revival of which has marked a tremendous setback for Muslim women throughout the world. Muhammad, the prophet and founder of Islam, preached kindness to women and showed great tenderness toward and respect for his wife. So when women are forced to cover their entire bodies in a *burka* to protect them from arousing lust in men, is the driving force religion, or is it sexism? And in its expression as terrorism, is Islamism an attack on the infidel—a "holy war," or *Jihad,* against Jews and capitalism—or is it an expression of political brotherhood?

Suffice it to say, religious fundamentalism is behind much of the extremist politics today. And religious hatred is as virulent as any other kind; fanaticism of any sort is dangerous. From mass bloodshed in the Bible and the slaughter of the Crusades to today's terrorist attacks in the United States and suicide bombings and Zionist retaliatory strikes in the Middle East, violence in the name of religion has a long history. The politics of the religious right has been scathingly analyzed in Kevin Phillips's (2004) best-selling portrait of the Bush family legacy, *American Dynasty.* In his alliance with the Religious Right, George W. Bush's emergence in national politics, as Phillips suggests, tapped religious forces akin to those promoting Sharon in Israel and fueling the rise of Islamic parties in Pakistan, Turkey, and elsewhere. Indignation over secularization is a force nurturing "true believers" the world over, as Phillips further argues (p. 212).

Religious oppression at its most extreme took place in Afghanistan, which fell under the control of Taliban zealots. The Taliban, allies of the United States in their earlier war with the Soviets, used their CIA training and weaponry to set up a fiercely violent regime in which educated women were persecuted; the teaching of Christianity became a capital offense; Hindus were ordered to wear an identifying label; and the largest Buddha statues in the world were ceremoniously blown up. Theologian Karen Armstrong (2001) puts this kind of religious fanaticism in context. "During the 20th century," she explains, "the militant form of piety often known as fundamentalism erupted in every major religion as a rebellion against modernity. . . . Fighting, as they imagine, a battle for survival, fundamentalists often feel justified in ignoring the more compassionate principles of their faith" (p. 48).

The World Trade Center, of course, was the prime symbol of capitalism, of the global economy. Anti-Semitism figured in as well in that in the terrorist's eyes, American capitalism is conceived of as Jewish finance capitalism (Petchesky, 2001). Although the American response to the mass destruction in New York City was far more nationalistic than sectarian in character, the anti-Arab backlash by the American people has taken on a character that could be construed as sectarian. The government's "war on terrorism," similarly, has taken on a character that is decidedly discriminatory. We return to this topic later in the chapter.

A social psychological phenomenon that surfaces in times of national crisis that is related to mass insecurity and even hysteria is the phenomenon of *displaced aggression* (Allport, 1954), as discussed in Chapter 1. This natural tendency to redirect one's personal discomfort toward a vulnerable source can readily be exploited by a nation's rulers. Through skillful use of propaganda, a people's righteous anger can be redirected away from criticism of the government and toward a vulnerable source such as criminals, immigrants, or terrorists. Clearly the all-time master of such redirection of anger was Hitler

(Mandel, 2002). How could Hitler have happened? Students of human behavior have been trying to answer that question for more than half a century, and probably never will. Certainly part of the answer lies in the severe economic crisis that Germany faced following the horrendous defeat of World War I. And part of it is likely familial—related to the rigid norms of obedience to authority, militarism, and denial of feelings characteristic of the German family during that period in history. Sectarianism came into play as well in that Jews were religiously and ethnically different and economically successful in times of hardship; accordingly, they easily could be targeted as scapegoats. In the concentration camps of their confinement, Jews joined others designated as different—known homosexuals, Roma (Gypsies), conscientious objectors, Jehovah Witnesses, persons with mental disabilities, and common criminals. The suffering of such individuals is now immortalized in the personal histories, pieces of clothing, photographs, and recordings displayed at the U.S. Holocaust Memorial Museum in Washington, DC. Box 5.3 provides a descriptive tour of this museum. The tour guide is a social worker, Tammy Pearson, who, with her 17-year-old son, embarked on a journey into the darkest corridors of modern human history.

Ethnocentrism

Ethnocentrism, briefly defined, is the taken-for-granted assumption that one's way is the only way or at least the best way. Because inevitably we view the world through the lens of our own culture, we are all ethnocentric to some extent. We cannot say we will rid ourselves of cultural bias any more than we can say we will part with the tastes we have acquired or the language we have learned. This lesson was not lost on the poet Tennyson who, speaking as the returning wanderer Ulysses, reviews his adventures in these words: "I am a part of all I have met" (Tennyson, 1979/1842, verse 1.6). We, likewise, are a part of our background and experiences.

Ethnocentrism relates to differences in values and in perceptions of values. Consider this statement, for example: "The Vietnamese do not value human life." During the war in Vietnam, this is what the American people were told about the slaughter of Viet Cong and civilians. Ethnocentrism plays into a natural distaste for the unfamiliar and foreign. Still, it can be generated or reinforced by powerful political interests. Economics may be both the cause and effect of conflict. Consider the role that competition over scarce resources has played in ethnic and racial conflict in the course of history—for example, in the annihilation and forced removal of America's native peoples, in slavery and segregation, in Israeli and Palestinian disputes over land and water rights, and in ethnic cleansing in Kosovo. It is a truth of social psychology that once people have been mistreated in this way, they are hated as a way to justify the mistreatment.

In a nation at war, the social climate relevant to foreigners is apt to change, to harden. The public in wartime, wracked by insecurity, is apt to be susceptible to scapegoating outsiders, especially those of the ethnic group of the designated enemy. Some may be citizens who just look like the enemy. Since the start of

5.3 A Visit to the U.S. Holocaust Memorial Museum

Tammy Pearson, MSW, of Cedar Falls, Iowa

Not only will a visit to the U.S. Holocaust Memorial Museum clear up any misinformation you may have about the Holocaust, but it also will engage you in a way that is everlasting. The time spent there will never leave you and will commit you to being a witness, bound to the responsibility that comes with it, to share what you have seen and learned with others. The experience will not only teach you about the means of the extermination but also about the victims behind the raw numbers. Because you will leave the museum as a witness, it is important to experience it all. To visit the Holocaust Museum is to be a witness to "man's inhumanity to man" but also to the strength of the human spirit, to resilience.

On June 7, 2001, I finally got to go to the U.S. Holocaust Memorial Museum. Although this visit was several years in the planning, once I was there, I stood staring at the front door and asking myself, "Why did I ever want to do this?" I was there to do research, I told myself, and because I care deeply about this horrible violation of humanity. The research role provided a way for me to distance myself, a top layer of protection for my emotional defenses. Attached to that was the duty to teach my 17-year-old son.

Placed among the other stately buildings in Washington, DC, the museum building is stylish and modern. The sidewalks in the area are teeming with tourists. Yet, because this was no ordinary museum, the sight of people (teens among them) casually exiting the building seemed suddenly incongruous. Was the teens' laughter a mask for their pain, the ultimate denial?

On entering the museum, my son became engaged almost immediately, mostly because of the personal qualities of the woman conducting the orientation. The museum's objective, as the guide explained, was not to teach us about 900 years of Jewish or European history; it was to concentrate on the cataclysmic events from 1933 to 1945, events that were executed in a "systematic" process. This knowledge is critical to an understanding of how the forces for genocide can build.

The museum also uses a process to systematically engage visitors. By physically walking among the photos and artifacts, listening to the audio accounts, and viewing the videos, one becomes personally engaged in mind and body. Exposed steel beams and brick walls provide an eerie quality to the experience. The exhibits begin on the fourth floor and wind down to the first, step-by-step, following the sequence of the events of the systematic extermination.

A basket held identification cards. We each chose one, a booklet that tells the story of a real person who lived during the Holocaust. It looks like a passport and on the front reads: "For the dead and the living we must bear witness," written over the United States crest. The identification card I would carry was #5395, Alida Nathans Wijnberg. On the first page was a small square photo of her and some vital statistics, such as her birth in Vries, Netherlands, on April 10, 1887. She was the oldest of eight children and born to religious Jewish parents. Her family owned a textile business, and it was her job to carry goods to the farmers in a suitcase that was attached to the handlebars of her bicycle. She married Samuel Wijnberg, and they had three sons and a daughter.

As I walked on, I read and learned about how the system gained its energy. It all began on February 27, 1933, when the Reichstag (German Parliament) was burned. Hitler blamed the communists, and President von Hindenburg invoked Article 48, at Hitler's insistence. Emergency orders thus went into effect; all individual and civil liberties, including the freedoms of speech, press, and assembly, were suspended. Other decrees issued at the same time instituted the death sentence. These emergency decrees became the legal

(continued)

5.3 *continued*

excuse for the concentration camps, camps that held not only Jews but also homosexuals, Romany people (Gypsies), and mentally ill and physically handicapped persons.

The exhibit of the "burning of the books" in Berlin on May 10, 1933, welded me to that spot. A picture shows a mountain of books engulfed in tall flames while a crowd of jeering onlookers cheered wildly. Next to the picture of the burning books is a quote from the Jewish poet Heinrich Heine, written a hundred years earlier, that reads, "Where one burns books, one will, in the end, burn people." A sad prophecy was unfolding.

I looked at Alida's identification card and turned to her next page. It told me that Alida's husband had died and that she and her children had continued to run the hotel until the Germans confiscated the property. The Wijnbergs were relocated to a shack with no running water; her son went into hiding, as did her daughter.

The Evian Conference of July 1938, as we learned, left no hope and no haven. By 1938, as many as 150,000 Jews had successfully fled Germany, but then the annexation of Austria in 1938 brought an additional 183,000 back into the Nazi orbit. There would be no escape for most Jews. The refugee segment displayed a photo of ships and told of the voyage of the *St. Louis*. This sickened and shamed me, as I have seen the same shoreline area of Miami as did the passengers of the *St. Louis*. They, of course, sailed the return voyage to their deaths after being turned away from Havana, Cuba, and other ports in North America.

Following the system, our journey took us next to the T-4 program. That was a program involving virtually all of the German psychiatric community. The fact that the doctors involved did not immediately become killers is yet more evidence of the deliberateness used in designing and implementing a system that led to genocide. They soon adopted the philosophy of "life unworthy of life," which led them to murder the mentally ill and physically handicapped patients in their care. Gas chambers were first developed at the killing centers for the handicapped, where incurably sick children were seen as a burden on the Volk (the German people).

The mobile killing squads single-handedly killed about one-fourth of all Jews in the Holocaust. We saw pictures of mass graves, one containing more than 7,000 people. It was a hastily dug trench on the outskirts of an eastern European town where an Einsatzgruppen unit of soldiers shot their victims while they stood, kneeled, or laid face down. So many bodies, piled in layers—it was so unnatural that one's mind could hardly take in the human images. Past the life-sized photos and captions, we arrived at a real freight car. This was an authentic, 15-ton Deutsches

America's war on terror, for example, many countries have become more wary of foreigners, including refugees. The United States, for example, admitted only 27,000 in 2002, less than half the number admitted in 2001 ("World Refugee Survey 2003," 2003). "More Than 13,000 May Face Deportation" (Swarns, 2003) was a recent headline from *The New York Times*. The European Union (EU) accepted far fewer, only an average of 10 percent of asylum seekers. (See Chapter 6 to learn more about the human rights violations of immigrant groups.) The anti-immigrant sentiment following September 11 has reverberated to include restrictions on the migration of highly skilled workers and ordinary laborers as well. This was not the case in Canada, however, at least initially: Many Pakistanis, Egyptians, Lebanese, and citizens from Muslim countries living in the United

Reichbahn freight car. It is positioned in the path of the exhibition route, as a bridge to the next segment of exhibits. My son and I stood together there for a long while. We talked softly of Elie Wiesel's (1982) ordeal that he described in his book *Night*. The reality gave me chills. Even worse, everything—the people and their suffering—had to be multiplied, as each train car carried as many as 80 to 100 people; each train carried between 1,000 and 2,000 people.

I was now on the last page of Alida Wijnberg's life. The Gestapo caught Alida during her attempt to go into hiding. She arrived in Auschwitz on October 12, 1942, where she soon perished. I felt myself looking for her in the next display. This exhibit was "Crematorium II," one of four such exhibits. The figures are of people and the process used to kill them, based on documents and the trial testimonies of SS guards.

A significant portion of the museum is designated for exhibiting information pertaining to rescues. Over this section are the words, "Whoever [shall] save a single life, saves an eternal world," from *The Talmud*. Short stories and many photos and clips were bound together in an arrangement. There were articles describing the saving of the Jews of Denmark, and telegrams from the War Refugee Board that appeared to offer too little too late. This segment shows the many people who were naturally compelled to help, claiming that it is more natural to help other humans than not to help them. Other displays were of people who were caught and killed for trying to help.

The last phase of the Holocaust Museum experience is for reflection, grief, and even mourning. After the intense journey through the exhibits, it provides a place to respect and acknowledge the cloud of witnesses above us. In this last room burns an eternal flame and a stone ledge on which to sit down and rest. Since the time of my witness, I have experienced a multitude of feelings, and I know that I am not alone. After years of studying the Holocaust—the literature, personal stories, and history—I finally can fathom the rationale, the purpose, behind the system of horror. I better understand because I was able to walk beside the evidence. I do not believe that we will ever be able to understand *why* the Holocaust happened, but one visit to the Holocaust Memorial Museum will provide those who care with a structure for learning and understanding *how* it happened.

Our visit to the past ended, ironically, via modern technology. Once back at our hotel, my son and I sent an e-mail to a dear friend. My son wanted to ask our friend, who is Jewish, if he had lost anyone in the Holocaust and to tell him that he looked for their family name on the wall of remembrance during our visit. He also wanted to ask our friend if he spoke Hebrew; but mostly, he said, he just wanted to tell our friend, he was sorry.

Note: For details of the Holocaust Memorial Museum, including haunting photographic displays, see http://www.ushmm.org.

States moved north of the border. But later, probably due to U.S. pressure, other Middle Easterners started being turned over to U.S. immigration authorities ("Canada Turns Away Pakistanis Fleeing U.S.," 2002).

Much of human migration from rich to poor countries is linked to economics—the need of industry for cheap labor and the need of migrants for self-sustaining work. Since Mexico borders directly on the United States, there is a constant flow of traffic northward. Families in Mexico depend on their relatives to send checks to help in their support. An estimated 1,500 people try to cross the 2,000-plus mile border at just one border town each day. According to an editorial in the *Chicago Tribune*, "The Deadly Immigration Impasse" (2003), the flow of illegal immigrants to the north has become an avalanche, and smuggling operations have become a multibillion-dollar industry. Incidents of deaths of would-be migrant workers abandoned in locked semi-trailers and rail cars reveal the desperation of Mexicans to find work.

Before September 11, plans were underway to negotiate immigration agreements, including an amnesty offer to Mexican residents to give them legal status as workers. After that fateful date, however, according to the *Chicago Tribune,* when "immigrant" became almost synonymous with "terrorist" in the minds of fearful Americans, all immigration talks ceased. There was one exception, however. The U.S. interest in Mexican oil generated a proposal to link U.S. willingness to legalize Mexican immigrants to a Mexican agreement to open its state-owned oil industry to foreign investment. The headline in Mexico's largest newspaper, which translates strikingly as "Blackmail," leaves no doubt about the Mexican response (Kammer, 2003).

As mentioned in the previous section on work, there is trouble on the horizon for Mexico in the form of competition from China. Although Mexico still maintains its position as the number two exporter to the United States after Canada, China is moving rapidly ahead (Smith, 2003). As factories move to China from Mexico in droves, emigration to the United States becomes an even more desperate option.

Latinos/Latinas

Demographic Facts

By 2000, the number of Hispanic Americans reached approximately 13 percent of the population (U.S. Census Bureau, 2000a), making them the largest minority group in the United States, and African Americans the second largest minority. By July 2003, the number of Hispanic Americans had climbed to 39.9 million, or about 14 percent of the population ("U.S. Hispanic, Asian Populations Booming," 2004). (Note: The word *Hispanic* is that used by the government in the collection of data, such as census data, and therefore is used in this book in a statistical context only. This term is not wholly representative, as it technically refers to persons of Spanish descent; yet many Latin Americans are of Portuguese or other ancestry.) Of these people of Spanish/Hispanic/Latino origin, in the 2000 Census report, 66.1 percent identified themselves as Mexican, 9.0 percent as Puerto Rican, 4.0 percent as Cuban, 14.5 percent as Central and South American, and 6.4 percent as Other Hispanic. Traditionally, Puerto Ricans identify themselves by class, not race (on a continuum of black to white), viewing skin color as unimportant.

On the whole, Latinos/Latinas are the least educated of all ethnocultural groups in the United States, with high dropout rates (Puerto Ricans have the highest) and a high school graduation rate of only 57 percent in 2000 ("FAQ's about the Latino Community," 2001). The proportion of Hispanics with a bachelor's degree (around 11 percent) was not significantly different from that of a decade earlier. This figure compares to 17 percent of black, 27 percent of white, and 47 percent of Asian American adults in the same age bracket

(Schmidt, 2003). The educational prospects improve substantially for the U.S.-born children of Latino immigrants, and some groups such as Cuban Americans and Dominican immigrants have done exceptionally well.

Recent immigrants are filling a high proportion of newly created jobs ("Immigrants Are Filling 3 of Every 10 New Jobs in United States," 2004). Latinos participate in the labor force in large numbers, mostly in laboring and service occupations (except for Cuban Americans). Large numbers of Mexican Americans and U.S. residents from Mexico have joined the military (despite the fact that the Mexican government has actively opposed the war against Iraq). Some have enlisted because there is less discrimination against them in the military than elsewhere, while others have done so to get a boost in their applications for citizenship. According to an article in *The Washington Post* (Jordan, 2003):

> There is a certain irony in the large Mexican American presence at Fort Bliss. The base was founded in 1848, just after the two-year U.S.-Mexican War which resulted in the United States taking about half of Mexico's territory. . . . Mexicans are taught in school that the war was an unjust land grab.

Cultural Factors

Traditional views of family and roles can be protective factors against the experience of poverty; at the same time, they make it more difficult to seek help. Protective factors identified in a study of 60 young, low-income, predominantly Mexican American women include a cohesive family of origin, adequate rule-setting by parents, and a strong social support system (Lindenberg et al., 1998).

Latino/Latina traditions sharply differentiate the roles of males and females (Alvarez & Ruiz, 2001; Medina, 2001). Women are expected to be the moral authority of the family and provide family connection and care for children, while men are expected to be the provider for the family as well as the disciplinarian and decision maker in financial matters. Women in traditional families are highly discouraged from using alcohol or drugs because of their critical role in child-rearing. Although there is great individual variance, many males relate strongly to the value of "machismo," that is, being brave, strong, a good provider, and dominant. Identification with these qualities may make it difficult to handle loss of employment (van Wormer & Davis, 2003).

Education and economic status are improving slightly among Hispanics, but again there is wide variation among subgroups. Poverty is still a major risk factor. Hispanic families have a 25.6 percent poverty rate, ranging from 31 percent for Puerto Ricans and Mexican Americans to 14 percent for Cuban Americans (U.S. Census Bureau, 2000a). As in any culture of poverty, this condition provides few opportunities to buffer the hardships of life, few resources to avoid harmful social and health-related consequences of drinking and using drugs, and greater vulnerability to social sanctions such as jail, prison, and discrimination (Alvarez & Ruiz, 2001).

Kinship (*familismo*) is highly valued, and extended family members commonly participate in child-rearing and other activities that support the family.

Although few have health insurance and Mexican Americans have a high teen birthrate, the infant mortality rate is relatively low compared to that among Anglo-Americans. This is probably due to the close family ties and nurturance provided to the pregnant women. Still, the stress of immigration, poverty, discrimination, isolation from extended family, and acculturation can cause dramatic effects and strain on the traditional Latino/Latina support system. These hardships may contribute to an attitude of fatalism, or the belief that life's problems are inevitable and must be accepted (Alvarez & Ruiz, 2001; van Wormer & Davis, 2003).

A major problem for Latinos in accessing social services is the language barrier. Even among the documented workers in the United States (those included in census data), 13.8 million Spanish-speaking people over age five do not speak English well (U.S. Census Bureau, 2000a). A commonly reported situation is that of Spanish-speaking clients talking to mental health professionals while their highly personal stories are being interpreted by their children or by maintenance personnel (O'Neill, 2003). Intensive recruitment of bilingual students to major in social work is underway. All across the United States, agencies and policy makers are taking steps to increase their capacity to serve Spanish-speaking clients.

Anti-Immigrant Harassment

Since September 11, the most blatant discrimination in the workplace has been against Arabs and others of Middle Eastern descent. According to a survey of workers, about 20 percent said Arab Americans were the employees most likely to be treated unfairly in the workplace (Armour, 2002b). That surpasses the number who said women or Hispanic workers were the most apt to be mistreated. Hundreds of discrimination claims have been filed with the federal government by Arab employees. The Council on American-Islamic Relations recorded just under 1,500 anti-Muslim incidents in the two months following the hijacked airplane attacks. Wipf and Wipf (2001) provide the following examples:

- In Illinois, 300 protesters yelled "USA!" as they tried to storm a mosque.
- A Molotov cocktail in Chicago destroyed an Arab American community center.
- Australians stoned a school bus carrying Muslim youngsters; a Lebanese church was also set afire.

Out of the fear that gripped America following the unprecedented hijackings and anthrax scare, the U.S. government was able to pass repressive legislation that would have been unthinkable pre–September 11. In conjunction with a major reorganization of federal law enforcement priorities, over 1,000 detainees were rounded up in a vast dragnet reportedly due to immigration violations. Some 40 militant groups were designated as terrorist organizations in a crackdown to identify possible terrorist sympathizers (Hentoff, 2003; Wilgoren, 2001). With close to unanimous support from Congress, the President signed into law the USA Patriot Act providing for expanded government powers of surveillance, intelligence sharing, and detention. Civil liberties affected are the right to freedom from discrimination based on religion and the right to habeas corpus and to a fair and speedy trial.

The anti-immigrant fervor, in fact, has extended to other groups of foreign workers in the United States, and the legal harassment of undocumented residents has encouraged an ever-expanding ring of illegal exploiters from smugglers to employers, feeding on the mass of vulnerable workers devoid of rights (Newman, 2002).

Where there has been an influx of Mexican laborers and factory workers, such foreign workers face abuse routinely, according to representatives from Iowa and Nebraska Latino outreach groups and civil rights agencies (Jerousek, 2003). Stories told by immigrant advocates depicted the following realities:

- Some plant workers who speak Spanish report that they are told they can speak only English while on break.
- A Mexican immigrant reports paying $100 a week to live in a trailer with 8 to 12 people, who are all being charged the same amount.
- A Latino man reports that he was promised pay after working on three construction projects. His employer accused him of stealing tools before the third project. The worker was arrested and never paid. (pp. 1A–2A)

Despite the harassment, the United States continues to absorb more than one million immigrants annually, including workers without legal documentation. Bringing in this additional labor force is key to America's economic growth, according to an article in *Business Week* (Baker, 2002). Given the aging of the baby boom population, the continuing influx of foreign laborers, especially persons with crucial technical and scientific talent, is in the interests of big business. Even labor leaders, reflecting a shift in policy, have spoken out in support of amnesty for undocumented workers, most of whom are Mexican. Residents from Muslim countries, however, are leaving in droves. Pakistanis, for example, are relocating to Canada where they feel more welcome than they do in the United States.

Summary and Conclusion

This was the chapter of "isms"—classism, racism, sexism, heterosexism, sectarianism, and ethnocentrism. Three obvious omissions—adultism, ageism, and ableism—are subjects of other chapters. Classism in the United States was discussed in terms of the ever-expanding gap between the rich and the poor, nonstigmatized welfare programs for the rich, and the war against the poor that is occurring simultaneously on two fronts—in the workplace, and through welfare reform geared to force the poor to take the jobs nobody wants, often at less than a living wage.

Racism, closely aligned to classism, was explored as a reality of conservative politics. Indeed racism can be regarded as being in the service of conservative politics, as its presence effectively obviates working-class solidarity. Racism clearly figures in the war on crime that has become a war on minorities; its presence is evidenced as well in the war on welfare that has become a war on single nonworking mothers. In recent times, use of a racial profile of another sort is applied in the war on terror. The statistics presented in this chapter and some that we will entertain in the next chapter reveal the omnipresence of racial and class oppression in American life.

Poverty in America, a major theme of Chapter 4, was also a consideration in this chapter as we entered the world of work and the worker in the global economy. The focus here was on the uneven distribution of resources, locally and globally. For man, woman, and child to live in poverty in the midst of plenty is one of the cruelest forms of oppression. This is classism because the control of the resources is in the hands of a few. Classism in today's world is expressed in the stunting of opportunity and enjoyment of life's bounties on the basis of class, while members of another class enjoy special benefits ranging from educational advantages to advantages in the way the tax structure is set up. The forces of racism and classism are especially pronounced in the impetus for welfare-to-work reform legislation. Coupled with the high unemployment rate for unskilled workers, the dreams of many American families must be put on hold. For the best expression of the human condition, we can return to the lines, cited at the beginning of this chapter, of famed African American poet Langston Hughes, who asked what happens to a dream deferred: Does it sag like a heavy load or does it explode? His words apply equally to the individual and the collective levels.

Institutionalized sexism is a reality the world over, arguably less on the North American continent than elsewhere. Sexual oppression is revealed in comparative data from international nongovernmental organizations and U.N. reports. Such reports chart the progress (and nonprogress) of women in various parts of the world in achieving social and economic equality. What the data on progress for girls and women reveal is that the half of humanity who do most of the world's work derive the least of the advantages from it. For economic development to become social development, women must be adequately represented at the policy and family decision-making level. Only in this way will domestic and international economic policies be instituted so as to protect the welfare of women and children.

Heterosexism, sectarianism, and ethnocentrism are other forms of social oppression that were discussed in this chapter. The extremes of heterosexism and homophobia were seen in hate crimes inflicted upon persons viewed to be sexually different. Ethnocentrism, in its extreme form, was seen to be expressed as anti-immigrant harassment following September 11. The example of sectarianism that is the most memorable is found in the reading in Box 5.3 concerning the historic persecution of European Jews.

This chapter, like the previous chapter, is written in the spirit of the Council on Social Work Education (CSWE, 2003) standard to prepare students "to alleviate poverty, oppression, and other forms of social injustice" and "to recognize the global context of social work practice" (p. 32). In light of the consequences of the global market imperatives, social work's ethical emphasis on social and economic justice assumes a rare importance. Social work is unique among the professions in its commitment to advocacy on behalf of the poor and dispossessed. Increasingly, a human rights focus is a part of this mission, and it is this focus to which we next turn our attention.

Thought Questions

1. How are racism and classism intertwined? Sexism and racism? Sexism and heterosexism?

2. Explain how classism can occur at all levels of society.

3. Study the chart in Box 5.1 on U.S. federal spending. How is the money spent? How could the money be better spent? Compare this chart to the government's pie chart.

4. Compare working conditions in the United States with those in other countries, both more progressive and less progressive countries. How could having an America labor party affect workers' rights and benefits?

5. Discuss the notion of the war against the poor. Refer to *Nickel and Dimed.*

6. How would you reform welfare reform if at all?

7. List three ways that the rich get richer (either locally or globally).

8. Make a case for or against the concept of "feminization of poverty."

9. Discuss some of the reasons for male/female pay inequities.

10. Compare heterosexism and homophobia as concepts. How are they manifest in the U.S. social structure?

11. Define sectarianism and relate it to religious fundamentalism.

12. What is the purpose of the U.S. Holocaust Museum? Relate this historical exhibition to the concept of displaced aggression.

13. Argue whether or not ethnocentrism is, to some extent, inevitable, or if we can avoid being ethnocentric as we visit foreign lands.

14. What form has anti-immigrant harassment taken after September 11?

15. Discuss some of the difficulties that Mexican Americans face in achieving "the American dream."

16. Discuss the meaning of Langston Hughes's poem, an excerpt of which begins this chapter.

References

Abramovitz, M. (2002, March). The combined impact of welfare reform, the recession, and the world trade center attack. *BCR Reports, 13*(1).

AFL-CIO. (2002, September 6). Poverty line is far below families' basic needs, new study reveals. Retrieved from http://www.aflcio.org

AFL-CIO. (2003). A real minimum wage raise or . . .? Retrieved from http://www.aflcio.org/issues politics/minimumwage

Allport, G. (1954). *The nature of prejudice.* Reading, MA: Addison-Wesley.

Alvarez, L., & Ruiz, P. (2001). Substance abuse in the Mexican American population. In L. A. Straussner (Ed.), *Ethnocultural factors in substance abuse treatment* (pp. 111–136). New York: Guilford.

Appleby, G. A., Colin, E., & Hamilton, J. (2001). *Diversity, oppression and social functioning: Person-in-environment assessment and intervention.* Boston: Allyn & Bacon.

Armour, S. (2002a, December 9). Job hunt gets harder for African-Americans. *USA Today,* p. B1.

Armour, S. (2002b, May 10). Reports of workplace bias still on rise since Sept. 11. *USA Today,* p. B1.

Armour, S. (2004, June 24). "Rife with discrimination": Plaintiffs describe their lives at Wal-Mart. *USA Today,* p. B3.

Armstrong, K. (2001, October 1). The true, peaceful face of Islam. *Time,* 48.

Associated Press. (2004, March 7). Buffett in Berkshire's annual report: Tax cuts favor corporations, wealthy. *Waterloo–Cedar Falls Courier*, p. A2.

Ayvazian, A. (2001). Interrupting the cycle of oppression: The role of allies as agents of change. In P. S. Rothenberg, *Race, class, and gender in the United States* (pp. 609–615). New York: Worth.

Baker, S. (2002, August 26). The coming battle for immigrants. *Business Week*, 138–140.

Barker, R. (2003). *The social work dictionary* (5th ed.) Washington, DC: NASW Press.

Bartlett, D., & Steele, J. (2003, February 3). The really unfair tax. *Time*, 46–47.

Bernstein, J., & Greenberg, M. (2001, January 1). Reforming welfare reform. *The American Prospect*, 10–15.

Bernstein, N. (2002, July 29). Side effect of welfare law: The no-parent family. *The New York Times*. Retrieved from http://www.nytimes.com

Billingsley, A., & Morrison-Rodriguez, B. (1998). The black family in the 21st century and the church as an action system: A macro perspective. In L. See (Ed.), *Human behavior in the social environment from an African perspective* (pp. 31–47). New York: Haworth Press.

Black jobless rate climbs. (2003, August 31). *Waterloo–Cedar Falls Courier*, p. G1. Reprinted from the *Chicago Tribune*.

Boshara, R. (2003, January/February). The $6,000 solution. *Atlantic Monthly*, 91–95.

Bremner, B. (2002, June 10). Cool Korea: How it roared back from disaster and became a model for Asia. *Business Week*, 56–58.

Broad, D. (1995). Globalization and casual labor: Marginalization of labor in Western countries. Paper presented at the International Social Welfare in a Changing World Conference, University of Calgary, Alberta, Canada.

Byrnes, N., & Lavelle, L. (2003, March 31). The corporate tax game: How blue-chip companies are paying less and less of the nation's tax bill. *Business Week*, 79–87.

Canada turns away Pakistanis fleeing U.S. (2002, January 31). CNN Online. Retrieved from http://www.CNN.com

Chicago Tribune. (2003, December 5). Research: Poverty hurts IQ. Reprinted in *Waterloo–Cedar Falls Courier*, p. A7.

Cohn, L. (2000, October 9). From welfare to worsefare? *Business Week*, 103.

Connolly, C., & Witte, G. (2004, August 27). Poverty rate up 3rd year in a row. *Washington Post*, p. A1.

Council on Social Work Education (CSWE). (2003). *Handbook of accreditation standards and procedures* (5th ed.). Alexandria, VA: Author.

Curphey, S. (2003, May 9). Safety net is weaker for unemployed women. *Women's e News*. Retrieved from http://www.womensenews.org

Danziger, S. (Ed.). (1999). *Economic conditions and welfare reform*. Kalamazoo, MI: Upjohn Institute.

Davis, T. J. (1999, January/February). Snowe warnings. *Secure Retirement*, 50–52.

Day, P. (2003). *A new history of social welfare* (4th ed.). Boston: Allyn & Bacon.

The deadly immigration impasse. (2003, June 7). *Chicago Tribune*, sec. 1, p. 10.

Dolgoff, R., & Feldstein, D. (2002). *Understanding social welfare* (6th ed.). Upper Saddle River, NJ: Prentice-Hall.

Dollard, J. (1988/1957). *Caste and class in a southern town*. New York: Routledge.

Dominelli, L. (2002). *Anti-oppressive social work theory and practice*. New York: Palgrave MacMillan.

Eby, C. (2002, June 12). Welfare reform has a darker side. *Waterloo–Cedar Falls Courier*, p. A1.

Ehrenreich, B. (2001). *Nickel and dimed: On not getting by in America*. New York: Metropolitan Books.

Ehrenreich, B. (2002, May). Chamber of welfare reform. *The Progressive*, 14–15.

Ehrenreich, B., & Hochschild, A. (2003). *Global woman: Nannies, maids, and sex workers in the new economy*. New York: Metropolitan.

Eisenhower, D. (1953, April 16). Speech delivered before the America Society of Newspaper Editors, Washington, DC.

FAQ's about the Latino community. (2001). National Council of La Raza. Online at http://www.nclr.org

Firestone, D. (2003, June 1). 2nd study finds gaps in tax cuts. *The New York Times*. Retrieved from http://www.truthout.org

Fiske, H. (2002, June 24). Welfare reform: Its effect on social workers and their clients. *Social Work Today*, 2(13), 8–11.

Food Research and Action Center. (2003, February 20). New publication assesses state records in using federal nutrition programs to alleviate hunger. Retrieved from http://www.frac.org

France, M. (2003, March 31). The rise of the Wall Street tax machine. *Business Week*, 84–87.

Francis, D. (2003, January 27). Upward mobility in real decline, studies charge. *Christian Science Monitor,* 21.

Free trade fuels rising poverty and growing rich-poor gap: World Bank's claims of success are challenged. (2001, October 11). Economic Policy Institute. Retrieved from http://www.citizen.org

Galbraith, J. (1992). *The culture of contentment.* Boston: Houghton Mifflin.

Galbraith, J. (1998, September 7/14). With economic inequality for all. *The Nation,* 24–26.

Gays comprise 5 percent of electorate in 2002, new poll finds. (2002, November 21). Human Rights Campaign. Retrieved from http://www.hrc.org

Gil, D. (1998). *Confronting injustice and oppression: Concepts and strategies for social workers.* New York: Columbia University Press.

Hager, G. (2001, April 9). More black workers face joblessness. *USA Today,* p. A9.

Hansberry, L. (1994/1958). *A raisin in the sun.* New York: Vintage Books.

Hanson, L. (2001, September 9). Racism world conference. National Public Radio; Weekend Edition.

Harrington, M. (1962). *The other America: Poverty in the United States.* Baltimore: Penguin.

The Hellenic EU presidency. (2003, March 30). Retrieved from http://www.eu2003.gr

Heller, A. (2002, August 12). More, not less "extremely poor": A wider measure of welfare reform. *Business Week,* 24.

Hentoff, N. (2003, February 28). Ashcroft out of control. *Village Voice.* Retrieved from http://www.villagevoice.com

Homeless families with children. (1999, June). National Coalition for the Homeless. Retrieved from http://nch.ari.net/families.html

hooks, b. (1993). *Sisters of the yam: Black women and self-recovery.* Boston: South End Press.

hooks, b. (2000). *Where we stand: Class matters.* New York: Routledge.

Huff, F. (1992, Winter). Upside-down welfare. *Public Welfare,* 36–40.

Hughes, L. (1967). A dream deferred. In L. Hughes (Ed.), *The panther and the lash: Poems of our times* (p. 14). New York: Knopf.

Immigrants are filling 3 of every 10 new jobs in United States. (2004, June 16). *Waterloo–Cedar Falls Courier,* p. A7. Reprinted from *Los Angeles Times.*

Japanese corporations bully workers into quitting. (1999, July 25). *Waterloo–Cedar Falls Courier,* p. A3. Reprinted from *Los Angeles Times.*

Jerousek, M. (2003, September 11). Immigrants face abuse routinely, activists say. *Des Moines Register,* pp. A1–2.

Jordan, M. (2003, February 28). Fighting "their war." *The Washington Post.* Retrieved from http://ist-socrates.berkeley.edu/~border/list

Kammer, J. (2003, May 17). Immigration and oil an explosive mix. Copely News Service. In *Effingham Daily News* (Illinois), p. A4.

Karger, H., & Stoesz, D. (2002). *American social welfare policy: A pluralist approach* (4th ed.). Boston: Allyn & Bacon.

Kijakazi, K., & Primus, W. (2000). Options for reducing poverty among elderly women by improving SSI. Center on Budget and Policy Priorities. Retrieved from http://www.cbpp.org

King, M. (1996, November 12). Suicide watch. *The Advocate,* 41–44.

Leander-Wright, B. (2003, March 7). Federal Reserve: Racial wealth gap has grown. United for a Fair Economy. Retrieved from http://www.ufenet.org

Lieberman, T. (2003, August 18). Hungry in America. *The Nation,* 17–22.

Lindenberg, C., et al. (1998). Risk and resilience: Building protective factors. *American Journal of Maternal Child Nursing, 23*(2), 99–104.

Link, R. (2002, February 15). Can re-authorization revitalize children's lives? Welfare reform through an international lens. *Electronic Journal of Social Work, 1*(1), 1–27.

Mandel, D. R. (2002). Instigators of genocide: Examining Hitler from a social psychological perspective. In L. S. Newman & R. Erber (Eds.), *What social psychology can tell us about the Holocaust: Understanding the perpetrators of genocide* (pp. 259–284). Oxford, UK: Oxford University Press.

Mantsios, G. (2001). Class in America: Myths and realities. In P. S. Rothenberg (Ed.), *Race, class, and gender in the U.S.* (pp. 168–181). New York: Worth.

Medina, C. (2001). Toward an understanding of Puerto Rican ethnicity and substance abuse. In L. A. Straussner (Ed.), *Ethnocultural factors in substance abuse treatment* (pp. 137–163). New York: Guilford.

Mullaly, R. (1998). *Structural social work: Ideology, theory and practice* (2nd ed.). New York: Oxford University Press.

Neubeck, K., & Cazenave, N. (2001). *Welfare racism: Playing the race card against America's poor.* New York: Routledge.

Newman, N. (2002, July 25). A war on immigrants to fight the war of terrorism? Lessons from the failed war on drugs. Retrieved from http://www.commondreams.org

O'Neill, J. (2003, June). Services in Spanish unavailable to many. *NASW News 48*(6), 4.

Oxford Modern English Dictionary (2nd ed.). (1996). New York: Oxford University Press.

Petchesky, R. (2001). Phantom towers: Feminist reflections on the battle between global capitalism and fundamental terrorism. *The Women's Review of Books.* Retrieved from http://www.wellesley.edu

Pharr, S. (2001). Homophobia as a weapon of sexism. In R. Rothenberg (Ed.), *Race, class, and gender in the United States: An integrated study* (pp. 143–152). New York: St. Martin's Press.

Phillips, K. (2004). *American dynasty: Aristocracy, fortune, and the politics of deceit in the house of Bush.* New York: Viking.

Pinkerton, J. (2003, January–February). A grand compromise. *Atlantic Monthly,* 115–116.

Piven, F. (2000, May 8). Welfare movement rises. *The Nation.* Retrieved from http://www.commondreams.org

Ratnesar, R. (1999, February 8). Not gone, but forgotten? *Time,* 30–31.

Reasons, C. E., & Hughson, Q. (1999). Violence against gays and lesbians. *Journal of Offender Rehabilitation, 30*(1–2), 137–150.

Reasons, C. E., & Hughson, Q. (2002). Violence against gays and lesbians. In C. E. Reasons, D. J. Conley, & J. Debro (Eds.), *Race, class, gender, and justice in the United States: A text reader* (pp. 100–114). Boston: Allyn & Bacon.

Reich, R. (2000). *The future of success: Working and living in the new economy.* New York: Vintage Books.

Remafedi, G., French, S., Story, M., Resnick, M., & Blum, R. (1998, January). The relationship between suicide risk and sexual orientation. *American Journal of Public Health, 88,* 57–60.

Ritter, J. (2002, December 12). Homeless hurt on several fronts. *USA Today.* Retrieved from http://www.usatoday.com

Rochlin, M. (2000). Heterosexual questionnaire. In K. van Wormer, J. Wells, & M. Boes, *Social work with lesbians, gays, and bisexuals: A strengths perspective* (p. 50). Boston: Allyn & Bacon.

Rothenberg, P. (2001). Introduction to Part II. In P. Rothenberg (Ed.), *Race, class, and gender in the United States* (5th ed., pp. 95–99). New York: Worth.

Sallah, M. (1994, April 17). In fertile land, a harvest of shame. *Waterloo–Cedar Falls Courier,* p. 1. Reprinted from the *Toledo Blade.*

Santiago, F. (2002, July 30). Welfare numbers hold steady, despite limits. *Des Moines Register,* p. W8.

Schiele, J. (1998). Cultural alignment, African American male youths, and violent crime. In L. See (Ed.), *Hunan behavior in the social environment from an African perspective* (pp. 165–181). New York: Haworth Press.

Schmidt, P. (2003, November 28). Academe's Hispanic future. *Chronicle of Higher Education.* Retrieved from http://chronicle.com/weekly

Schram, S. (2002). *Praxis for the poor: Piven and Cloward and the future of social science in social welfare.* New York: New York University Press.

Schwartz-Nobel, L. (2003). *Growing up empty.* New York: HarperCollins.

Seabrook, J. (1991, June 28). The unpeople. *New Statesman and Society,* 15–16.

Seccombe, K. (1999). *"So you think I drive a Cadillac?" Welfare recipients' perspectives on the system and its reform.* Needham Heights, MA: Allyn & Bacon.

Sklar, H. (2001, August 29). Minimum wage—It just doesn't add up. Retrieved from http://www.commondreams.org

Smith, G. (2003, June 2). Wasting away: Despite SARS, Mexico is still losing export ground to China. *Business Week,* 42–43.

Statistics Canada. (2003). 1990s a good decade for the rich. CBC News. Retrieved from http://www.cbc.ca

Stein, J. (2003, January 20). The real face of homelessness. *Time,* 52–57.

Stromberg, V. (2001, May 11). Letter to the editor. *Madre.* Retrieved from http://www.madre.org

Swarns, R. (2003, June 7). More than 13,000 may face deportation. *The New York Times.* Retrieved from http://www.NYTimes.com

Tax Policy Center. (2002). Tax facts. Retrieved from http://www.taxpolicycenter.org

Tennyson, A. L. (1979/1842). Ulysses. In *The Oxford Dictionary of Quotations* (3rd ed., p. 544). Oxford, UK: Oxford University Press.

Tice, C. J., & Perkins, K. (2002). *The faces of social policy: A strengths perspective.* Pacific Grove, CA: Brooks/Cole.

United Nations. (2003). *The world's women 2000: Trends and statistics.* New York: Author.

United Nations Development Fund for Women (UNIFEM). (2000). *Progress of the world's women 2000.* New York: United Nations.

United Nations Development Programme (UNDP). (2002). Human development report. Retrieved from http://www.undp.org

U.S. Census Bureau. (2000a). *Overview of race and Hispanic origin.* U.S. Department of Commerce, Economics and Statistics Administration. Retrieved from http://www.census.gov

U.S. Census Bureau. (2000b). Profile of selected economic characteristics: 2000. U.S. Census Bureau. Retrieved from http://factfinder.census .gov/home/en/datanotes/expsf4.htm

U.S. Hispanic, Asian populations booming. (2004, June 15). *USA Today*, p. A2.

U.S. signs free trade pact with Chile. (2003, June 9). *The New Zealand Herald.* Retrieved from http://www.nzherald.co.nz

van Wormer, K. (2004). *Confronting oppression and restoring justice: From policy analysis to social action.* Alexandria, VA: Council on Social Work Education.

van Wormer, K., & Davis, D. R. (2003). *Addiction treatment: A strengths perspective.* Belmont, CA: Brooks/Cole.

van Wormer, K., Wells, J., & Boes, M. (2000). *Social work with lesbians, gays, and bisexuals.* Boston: Allyn & Bacon.

Wanted: A new regional agenda for economic growth. (2003, April 26). *The Economist,* 27–29.

War Resisters League. (2004). Where your income tax money really goes. Retrieved from http://www.warresisters.org/piechart.htm

Watson, D. (2003, May 7). Record number of US children in extreme poverty. Retrieved from http://www.wsws.org

Waugh, P. (2003, May 12). Poverty levels have grown under Labour. *The Independent.* Retrieved from http://www.independent.co.uk

Weisman, J. (2003, September 27). Poverty rose, income fell in past year. *Washington Post,* p. A01.

Welch, W. (2003, June 3). Tax cuts to take effect by summer. *USA Today.* Retrieved from http://www.usatoday.com

Wiesel, E. (1982). *Night.* New York: Bantam Books.

Wilgoren, J. (2001, November 25). Swept up in a dragnet, hundreds sit in custody and ask, "Why?" *New York Times,* p. B5.

Wipf, J., & Wipf, P. (2001). Anti-immigrant sentiments soar. *Immigration Issues.* Retrieved from http://immigration.about.com/library

World Health Organization (WHO). (2000). Gender, health, and poverty (Fact Sheet #251). Geneva: Author.

World refugee survey 2003. (2003, June 8). *U.S. Newswire.* Retrieved from http://www.hvea.org

Young, I. M. (1990). *Justice and the politics of difference.* Princeton, NJ: Princeton University Press.

Zastrow, C. (2004). *Introduction to social work and social welfare: Empowering people* (8th ed.). Belmont, CA: Brooks/Cole.

CHAPTER

6

Where, after all, do universal human rights begin? In small places, close to home—so close and so small that they can't be seen on any map of the world. Yet they are the world of the individual person.

ELEANOR ROOSEVELT, 1958

Human Rights and Restorative Justice

© Rupert van Wormer

All justice reform, whether in the standard justice system or through restorative justice initiatives, must be contextualized within the broader recognition of people's human rights. The template for human rights is the United Nations (U.N.) Universal Declaration of Human Rights. The rights spelled out in that document are multidimensional: They relate to economic security, rights before the courts of law, and cultural protections for minority populations.

In the preceding chapter we considered the economic dimension. That economic rights are even included along with political and civil rights under the rubric of human rights may come as a surprise to many Americans (Wronka, 1998). Part of the reason may be because, as Gil (1998) informs us, the Bill of Rights of the U.S. Constitution guarantees civil and political rights only. The U.N. Universal Declaration of Human Rights, in contrast, provides for civil and political rights supplemental to comprehensive economic rights.

In any case, this chapter begins where the previous chapter left off, with an overview of civil rights as legal rights. The principal concern of this chapter, however, is with the domestic side of human rights, most especially with legal rights and wrongs.

The key aspects of criminal justice—crime, courts, and corrections—are part of the fabric of American society, indeed, of virtually any society. The idea that criminal justice systems are organic and rooted in society is an underlying assumption of this volume. In the pages ahead, we look at the criminal justice process with special emphasis on one undeniable dimension in the United States: racism—racism embodied in the law, and in the sanctions imposed by the law. The "ultimate sanction," the death penalty, will be examined against a human rights backdrop. Infused with ideology and emotion, the U.S. criminal justice labyrinth does not offer a pretty picture, but rather one marred by the public's seemingly insatiable appetite for vengeance.

Drawing on the Universal Declaration of Human Rights as a framework, we consider such issues as war and peace, terrorism, war crimes, and violence of the most brutal sort resulting in maiming and death, which is systematically practiced in many parts of the globe. Topics for special consideration are the human rights violations of slavery and mass rape as weapons of war. Then we turn our attention to trends within the U.S. criminal justice system with an examination of crime rates, mass incarceration, the war on drugs as a war on minorities, and the death penalty, which is state-sanctioned violence against the person. In our discussion of human rights violations taking place in U.S. prisons, we will rely on facts and figures from investigations by Amnesty International (AI) and other nongovernmental organizations (NGOs) such as Human Rights Watch. Human rights violations throughout the world are described in this chapter.

The chapter ends with a description of promising restorative justice initiatives and a plea for sentencing reform. Many of the solutions to problems related to personal and international conflict the world faces today can be found in the centuries-old principle of restoring peace and justice.

Introduction

Most social workers, if asked to summarize the value base of their practice, would probably use the term *social justice* rather than *human rights* (Ife, 2001). Social justice, in fact, is the second of the core social work values listed in the National Association of Social Workers (NASW) *Code of Ethics* (see Appendix B). *Human rights,* a term that I will argue has more clout than *social justice* (the referents of which are extremely vague), is included in the International Federation of Social Workers (IFSW) and the International Association of Schools of Social Work (IASSW; 2004) *Code of Ethics* (see Appendix C—namely, Section 2, Definition of Social Work; Section 3, International Conventions; and Section 4.1, Human Rights and Human Dignity). The majority of the nation members of IFSW (e.g., Australia, Britain, Denmark, France, and Turkey) include a reference to human rights. The United States has not yet done so but, as an active member of IFSW, can be expected to do so in the future. (See http://www.ifsw.org to compare the various codes.)

To learn how widely or rarely the human rights concept is used in social work, I searched the indexes of the leading introductory social welfare/social work texts in the field. *Human rights* was indexed in the introductory texts only by DiNitto (2003) and Jansson (2001), and then discussed only in a historical context. (Others consulted were Dolgoff and Feldstein, 2003; Johnson, Schwartz, and Tate, 1997; Karger and Stoesz, 2002; Kirst-Ashman, 2003; Mandiberg, 2000; Popple and Leighninger, 2002; Suppes and Wells, 2003; and Zastrow, 2004.) The international social work texts of Dominelli (2002), Healy (2001), and Ramanathan and Link (1999), as I expected, did contain multiple references to global human rights documents. The message seems to be that for ordinary, home-based social work practice and policy-making efforts, any reference to universal standards as codified in international law is irrelevant, implying that students of U.S. social welfare or social work need not view their government's policies within the context of global standards.

This situation is rapidly changing, however—an observation that is based on four developments: the Council on Social Work Education (CSWE; 2003) requirement that social and economic justice content be grounded in an understanding of human and civil rights and the global interconnections of oppression (Standard 4.2); NASW's (2003c) policy statement endorsing a human rights focus; NASW's alliance with Canada as joint members of IFSW; and the increasing globalization of the social work profession that parallels the globalization of just about everything else. A recent Internet search of *Social Work Abstracts* revealed 107 records on the subject of human rights: Among the topics covered were treatment of mental health patients, the needs of women with disabilities, gay/lesbian rights, and survivors of torture and war. Many of the sources were from the United States as well as the United Kingdom, Canada, and India.

The social work profession has a long tradition of promoting social justice activities. Traditionally, social workers as social democrats condemned gross inequalities of income, opportunities, affirmative action, and living conditions.

Consistently, the state has been favored as the arena for governing the economic process rather than, as often occurs today, looking to the global economic market as the shaper of the political structure (Mullaly, 1997). In holding the state accountable to standards as codified in international law, the effectiveness of the social work mission will be enhanced.

The human rights value base, as articulated in various legal documents, parallels the values of our profession, and social workers in the United States, following the path of the international social work community, are only on the threshold of this realization. NASW (2003c) has taken a decisive step toward moving the profession forward by issuing the following policy statement:

> Social work can be proud of its heritage. It is the only profession imbued with social justice as its fundamental value and concern. But social justice is a fairness doctrine that provides civil and political leeway in deciding what is just and unjust. Human rights, on the other hand, encompasses social justice, but transcends civil and political customs, in consideration of the basic life-sustaining needs of all human beings, without distinction. (p. 211)

Another milestone has occurred in the publication of the definitive *Social Work and Human Rights: A Foundation for Policy and Practice* by Elisabeth Reichert (2003). This book helps us connect the dots between values set forth in the NASW *Code of Ethics* and human rights documents. For the occasion of writing the present book, I invited Reichert to share with us her understanding of human rights and of social work as a human rights profession. She generously shares her expertise in Box 6.1.

The United Nations (U.N.) Universal Declaration of Human Rights

In *A World Made New: Eleanor Roosevelt and the Universal Declaration of Human Rights,* Mary Ann Glendon (2001) takes us step-by-step into the political history that culminated in one of the greatest documents of all times. Clearly ahead of its time, this document—which has been called "a Magna Carta for all humanity"—had as its basic assumption, according to Glendon, the belief that the causes of atrocities and armed conflict are rooted in poverty and discrimination. In addition, this international human rights document assumes that civil and political rights cannot be assured in the absence of economic rights (Gil, 1998).

In the aftermath of the Nuremberg war crimes trials that prosecuted leading Nazis under the novel charge of crimes against humanity, in order to ensure that the horrors of the Holocaust would never happen again, the framers of the U.N. Declaration set to work. President Truman appointed Eleanor Roosevelt as U.S. delegate to the United Nations. No person could have been better qualified to support the late President Franklin Roosevelt's Four Freedoms—freedom of speech and expression, freedom to worship, freedom from want, and freedom from fear of aggression (as outlined in his 1941 State of the Union address)—than was his wife, Eleanor. This reserved but courageous woman chaired the

6.1 On Human Rights

Elisabeth Reichert, MSSW, PhD,
Southern Illinois University at Carbondale

Human rights have gone global not because it serves the interests of the powerful but primarily because it has advanced the interest of the powerless.

Ignatieff, 2001, p. 7

What Are Human Rights?

The concept of human rights has occupied social workers, educators, philosophers, lawyers, and politicians for ages. The proposition that all individuals who inhabit the planet Earth share inherent privileges and rights has great attraction. This commonality among all who reside on the planet, regardless of country or nationality, aims to bring individuals closer together than they might otherwise be. After all, if someone residing in the United States acknowledges that someone residing in Russia or China has the same right to a safe, nonviolent environment, this link can lead to better cooperation in resolving key issues affecting the human existence.

Human rights cover domestic, as well as international, circumstances. Unless individuals, communities, corporations, governments, and other groups recognize human rights at home, promotion of human rights on a broader level appears meaningless or, at best, superficial. The most appropriate place to begin the study and application of human rights is within one's own environment. Only after the individual, entity, or group thoroughly understands human rights in a local sense can human rights be expanded to a broader spectrum of circumstances.

Definition of Human Rights

Although no single definition can possibly cover the entire gamut of what human rights involve, the idea of human rights can generally be defined as:

those rights, which are inherent in our nature and without which we cannot live as human beings. Human rights and fundamental freedoms allow us to fully develop and use our human qualities, our intelli-

gence, our talents and our conscience and to satisfy our spiritual and other needs. They are based on mankind's increasing demand for a life in which the inherent dignity and worth of each human being will receive respect and protection. (United Nations [U.N.], 1987)

People from different backgrounds readily endorse the concept of human rights, which refers to those rights that every human being possesses and is entitled to enjoy simply by virtue of being human (Ife, 2001).

Universal Declaration of Human Rights

The starting point in understanding human rights lies within the U.N. Universal Declaration of Human Rights. Most nations, including the United States, have approved this 1948 document, which lists specific human rights. The Declaration is not legally binding on any country that approves it, yet approval of the Declaration by a country indicates, at a minimum, a commitment to satisfying the specified rights.

The Universal Declaration contains three distinct sets or generations of human rights. The first set or generation lists political and individual freedoms that are similar to what Americans view as human rights. The right to a fair trial, freedom of speech and religion, freedom of movement and assembly, and guarantees against discrimination, slavery, and torture fall within these political and civil human rights (U.N., 1948, Articles 2–15).

Although much of the Universal Declaration addresses political and individual freedoms similar to those contained in the U.S. Constitution and its Bill of Rights, the Universal Declaration goes further. Reading beyond the initial set of human rights in the Declaration reveals another set of human rights that addresses economic and social welfare concepts. This set of rights attempts to ensure each resident of a country an adequate standard of living based on the resources of that country. Under this second set of human rights, everyone "has the right to a standard of living adequate for the health and well-being of himself and of his family, including food, clothing, housing and medical care and necessary social services." In addition, "motherhood and childhood are entitled to special care and assistance," and everyone has the right to a free education at the elementary level (U.N., 1948, Articles 16–27).

Americans applaud themselves for their strong commitment to the first set of human rights enumerated in the Universal Declaration, but within the second group of human rights, America frequently comes up short. Compared to many other countries, the United States fails to fulfill its obligation to promote economic and social human rights (Reichert & McCormick, 1997). For instance, our failure to provide adequate health care for all expectant mothers and children violates the same Universal Declaration of Human Rights that U.S. political leaders continually use to denigrate China, Cuba, Iraq, and other countries. The infant mortality rate, meaning the death of children in the first year of their lives, is higher in the United States than in any other industrialized country (United Nations Development Programme, 2003). Within the United States itself, disparity in infant mortality rates exists among racial groups, with African American infants suffering a mortality rate more than twice that of non-Hispanic whites (U.S. Department of Health and Human Services, 2000). While this poor ranking in infant mortality may not be entirely due to the lack of adequate health care, the failure of Americans to ensure health care to all residents most likely plays a role.

A third and final set of human rights involves collective rights among nations. This set of rights is the least developed among the three types of human rights. Under the 1948 Declaration, everyone "is entitled to a social and international order in which the rights and freedoms" listed in the document can be fully realized (U.N., 1948, Articles 28–30). Essentially, promotion of collective human rights requires intergovernmental cooperation on world issues, including environmental standards relevant to clean air, soil, and water. Industrialized countries should not take advantage of less economically developed countries by exploiting resources.

Clearly, as defined by the Universal Declaration, human rights cover much more than political rights. Social welfare benefits are as important a human right as the right to live without discrimination. The Declaration also provides that "everyone" is entitled to all the rights and freedoms listed in the Declaration without distinction.

Universality and Indivisibility

The concept of universality underpins human rights. Every individual has a claim to enjoyment of human rights, wherever the individual resides. For example, human rights include adequate health care and nutrition for everyone. Perhaps a country's resources are insufficient to provide universal health care and food, and therefore, not everyone receives adequate care and nutrition. However, because health care and food are integral to human rights, governments have an obligation to provide a framework for ensuring the delivery of these rights.

Not all human rights are so clear-cut as the examples previously given, which can result in reluctance to promote a particular human right. The notion of universality may clash with particular cultures, laws, policies, morals, and regimes that fail to recognize a particular human right in question. In some countries, employment and other forms of discrimination against gays and lesbians is allowed because cultural or religious norms permit this type of discrimination. Such discrimination violates human rights principles even though human rights require sensitivity to culture and religion. This clash between human rights and cultural or religious norms raises a basic question: Which should prevail, the cultural or religious norm or the human right? If human rights apply to everyone, then the human right must prevail. Of course, the issue is not so concrete. Who defines a human right? Who benefits from the definition? Who loses from the definition? Whose voices are being heard in enforcing human rights? Who defines culture and cultural norms? Does one government have the right to tell

(continued)

6.1 *continued*

another government that its policies violate a human right? In the case of disagreement over interpretation of a human right, who decides? The infusion of human rights into a society often requires great consideration.

In addition to universality, the other concept important to human rights is that of indivisibility. The concept of indivisibility refers to the necessity that government and individuals recognize each human right and not selectively promote some rights over others. As noted previously, the United States tends to recognize political and civil human rights over social welfare rights. For instance, the United States does not guarantee health care to all its citizens but guarantees (at least on paper) due process in criminal trials. Yet, without adequate health care, an individual may fail to attend to an illness that becomes life-threatening or debilitating. Impaired health reduces an individual's enjoyment of other human rights. Can the right to due process then be more important than the right to adequate health care, especially where the individual has never been arrested for any crime? Ironically, individuals detained in jail or prisons in the United States are guaranteed health care, something other individuals are not.

After the Universal Declaration, numerous other documents addressing specific areas of human rights have come into existence, including the International Covenant on Civil and Political Rights; the International Covenant on Economic, Social and Cultural Rights; the Convention on the Rights of the Child; and the Convention on the Elimination of All Forms of Discrimination against Women (CEDAW). However, the starting point for any contemporary human rights discussion remains the Universal Declaration.

Human Rights and Social Work

While social workers must have knowledge of human rights to apply human rights principles to their practice, knowledge alone may not provide a sufficient basis by which to connect human rights to social work practice. Social workers who are familiar with the Universal Declaration, for example, might view human rights as too theoretical or legalistic, which can create difficulties in connecting the concept to their practice. However, a relatively straightforward way exists by which social workers in the United States can re adily see the connection between human rights and their profession. The NASW *Code of Ethics* under which most U.S. social workers practice contains numerous references to human rights. Provisions of the *Code* essentially require adherence to human rights principles, without actually using the term *human rights*. By identifying the *Code* as a human rights document, social workers can better understand why their profession is a human rights profession and apply human rights to practice.

The importance of human rights to the social work profession cannot be overstated. In confronting social issues, human rights provide an important link between the individual and the broader spectrum of

Human Rights Commission during its first crucial years. From that vantage point, she focused her attention and lobbying efforts on the creation of international law for the promotion of human rights. The resulting document, which forged an uneasy path of compromise between the warring doctrines of capitalism and communism and between East and West, was largely Roosevelt's per-

society. As an example, human rights do not view the battering of women as a problem of a particular individual. Instead, human rights define such battering as a structural and political problem. A woman has a human right not to be battered, regardless of cultural norms or other accepted practices allowing or justifying the battering (Bunch, 1991). This classification of domestic violence into a human rights issue communicates to victims of domestic violence that they are human beings entitled to protection, and not simply "sick" individuals in need of treatment (Witkin, 1998). Reframing a social problem like domestic violence into a human rights issue also creates an international context in which to combat domestic violence. International pressure may induce governments to actively try to prevent domestic violence, knowing that to do otherwise can result in allegations of violating human rights.

Human rights issues, such as freedom from physical abuse and a right to medical care and housing, clearly fall within the ethical responsibilities of social workers. By emphasizing the human rights aspect of social work, social workers can enhance their own fulfillment of ethical responsibilities. Social workers who connect human rights issues with ethical principles can also better identify issues that go beyond individual circumstances. For instance, from a human rights perspective, a social worker would not view domestic violence simply as an issue involving the dynamics of the individual or couple, but also as an issue that operates on a national or international scale. If it is a human right to be safe and secure, then this right would apply to everyone at any place and at any time, irrespective of circumstances.

Individuals alone may not always be capable of overcoming oppression, especially when obstacles arise from broader structural difficulties. Adopting a human rights perspective can help social workers more readily identify structural difficulties in planning appropriate interventions.

Human rights are continually evolving, especially at the grassroots level. Tensions caused by differing viewpoints on human rights will always exist. Issues of culture, religion, and power will always be part of the struggle for human rights. Unquestionably, social workers everywhere have a unique role to play in promoting further development of human rights in every society.

REFERENCES

Bunch, C. (1991). Women's rights as human rights: Toward a revision of human rights. In C. Bunch & R. Carrillo (Eds.), *Gender violence: A development and human rights issue* (pp. 3–18). New Brunswick, NJ: Center for Women's Global Leadership.

Ife, J. (2001). *Human rights and social work: Towards rights based practice.* Cambridge, MA: Cambridge University Press.

Ignatieff, M. (2001). *Human rights as politics and idolatry.* Princeton, NJ: Princeton University Press.

Reichert, E., & McCormick, R. (1997). Different approaches to child welfare: United States and Germany. *Journal of Law and Social Work, 6*(2), 17–33.

United Nations (U.N.). (1948). *Universal declaration of human rights.* New York: Author.

United Nations (U.N.). (1987). *Human rights: Questions and answers.* New York: Author.

United Nations Development Programme. (2003). *United Nations human development report.* Retrieved from http://hdr.undp.org

U.S. Department of Health and Human Services, Centers for Disease Control. (2000). Fact sheet. Retrieved from http://www.cdc.gov.nchs/releases/00facts/infantmo.htm

Witkin, S. (1998). Editorial: Human rights and social work. *Social Work, 43,* 197–201.

Source: E. Reichert, *Social Work and Human Rights: A Foundation for Policy and Practice* (2003). New York: Columbia University Press. Reprinted by permission of Elisabeth Reichert.

sonal gift to the world. In 1948, marking a milestone in human relations, the General Assembly of the U.N. unanimously adopted the Universal Declaration of Human Rights.

Read the complete Declaration in Appendix A of this text. As you read through the 30 articles, keep in mind that collectively they are about the ways in which a state treats (or should treat) its citizens. The standards provided in the Declaration relate not to the violation of individuals in personal crime but to violations sanctioned by the state such as in police torture of suspects. Nongovernmental organizations (NGOs) such as Amnesty International and Human Rights Watch conduct research on such violations and report their findings to the U.N.

Although originally nonbinding, the principles immortalized in the Declaration increasingly have acquired legal force, mainly through their incorporation into the laws of individual nations. Today, in the United States, the principles laid down in this document compose what is called, in legal jargon, customary international law. Following a federal decision in 1980 that ruled against a torturer in Paraguay, governments are beholden to universal principles (Wronka, 1999).

One serious flaw in obtaining justice in the United States under the auspices of the U.S. Declaration is the fact that the United States has ratified only that portion of the document that is consistent with the U.S. Constitution, in other words, the recognition of political and civil rights. In 1977, then U.S. President Jimmy Carter, hoping to correct this omission, signed the U.N. International Covenant on Economic, Social, and Cultural Rights. This document, which has been signed by 145 nations, still awaits U.S. Senate ratification (Food First, 2002). The wait may be a long one.

As a global profession, social work is concerned with economic and social rights as well as with civil rights. (When people are hungry, in fact, their concern with personal liberties is apt to be slight.) As a global profession, social work can be expected increasingly to look to human rights documents such as the Universal Declaration as a blueprint for policy practice. The standard is there. Consider Article 25, for example:

1. Everyone has the right to a standard of living adequate for the health and well-being of himself and of his family, including food, clothing, housing and medical care and necessary social services, and the right to security in the event of unemployment, sickness, disability, widowhood, old age or other lack of livelihood in circumstances beyond his control.
2. Motherhood and childhood are entitled to special care and assistance. All children, whether born in or out of wedlock, shall enjoy the same social protections.

Three categories of rights are provided in the Declaration: economic and cultural rights; protection against discrimination based on race, color, sex, language, religion, and political opinion; and civil and political rights against the arbitrary powers of the state. Those articles of the Declaration concerned with economic, social, and cultural rights range from the less urgent rights of "rest, leisure, and reasonable limitation of working hours and periodic holidays with pay" (Article 24) to the more fundamental rights of food, housing, health care, work, and social security (Article 25). The fact that these rights are included nowhere in the U.S. Constitution (though they are in many European constitutions) has hindered the American people in their claims to basic social and economic benefits.

Alisa Watkinson (2001), writing from a Canadian perspective, argues that the inclusion of human rights documents and legal decisions arising from them is an essential part of social work education. Human rights laws, moreover, as Watkinson indicates, "provide a valuable theoretical and practical base for assisting in social change" (p. 271). Because Canada was a signatory (unlike the United States) to the Covenant on Economic, Social and Political Rights, social workers in that country can use the document as a touchstone by which to examine social policy and to hold the government accountable. All the provinces in Canada as well as the federal government, in fact, have human rights legislation that is administered by a Human Rights Commission. For Canadian social workers, as Watkinson argues, human rights laws can be a valuable tool for advocacy for social and economic justice within the era of globalization.

NASW (2003c) strongly promotes U.S. ratification of the Universal Declaration in its entirety, as well as other critical U.N. treaties such as the Covenant on Economic, Social and Cultural Rights, and the Convention on the Rights of the Child. NASW also urges passage of the Convention on the Elimination of All Forces of Discrimination against Women which President Jimmy Carter signed but which the Senate never has ratified.

The International Federation of Social Workers (IFSW) has established a Human Rights Commission to ensure that the organization maintains a human rights orientation in all its activities. The Commission advocates for the release of social workers who are incarcerated because of their work and others at risk of torture or death throughout the world. The Commission works closely with the U.N. Commission on Human Rights (Johannesen, 2003). The IFSW commission also has an official liaison to Amnesty International (Healy, 2001).

In his lead editorial, the editor of *Social Work,* Stanley Witkin (1998), recommended using a human rights lens to new social problems such as violence against women. Rather than viewing such violence as a relationship or psychological issue, social workers can reframe the antiwoman attacks from a human rights perspective. Such reframing, as Witkin suggests, brings the force of international law to bear on governments that allow for such violence and encourages the development of resources such as shelters for abuse victims.

The rights contained in the Declaration and the two covenants have been further elaborated in such legal documents as the International Convention on the Elimination of All Forms of Racial Discrimination (adopted by the U.N. General Assembly in 1969), which declares dissemination of ideas based on racial superiority or hatred as being punishable by law; the Convention on the Elimination of All Forms of Discrimination against Women (adopted by the General Assembly in 1979), covering measures to be taken for eliminating discrimination against women in political and public life, education, employment, health, marriage and family; and the Convention on the Rights of the Child (adopted by the General Assembly in 1989), which lays down guarantees in terms of the child's human rights. Of these important initiatives, the United States has ratified only the Elimination of All Forms of Racial Discrimination.

In 2002, a major milestone was reached when, at a ceremony at the U.N., the last two of the 60 nations needed to formally ratify the treaty on the

International Criminal Court became a reality. The creation of this new war-crimes tribunal, the world's first permanent war-crimes tribunal, has been hailed by human rights activists but strongly opposed by the United States (Lederer, 2002). The U.S. objection is based on the fear that American citizens could be subjected to politically motivated prosecutions.

America's reluctance to be judged in accordance with international law cannot shield it from the scrutiny of NGOs such as Amnesty International (AI) and Human Rights Watch. A significant development in recent years is the fact that AI and Human Rights Watch investigations are given much more media attention than in the past in their documentation of human rights abuses. AI today devotes much attention to prison conditions, the "cruel, inhuman or degrading treatment or punishment" mentioned in Article 5 of the U.N. Universal Declaration of Human Rights (refer to Appendix A).

Each year AI presents its findings on the countries of the world in terms of violations of citizens by the state. Special attention is paid to the incarceration of persons for political reasons and the mistreatment of individuals accused of a crime. More than any other human rights monitoring organizations, AI (like Human Rights Watch) can make a reasonable claim to being politically nonpartisan. Accordingly, its fastidious research findings give meaning to the concept of universal standards of humanitarianism.

Human Rights Violations Worldwide

In its 2003 report, Amnesty International (AI) notes that the war on Iraq, which dominated the international agenda, diverted attention from other human rights issues. Irene Khan (2003), AI's secretary, offered a general message in the introduction to AI's annual report, which contained an extensive accounting of gains and setbacks for human rights in 151 countries and territories. As her theme, Khan chose the wars that have been conducted across the world, from Burundi to Israel to Afghanistan to Iraq, in the name of security and counter-terrorism. Khan does not equivocate; she articulates AI's unyielding commitment to the premise that human rights are not a luxury for good times but a standard for all times. Here is her message in part:

> The focus on national security has diverted attention from some very real threats that affect the lives of millions of people. The real sources of insecurity for many people lie in the failure to halt the unimpeded flow of small arms, to eradicate extreme poverty and preventable diseases, to arrest and treat the spread of HIV/AIDS, and deal with the social dimensions of globalization. Real security will remain illusory, especially for the poor, so long as police, courts and state institutions in many countries remain inept or corrupt. Many women will continue to feel insecure as long as they are unprotected from violence in their home and communities. Amnesty International's campaign on Russia has highlighted the failure of the parliament to adopt legislation to criminalize domestic violence, despite 50 drafts, in a country where some 14,000 women die at the hands of their partners or family members each year.

Governments are not entitled to respond to terror with terror. They are obliged at all times to act within the framework of international human rights and humanitarian law. The people who organize and perpetrate bombings of buses in Tel Aviv or a discotheque in Bali, who ambush and kill civilians in Burundi, or who take hostages in a theatre in Moscow must be brought to justice in accordance with standards of fair trial. So too must the Israeli soldiers who carry out unlawful killings in the Occupied Territories, the Indonesian police who torture in Aceh and Papua, the Russian security forces who rape villagers in Chechnya.

The United States comes in for criticism in this AI report for its detentions of prisoners of war in defiance of international law; according to the report, the United States turned "a blind eye to reports of torture or ill-treatment of suspects by its officials and allies, and sought to undermine the International Criminal Court through bilateral agreements. In the process, it undermined its own moral authority to speak out against human rights violations in other parts of the world" (p. 2 of 3).

The War on Terrorism

Social work and the peace movement have a longstanding connection. Jane Addams, the founding mother of social work, was a pacifist who saw herself as a citizen of the world. She believed that violence was used because people lacked knowledge of other ways to fight injustice (Farrell, 1967). Social work has continued to have a strong peace movement within its ranks. Social workers, as Verschelden (1993) tells us, have a moral responsibility to work toward redirections in federal spending—away from militarism and globally toward the creation of a safe and just environment. "Promoting peace and social justice and resisting nuclear war are consistent with the central values of the social work profession, which stress self-determination, human rights, and social equity" (Van Soest, 1995, p. 1814).

Under the U.S. Patriot Act of 2001, the Attorney General of the United States was given unprecedented powers to detain noncitizens on national security grounds. Under this act, noncitizens suspected of terrorist acts could be held in custody indefinitely (Human Rights Watch, 2002a). New orders by the president permitted military jurisdiction over noncitizens and military commissions to hear cases that were not subject to the rules governing due process safeguards required at regular military courts-martial. Such safeguards as presumption of innocence, protection against forced confessions, and the right of appeal would no longer apply. By November 2001, more than 1,100 people, mostly Arabs and Muslim men, had been detained in this fashion. These steps taken after September 11 were an erosion of key values including the rule of law according to the Human Rights Watch World Report.

Civil liberties do not count for much in a warfare state; the rights of people who look like the enemies count for little as well. Just as peace and social justice are interdependent (NASW, 2003e), so the impact of war is brutalizing on all those who are caught in its web. Not only the tragic loss of life and traumatized lives, but the enormous drain on the world's dwindling natural resources are anti-thetical to global social welfare and security as well as to the central purpose of the social work profession (NASW, 2003e). Even in the face of overt terrorist attacks on our country, it is vital that we work through international organizations to reduce violence against innocent civilians. "Full participation with such organizations as the U.N., the World Health Organization and the World Court are," as the NASW policy statement contends, "critical first steps in such an effort" (p. 268). In 2002, the first permanent World Court, the International Criminal Court (ICC), got the international backing it needed to investigate and prosecute individuals accused of genocide or other wars against humanity (Lederer, 2002). Such a truly international tribunal ideally would hold all countries accountable to standards of international law. Following September 11, a war mentality has ensued. In an article entitled "The Troubling New Face of America," recent Nobel Prize recipient Jimmy Carter (2002) expressed his concern:

> Fundamental changes are taking place in the historical policies of the United States with regard to human rights, our role in the community of nations and the Middle East peace process—largely without definitive debates (except at times within the administration). (p. A31)

In fact, however, wars and terrorism invariably have a dramatic effect on the systems of law and justice. In the American Civil War, President Lincoln cur-tailed many of the citizens' constitutional rights, an act for which he was greatly criticized. Restrictions on freedom of the press have characterized more recent antiterrorist operations. In the national interest, many of the traditional civil lib-erties are suspended. Britain, for example, responded to the Irish Republican Army's (IRA) bombing attacks with repressive measures that resulted in claims of human rights violations (Fairchild, 1993). Imprisonment of suspected terror-ists without trial, searches and seizures without warrants, and suspension of the right to remain silent under questioning ensued. Amnesty International (1999) detailed allegations of ill-treatment bordering on torture in Britain by police officers and private security guards. This human rights organization also pub-lished a report on political killings of IRA suspects by government officials in Northern Ireland. The Patriot Act passed in 2001 thus takes its place in a long line of actions associated with fear of internal strife. In the United States, in 2003, efforts to tighten Homeland Security paralleled mobilization for a "pre-emptive strike" on an enemy nation and assassination of national leaders who posed a threat.

War Crimes

During wartime, the standards of ordinary conduct concerning respect for human life, personal dignity, and personal property give way. Under the exigen-cies of war, horrible crimes against humanity are sometimes tolerated in the interests of defeat of the enemy or in wreaking revenge for atrocities inflicted by the other side. In wartime, the enemy is demonized; soldiers are trained to kill, and normal inhibitions against violence, including genocide, are loosened. From their outset, according to the encyclopedia, war-crime trials were dismissed by critics as "victor's justice" because only individuals from defeated countries were prosecuted.

What constitutes a war crime? How can it be differentiated from ordinary combat? *War crimes* are acts of war determined to be characterized as atrocities by international oversight bodies. According to the entry "war crime" in the *Encyclopaedia Britannica* (2003), the term *war crime* has been used in a very imprecise fashion; modern definitions are more expansive than earlier, criminalizing atrocities by civilians as well as by military personnel. Included under the rubric of war crimes are *crimes against humanity,* or the political, racial, and religious persecution of civilians.

Genocide—the attempt to wipe out an entire population or ethnic group, such as in Nazi Germany, Nigeria, Cambodia, Rwanda, and Yugoslavia—is the most obvious form of crime against humanity. Throughout history, most nations have "turned a blind eye" to genocidal campaigns, only becoming involved as refugees have migrated across borders. Despite the U.N. Genocide Convention in 1948, the West has remained as reluctant to respond to genocidal campaigns as it was initially regarding the situation of Turkish Armenians and the Nazi-led Holocaust (Power, 2002). Sometimes nations that have been involved in persecutions of their people (such as Saddam Hussein's massacre of Iraqi Kurds) have continued to receive military and other assistance, as Power suggests.

Since World War II, war-crime trials have been conducted by international tribunals in Nuremburg, Tokyo, and, more recently, The Hague (regarding Rwanda and former Yugoslavia). In none of these trials were individuals relieved of criminal liability for war crimes committed under orders from authorities ("War Crime," 2003). The general procedure set by the Nuremburg trials is the hearing of cases against the smaller number of principals responsible for the atrocities. The advantages of an international tribunal are in the worldwide message that such violence is widely condemned and in the image of impartiality. The "power of shame" can play a role both as an enforcement tool and in helping to impart justice to the victim population.

An exciting development today is the establishment of a permanent world criminal tribunal, the ICC described earlier. The ICC, which will have jurisdiction over crimes against humanity committed by ratifying states and nationals of those states, will be based in The Hague (Human Rights Watch, 2003b). As of May 2003, 90 countries have ratified this treaty. Unfortunately, the United States under the Bush administration has expressed strong opposition to the existence of the world court and has withdrawn the U.S. signature on the treaty (Human Rights Watch, 2003b). Moreover, special arrangements were made with the U.N. to protect U.S. "peacekeepers" from accountability to the international body for human rights violations. Despite this U.S. opposition, however, the establishment of such a world court of justice, a dream ever since the U.N. was established, is a major victory for world peace and human rights.

Amnesty International (AI) has played an important role in lobbying for the ICC (Pittaway, 2003). To learn of the human rights violations in any particular country, simply go to AI's annual report, contained in most academic libraries, or on the Internet to http://www.amnesty.org and under search, type in the name of the country. Type in Turkey, for example, and you get: "Turkey: End Sexual Torture against Women in Custody!" The report describes the plight of Kurdish women in police custody among other abuses. Check out the USA and you will find among the violations the detention without charge of over 600 foreign nationals captured in Afghanistan and held at Guantanamo Bay, Cuba. Other topics covered include detentions of Muslim men of Arab descent in the United States, conditions in supermax prisons, and the death penalty. Under violations by the Canadian government, you will find a description of police violence against Native Canadians and denial of rights to asylum seekers. And so we could go on and on.

Rape in War

Another recent development of consequence is the belated recognition of rape of the enemy's women—a common occurrence during and after a war—as a war crime. The International War Crimes Tribunal in The Hague took a revolutionary step when three Bosnian soldiers were convicted of rape and sexual enslavement as crimes against humanity. The judgment followed years of lobbying by women's rights groups (Pittaway, 2003). Women's rights activists participated in every major U.N. preparatory meeting on the ICC (Human Rights Watch, 2002b).

Now, the new International Criminal Court (ICC), which will replace the U.N. tribunals that have been convened on strictly an ad-hoc basis, has officially (in statutes seven and eight) declared rape in a conflict situation to be a war crime and a crime against humanity. The ICC provides witness and victim protection and the possibility of redress for the wrongs done. Counseling and other assistance will be provided through the Victims and Witnesses Unit (Human Rights Watch, 2003b).

To put this development in perspective, I will draw on the feminist literature on the psychology of rape in war. What we learn from the literature is this universal truth: Rape of the enemy's women is so much a part of war and its aftermath that under conditions of military occupation, it is more remarkable in its absence than in its presence. The rape that accompanies war involves both a tremendous act of aggression and humiliation against a conquered people and a reward to soldiers who are encouraged by their officers to loot a village and rape the women at will. Rape is the act of patriotism, misogyny, and lust rolled into one. In the name of victory and the power of the gun, war provides men with a tacit license to rape (Brownmiller, 1975). In her analysis of rape in warfare, Brownmiller (1993) forcefully concludes:

> Sexual sadism arises with astonishing rapidity in ground warfare when the penis becomes justified as a weapon in a logistical reality of unarmed non-combatants, encircled and trapped. Rape of a doubly dehumanized object—as woman, as enemy—carries its own terrible logic. In one act of aggression, the collective spirit of women *and* of the nation is broken, leaving a reminder long after the troops depart. And if she survives the assault, what does the victim of wartime rape

become to her people? Evidence of the enemy's bestiality. Symbol of her nation's defeat. A pariah. Damaged property. A pawn in the subtle wars of international propaganda. (p. 37)

Notably, in the battles of ancient Greece, the Crusades, the U.S. Civil War, World Wars I and II, and Vietnam, rape was utilized as a physical and psychological weapon of war (Wing & Merchan, 1993). Within this context, it is not surprising to hear of mass rapes by all factions in the Bosnian and Rwandan conflicts. In Haiti, too, military rapists targeted women in terrorism preceding the recent government overthrow. Compounding the injury to the victims, the husbands often transfer their feelings of revulsion from the enemy to their victimized wives. Such rejection of women as defiled beings is consistent with traditional patriarchal ideology that universally demands that women should not allow more than one man to have access to their bodies (Wetzel, 1993).

Law professor Adrien Wing, herself a descendant of Confederate General Beauregard and of one of his slave-mistresses, draws a gripping parallel between the ethnic cleansing and forced impregnation in Bosnia and the history of rape and miscegenation in the American South (Wing & Merchan, 1993). On six key attributes related to what Wing and Merchan call "spirit injury" or "the slow death of the psyche, of the soul, and of the identity of the individual" (p. 2) and of the group, the early American South and Bosnia share a common ground. These traits are: rape as defilement not only of the individual woman but of a whole culture; rape as silence as the women internalize their experience of oppression, rendering them more vulnerable to males within their own group; rape as sexuality, with raped women seen as promiscuous and impure; rape as emasculation of men due to their sense of helplessness to protect their wives and daughters; rape as trespass on the "property" rights of men, most pronounced under slavery where the women were the property of their white masters, as were the racially mixed offspring; and rape as pollution of the victim and of her children born as a result of nonconsensual sex.

Rape as an instrument of war is clearly a violation of international law and its proscriptions against war crimes, taking of hostages, torture, and violation of human dignity (Wing & Merchan, 1993). Deplorably, although torture has been prosecuted as a war crime, only recently has war-rape been considered anything more than an inevitable by-product of war. Now at last, however, women's rights are being seen as human rights. Justice and accountability for past abuses increasingly are seen as bedrock issues for human rights organizations everywhere, and as a vital protection against future abuses. That the ICC has come into force today as a potentially powerful instrument for protecting women's rights is a testament to the mass networking and courage of women's rights activists throughout the world (Human Rights Watch, 2002b).

Women, War, and Peace

The title for this section is taken from a book by Elisabeth Rehn of Finland and Ellen Johnson Sirleaf of Liberia. Commissioned by the U.N. Development Fund for Women (UNIFEM), Rehn and Sirleaf (2002) conducted an independent expert assessment on the gender dimensions of conflict. This effort parallels a new impetus by the U.N. Security Council to attend to the needs of war-affected women.

Women, War and Peace documents in graphic detail the injustices inflicted upon the bodies and lives of women stemming from the horrors of war and its aftermath. Women in war zones throughout the world shared the impact of aimed conflict on their families. They told how militarization affected their sons, their husbands, and their brothers—turning them into different, often explosive and violent people. They described the unaccustomed roles they were required to fill as the peacetime infrastructure was destroyed. In the upheaval that follows war, women are especially vulnerable, as the social and legal institutions are weakened. The status of women in Afghanistan, for example, is as precarious as ever; many still have not felt secure enough to remove the burka, and some of the new girls' schools have been set on fire. Rehn and Sirleaf generalize their findings in the book's introduction:

> While more men are killed in war, women often experience violence, forced pregnancy, abduction and sexual abuse and slavery. Their bodies, deliberately infected with HIV/AIDS or carrying a child conceived in rape, have been used as envelopes to send messages to the perceived enemy. (p. 1)

The injury to women and their families can be seen as well in uprootedness; mental trauma; lack of food, potable water, and electricity; health problems stemming from exposure to chemicals such as uranium; violence and sexual assault in refugee camps; and the numbers resorting to sex work to feed their children. Eighty percent of the world's refugees are women and children.

Although 75 percent of the world's war casualties today are civilians, more men than women die in war. After the first Gulf War, divorce rates skyrocketed in communities surrounding large army bases (Zamichow & Perry, 2003). Domestic violence increased in Marine communities. About 15 percent of veterans experience emotional problems stemming from the trauma of warfare. Veterans of the Iraq war are reporting sleeping and drinking problems and a sense of alienation (Zamichow & Perry, 2003).

Rehn and Sirleaf credit the U.N. for its expression of political commitment to women's special needs in war-torn societies. But women need to be at the forefront of peacemaking, humanitarian relief efforts; the resources allocated to the relief efforts are entirely inadequate, and greater high-level support to effectively address the gender dimensions of war and peace is required.

One model program that could be emulated elsewhere is the International Rescue Committee (IRC) in Sierra Leone. This group aids the victims of war. Susan Koch (2003), a global health expert, describes the remarkable work performed by this organization. Originally founded by Albert Einstein, the IRC conducts a reunification project in war-torn Sierra Leone to reunite abducted girls and their families or to help them get educated for a new life if family members cannot be found. The matter of reunification is problematic because typically the girls who were kidnapped were sexually abused and used as sex slaves. Some families might refuse to take them back, seeing them as tainted or as changed. The IRC works to locate the families. Videotapes are made of the girls talking about how much they want to come home, and the families see these tapes. Then, if they are receptive, family members are videotaped saying how much they miss their daughter. To date, there have been 60 successful reunifications.

Violations of Women Domestically

Ponder the following headlines:

- "Kadra: Female Genital Mutilation Exposed," *MS* (Bakke, 2001)
- "Pakistan's Fiery Shame: Women Die in Stove Deaths," *Women's E News* (Terzieff, 2002)
- "Afghan Women Remain Victims of Hope Unfulfilled," *Toronto Star* (Landsberg, 2002)
- "The Lack of Equal Rights for African Women is a Central Cause of the Rapid Transmission of HIV/AIDS on the Continent" (UNIFEM, 2003)
- "Sierra Leone: Human Rights Watch Details Sexual Atrocities in Civil War" (United Nations [U.N.], 2003b)
- "Book Credits Women's Shelters for Saving Men's Lives," *Waterloo–Cedar Falls Courier* (A. Wind, 2000)

Ever since Afghanistan came on our radar screen as the homeland of woman-hating, American politicians have been more sensitized to the rights of women: So wrote Ellen Goodman (2002) in her editorial carried by the *Baltimore Sun.* Yet the United States stands alone among Western nations in its reluctance to ratify the U.N. Convention on the Elimination of All Forms of Discrimination against Women. President Jimmy Carter signed it, but the U.S. Senate has never ratified it. Conservatives, as Goodman suggests, worry about the destruction of the family. If the United States would join other nations in endorsing this treaty, it would provide a tool for women fighting for their lives across the world. "Women from Colombia to Rwanda have used the treaty as a standard to rewrite laws on inheritance and domestic abuse, to change the patterns of education and employment," Goodman states (p. 15A).

The Beijing Fourth World Conference in 1995 marked a milestone in women's rights history as women of the world let go of their cultural differences and stood united against antiwoman violence, whether in the home or community. Still the horror stories persist—the infanticides in China of unwanted girls, the public stoning of rape *victims* in Pakistan (*Time,* 2002). There is a saying in Russia, "If he loves you, he beats you" (Basu, 1999). Russian men who beat or rape their wives or partners are unlikely to face prosecution. With a population nearly half the size of the United States, Russian women are murdered by family members at ten times the American rate. The highest suicide rate for women in the world occurs in China. World Bank researchers found that young, rural Chinese women are killing themselves at an alarming rate of 500 per day (Lamb, 1999). Arranged marriages are still common there, and the young brides are expected to wait on their mothers-in-law as servants.

Although domestic violence is the leading cause of female injury in almost every country in the world, typically it has been defined by the state as a private matter or simply ignored. According to a World Health Report based on 48 surveys from around the world, between 10 and 69 percent of women report having been physically assaulted by a partner. In the United States, 22 percent report domestic violence (Lite, 2002). Such violence is now regarded by the U.N. as a worldwide public health problem. In its comprehensive report entitled *The World's Women 2000,* the U.N. (2003b) listed the following trends and statistics:

▮ Physical and sexual abuse affect millions of girls and women worldwide—and are known to be seriously underreported.

▮ In some African countries, more than half of all women and girls have undergone female genital mutilation, and the prevalence of this practice is not declining.

▮ Women and girls comprise half of the world's refugees and, as refugees, are particularly vulnerable to sexual violence while in flight, in refugee camps, and during resettlement.

▮ Despite calls for gender equality, women are significantly underrepresented in governments, political parties, and at the United Nations.

Though in the past violence against women in the home was viewed as a private matter, today the international community has recognized such violence against women as a human rights issue and holds the state responsible for taking steps to protect women (Amnesty International [AI], 2001).

In honor of International Women's Day in 2000, U.N. Children's Fund (UNICEF; 2000) executive director Carl Bellamy praised UNICEF-supported efforts by women's organizations campaigning against "honor killing." *Honor killing* is the ancient practice in which men, often brothers, kill female relatives who have disgraced the family through sexual activity, even rape victimization. In Jordan, according to the UNICEF report, around 23 such murders occur per year; another 300 took place in 1997 in Pakistan and Yemen, and 52 in Egypt. Hundreds of women in Bangladesh have been subjected to acid attacks, while in India more than 5,000 women are killed each year because their in-laws consider their dowries inadequate. One story had a happy ending, however. According to a British Broadcasting Company (BBC) news report, a bride-to-be took the step of calling the police after the groom asked her father for more dowry money and then assaulted him minutes before the wedding (Rao, 2003). Her case was taken seriously. The bride, Nisha Sharman, who has received widespread support and favorable media coverage, has become quite a celebrity in India.

In honor of International Women's Day the following year, AI (2001) published the report *Broken Bodies, Shattered Minds.* This document was a complement to earlier reports of sexual abuse of women in custody and the use of sexual violence as a weapon of war. In providing the results of investigations of abuses committed by private individuals, acts of torture against women in the home, this report shows that women at risk of violence require protection, whether through refugee services that grant them the right of political asylum or safe places such as women's shelters in their own countries. All across the North

American continent, states are reducing funding for shelters and victim-assistance programming. In Canada, cutbacks in funding have already led to tragic results with a significant increase in murders of women by their abusers (Landsberg, 2003).

Gays, Lesbians, and Human Rights

At present, no human rights document exists that specifically addresses gay/lesbian/transgender rights other than in the context of HIV-AIDS (Reichert, 2003). In virtually every country of the world, sexual minorities are vulnerable to mistreatment without recourse. In his World Values Survey, Ronald Inglehart compared attitudes concerning homosexuality (Florida, 2003). Countries where large majorities are intolerant of gays (e.g., Egypt, Bangladesh, Iran, and China) tend to be economically unstable and under authoritarian rule. In advanced democracies such as Britain, Germany, and Canada, only a quarter or less of the people reject gays. In the United States, according to the World Values Study, 32 percent reject gays.

The laws both reflect and shape public opinion, as we saw in Chapter 1. The recent Supreme Court decision striking the antisodomy laws that criminalized sexual practices associated with male homosexuality in 13 states (most in the South) is a landmark decision for U.S. law (Biskupic, 2003). The court ruled that the Constitution's guarantee of individual liberty protects individuals who engage in sexual relationships in the privacy of their homes. Two aspects of the ruling are highly significant. First, it completely overturned *Bowers v. Hardwick,* which 17 years ago endorsed Georgia's antisodomy law. But just as remarkably, Justice Kennedy, writing for the majority, drew upon international law; he noted that the European Court of Human Rights and other nations recognize the right of gay and lesbian adults to engage in intimate, consensual conduct.

Future bridges to be crossed in the United States concern the need for gays, lesbians, bisexuals, and transgender people to have the full rights and protections of citizenship, including the right to marry, the right to adopt children, and protection from discrimination in employment and the military. Recently, NASW and its Massachusetts chapter filed a legal brief to argue that gay and lesbian couples have the right to marry under the state's constitution. The Massachusetts Supreme Judicial Court's decision to end the exclusion of same-sex couples from marriage was a historic decision with national ramifications (Stoesen, 2004). One outgrowth of this decision was that public officials from San Francisco to Portland, Oregon, to New York City began performing same-sex marriage ceremonies. After watching television images of gay marriages in San Francisco, the 81-year-old monarch of Cambodia decided that same-sex weddings should be allowed in Cambodia as well. (BBC, 2004.) (The photo that opens this chapter shows couples in the Portland lineup.)

With reference to the military, Human Rights Watch has called on the United States to lift the ban on gays and lesbians serving openly in the military, as other democratic nations have done (The Data Lounge, 2003). Australia,

The Civil Rights Movement of the 1960s aroused the consciousness of many other minority groups as well. The cultural contribution of gays and lesbians has been enormous.

Britain, Canada, and Israel are among the nations that welcome gays and lesbians into the military (Alexander, 2003). From the following personal account (provided to me in personal correspondence in August 2003) by an individual on active duty in the U.S. Navy, we get an insider's view of the effect of the present U.S. policy:

> I have been aboard ships at sea twice in my career where one, or several, homosexuals have been "uncovered." The reaction to this discovery is swift. First, the person is taken immediately into custody and placed under guard. Secondly, the person is removed from the ship at the absolutely earliest possible opportunity and taken to the closest installation where an investigation is conducted.
>
> The reason for such swift action is a sad commentary on our society. The person is placed in custody for the protection of the individual himself. Retaliation against alleged homosexuals at sea is often swift and inevitably violent.

The question we need to consider is: To what extent do discriminatory policies encourage persecution of sexual minorities? We also need to ask: What kinds of protections are provided in other countries? In 2001, the Netherlands, which had already welcomed gays and lesbians into the military, became the first nation to give gay and lesbian partners full marriage rights without restriction

(Deutsch, 2001). Belgium followed suit. Other countries such as Germany and Norway allow for same-sex partnerships with certain but not all advantages of marriage. In 2003, Canada took a major step forward in announcing it will change its law to allow same-sex marriage; it is only the third country to do so (McClelland, 2003). In the United States, homosexual marriage lacks full recognition in all 50 states. Vermont recognizes civil unions of same-sex couples with full benefits within the state. In an editorial in *Time* magazine entitled "The Conservative Case for Gay Marriage," Sullivan (2003) makes a convincing case for bringing gay men and lesbians into the institution of marriage, an institution that fosters responsibility, commitment, and (I would add) respectability. Legal commitment breeds stability, which is vital for society and for the children who are often involved. (The 2004 election marked a major setback in this regard.)

Criminal Justice in the United States

Although the U.S. human rights tradition is weak in terms of providing economic rights and security to its citizens, its provision of individual rights and freedoms over the arbitrary abuse of power by the state is an area in which most Americans are justifiably proud. The concepts of human rights, liberty, and equality are deeply engrained in American history; their roots go back to the founding of the American Republic. Out of the revolt against the British colonizers came various documents expounding on "the rights of man," including the Declaration of Independence that held life, liberty, and the pursuit of happiness as self-evident and, later, the U.S. Constitution (Reichert, 2003). The first ten constitutional amendments, the Bill of Rights, specify certain civil and political rights and protections: the basic freedoms of religion, speech, and the press; the right to counsel in all criminal cases; guarantees against unreasonable search and seizure and against violations of due process in criminal proceedings; the right to a speedy, fair trial and an impartial jury; and the prohibition of cruel and unusual punishment.

In America, there are two strains of thought and tradition. These are at war with each other in some ways, but are juxtaposed or blended in other ways. One strain is the respect for individual rights and dignity, as discussed previously, and the other is the punitive tradition.

Punitiveness is a cardinal American value that is difficult for U.S. citizens to explain to outsiders. The death penalty, harsh mandatory sentencing laws for drug users and dealers, the exposure of inmates to violence within the prison—these are just a few examples that come to mind. The absence of prevention measures (e.g., strict gun control laws, censorship of violence in video games and mass media portrayals, and affordable substance abuse treatment) also sets the United States apart from other industrialized nations. The seeming paradox of tough punishments in some areas and laissez-faire, devil-may-care policies in others can be explained, however, in light of the legacy of the past, namely, the Calvinistic creed. The early Puritans, we must remember, were religious dissenters; they were regarded as strange and fanatical in their day. Their creed, on which this nation was founded, was strong on earthly punishments for crimes related to sloth and lust and weak on forgiveness and compassion. The strong work ethic prevails, as does intolerance for the nonproductive and criminal. The desire for redemption, the cleansing of sin, is not so much the opposite of the punitive thrust as its correlate. The early penitentiaries were designed for penitence, mostly through solitude and meditation.

By any standard, the United States is considered a highly punitive nation. Although the crime rate has been dropping palpably for years, media-generated horror stories have instilled fear and anger in the American public and led to a prison-industrial complex such as the world has never known. Political leaders compete with each other for who can be the toughest on crime. For a male candidate for political office, a personal history of military heroism in combat is a highly prized trophy that can be utilized again and again to score points on the campaign trail. Whipping up fear of illegal drugs, and mobilizing the public to support drastic measures to combat such crimes, is a well-known tactic by right-wing politicians wishing to distract attention away from the real problems.

During the 1960s, rehabilitation was the primary goal of corrections. Programs in counseling, education, and training were set up for the purpose of "correcting" inmates' behavior to help them lead law-abiding lives upon their return to society (Welch, 1996). The enthusiasm, however, was short-lived. Research findings that seemed to point to the ineffectiveness of treatment were used by conservatives to disparage the belief that criminals could be rehabilitated; over the next two decades, punishment came back in full force. Gradually, ideals were forgotten, and the reformatories and custodial prisons were merged into the medium-security design that we have today.

Human rights concerns enter the picture when the severity of the punishment is out of proportion to the offense and when there is inequity in how the laws are made and enforced. In the United States, both of these conditions apply. First, mandatory minimum sentencing has removed judicial discretion and created a system in which drug offenders, in many cases, are serving more time in prison than are violent offenders. Second, race, citizenship status, and economic resources dramatically influence (as always) how different groups of people experience the American system of justice (Miller & Schamess, 2000). And third, human rights abuses occur on a regular basis within the U.S. prison system; the erosion of offenders' constitutional rights is unceasing (Whitlock, 2001). The much publicized incidents of savage brutality against Iraqi prisoners at Abu Ghraib are only more extreme versions of the kind of physical and sexual abuse of their counterparts in the United States. In Pennsylvania and some other states, for example, inmates are routinely stripped in front of other inmates; in Arizona, male inmates are forced to wear pink underwear (Butterfield, 2004).

See Box 6.2 for the facts at a glance. This box contains information from the Bureau of Justice Statistics (BJS). Data presented have been gathered from the U.S. Department of Justice in the National Crime Victimization Survey for 2001 and the FBI's Uniform Crime Reports based on crimes known to the police for the same year. Box 6.2 reveals some very interesting trends and has some important political implications. The fact that crime rates are down, significantly down, while the incarceration rate continues to rise is reflective of the punitiveness of the times. Also, the decline in the number of men murdered by partner

6.2 **U.S. Criminal Justice Statistics**

Overview of Crime Rates

- Violent crime has decreased about 50 percent since 1994 and has reached its lowest level; it has decreased for all races.
- Between 1993 and 2000, homicides were down by 42 percent.
- Guns were used in 66 percent of homicides.
- Persons 12 to 24 years of age sustained the most violent victimization.
- Most male victims (55 percent) were victimized by strangers; most females, by intimates or friends.
- Two-thirds of victims of violence by an intimate reported that alcohol had been a factor; about one in five of those involving alcohol also involved drugs.
- Almost half of murder victims were African American.
- Hispanics were victims of overall violence at some-what higher rates than non-Hispanics.
- American Indians have a murder rate only one-fifth that of African Americans, but they are twice as likely as blacks to be victims of rape or assault.
- Property crime rates have continued to decline.

Source: Bureau of Justice Statistics, *Press Release: Nation's Violent Crime Victimization Rate Falls 10 Percent* (2002). Retrieved from http://www.ojp.usdoj.gov/bjs

Intimate Partner Violence (homosexual relationships are included)

- 1,247 women and 440 men were killed by an intimate partner in 2000.

- 85 percent of victimizations and 72 percent of murders by intimate partners in 2001 were against women.
- The rate of intimate violence against both men and women fell significantly.
- Between 1976 and 2000, the number of males killed by an intimate partner declined from 1,357 to 440; the number of female murder victims declined only from 1,600 to 1,247.

Source: BJS, *Intimate Partner Violence, 1993–2001* (2003). Washington, DC: U.S. Department of Justice.

Corrections

- There were 2 million prisoners in the United States in 2002; the number represents an increase in the federal prisons and local jails.
- In large states such as Illinois, California, and Texas, due to new parole policies, the numbers declined.
- The rate of incarceration in the United States is the highest in the world.
- An estimated 4.8 percent of all black males in the population were in prison or jail, compared to 1.7 percent of Hispanics and 0.6 percent of whites.
- The percentage increase in women inmates continued to surpass that of male inmates.

Source: BJS, *Prison Statistics* (2003). Washington, DC: U.S. Department of Justice.

violence is not matched by a comparable decline in the number of homicides of female intimates. I have written about this phenomenon elsewhere (van Wormer, 2001). My theory is that although women's shelters are giving battered women an alternative to violence, a chance to escape, many do not escape, as the statistics on female intimate homicide tragically bear out.

Juvenile Justice

The first juvenile court was founded in 1899 to provide nonpunitive treatment for children who were in trouble with the law or were victims of child abuse and neglect. Although the provision of civil rights protections to juveniles was a progressive and much-needed development, in the intervening years, the philosophy of the juvenile court has moved in the direction of greater legalization. Since the 1980s, increasingly, the impetus toward treatment and diversion has given way in most states to legislation allowing for reduction in the age of criminal responsibility for serious crimes. In 2000, according to The Sentencing Project (2001), the United States prosecuted 200,000 youths under the age of 18 in adult criminal court. Many of the transfers to adult court were for non-violent drug-related and property crimes, and the majority of those prosecuted were African American.

In light of the extreme punitiveness and racism evident in current juvenile justice policies, NASW (2003d) issued a policy statement recommendation that the processing and treatment of children and youths who enter the juvenile justice system be differentiated from the treatment of adults in every phase of contact. Further recommendations are for oversight to ensure nondiscrimination of minority and indigent youth, the provision of family services, and a reliance on restorative justice practices including restitution and community service. (See the section on restorative justice later in this chapter.)

The United States, one of two nations to refuse to sign the Convention on the Rights of the Child (U.N., 1990), is in clear violation of a number of its principles. Article 3, for example, states that in all actions concerning the child, including in courts of law, the best interest of the child shall be a primary consideration. And Article 37 states that no child shall be subjected to cruel, in-human, or degrading treatment or punishment.

Handguns

Use of guns in America is another point of interest. The high rate of gun-related deaths in this country is in sharp contrast with the rates found in other industrialized countries. Consider the fact that in 1998 (the most recent year for which statistics are available), handguns murdered:

- 373 people in Germany
- 151 people in Canada
- 57 people in Australia
- 19 people in Japan
- 54 people in England and Wales
- 11,789 people in the United States (provided by the Brady Campaign, 2003)

Keep in mind that this gun-related homicide figure for the United States does not include suicide by guns. Firearms are used in more suicides than homicides. In 1998, 57 percent of all U.S. gun deaths were suicides (Murphy, 2000).

Research shows, moreover, that the mere presence of a gun in a household heightens a household member's likelihood of gun suicide (Dahl, 2003). The majority of all suicides are committed with a gun. Elderly men have a strikingly high rate of gun suicides (check the figures for gun-related deaths on http://www.jointogether.org). According to a study from the Harvard School of Public Health (Hemenway, 2002), there is an association between gun ownership and suicide rates when regions with high levels of gun ownership are compared with regions with low levels. National surveys suggest that almost half of U.S. households have at least one gun (Macionis, 2004).

Whereas most other industrialized nations have strict gun control laws, the $1.4 billion U.S. gun industry has used lethality as a marketing tool in its production of even more deadly guns. (See *Making a Killing* by Tom Diaz, 1999, a former member of the National Rifle Association. See also the Oscar-winning documentary film *Bowling for Columbine,* in which director Michael Moore takes us on a journey through the United States and Canada in search of answers as to why more than 11,000 people die of gun violence each year in the United States but not in neighboring Canada.)

Corrections

The prison industry, especially in its privatized dimension, is a significant force in blocking criminal justice reform. As more private prisons are built, more lobbying of politicians will take place to keep the prison construction going and to keep the beds full. "Build it and they will come," goes the popular slogan. As Angela Davis (1998) stated:

> The prison industrial complex has . . . created a vicious cycle of punishment which only further impoverishes those whose impoverishment is supposedly "solved" by imprisonment.
>
> Therefore, as the emphasis of government policy shifts from social welfare to crime control, from a caretaking to a punishment bent, the prisons have become vast warehouses for the poor and unemployed, and most especially, for African American and Latino males. The war on drugs has become, in reality, a war on poor men and women of color. (p. 3)

War on Drugs

First declared by President Ronald Reagan as a public relations strategy to rally middle America against inner-city crime, America's war on drugs has been fought with greater and greater zeal (and economic support) by each successive administration. There have, of course, been drug prohibitions throughout American history, with the drug of focus (whether opium, alcohol, marijuana, or crack cocaine) being associated with a certain immigrant or minority group (van Wormer & Davis, 2003). The patent medicines of the 19th century are the illegal drugs of today. In the early 20th century, America talked of demon rum in much the same way we talk of use of illegal drugs at the present time—as a dangerous and corrupting vice.

Today's zero tolerance of certain drugs has culminated in a war on drugs of vast proportions: A military crusade in drug-supplying countries is matched on the home front by the incarceration of over one million people for drug-related crimes. Meanwhile, the sale of illegal drugs has become an underground enterprise entailing high risks, violence, corruption, and unconscionable profits.

To put the U.S. drug war in perspective, let us hear from the British (*The Economist,* 2001):

> Moral outrage has turned out to be a poor basis for policy. Nowhere is that more evident than in the United States. Here is the world's most expensive drugs policy, absorbing $40 billion a year of taxpayers' cash. It has eroded civil liberties, locked up unprecedented numbers of young blacks and Hispanics, and corroded foreign policy. It has proved a dismal rerun of America's attempt in 1920–1933 to prohibit the sale of alcohol. That experiment—not copied in any other big country—inflated alcohol prices, promoted bootleg suppliers, encouraged the spread of guns and crime, increased hard liquor drinking. (p. 4)

That the national antidrug policy has not been a success is a generally acknowledged fact. Consider the following: Afghanistan has resumed its opium poppy trade since the overthrow of the Taliban regime; the percentage of American teens who have used marijuana is 41 percent compared to 16 percent of teens in the EU; there is no decline in the supply of cocaine from Latin America and drugs that continue to flow north of the border; and HIV/AIDS and hepatitis continue to be spread through the sharing of dirty needles (van Wormer & Davis, 2003).

Even though drug use is spread fairly evenly across the population, three-fourths of those locked up are minorities. There are, in fact, more African American males behind bars than in programs of higher education (Crockett, 2002). At the end of 2002, an estimated 12 percent of African American males and 4.3 percent of Latino males between the ages of 25 and 29 were incarcerated as compared to 1.6 percent of whites in the same age group (BJS, 2003). Although their drug use is not substantially higher than other racial groups, African Americans comprise 59 percent of those convicted for drug offences (Drug Policy, 2003). African Americans convicted of drug offenses serve extremely long mandatory minimum sentences for crimes such as selling only five grams of crack cocaine.

The high rate of incarceration has decimated inner-city families and taken a double toll on children—first in taking their parents away, and second in terms of the stigma they bear for having a parent in prison. Half of the 1.5 million kids with a parent in jail or prison, in fact, will commit a crime before they turn 18 (Drummond, 2000).

America's drug war, according to *The Economist* (2001), prevents policing not only in encouraging corruption (e.g., taking bribes and lying on the witness stand to put gang members behind bars) but also in the legal seizure of property from those arrested for drug use. Another undesirable effect, according to this British magazine, is the erosion of constitutional rights. With virtually everyone a suspect, all citizens must be observed, checked, screened, and tested. Law enforcement has become increasingly militarized: SWAT teams perform drug raids, sometimes getting innocent people by mistake, and officials have the power to sniff with canines and search almost at will.

Police search a man's belongings. The criminal justice system's attempt to stop illicit drug use has been largely unsuccessful.

Civil liberties also have suffered in terms of the mandatory sentencing laws enacted in 1986, which take sentencing discretion away from judges and place it in the hands of prosecutors. Only by providing prosecutors with information needed to prosecute other offenders may defendants get their sentences reduced. Wives and girlfriends of drug dealers, accordingly, are often sentenced as conspirators. Because they typically lack information about the drug-trafficking operation that the prosecutors seek, these partners of the traffickers often wind up with longer sentences than the men who implicated them.

Although the percentage of women in U.S. prisons is only 6.1 percent of all prison inmates, their numbers have doubled since the 1980s. The increase was related to drug law violations. In the United Kingdom, the female prison population has more than doubled since 1993. A high proportion of female prisoners are from foreign ethnic groups, mostly coming into the country as "drug mules," according to a BBC (2003) report entitled "Inside Highpoint Prison."

In Canada, the incarceration rate has declined as the community supervision rate has increased (Statistics Canada, 2002). Although highly criticized by U.S. officials, Canada is moving in the direction of the pragmatic harm reduction model that is practiced in much of Western Europe. Marijuana decriminalization is well underway. Recently, for example, to curb the spread of hepatitis C, a needle-exchange program in Prince George, British Columbia, began giving out clean crack pipes to addicted individuals. Other Canadian cities also have crack-pipe exchanges ("British Columbia Needle-Exchange Program Includes Crack Pipes," 2003).

The focus of the harm reduction approach is on saving lives through monitoring rather than forbidding drug use. In Europe, it took the AIDS epidemic of the 1980s to catapult harm reduction strategies into prominence. With these strategies, drug use is defined as a public health rather than a criminal justice problem, and the behavior of the drug user is closely monitored at methadone and other clinics where a safe supply is provided under medical supervision. Several U.S. cities, including Baltimore and Seattle, utilize such progressive policies, at least with regard to needle-exchange and methadone maintenance programs. (See van Wormer & Davis, 2003, and Chapter 9, this volume.)

European programming has been especially successful in reaching the hardcore addicts like no other program can. Pharmaceutical heroin is administered to such addicts in a clinic in Berne, Switzerland. According to *The Economist* (2001), patients receiving such treatment quit using cocaine, which most had used in addition to the heroin; the crime, prostitution, and suicide rates all dropped precipitously. Heroin maintenance is practiced in the United Kingdom and the Netherlands, as well.

As many social workers are aware, the harm to society from the war on drugs is often greater than the harm from the drugs themselves. And treatment offerings are highly inadequate, even for clients with strong insurance policies. NASW (2003a) recommends that the ineffective war on drugs be replaced with a comprehensive public health approach, including adequate financing and harm reduction strategies, and that social workers advocate for such policies.

Fortunately, as states, in the throes of huge deficits, face the necessity of budget cuts, there are moves underway to reverse some of the harsh sentencing laws. To curb correction costs, states are modifying mandatory sentencing laws and funding drug courts for intensive community treatment (Justice Policy Institute, 2003). Social workers and social work educators are thus advised to provide their legislators with Fact Sheets providing the latest data concerning treatment effectiveness studies and sentencing reform. (To present evidence of drug court versus imprisonment cost savings, check out the Drug Policy Alliance at http://www.drugpolicy.org.)

Human Rights Violations of Prisoners

Prison labor, as Davis (1998) indicates, competes very successfully with "free world" labor, making huge profits for corporations such as IBM, Texas Instruments, travel agencies, and credit card companies. With prison labor, there is no union organizing, no health benefits, and no need to worry about strikes or paying at or above the minimum wage. From the inmate point of view, the opportunity to work at a real job is a plus.

Labor exploitation is clearly an area of human rights concerns. In 1979, to ensure a cheap labor pool, Congress began a process of deregulation that allowed private corporations to exploit the captive labor market for profit. Modern-day prison labor bears a frightening resemblance to slavery that few people acknowledge. With wages as low as 11 cents an hour in some places and no benefits or vacations, the prisoners must choose between taking low-paying jobs or serving longer sentences, since "good time" policies subtract days from one's total sentence for good behavior and days worked. Such prison labor practices bear a striking resemblance to slavery that is more than coincidental. In fact, involuntary servitude as punishment for crime is *legal* under the U.S. Constitution (Thirteenth Amendment), but not under the U.N. Universal Declaration of Human Rights (1948, Article 4), which, as a more comprehensive document, outlaws slavery of all forms.

According to Human Rights Watch (2001), the United States has made little progress in embracing international human rights standards at home. Serious human rights violations have been most apparent in the criminal justice system, according to the report (http://www.hrw.org). Police brutality, discriminatory racial disparities in incarceration, abusive conditions of confinement, and state-sponsored executions, even of juvenile offenders and mentally handicapped persons, were singled out as obvious violations. The pronounced sentence discrepancies between persons convicted of selling crack cocaine, who are highly apt to be inner-city African Americans, and those selling the more expensive powder variety of cocaine are reflected in the disproportionately high incarceration rate of African Americans for drug-related crimes.

As we review conditions in the U.S. prison system, we need to bear in mind Article 5 of the U.N. Universal Declaration of Human Rights that states: "No one shall be subjected to torture or to cruel, inhuman, or degrading treatment or punishment." This standard, which seems to be identical to that of the U.S. Bill of Rights, is in fact a higher standard than that in the United States because of the word *or*. In the United States, the application of the Eighth Amendment's prohibition against "cruel and unusual punishment," according to an article in the *Harvard Environmental Law Review* (Geer, 2000), requires that both elements apply at once—cruel *and* unusual. In a recent Supreme Court ruling, the majority determined that if the cruelty is usual, then it is constitutional!

Under international guidelines, conditions in U.S. prisons easily qualify as "cruel and inhuman." Mentally ill inmates are often placed in solitary confinement as troublemakers. In 2003, in fact, between 200,000 and 300,000 men and women with serious mental illnesses were incarcerated in U.S. prisons—more than three times the number confined in mental institutions, according to a shocking investigative report by Human Rights Watch (2003a). Supermax prisons in Ohio, Illinois, Wisconsin, and elsewhere keep inmates in constantly lit solitary confinement. Such social isolation leads many of those so confined to attempt suicide as their only means of escape. As noted in the Human Rights Watch report:

> In the most extreme cases, conditions are truly horrific: mentally ill prisoners locked in segregation with no treatment at all; confined in filthy and beastly hot cells; left for days covered in feces they have smeared over their bodies; taunted, abused, or ignored by prison staff; given so little water during summer heat waves that they drink from their toilet bowls. (p. 2)

The incarceration industry generates $30 billion a year in the United States (Mundow, 2001). Private corporations now compete with state governments for lucrative prison contracts. Major correctional corporations are large political lobbying groups; profits are tied in to the incarceration boom. Their representatives lobby for keeping the prisons full through abolishing parole, placing restrictions on lawsuits, and setting maximum and minimum sentencing guidelines. When private companies run prisons, they hire minimum-wage workers to reduce costs. Their economic incentive is to keep the beds full by any means. The prison-industrial complex is expanding in Europe, especially in the United Kingdom. One major advantage for the government in having privately owned and operated prisons is that it exempts the state from lawsuits in the cases of maltreatment and wrongful death. (See Coyle, Campbell, & Neufeld, 2003, *Capitalist Punishment: Prison Privatization and Human Rights.*)

In 1994 the United States ratified the Convention against the Torture and Other Cruel, Inhuman or Degrading Treatment or Punishment. The U.S. government only signed this treaty with the stipulation that individuals would be given no more rights than those provided by the U.S. Constitution. This restriction has important implications for prisoners who are mistreated in the custody of the state. While women in prison have been subjected to gross violations at the hands of correctional officers (especially males), incarcerated men have often found themselves in grave danger from fellow inmates.

Behind bars, flagrant violations of international law take the shape of the sexual abuse of female inmates by male correctional officers and male rape by other inmates in U.S. prisons. We will consider each in turn, drawing on facts from the human rights NGOs.

Men in Prison

Prisons are brutalizing institutions. In all-male places of confinement, men are subject to constant power games; the premium is on toughness. Within the walls of prison, violence and the threat of violence is a constant, much of it racially motivated. Few law-abiding citizens are aware of the brutalities that routinely take place behind the barbed-wire fences, especially to inmates who are not "street wise."

In their exhaustive investigation of custodial sexual abuse in the U.S. prison system, appropriately entitled "No Escape," Human Rights Watch (2001) presented the horror stories collected from over 200 prisoners spread among 37 states. Sample narratives tell of the kind of fate that befalls inmates with perceived feminine characteristics. The narratives are harrowing. For example:

> I've requested protective custody only to be denied. It is not available here. He [the guard] also said there was nowhere to run to, and it would be best for me to accept things. . . . I probably have AIDS now. I have great difficulty raising food to my mouth from shaking after nightmares or thinking too hard on all this. . . . I've laid down without physical fight to be sodomized. To prevent so much damage in struggles, ripping and tearing. Though not in fighting, it caused my heart and spirit to be raped as well. Something I don't know if I'll ever forgive myself for. (p. 2 of 7)

Suicide attempts by rape victims in prisons are common. Part of the reason is the fear they have lost their manhood and been made into homosexuals. Yet the perpetrators are heterosexuals who perceive their prey as substitute women. As we hear from a Florida prisoner:

> Mostly young youthful boys are raped because of their youth and tenderness, and smooth skin that in the mind of the one during the raping he thinks of the smooth skin and pictures a woman. . . . Prisoners even fight each other over a youth without the young man knowing anything about it to see who will have the boy first as his property. (p. 3 of 4)

Young white inmates are typical targets; whites represent the racism in the system, and they are also considered to be weak and cowardly. Some victims of mass sexual assault seek out a protector and become the "property" of this inmate. Forced to satisfy the protector's sexual needs, they also may be given a female name, "rented out" for sex, and forced to do scrubbing and cleaning.

Recommendations by Human Rights Watch are: putting an end to double (and triple) celling, providing protection through the federal courts, repealing the Prison Litigation Reform Act that protects prisons from lawsuits, putting pressure on the states by Congress to either protect prisoners or have federal funding withdrawn, and providing protective custody units that are not punitive in nature. (Read the full report at http://www.hwr.org/reports/2001.)

Results of an empirically based survey revealed that 21 percent of inmates in seven prisons had experienced at least one episode of pressured or forced sex within the prison (Human Rights Watch, 2002b). Staff generally ignored such attacks. Violations by correctional officers included punitive use of electrical stun devices and confinement of inmates in total isolation for 23 hours per day in maxiprisons.

Women in Prison

The U.N. standards for prison treatment carry less legal weight than treaties, but nevertheless they carry moral power. Relevant to women who are imprisoned is the U.N. Standard Minimum Rules for the Treatment of Prisoners. Rule 53(3) provides that women should be attended and supervised only by women officers. In the United States, however, nondiscrimination guidelines have removed most restrictions on women working in men's prisons. Accordingly, more often than not, women incarcerated in the United States are guarded by men; uniquely in this country, men are sometimes placed in contact positions over female inmates (van Wormer, 2001). Seventy percent of guards in U.S. federal women's institutions are men; in contrast, in Canada, 91 percent of officers in women's facilities are women (AI, 1999). Violations in the form of sexual harassment have been reported in virtually every state. The worst violations have come from privatized prisons; these prisons are staffed by poorly trained and poorly paid correctional officers.

The stories of rape, revenge deprivations, forced nudity in lockup, pregnancies in a closed system where only males were the guards, forced abortions, and solitary confinement of complainants and witnesses to the abuses barely received notice until the late 1990s. It was thanks to the facts revealed in a string of lawsuits that organizations such as AI were able to run investigations of their own.

A major setback to the civil rights of inmates came when the Prison Litigation Reform Act was passed in 1995. This act limits judicial supervision of prisons and thereby reduces the civil rights of inmates. The difficulty of litigation notwithstanding, substantial settlements have been awarded in a number of high-profile cases.

Female immigrants, including refugees in detention, are another group of women who have suffered serious human rights violations. Even before the war on terrorism was declared, brutal treatment of detained political refugees was the norm. Yet, because the detainees are not U.S. citizens, they are considered to be outside the jurisdiction of the protections of the U.S. Constitution. They are not, however, outside the scope of international law.

The Death Penalty

One of the most extreme forms of brutality is represented by state-assisted murder, better known as the death penalty. Most major democracies and dozens of other countries have abolished the death penalty. The support by the American public and politicians of this form of punishment is one of a kind with the harsh welfare cutbacks and "the race to incarcerate."

In 2002, at least 1,526 people were executed in 31 countries, according to figures known to Amnesty International (AI; 2003). The overwhelming majority of executions took place in China. Over 100 were in Iran and 71 in the United States. At the end of 2002, 76 countries, according to AI's annual report on executions, abolished the death penalty for all crimes, while 15 held it for exceptional situations such as war crimes. A further 20 countries were abolitionist in practice. The official policy of the EU is to promote the abolition of the death penalty throughout the world (*The Economist*, 1999). There are encouraging developments, such as the moratorium on executions in the state of Illinois due to the large number of individuals on death row found to be innocent, and the same in the state of Maryland due to the outcome of a study showing racial and geographic bias in the imposition of sentencing.

Capital punishment has been abolished by all the major democracies except the United States, Japan, and India. For large parts of the world, capital punishment is now regarded as barbaric and unnecessary. The way the death sentences are carried out in Japan and China are especially brutal. For 10 to 20 years, convicted murderers live in solitary confinement; then suddenly, with no warning, the cell doors swing open and they are led out and hanged. Families receive no prior notice as well (*The Economist*, 1999). In China, convicts are shot in the head immediately after sentencing; a bill for the bullet is sent to the family. In the Middle East, women frequently are publicly stoned to death for adultery.

Most of the states in the United States that have the death penalty have abandoned the electric chair and hanging in favor of the more sanitized version, lethal injection. More states also now have life sentences without parole as an alternative to the death penalty; this has helped to reduce the numbers being sent to death row. The concern about miscarriages of justice—107 death row inmates have had to be released since 1973—has caused a deep wariness about this final solution (*The Economist*, 2003).

Still, opinion polls show the majority of Americans support the death penalty. To understand the reason for the death penalty's appeal, a national survey was undertaken by a *Washington Post*–ABC News poll (Morin & Deane, 2001). The poll showed that in the wake of falling crime rates, overall support for the death penalty has declined to 63 percent from 77 percent five years ago. When asked if the choice was death or life without parole, the numbers fell even further to 46 percent. A minority, only 43 percent, accepted the argument that the death penalty is a deterrent to crime. (This rejection of the deterrence argument is, perhaps, a reflection of the fact that the states with the highest execution rates also have the highest murder rates, and vice versa. In Canada, since 1976 when the death penalty for murder was abolished, the murder rate has declined by 42 percent [AI, 2003].) Another argument that no longer carries weight is the cost argument. A Gallup poll found that only 20 percent of those supporting the death penalty cited the high fiscal costs of imprisonment as the reason for their support (Jones, 2001). (Due to the huge expense of the trials and confinement on death row, a price tag of $2 million per execution beyond what life in prison would cost is the norm [Death Penalty Information Center, 2000].)

How about the unfairness factor with regard to race? Only 37 percent of respondents accepted the argument that the death penalty was discriminatory by race in the *Washington Post*–ABC News survey. Two factors emerged as decisive: closure for the victim's families, and revenge—the "eye-for-an-eye" concept of justice.

The racism argument, so widely rejected in the poll, is, in fact, a reality. Of the 845 prisoners executed between 1977 and 2003, 80 percent were for murders involving white victims (AI, 2003). Of all murders in the United States during that period, about half were black and half were white. African Americans were disproportionately represented on death row in 2003. While they make up 12 percent of the population, they made up 40 percent of death row inmates and one in three of those executed. Although not considered in opinion polls, class is a factor in who gets executed as well. The fact that about 90 percent of people on trial in capital cases cannot afford their own attorney is indicative of the financial status of these individuals (NASW, 2003b). For a gripping account of an African American teenager who was sentenced to death row, a sentence that was later commuted to life, and who is today a professor of social work at The Ohio State University, see *To Ascend into the Shining World Again* by Rudolph Alexander, Jr. (2001).

I want to say a word about the now-rejected deterrence argument as well. In public testimony before the Iowa legislature when Republicans tried to reintroduce the death penalty, I made an argument that seems to go against common sense. Far from being a deterrent to crime, I argued, the death penalty can be an attraction to certain persons who are both suicidal and antisocial. My evidence consisted of 20 cases of criminals, including Gary Gilmore (the first person executed when capital punishment was restored in 1977), who committed their murders in hopes of dying themselves in a very dramatic way. Most of the cases of suicide-murder that I found involved men who wanted to die but did not have the nerve to pull the trigger themselves (see van Wormer, 1997). The phenomenon, suicide-by-cop, in which individuals deliberately set up situations that will lead the police to kill them, is a circumstance of which police officers are well aware.

NASW (2003b), in its handbook of policy statements, takes a strong position against the practice of capital punishment: "NASW's broad ethical principle that social workers respect the inherent dignity and worth of each person prohibits support of the death penalty. . . . This ethical principle also applies to efforts by social workers to enhance clients' capacity and opportunity for change" (p. 30).

Sister Helen Prejean, spiritual leader and social activist and the author of *Dead Man Walking* (Prejean, 1994), spearheaded the national campaign for a moratorium on the death penalty (check out http://www.Moratorium Campaign.org). In common with social work values is the belief by members of this campaign that it is wrong to take human life, but beyond that, in human redemption. The prime example of a life totally turned around was that of Karla Faye Tucker who was executed in 1998 in Texas. Few doubted that her repentance was real, least of all her pastor who married her in prison. Not only was Tucker able to forgive her tormenters—those Texans cheering on her execution—but more strikingly she was able to forgive herself for the senseless murders she had committed (van Wormer, 2001). Many anti–death penalty activists such as Sister Helen Prejean, as well as conservative religious leaders, took up her cause. In the end, however, then Governor George W. Bush refused to stay her execution.

Tucker's death may or may not have provided a sense of closure to the victims' families. This element of capital punishment has been played up extensively in the media to the extent that the public believes the killing of the murderer of their child or relative somehow helps the family recover from the loss. Members of the organizations Murder Victims' Families for Reconciliation and Journey of Hope feel otherwise, however (Moratorium Campaign, 2002). The organization Journey of Hope: From Violence to Healing conducts a national speaking tour of people who have lost loved ones to murder but oppose the death penalty. The supposed cathartic power of watching their loved one's murderer die is a myth, they say. You have to let go; hate can literally destroy you. "You become what you hate" is their slogan. The teachings of these groups are generally are ignored by prosecutors and the media, however, who have other agendas. Victims' needs, accordingly, tend to be narrowly defined in terms of retribution and "closure" from state-sponsored vengeance. According to spokespersons for Journey of Hope, the mainstream philosophy corresponds to the principles of "restrictive" justice.

Restorative Justice

Overview

In an aboriginal peacekeeping circle, members of the community open the session with a prayer and reminder that the circle has been convened to discuss the behavior of a young man who assaulted his sister in a drunken rage; an eagle feather is passed around the circle, held by each speaker as the person expresses feelings about the harmful behavior. This process is about reconciliation and the healing of wounds. It is about restoring the balance or the sense of justice that was lost.

Social workers in the field of corrections certainly need to know about restorative justice. In Canada, perhaps due to the influence of First Nations people, restorative justice principles are well known. In the United States, restorative justice practices have made inroads within the criminal justice field (a March 2004 search of *Criminal Justice Abstracts* revealed 253 relevant articles, while a search of *Social Work Abstracts* revealed only 4). The most promising developments in the United States are taking place in the states of Minnesota, Vermont, and Hawaii. Social work students at Bluffton College, a Mennonite college in Ohio, take a course in restorative justice theory.

So what is restorative justice? And what is its connection with human rights? *Restorative justice* is a broad term that refers to various strategies for finding resolutions to criminal and human rights violations. Both an ideal principle (providing justice to the offender, victim, and community) and a method of dispensing justice when a violation has been committed, this form of justice can be considered a form of social justice because of its fairness to all parties. Restorative justice is highly relevant to social work in terms of its focus on: healing, face-to-face communication, spiritual qualities (in allowing for expiation for guilt), and underlying assumption that if you seek the good in people, you will more than likely find it. The four basic kinds of restorative justice are victim-offender conferencing, family group conferencing, circle sentencing, and reparations. Whereas victim-offender conferencing operates most generally at the micro level, reparations can extend to what sociologists might call the macro-macro level. We will return to a discussion of reparations later in this chapter; reparations is the form of justice most closely linked to human rights.

On the international stage, the thrust for a restorative justice vision has been embraced through the role of the United Nations. In consultation with NGOs, the U.N. has established formal standards or guidelines for countries to use in restorative justice programming (Van Ness, 2002). The United States, however, has not officially endorsed these procedures.

The variety of initiatives that fall under this rubric have their roots in the rituals of indigenous populations from across the globe, especially those in Canada and New Zealand. (Canadian Mennonite probation officers played an important role as well.) This form of justice has as its purpose the repairing of the harm that has been done to the victim, community, and offender himself or herself. Note that the starting point is always the *victim*. From the offender's standpoint, restorative justice condemns the criminal act but not the actor and holds the offender accountable to the community (Umbreit, 2000). The restorative justice process can take place either in addition to or instead of standard judicial proceedings. This three-pronged approach—to the needs of victim, offender, community—gives individuals and families most directly affected by wrongdoing the opportunity to be involved in the resolution process. Providing a possible antidote to punitive politics, restorative justice theory can be applied in a wide variety of contexts ranging from the most extraordinary forms of injustice considered by the national courts to the types of issues considered in the meeting room of neighborhood schools.

In many U.S. states, representatives of the victims' rights movement have been instrumental in setting up programs in which victims/survivors may confront their violators. For both victim and offender, restorative justice protects individual rights by providing options that no mere legalistic resolution could offer; participation is strictly voluntary. With regard to the matter of reparations for violations of human rights to whole classes of people, the restorative justice process is the method of choice for addressing the wrongs that have been done, both by individuals and by the state.

The standard variety of justice goes as follows: For the offender charged with a crime, the goal is to "beat the rap." The process of adjudication typically involves "copping a plea" to a lesser charge through a deal between prosecutor and defense attorney or participation in the adversarial arena, the modern equivalent of trial by combat. Consistent with its origin in trial-by-combat, the adversary system is built on dueling as opposed to negotiation and compromise. In civil cases, the plaintiff's lawyers, paid on a contingency basis, share up to 40 percent of the winnings. In both civil and criminal cases, one party wins; the other party loses. This form of justice, common in most of the Western and non-Western world, is retributive justice. The ultimate form of retribution is found in the death penalty.

In contrast, the campaign for restorative justice advocates alternative methods to satisfying the victim's needs other than through harsh punishment. Accountability to the victim, however, is indispensable here, as is accountability to the community. Restitution is often involved in situations of property offenses, for example. But restitution can go far beyond mere monetary compensation.

The criminal justice literature is almost exclamatory regarding this new development. Restorative justice has variously been called "a new model for a new century" (van Wormer, 2001, 2004), "a paradigm shift" (Zehr, 1997), and "a revolution" (Barajas, 1995). There are now more than 1,000 such programs operating throughout North America and Europe, according to the international survey done by the Center of Restorative Justice and Peacemaking (Umbreit, 2000). In Germany alone, there are 400 victim-offender mediation centers. Many programs operate inside U.S. and Belgian prisons. Belgium now has a restorative justice coordinator in each of its 30 prisons who arranges conferences between victims and inmates (McGeorge, 2003). There is also a significant restorative justice focus in the Australian prison system, while practically the whole criminal justice system in New Zealand, following Maori tradition, utilizes a restorative conferencing format. In New Zealand, the child welfare system has come to rely on family group conferencing as a means of drawing on community and the extended family for help in cases of child abuse and neglect (Restorative Justice Website, 2002). In their work with families, social workers find that the spirituality components, nonbureaucratic processes, and reliance on mutual aid of family conferencing are compatible with the values and traditions of the Latino community (Gutiérrez & Suarez, 1999) as well as with African-centered principles (Carter, 1997). Indigenous populations, such as North American Native tribes, incorporate spiritual leaders into the healing process. In aboriginal culture, all life is viewed as sacred; disruptive acts typically are viewed as signals of relational disharmonies.

Social workers in Hawaii have been quietly incorporating Native Hawaiian culturally based tradition into their human service interventions. The impetus for introducing the culturally specific programming came in the 1970s when it was noted that Native children were not responding to the standard forms of psychotherapy provided. Hurdle (2002) chronicles how social workers in collaboration with Hawaiian elders worked to revitalize the use of *ho'oponopono,* an ancient Hawaiian conflict resolution process. This model is embedded in the traditional Hawaiian values of extended family, respect of elders, need for harmonious relationships, and restoration of good will or *aloha.* The process is very ritualistic and follows a definite protocol. With the leader in tight control of communication, the opening prayer leads into an open discussion of the problem at hand. The resolution phase begins with a confession of wrongdoing and the seeking of forgiveness. Uniquely, as Hurdle relates, all parties to the conflict ask forgiveness of each other; this equalizes the status of participants. This process effectively promotes spiritual healing and can be used in many contexts. On the small island of Guam, restorative practices adopted from the Chamorro (Guam's major indigenous group) are infused into official social institutions such as the legal and educational structures. Restorative awareness presentations are provided on a regular basis ("Restorative Practices in Guam," 2004).

In communities across North America, an unusual coalition of idealistic lawyers, religious leaders, and even conservative victims' advocates are at the helm of this restorative justice policy movement. Among these movers and shakers is a remarkable woman whom I interviewed personally. Her name is Linda Harvey. From the interview and documents she provided, I have gleaned the following description of her work.

"I have a passion for the restorative justice philosophy because it is about the healing of relationships and harm. I believe that I am doing the ministry of reconciliation to which God is calling all of us." So says Linda Harvey (2001), social worker, devoted Catholic, and founder of Transformation House in Lexington, Kentucky. Transformation House provides assistance to victim survivors who are struggling with the emotional devastation resulting from the homicide of a family member. Operating under independent auspices, this program is not derived from the criminal justice system. It builds on personal relationships and relies on the goodwill of public officials such as the prison warden. Harvey's vision for promoting reconciliation has included working closely with incarcerated women, especially those who have killed their abusers (L. Harvey, personal communication to van Wormer, November 27, 2001). For such women and others at the Pee Wee Valley Correctional Institute, Transformation House provides a series of educational classes and seminars. The dual focus of the classes and seminars is to help women take responsibility for what they have done and to experience catharsis and healing (Restorative Justice Website, 2001). During the seminar, a panel of victims and survivors share their stories of grief and loss with the inmates.

Transformation House, for Linda Harvey, was the culmination of a dream. The idea started with a vision to bring death row inmates together with their victims' families. In 1999, when Harvey brought together Patsy Smith, whose mother had been murdered, with an inmate at the women's prison who had been convicted as an accomplice in the mother's death, the meeting turned out to be a powerful healing experience for both parties. According to the newspaper's account:

> For Smith, the meeting challenged her faith and gave her the chance to live it out. It was a time for facing her sorrow and anger. It was what her mother would have wanted her to do, she said. She was also finally able to hear that her mother had died a few minutes after midnight. (Kimbro, 1999, p. A1)

For more information on Linda Harvey and other restorative justice pioneers, see the International Centre for Justice and Reconciliation at http://www.restorativejustice.org. See Box 6.3 to read a personal account of the process from inmate Jackie Marple.

Harvey's work is an example of victim-offender conferencing within prison walls. Most cases of victim-offender work are not that extreme, however; most involve property offenses. The most extensive and comprehensive studies of the impact of restorative justice interventions to date have been conducted at the Center for Restorative Justice and Peacemaking in Minnesota under the leadership of Mark Umbreit. The center is associated with the University of Minnesota's School of Social Work. In one of the most comprehensive studies, data were collected from four Canadian victim-offender mediation programs on 4,445 offenders, mostly adults, who were referred to the programs (Umbreit, 1996). Approximately 75 percent of the victims and the offenders who were interviewed reported satisfaction with the process. Ninety percent from both groups felt they had been treated fairly. Members of a comparison group who did not participate in mediation were significantly less satisfied with the handling of their cases.

Umbreit's summary (1998) reported that for victims, the possibility of receiving restitution appeared to initially motivate them to enter the mediation process. After mediation, however, they reported that meeting the offender and being able to talk about what happened was more satisfying than receiving restitution. Even in cases of extreme violence, victims and offenders often highlighted their participation in mediated dialogue as a powerful and transformative experience that helped them express personal pain, let go of their hatred, and, finally, heal.

6.3 One Inmate's Story

Jackie Marple

I was 22 years old on December 26, 1992. After suffering a lifetime's worth of abuse and neglect at the hands of both my parents, while also acting under the effects of post-traumatic stress disorder (PTSD), I made the unrealistic attempt to put a stop to my parents' abuse of my nephew who was 2½ years old. A gun battle ensued and once the smoke cleared, both my parents lay dead on our living room floor. I drove my nephew home to my sister's apartment. Then, after coming to my senses, I turned myself into the police.

Two years later, after a lengthy stay in the county jail, I pled guilty to two counts of manslaughter one. I was sentenced to 20 years' imprisonment. I was later found by the court to have been a victim of domestic violence and abuse at the hands of my parents. I was finally sentenced for my crimes on November 14, 1994. I have remained in prison ever since.

Prison is an awful place. However, there are times when I am given the opportunity to help a fellow human being, to show the world that my status as an inmate has not stripped me of my ability to show compassion and understanding for my fellow man. To the contrary, I cherish these moments most of all, as they allow me to be truly free once again. Not long ago I, along with several of my fellow inmates, was asked to take part in the Impact of Crime on Victims Seminar. We were unsure of what we were getting ourselves into. We soon discovered that we were to be taken on a roller coaster ride of healing and self-forgiveness as well as an understanding of restorative justice. We heard the true stories of surviving [relatives of] victims of homicide, and by the end of the seminar, we all walked away with the realization that it's okay to feel pain and remorse about our crimes, but most of all it's okay to forgive ourselves. The Transformation House team did a wonderful job of presenting their message of unconditional love and self-healing. I will not soon forget the lessons they taught me.

Source: *Transformation House Mendings, 1*(1), p. 3 (Summer 2002). Reprinted by permission of Jackie Marple and Transformation House.

Healing through Reparations

Healing for the woundedness of whole populations of people is the ultimate goal of reparative justice. Whereas the other methods of restoring justice generally relate to wrongdoing within a personal or criminal justice context, *reparative justice,* as the term is used here, refers to reparations for violations of human rights where the state is the culprit. Reparations may be in the form of cash or territorial payments as material compensation for historical wrongs done. Reparation with or without an apology is an admission of past wrongdoing and a recognition by perpetrators or their descendants of the need to amend for past wrongdoing. In *The Guilt of Nations,* Barkan (2000) traces the new global trend of restitution for historical injustices, a trend based on the belief that nations as moral beings must acknowledge their past wrongdoing if they are ever to get beyond it.

When reparations were made in 1988 by the U.S. Congress to Japanese Americans for wrongs inflicted upon them after war was declared on Japan (including confiscation of their property and confinement in concentration camps), a precedent was set for other mistreated groups to seek compensatory measures. Among them are the Native American claims for broken treaties and brutal practices forcing assimilation. Australian aboriginal peoples are currently organizing to receive reparations for their "stolen childhoods." The reference is to the forced removal of mixed-race children from aboriginal mothers and their placement in orphanages or white homes. In Japan in 2000, a tribunal held in Tokyo was convened by various women's rights groups to hear testimony from Japanese and Korean women survivors who had been forced to be sexual slaves or "comfort women" of the World War II Imperial Army (Steinem, 2002). In the United States, the African American movement for reparations incurred by the ancestors of persons brought to American and sold as slaves has been widely publicized. This effort gained ground after the U.N. Conference against Racism, which was held in Durban, South Africa, in 2001, issued a document defining slavery as a crime against humanity (Ogletree, 2002). Compensation claims that parallel the class-action lawsuit focusing on international profiting from South Africa's apartheid are requesting that money be set aside in a trust fund for the poorest members of the African American community. If granted, money will come not from the U.S. government but from corporations such as Aetna and Union Pacific railroad that likely benefited from slavery (Roosevelt, 2003).

Where there has been victimization and possible trauma, rituals are needed to "heal the damaged souls of the people, to help them find ways to transform hatred into sorrow or forgiveness, to be able to move forward with hope rather than wallow in the evil of the past" (Braithwaite, 2002, p. 207). On a global scale, the most astonishing example of public truth-telling and catharsis for crime took place in South Africa before the Truth and Reconciliation Commission. The core purpose of the national inquiry was to promote national unity through public disclosure of the nature and extent of the human rights violations under apartheid. Victims of the apartheid regime testified, and ex-officials who had committed unspeakable crimes under the former government were forced to own up to these crimes. In exchange for taking responsibility for the wrongs inflicted on black and mixed-race people, the former officials were offered amnesty.

"Without Memory, There Is No Healing. Without Forgiveness, There Is No Future." This is the title of an article by Colin Green (1998) on how the Truth and Reconciliation Commission hearings on human rights abuses under the evils of apartheid attempted to reconcile former victims and oppressors in that country. Cited in the article, Archbishop Desmond Tutu declared:

> There's something in all of us that hungers after the good and true, and when we glimpse it in people, we applaud them for it. We long to be just a little like them. Restorative justice is focused on restoring the personhood that is damaged or lost. (pp. 5–6)

Less widely known are events taking shape in Rwanda, riven by a genocide in 1994 that claimed an estimated half a million lives. Because women are believed by many to be better at forgiveness and reconciliation, women are guaranteed a minimum of 30 percent of governmental seats of power. The purpose is to ensure a greater role of women in the postconflict period, a period that has witnessed deep change in social attitudes toward women (U.S. Institute of Peace, 2003). The most comprehensive and useful collection of studies on restorative justice is available online at http://www.restorativejustice.org.

Summary and Conclusion

Human rights, harm reduction, and restorative justice are the three key models that were explained in depth in this chapter. A notion of human rights is the cornerstone for both of the other two models, harm reduction and restorative justice, as we have seen in this chapter. Harm reduction is an antidote to the war on drugs, a way of protecting drug users from the law and themselves until they can find healthier ways of coping with life. Restorative justice approaches provide alternatives to prison in some cases and help convicts repair the harm they caused in others. At the societal level, reparations are being sought by minority and indigenous populations for past wrongs done to their people through war crimes such as genocide, slavery, removal of their children, and other extreme human rights violations.

One theme that emerged in the writing of this chapter is how much U.S. policy makers (whether politicians or social workers) can learn from international sources, including nongovernmental organizations such as Human Rights Watch and Amnesty International. The very concept of human rights is a global concept based on the universal principles of justice and security. Seen from a human rights perspective, the United States is strong in the area of political and civil rights but remiss in providing economic rights including health care and housing. The importance of a human rights perspective for the social work profession was stressed in Box 6.1, a contribution written by Elisabeth Reichert.

This chapter is informed by the U.N. Universal Declaration of Human Rights, the body of which is included in Appendix A. This remarkable document from which so many other remarkable documents and treaties have sprung can serve as a template against which to measure the level of civilization of a given country. Within this framework, we considered the treatment of women globally and the treatment of various minority groups. To say that war, in its preparation and glorification, has a dampening effect on citizens' human rights is an understatement. Civil liberties do not count for much in a nation at war or in a warfare state.

In our overview of the U.S. criminal justice system, the negatives in the ruthless war on drugs and pervasive racism were pointed out. Positives that were reviewed include the introduction of the harm reduction model and restorative justice strategies.

The theme of gender emerged once again in the discussions of women and crime (women in confinement) and female victimization under conditions of war. Unlike incarcerated men who engage in endless power struggles, women in prison seem to be more interested in reproducing family-type ties for their emotional survival. The section on war and rape described specific human rights violations suffered by women universally in war-torn areas. This chapter has viewed such violations of women as a deliberate component of military strategy. The role of rape and sexual bondage in altering the ethnic and racial composition of a people has been seen historically in American slavery and more recently in the ethnic conflicts in Bosnia and Rwanda.

Gay and lesbian rights are only in their infancy. Promising developments have taken place in two European countries and Canada, however, with full marriage rights being provided to gays and lesbians—something that would have been considered almost laughable even a decade ago. Now that the example has been set, other nations will follow in this area, as well as in other humane and pragmatic pursuits. The pattern is this: First the unthinkable becomes thinkable, and then there are actions and counteractions. Where this will lead us, only time will tell.

Thought Questions

1. Define human rights as a concept that goes beyond social justice.
2. Discuss the relevance of a human rights perspective to the social work profession.
3. Study the U.N. Universal Declaration of Human Rights in Appendix A. Mark the basic divisions or generations of human rights.
4. What is the significance of the International Criminal Court? Discuss possible reasons for the United States' refusal to join it.
5. What is the role of Amnesty International in regard to human rights?
6. What is a war crime? How is a war crime legally different from ordinary combat? What is a war-crime tribunal? Give examples.
7. Discuss the phenomenon of rape in war. What is "spirit injury" as defined by Wing and Merchan?
8. Discuss the special suffering of women in wartime.
9. Study the newspaper headlines listed in the section "Violations of Women Domestically" and discuss their ramifications.
10. Differentiate the U.S. Bill of Rights from the Universal Declaration.
11. What is controversial about the U.S. Patriot Act that followed September 11?
12. Analyze the meaning of the statistics provided in Box 6.2.
13. Debate America's concept and operation of a war on drugs. Draw on global comparisons. What is harm reduction?
14. How is incarceration big business in the United States?
15. Compare issues of men in prison with those of women in prison.
16. Debate pros and cons of the death penalty.
17. What is suicide murder? How does this relate to the death penalty?
18. Define restorative justice. What are the basic types? What is the relevance of social work?
19. Relate reparations to crimes against humanity.

References

Alexander, D. R. (2003, June 9). U.S. gay military ban denounced in army journal. The Gay.com Network. Retrieved from http://www.UK.gay.com/headlines

Alexander, R., Jr. (2001). *To ascend into the shining world again.* Westerville, OH: TheroE Enterprises.

Amnesty International (AI). (1999). *Not part of my sentence: Violations of human rights of women in custody.* New York: Author.

Amnesty International (AI). (2001). *Broken bodies, shattered minds: Torture and ill treatment of women.* New York: Author.

Amnesty International (AI). (2003). *Death by discrimination–The continuing role of race in capital cases.* New York: Author.

Bakke, K. (2001, June/July). FGM exposed. *MS.,* 21.

Barajas, E. (1995). *Moving toward community justice.* Topics in Community Corrections. Washington, DC: U.S. Department of Justice.

Barkan, E. (2000). *The guilt of nations: Restitution and negotiating historical injustices.* New York: W. W. Norton.

Basu, R. (1999, January 5). Domestic violence in Russia reminds Iowan of need for vigilance. *Des Moines Register,* p. M5.

Biskupic, J. (2003, June 27). Decision represents an enormous turn in the law. *USA Today,* p. A5.

Bloch, H. (2002, May 27). Charging rape, facing prison. *Time,* 20.

Brady Campaign. (2003). Brady Campaign to Prevent Gun Violence. Retrieved from http://www.bradycampaign.com

Braithwaite, J. (2002). *Restorative justice and responsive regulation.* Oxford, UK: Oxford University Press.

British Broadcasting Company (BBC). (2003, June 9). Inside Highpoint Prison. *BBC 1.* Retrieved from http://www.bbc.co.uk

British Broadcasting Company (BBC). (2004, February 20). Cambodian king backs gay marriage. BBC News. Retrieved from http://newsvote.bbc.co.uk

British Columbia needle-exchange program includes crack pipes. (2003, June 25). Join Together Online. Retrieved from http://www.jointogether.org

Brownmiller, S. (1975). *Against our will: Men, women and rape.* New York: Bantam.

Brownmiller, S. (1993). Making female bodies the battlefield. *Newsweek,* 37.

Bureau of Justice Statistics (BJS). (2003). *Prison and jail inmates at midyear 2002.* Washington, DC: U.S. Department of Justice.

Butterfield, F. (2004, May 8). Mistreatment of prisoners is called routine in U.S. *The New York Times.* Retrieved from www.nytimes.com/2004/05/08/national

Carter, C. (1997, September/October). Using African-centered principles in family preservation services. *Families in Society, 78,* 531–538.

Carter, J. (2002). The troubling new face of America. *Washington Post,* p. A31.

Council on Social Work Education (CSWE). (2003). *Handbook of accreditation and procedures* (5th ed.). Alexandria, VA: Author.

Coyle, E. A., Campbell, A., & Neufeld, R. (2003). *Capitalist punishment: Prison privatization and human rights.* London: Zed Books.

Crockett, S. A. (2002, August 30). Study: More African-American men incarcerated than in college. Black Entertainment Television. Retrieved from http://www.bet.com/articles

Dahl, D. (2003, June 4). Guns in home endanger household members, study says. Join Together Online. Retrieved from http://www.jointogether.org

The Data Lounge. (2003, January 29). Pentagon ban criticized in rights report. Retrieved from http://www.datalounge.com

Davis, A. (1998). Masked racism: Reflections on the prison industrial complex. *Colorlines, 1*(2). Retrieved from http://www.arc.org/c_lines

Death Penalty Information Center. (2000, November 10). Facts about the death penalty. Retrieved from http://www.deathpenaltyinfo.org

Deutsch, A. (2001, March 31). Dutch gays to wed as law changes. *Des Moines Register,* p. A1.

Diaz, T. (1999). *Making a killing: The business of guns in America.* New York: New Press.

DiNitto, D. (2003). *Social welfare: Politics and public policy* (5th ed.). Boston: Allyn & Bacon.

Dolgoff, R., & Feldstein, D. (2003). *Understanding social welfare* (6th ed.). Boston: Allyn & Bacon.

Dominelli, L. (2002). *Feminist social work: Theory and practice.* Hampshire, UK: Palgrave.

Drug policy. (2003). Overview. Retrieved from http://drugpolicy.org/race

Drummond, T. (2000, November 6). Mothers in prison. *Time,* 105–107.

The Economist. (1999, May 15). The cruel and ever more unusual punishment. Retrieved from http://www.economist.com

The Economist. (2001, June 26). Illegal drugs: Stumbling in the dark. Retrieved from http://www.familywatch.org/library

The Economist. (2003, March 22). The needle paused. *The Economist,* 29.

Encyclopaedia Britannica. (2003). War crime. Retrieved from http://search.eb.com/eb/article?eu=78081

Fairchild, E. (1993). *Comparative criminal justice systems.* Belmont, CA: Wadsworth.

Farrell, J. (1967). *Beloved lady: A history of Jane Addams' ideas on reform and peace.* Baltimore: John Hopkins University Press.

Florida, R. (2003, May 1). Gay-tolerant societies prosper economically. *USA Today,* p. A13.

Food First. (2002). Hunger, a growing epidemic in America. *Food First Fact Sheet.* Retrieved from http://www.FoodFirst.org

Geer, N. (2000). Human rights and wrongs in our own backyard—A case study of women in U.S. prisons. *Harvard Environmental Law Review, 13.* Retrieved from http://www.lexis-nexis.com/universe/doc

Gil, D. (1998). *Confronting injustice and oppression: Concepts and strategies for social workers.* New York: Columbia University Press.

Glendon, M. (2001). *A world made new: Eleanor Roosevelt and the Universal Declaration of Human Rights.* New York: Random House.

Goodman, E. (2002, July 14). Justice for women. *The Boston Globe.* Retrieved from http://www.boston.com

Green, C. (1998, January 11). Without memory, there is no healing: Without forgiveness there is no future. *Parade,* 5–7.

Gutiérrez, L., & Suarez, Z. (1999). Empowerment with Latinas. In L. M. & E. A. Lewis (Eds.), *Empowering women of color* (pp. 167–186). New York: Columbia University Press.

Harvey, L. (2001). Leading edge: Linda Harvey. The International Center for Justice and Reconciliation Web. Retrieved from http://www.restorativejustice.org/rj3

Healy, L. (2001). *International social work: Professional action in an interdependent world.* New York: Oxford University Press.

Hemenway, D. (2002, December 9). Level of handgun ownership, not key mental health indicators, increases likelihood of suicide. Retrieved from http://www.jointogether.org

Human Rights Watch. (2001). *No escape: Male rape in U.S. prisons.* New York: Author.

Human Rights Watch. (2002a). Human Rights Watch world report: United States. Retrieved from http://www.hrw.org/wr2k2/us.html

Human Rights Watch. (2002b, July 1). International justice for women: The ICC marks a new era. Retrieved from http://www.hrw.org

Human Rights Watch (2003a). *Ill-equipped: U.S. prisons and offenders with mental illness.* New York: Author.

Human Rights Watch (2003b). The international criminal court. Retrieved from http://www.hrw.org

Hurdle, D. (2002). Native Hawaiian traditional healing: Culturally based interventions for social work practice. *Social Work, 47*(2), 183–192.

Ife, J. (2001). *Human rights and social work: Towards rights-based practice.* Cambridge, England: Cambridge University Press.

International Federation of Social Workers (IFSW). (2004). IFSW: Ethics of social work—Principles and standards. Adopted by the IFSW-IASSW General Meeting, Adelaide, Australia, August 2004.

Jansson, B. (2001). *The reluctant welfare state* (4th ed.). Belmont, CA: Wadsworth/Thomson Learning.

Johannesen, T. (2003, March 6). Positioning social work: A human rights profession in the era of globalization. Paper presented at University of Northern Iowa, Department of Social Work, Cedar Falls, IA.

Johnson, L., Schwartz, C., & Tate, D. (1997). *Social welfare: A response to human need* (4th ed.). Boston: Allyn & Bacon.

Jones, J. (2001). Two-thirds of Americans support the death penalty. Retrieved from http://www.gallup.com/poll

The Justice Policy Institute. (2003, January 6). States rely on sentencing reform to address fiscal crises. Retrieved from http://www.justicepolicy.org/cutting2

Karger, J., & Stoesz, D. (2002). *American social welfare policy: A pluralistic approach.* Boston: Allyn & Bacon.

Khan, I. (2003). Security for whom? A human rights responsibility. Amnesty International. Retrieved from http://web.amnesty.org/report2003/message-eng

Kimbro, P. (1999). Criminals meet with victims, learn impact of crimes. *Lexington Herald-Leader,* p. A1.

Kirst-Ashman, K. (2003). *Introduction to social work and social welfare: Critical thinking perspectives.* Belmont, CA: Brooks/Cole.

Koch, S. (2003, May 15). Women, war, and peace. Paper presented at the May Institute, "Peace,

Human Rights and U.S. Foreign Policy,"
University of Northern Iowa, Cedar Falls, IA.

Lamb, L. (1999, December 18). No exit here:
Oppressed by tradition and politics. *Utne Reader.*
Retrieved from http://www.utne.com

Landsberg, M. (2002, September 8). Afghan women
remain victims of hope unfulfilled. *Toronto Star,*
p. A2.

Landsberg, M. (2003, February 22). Assaults on
women continue while Tories do nothing. *Toronto
Star,* p. L1.

Lederer, E. (2002, April 12). U.N. creates new war-
crimes tribunal. Associated Press. Printed in *The
Daily Iowan,* Iowa City, Iowa.

Lite, J. (2002, October, 3). Report indicates gender-
related violence is global. *Women's E News.*
Retrieved from http://www.womensenews.org

Macionis, J. (2004). *Society: The basics* (7th ed.).
Upper Saddle River, NJ: Prentice-Hall.

Mandiberg, J. (2000). *Stand! Introduction to social
work: Contending ideas and opinions.* Madison,
WI: Coursewise Publishers.

McClelland, C. (2003, June 17). Canada to allow
same-sex marriage. *The Washington Post.*
Retrieved from http://www.washingtonpost.com

McGeorge, N. (2003, May). Restorative justice and
the EU. *Around Europe.* Quaker Council for
European Affairs, Brussels, Belgium.

Miller, J., & Schamess, G. (2000). The discourse of
denigration and the creation of "other." *Journal of
Sociology and Social Welfare, 27*(3), 39–62.

Moratorium Campaign. (2002). We become what
we hate: Murder victims' families and the death
penalty. Retrieved from http://www
.moratoriumcampaign.org

Morin, R., & Deane, C. (2001, May 3). Support for
death penalty eases. *Washington Post,* p. A09.

Mullaly, B. (1997). *Structural social work: Ideology,
theory, and practice* (2nd ed.). Toronto: Oxford
University Press.

Mundow, A. (2001, May 12). The business of prison.
The Irish Times. Retrieved from http://www
.greaterdiversity.com

Murphy, S. (2000). Deaths: Final data for 1998.
National Vital Statistics Reports, 48(11). Retrieved
from http://www.jointogether.org

National Association of Social Workers (NASW).
(2003a). Alcohol, tobacco and other substance
abuse. In *Social work speaks: National Association
of Social Workers policy statements 2003–2006*
(pp. 20–27). Washington, DC: NASW Press.

National Association of Social Workers (NASW).
(2003b). Capital punishment and the death
penalty. In *Social work speaks: National Association
of Social Workers policy statements 2003–2006*
(pp. 28–31). Washington, DC: NASW Press.

National Association of Social Workers (NASW).
(2003c). International policy on human rights. In
*Social work speaks: National Association of Social
Workers policy statements 2003–2006* (pp.
209–217). Washington, DC: NASW Press.

National Association of Social Workers (NASW).
(2003d). Juvenile justice and delinquency prevention. In *Social work speaks: National Association of
Social Workers policy statements 2003-2006* (pp.
218–223). Washington, DC: NASW Press.

National Association of Social Workers (NASW).
(2003e). Peace and social justice. In *Social work
speaks: National Association of Social Workers policy statements 2003–2006* (pp. 265–269).
Washington, DC: NASW Press.

Ogletree, C. J. (2002, August 16–18). The case for
reparations. *USA Weekend,* pp. 6–7.

Pittaway, E. (2003). A court to defend those raped in
war. *The Sydney Morning Herald.* Retrieved from
http://www.smh.com.au

Popple, P. R., & Leighninger, L. (2002). *Social work,
social welfare, and American society* (5th ed.).
Boston: Allyn & Bacon.

Power, S. (2002, Spring). Raising the cost of genocide.
Dissent, 49(2), 69–77.

Prejean, Sister H. (1994). *Dead man walking.* New
York: Vintage Books.

Ramanathan, C., & Link, R. (Eds.). (1999). *All our
futures.* Belmont, CA: Wadsworth.

Rao, R. (2003, May 14). Dowry demand lands groom
in jail. BBC News. Retrieved from
http://news.bbc.co.uk

Rehn, E., & Sirleaf, E. J. (2002). *Women, war and
peace: The independent expert's assessment on the
impact of armed conflict on women and women's
role in peace-building.* New York: U.N.
Development Fund for Women.

Reichert, E. (2003). *Social work and human rights: A
foundation for policy and practice.* New York:
Columbia University Press.

Restorative Justice Website. (2001). Transformation House. Retrieved from http://www.restorative justice.org

Restorative Justice Website. (2002, October). New Zealand expands official recognition. Retrieved from http://www.restorativejustice.org

Restorative Justice Website. Restorative practices in Guam. (2004). Retrieved from http://www .restorativejustice.org

Roosevelt, M. (2003, June 9). A new war over slavery. *Time.* Retrieved from http://www.time.com

The Sentencing Project. (2001). *Prosecuting juveniles in adult court.* Retrieved from http://www .sentencingproject.org/brief/juveniles.html

Statistics Canada. (2002, October 30). Adult correctional services 2000/01. Retrieved from http://www.statcan.ca/Daily/English

Statistics, facts, and quotes. (2003). Brady Campaign to Prevent Gun Violence. Retrieved from http://www.ichv.org

Steinem, G. (2002, December). Flashes of hope from South Korea. *MS.,* 23.

Stoesen, L. (2004, January). Gay marriage rights upheld. *NASW News,* 6.

Sullivan, A. (2003, June 30). The conservative case for gay marriage. *Time.* Retrieved from http://www.time.com

Suppes, M., & Wells, C. (2003). *The social work experience: An introduction to social work and social welfare* (4th ed.). New York: McGraw-Hill.

Terzieff, J. (2002, October 27). Pakistan's fiery shame: Women die in stove deaths. *Women's E News.* Retrieved from http://www.womensenews.org

Time. (2002, May 20). Blaming the victim. Retrieved from http://www.time.com/time/asia

Umbreit, M. (1996). Restorative justice through mediation: The impact of programs in four Canadian provinces. In B. Galaway & J. Hudson (Eds.), *Restorative justice: International perspectives* (pp. 373–385). Monsey, NY: Criminal Justice Press.

Umbreit, M. (1998). Restorative justice through victim-offender mediation: A multisite assessment. *Western Criminology Review 1*(1), 24–30.

Umbreit, M. (2000). *Family group conferencing: Implications for crime victims.* Office for Victims of Crime. Washington, DC: U.S. Department of Justice.

United Nations (U.N.). (1948). *Universal declaration of human rights.* Resolution 217A(III). New York: Author.

United Nations (U.N.). (1990). *Convention on the rights of the child.* New York: Author.

United Nations (U.N.). (2003a). Human rights watch details sexual atrocities in civil war. *UN Wire.* Retrieved from http://www.unwire.org

United Nations (U.N.). (2003b). The world's women 2000. United Nations Statistics Division. Retrieved from http://www.unstats.un.org/

United Nations Children's Fund (UNICEF). (2000, March 7). UNICEF executive director targets violence against women. Retrieved from http://www.unicef.org

United Nations Development Fund for Women (UNIFEM). (2003, May 13). The lack of equal rights for Africans is a central cause of the rapid transmission of HIV/AIDS on the Continent. Retrieved from http://www.unifem.org

U.S. Institute of Peace. (2003, December). Rwanda's women, ten years later. *Peace Watch, 10*(1), 10.

Van Ness, D. (2002, May). U.N. Crime Commission acts on basic principles. Restorative Justice Online. Retrieved from http://www .restorativejustice.org

Van Soest, D. (1995). Peace and social justice. *Encyclopedia of social work* (19th ed., pp. 95–100). Washington, DC: NASW Press.

van Wormer, K. (1997). *Social welfare: A world view.* Belmont, CA: Wadsworth.

van Wormer, K. (2001). *Counseling female offenders and victims: A strengths-restorative approach.* New York: Springer.

van Wormer, K. (2004). *Confronting oppression, restoring justice: From policy analysis to social action.* Alexandria, VA: Council on Social Work Education.

van Wormer, K., & Davis, D. R. (2003). *Addiction treatment: A strengths perspective.* Belmont, CA: Brooks/Cole.

Verschelden, C. (1993). Social work values and pacifism: Opposition to war as a professional responsibility. *Social Work, 38*(6), 765–769.

"War crime." (2003). *Encyclopaedia Britannica.* Retrieved June 24, 2003 from http://search.eb.com/eb/article?eu=78081

Watkinson, A. M. (2001). Human rights laws: Advocacy tools for a global civil society. *Canadian Social Work Review, 18*(2), 267–286.

Welch, M. (1996). *Corrections: A critical approach.* New York: McGraw-Hill.

Wetzel, J. (1993). *The world of women: In pursuit of human rights.* London: McMillan.

Whitlock, K. (2001). *In a time of broken bones: A call to dialogue on hate violence.* Philadelphia: American Friends Service Committee.

Wind, A. (2000). Book credits women's shelters for saving men's lives. *Waterloo–Cedar Falls Courier.* Retrieved from http://www.sonic.net~doretk

Wing, A., & Merchan, S. (1993). Rape, ethnicity, and culture: Spirit injury from Bosnia to Black America. *Columbia Human Rights Law Review, 25*(1), 1–46.

Witkin, S. (1998, May). Human rights and social work. *Social Work, 43,* 3.

Wronka, J. (1998). *Human rights and social policy in the 21st century.* Lanham, MD: University Press of America.

Wronka, J. (1999). Introducing the knowledge of people living in poverty into an academic environment: A challenge for the year 2000. Paper presented at the Fourth World University Conference, Sorbonne, Paris, April 23–24.

Zamichow, N., & Perry, T. (2003, June 25). Home is where the hurt is. *Los Angeles Times,* p. A1.

Zastrow, C. (2004). *Introduction to social work and social welfare* (8th ed.). Belmont, CA: Brooks/Cole.

Zehr, H. (1997). Restorative justice: The concept. *Corrections Today, 59*(7), 68–71.

Social Work across the Life Cycle

Protecting people and the natural environment through sustainable development is arguably the fullest realization of the person-in-environment perspective.

NASW, *SOCIAL WORK SPEAKS*, 2003, P. 120

Human Behavior and the Social and Physical Environment

© Rupert van Wormer

With this chapter, we begin the second of the two parts of this book. Whereas Part I has dealt more or less with the structure of social welfare systems, Part II unites policy and practice across the life span of human behavior. It is appropriate, therefore, to begin with an introduction into the bio-psycho-social and spiritual realms of life, to study what Saleebey (2001) terms "the nature of the relationship between the body, mind, soul, and the environment," a relationship that "is, at worst, a confusion, and at best, a thrilling intricacy" (p. 92).

Central to the core curriculum of social work is a course (often two courses) called "human behavior and the social environment" (usually abbreviated as HBSE). The Council on Social Work Education (CSWE; 2003) *Handbook of Accreditation Standards and Procedures* offers the following description of this course:

> Social work education programs provide content on the reciprocal relationships between human behavior and social environments. Content includes empirically based theories and knowledge that focus on the interactions between and among individuals, groups, societies, and economic systems. It includes theories and knowledge of biological, sociological, cultural, psychological, and spiritual development across the life span; the range of social systems in which people live (individual, family, group, organizational, and community); and the ways social systems promote or deter people in maintaining or achieving health and well-being. (p. 35, sec. 4.3)

Missing from this definition is the word *physical,* as in physical environment. However, social work is making some strides, albeit slowly, in conceptualizing human behavior within this larger context; attention to global phenomena requires it.

This book is about social welfare and the profession most closely associated with social welfare—social work. Social workers must have a solid grounding in the science of human behavior and understand the biological, psychological, social, and spiritual needs of people at various stages of development. Social workers also need to know how aspects of the environment and the social welfare system give rise to desirable and undesirable patterns of behavior. The knowledge of human behavior required to work in some aspect of the social welfare system is knowledge that relates to the human condition—to the corrosive effects of oppression and how people can overcome them or why so many cannot do so. As social workers and as students of human behavior, we are obligated, as Saleebey (2001) notes, "to understand, as best we can, those forces that shape and drive, constrain and obstruct, the human experience" (p. 1).

The science of human behavior is so complex as to defy our ability to do it justice, and so vast as to defy our imaginations to even try. Fortunately, our scope is limited here, in this book and chapter, to those aspects of human behavior most relevant to social welfare programming and policy. Cognizant of the notion of interactionism, we are dealing with society and self in constant interaction, with the person-in-the-environment and the environment-in-the-person. We are thus dealing with social dynamics even as we explore the biological and psychological dimensions of human existence.

Life is fraught with horrendous obstacles as people struggle to meet their basic needs. Insecurity and greed are two common pitfalls, pitfalls leading to oppression and war. Yet "from out of the ashes of oppression and destruction," as Saleebey (2001) eloquently states, "we still may witness the flourishing of the human spirit" (p. 7). At the least, as this insight offered by William Faulkner (1964/1936) (speaking of the suffering of women) indicates, people manage "to endure and endure, without rhyme or hope of reward—and then endure" (p. 144). What are the biological attributes and constraints that make survival possible? What is the message of the global environmental crisis for the world? What kind of environment is amenable to or destructive of psychological growth and development? What is the role of social forces in perpetuating our social system and what is the impact of the spiritual dimension on human behavior? Because these questions are too broad to be any more than touched on, that is what this chapter will do—touch on the fundamentals of human behavior germane to the study of social welfare systems. We start with some of the basic concepts from the social work human behavior literature.

Concepts of Human Behavior and the Social Environment

To social workers, knowledge of the concepts of human behavior and the social environment (HBSE) is not just a matter of learning the nomenclature; it is the foundation on which their change efforts will rest. Solutions to problems often depend on how they are defined and how the concepts are used. The risk to social workers who so often work at the individual level—doing assessments, treatment, and so on—is in the tendency to seek the root of the problem (such as unemployment) in individual pathology rather than in structural or interactional factors.

> The tendency to dichotomize person and environment through use of such oppositions as micro vs. macro practice is artificial. Once the split is made, the personal dimension becomes emphasized over the environmental dimension of the construct. (Besthorn & Canda, 2002)

Keep this tendency to err on the side of the individual determinism in mind as we review the fundamental HBSE concepts.

Sustainability

A term that came into prominent usage with the publication of the Brundtland Report (United Nations [U.N.] World Commission, 1987), *sustainability* is most often defined as meeting of the needs of the present generation without compromising the ability of future generations to meet their needs.

Person-in-Environment

Person-in-environment is another way of stating the basic conceptual framework of social work practice (and of social psychology), that the person and environment are in constant interaction. From a biological standpoint we must attend to factors of health, nutrition, the potential for disease, and the *physical* environment. Note the emphasis on the word *physical*. Social work has been remiss, although not as remiss as comparable professions, in its failure to recognize the interconnectedness of humankind and nature, or in failing to speak of nature at all.

Ecosystems Theory

As defined in Chapter 1, this multidimensional approach of viewing reality brings our attention to the interrelatedness of phenomena in the universe. Cause and effect are viewed as intertwined and inseparable. This is the related concept of *interactionism*: The parts of the whole are seen as being in constant interaction with other parts. Viewed in its totality, we say, "The whole is more than the sum of its parts." Just as the emotional health of the growing child requires a nurturing environment, so the health of the larger whole is essential to the health of the parts. Because the notion of *ecosystem* is a concept that originated in the biological science of ecology "pertaining to the physical and biological environment" (Barker, 2003, p. 137), it offers a useful conceptual lens for the discussion of human behavior in the social and physical environment.

Bio-Psycho-Social-Spiritual Model

The *bio-psycho-social-spiritual approach* allows the social worker to view the person holistically, as both an individual with inner biological drives and as a social and cultural being who may or may not have a sense of the sublime. Each component in the system—whether biological, psychological, social, or spiritual—is intertwined with every other component. The bio-psycho-social-spiritual framework itself can be viewed as part and parcel of ecosystems theory. It reminds social workers that even in individual micro-level intervention, a holistic, environmental approach will enhance understanding.

Let us apply this holistic approach to a 35-year-old client, Bill, who has an alcohol or other drug addiction. From a *biological* standpoint, this individual probably had a genetic predisposition that was problematic: Perhaps his father and grandfather were both alcoholics, and his aunt was bulimic. At an early age, Bill was diagnosed with hyperactivity. *Psychologically*, Bill had never grieved the loss of a brother in early childhood, a brother toward whom he had borne an unconscious sense of guilt. He survived the same illness that took the life of his younger brother. *Social* factors that affected Bill were feelings of isolation from his parents and overidentification with a high risk–taking peer group. The *spiritual* side of Bill's life had consisted of steady and early church attendance with his grandmother.

From a strengths perspective, essential to social work practice, Bill was physically strong and healthy when sober, psychologically sensitive and capable of insight and empathy with others; socially he was outgoing; and there were spiritual longings that could be tapped into as a resource for recovery and healing.

Now we will explore each aspect of the bio-psycho-social-spiritual model separately. The four interrelated parts of this model furnish the organizational scheme for this chapter. The biological component is presented in two parts—the external physical realm of the world around us, and the inner physiological world. These two worlds are interconnected in that human physical problems often emanate from environmental abuses; among them are birth defects, cancer, respiratory problems, and lead and radiation poisoning. It is imperative that social welfare professionals be guided by sustainable social development concepts to contribute to policy decisions needed in this time of unprecedented global challenge.

We now turn our attention to the environmental portion of the person-in-the-environment configuration. Because it is not dealt with elsewhere in this book, and because the health of our physical surroundings is a joint local and global concern, the bulk of our attention is centered here.

The Physical Environment

With publication of *Silent Spring*, Rachel Carson (1962) presented shocking data on the biological impact of chemical pollution that raised the consciousness of the world. Carson's work was so catalytic because it linked conservation of nature to human health (Dorsey & Thormodsgard, 2003). The title of her painstakingly documented book refers to the silencing of songbirds due to the spraying of insecticides and herbicides.

To consider human behavior in the social environment, without consideration of the impact of the physical environment on human behavior, is to omit a vital part of the equation. A full understanding of human functioning requires assessment of the physical and social environments concurrently—the physical environment includes the natural world of animals, plants, and land forms (Besthorn & McMillen, 2002). Yet conventional ecological/system models of social work have, for the most part, divorced human behavior from the physical environment. Such constructs, as Besthorn and McMillen (2002) suggest, have defined the person-in-environment only narrowly, with little or no recognition of an individual's rootedness in the natural realm. In light of the impact of the increasing environmental degradation on poor people the world over, a person-in-nature focus cannot be separate from social work's conceptualization of social justice. Such a holistic consideration effectively incorporates the macro realm with the micro and the personal (health and living standards) with the political (corporate power and public calls for governmental regulation).

Central to the study of HBSE is human growth and development. Both globally and locally a toxic environment is associated with reproductive disorders, spontaneous abortions, and malformed limbs. Consider the effect of Agent Orange sprayed by U.S. forces during the Vietnam War to defoliate forests to deny the enemy cover. Today, one in every 10 children in affected villages suffers from a serious birth defect, according to an article in *U.S. News and World Report* (Satchell, 1999).

Hardest hit by environmental problems are countries on whose soil wars are fought, poor nations of the world, and women within those nations who work closely on the land. The most common environmental problems include rural land degradation that pushes people into overpopulated cities (e.g., in Mexico), fertile soils rendered barren by drought (as in Ethiopia) and by monocropping, depletion of water through intensive irrigation (e.g., in the U.S. West), and pollution of freshwater resources (extensive in Russia) (Brown, 2001; Kluger & Dorfman, 2002). In most communities, women are the first to experience the effects of environmental damage, whether through the children they bear or in their responsibilities related to providing food and water for their families.

In a strong policy statement on the environment, the National Association of Social Workers (NASW; 2003) urges that citizens of the world embrace a moral code that recognizes the vulnerabilities of the natural environment. The position of NASW is that:

> Global justice cannot exist unless all people of the world share the Earth's resources. Global justice cannot exist when a minority of people in technologically developed countries consume a disproportionate share of the available resources. (p. 120)

The Environmental Crisis

As most environmentalists are painfully aware, human activities—burning fossil fuels, emitting pollutants from industry, and clearing forests that are the habitats for plant and animal species—now match or even surpass natural processes as agents of change. The first comprehensive study of the issue by the world's scientists, the Global Biodiversity Assessment (a U.N. report), estimates that more than 30,000 plant and animal species now face possible extinction (Associated Press, 1995). Since 1810, nearly three times as many bird and animal species have disappeared as in the previous two centuries. The U.N. report decries the loss of genes, habitats, and ecosystems. Evidence of the intensifying conflict between the economy and the ecosystem can be seen in the dust bowl emerging in China; the burning rainforests in Indonesia; the collapsing cod fishing industry in the North Sea; the falling crop yields in Africa; and the falling water tables in India (Brown, 2001). Hoff and McNutt (1994) decry the loss of something else as well—the loss of beauty:

> Perhaps the most dramatic way to express this interdependency, this imbeddedness in nature, is to say that, if we destroy our environment we destroy ourselves—our irreplaceable source of sheer physical sustenance, as well as the source of our imaginative capacities for experiencing the penultimate realities of the good, the true, and the beautiful. (pp. 4–5)

In September 2002, national leaders from around the world met in Johannesburg, South Africa, for the World Summit on Sustainable Development to address one of the most fundamental issues facing the human race at the dawn of the new century: Will the global economy make an adjustment to the contemporary biological imperatives? Korten (1999), formerly a social development worker in Africa and Latin America, uses the term *the new biology* (p. 9) to represent a paradigm shift from a belief that modern technologies such as genetic engineering will help sustain our resources to a recognition that environmental collapse will also produce economic collapse and endanger the life-giving properties of Mother Earth. The shift, as Korten sees it, is from a machine metaphor to an organism metaphor. In his book *The Post-Corporate World,* Korten envisions a world that moves beyond corporate control and makes the welfare of human beings the first priority—a priority foreign to capitalism. Continuing with business as usual, warns Korten, will ultimately lead to economic, social, and environmental collapse.

Korten's statement about environmental collapse is echoed in cautionary reports by nongovernmental organizations. A study by the World Wildlife Fund, for example, resulted in a compiled report based on scientific data from across the world that argued that the human race is plundering the planet at a pace that outstrips its capacity to support life (Townsend & Burke, 2002; World Wildlife Fund, 2002). Evidence offered in the report reveals that the seas are becoming emptied of fish, while forests—which absorb carbon dioxide emissions—are being depleted. One third of the natural world, in fact, has been destroyed by humans over the past three decades, according to the World Wildlife Fund report.

Although global economics and environmental concerns are often depicted as being at loggerheads, the health of the natural environment is vital to a healthy economy. According to Gardner (2002) of the Worldwatch Institute, the value of "nature's services" can actually be quantified. The soil-holding capacity of tree roots and the flood protection offered by mangroves have direct economic benefits, for example, while the consequences of a human-generated disruption of climate—ranging from cataclysmic weather events to insect plagues—represent severe economic losses. This fact has not been lost on insurance companies, roiling from increased damage claims stemming from natural disasters. Island nations and the Louisiana coastal areas face economic ruination from the rising seas. These phenomena, as Gardner indicates, were of no surprise to scientists. Yet the loss of some 27 percent of the world's coral reefs, another product of global warming and pollution, shocked even them. The impact is seen in fish loss and beach erosion, and probably in other ways that have not yet been realized.

The Earth can be conceived of as a giant ecosystem—a change in one part of the system reverberates throughout the whole. The founder of the Worldwatch Institute and author of *Eco-Economy,* Lester Brown (2001), urges a reversal in our thinking, accordingly: We need to regard the economy as a part of the environment, rather than vice versa, and restructure the global economy to make it compatible with the Earth's ecosystem. To envision the extent of the destruction in store for us as a world community, Brown has us imagine what would happen if China were to have a car for every adult, American style. That would require 80 million barrels of oil a day. If China produced and used paper at American rates, all the forests would disappear. One can easily see, in this example, the environmental economic interconnectedness and, of course, global interconnectedness as well. Clearly, at our present rate of industrialization, economic development is not sustainable development. Instead of living in harmony with nature, our notion of progress is more often played out as a war against nature.

War against Nature and Mother Earth Concepts

Imagine these dual (and dueling) concepts along a continuum. On one end is the notion that nature can be, must be, subdued—the notion that permeates Western thought. Bateson (1972) summarized this legacy in terms of the following core beliefs: progress derives from taming the natural elements; economic determinism is the key to progress; and we must control nature, the enemy. At the opposite end of the continuum is the Mother Earth conceptualization. This conceptualization is epitomized in the belief systems of poets, Native peoples, as well as the inhabitants (both indigenous and nonindigenous groups) of Norway. The sense of nature as teacher and nurturer is biblical:

> But ask now the beasts, and they shall teach thee;
> And the fowls of the air, and they shall tell thee;
> Or speak to the earth, and it shall teach thee. (*Bible,* Job 12:7–8)

Influenced by the birth of rationalism (1500s–1800s), the older, organic worldview of nature was replaced by a modern, scientific worldview (Warren, 2000). The new images of mastery and domination complemented the economic processes of commercialism and industrialization. Nature became viewed not as intrinsically valuable but as an end in itself, as something to be cultivated, exploited.

Social work educator Thomas Keefe (2003) shares his childhood reminiscence:

> From when I was six years old until I was nine, we had a woods in back of our house that lined the back yards of our whole street, the last street in the neighborhood. From my young perspective it seemed a very large woods. It was old growth eastern forest populated with box turtles the color of the earth, gray squirrels, fleet rabbits, pesky ticks, and a small band of kids. The woods taught me to explore, to challenge fear, to appreciate the seasons, and to just be among the trees and bushes either by myself or following my dog who often led me to some new discovery. Bulldozers and chain saws came to our woods one day; our band was hostile. After the workers went home in the evenings, we pulled bulldozer sparkplug cords, hid tools, pulled up surveying stakes, and landed in a world of trouble. Later, the workers carved wooden whistles for us kids from the felled oak and larch branches. Foundations were dug. Houses went up. Progress. People needed houses. But since that time, for me, progress and peoples' needs have seemed to rest on a great and vile pillaging of something loved. I wonder if I had not known that loss, would I not be even more lost today . . . in an illusion of progress without cost, and a world of no needs but human needs. (p. 1)

In this quotation, the child can see what the modern adult cannot—the beauty of nature, the lessons of life found in the "forest primeval," and the loss that clearing of the forest represents. Sympathizers with the feelings represented in this passage would be interested to learn of the Chipko or tree-hugging movement in India. Vandana Shiva, physicist and ecofeminist, argues that Western development is really "maldevelopment" and that when old-growth forests are replaced with commercial, monocultural plantations, important women-nature interconnections as well as ecological connections are lost (Warren, 2000).

Native Americans, Native Canadians, and many other indigenous peoples share a notion of oneness with the universe. Viewing themselves as one with the Earth and its creatures, these people see all species as being interrelated in a web of life. Historically, Native tribes had no notion of land ownership; they valued their resources and did not waste them. Blue and Blue (2001) articulate this consciousness: "In the First Nations' sense, prayer usually involves the Father Sun, Mother Earth, and the four compass directions as well as the Creator" (p. 69). Central to the Native belief system is reverence for the plant order and animal order. "The spiritual essence of the First Nations' people comes from the earth, comes from this land" (p. 79).

The European and American exploitation of the buffalo for their hides was perceived as a sacrilege by the Native people of what is now the Midwest. The mass and reckless slaughter of buffalo is realistically portrayed in the epic drama starring Kevin Costner, *Dances with Wolves*. Such slaughter typifies the new settlers' relationship with nature; they sought to subdue it and enjoy it for their immediate pleasure.

A major event in Native American history was the long-awaited opening in September 2004 of the Smithsonian Institute's National Museum of the American Indian in Washington, DC. Designed and operated by tribal members, this living museum features music, dancing, and contemporary art. Themes of nature are threaded all through the display areas (Lacayo, 2004). Constructed in harmony with nature, the tan-colored building is layered in rounded levels of limestone to depict the curves of the earth, sun, and moon. The three permanent exhibits demonstrate the relationship between humans and the spiritual realm, the survival of Native people against the forces of conquest, and Indian life in today's world. Four million people are expected to visit the new museum annually. (See the web site at http://www.nmai.si.edu.)

War and the Environment

Unlike the deliberateness of the war on nature where the goal is the taming of nature for human consumption, wars against people may or may not deliberately attack the environment as a part of a military "bring-the-enemy-to-its-knees" campaign. "It is a curious feature of our existence," notes popular author Bill Bryson, "that we come from a planet that is very good at promoting life, but even better at extinguishing it" (quoted in Challender, 2003, p. 5).

Throughout history, the environment has been one of the war's worst casualties: Romans spread salt of the fields of Carthage; Sherman's troops marched through Georgia; the United States defoliated Vietnam's jungles; and Hussein set fire to the oilfields in Kuwait. Long after the wars are over, major unanticipated effects may occur. Fischer (1993) reminds us of the "Just Cause" invasion of Panama in 1989 that, along with imposed U.S. sanctions, broke the economy, causing the people to turn to the land and take the forests. Just as war leads to environmental decimation, so does depleting the environment produce ethnic and territorial conflict. Waves of refugees fleeing war zones further ravage environmental resources.

During the Gulf War, the white mountain peaks of Iraq's northern mountains turned black, and the burning oil inferno in Kuwait blackened the skies, polluted waterways, and wiped out lower-level animal life for years thereafter. Six million barrels of oil were spilled into the sea ("The Spoils of War," 2003). In Afghanistan, landmines continue to destroy human and other animal life, and the uncontrolled use of resources, such as the cutting of forests for firewood, by six million refugees from the bombings has depleted the land of forest cover ("The Spoils of War"). Bulldozers and tanks have wreaked havoc on Palestine and prevented the people from disposing of sewerage properly. Damage to the water system has been the result.

The North Atlantic Treaty Organization (NATO) bombs that demolished the bridges of the Danube in the late 1990s did more than close the passageway to road traffic. They filled the river with debris and possibly unexploded bombs that will take years to clear (Booth, 1999). Today, according to Australian physician Helen Caldicott (2002), author of *The New Nuclear Danger: George W. Bush's Military-Industrial Complex,* the United States, with its massive arsenal of weapons of mass destruction, is the most subversive threat to world peace and the environment. The use of depleted uranium in recent wars is a case in point. Such toxic weaponry constitutes a weapon of mass destruction in terms of destruction of human life and radioactive contamination of the environment. Such weaponry goes on killing for years after a war has ended, killing the victors as well as the defeated. The chemically toxic and radioactive depleted uranium dust that is inflicting children in Iraq with leukemia and all sorts of physical deformities has entered the water table and fauna and flora and will still be polluting our Earth for endless generations (Elston, 2003). Depleted uranium vaporizes when it hits a target; once released, the particles are easily spread by the wind. This product is used by the military because of its high density, which enables it to penetrate heavy armor and military vehicles. Depleted uranium, as Elston indicates, is strongly suspected as a cause of *Gulf War Syndrome,* the term used to describe an assortment of health problems that have affected many members of the military who fought in recent wars. (For more information, visit the National Gulf War Resource Center at http://www.ngwrc.org.)

In light of the global consequences of war for the physical and social environment, the Sierra Clubs of North America have issued statements on behalf of disarmament, and reduction in dependence on oil and fossil fuels (foreign and domestic). The Sierra Clubs urge a move to a clean energy economy, greater fuel efficiency, and use of renewable sources of energy (May, 2002).

To Norwegians, adoration of nature is a vital ingredient in their national identity. Arne Naess, the founder of the deep ecology movement (which combines a love of the Earth and Earth's creatures with spirituality), spends a great part of his time in a rustic, geographically isolated mountain cabin (Eriksen, 1998). This is the national custom: More than half the population of Norway has ready access to a cabin where they spend their weekends and extensive holidays communing with nature. In an article entitled "Norwegians and Nature," Eriksen describes this other face of a modern European country—a face tied to Norway's dramatic landscape, especially in its wintry incarnation. Simplicity is a virtue in all areas of cabin life—this means no TV, computer, or indoor plumbing. The cabin is a starting point for hiking or cross-country skiing into the woods. Children in Norway learn to ski as soon as they learn to walk. The schools arrange annual ski days. In my work as an alcoholism counselor in Norway, I found that while Norwegians generally rejected a belief in God, they were comfortable with the concept of a Presence in nature. There they sought their Higher Power.

Ecofeminism and Sustainability

Besthorn and McMillen (2002) define ecofeminism as an environmental philosophy that originated with French feminism as a reaction to the "twin oppressions of women and nature within the dominance structure of patriarchal social conventions" (p. 224). The involvement of women in environmental politics bolstered this movement. Ecofeminism asserts that the dualistic division between humankind and nature is a false one, and that famine and overpopulation are rooted in oppressive power structures.

Ecofeminists view human oppression and oppression of nature as being inextricably linked. Besthorn and McMillan's recommendation is for an expanded ecological social work model of social justice; such a model is directed toward ending oppression in all its forms—social, political, economic, and environmental. Hoff and McNutt (2002) concur: Social policy making requires a new paradigm to guide progress toward building a caring, sustainable social development. Such a policy involves restoration and preservation of the natural environment.

The sustainability movement strives not only for replenishment of natural resources and "saving the Earth" but also, beyond that, for moving in the direction of a human rights focus—the rights to potable water, nutritious food, and arable land (Hawken, 2003).

On the eve of the World Summit on Sustainable Development in Johannesburg, U.N. Secretary-General Kofi Annan contrasted raw economic development with sustainable development: "Development that takes little account of sustainability is ultimately self-defeating. Prosperity built on the despoliation of the natural environment is no prosperity at all" (p. A19).

Sustainability entails an economic and political order that is in harmony with the biological resource base of society. Such conferences as the Rio de Janeiro Earth Summit in 1992 and the World Summit on Sustainable Development in Johannesburg in 2002 were inspired by the principle that only through global partnership and careful future planning can sustainable development become a reality and the steady degradation of the Earth's environment be reversed (U.N. Press Release, 2002).

In 1994, the International Conference on Population and Development in Cairo put the spotlight on the desperate need to curb overpopulation. Solutions were seen in expanding access to family planning, stress on education for girls, and improving women's and children's health and literacy. Protecting the environment, slowing population growth, and preventing poverty are now recognized as interlinked priorities. Unfortunately, in the United States, population policy is intertwined with political and religious division over abortion (Hoff & McNutt, 2002). This controversy has hovered over foreign aid funding for family planning programming as well. The link between sustainability and women's issues must be recognized.

This link was articulated for the first time by an international body at the Population Conference in 1994 and later at the World Summit for Social Development held in Copenhagen in 1995. At these conferences, the terms of the discourse shifted. At this juncture, the link between women's issues and sustainability was recognized: Not only were women on the agenda, but women also helped to set the agenda (U.N., 1995; Worldwatch Institute, 2002).

The well-publicized involvement of the world's citizenry at each recent international forum has bolstered the understanding of the human dimension of the environmental crisis. In Rio, for example, 20,000 concerned citizens and environmental activists from around the world outnumbered official representatives by at least two to one. The same was true at Cairo and was even more striking at the Women's Conference in Beijing. At these conferences, members of nongovernmental organizations (NGOs), rather than official delegates, captured the imagination of the world. Many of the organizations represented— for example, Greenpeace, Amnesty International, International Planned Parenthood, and Friends of the Earth—are themselves international. And according to French (1995), the participation of the world scientific community also has been crucial in providing the data to inform the world of the need for renewable energy sources, a very important development to counterbalance the lobbying efforts of oil and coal companies.

Over the past two or three decades, the world community has responded to the environmental challenge through the signing of numerous treaties protecting the oceans, the land (from desertification), the air (from pollution in Europe and in polar regions), and endangered species of wild flora and fauna (Annan, 2002). Yet for all the advances in helping reduce carbon emissions here, in helping protect water loss there, the reality remains: The relentless pace of global ecological decline shows no sign of abating. Income inequality continues to rise; pressures from the global market still benefit the rich at the expense of the poor; and much of the world is in a continual state of warfare. There is no recognition of pending environmental disaster, in other words— and no remedy is, as yet, in sight.

In summary, our societies are paying a high price for having followed policies of economic development that operate at the expense of social development and the protection of nonrenewable resources. The smog of Eastern Europe, eroded hillsides of Nepal, toxic waste sites of Russia, and denuded forests of Brazil and the Pacific West Coast testify to the massive destruction. Yet today, fortified by U.N. summits and much grassroots energy surrounding these international events, a new paradigm may lead to a reappraisal of the traditional focus on growth, progress, and "modernization" as ends in themselves. The notion of sustainable development is here to stay.

Water

Lack of sanitation and clean water are primary concerns of the Global South and, in some instances, of communities in the Global North, though on a much smaller scale. Only 2.5 percent of water is fresh, and only a fraction of that is accessible (Kluger & Dorfman, 2002). Global consumption of water is doubling every 20 years, twice the rate of population growth. Worse, as Barlow and Clarke (2002), authors of *Blue Gold,* indicate, toxins from cities, factories, and farms have polluted more than half of the world's rivers. The algae buildup that results from chemical contamination suffocates ocean life. Rivers, lakes, and wetlands have become repositories for excess agricultural nutrients (Brown, 2001). According to a University of Iowa report, 23 percent of wells tested in Iowa contained nitrates from fertilizer and sewage above the health limits allowed ("New Study Shows Nitrate Contamination in Wells," 2003).

Economic mismanagement, global warming, factory farming, and population growth are responsible for this worldwide water crisis, according to the World Water Development Report, a 600-page assessment of the world's most precious resource by the U.N. (Weiss, 2003). Over one billion people, mostly in poor countries, do not have access to safe water. Water scarcity is of special concern for women and children. Women and girls spend up to 43 hours per week collecting and gathering water (Warren, 2000). Because of depletion of the water supply, women must walk further for water or risk their and their family's health in fetching unsanitary water. Tragically, water is viewed by international banking associations as a human need rather than a human right.

The distinction between *need* and *right* is crucial, as Barlow and Clarke (2002) point out. A human need (e.g., health care) can be provided through private business. Accordingly, a handful of transnational corporations financed by the World Bank and IMF are reaping enormous profits through their delivery and sales of private water and wastewater services. The bottled water industry, one of the fastest-growing and least-regulated industries in the world, is depleting aquifers for profit. In allowing the commodification of the world's freshwater supplies, we are losing the capacity to avert the looming water crisis, as Barlow and Clarke argue. Hope is found in organized political resistance to water privatization by a coalition of environmentalists, indigenous human rights groups, and antipoverty activists.

Air

In satisfying the energy needs of the burgeoning human population, humans are likely affecting the climate of the entire planet. The same pollution—primarily from fossil fuels—that causes warming of the atmosphere is also causing respiratory illness (Kerry, 2002). Poor children in urban areas are at special risk of developing asthma related to poor air quality (Hoff & McNutt, 2002). To address global warming, the Kyoto Protocol was endorsed by 160 nations for the purpose of controlling greenhouse gas concentration levels. Unfortunately, ignoring the world outcry, President George W. Bush unsigned the United States from this treaty ("Alarm after U.S. Abandons Environment Treaty," 2001).

Most scientists agree that so-called greenhouse gases such as carbon dioxide and methane are depleting the ozone layer of the atmosphere. The amount of carbon pumped into the air by fossil fuel burning rose slightly in 1994, while deforestation released additional billions of tons of carbon into the atmosphere. The emissions released in the atmosphere surpass the rate at which the world's oceans and forests can absorb the chemical (Roodman, 1995). A PBS broadcast, "Earth on Edge," provided evidence of global warming as seen in the destruction of coral reefs in the Southern Hemisphere, accordingly (Moyers, 2001). Fishing industries are on the brink of collapse. Trees and other plants counter the carbon dioxide in the atmosphere and replace it with oxygen. Destruction of the Earth's vegetation is thus extremely damaging to life on Earth, affecting the very air we breathe. As more pollution enters the atmosphere, sun rays become more penetrating. The recent rise in skin cancer rates may be related to this fact ("Oh, Oh! 'Ozone Hole' Is Back," 2003).

Air pollution in Eastern Europe was so shockingly high during the 1980s and 1990s that trees and grass are stained with soot. In some areas of Poland, children are taken down in mines periodically to escape the buildup of gases in the air. The grassroots initiative called "Clean up Poland" has expanded across the nation to involve millions in the ongoing campaign to clean up wastes. Polish waterways are still heavily polluted with industrial wastes, however, and Mexico City suffers from some of the worst air pollution of any city in the world. Recently, attention was turned to China. The "Asian brown cloud," which is estimated to be two miles thick, may be responsible for hundreds of deaths a year (Kluger & Dorfman, 2002). In the United States, Canada, and Western Europe, a great deal has been done to prevent the kind of "killer smogs" that paralyzed cities in the 1950s. Air pollution, however, reaches every place on Earth, and one country's neglect is paid for, in one way or another, by the entire world.

Soil

In *A Thousand Acres* by Jane Smiley (1991), the narrator depicts her love affair with the Iowa wetlands teeming with life—"sunfish, minnows, nothing special, but millions or billions of them: I liked to imagine them because they were the soil, and the soil was the treasure, thicker, richer, more alive with a past and future abundance of life than any soil anywhere" (pp. 131–132).

Poet and environmentalist Wendell Berry (1977), in his classic work on agriculture, *The Unsettling of America*, states that if we regard plants as machines, we wind up with huge monocultures (corn and soybeans), and if the soil is regarded as a machine, then its life, its involvement in living systems and cycles, must perforce be ignored. If, like the strip miners and the "agribusiness" interest groups, we look on all the world as fuel or as extractable energy, we can do nothing but destroy it. And ultimately, what we turn against, turns against us.

Soil is the source of life. Food chains are the living channels that conduct energy upward; death and decay return it to the soil (Leopold, 1966). In his collection of essays called *A Sand Country Almanac* originally published in 1949, Aldo Leopold defined *fertility* as the ability of the soil to receive, store, and release energy. Agriculture, by overdrafts on the soil, or by too radical a substitution of domestic for native species in the superstructure, explains Leopold, may derange the channels of flow or deplete storage. Soil that is depleted of its storage or of the organic matter that anchors it washes away faster than it forms. This is erosion.

Berry (1993) goes further and talks of *land abuse.* Any form of land abuse—a clearcut, a strip mine, an overplowed or overgrazed field—is a dire threat to the Earth's ecosystem. Land abuse goes back to early American history. In *Grassland,* Richard Manning (1995) offers a critique of modern agricultural practices that began with procedures used on the rich prairies of early America. European Americans transformed a land that supported 50 million bison into one that supports about 45 million cattle. As for the soil, the cattle have eaten plants right to the dirt, killing saplings that could have controlled erosion. Whereas bison migrated with the seasons, allowing the plant life to be replenished, the cattle stay permanently on the land. Plowing, too, has taken its toll, turning long-evolved plant communities into a system of monocrop farming.

To force some life out of the depleted soil, farmers use an incredible amount of chemicals—many of them highly toxic—which seep into the rural waterways, drinking water, soil, and air. The average size of cropland is shrinking commensurate with population growth. This fact is especially pronounced in Nigeria, where rapid population growth has outrun grain production, in India, and in Bangladesh where land is divided each generation among heirs (Brown, 2001).

A popular myth is the belief that a green revolution through the wonder of fertilizers and pesticides could feed the world. Worldwide, farmers use 10 times more fertilizer and spend 17 times as much on pesticides as in 1950 (Brown, 2001). The problem is that after a few years of treating (mistreating) the soil in this way, the increased yields taper off and soil erosion and water pollution hinder further food production.

The threat to human health and to the health of other animals, earlier documented so graphically in Rachel Carson's (1962) *Silent Spring,* still persists in the United States today. In Iowa, pesticides are showing up in the state's wells and streams, and at least a million fish have been killed by manure spills over the past few years (Applegate, 1999). Researchers are studying whether or not a pesticide called dieldrin is responsible for the high rate of Parkinson's disease found in farmers in Iowa, Minnesota, Nebraska, and the Dakotas (Iowa Grain Quality Initiative, 2001). It is not just farmers, however, who are responsible. According to state officials, home owners in Iowa apply three times more pesticides on lawns, per acre, than farmers do on cropland (Beeman, 1994). Then there are golf courses, which represent the most artificially managed acreage in existence.

Without soil, we are without food. Soil loss has a lot to do with unsustainable agricultural practices. Every year, from every plowed acre in Kansas, an average of two to eight tons of topsoil wash away (Sanders, 1999). Ninety percent of U.S. cropland is losing soil with conventional farming practices (Land Institute, 2002). Conventional practices are inefficient in terms of land usage. Only a tiny fraction of pesticides reach their targets, for example, and insects, having developed resistance, are destroying crops at an increasing rate. Loss of biological diversity has become acute. Diversity, such as that found in the Land Institute's prairie, features a diversity of species. Such an ecosystem maintains its own health: Some plants thrive in dry years, others in wet; some in sun, others in the shade.

The theory behind organic agriculture lies in creating a healthy environment free from synthetic fertilizers, pesticides, and herbicides and avoidance of monocropping. Farmers' markets help the community by providing fresh produce to the local area and supporting the local economy. Thanks to refrigerated trucks and subsidized highways, the average food item travels 1,500 miles from the farms to our tables, 25 percent farther than in 1980 (Roosevelt, 2003). Fruits and vegetables lose nutrients and flavor along the way. In Iowa, the "Buy Fresh, Buy Local" campaign urges people to strengthen regional markets for locally grown foods and to choose food from farmers who avoid or reduce their use of chemicals and antibiotics. The campaign has successfully convinced local restaurants, universities, and grocery stores to purchase locally grown or raised food. (Visit http://www.foodroutes.org to learn how the "Buy Fresh, Buy Local" campaign is reintroducing Americans to knowledge concerning their food and the farmers who produce it.)

Good news for organic farmers has come from an unlikely source: McDonald's. Giving formal recognition that heavy use of growth-stimulating hormones and bacteria-controlling antibiotics is a threat to human health, McDonald's asked their meat suppliers (especially of chicken) to phase out these practices (Greider, 2003). It is generally believed that change at the demand level will have a major impact on livestock production nationwide.

Industrialized agriculture puts food on the table, but at a price—both to the farmers and to all the species that depend on the land. Farmers follow what they were taught at the land grant colleges—using artificial fertilizer and irrigation systems. Yet, this scenario is typical: Beef sells for less than the cost of raising it, and there is a glut of wheat (Sanders, 1999). While small farmers go bankrupt, the giant corporations thrive as the major beneficiaries of modern agricultural policies.

Large farms, with more land in production and more crops to sell, are in a position to benefit from subsidies. While they deplete the soil with monocropping, overproduction, and heavy use of chemicals, the large farmers produce at a lower cost, eventually driving traditional farmers out of business. And when the family farm goes, so does the local hardware store, the farm equipment store, the local school, and the café. Food prices are kept artificially low by the government; today U.S. farmers sell their products for low prices in a market glutted with food. They operate an intensified farming system that requires capital that must be borrowed at high interest rates. Families forced off the farm often end up in factory work or domestic labor. During the first seven years of the North American Free Trade Agreement (NAFTA), all three participating nations saw commodity prices and farmer incomes plummet (Halweil, 2002).

For the farm family, the loss of a farm is the loss of a whole way of life. The connection to the land is often a legacy from parents or grandparents, a family heritage that links family members to the wider community. Financial failure,

All over America farmers are selling fresh produce at farmers' markets such as this one in Iowa.

therefore, leaves farmers with a sense of personal failure and public shame. The 1984 movie *Country* movingly depicts the tragedy befalling an Iowa family after the banks foreclose and the father suffers a breakdown.

What is happening in the United States is being replicated around the world. In Australia pressures on farmers to stay afloat give them little choice but to pursue short-term efficiency at the expense of sound ecological policy. Land degradation from overgrazing is taking an economic toll in lost rangeland (Brown, 2001). In Europe the standardization demanded by modern agricultural methods is diminishing the number of species and varieties grown (Vellvé, 1993). In Asia rural villages are dying as cities become overpopulated due to developing agricultural technology, and rural values and support systems are eroding as well. Overgrazing in China, for example, has created a disastrous dust bowl situation in northern areas while irrigation is depleting the aquifers of much-needed water (Brown, 2001). From 1996 to 2001, Canada lost 22 percent of its farmers. The farm crisis has decimated rural communities while profits have gone to transnationals. The farm crisis in Canada, as elsewhere, is a result of intentional restructuring policies designed to meet market demands and promote the interests of large agribusiness corporations (Qualman, 2002).

Environmental Racism

Poverty and the environment are mutually reinforcing; as the world's poor have stretched their environmental resources to the maximum for the sake of survival, they have used up their natural capital and thereby become further impoverished. Although all humans are affected by environmental degradation, women, people of color, children, and the poor throughout the world experience the harms from it disproportionately (Warren, 2000). By the same token, while all children are at risk of environmental hazards, poor children in poor neighborhoods are at the greatest risk of developing health problems due to exposure to contaminants.

Incinerators, toxic waste dumps, and contaminated air, drinking water, and rivers are located disproportionately in African American neighborhoods and on Indian reservations. Enforcement of environmental laws, significantly, is far less vigorous in communities of people of color than in white communities. Most of the companies spewing the toxins that contaminate the communities receive massive tax incentives from state government and deny culpability for the illnesses that result from exposure to the toxins. Because American Indian lands are self-governed, many of the states' waste management laws can be ignored by commercial waste operations. Tribes are offered financial incentives to allow their land to be used as a toxic dumping ground (Warren, 2000).

In his collection of essays on environmental racism, sociologist Robert Bullard (1994) documented the glaring disparities in who pays the price for the nation's extravagant use of energy. Contained in his book *Unequal Protection* is the story of Louisiana's "Cancer Alley." Here, in the lower Mississippi River valley where more than a quarter of the nation's chemicals are produced, incredibly high cancer rates are found. Activists from NGOs such as Greenpeace have organized to expose this fact and have revealed to the world the severe health problems of children living near the industrial sites. In Louisiana, the pollution is so life-threatening that whole communities are fighting for relocation. Environmental groups are taking industries to court based on Title 6 of the Civil Rights Act, which guarantees equal protection under the law (Monsho, 2001). Built from the grass roots up, the environmental justice movement is an effort with long-term implications for changing national policies.

Another focal point of environmental concern has taken place in Anniston, Alabama, where a recent court settlement confirmed the damage done by industry-polluted waterways. Monsanto polluted the soil and water in their production of cancer-causing PCBs (polychlorinated biphenyls), which were used in insulation for electrical equipment. Human exposure to PCBs comes through eating contaminated fish. Residents of the largely black and low-income Anniston neighborhood won a settlement of $42.8 million in their class-action suit against the company (Environmental Justice Resource Center, 2001). Production of PCBs was banned in the 1970s.

Promising Developments

Measures of the gross domestic product (GDP) gauge economic growth in terms of production and sales of merchandise; no accounting is made of the loss of resources. Defense spending can make a nation at war look very productive on paper. Social policy, as Hoff and McNutt (2002) suggest, should move us from a model that promotes cleanup of the toxic wastes of industrial capitalism to a proactive model for environmentally sustainable practices. We, as citizens of the world, must advocate for the following governmental policies.

Ratification of Relevant Environmental Treaties   Environmental treaties that need to be ratified include those such as the Convention on Biological Diversity, which promotes conservation of natural resources, and the Kyoto Protocol, which is designed to counter human-induced climate change. Both the events of September 11 and recent empirically based evidence of global warming related to heavy consumption reinforce the case for accelerating the transition to a more efficient energy system that is based on alternative, regional resources. The European Union (EU) is making strides toward achieving its Kyoto target by enhancing energy efficiency (Dunn & Flaven, 2002). Carbon emissions in the EU have already dropped significantly; for example, in Germany, they have dropped by 19 percent owing to the decline in coal use in former East Germany. Non-EU nations such as China, Mexico, and India also have set national goals to increase renewable energy.

Reorientation of National Health Policy   The national health policy needs to be reoriented toward prevention—a public health approach. Hoff and McNutt (2002) recommend such a policy to reduce the presence of cancer-causing substances in the environment. Ordinary citizens can do much to uncover the truth about such things as the impact of landfills and the effects of water pollution in their region by using federal and state freedom-of-information laws. The public can use such laws to request all documents (e.g., from the state Department of Environmental Protection) pertaining to the issue at hand, and then expose any revelations of concern to the public through the media.

Support for Organically Based and Diversified Agriculture   Organic milk is healthier because it comes from cows that are not treated with antibiotics and synthetic growth hormones (Buechner, 2003). Vandana Shiva has set an eco-friendly standard in India through her organization Navdanya (Nine Seeds), which encourages farmers to form their own seed banks in order to produce hardy varieties of crops that can be grown with natural fertilizer (Ganguly, 2002). Shiva's work, like that of the Land Institute in Kansas, shows that traditional methods can produce high yields at little cost to the environment.

Worldwide, instead of encouraging mass food production by any means, governments should eliminate pesticide subsidies and tax the use of harmful chemicals instead. Denmark, Norway, and Sweden all do this at the present time (Halweil, 2002).

Promotion of Viable Alternative Energy Sources The average American's car is driven nearly 12,000 miles every year (American Automobile Association [AAA], 2003). With fossil fuels (coal, oil, and natural gas) being unable to meet our current demands, we must seek alternatives to our present reliance on them. According to Lester Brown (2001), Denmark is farther along than any other nation in the shift to the reuse/recycle model—the new "eco-economy." The eco-economy, ideally, will be powered by sources of energy that derive from the sun, wind, and geothermal energy within the Earth. Denmark has stabilized population growth, banned the use of coal-fired power plants and of nonrefillable beverage containers, promoted fuel efficiency in cars, and is now getting 15 percent of its electricity from wind. "In addition, [Denmark] has restructured its urban transport network; now 32 percent of all trips in Copenhagen are on bicycle" (p. 82). Brown also commends South Korea for its successful reforestation program, and Costa Rica and Iceland for their plans to shift entirely to the use of renewable energy in the decades ahead.

An article on pedestrian cities describes how Copenhagen, Denmark, became one of the world's great pedestrian cities (Makovsky, 2002). Copenhagen's success was 40 years in the making. City planners did the following: converted streets into pedestrian-only thoroughfares; gradually eliminated parking spaces; turned parking lots into public squares; populated the core of the city; and made bicycles available for $2.50 per day. The bikes can be left at any of the more than 100 bike stands, and money is refunded.

Unlike with oil, nearly all countries can tap into wind power to generate electricity. Denmark and Germany are now building offshore wind farms (Brown, 2003). Denmark gets a higher percentage of its electricity from wind with each year that passes. The energy future, as Brown dramatically states, belongs to wind.

Restructuring of Transportation Practices Denmark is not the only country that relies on bicycle transport. The Netherlands, Germany, and China also have a high ratio of bikers to drivers. More and more local governments are recognizing that bikes reduce pollution and traffic (Gardner, 1998). In the United States and Canada, bicycles are rarely used for trips to work. Most bike trails are strictly recreational. Since housing tends to be miles away from work, commuting by car is often the only way to get there. The city of Portland, Oregon, however, has been a leader among U.S. cities in providing extensive light-rail from housing developments to the city center. A survey of light-rail ridership that included the cities of Los Angeles, Denver, Washington, DC, and Salt Lake City showed that most rail passengers left their cars at home ("Rail Ridership Exceeds Expectations, Study Says," 2003).

The very cars and trucks that made massive urbanization possible are now contributing to the deterioration of cities (Brown, 2001). To alleviate central city congestion, some cities such as London, Singapore, and Trondheim are charging motorists who drive to the city centers. The U.S. federal budget allocations, unfortunately, are biased toward the construction of highways over rail transport.

© Rupert van Wormer

Portland, Oregon leads the way in urban transport. Such developments reduce air pollution while alleviating traffic congestion.

If you talk to tourists who have visited Europe or Japan, you will hear of the convenience of high-speed rail travel. The Eurostar from London to Brussels, for example, can travel up to 186 miles per hour. In the United States, in contrast, passenger trains were driven out of business, and huge, heavily polluting trucks have displaced railroads as carriers of most high-value freight. According to a recent study by economists from the Brookings and American Enterprise institutes, for every passenger mile traveled, public transportation uses about half the fuel of private modes of travel (Layton, 2002). Private vehicles emit 95 percent more carbon monoxide, and about twice as much carbon dioxide and nitrogen oxide, than public vehicles for every passenger mile traveled. Two tracks of rail can carry as many people in an hour as 16 lanes of highway—with far less energy and pollution (Lowe, 1994). Readily available mass transportation, moreover, alleviates poverty by connecting jobs and homes to transit as well as providing mobility for elderly people no longer able or willing to drive.

Ian Roberts (2003) argues convincingly that America is pathologically addicted to oil. This fact he attributes partly to the growth of the car industry— in the 1930s, General Motors bought up America's tramways and then closed them down—but mainly to urban planners for creating a situation of urban sprawl. In his words:

> Throughout the 1920s and 1930s, America "road built" itself into a nation of
> home-owning suburbanites. In the words of singer Joni Mitchell: "They paved par-

adise and put up a parking lot." Cities such as Los Angeles, Dallas, and Phoenix were moulded by the private passenger car into vast urban sprawls which are so widely spread that it is almost impossible to service them economically with public transport.

As the cities sprawled, the motor manufacturing industry consolidated. Car-making is now the main industrial employer in the world, dominated by five major groups of which General Motors is the largest. The livelihood and landscape of North Americans were forged by car-makers. (p. 2)

Some positive steps have been taken; for example, the cities of Portland, San Diego, Baltimore, St. Louis, Denver, and Dallas have installed new, or expanded former, light-rail systems. In nearly every instance, the daily use of these trains has been much greater than what was projected. More typical than these cities with intracity rail transit systems, however, are cities that spend decades dealing with discussions, proposals, planning processes, referendums, and so on, only to end up building yet more multilane highways and overpasses. As highways expand, the problems of urban sprawl, pollution, and congestion continue to grow.

Today, there is much social activism on behalf of our environment and future generations. Social activists also seek to end discriminatory practices such as locating highly polluting factories in low-income, populated areas. A surprising ally in the cause of environmental protection is the Evangelical Environmental Network—a group of fundamentalist Protestants who cite the Old Testament teachings concerning the need to acknowledge the presence of God in the land and proscriptions against waste. Jewish and Muslim scholars concur in this view ("Religious Scholars Say God Decrees: 'Thou Shalt Conserve,'" 2001).

For social workers, opposing environmental degradation is a crucial social justice issue, one closely bound to global interconnectedness: Air and water pollution know no national boundaries. Confronting this issue should be, as Kahn and Scher (2002) suggest, an essential part of generalist social work practice in the new millennium. To this end, the curriculum at Ramapo College in New Jersey has placed a focus in their HBSE courses on the integration of natural and human needs and on research into evidence of environmental racism concerning African Americans, Pacific Islanders, and Latino farm workers (Kahn & Scher). The HBSE component of the curriculum, as Besthorn and Canda (2002) indicate, is an ideal place to begin revisioning the social environment to encompass a deep ecological awareness.

Biological Components in Human Behavior

In the previous section, we considered the importance to all life of having a healthy atmosphere—clean air and water, and uncontaminated and abundant plant and marine life. We also considered the reverse: the tremendous health consequences of pollution—the human-made despoliation of the air we breathe, the water we drink, and the food we eat.

This section provides a brief overview of the biological attributes that are most relevant to social work at the individual level—the physiological dimension. For social work practice as it is carried out in most industrialized nations (e.g., in child welfare departments, schools, mental health centers, and nursing homes), the practitioner must have knowledge of psychopathology, substance abuse, mental illness, and health problems and disease in general. New knowledge about the genetic and biochemical links to individual problems and exciting discoveries about the dynamics of the brain (e.g., from magnetic resonance imaging, or MRIs) have provided an awareness of the link between inner and outer—between the inner workings of the mind and outer behavior. For example, using MRIs, scientists have learned that the brains of schizophrenics differ from those of people without the disease; schizophrenics have smaller frontal lobes, the part of the brain responsible for planning and decision making (Park, 2003).

The truth of interactionism is shown most strikingly in studies of the impact of sensory input in changing the brain. Among musicians and blind Braille readers, for example, years of tactile movements of a certain sort are reflected in brain functioning, a difference that can be viewed thanks to the new technologies. The implications of Schwartz and Begley's book *The Mind and the Brain: Neuroplasticity and the Power of Mental Force* (2002) are profound: The brain has the ability to rewire itself. This phenomenon has been revealed in experimentation with stroke victims and dyslexics, and even in thinking exercises as described by Schwartz and Begley in their groundbreaking research.

Such new insights, as Schwartz and Begley (2002) contend, herald a revolution in the treatment of strokes, depression, addictions, obsessive-compulsive disorders, and even psychological trauma. What we have learned from the recent research explains why certain therapies are effective—for example, work with stroke victims in redirecting activities to undamaged regions of the brain and cognitive therapy for alcoholics and for persons suffering from obsessive-compulsive disorders or depression to help them replace irrational thoughts and obsessions with healthy thoughts. Self-help groups like Alcoholics Anonymous have relied on such approaches for years (e.g., teaching slogans such as "easy does it" and "one day at a time" to suppress the addict's tendency to catastrophize events); we knew such methods worked, but we did not know why. Now we do know why. Recent discoveries also have further reinforced our awareness of the interconnectedness of the biological and psychological dimensions of human behavior. This interconnectedness is most obvious in the effect of psychotropic medications on mental disorders such as psychosis.

Less intriguing perhaps, because it is more out of our control, is the role of intrauterine and genetic factors including hormones in human behavior. Intrauterine exposure to testosterone, for example, can masculinize a child, affect the development of sexual orientation, and even affect aspects of learning. In one study of spatial abilities, lesbians performed as well as straight men ("Gay Men's Brains Work Like Women's, Study Says," 2003). More obvious are the effects of intrauterine exposure to high levels of alcohol, which can cause irreversible brain damage and is the leading known cause of mental retardation.

The genes we inherit from our parents determine much of what we are and look like. Temperament (e.g., timidity or a tendency toward aggression) is highly hereditary as well (Harris, 1998). Genes also have been implicated in predispositions to certain diseases—alcoholism, asthma, breast cancer, hypertension, schizophrenia. But nature and nurture, as Saleebey (2001) suggests, go hand-in-hand. How people react to our innate characteristics determines, to a large degree, their significance and meaning.

Biochemical abnormalities associated with chemical abuse trigger mechanisms that demand more of the harmful substances; this is the phenomenon known as addictive craving. The addicted brain, we now realize, is significantly different from the normally functioning brain. Through long-term drug misuse, the depletion of the brain's natural opiates creates a condition ripe for the kind of relentless craving that is known to all "who have been there." Compounding the problem of molecular alterations in the brain (experienced as a general malaise) is the fact that each time a neurotransmitter such as dopamine floods a synapse through the introduction of a powerful drug like crack or meth into the body, circuits that trigger pleasure are indelibly imprinted in the brain. So when the smells, sights, and sounds associated with the memory are experienced, these feeling memories are aroused as well. So palpable, in fact, are these feeling memories that researchers can now compare the brain of the addict in a state of craving (elicited by these behavior feelings) with the brain of the addict in a stationary state (van Wormer & Davis, 2003).

Society's response to illness and disease—the safety net available to help people who are incapacitated physically or mentally—is often taken as a measure of a society's level of civilization. Caring societies have remedies in place to alleviate individual suffering so that rich and poor alike receive the help they need in times of grave difficulty. In Chapter 9, we explore the health/mental health care policy ramifications in some depth.

Biology and psychology are intimately linked inasmuch as the mind is a part of the body. Studies have established links, for example, between the incidence of depression and several other diseases, including cancer, Parkinson's disease, epilepsy, stroke, and Alzheimer's disease (Lemonick, 2003). With recognition of this link between mind and body, we move to a consideration of psychological factors in human behavior. The psychological aspect of being encompasses our dreams and visions, as well as our will to keep going against all odds or, conversely, to give up at the first sign of defeat.

The Psychological Domain

Psychology examines human behavior from the viewpoint of the individual. Emphasis is placed on learning, drives, and motivation. Psychological variables interact with innate, biological tendencies to produce personality characteristics. On the school ground, for example, recess is a dreaded time for shy and unathletic boys. Some children are aggressive and tend to dominate the schoolyard, while others retreat to the background. Social variables thus come into play, reinforcing psychological predispositions to encompass what we know as personality. How people handle the vicissitudes of life, how they build up defense mechanisms to cope with adversity and defeat—these are defining characteristics of personality, the traits we know as character.

Given the same set of circumstances, why does one person sink and another swim? William Shakespeare (1970/1599), whose genius showed in his intuitive grasp of psychology, grappled with this question in his historical tragedies. Drawing on historical and fictional characters, Shakespeare brilliantly related his heroes' deeds to their personal mind-sets and predispositions. Thus we hear from Cassius in *Julius Caesar:*

> Men at some time are masters of their fates;
> The fault, dear Brutus, is not in our stars,
> But in ourselves, that we are underlings. (Act I, scene ii)

Three centuries before Freud, Shakespeare drew our attention to the role that the unconscious mind plays in human behavior. Guilt, a key theme of *Macbeth,* is revealed in the behavior of Lady Macbeth, who could not stop washing her hands following the murder of Duncan, and who asks, "Will not all great Neptune's ocean wash this blood clean from my hand?" (Shakespeare, 1970/1605, Act II, scene i).

Our concern in this section is with psychological aspects of human behavior as exemplified in issues of personal trauma and resilience, as people endure ordinary and extraordinary crises across the life span. We start with the concept of developmental psychology, which concerns human growth and development from childhood to old age. Most HBSE courses draw on the theory of psychological development proposed by Erik Erikson (1950), whose contribution is highly compatible with social work theory.

In his formulation, Erikson focuses on how individual personalities evolve throughout life as a result of the interaction between biologically based maturation and the demands of society (Zastrow & Kirst-Ashman, 2004). At each *stage of development,* from birth to old age, there is a crisis to be resolved. For the practitioner, knowledge of psychological milestones that are normally achieved (e.g., when leaving adolescence and entering young adulthood) is important in individual evaluations. In Erikson's conceptualization, at each juncture of life, an individual must resolve the crisis relevant to that developmental stage before moving on to the next stage. Unresolved crises from the past, such as issues from early childhood, can come back to haunt people later in life. The stages are as follows:

1. Basic trust versus mistrust—birth to 18 months
2. Autonomy versus shame and doubt—18 months to 3 years
3. Initiative versus guilt—3 to 6 years
4. Industry versus superiority—6 to 12 years
5. Identity versus role confusion—adolescence
6. Intimacy versus isolation—young adult
7. Generativity versus stagnation—maturity
8. Ego integrity versus despair—old age

Psychologist Abraham Maslow (1970), another major contributor to development theory, constructed a paradigm of needs, each of which has to be fulfilled successively before the next level of higher needs can be achieved. In Maslow's *hierarchy of needs* (see Figure 7.1), the basic physical needs of human

Figure 7.1 | Maslow's Hierarchy of Needs

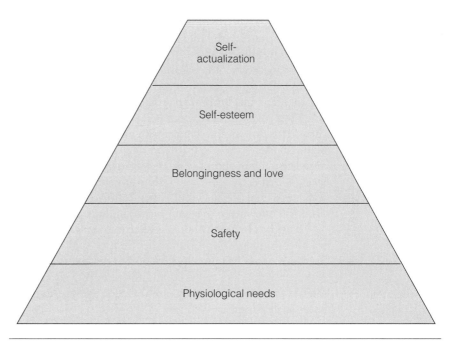

survival must be met before the higher-level needs—safety, belongingness and love, esteem, and self-actualization—can be realized. Self-actualization refers to a person's achievement of his or her highest potential as a human being. Because each person in Maslow's conceptualization tries to satisfy these needs in ascending order, high self-esteem is not likely to occur in the absence of love, nor is self-actualization likely to happen without a certain degree of financial security. The stage of self-actualization is not permanent. Given the uncertainties in life, one can lose one's balance at any moment and be reduced to the lower rungs of the ladder, struggling at the level of mere survival.

Maslow's theory is psychological in its emphasis on the individual's being driven by impulses toward an identifiable goal. The concepts of esteem and self-actualization are not aggregate concepts, certainly. Strength, from this perspective, comes from one's own inner resources, not from rootedness in the community. Dominelli (2002) critiqued Maslow's model, pointing out its neglect of social attributes (e.g., race and gender) and of the influence of capitalism (e.g., in manufacturing need through the marketing of commercial products that may be downright harmful). These points are well taken. Maslow's paradigm, moreover, reflects the value of individualism in mainstream U.S. culture. Other cultures are more collectively oriented; traditional American Indian culture, for example, is geared toward group and spiritual satisfaction rather than elevation of self. Still, because of its relevance to social welfare, Maslow's conceptualization of human needs is commonly cited in the social work literature. With slight modification (such as linking self-actualization to generativity, or giving to others and posterity), the hierarchy-of-needs construct can offer a holistic guide to personal fulfillment.

The hierarchy of needs offers a paradigm for viewing a society's level of success in meeting its people's needs, or the needs of any group, in society. Take, for instance, a community with a high crime rate: People may have no trouble getting their physical needs met, and yet they may experience serious safety concerns. This does not preclude residents in the community from having a sense of belongingness and love from their families, but they will still experience hostility in the neighborhood (e.g., if gang-related violence proliferates). At the micro level (which is clearly how Maslow intended for his model to be applied), physical needs may be met, but other factors (e.g., physical or sexual abuse) can diminish one's sense of safety, belongingness, self-esteem, and self-actualization.

Maslow's hierarchy of needs, like Erikson's developmental stages, lends itself to a consideration of both the healthy and unhealthy in human affairs. Furthermore, it has more potential than Erikson's model, which is age-based, to represent setbacks caused by adulthood socialization and traumatization (e.g., long-term family violence, the horrors of warfare, and more immediate experiences such as rape).

Now we move from paradigms to a study of actual human behavior under conditions of mass experimentation and terrorization. In one of the most extraordinary social-psychological documents of all time, Bettelheim (1943) recounted in graphic detail the behavior of inmates in the wartime concentration camps at Dachau and Buchenwald. We will apply the insights we draw from the Bettelheim study, based on situations of extreme disempowerment through psychological abuse and torture in the concentration camps, to more domestic situations such as kidnapping and battering. The focus will be on how victim behaviors that strike outsiders as bizarre and counterproductive can make perfect sense when viewed from the inside. While reading these case histories, consider the ways in which we use psychological defenses to maintain our emotional balance and, indeed, our very sanity.

Bettleheim's Concentration Camp Study

From the moment of their arrival, the persons herded into the German concentration camps were deprived of all means of meeting their biological needs. As they watched their fellow inmates being beaten and killed, their sense of safety was nonexistent. Following Maslow's theory, we could say that all their means of meeting the basic needs that human beings have were violated.

The socialization process into the rules and norms of concentration camp life began almost instantly. The prisoners did not know exactly why they were incarcerated or for how long. They were cut off from all contact with the outside. They suffered extreme malnutrition, and yet were forced to perform hard labor. The goals of the Gestapo, as Bettelheim saw it, were to break the prisoners as individuals, provide a laboratory for human experimentation, and spread terror through the wider population.

The first stage of imprisonment, Bettelheim termed "the initial shock." During this period of being taken into police custody, all new prisoners were in shock. Their survival rates depended, in part, on their interpretation of the situation. The nonpolitical middle-class prisoners who were in the minority were the least able to withstand the initial shock, as they had never opposed Nazism. Some who committed suicide were in this group. Members of the upper classes, who felt superior, and of the lower classes, who were surprised to be in "good company," fared better.

Torture took place during the next stage—entry into the camp. Initiation rituals consisted of forcing inmates to curse their God and defile themselves in various ways.

The most important psychological truth we can learn from this study, in my opinion, comes from the final stage of imprisonment; it has to do with the difference in attitude between the new prisoners and the prisoners who had served more than a year in the camp. The seasoned prisoners seemed little concerned with life on the outside; only what took place in the camp was real. "There was every indication," Bettelheim wrote, "that the prisoners who had reached [this later stage] were afraid of returning to the outer world" (p. 437). Further, they had learned to direct aggression against themselves, which was safe. The longer-term prisoners talked little of their past lives and seemed to be out of touch with reality. They "lived, like children, only in the immediate present" (p. 443). They fought with each other one minute, only to become close friends a few minutes later. Regression to childhood seemed apparent in their attitudes and interactions.

Bettelheim defined this final adjustment to life in the camp as the internalized acceptance of the values of the Gestapo. This transition was displayed in acts such as inmates' emulating the guards' dress and behavior, taking pride in standing well at attention, and espousing belief in the superiority of the German race.

The truths revealed in this study of a cruel and extreme situation can be generalized to some other situations. Though some of these situations are more individualized, they are not necessarily less cruel or extreme.

Kidnap Victims and Hostage Situations

When 14-year-old Elizabeth Smart was kidnapped from her suburban bedroom and marched at gunpoint miles into the woods and held for many months, she made no effort to get help. When the police came to rescue her, she denied her identity. Her father later explained to reporters that she had been brainwashed (Browning, 2003).

The term *brainwashing* refers to the deliberate attempt to control someone's mind. The Chinese communists used this term to describe their partially successful attempts to get American prisoners of war to believe in communism and denounce the United States (Browning, 2003). The case of Patty Hearst, heir to a huge newspaper fortune, who became a member of the violent political gang that kidnapped her is often considered an example of brainwashing. Beaten and raped while confined to a dark closet, Hearst later served time in prison for bank robbery (Miller, 2002).

In fact, neither of these kidnapping cases constitutes instances of brainwashing. There appeared to be little systematic effort to indoctrinate the kidnap victims. A more relevant explanation for the overly compliant behavior of Elizabeth Smart and the conversion experience of Patty Hearst is what we can refer to as the *survivor syndrome*. This phenomenon occurs in situations of terror, disorientation, and absolute dependence on one's captors. The survivor syndrome is characterized by feelings of attachment and gratitude for small favors that may be provided. In the first instance of extreme helplessness, one's behavior may change for self-protection and to meet one's biological needs. The sexual exploitation that occurred with these teen victims would have played havoc with the emotions of these young captives.

The manifest personality changes seen in survivors (e.g., of the concentration camps or of marriages built on alternating violence and kindness—see the next section) and the eventual bonding of victims with their captors may be hard to explain to outsiders, but they are normal responses to situations of extreme powerlessness and uncertainty. The survivor syndrome, which is similar to the phenomenon known in the literature as the "Stockholm syndrome" (referring to a hostage situation in Sweden in which the hostages bonded with their captors to some extent), explains why even severely abused children love and may be fiercely loyal to their parents, and why women exposed to intermittent kindness by their captors—within the context of a life-and-death situation from which there is only limited possibility of escape—may bond with their captors, and even testify on their captors' behalf in court proceedings (Wallace, 1999).

The Captivity of Battered Women

I purposely use the word *captivity* here, avoiding the term *battered women's syndrome*, in order to stress the situational aspect of domestic violence. Male batterers, consciously or unconsciously (due to their own psychological insecurity), oppress their partners by isolating them from loved ones, making constantly demeaning remarks, and instigating calm periods punctuated by periods of frightening violence. The widely used Power Wheel from the Duluth Domestic Intervention Project includes the following strategies of dominance: intimidation; emotional abuse; isolation; and minimizing and blaming, using children, male privilege, economic abuse, and coercion as leverage. Along the rim of the wheel are the words *physical* and *sexual violence.* The Duluth Power Wheel accurately reflects the system of privilege that perpetuates violence and the dynamics of maintaining that power. (See the Power Wheel at http://www.domestic violence.org/wheel.html.) The Power Wheel is an effective heuristic device for helping survivors to externalize their maltreatment. In battering men's groups, however, presentation of the Power Wheel reportedly mystifies many of the participants. Most of the men who are court-ordered to treatment often, paradoxically, see themselves as the victims (van Wormer & Bednar, 2002).

Power abuse by a man of a woman is often about cultural attitudes pertaining to expected roles for women. Our concern here, however, is with the psychology of male battering. Typically suffering from underlying feelings of insecurity, batterers often display jealousy and possessiveness of their partners. Male abusers, as Marano (1993) suggests, may go into a rage when their wives go out with friends. Immigrant wives may be discouraged from learning the language of the new country or from driving to keep them dependent and easier to control.

Imagine the impact on the victimized party in such a relationship after years of put-downs, beatings, and threats of violence or murder if the victim tries to leave. Some stay in these abusive situations out of fear of the risks involved in escape—risks that are very real. Another rational reason for staying in such relationships may be, at least in part, an economic one (James & Harris, 1996; O'Brien, 1999). Foreign women may fear deportation.

In my work with a group of battered alcoholic women, over and over I heard comments like, "But I love him"; "He needs me"; "I was safe, but I went back to him again and again"; and "I had some nice men friends, but they bored me." I did not see economic motives in that group. Some of the group members said they supported their partners, or loaned or gave money or cigarettes to them. Often deep, underlying motives keep such women hooked to their abusive partners—motives I attribute to situations of long-term and severe psychological mistreatment. The physical wounds of repeated beatings may heal; the psychological wounds may not. Anna Quindlen (1998), in *Black and Blue,* articulates the captivity of being battered and the helplessness that ensues:

> Nobody got to see the hitting, which was really the humiliation, which turned into the hatred. Not just hating Bobby, but hating myself, too, the crying self that was afraid to pick up the remote control from the coffee table in case it was just the thing that set him off. (pp. 10–11, 210)

Deeply disturbing and violent events can leave an indelible mark on the human psyche. Typical problems that bring women survivors of long-term violence into treatment include problems in new relationships, inability to sleep, depression, and addiction disorders. Survivors' psychological defense mechanisms cause them to repress overwhelming emotions and thoughts related to trauma. The unconscious knows, however, even when memory does not.

Some commentators still blame the victim for staying in abusive relationships. Terms such as *codependent* and *enabler* are often applied indiscriminately to women who are not yet strong enough or angry enough to escape the abuse: "The first time he beat me, it was his fault; the second time, it was my fault for staying" ("Enabling Concept," 1986, p. 6). The challenge to feminist theorists is how to explain the often-irrational attachment of battered women to their abusers.

If we agree with the psychological truths that were revealed in the Bettelheim concentration camp study and the long-term kidnapping examples, we can come to understand how prisoners get institutionalized and seem to lose their ability to make decisions for themselves. Basically, we can understand the victim's identifying with the powerful individuals who can exact terrible punishments and withhold the necessities of life as a regression to a dependent childlike state. This response is not gender-specific; it is a human response. In positions of vulnerability (e.g., old age), men as well as women can and clearly do experience battering in relationships.

Fortunately, with help and support, such as that offered through professional counseling, after the danger has ceased, the long journey toward freedom and healing can begin. Following Maslow, the transition is from the level of safety to the level of love and belongingness. Social workers are apt to encounter women who have been battered when working in emergency rooms or women's shelters and (less obviously) through child abuse investigations and work with clients at substance abuse treatment centers. Always, in the information-gathering process with any client, women should be asked about abuse.

In her interviews with women who had left battering situations, Schechter (2002) posed a question that is rarely asked of survivors of abuse: "What helped you get out of the situation?" The typical response was: "Another human being who cared." From an empowerment perspective, counselors can help women discover inner strengths they never knew they had, and help them understand that behaviors that might seem maladaptive to outsiders actually are a means of survival—that in no way are they to blame for the abuse or for their response to it. Empowering interventions can help women move from a self-concept of victim to viewing themselves as survivors.

Post-Traumatic Stress Disorder and War

Chronic post-traumatic stress disorder (PTSD) affects 5.2 million Americans—including 30 percent of all combat veterans—who have endured a traumatic event like combat, rape, or a natural disaster, according to the National Mental Health Association (Coolican, 2004). The American Psychiatric Association's (APA; 2000) *Diagnostic and Statistical Manual of Mental Disorders,* fourth edition, text revision (DSM-IV-TR), lists the major symptoms of PTSD as: denial of event, numbing, flashbacks, intrusive thoughts, guilt feelings, sleep disturbances, jumpiness, and preoccupation. Such compulsive reexperiencing of pain may be regarded as an unconscious attempt to integrate and heal the past. (The concept of PTSD was originally called post-Vietnam syndrome, but then was broadened to include survivors of other traumatic experiences such as rape.)

War experiences, singularly, are fraught with trauma-inducing events. Veterans in treatment for conditions such as alcoholism or other drug addictions, sleeping problems, recurrent nightmares, depression, and physical wounds often suffer from psychological trauma. An experimental program at the University of Washington School of Medicine for veterans suffering from nightmares and other symptoms is prescribing the prescription drug Prazosin. Although results are preliminary, many of the 1,000 patients are now sleeping normally for the first time in years (Coolican, 2004). The drug apparently works by cutting down on an adrenalinelike compound that floods the brain of war-traumatized veterans at night.

Social workers, in their work with persons who have survived horrifying experiences, can provide crisis intervention as soon as possible in hopes of preventing traumatic reactions. Social workers have a long history of working with trauma. The Smith College School for Social Work, in fact, was founded more than 85 years ago to respond to the "shell-shocked" veterans of World War I. Today the school still offers training in interventions to respond to trauma wherever it is found.

Trauma prevention is another area of social work clinical activity. After September 11, for example, volunteers went to New York City from all over the United States to provide supportive counseling to survivors. Work with rape victims, battered women soon after an assault, and children who have experienced or witnessed violence is important to prevent long-term psychological damage. We do not know the degree of effectiveness of such counseling, but recently a study on this topic was published in the *Journal of the American Medical Association.* The study involved a cognitive behavioral intervention group (and a control, or wait-list, group) of school children who suffered from anxiety and/or depression following victimization by experiencing or witnessing severe family violence. After three months, the researchers found that a large majority of the students who were given immediate therapy had fewer signs of violence-related distress when compared to the delayed-treatment group. The latter group, however, also improved after therapy (Stein et al., 2003).

In an earlier study of college rape victims, Schwartz and Dekeseredy (1997) discovered that the initial response to a rape victim has more impact on her eventual recovery than anything else. I suspect this has to do with the impressionable state of mind during the time period immediately after the terrifying event. Neurobiologists, who are pioneering studies using brain imaging technology to learn how traumatic events are imprinted on the brain through altered brain chemistry, now know that there is an organic basis to psychological trauma (Jackson, 2003). Anecdotal reports provided in Jackson's article on trauma indicated that patients who were in Manhattan on September 11 and who were on psychotropic medication such as Prozac appeared to cope remarkably well in the wake of the attack. Speculation was that the neurochemical response in these people was diminished. Interestingly, in most of the wars throughout history, soldiers have sought to dull their senses through use of alcohol and any other available drugs.

The unconscious mind, as dream analysis reveals, has no sense of time, and past and present are interlocked (van Wormer, 2001). Often adults, accordingly, seek counseling for symptoms such as nightmares, depression, or phobias that stem from childhood or young adult traumas. Sometimes the events related to the traumatic experience have been repressed.

Every time a new war breaks out and the images of it blast forth from the television screen, veterans of previous wars report that they start experiencing symptoms of anxiety. As the conflict in the first Gulf War escalated, for example, some Vietnam veterans became increasingly agitated. Nightmares, retreat from society, and even suicide attempts resulted (Kobrick, 1993). The psychological

toll from the war in Iraq is anticipated to be substantial. The suicide rate is somewhat higher than that of previous wars, and one in six veterans is expected to
suffer symptoms of combat stress, according to military experts. The high
human cost of the Iraq war is related to the enormous insecurity of constant
exposure to bomb threats and situations of close combat and the witnessing of
maiming and death. Mental health professionals at Veterans Administration outreach centers, many of them survivors of combat themselves, are establishing
support groups to deal with postwar emotional crises (*Biloxi Sun Herald,* 2004).

Social Aspects of Human Behavior

In Wartime

This discussion of war trauma has brought us into the area that is at the intersection between biological and psychological causation. Now we move into a
consideration of the *social* dimension of human behavior. Civilians directly
frightened by bombings can have their reservoirs of strength thrown out of
whack; the effects can be long-lasting. Images of today can bring back the terrors
of yesterday. During the televised bombings of Iraq, for example, the horrors of
World War II bombings of German civilians resonated with the older generation
of Germans. Helping to stir the long-buried memories of the suffering endured
during the allied bombardment, in which 161 German cities were obliterated
and hundreds of thousands of civilians killed, was the publication of *The Fire* by
Joerg Friedrich (2002). Response to this first comprehensive account of what
happened to the towndwellers marks the first time many Germans were openly
considering themselves as victims rather than just perpetrators of war (Rhoads,
2003). Many who were children at the time were severely traumatized. Partly
because of their awareness of the horrors of civilian bombings, as a nation, the
German people stood vehemently opposed to the U.S.-led attack on Iraq.

In times of mass fear, the adrenaline is high; the part of the brain that is gov-
erned by fight or flight instincts becomes mobilized for aggressive action
(Jackson, 2003). Politicians know that when the masses feel threatened, they can
easily be programmed for hostility against the enemy. Experts cited by Jackson
refer to the attack on Iraq as an event "preceded by a host of trauma-generated
events" (p. 22).

What we are touching upon here is one of the universal truths of mass behavior. Gustave Gilbert (1947), a German-speaking intelligence officer and psychologist, provided the following quote from the Nazi Air Marshall Hermann Goering
who was interviewed by Gilbert at a recess during the Nuremburg trials:

> Of course the people don't want war. But after all, it's the leaders of the country
> who determine the policy, and it's always a simple matter to drag the people along
> whether it's a democracy, a fascist dictatorship, or a parliament, or a communist
> dictatorship. Voice or no voice, the people can always be brought to the bidding of
> the leaders. That is easy. All you have to do is tell them they are being attacked, and
> denounce the pacifists for lack of patriotism, and exposing the country to greater
> danger. (p. 278)

The impact of war reverberates throughout the society; the family system is badly shaken by the continued anxiety of knowing their loved ones are in a hostile place and subjected to daily horrors. Although in past wars, much hostility by family members was directed toward peace protesters, much of the anger generated by the war in Iraq, uniquely, has been vented against the U.S. government. In a move unprecedented in American history, a group of American military families of soldiers stationed in Iraq have formed a "Bring Them Home Now" protest group. "My son will not return, but we want these other children to return to their families," said the leader of the group (Dart, 2003, p. B2).

Social workers in the military work with family members of veterans returning from war when a crisis (e.g., domestic violence or alcoholism) brings them into treatment. Prevention work, however, is more to the point. When men and women return from service overseas, the family system experiences a shock. The family has survived without the soldier; now they must step aside from these roles. Family members need to be prepared for readjustment; additionally, they need to be educated to understand the reality of war trauma, the need to talk about some very painful things that may make it impossible for the veteran to just "say good-bye to all that."

Mental health professionals must be prepared for the healing of wounds of returning soldiers, their families, and the families of soldiers who never come home. Many of the wounds caused by the wretched business of war, however, can never be healed. There can be no closure. Recently, I was a guest at a poetry writing group (Southern Kentucky Poetry Salon) in Bowling Green, Kentucky. The following poem, read matter-of-factly by Bowling Green physician Eugene Terry Tatum (2003), had a palpable impact on group members who, for one moment following the reading, were uncharacteristically silent.

"CLOSURE"
by Eugene Terry Tatum

Some slick shrink
Coined a term
Loved by the media
Hated by those who grieve
"Does this give you closure?"
They asked breathlessly
Shoving a microphone
In the faces
Of those left behind
In Oklahoma City
After McVeigh went to sleep.

They could have asked the same
Of me when my father
Didn't come back from the war
And they handed my mother
A neatly folded flag and a medal
Except I stayed at home.
Even as a teenager

> I knew that "closure" wasn't hiding
> In that piece of cloth
> I will only find it
> When they close the lid on me.

(Printed with permission of Eugene Terry Tatum.)

When I wrote to the author for permission to print his poem, he provided the following background:

> My father, Lawrence Byron Tatum, was an Air Force pilot in the Vietnam War. I worshipped him because I honestly thought he was the best dad in the world (I still do). When his plane was shot down, and he was missing in action for years, we were one of the thousand or so American POW/MIA families of the war. We didn't know whether he was dead or alive. Finally, some time after the end of the war, after all the POWs returned and my father wasn't one of them (we watched every face stepping off the plane), he was finally recognized as KIA (killed in action). His body was never found. So, in finest military tradition, a ceremony was held at the cemetery of the U.S. Air Force Academy in my father's honor, with a flag presented to my mother. As an angry and grieving teenager (almost an adult by then), I didn't see much use in their official ceremony of "closure" so I didn't attend. I mourned him in my own way, and still do. So now, as Paul Harvey likes to say, "you know the rest of the story." (personal correspondence to van Wormer, August 18, 2003)

Social Components in Addiction

Let us reflect for a moment on what the social component of the bio-psycho-social-spiritual model of human behavior entails. In *Addiction Treatment: A Strengths Perspective* (van Wormer & Davis, 2003), my coauthor and I chose to divide the book into three major sections, the first to discuss the biological factors in addiction—genetic components and physiological aspects of alcohol and other drug consumption, the second to cover the psychological correlates of heavy drug use—the unhealthy thought processes and feelings, and then the third to discuss the social component:

> The *social* component in addiction relates to *where* as opposed to *why*—where does the addictive activity take place and where is the impact felt? The peer group and family may be involved, respectively. One factor we should never lose sight of is social class. As Harrison and Luck (1996) remind us, the disadvantaged are more likely to suffer alcohol-related problems, even when drinking at the same level as more economically privileged groups, because they lack the material resources and often the social supports available to others.
>
> Interactionism is a major component of the biopsychosocial model of addiction. In the language of systems theory, the basic principle of interactionism is that cause and effect are intertwined. Interactionism is seen most vividly in the dynamics of the family system. Much has been written about "the alcoholic family." The set of demands imposed upon the family members of an alcoholic or addict can be awesome, both emotionally and financially. Each family will have its own peculiar style of adaptation and coping, whether through blaming, denial, and/or over-protecting.

> Because the family is a system, one member's malfunctioning throws the whole family's functioning out of whack. While the addict himself or herself remains to some extent "out of things," family members may take the tension out on each other. (pp. 12–13)

In the addiction treatment book, we included not only factors like social class and family dynamics but also societal policies addressing the treatment of persons with substance abuse problems and the government's attempts to eradicate the supply of drugs and interdict the dealers.

In contrast to micro practice, which involves working with an individual to enhance his or her functioning, mezzo practice is oriented toward the family and other small groups. Social workers engaged in macro practice are directing their interventions toward social institutions and the services they provide. The social system encompasses both mezzo and macro phenomena, or virtually everything with which social work is concerned. And even when social workers do individual assessments, their focus is on relationships, support systems, family ties, and the like. When helping an individual with *social* adjustment, the social worker may work with the family unit and focus on communication patterns and boundary issues to enhance family functioning. Alternatively, or simultaneously, social workers may locate the root of the problem in political or economic realities and intervention may take place at the community level or alone. Advocacy for legislative initiatives may be involved, for example, to establish a halfway house for meth-addicted mothers.

The study of HBSE rarely reaches what I would call the *macro-macro* level of understanding. This level I define as global impacts on mass behavior. Yet, as Morell (2002) rightly maintains, the new globalization and its attendant values now provide the overarching context for human development in today's world. What is especially lacking in HBSE courses, as Morrell further notes, is critical analysis of such global realities as commercial culture and rampant consumerism. Consumption provides a frame of reference for relationships; the social environment is heavily corporate, a fact that often is taken for granted. Students who become social workers will confront these issues and their residue, so the HBSE curriculum cannot gloss over them.

As we pursue human behavior across the life span in the remaining chapters of this book, our concern remains at this level, with the social dimension of human behavior. Issues like the treatment of children and the elderly in society, and the conundrum of health care policies are decidedly social. But before we continue exploring the third part of the bio-psycho-social-spiritual model, we will examine the far more elusive spiritual realm.

The Spiritual Realm

When we talk about the sanctity of life, we are moving beyond the realm of the knowable into the realm of the spiritual. Throughout history, men and women have experienced a dimension of the spirit that seems to transcend the mundane world (Armstrong, 1993). Spirituality is often defined in terms of its opposite—materialism.

So far in this text, we have learned of the link between justice and spiritual-ity in First Nations people's healing ceremonies as well as in the First Nations people's and Norwegians' sense of a Presence in nature. The first discussion was in the section on restorative justice, a concept compatible with the teachings of all the major religions (Zehr, 1995). The second discussion was contained in this chapter as we explored the environmental crisis and the concept of sustainable development. As expressed by Blue and Blue (2001), "The spiritual essence of the First Nation's people comes from the earth, comes from this land" (p. 79).

A small but growing movement within social work, deep ecological social work, echoes this theme. As eloquently described by Besthorn (2002):

> Deep-Ecological spirituality recognizes that humans share a common destiny with the earth. It celebrates an ongoing cultivation of a deeper identification of self with the whole of the cosmic order. From this vantage point, self-interest becomes identical with the interest of the whole. Humanity and nature cannot be separated—the sacred is in and of both. (p. 4)

The challenge for social work is to contribute to an alternative vision of the good life, to make a common cause together by beginning to redefine social work's existing ecological awareness to incorporate environmental, spiritual, and polit-ical dimensions.

Social workers along with their clients face daunting challenges today in a world shaken by terrorism, religious divisiveness, and mass disillusionment over scandals in the Catholic Church. In helping clients cope with the daily cruelties and chronic stresses of life, spirituality and empowerment practice are viewed as companion forces. Disempowered people, as Ortiz and Smith (1999) suggest, often need a purpose that transcends their mere existence. They, like all of us, need to find a meaning in life. Involvement in organized religion can provide much-needed social and material support—witness the historic role of the African American church, which was the midwife of the civil rights movement. The African American church is recognized as the backbone of the black community and the preserver of African American heritage. Spirituality, the belief in a power greater than oneself, and the importance of the spiritual dimension in finding a sense of meaning in life are considered key components in the Afrocentric world-view. The African American family is under assault today from the negative con-fluence of economic and social forces. Yet, as Billingsley and Morrison-Rodriguez (1998) note, the black church in its role as a social institution has the ability to strengthen the black family and promote social organization.

Edward Canda (2002), founder of the Society for Spirituality and Social Work, conducted a survey of 402 persons living with the chronic and ultimately fatal disease, cystic fibrosis. A significant majority said it was appropriate for practitioners to raise the topics of spirituality and religion. The study, as Canda suggests, highlights the need to address spirituality in all its diverse beliefs and rituals as a strength in situations of disabilities and health challenges. In an inter-esting postscript to the study, Canda reveals his choice to go public about his own disability in order to advocate for people with cystic fibrosis. Based on his own story and extensive research that has provided evidence of spiritual growth through adversity, Canda recommends that clients receive assistance in addressing these challenges through self-reflection, therapeutic dialogue, and collaboration with relevant clergy and other spiritual friends and mentors.

Summary and Conclusion

Consistent with my belief that society and self are in constant interaction, I chose to include in this text on social welfare a chapter that explored the inner psyche as well as the outer circumference of human existence. The bio-psycho-social-spiritual framework of social work offered a natural organizational scheme for this chapter. A major argument of this presentation was that the person-in-environment conceptualization of social work must include the physical as well as the social environment.

Because of the consistent neglect of matters in our surroundings—the air we breathe, the soil that provides plants and nourishment, the water for our sustenance—the majority of this chapter was devoted to sustainable development. A second (but not secondary) reason for the environmental emphasis is related to social justice both regionally and internationally. No other phenomenon better illustrates the impact of global interconnectedness than does our use and abuse of natural resources. Even wars often have their roots in disputes over territory, access to the sea, and greed for oil. Wars leave in their paths environmental trauma as well as personal trauma.

Our discussion of the destructiveness of war linked the personal with the political.

In fact, each component of human behavior discussed in this chapter is linked to every other component so that micro and macro are intricately intertwined. Governmental policies concerning the environment affect the health of humans and other species, what form that life takes, and ultimately, whether there is life at all. Biological and psychological dimensions of human behavior are intricately linked with each other as well: Consider, for example, an adolescent struck by mental illness whose aberrant thought patterns are later alleviated through use of antipsychotic medication. Consider also the impact on the family in which a member has a mental illness, or any illness, and the effect this family's wrestling with disease may have on the spiritual life of the family members.

Admittedly, this chapter covered an inordinate amount of ground. Yet, if it whets the appetite of readers to learn more about some of the human and nonhuman phenomena touched on here, then the effort will have been worthwhile.

Thought Questions

1. What does this chapter add to the person-in-environment configuration of social work theory?
2. Discuss the impact of Rachel Carson's *Silent Spring*.
3. Discuss the effect of pollution on the climate, land, crops, and fresh bodies of water.
4. Differentiate between the war-against-nature and Mother-Earth concepts.
5. Discuss Keefe's childhood reminiscence and what it says about progress.
6. What can we learn from First Nations people concerning respect for our planet?
7. Discuss several ways that wars ravage the environment. What do chemicals such as depleted uranium do to people?
8. Define and discuss the concepts ecofeminism and sustainable development.

9. Discuss the global dependence on fossil fuels, and propose ways this can be alleviated.

10. Compare new methods of farming and the economic and environmental impacts of each.

11. Argue the case that environmental racism is a reality. Refer to specific situations.

12. Discuss promising developments for environmental sustainability. How could investment in mass transportation (e.g., trains and streetcars) help?

13. With reference to human biology, discuss the revolution in brain research and what this says to us about personality.

14. Give examples showing how the biology and psychology of human behavior are intertwined.

15. Select several of Erik Erikson's stages of development and discuss them in terms of resolving key issues across the life span.

16. Using Maslow's hierarchy of needs, discuss the social class structure in the United States.

17. Summarize Bettelheim's classic study on the human behavior of prisoners in the German concentration camps. What does this say about the socialization process?

18. Relate the psychology of being a kidnap victim to Bettelheim's findings.

19. How can battered women be considered captives? What does the concept of the survivor syndrome explain?

20. Define PTSD and relate it to situations of war and rape.

21. Review Goering's observation about manipulation of the public in preparation for war. Does it have any relevance today?

22. Discuss the impact of war on family members. Refer to the poem "Closure."

23. Why is it important for social workers to acknowledge the spiritual dimension?

24. How can social workers help people achieve spiritual healing?

References

Alarm after U.S. abandons environmental treaty. (2001, March 29). Cable Network News (CNN). Retrieved from http://www.cnn.com

American Automobile Association (AAA). (2003, September/October). Here and there. Retrieved from http://www.homeandawaymagazine.com

American Psychiatric Association (APA). (2000). *Diagnostic and statistical manual of mental disorders* (text revision; DSM-IV-TR). Washington, DC: Author.

Annan, K. (2002, August 26). Beyond the horizon. *Time*, A18–19.

Applegate, L. (1999, March 4). Is it time to find out what's in our water? *The Des Moines Register*. Retrieved from http://www.earthweshare.org

Armstrong, K. (1993). *History of God*. New York: Ballantine.

Associated Press. (1995, November 14). U.N. report tabulates human destruction. *Waterloo–Cedar Falls Courier*, p. A6.

Barker, R. L. (2003). *The social work dictionary* (5th ed.). Washington, DC: NASW Press.

Barlow, M., & Clarke, T. (2002). *Blue gold: The fight to stop the corporate theft of the world's water*. New York: New Press.

Bateson, G. (1972). *Steps to an ecology of mind: Collected essays in anthropology, psychiatry, evolution, and epistemology*. San Francisco: Chandler.

Beeman, P. (1994, March 20). Earthly issues await action. *Des Moines Register*, p. B1.

Berry, W. (1977). *The unsettling of America: Culture and agriculture*. San Francisco: Sierra Club Books.

Berry, W. (1993, March/April). Decolonizing rural America. *Audubon*, 100–105.

Besthorn, F. H. (2002, February 15). Toward a deep ecological social work: Its environmental, spiritual, and political dimensions. Paper presented at the University of Northern Iowa, Cedar Falls, IA.

Besthorn, F. H., & Canda, E. R. (2002). Revisioning environment: Deep ecology for education and teaching in social work. *Journal of Teaching in Social Work, 22*(1/2), 79–101.

Besthorn, F., & McMillen, D. P. (2002). The oppression of women and natives: Ecofeminism as a framework for an expanded social work. *Families in Society, 83*(3), 221–232.

Bettleheim, B. (1943). Individual and mass behavior in extreme situations. *Journal of Abnormal and Social Psychology, 38*, 417–452.

Billingsley, A., & Morrison-Rodriguez, B. (1998). The black family in the 21st century and the church as an action system: A macro perspective. *Journal of Human Behavior in the Social Environment, 1*(2/3), 31–47.

Biloxi Sun Herald. (2004, September 20). Vets find stress hard to shake. Retrieved from http://www.military.com

Blue, A. W., & Blue, M. A. R. (2001). The case for aboriginal justice and healing: The self perceived through a broken mirror. In M. L. Hadley (Ed.), *The spiritual roots of restorative justice* (pp. 57–79). Albany, NY: State University of New York Press.

Booth, W. (1999, July 29). War debris in Danube chokes off trade route. *Washington Post*, p. A23.

Brown, L. R. (2001). *Eco-economy: Building an economy for the earth.* New York: W. W. Norton.

Brown, L. R. (2003). Wind power set to become world's leading energy source. Earth Policy Institute. Retrieved from http://www.earth-policy.org

Browning, M. (2003, March 14). Brainwashing agitates victims into submission. *Palm Beach Post.* Retrieved from http://www.rickross.com/reference/brainwashing/brainwashing32.html

Buechner, M. (2003, July 14). A new cash cow. *Time.* Retrieved from http://www.time.com

Bullard, R. (1994). *Unequal protection: Environmental justice and communities of color.* San Francisco: Sierra Club Books for Children.

Caldicott, H. (2002). *The new nuclear danger: George W. Bush's military-industrial complex.* New York: New Press.

Canda, E. R. (2002). The significance of spirituality for resilient response to chronic illness. In D. Saleebey (Ed.), *The strengths perspective in social work practice* (3rd ed., pp. 63–79). Boston: Allyn & Bacon.

Carson, R. (1962). *Silent spring.* Boston: Houghton Mifflin.

Challender, M. (2003, May 11). History's tidbits satisfy the curious. *Des Moines Register*, p. OP5.

Coolican, J. P. (2004, January 4). Old drug may quiet the nightmares of war. *Des Moines Register*, p. A11.

Council on Social Work Education (CSWE). (2003). *Handbook of accreditation standards and procedures* (5th ed.). Alexandria, VA: Author.

Dart, B. (2003, August 14). Some U.S. military kin denounce Iraq occupation. *Atlanta Journal-Constitution*, p. B2.

Dominelli, L. (2002). *Anti-oppressive social work theory and practice.* Hampshire, UK: Palgrave.

Dorsey, E., & Thormodsgard, M. (2003, January). Rachel Carson warned us. *MS*, 43–45.

Dunn, S., & Flaven, C. (2002). Moving the climate change agenda forward. In Worldwatch Institute (Eds.), *State of the world 2002* (pp. 24–50). New York: W. W. Norton.

Elston, S. (2003, February 3). Depleted uranium keeps killing. *Western Catholic Reporter.* Retrieved from http://www.wcr.ab.ca

Elston, S. (2003, August 1). Increasing evidence depleted uranium causes great harm. *Your Earth.* Retrieved from http://www.straightgoods.com

"Enabling concept" cannot be applied to battered women. (1986, November/December). *Networker*, 6.

Environmental Justice Resource Center. (2001, November 27). Chemical assault on an African American community. Retrieved from http://www.ejrc.cau.edu

Eriksen, T. (1998, March). Norwegians and nature. *The Norseman*, 10–15.

Erikson, E. (1950). *Childhood and society* (2nd ed.). New York: W. W. Norton.

Faulkner, W. (1964/1936). *Absalom, Absalom!* New York: Modern Library.

Fischer, E. (1993). War and the environment. In J. Allen (Ed.), *Environment 93/94* (12th ed., pp. 73–88). Guilford, CT: Dushkin.

French, H. (1995, May). Forging a new global partnership to save the earth. *USA Today* (magazine), 76–80.

Friedrich, J. (2002). *The fire (Der brand).* Berlin: Propyläen.

Ganguly, M. (2002, August 26). Heroes; Vandana Shiva. *Time* (bonus section), A34.

Gardner, G. (1998, November). Pedal pushers: When cities take bicycles seriously. *The Rotarian*, 8.

Gardner, G. (2002). The challenge for Johannesburg: Creating a more secure world. In Worldwatch Institute (Eds.), *State of the world 2002* (pp. 3–23). New York: W. W. Norton.

Gay men's brains work like women's, study says. (2003, March 26). Gay.com. Retrieved from http://uk.gay.com/headlines/4032

Gilbert, G. (1947). *Nuremburg diary.* New York: Farrar, Straus.

Greider, W. (2003, August 18). Victory at McDonald's. *The Nation,* 8–10, 36.

Halweil, B. (2002, August 26). Farming in the public interest. In Worldwatch Institute (Eds.), *State of the world 2002* (pp. 51–74). New York: W. W. Norton.

Harris, J. R. (1998). *The nurture assumption: Why children turn out the way they do.* New York: Touchstone.

Harrison, L., & Luck, H. (1996). Drinking and home-lessness in the U.K. In L. Harrison (Ed.), *Alcohol problems in the community* (pp. 115–140). London: Routledge.

Hawken, P. (2003, May–June). Dreams of a liveable future. *Utne,* 50–54.

Hoff, M., & McNutt, J. (Eds.). (1994). Introduction. In *The global environmental crisis: Implications for social welfare and social work* (pp. 1–11). Aldershot, England: Avebury.

Hoff, M., & McNutt, J. (2002). Social policy and the physical environment. In J. Midgley, M. B. Tracey, & M. Livermore (Eds.), *The handbook of social policy* (pp. 461–475). Thousand Oaks, CA: Sage.

Iowa Grain Quality Initiative. (2001, January 14). Iowa farmers at risk for disease, newspaper reports. Retrieved from http://www.extension.iastate.edu

Jackson, K. (2003, June). Trauma and the national psyche. *Social Work Today,* 20–23.

James, S., & Harris, B. (1996). Gimme shelter: Battering and poverty. In D. Dijon & A. Withorn (Eds.), Crying out loud: Women's poverty in the United States (pp. 57–65). Boston: South End Press.

Kahn, M., & Scher, S. (2002). Infusing content on the physical environment into the BSW curriculum. *Journal of Baccalaureate Social Work, 7*(2), 1–14.

Keefe, T. (2003). The bio-psycho-social-spiritual origins of justice. *Critical Social Work, 3*(1), 1–17.

Kerry, J. (2002, August 26). Bush takes a backseat. *Time,* A49.

Kluger, J., & Dorfman, A. (2002, August 26). The challenge we face. *Time,* A4–A11.

Kobrick, F. (1993). Reaction of Vietnam veterans to the Persian Gulf War. *Health and Social Work, 18,* 165–171.

Korten, D. C. (1999). *The post-corporate world: Life after capitalism.* San Francisco: Berrett-Koehler.

Lacayo, R. (2004, September 20). A place to bring the tribe. *Time,* 68–70.

Land Institute. (2002). Natural systems agriculture. *Land Institute Newsletter,* 1–2.

Layton, L. (2002, July 17). Study lists mass transit benefits. *Washington Post,* p. B5.

Lemonick, M. D. (2003, January 20). The power of mood. *Time,* 67–72.

Leopold, A. (1966). *A Sand County almanac.* New York: Sierra Club/Ballantine Book.

Lowe, M. (1994, November/December). Back on track. *Utne Reader,* 48–52.

Makovsky, P. (2002, August/September). Pedestrian cities. *Metropolis Magazine.* Retrieved from http://www.metropolismagazine.com

Manning, R. (1995). *Grassland.* New York: Viking Penguin.

Marano, H. (1993, November/December). Inside the heart of marital violence. *Psychology Today,* 50–53, 76–78, 91.

Maslow, A. (1970). *Motivation and personality.* New York: Harper & Row.

May, E. (2002, December 11). Sierra Club in the U.S. press release. Retrieved from http://www.sierraclub.ca

Miller, M. (2002, February 4). From villain to victim: In 1976, prosecutors tore Hearst's credibility to shreds. *Newsweek,* 29.

Monsho, K. A. (2001). Living in cancer alley: Fighting environmental racism. *HealthQuestMag.Com.* Retrieved from http://www.healthquestmag.com

Morell, C. (2002). Human behavior and commercial culture: Bringing the new global economy in HBSE. *Journal of Progressive Human Services, 13*(2), 27–42.

Moyers, B. (2001). Earth on edge. PBS (Public Broadcasting Service).

National Association of Social Workers (NASW). (2003). Environmental policy. In NASW, *Social work speaks: National Association of Social Workers policy statements 2003–2006* (pp. 116–123). Washington, DC: NASW Press.

New study shows nitrate contamination in wells. (2003, August 23). *Des Moines Register,* p. B1.

O'Brien, P. (1999, December). Book review: More than victims: Battered women, the syndrome, society, and the law. *American Political Science Review, 93*(4), 974.

Oh, oh! "Ozone hole" is back. (2003, September 9). Columbia Broadcasting Company (CBS). Retrieved from http://www.cbsnews.com

Ortiz, L. U., & Smith, G. (1999). The role of spirituality in empowerment practice. In W. Shera & L. M. Wells (Eds.), *Empowerment practice in social work* (pp. 307–319). Toronto: Canadian Scholars' Press.

Park, A. (2003, January 20). Postcards from the brain. *Time*, 94–97.

Qualman, D. (2002, December 2). Canadian study shows "structural adjustment" of ag. policies reap devastating effects for farmers. *Agribusiness Examiner*, No. 205.

Quindlen, A. (1998). *Black and blue.* New York: Dell.

Rail ridership exceeds expectations, study says. (2003, July 8). *Metro Magazine.* Retrieved from http://www.metro-magazine.com

Religious scholars say God decrees: "Thou shalt conserve." (2001, July 5). Associated Press. *Waterloo–Cedar Falls Courier*, p. A1.

Rhoads, C. (2003, February 26). Behind Iraq stance in Germany a flood of war memories. Retrieved from http://www.rense.com

Roberts, I. (2003, January 18). Car wars. *The Guardian.* Retrieved from http://www.guardian.co.uk

Rogge, M. (1994, March 20). Environmental injustice: Social welfare and toxic waste. In M. Hoff & J. McNutt (Eds.), *The global environmental crisis: Implications for social welfare and social work* (pp. 53–74). Aldershot, England: Avebury.

Roodman, D. (1995). Carbon emissions resume rise. In L. Brown, N. Lenssen, & H. Kane (Eds.), *Vital signs 1995* (p. 66). New York: W. W. Norton.

Roosevelt, M. (2003, November 3). Fresh off the farm. *Time*, 60–61.

Sachs, I. (1995, March). Dismantling the mechanism of exclusion. *UNESCO Courier* (pp. 9–13). New York: United Nations.

Saleebey, D. (2001). *Human behavior and social environments: A biopsychosocial approach.* New York: Columbia University Press.

Sanders, S. (1999, March–April). Lessons from the land institute. *Audubon*, 76–79.

Satchell, M. (1999, April 26). Questions in a village: Did Agent Orange cause Vietnamese birth defects? *U.S. News & World Report*, 62.

Schechter, S. (2002, September 21). Family violence. Presentation given at the University of Northern Iowa, Cedar Falls, IA.

Schwartz, J., & Begley, S. (2002). *The mind and the brain: Neuroplasticity and the power of mental force.* New York: HarperCollins.

Schwartz, M., & Dekeseredy, W. S. (1997). *Sexual assault on the college campus: The role of male peer support.* Thousand Oaks, CA: Sage.

Shakespeare, W. (1970/1599). Julius Caesar. In *The Complete Works of William Shakespeare* (pp. 719–743). London: Spring Books.

Shakespeare, W. (1970/1605). Macbeth. In *The Complete Works of William Shakespeare* (pp. 922–944). London: Spring Books.

Smiley, J. (1991). *A thousand acres.* New York: Knopf.

The spoils of war. (2003, March 29). *Economist*, 71–72.

Stein, B., Jaycox, L., Kataoka, S., Wong, M., Tu, W., Elliott, M., & Fink, A. (2003). A mental health intervention for schoolchildren exposed to violence: A randomized controlled trial. *Journal of the American Medical Association, 290,* 603–611.

Tatum, E. T. (2003, May 22). Closure. Unpublished poem shared with poetry group in Bowling Green, KY.

Townsend, M., & Burke, J. (2002, July 7). Earth will expire by 2050. *Guardian Unlimited.* Retrieved from http://www.observer.co.uk

United Nations (U.N.). (1995). *The world's women 1995.* New York: United Nations Development Programme.

United Nations (U.N.) Press Release. (2002, September 4). Sustainable development summit concludes in Johannesburg. Retrieved from http://www.un.org

United Nations (U.N.) World Commission on Environment and Development. (1987). *Our common future.* Oxford: Oxford University Press.

van Wormer, K. (1997). *Social welfare: A world view.* Belmont, CA: Wadsworth.

van Wormer, K. (2001). *Counseling female offenders and victims: A strengths-restorative approach.* New York: Springer.

van Wormer, K., & Bednar, S. (2002). Working with male batterers: A restorative-strengths perspective. *Families in Society, 83*(5/6), 557–565.

van Wormer, K., & Davis, D. R. (2003). *Addiction treatment: A strengths perspective.* Belmont, CA: Brooks/Cole.

Vellvé, R., (1993, March/April). The decline of diversity in European agriculture. *Ecologist*, 64–69.

Wallace, H. (1999). *Family violence: Legal, medical, and social perspectives* (2nd ed.). Boston: Allyn & Bacon.

Warren, K. J. (2000). *Ecofeminist philosophy: A western perspective on what it is and why it matters.* Oxford, England: Rowan & Littlefield.

Weiss, R. (2003, March 5). Threats posed by water scarcity detailed. *Washington Post,* p. A3.

World Wildlife Fund (2002). Living planet report 2002. Retrieved from http://www.panda.org /downloads/general/LPR_2002.pdf

The Worldwatch Institute. (2002). *State of the world 2002.* New York: W. W. Norton.

Zastrow, C., & Kirst-Ashman, K. K. (2004). *Understanding human behavior and the social environment* (5th ed.). Belmont, CA: Wadsworth.

Zehr, H. (1995). *Changing lenses.* Scottsdale, PA: Herald Press.

Your children are not your children.
You may give them your love but not your thoughts,
for they have their own thoughts.
You may house their bodies but not their souls,
for their souls dwell in the house of tomorrow,
which you cannot visit, not even in your dreams.
You may strive to be like them,
but seek not to make them like you.

KAHIL GIBRAN, 1923, P. 17

Child Welfare

© Rupert van Wormer

The term *child welfare* is used here not in the narrow sense of "a specialized field of practice," but in its literal meaning of the general well-being of children. Underlying assumptions of this chapter are, first, that children are the most powerless members of the human community and, second, that the primary source of help and nurturance for children is the family. Many families, however, cannot do the job they were meant to do, so some form of help or even substitutive care has to be provided. In societies that have formal, *residually* based social services, intervention occurs only when there is a lapse in care so serious that it comes to the attention of the authorities. In societies with *institutionally* based programming, all families with children have access to family allowances, extensive parental leave for infant care, subsidized child care, and universal health care. In nonindustrialized societies, care for children is provided by the whole community, with grandparents, and great-aunts and -uncles, and so on all playing an active role in bringing up a child.

Central to the treatment of children is the societal notion of childhood itself. This chapter traces the historical development of the concept of childhood and of child welfare services in Western society. In providing this overview, we will address Ann Hartman's (1990) provocative rhetorical questions: "What is happening in this country? How is it that this society, which is supposed to be so child-centered, can be guilty of such unconscionable neglect?" (p. 118). Our children are our future and the future of the world. When we do not pay for children's well-being at the front end, we pay a larger price later in intergenerational ignorance, poverty, and crime.

As in other chapters, we will look beyond American society. In many countries, what we find is that under taxing conditions such as plague, grave economic crisis, overpopulation, and war, the standards of child welfare are worsening. From around the world, here are the images:

- Disabled orphans in Russia, many the victims of nuclear radiation and industrial pollution
- Serious decline in the numbers of female children in China and India
- Street children of Brazil shot by police officers
- Child refugees roaming the earth, many traumatized by war
- Children on the streets of New York City shot by stray bullets
- Children starving in Ethiopia and North Korea
- Child warriors forced to engage in horrible acts of slaughter in Liberia
- Huge death toll and maimings among the children in Iraq related to earlier United Nations (U.N.) sanctions and war

Then here are the statistics:

- More than 150 million children in poor countries of the world are underweight.
- Since 1990, more than 2 million children have been killed and 6 million seriously injured in wars.
- One child in eight is believed to be engaged in the worst forms of child labor.
- More than 14 million children under 15 years of age have lost one or both parents to AIDS. (United Nations Children's Fund [UNICEF], 2003b, p. 78)

This chapter will go beyond the statistics to examine issues that know no geographical boundaries. Much of the material is highly disturbing. We start with a historical overview of the notion of childhood and the treatment (and exploitation) of children. Before considering the contemporary realities (child poverty, abuse, etc.), we will consult the standards for how children should be treated, their rights as codified in international law. Enacted in 1990, the U.N. Convention on the Rights of the Child provides us with a framework from which to examine the progress of nations in meeting human rights standards concerning the treatment of children. Worldwide, despite the Convention, violations of children's rights continue to occur, violations ranging from genital mutilation and infanticide of girl babies, to the exploitation of children as soldiers and prostitutes, to the more mundane forms of abuse within the family.

Where are the child protections? The provision of services to children, the child welfare system, is the next subject of this chapter. We will explore areas of traditional social work practice, such as family preservation, kinship care, child protective services, juvenile court, and school social work. The boxed reading describes roles for social workers in helping gay and lesbian youth. The chapter ends with some thoughts on what we can learn from innovations abroad.

History of Childhood and Child Welfare

Without a historical perspective that traces the relation of economic forces, from feudalism and postindustrial capitalism to the development of child and family welfare policies, a nation's treatment of children cannot be understood or evaluated. Moreover, without grasping the power of cultural proclivities that bear on the treatment of infants and children, the question of how we can "be guilty of such unconscionable neglect" (Hartman, 1990) leads only to bewilderment. So, let us look at culture.

A society's attitude toward the treatment of children is part of its whole texture of values, and this one cultural attribute can be regarded as a clue to the cultural whole. Thus, in the United States, we see Anglo-Saxon punitiveness reflected in strict child-rearing patterns, the harsh sentencing of juvenile delinquents, the creation of conditions that are conducive to poverty, and the ubiquity of military role models for youth.

In contrast, the egalitarianism and kindness evidenced in Norwegian society today hark back to the Viking Age, a time when regional assemblies passed statutes that provided for relief to destitute persons (Selbyg, 1987). These statutes became incorporated into the first national civil code in the 13th century. Also in the 13th century came recognition of the fact that society cannot react to juvenile law-breaking with the same severity reserved for adult law-breaking. In 1621, Norwegian law provided for public guardians to assume responsibility for youngsters not adequately cared for by their parents (Flekkoy, 1989). The evils inherent in the merciless factory system inevitably followed, but they were met by subsequent reforms. Similarly, in Sweden, solicitude for its people has not stopped with care for the aged, the physically handicapped, the mentally sick, and the criminal. Children have been well cared for also (Berfenstam, 1973). Ellen

Key, an author and journalist who wrote in 1900, advocated a free upbringing for children, and her work has been exceedingly influential in terms of Scandinavian cultural values regarding the care and upbringing of children.

There are conflicting estimates of when the notion of childhood as a special developmental stage began and of precisely when and where institutionalized child welfare began. "The whole concept of childhood as a special, unique phase of human development," argued Richette (1969), "is a twentieth century idea" (p. 56). Before that, children were considered the chattel of their parents (Aries, 1965). A gradual transition toward the notion of children as individuals with rights took place, probably, around the end of the 19th century.

In his article "Our Forbears Made Childhood a Nightmare," DeMause (1975) reviewed the facts concerning the horrors that children once endured. The further back in history one goes, according to DeMause, the lower the level of child care, and the more likely children were to have been killed, abandoned, whipped, sexually abused, and terrorized by their caretakers. Battering, which was recommended in all the early child-rearing tracts, began in infancy. The sexual use of children, well documented in ancient Greece and Rome, was so ingrained in the male culture that slave boys were commonly kept for sexual use by older men.

The killing of children is a constant and important feature of human social history (Chase, 1975). Child sacrifice was common in ancient and biblical times. Infanticide served as a means of rendering sacrifice to the gods, as a eugenic device to weed out the sickly and deformed, as a tool of population control, and as the last resort of unmarried mothers. In China, the killing of infant girls was the norm. In Japan's feudal era, farmers killed their second or third sons at birth. Infanticide was a regular feature of Eskimo, Scandinavian, Polynesian, African, American Indian, Australian Aborigine, and Hawaiian cultures. The taboo, concludes Chase, has not been so much to forbid the act, as to avoid mentioning it. Until the relatively recent "discovery" of child abuse and neglect, in fact, there has long been a norm of silence concerning the maltreatment of children.

Aries (1965) documented some of the sadistic punishments carried out against children in England during the 17th and, especially, the 18th and 19th centuries. Deliberate pain was inflicted to teach school lessons, social norms, and even self-control. Both in England and in early America, disobedient children were flogged and executed, traditions that reflected the harshness of a society that was aggressive as well as punitively religious. Although today children in North America and Britain have some protection against extreme physical abuse, they are not protected to the degree that adults are, against ordinary forms of violence—slapping, hitting, and so on.

The most pervasive form of abuse against children has come, not directly from a source such as the family, but indirectly through the cruelty in the social order. A society in which survival-of-the-fittest rather than justice and equality has been the predominant cultural mode could not fail to be oppressive toward children. For, as we will see in the remainder of this chapter, when families suffer, children invariably suffer also.

Early settlement workers understood that the well-being of children and their families depended on stable work and adequate income, and that special reforms would have to be pursued in an integrated rather than fragmented manner (Gil, 1998). The child-saving and child-rescue movements of the 19th century eventually crystallized into a system of services that emphasized removal of children from the home as a solution to family and cultural problems. Although many states established orphanages during the early 19th century, current child welfare policy did not get underway until the 1870s.

For the beginnings of institutionalized child welfare, Hegar (1989) and Moe (1990) point to Norway's Child Welfare Act of 1896. This protectionist act was the first in history designed to protect children from punishment, abuse, and exploitation by adults. However, across the Atlantic, several years before this, the seeds of the Canadian "child's movement" already were being sown. Out of this movement sprang the first Children's Aid Society in Canada in 1891, as well as the promotion of legislation in Ontario that protected children living with their own families and those who were abandoned or orphaned (Swift, 1991). As early as 1888, the province was given the right to oversee the child's environment if deemed in the child's interest. Shortly thereafter, more specific legislation was passed to prevent cruelty to children.

In the United States, spawned by a response to industrialization and urbanization, which often left children unprotected and homeless, the first separate juvenile court was established in 1899 in Chicago. Not a criminal court, this institution theoretically considered the needs of children in trouble and those who were neglected by their parents. In fact, children under the jurisdiction of the court were often removed from their homes and placed in institutions. Parents had no right to voice objections. The significance of these developments, and of parallel developments throughout Europe, was in the newly carved out role for the state, an undertaking that was eventually to transform philanthropic child-saving into public child welfare. This was the birth of the idea that all children are the special concern of the state. The role of the state in child education expanded simultaneously.

In the 1890s, New York City was filled with children begging on the streets. Many others lived in orphanages. Pioneers in human services and the ministry devised a plan to put such children on trains to farm states like Iowa and Kansas where they would have clean living and could work on the farms (Dominick, 2002). Children were lined up on train station platforms or at local theaters. Adults chose the ones they wanted. Altogether about 200,000 children rode the "orphan trains" until the program ended in 1929. Today, thanks to the Internet, former orphan train riders, many of whom now are quite elderly, are reuniting with long-lost siblings and talking about their dramatic experiences for the first time.

France found another solution to the problem of unwanted children. In a very old edition of *Popular Mechanics,* I came across a curious headline, "A Baby Raffle in Paris" (1912, p. 19). The management of a foundling hospital, according to the news report, held a raffle as a means of finding homes for a large number of its charges, and to raise money.

About the same time in Canada, thousands of Aboriginal children were being removed from their families and placed in more than 100 residential schools to "civilize" them. Malloy (1999), who was granted access to secret government documents, uncovered a legacy of death, malnutrition, and sexual abuse of the youngsters. It was not until the 1990s, when former residents of the schools came forward, that the extent of the sexual abuse of both boys and girls, often by priests, came to light.

In 1978 in the United States, the Indian Child Welfare Act was passed. The passage of this act was for the purpose of reversing the pattern of placing Indian children in non-Indian foster and adoptive homes or boarding schools. This act tightened the legal protection given biological parents and relatives in child custody matters. Tribal courts under this law were recognized as the authority in child welfare decisions (van Wormer, 1997).

In Australia, too, Aboriginal children of mixed blood had been forcibly removed from their families. Their removal was highly secretive; many were put up for adoption by white families or placed in foster care or in institutions before being sent out to work as domestics (Patrick, 2000). The majority of children removed from their homes were girls. This practice of forced removal took place between 1900 and 1960. Fittingly, the term *stolen generation* has gained currency to define the tragedy that befell these children ("Dictionary Recognizes Stolen Generation," 2001). Social workers, unfortunately, were involved in this child removal process. Today, the survivors are demanding reparations from the Australian government.

More recently in Romania, many children have endured an inhumane existence, a legacy from a cruel past when sick and disabled children were left to vegetate or die. As described by Ron Roberts (2001), after a visit to such caring institutions:

> The children were taught Montessori principles, and their rooms were cheerful and immaculate. At least two of the children came from settings where they were locked in rooms all day and had food shoved under the door. Their fear and ignorance convinced them that contact with the children was too risky. The mommas took wonderful care of these abused and sick children. (p. F2)

In the United States, due to the economic circumstances of poor families, child labor emerged as a primary social problem (Karger & Stoesz, 2002). The absence of public relief compelled children to work full shifts in coal mines and textile mills. Child labor was finally prohibited over the protests of capitalists. The greatest boost to child welfare in general was the establishment of Aid to Families with Dependent Children (AFDC), a preventive measure enacted under the auspices of the Social Security Act. Significantly, both family relief and child welfare services were to be administered by the states through public welfare departments.

France, despite the earlier example of the baby raffle, has a history of child protection that extends as far back as the 1800s. During that time, a slew of bills were enacted decreeing standards to protect children from child labor and mistreatment and to provide suitable housing and education (Hegar, 1989). Similarly, by the 1880s in Great Britain, the groundwork had been laid for an expanded state role in child welfare; and during World War I, the work of family service units was begun when conscientious objectors cared for disorganized, bombed-out families in English cities. Today, a universally operated program is the public health nurse visitation (in the United Kingdom [U.K.] and Ireland) to the homes of all new mothers to provide instruction in child care. Many European countries also have such preventive programs.

Consistent with the residual concept of welfare, primary responsibility for children in the United States rests with their parents, with state intervention as a backup (Karger & Stoesz, 2002). The role of the federal government has declined, as has the funding for child welfare programs. In fact, the trend in most countries today is toward reduced funding for social services, and this has serious implications for child welfare. Likewise, the parallel trends toward developing international free trade agreements and reducing labor have had serious ramifications for the well-being of many nations' children. The issue of children's rights is just as related, both directly and indirectly, to economic factors as it is to cultural traditions.

The United Nations Convention on the Rights of the Child

Because of children's vulnerability and near total dependence on their parents or guardians, and because children are often viewed as the property of their parents, the potential for rights abuses is rampant. In many parts of the world, in fact, children have no rights at all. The individual states in the United States have laws protecting children from abuse and neglect and, in situations of adoption disputes, laws requiring that the child's interest be taken into consideration.

In 1989 while I was working in Norway, the U.N. Convention on the Rights of the Child was passed by the U.N. General Assembly; it was scheduled to go into effect the following year. This landmark document, which was almost immediately ratified across the world, provided that children have the right to due process in court, the right to be protected from violence and exploitation, and the right to health and nutrition. The passing of the Convention was historic in that it was the first human rights document to focus specifically on the rights of children. Norway, like many other nations (e.g., Vietnam, Malaysia, and Mexico), rapidly revised their policies to be in compliance with international law. (Norway's adjustments were in the area of tightening due process procedures in juvenile hearings.) In a recent special session, the Committee on the Rights of the Child issued conclusions on reports from Germany, the Netherlands, and Japan. The Committee welcomed the proactive measures taken by these countries in the areas of protecting child asylum seekers and children with disabilities, and combating child abuse (International Federation of Social Workers [IFSW], 2004).

Norway and Sweden had previously outlawed all forms of physical violence against children. Article 19 of the Convention requires state parties to the Convention to take legislative measures against such practices. In Canada, the provincial governments and members of Parliament have faced intensive lobbying to protect children, as adults are protected, from assault. Now the pressure has intensified due to the support of international law. Children's rights are gradually being expanded in Canada as a result of recent human rights cases in which the U.N. Convention has been a prominent feature in the deliberations (Watkinson, 2001).

To date, all nations have ratified the Convention except for two: Somalia and the United States. Former President Clinton signed the Convention in 1993, but it has never been ratified. Among the objections to ratification are: fear of increased state interference in family life; the failure of the Convention to preserve the rights of both "born and unborn" children; restrictions on governments in regard to executing children; the requirement for universal health care for children; the proscription against inflicting violence on children (hitting, spanking, etc.); and the proscription against recruiting children under the age of 18 into the military (Reichert, 2003; van Wormer, 2004).

Read the entire Convention on the Rights of the Child (go to http://www.hrweb.org/legal/child.html) to appreciate the remarkable qualities of this far-reaching document. Rights specified in the Convention cover three major areas: entitlements related to material provisions; protections (e.g., from labor exploitation) to safeguard children's well-being; and affirmative rights related to privacy, culture, religion, and language. Having just returned from Korea where children, under enormous pressure to achieve entry into elite universities, study relentlessly from dawn to midnight, I was impressed with Article 31: "States recognize the right of the child to rest and leisure, to engage in play and recreational activities appropriate to the age of the child and to participate fully in cultural life and the arts" (U.N., 1989).

Founded well before the Convention on the Rights of the Child was conceived, to help children after World War II in Europe, the United Nations Children's Fund (UNICEF) works with national governments to protect children's rights and publishes a progress report each year, *The State of the World's Children* (see http://www.unicef.org). In a recent press release, UNICEF (2003a) praised Kenya for its progress in providing free education to all its children and Afghanistan for making some strides in getting girls to school, but nevertheless noted that of the 2.1 billion children in the world, half still live in abject poverty.

Child Poverty

When poverty engulfs a family, the youngest are the most affected—they are at high risk of permanent developmental damage, susceptibility to disease, and early death. There is also resilience. In *Angela's Ashes,* Frank McCourt (1996) takes us back to his oppressive Irish roots:

> People everywhere brag and whimper about the woes of their early years, but nothing can compare with the Irish version: The poverty; the shiftless loquacious alcoholic father; the pious defeated mother moaning by the fire; pompous priests; bullying schoolmasters; the English and the terrible things they did to us for eight hundred long years. (p. 11)

On the American continent, bell hooks (1993) eloquently reflects on the pain of her upbringing:

> Black people are indeed wounded by forces of domination. Irrespective of our access to material privilege we are all wounded by white supremacy, racism, sexism, and a capitalist economic system that dooms us collectively to an underclass position. Such wounds do not manifest themselves only in material ways, they affect our psychological well-being. . . . (p. 11)

Approximately 17.6 percent or one in six children in the United States lives in poverty (U.S. Census Bureau, 2004). This represents an increase of about one percent from the previous year. In 2000, there had been a small drop in the child poverty figures, a fact probably related to the previous rise in employment opportunities, the increase in overtime work, and the higher percentage of parents holding two or even three jobs between them. The recent increase in child poverty has occurred despite the fact that 77 percent of the poor live with a family member who works at least part-time; this compares to 60 percent in the early 1990s (Children's Defense Fund, 2002). What this means is that more children are at home alone. The lack of child care provisions compounds the problem. Also, whereas just 30 years ago full-time work at the minimum wage lifted a family out of official poverty, today it does not. Parallel developments have taken place in the United Kingdom (Save the Children, 2004) and Canada ("Higher Child Benefits Needed to Counter Persistent Poverty," 2003).

The relationship between a family's loss of welfare benefits under Temporary Assistance for Needy Families (TANF) and children's suffering from ill health and inadequate food has been documented by medical researchers (Children's Defense Fund, 2002). The six-city U.S. study showed that in families bumped from the welfare rolls, children were more likely to have been hospitalized and not to have been properly fed. Nearly one in three black children and more than one in four Hispanic children are poor, compared to 13 percent of non-Hispanic white children (UNICEF, 2001). The number of black children who live in extreme poverty (in families with an income under $7,000) is at its highest level since the government began collecting such statistics.

Homelessness also has increased tremendously among young women and their children as a result of welfare reform. Not since the Great Depression have this many children—hundreds of thousands of them—had no place to call home (Quindlen, 2001).

Even before unemployment continued to rise, two alarming trends were identified in a joint RAND Corporation/University of California report. The first of these findings was that in many poor, especially African American, families, children are being moved into relatives' homes while their parents work (Watson, 2002). This fact was reflected in the seemingly optimistic figures that showed a decline in single-parent households. The second trend identified was that welfare reform is forcing women into marriages that are likely to break up later. We can speculate further that, without economic aid, battered women are more apt to stay in violent marriages.

The number of children left behind when mothers are incarcerated through mandatory sentencing policies for drug offenses exacerbates the poverty picture. The racial disparity in sentencing policies and law enforcement places a disproportionate burden on caregivers in the black community (Smith & Young, 2002).

The impact of welfare reform, in short, is the ignoring of children's needs for short-term economic gains. In all likelihood, the long-term costs will be seen in increased expenditures for health care, foster care, special education, and child protection services. Reducing child poverty, on the other hand, would be cost-effective in reducing the waste of government resources. The payment of a child benefit (known as a family allowance) to all families, as is done in most other industrialized nations, would ensure that basic necessities were provided without reducing the work incentive.

As this section has shown, children are being increasingly neglected through lack of provision for their well-being. Now we turn to another issue of increasing concern: the direct exploitation of children.

Exploitation of Children

Child Labor

Impoverished children find many creative and desperate ways to survive. Viewed outside the context of despair and misery, the survival strategies make little or no sense. The exploitation of children, likewise, takes shape within the context of human misery, and against a background of what Erik Erikson (1963) calls the "prolonged inequality of child and adult, as one of the facts of existence which makes for exploitability" (p. 422).

Before discussing the matter further, it is important to distinguish between *child work* and *child labor*. Child work, as defined by the International Labor Organization (ILO), refers to adult-guided activities whose focus is the child's learning of vocational or cultural skills. Child labor, in contrast, as it is used here, does not refer to after-school work such as at a car wash, but rather to "any economic exploitation or work that is likely to be hazardous or interferes with the child's education, or is harmful to the child's health or physical, mental, spiritual, moral, or social development" (U.N., 1989, Article 32). A pejorative term, *child labor* includes activities that are potentially hazardous, interfere with education, and represent clear exploitation of the child. As a truly comprehensive document, the Convention on the Rights of the Child recognizes the right of children to be protected from economic exploitation and from performing work harmful to their health.

According to the ILO, some 250 million children between the ages of 5 and 14 are working illegally on farms and in sweatshops (UNICEF, 2003a). The elimination of child labor and its replacement with universal education would be enormously cost-effective in the long run, states the ILO. In the United States, it is generally believed there are almost 1.5 million children working illegally on farms and in sweatshops.

Why would parents allow their children to be victimized as child-slaves? Why would the state look the other way? The answer to both questions is the same: money. Families living in extreme poverty may feel compelled to exploit their children's labor for the family's survival. Parents who hardly can feed themselves may find it nearly impossible to refuse a man's cash payment in exchange for sexual acts with one of their daughters (Sachs, 1994). As environmental stress associated with global trade pushes rural families toward ruination, children become economic liabilities. In desperation, such children may be sold to a sweatshop or brothel. The recent boom in these forms of child labor is endemic in countries with a rapidly widening gap between the rich and the poor and with an export-oriented economy. Heightened competition in the global marketplace, enormous debt burdens by countries and individuals, and bloated military budgets have pushed families to look to their children as a financial resource (UNICEF, 2003a). Children are in demand—both boys and girls—as factory workers, as their nimble fingers, docility, and inexpensive upkeep make them valuable commodities. They also are in demand as sex objects for the tourist trade.

To protect children from such vile forms of exploitation, Otis (1995) recommends compulsory education for all children, the establishment of governmental organizations to expose conditions and coordinate activities to rectify them, and boycotting of goods produced by child labor. Making child labor a focus of child advocacy activity, as in the early days of our social work heritage, could do much to better the lives of children (Otis, Pasztor, & McFadden, 2001). In 2002, a promising step was taken when the U.S. Congress unanimously approved an amendment cosponsored by Senator Tom Harkin to make the elimination of the worst focus of child labor and trafficking in children a major goal in future trade negotiations (Associated Press, 2002).

Child Prostitution

Parents throughout Southeast Asia and from other impoverished countries, often out of desperation to survive, press their daughters into prostitution. In India, for example, the Banchharas, one of the lowest-ranking castes, have been identified by human rights groups as a group that uses prostitution as its primary source of revenue (Majumdar, 2002). By tradition, the eldest daughter in the family becomes a prostitute at age 12. As Indian laws increasingly prohibit the practice, girls are being sent to West Asian countries.

Sex is a multibillion-dollar industry, and today in places as geographically diverse as Brazil, Colombia, and Russia, the trade in children's bodies is booming. Street children in St. Petersburg, Russia, most of them runaways, often work as prostitutes or in the porn industries (Müller, 2003). Street children are victims and victimizers both; they are pushed out of their homes by family poverty and neglect, while pulled into a life on the streets by the availability of work and income. At once attracted and repelled by their lifestyle, these children tend to be boys, and their numbers are increasing dramatically worldwide. Known as *runaways* or *homeless children* in the United States, as *street sparrow* in Zaire, *pelone* in Mexico, and *gamine* in Colombia, such children are identified by the U.N. as street children. *Street children* are defined as minors who earn their living by working on the streets or as children who reside on the streets full-time (Peralta, 1995). It is estimated that over 100 million children live on the streets worldwide, about half of them in Latin America (United Nations Development Programme, 2000). Street children such as those in Brazil are subject to constant police violence and abuse (Human Rights Watch, 2003).

In a comparative study of children who inhabit the streets in the United States, India, and Colombia, Viswanathan and Arje (1995) perceive the economic conditions as paramount: The plight of the street children, according to these authors, is shaped by poverty, gender, and child labor conditions. In the United States, children of all social classes gravitate to the streets, often to escape situations of abuse and neglect in their homes, and are drawn into deviant subcultures. In Colombia, on the other hand, children are on the street more to ease family economic burdens; and on the street, they are active participants in the underground economy, especially drug traffic. The large majority of street children in Colombia and in other parts of Latin America maintain some continuing relationship with their families. In India, on the other hand, girls whose parents could not afford to keep them are often entrapped in brothels and prostitution as a way of life.

Child prostitution, according to an article in *Lancet,* is not only a cause of death and high morbidity but also a gross violation of human rights. Hundreds of thousands of children, according to estimates, have engaged in the sex trade in India, the United States, Brazil, Thailand, and China. Of children rescued in Southeast Asia, more than half are infected with HIV/AIDS (Willis & Levy, 2002). Sex tourism is especially on the rise in Central and South America. Internationally, the trafficking of street children or children sold by their parents to pay off debts has become a flourishing industry. Declining economic conditions for the poor in Mexico stemming from the effects of the North American Free Trade Agreement (NAFTA) have increased such exploitation, according to a study conducted by Estes and Weiner (interviewed by Valliantos, 2000). In the coastal districts of Sri Lanka, an estimated 36,000 boys are exploited as prostitutes (UNICEF, 2003b).

Child Soldiers

In wartime, girls and women are at high risk of rape and, in many parts of the world, forced prostitution. In Uganda, for example, a rebel group curiously called "the Lord's Resistance Army" has captured thousands of children over the past decade, about 40 percent of them girls, to serve as sex slaves. The boy soldiers and some of the girls as well become indoctrinated killers (Friedlin, 2002). The babies that the girls have are also captives. Some of the children escape; others are so brainwashed that they lose all desire to leave. World Vision, a Christian aid organization, runs a rehabilitation camp in Uganda for rescued child soldiers. At the camp, the children are cared for, educated, and counseled while volunteers search for their families (Baldauf, 2002).

In violation of international law, child soldiers have long been fixtures in Africa's lingering civil wars. About 300,000 children are fighting in 30 nations, a third of them in sub-Saharan Africa (Raghavan, 2003). United Nations aid workers are noticing a disturbing trend: Drugged children are being sent to the front lines. Colombia and Myanmar have over 77,000 child soldiers, many as young as 8 years old (*UN Wire*, 2004). Northern Ireland and Israel also have been on the list of countries in which children are recruited as soldiers and messengers. Worldwide, poverty and the proliferation of small and cheap weapons have created this situation in which children with parental permission have become prized for their fighting abilities (McManimon & Stohl, 2001). The recruitment of children for war has some key advantages. Boys will do things like torturing whole families and burning houses that men would shy away from, and the children's belief in magic renders them remarkably fearless. The violence done to small boy recruits defies description; this abuse helps train them for savagery. Girls often serve as sex slaves.

A sad fact in the brutalization of children is that the brutalized learn to enjoy the killing. Belief in magic and use of drugs seem to subdue fears and inhibitions. Children brag about raping and killing members of whole families and about the sense of exhilaration they felt as they looted the families' things (Masland, 2003). Except for Palestinian youth growing up under occupation, political ideology usually does not enter the picture. In many places, picking up a gun is simply the best survival option available. A child soldier gets a bright-colored uniform, shoes, and a weapon—symbols of power and status. In addition, the child gets three meals a day and medical care.

Under the auspices of the U.N. Children's Fund, limited programs are preparing ex–child soldiers to resume school and ordinary life. When the children arrive in these program's camps, according to reports, they are aggressive, refuse to listen to adults, and try to rape female staff members. The children blame their nightmares on the staff for "taking away their powers."

Child labor, children in prostitution, child soldiers, and street children are all examples of the abuse and neglect of children on a mass scale, often committed by the social system itself. Other forms of abuse and neglect, however, occur at both the global and the familial level. We will discuss these forms of child abuse next.

Child Abuse and Neglect

Genital Mutilation

As stated in the U.N. Convention on the Rights of the Child (U.N., 1989):

> Children have a right to protection from all forms of physical or mental violence, injury or abuse, negligent treatment, maltreatment, or exploitation, including sexual abuse, while in the care of parents, legal guardians, or any other person who has the care of the child. (Article 19)

When we think of child abuse, we usually think of acts of violence performed by sick or sadistic individuals outside the norms of mainstream society. In many parts of the world, however, child abuse is culturally prescribed. One such practice that has involved millions of girls is known as *genital mutilation*. International health authorities have found the most extensive evidence of this custom on the African continent and Arabian Peninsula (Steinem & Morgan, 2002). A high rate of mortality is suspected to occur.

Drawing on indigenous sources, DeMause (2002) graphically describes the procedure of genital mutilation:

> The girl's sexuality is so hated that when she is five or so, the women grab her, pin her down, and chop off her clitoris and often her labia with a razor blade or piece of glass, ignoring her agony and screams for help, because, they say, her clitoris is "dirty," "ugly," "poisonous," "can cause a voracious appetite for promiscuous sex," and "might render men impotent." The area is then often sewn up to prevent intercourse, leaving only a tiny hole for urination. The genital mutilation is excruciatingly painful. (p. 341)

This practice is frequently described erroneously as "female circumcision," a puberty ritual. Yet the degree of damage, both psychological and physical, is not comparable to that involved in the African custom of male circumcision. Although it may be considered abusive in its own right, male circumcision is not, as Steinem and Morgan (2002) point out, performed for the purpose of destroying its victim's capacity for sexual pleasure.

Although some African countries such as Sudan, Egypt, Ghana, and Guinea have banned genital mutilation in recognition of Western sensibilities, generally the laws are not enforced. Estimates are that a staggering 137 million women have been abused in this way ("Female Genital Mutilation: Is It Crime or Culture?" 1999). Recently the U.N. General Assembly's Special Session on children set a goal to work toward ending female genital mutilation (Bellamy, 2003). As well as being a violation of human rights, this practice increasingly is recognized as making women and girls vulnerable to contraction of HIV/AIDS and other sexually transmitted infections.

Other Global Forms of Child Violence

Even apart from the deliberate involvement of children in abusive practices such as genital mutilation, millions of children are having their rights violated every day, indirectly through poverty, and more directly through war, as we saw earlier. A psychological study of 1,300 children showed that 70 percent of Palestinian children in the West Bank and 30 percent of children in Jewish settlements were suffering from post-traumatic stress disorder (PTSD) following exposure to months of bloodshed (Plushnick-Masti, 2002). There is no reason to believe that the harm done to children in Afghanistan, Iraq, or Northern Ireland is any less severe.

As violence strikes at women through human rights abuses, their children, both born and unborn, often bear the consequences. In some regions of the world, infants are stillborn due to their mothers' malnutrition and domestic violence (UNICEF, 2001). Sexual oppression, too, rears its ugly head in a statistical anomaly: In parts of Southeast Asia, there are far more births of males than of females. Griswold (2003), a journalist reporting on life in the Taliban-controlled area of Pakistan, for example, provides this description of an interview he had with a young mother: "How many children does she have now? 'Two,' she says. 'Three if you count the girl'" (p. 62).

In China, where the natural sex ratio should be 105 males per 100 females, the number is now a lopsided 116.9 males to 100 females (Gittings, 2002). Infanticide is no longer responsible for this disparity, as in the past; now it is due to prenatal sex selection. The Chinese "one-child" policy, coupled with modern technology (ultrasound tests), favors the selection of male children over female ones. Chinese men are now paying up to $4,000 for kidnapped Vietnamese women to marry.

India has a similar shortfall of women despite a government ban on ultrasound. Young Indian men are having difficulty finding wives (the girl/boy ratio has dropped to 927 per 1,000, and far less in certain regions), so prosperous men are buying girls from poor villagers (Kennedy, 2004). Such children become part of a mass trafficking trade to meet the demand for brides, many of whom must provide sexual favors to all the men in the family.

Family violence in Great Britain is pronounced, according to an article by Rice-Oxley (2003). Estimates from the past 30 years are that one child has died every week from an adult's cruelty. In contrast to Britain where hundreds of infanticides have been recorded since 1981, in Sweden only four cases of infanticide have been recorded during the same period. In light of such facts, and due to a recent outcry precipitated by the death of an 8-year-old immigrant child who was killed even after the authorities had been notified, the British system is being overhauled so that all children will be monitored for abuse and neglect.

Child Abuse and Neglect in the United States

Child abuse, in the sense of the deliberate infliction of pain on a child by an adult, can be conceived of as extending along a continuum, with mild hitting (euphemistically called spanking or smacking) at one end, and life-threatening assault at the other. This conceptualization is controversial because it treats mild assaults and violent beatings as being different only in degree rather than in kind. The reason this makes the notion controversial is that in our society, whereas physically striking an adult is widely condemned and illegal, striking a child is a culturally normative behavior. According to a recent national survey, for example, 61 percent of American parents of children under age 7 viewed spanking as a form of regular discipline to be appropriate (Springen, 2000).

The National Association of Social Workers (NASW; 2003) opposes all forms of physical punishment of children, whether in the home or at school. One of the roles that child welfare workers (and women's shelters counselors) play is to teach parents nonviolent forms of discipline. Among the reasons given in the NASW policy statement are: Such punishment causes fear and anger, teaches aggression, is ineffective in curbing misbehavior, stunts moral development, and can get out of control and lead to injury. The NASW position is consistent with that of the International Federation of Social Workers (IFSW), which opposes corporal punishment globally, and with the positions of many other nations that have outlawed child assault over the past two decades ("Europe Turns against Smacking," 2000). To date, the countries that have outlawed child assault by parents or others include Austria, Belgium, Bulgaria, Croatia, Cyprus, Denmark, Finland, Germany, Israel, Italy, Norway, and Sweden. Anglo-American nations are far more reluctant than other industrialized nations to promote interference with the privacy of the home. Recently, in the United Kingdom, the House of Lords refused to give children the same protection against violence that is enjoyed by adults, although they did offer some protection against striking that causes bruising or reddening of the skin (Cowell, 2004). The Canadian Supreme Court has offered a similar halfway measure (Canadian Broadcasting Company, 2004). Private schools in the United Kingdom and both public and private schools in 23 U.S. states (mostly in the South) are accorded the right to use physical discipline (Osunsami, 2002).

Unlike child abuse, child neglect is an act against a child of omission rather than commission; typical examples are failure to feed or clothe a child and exposing a child to the elements under unsafe conditions. For an overview of life-threatening forms of violence and neglect, the National Clearinghouse on Child Abuse and Neglect (2004) provides the following facts:

- Approximately 1,400 children were known to have died from abuse or neglect in 2002.
- Because of underreporting, estimates are that more than 2,000 children die each year due to abuse or neglect.
- A total of 168 of the child victims had contact with child protective services within 5 years before their deaths.
- American Indian and Alaska Natives had twice the victimization rate as whites.
- Infant boys had the highest rate of fatalites; three-quarters of children who were killed were younger than 4 years old.
- Physical abuse was involved in about a quarter of the cases and neglect in about half the cases. (See the full report at http://www.acf.hhs.gov)

Commenting on similar figures from the previous year, the president of the Children's Defense Fund, Marian Wright Edelman (2003), expressed shock and outrage that we as a culture continue to allow such a death toll. The solution, she wisely suggests, is to extend greater federal and state support to children and families who come to the attention of the child welfare system. We need nurturing homes for children in need and, as Edelman recommends, better-trained caseworkers.

More to the point, however, would be to greatly reduce the caseloads that workers carry. No doubt the primary reason that more than 500 children whose cases had been reported to the authorities still died was because the authorities were too bogged down in overwork to help. Caseloads in Iowa have grown so large due to state budget cuts (as high as 80 to 100 families per worker) that some caseworkers are leaving the field. Meanwhile, the number of abuse victims has increased significantly (Rood, 2002). A nationwide Brookings report on the human services workforce confirmed a high dissatisfaction and burnout rate due to heavy workloads and excessive regulation (O'Neill, 2003).

We cannot leave this section on systemic mistreatment of children without addressing the fate of immigrant children who, fleeing persecution in their families and countries, travel to the United States unaccompanied and beg for asylum. Up to 80,000 children come from all over the world, but mostly from Latin America, seeking help (Knight, 2004). Most are deported within 72 hours, but the thousands who are allowed to stay languish in juvenile jails and adult prisons alongside young violent offenders. In 2003, for example, one third of children seeking asylum were detained in juvenile jails; many were shackled and handcuffed, isolated, and physically abused (Knight). Without laws to protect them, many remain in custody for years. Amnesty International and the Justice Department are investigating the treatment of immigrant youth and other non-delinquent youth who are confined in such facilities. (Refer to Chapter 6 for more on human rights violations against children.)

Child Sexual Abuse

Child sexual abuse is generally understood to refer to forced, tricked, or manipulated contact with a child by an older person (usually five or more years older) for the purpose of the sexual gratification of the older person (Conte, 1995). Child sexual abuse includes incest, sexual molestation, sexual assault, and exposing the child for purposes of pornography or prostitution. Although there has been concern with sexual abuse of children previously in history—in 19th-century France and at the turn of the century when the French brought the issue out in the open—for the most part, there has been a conspiracy of silence concerning its very existence. For personal, societal, and political reasons, it has always been more expedient for society to deny this problem than to face it head on. This unhappy synergy is well illustrated by the spate of clergy sexual abuse cases that has been highlighted in American news reports. By mid-2002, 50 U.S. priests suspected of molesting minors had either resigned or been dismissed from duty, and many cases were pending (Bayles, 2002). Hundreds more have been accused. Such abuse is not new, nor is it confined to the United States. In a poignant case from Ireland, the Irish actor Malachy McCourt (2001) recalls how he drowned his pain in alcohol to help him forget disturbing incidents with three different priests:

> In Limerick, I could no longer successfully suppress feelings I'd ignored my whole life; couldn't seem to clean out the rage and bitterness and depression that were clogging my soul and spirit. At intervals, the whiskey let me forget for a bit, but then I'd slide deeper into the slough, when sobriety returned.
>
> It was this time in Limerick, too, that memories of being molested sexually came flooding back. I was about eleven when one of the priests told me he would test my ability to resist sin, and then he fiddled with me, all the time lecturing me

on the punishments that awaited me in hell and the lashings with cat-o'-nine tails I deserved. (p. 166)

The scandal has been so far-reaching in the United States that an attitude of cynicism concerning the once-venerated priesthood has developed, and the number of young men entering Catholic seminaries consequently has declined. A growing number of state legislatures are changing their laws to make it a crime for church officials not to report sexual abuse of minors (Bayles). To read excerpts from personal narratives of women who were molested by their priests when they were in their teens, see van Wormer and Berns (2004). Looming through these narratives are two themes—the crushing loss of religious faith, and the intense loneliness that comes from being forced to keep the dread secret quiet.

Cases of clergy abuse have been prominent news stories because the incidents were hidden for so long and because they shock our sensibilities. In most cases of childhood sexual abuse, the predators are fathers, stepfathers, other relatives, or friends of the family. Of the reported family cases of abuse and neglect, about 10 percent involve sexual abuse (National Clearinghouse on Child Abuse and Neglect, 2004). Sexual abuse includes not only sexual intercourse but also oral-genital contact, fondling, indecent exposure, and pornographic exploitation. In child sexual abuse, the child is used as an object for the immediate gratification of the older person. Over 90 percent of child molesters are males (Zastrow, 2004). Boys, unlike girls, are more likely to be abused by non-family members.

What is the impact of childhood sexual abuse? A history of such abuse predisposes the female child to a pattern of later victimization, early teen pregnancy, and alcohol and other drug abuse (van Wormer, 2001). A growing body of research, including an intriguing study by the Alan Guttmacher Institute, indicates that childhood sexual abuse is a potent factor in teenage childbearing (reported in *NASW News,* 1995). According to one study, up to two-thirds of teen mothers say they had sex forced on them earlier by older men; another study of almost 200,000 births by teenage mothers revealed that 70 percent of the children were fathered by adults. Such findings put a different angle on the early teenage pregnancy phenomenon that is so persistent in the United States. Accumulating evidence has revealed that young teen girls who get pregnant are often suffering from earlier traumas that have led them to self-destructive links with older men. Sometimes the pregnancy is the result of rape. In any case, provision of psychological counseling would seem to be more effective in altering undesirable behavior patterns than cutbacks in welfare benefits.

Incest within the immediate family is apt to be far more traumatic for the child than other forms of sexual abuse. In cases of incest, all the relationships within the family are poisoned. Assuming the perpetrator is the father, the father's denial becomes the mother's also; the child, who now has the power to destroy the family and threaten the marriage, is initially called a liar. The movie *Bastard out of Carolina,* based on an autobiography by Dorothy Allison (1993), accurately portrays the depth of the hurt inflicted on all concerned by the beatings and rape perpetrated by a family member (in this case, a stepfather). Dealing with the same subject, Jane Smiley's (1992) novel *A Thousand Acres* retells Shakespeare's *King Lear* with a twist. The novel (and the later movie version) artfully delves into the intense sibling divisions caused not by the childhood violations but by their suppression.

The child welfare worker or therapist faces an awesome challenge in crisis intervention under the circumstances of incest in the family. The choices are grim. If the child is placed in foster care, she may feel further victimized; and as Zastrow (2004) indicates, such an action is likely to become known to the community, after which all the family members will be shunned. In recent years, an alternative approach has been to remove the violator from the home for a long period of time and then, through intensive counseling, help the family become reunified. Given the heavy caseloads that most child welfare workers bear and the lack of funding for referral to relevant therapy services, however, it is doubtful that this intervention will be effective.

Why the Child Welfare System Is Failing Our Children

The child welfare system does not operate in a vacuum. The expectation that the child welfare system can "pick up the slack" from an inadequate social welfare system is wishful thinking. Following Maslow's (1970) hierarchy of needs as discussed in Chapter 7, we can see that the starting point for achievement of self-actualization and esteem rest on a foundation of fulfillment of one's basic needs and development of a sense of security. In order to do their jobs adequately and ensure that children receive the care they need, child welfare workers need the following:

- Available long- and short-term substance abuse treatment provisions for all family members
- Close working relationships with school social workers and guidance counselors
- Separation of the policing and therapy functions in order to develop trust with family members
- Subsidized preschool for all children
- Access to intensive mental health services as needed so that children do not have to be sent into foster care before they are eligible for such services
- Support of a welfare system that includes adequate income, quality child care, universal health care, and affordable housing
- Public health nurse visitation to the homes of all new parents

To the extent that these provisions are lacking, the child welfare system is doomed to failure, and child welfare workers will continue to receive much criticism when a child is severely abused or killed.

To learn how good a child welfare system can be, and to appreciate how crucial societal supports are, we can travel northeastward across the Atlantic to Sweden. Khoo, Hyvönen, and Nygren (2002) have made the journey easy for us.

In a comparative study based on focus groups of Swedish and Canadian child welfare workers, these Swedish researchers determined similarities and differences in professional intervention in cases of child maltreatment. The Canadian child protection system, described as one where only the most needy children are eligible for a limited range of services, is roughly comparable to the U.S. system, although more advanced in terms of health care, paid childbirth leave policies, and social welfare provisions. This is what the researchers found: In Sweden, children have more clearly defined rights to satisfactory life conditions and more protections from physical punishment. The Swedish approach is more holistic, and most of the clients are voluntary. This means:

> [There is a] greater willingness of the state to intervene in the private realm of the family—providing supportive measures such as adequate housing, decent day care, mental and dental services for children, and economically viable parental leave from the workforce.

If we are truly serious about reducing incidents of abuse and neglect, we need to address the clear connection between poverty and abuse/neglect. As David Gil (1998), an expert on injustice and oppression, states:

> My studies of child abuse and neglect led me to conclude that the abuse inflicted upon children by society exceeded in scope and destructive consequences their abuse and neglect by parents. . . . I also realized that abuse of children by their parents is frequently associated with abuse of the parents by society. (p. 109)

The societal abuse to which Gil was referring includes unemployment, poverty, discrimination, ill health, and work stress—events that are related to injustice and oppression in society.

Children's well-being is directly related to the family's standard of living and ability to provide food, clothing, shelter, and the time necessary for child care. The well-being of children is indirectly related to parental stress inasmuch as economic and other forms of hardship are apt to be displaced onto vulnerable family members. In the United States, for example, the adoption in 1996 of welfare "reform" (the Personal Responsibility and Work Opportunity Reconciliation Act, PL 104-193) has caused higher levels of poverty and child neglect by forcing mothers on welfare to work without adequate child care provisions (Littell & Schuerman, 1999).

There are some promising developments afoot, however, that provide hope for the future. The next section examines some of these.

Promising Developments

Kinship Care

The practice of subsidizing family members to provide care for children in need, which was written into law in New Zealand, has had a significant influence on U.S. foster care policy (Ernst, 1999). Accordingly, in the United States, kinship care has become the fastest-growing child placement program in child welfare (Hawkins & Bland, 2002). The idea for this formalized system of care rapidly gained ground in the 1980s as the demand for homes in which to place children in need of care far exceeded the number of available registered foster homes (Ingram, 1996). A second factor contributing to the promotion of relative foster care was the growing recognition of the benefits of family care and the stabilizing effect extended family can have on placement. An additional incentive for providing kinship care is the desire by all parties to avoid placement of children outside of their own racial or ethnic communities. Now all states require that workers give priority consideration to relatives when making decisions about a child's out-of-home placement (Samantrai, 2004).

Formal kinship care often involves placement, generally of an African American child, with his or her grandmother. Grandmothers, to help in this way, often need financial assistance, which is provided with this program. Key advantages of such an arrangement are its relative permanence and stability, the familiarity of the child with the setting and relatives, continuity in schooling, and the absence of stigmatizing family removal (Greeff, 1999). Research indicates that children in kinship care remain 30 percent longer than children in other forms of care (Wulczyn, Harden, & George, 1997). Although this program may be more costly to the state, the advantage of the stability of an extended stay in the home of caring relatives should not be overlooked. The Adoption and Safe Families Act of 1997 (PL 105-189) has called for more extensive evaluation of the use of kinship care.

Shared Family Care

Inspired by the Danish whole family placement program in which troubled families receive six to eight weeks of constant supervision and guidance, the Shared Family Care Program was established in Colorado Springs. An article in Colorado's *The Gazette* (Sampson, 2000) describes this remarkable whole family placement program. Instead of splitting up the family while it gets help, as the article informs us, the local social service agency is moving entire families into foster care. Unlike Denmark's foster care arrangement in which families are mentored by professionally trained social workers, these families move in with a mentor family, hopefully to absorb parenting skills from their hosts. The beauty of this program, according to the article, is that it enables families who have minimal support systems to get the resources and skills they need to move toward self-sufficiency. It ensures that children are protected while parents learn the parenting skills they need (Samantrai, 2004). This practice of opening one's home to unrelated dependent adults has been in operation for centuries in Europe (Barth, 1994).

Shared family care programs are now available in ten states. Results from the small studies that have been done are promising: Children whose parents complete the program are only half as likely to reenter the child welfare system as are those families reunited after foster care (Bower, 2003). Five types of shared family care arrangements in the United States, as singled out by Barth, are: (1) residential programs for children that also offer residence and treatment for their parents, (2) drug and alcohol treatment programs for adults that also provide treatment for children, (3) drug treatment programs for mothers and children, (4) residential programs for pregnant and parenting mothers, and (5) foster family homes that offer care of teen parents and their children. Although funding for such whole family program designs has not been widely available in America, as in Europe, this form of family presentation holds much promise for future development.

Other Empowering Approaches

The universal paradox is whether to risk erring on the side of the child or on the side of the family. Perhaps the issue is not either/or but both/and, as Wharf (1995) helpfully suggests. Maybe it is not an issue of whether you should protect the child or support the family but rather how to provide a means of empowerment for all persons in the equation. Such a balance can be achieved, according to Wharf, through the building of mutual aid associations and group and community approaches to provide the maximum benefit for all family members.

Formulated on the North American continent and originally directed toward women and other minority groups, the principle of empowerment is the cornerstone of community-centered innovations. Carter (1997), for example, describes how African American–centered family services and the use of a strengths perspective can protect children and empower families within the natural context of their home communities. Incorporating natural networks that exist within African American communities (e.g., the church and child care cooperatives) can strengthen high-risk families and prevent removal of children by child welfare authorities.

A rare find in the literature is the description of an artificially designed community, now called "Generations of Hope," that houses 13 families—most headed by foster parents, especially senior citizens (Eheart, 1997; Eheart & Power, 2001). The "village" is located on a former Air Force base in Rantoul, Illinois. Generously funded by the state of Illinois, this experiment in community living is generally considered a successful model expected to be emulated soon in Ohio and elsewhere.

Another model of child protection that is premised on increasing partnerships with families through community involvement is found in Iowa (Salus, 1999). Placing less emphasis on the incident in question and more on the family's strengths and concerns, social workers who work for the Iowa Department of Human Services learn competencies for strengths-based assessment in workshops and trainings that are offered statewide. Instead of using a problem-solving focus (e.g., asking "What could you have done differently?"), workers are encouraged to ask solution-focused questions such as, "After all you've been through, how did you find enough strength to keep pushing on?" Such questions are geared toward extracting positive rather than negative responses.

From a strengths perspective, social workers help families find a way to get their needs met.

In Oregon, similarly, workers performing casework assessments have shifted from looking at problems to focusing on how to help families (National Institute of Justice, 1997). The Family Unity Meeting evolved as a partnership between professionals and family members. The Oregon model has many similarities with family group conferencing, but developed independently of it.

Hawaii, with its universal health care and its generously funded programs, has been described in the Canadian *Globe and Mail* as the one that "child welfare workers in Canada point to [as an example the] country . . . must replicate if it is to attack the roots of delinquency, crime . . . and wasted human potential" (Gadd, 1997, p. A1). The Hawaiian program cites an almost unbelievable success rate in preventing child abuse and neglect—99 percent. Called Healthy Start, this state-funded program is basically an early-intervention program that turns potentially bad parents into good ones. It achieves this, according to the article, "not by lecturing, punishing or advising, but by providing the nurturing care that most of them [the parents] never had" (p. A1).

In rural regions of the world, outside the parameters of formal child welfare systems, grassroots approaches often arise to meet the needs of children. Midgley and Livermore (2004), writing in the new NASW collection *Lessons from Abroad*, bring our attention to the Integrated Child Welfare Services Scheme in India. Social workers use community organization techniques to motivate parents and local leaders to establish day care centers for young children where the children are fed and given preschool education; health care services are also provided. Such an investment in the social capital of the villages' children, as Midgley and Livermore point out, is more cost-effective than remedial child protective and residential services implemented after the fact. Funding for such programming is available through international organizations such as UNICEF.

Common to all these innovations is their reliance on the strengths/empowerment framework in working with, not against, families in the fulfillment of mutual goals. The strengths perspective as conceptualized by Saleebey (2002), along with the empowerment perspective as formulated by Simon (1994) and Gutiérrez and Lewis (1999), is rapidly emerging as the most powerful framework for counseling and other interventions in North America. The model is quite simple, its realization much more complex, but yet its formulation is an American offering that should serve to embrace child welfare practice internationally.

School Programming

If we believe new research findings showing that most of the child's brain development occurs before the age of 3 and that early trauma can arrest such development, then early childhood education, especially for disadvantaged children, is a must (Starr, 2002). Studies show that top-notch programs yield a payback of nearly $4 for every $1 invested in poor children's prekindergarten years. Exemplary programs are being set up in Kentucky, New Jersey, and North Carolina. Head Start has, of course, been providing mentally stimulating programming for years. Teachers and social workers work closely with parents to ensure that young children get the educational and emotional start they need. Regrettably, there is talk of cutbacks at the federal level. In the U.K., children's social services are currently being revamped. Every child is to have a tracking number for cross-agency exchange of information. Free nursery school education and hundreds of Sure Start programs modeled on Head Start are being set up in poor neighborhoods (*The Economist*, 2003).

Older children, especially during the turbulent adolescent years, require a nurturing and personal setting of a kind provided in European schools but rarely in American mega–junior high and high schools. The advantages of small schools are that attention can be provided to kids who engage in bullying; drug use is reduced, as there are fewer drug users who can establish their own peer groups; and greater opportunities for school leadership and athletic accomplishments exist. Catholic schools have served diverse populations in low-income areas with success for years.

Studies show that small public schools have higher attendance rates and lower dropout rates, benefits that are especially pronounced in lower-income communities (Ark, 2002). The Met High School in Providence, Rhode Island, has reduced the dropout rate significantly and helped motivate children to

Social workers at Head Start, Waterloo, Iowa. One of America's most successful anti-poverty programs Head Start helps prepare children for school.

learn. Schools in Chicago and Philadelphia have seen equally promising results. Ark describes results in midtown Manhattan, which has reorganized its structure into a consortium of small schools, each with no more than 300 students: "Metal detectors have been replaced with teachers who know every student's name, and incidents of violence have plummeted" (p. 56).

Work with Gay and Lesbian School Youth

A common phenomenon of the American junior high and high school is bullying of youth whose dress and/or behavior are seen as gender-inappropriate. In research conducted by Olweus (2001), boys who were bullies at ages 13 to 16 were more likely than other youth to be connected with a crime by age 24. Some research suggests that up to 20 percent of victims suffer long-term effects, ranging from failing grades to suicidal thoughts to violence (Jonsson, 2004).

How do gay, lesbian, bisexual, and transgender youth fare in the typical high school environment? And what roles can school social workers play in providing a safe environment for such kids? These issues are addressed in Box 8.1.

8.1 Protecting GLBT Youth: The Role of Social Workers in Schools

When I think of what society and social workers can do to help gay, lesbian, bisexual, and transgender (GLBT) youth, my mind turns to schools for children who are deemed to be different. Especially regarding gender role expectations, school can be a toxic environment. The focus of this article is on the role social workers can play in creating a safe school environment for kids of all sexual orientations.

Hatred in the Hallways

In May 2001, the Human Rights Watch issued its comprehensive report aptly titled "Hatred in the Hallways." This report offered the first comprehensive look at the human rights abuses suffered by GLBT students at the hands of peers. Often, teachers and administrators look the other way. Interviews with 140 youths and 130 teachers, administrators, counselors, parents, and youth service providers in seven states, combined with data from state surveys, reveal the following facts:

- The average high school student in Des Moines, Iowa, hears an antigay comment every 7 minutes.
- Youths identifying as lesbian, gay, or bisexual report a rate of alcohol/drug use more than 3 times that of their peers; the rate for use of injected drugs is 9 times as high.
- Approximately one-third of students report recent participation in unsafe sex.
- Although the exact numbers are unknown, a substantial percentage of homeless youths are gays and lesbians forced out of their homes because of "lifestyle" issues.
- Gay, lesbian, and bisexual youths are more than three times as likely as other youths to report that they attempted suicide; being perceived as gay or lesbian and harassed on that basis appears to be the key factor.
- The failure of most states to protect the rights of gay and lesbian teachers has serious ramifications in the lack of role models for youths.

The high rates of attempted suicide and use of alcohol and other drugs by sexual minority youths clearly constitute a form of escape from an unbearable situation. Unlike members of other minority groups, who have family and church as buffers, gays and lesbians face rejection on every front. Self-hatred is a likely consequence.

Children growing up gay and lesbian in strict religious families are most apt to experience dissonance between their spirituality and sexuality. The guilt feelings of a religious child can be overwhelming. Suggested reading is *Prayers for Bobby: A Mother's Coming to Terms with the Suicide of Her Gay Son* (Aarons, 1996), which depicts a mother's journey from religious fanatic—she taped Bible verses on her gay son's bathroom mirror—to pro-gay activist following her son's tragic death. This biography offers a strong cautionary note to parents and extremist religious groups bent on changing children's sexual orientation.

The jock culture of high school creates a climate in which males, insecure in their own masculinity, attack other males whom they perceive as feminine. Similarly, girls whose sex-role behavior is nonnormative may be exposed to relentless taunting by others in search of scapegoats. Preventive measures, therefore, need to be aimed at all school youths to help them with sexual identity issues. Although individual counseling is needed for GLBT youth (to help them adjust to their sexual orientation and cope with peer pressure), such counseling is needed even more for bullies to find the source of their displaced hostility and help them change their behavior (van Wormer, Wells, & Boes, 2000).

Roles for Social Workers

School shootings across the United States, such as the one at Columbine High School in Colorado, often originate in the bullying of male students perceived as weak or nonmasculine in some way. Due to public concern over the deadly school incidents, federally funded block grants have been made widely available for a variety of school programs to provide safety for all students. Social workers have been hired with such grant money to conduct sensitivity training in schools for teachers and parents. Peer-mediation programs, in which students assist other students in resolving conflict situations, have been successfully implemented. The goal of these initiatives is to change the school culture from heterosexist to accepting, while making it known that antigay harassment will not be tolerated.

Two organizations of which social workers should be aware are the Gay, Lesbian, and Straight Education Network (GLSEN) and Parents, Families, and Friends of Lesbians and Gays (PFLAG). The largest national organization to fight antigay bias in America's schools, GLSEN conducts national surveys on school harassment and has chapters in 85 communities (http://www.glsen.org). The inclusive support group PFLAG (http://www.pflag.org) also functions as an advocacy group. Chapters support safe youth groups, conduct parent panels, and speak at local schools. In addition, PFLAG goes to legislators, employers, and school board members to support policies and laws to give sexual minorities the same rights as heterosexuals. Among the most well-known PFLAG members are Judy Shepard, mother of Matthew Shepard (who was savagely murdered in a homosexual hate crime in Laramie, Wyoming), and Cher, whose daughter Chastity Bono (from her first husband, the late Sonny Bono) has come out as a lesbian. Safe schools programs have been implemented by 150 chapters of PFLAG nationwide; often, they are linked to gay-straight alliances in local communities.

As the NASW (2002) seven-page practice update on creating safe schools states, social workers can play active roles in creating safe schools and preventing school-based violence. Social workers who practice in schools or community-based settings can work with students individually or in group settings to help develop their social skills, and they can provide consultation and inservice training to teachers and administrators. The NASW update, however, does not mention the key link between school violence and gender identity issues, which often prompts behaviors such as name-calling, rumors, and scapegoating.

Guidelines for helping to make schools safe for all youths include the following:

- Promote the introduction of school programs to prevent bullying and verbal abuse of students who are deemed different.
- Organize workshops on sexual orientation for student leaders, faculty, and administrators.
- Provide school-based support for gay/lesbian youths and their families.
- Facilitate gay-straight alliances and PFLAG groups.
- Promote the use of gay, lesbian, and bisexual panels from a nearby college or university.
- Ensure that the school library has ample books and periodicals that address issues of homosexuality and bisexuality.
- Host informal rap sessions for interested parties to explore sexual identity issues.
- Link students and their families to helpful community resources.
- Maintain strict confidentiality in all services provided.
- Support education geared to safer sex and the prevention of high-risk behaviors, including substance abuse, which is closely associated with unsafe sex.
- Advocate for the state's Department of Education's antidiscrimination law to include protection of GLBT students.
- Get involved in writing grants for Safe and Drug-Free Schools Programs. (Information is available at http://www.ed.gov/offices/OESE/SDFS/actguid/.)

REFERENCES

Aarons, L. (1996). *Prayers for Bobby: A mother's coming to terms with the suicide of her gay son.* San Francisco: Harper.

Human Rights Watch. (2001). Hatred in the hallways: Violence and discrimination against lesbians, gay, bisexual, and transgender students in the U.S. schools. Available at http://www.hrw.org/reports/2001/uslgbt/

National Association of Social Workers (NASW). (2002). Children, families, and schools: Practice update. Available at http://www.naswdc.org

van Wormer, K., Wells, J., & Boes, M. (2000). *Social work with lesbians, gays, and bisexuals: A strengths perspective.* Boston: Allyn & Bacon.

Source: K. van Wormer, *Social Work Today,* June 10, 2002, pp. 20–21. Reprinted with permission of *Social Work Today,* © Great Valley Publishing Co.

Summary and Conclusion

In the shattering Depression documentary *Let Us Now Praise Famous Men,* James Agee (1939) grasped the essence of life accordingly, "In every child who is born, under no matter what circumstances, and of no matter what parents, the potentiality of the human race is born again" (p. 263). Under conditions of dire poverty, however, children's growth is stunted (literally and figuratively) so that they never can achieve their potential.

That child welfare practice is a gauge by which we can observe the values of a society is a basic assumption of this book. This chapter surveyed across the continents some of the worst forms of societal mistreatment of its youngest members. We viewed child cruelty both historically and with regard to its vestiges today—children as sex slaves, child soldiers, child laborers, and child prostitutes. Despite the promises and the nearly universal ratification of the U.N. Convention on the Rights of the Child, children's rights are widely disregarded throughout the world. In all parts of the world, the health and lives of children are threatened when a given society discriminates on the basis of race, ethnicity, and gender. In many places, children's lives are endangered because their families are at risk for genocide, political persecution, or grinding poverty.

From the standpoint of the United States, a country with professional child welfare services, I described some of the challenges that child welfare workers face on a daily basis, while being torn between inadequate social structures and children from abusive and neglectful families in dire need of help. For all its talk of "family values," the United States is not a family-friendly society. In contrast, in Sweden and Norway, a year of maternity leave at nearly full salary is provided to ensure that one parent will stay home with the child. Child care fees are set on a sliding scale, and the standards of public day care are extraordinarily high. At the heart of such policies is the premise that the whole community thrives when families and children thrive.

From a positive angle, in this chapter, we surveyed some examples of innovative programming that are improving the lives of children. Such programs help children by boosting their families and helping them tap into community strengths and resources. For situations of child abuse and neglect, some of the best preventatives, however, may be a reduction in macro-level stress on families, especially single-parent families. All families require bolstering through provision of health care, day care, and jobs that pay an adequate wage. A program of parent education for all parents-to-be and a program of periodic public health nurse home visits to monitor the progress of children are invaluable in ensuring children's health. The next chapter addresses health and mental health care in more detail.

Thought Questions

1. What is the lesson of DeMause's article, "Our Forebears Made Childhood a Nightmare," discussed in this chapter?
2. Discuss some of the horrors children faced in the past.
3. Discuss this statement: "Child welfare practice is a gauge by which we can observe the values of a society." Give some examples from various times and places.
4. Describe the early orphanages and the "orphan train." Was this an acceptable solution to the social problems of the day?
5. What is the system of family allowances? How does it relate to child welfare?
6. What is the significance of the U.N. Convention on the Rights of the Child? How does it influence policy internationally? Give examples.

7. Name three ways the United States is in violation of the principles of the Convention.
8. Compare poverty in the United Sates with the situation in some African countries. Explain how reducing child poverty in the United States would be cost-effective.
9. Describe the difference between *child work* and *child labor*. Give some examples from around the world of child labor. What are some recommendations for reform?
10. Relate child prostitution to child soldiers and wartime in general.
11. How can children be programmed for war? Discuss the life of boy soldiers.
12. Discuss the findings on studies of street children. What draws them to the streets? Are there any remedies?
13. What does the U.N. Convention on the Rights of the Child say about violence against children? What are the implications for parents?
14. Discuss different ways of viewing physical punishment of children throughout the world.
15. What is the connection between economic stress and child abuse? What is NASW's position on violence against children? How is this controversial?

16. Define child neglect ⸱ types. How do variou⸱ uations of abuse?
17. Compare priest sexual ⸱ of sexual abuse.
18. What is PTSD (refer to C ⸱ how does it relate to sexual abu⸱ ⸱what do we learn from substance abuse treatment centers about the prevalence of PTSD in clients? How about the problem of early pregnancy?
19. How is the child welfare system failing our children? What are some successes?
20. Discuss the advantages and disadvantages of the family preservation movement. How might it be improved?
21. What can we learn from New Zealand and Denmark in terms of helping families with problems?
22. Discuss the role of the social worker in helping to protect gay and lesbian youth in our schools.
23. Agree or disagree with the following statement and back up your arguments: "For all its talk of 'family values,' the United States is not a family-friendly society." Relate U.S. practices to Scandinavian practices.

References

A baby raffle in Paris. (1912, January). *Popular Mechanics*, 19.

Agee, J. (1939). *Let us now praise famous men*. New York: Ballantine Books.

Allison, D. (1993). *Bastard out of Carolina*. New York: Plume.

Aries, P. (1965). *Centuries of childhood: A social history of family life*. New York: Vintage Books.

Ark, T. V. (2002, February). The case for small high schools. *Educational Leadership* 59(5), 55–59.

Associated Press. (2002, May 23). Harkin statement on unanimous Senate approval of child labor amendment. Retrieved from http://www.senate.gov

Baldauf, S. (2002). Aid flows to Afghanistan, in drips. *Christian Science Monitor, 1*, 10.

Barth, R. P. (1994). Shared family care: Child protection and family preservation. *Social Work, 39*(5), 515–524.

Bayles, F. (2002, July 5–7). States add clergy to sex-abuse laws. *USA Today*, p. A1.

Bellamy, C. (2003, March 8). To the symposium on female genital mutilation in Berlin. UNICEF. Retrieved from http://www.unicef.org

Berfenstam, R. (1973). *Early child care in Sweden*. London: Gordon & Breach.

Bower, A. (2003, February 17). Sharing family values, *Time*, 62–63.

...an Broadcasting Company (CBC). (2004, January 30). Supreme Court upholds spanking law. CBC News. Retrieved from http://www.cbc.ca

Carter, C. S. (1997). Using African-centered principles in family preservation services. *Families in Society 78*, 531–538.

Chase, N. (1975). *A child is being beaten.* New York: McGraw-Hill.

Children's Defense Fund. (2001, December). Facts and FAQs. *Fair Start—FAQs.* Retrieved from http://www.childrensdefense.org

Children's Defense Fund. (2002, July). New findings show direct link between loss of TANF benefits and children suffering. *Fair Start—FAQs.* Retrieved from http://www.childrensdefense.org

Conte, J. (1995). Child sexual abuse overview. In NASW, *Encyclopedia of social work* (19th ed., pp. 402–408). Washington, DC: NASW Press.

Cowell, A. (2004, July 6). The House of Lords restrains the hand that hits the child. *New York Times*, p. 6.

DeMause, L. (1975, April). Our forebears made childhood a nightmare. *Psychology Today*, 85–88.

DeMause, L. (2002, Spring). The childhood origins of terrorism. *Journal of Psychohistory 29*(4), 340–348.

Dictionary recognizes stolen generation. (2001, July 12). Australian Associated Press. Retrieved from http://www.australiannews.com

Dillon, S. (2003, April 30). Report finds number of black children in deep poverty rising. *New York Times.* Retrieved from http://www.nytimes .com

Dominick, A. (2002, December 22). When orphan trains came to Iowa. *Des Moines Register*, p. OP7.

The Economist. (2003, September 13). Suffer the little children. *Economist*, 51.

Edelman, M. (2003, February). Faheem's story: When will there be no more "next time"? *Child Watch.* Retrieved from http://www.childrensdefense.org /childwatch

Eheart, B. (1997, May). Homes for foster children. *Kiplinger's Personal Finance Magazine, 51*(5), 143–144.

Eheart, B., & Power, M. (2001). From despair to care: A journey of the old and the young at Hope Meadows. *Children and Youth Services Review, 23,* 691–718.

Enright, T., & Burton, B. (2002, May 23). Harkin statement on unanimous Senate approval of child labor amendment. Retrieved from http://harkin .senate.gov/news

Erikson, E. (1963). *Childhood and society* (2nd ed.). New York: W. W. Norton.

Ernst, J. S. (1999). Whanau knows best: Kinship care in New Zealand. In R. Hegar & M. Scannapieco (Eds.), *Kinship foster care: Policy, practice, and research* (Chapter 8). New York: Oxford University Press.

Europe turns against smacking. (2000, January 18). BBC News. Retrieved from http://www.nospank .org

Female genital mutilation: Is it crime or culture? (1999, February 13). *Economist*, 45–46.

Flekkoy, M. (1989). Child advocacy in Norway: The ombudsman. *Child Welfare, 68*(2), 113–122.

Friedlin, J. (2002, June 14). Girl soldier tells of rape, forced killing. *Womens Enews.* Retrieved from http://www.feminist.com

Gadd, J. (1997, October 18). Paradise found for child welfare. *Globe and Mail*, p. A1.

Gibran, K. (1923). *The prophet.* New York: Random House.

Gil, D. (1998). *Confronting injustice and oppression.* New York: Colombia University Press.

Gittings, J. (2002, May 13). Growing sex imbalance shocks China. *The Guardian.* Retrieved from http://www.guardian.co.uk

Graham, J., Swift, K., & Delaney, R. (2000). *Canadian social policy: An introduction.* Scarborough, Ontario: Prentice-Hall.

Greeff, R. (1999). Kinship, fostering, obligations, and the state. In R. Greeff (Ed.), *Fostering kinship: An international perspective on kinship foster care* (pp. 17–19). Aldershot, England: Ashgate.

Griswold, E. (2003, September). Where the Taliban roam. *Harpers*, 57–65.

Gutiérrez, L., & Lewis, E. A. (Eds.). (1999). *Empowering women of color.* New York: Colombia University Press.

Harman, D. (2002, August 27). Hard return for Uganda's lost children. *Christian Science Monitor*, 1.

Hartman, A. (1990). Children in a careless society. *Social Work, 35*(6), 483–484.

Hawkins, C., & Bland, T. (2002, March/April). Program evaluation of the CREST project: Empirical support for kinship care as an effective approach to permanency planning. *Child Welfare, 81*(2), 271–292.

Hegar, R. (1989). The rights and status of children: International concerns for social work. *International Social Work, 32,* 107–116.

Higher child benefits needed to counter persistent poverty. (2003, July 7). News alerts from Campaign 2000. Retrieved from http://action.web.ca

hooks, b. (1993). *Sisters of the yam: Black women and self-recovery.* Boston: South End Press.

Human Rights Watch. (2003). Street children. Retrieved from http://www.hrw.org

Ingram, C. (1996). Kinship care: From last resort to first choice. *Child Welfare, 75*(5), 550–566.

International Federation of Social Workers (IFSW). (2004, February 23). U.N. Committee on the Rights of the Child. *IFSW Update 2/2004,* 8–9.

Jonsson, P. (2004, May 12). Schoolyard bullies and their victims: The picture fills out. *Christian Science Monitor,* 1, 3.

Karger, H. J., & Stoesz, D. (2002). *American social welfare policy: A pluralist approach* (4th ed.). Boston: Allyn & Bacon.

Kennedy, M. (2004, Spring). Cheaper than a cow. *MS.,* 50–53.

Khoo, E., Hyvönen, U., & Nygren, L. (2002). Child welfare or child protection. *Qualitative Social Work, 1*(4), 451–471.

Knight, D. (2004, March 15). Waiting in limbo, their childhood lost. *U.S. News & World Report,* 72–74.

Littell, J. H., & Schuerman, J. R. (1999). Innovations in child welfare: Preventing out-of-home placement of abused and neglected children. In D. E. Biegel & A. Blum (Eds.), *Innovations in practice and service delivery across the lifespan* (pp. 102–123). New York: Oxford University Press.

Lopez, S. (1999, December 13). A safe place to be till the folks calm down. *Time,* 6.

Majumdar, S. (2002, May 4). Preteens in Indian caste forced into prostitution. *Women's Enews.* Retrieved from http://www.womensenews.org

Malloy, J. (1999). *A national crime: The Canadian government and the residential school system, 1879 to 1986.* Winnipeg Canada: University of Manitoba Press.

Masland, T. (2003, May 13). Voices of children: We beat and killed people. *Newsweek,* 24–29.

Maslow, A. (1970). *Motivation and personality.* New York: Harper & Row.

McCourt, F. (1996). *Angela's ashes: A memoir.* New York: Scribner.

McCourt, M. (2001). *Singing my him song.* New York: Perennial.

McManimon, S., & Stohl, R. (2001, October). Use of children as soldiers. *Foreign Policy in Focus, 6*(36). Retrieved from http://www.foreignpolicy-inFocus.org

Midgley, J., & Livermore, M. (2004). Social development lessons from the global South. In M. C. Hokenstad & J. Midgley (Eds.), *Lessons from abroad: Adapting international social welfare innovation* (pp. 117–135). Washington, DC: NASW Press.

Moe, A. (1990). *Tilsyn I forebyggende barnevern.* Tondheim, Norway: University of Trondheim.

Müller, W. (2003, September). The street kids of St. Petersburg. *World Press Review,* 42–44.

NASW News. (1994, October). Economic abuse. *NASW News,* 9.

NASW News. (1995, October). Teens and age difference. *NASW News,* 13.

National Association of Social Workers (NASW). (2003). Physical punishment of children. *Social work speaks: NASW policy statements 2003-2006* (pp. 276–279). Washington, DC: NASW Press.

National Clearinghouse on Child Abuse and Neglect. (2004). Summary of key findings from calendar year 2002. Retrieved from http://www.acf.hhs.gov

National Institute of Justice. (1997). Child abuse intervention strategic planning meeting. U.S. Department of Justice. Retrieved from http://www.ojp.usdoj.gov

Olweus, D. (2001, March). Bullying at school: Tackling the problem. *OECD Observer,* 24–26.

O'Neill, J. (2003, June). Child welfare reform is called essential. *NASW News,* 9.

Osunsami, S. (2002, November 8). Black and blue: Teachers in nearly half the country can use corporal punishment. ABCNews.com. Retrieved from http://www.abcnews.com

Otis, J. (1995). Child labor. In NASW, *Encyclopedia of social work* (19th ed., pp.197–212). Washington,DC: NASW Press.

Otis, J., Pasztor, E. M., & McFadden, E. J. (2001, September/October). Child labor: A forgotten focus for child welfare. *Child Welfare, 80*(5), 611–623.

Patrick, E. (2000, August/September). Australia's stolen generation. *Ms.*, 38.

Peralta, F. (1995, July 29–August 1). Street children of Mexico City. Paper presented at the International Social Welfare in a Changing World Conference, Calgary, Alberta, Canada.

Plushnick-Masti, R. (2002, July 3). Study: High stress among Mideast kids. *Star-Telegram.com.* Retrieved from http://www.dfw.com

Quindlen, A. (2001, March 12). Our tired, our poor, our kids. *Newsweek,* 80.

Raghavan, S. (2003, June 8). Child soldiers: They are good and obedient killers; will U.N. force in Africa fight them? *Herald.com.* Retrieved from http://www.miami.com

Reichert, E. (2003). *Social work and human rights: A foundation for policy and practice.* New York: Colombia University Press.

Rice-Oxley, M. (2003, September 16). Child abuse tragedy spurs British overhaul of social services. *Christian Science Monitor,* 7.

Richette, L. (1969). *The throwaway children.* New York: Delta.

Roberts, R. (2001, June 10). Romanian children endure inhumane existence. *Waterloo-Cedar Falls Courier,* p. F2.

Rood, L. (2002, December 29). Progress hard to spot since Duis' tragic death. *Des Moines Sunday Register,* p. A4.

Sachs, A. (1994). The last commodity: Child prostitution in the developing world. *World Watch, 7*(4), 24–30.

Saleebey, D. (Ed). (2002). *The strengths perspective in social work practice* (3rd ed.). Boston: Allyn & Bacon.

Salus, M. (1999). *Strengths-based assessment process: Training manual.* Iowa Protective Training Academy, Cedar Falls, IA.

Samantrai, K. (2004). *Culturally competent public child welfare practice.* Belmont, CA: Wadsworth.

Sampson, O. (2000, October 1). Foster family plan expected to spread. *The Gazette* (Colorado Springs, CO). Retrieved from http://www.gazette.com

Save the Children. (2004, March 3). UK child poverty figures still unacceptable. Retrieved from http://www.savethechildren.org.uk

Selbyg, A. (1987). *Norway today.* Oslo: Norwegian University Press.

Simon, B. L. (1994). *The empowerment tradition in American social work: A history.* New York: Colombia University Press.

Smiley, J. (1992). *A thousand acres.* New York: Fawcett.

Smith, C. J., & Young, D. S. (2002, February 26). The multiple impacts of TANF, ASFA, and mandatory drug sentencing for families affected by maternal incarceration. Presented at Council on Social Work Education Annual Program Meeting, Nashville, TN.

Springen, K. (2000, October 16). On spanking. *Newsweek,* 62.

Starr, A. (2002, August 26). The importance of teaching tots. *Business Week,* 164–166.

Steinem, G., & Morgan, R. (2002, Spring). Female genital mutilation. *Ms.,* 42–44.

Swift, K. (1991). Contradictions in child welfare: Neglect and responsibility. In C. Baines, P. Evans, & S. Neysmith, (Eds.), *Women's caring: Feminist perspectives on social welfare, 74*(1), 71–91.

UNICEFUSA. (2003a). Child labor. U.S. fund for UNICEF. Retrieved from http://www.unicefusa.org

UNICEFUSA. (2003b). Fighting child sexual trafficking. U.S. fund for UNICEF. Retrieved from http://www.unicefusa.org

United Nations (U.N.). (1989). *Convention on the rights of the child* (U.N. Document A/res/44/23). New York: Author.

United Nations Children's Fund (UNICEF). (2001). *State of the world's children 2001.* New York: United Nations.

United Nations Children's Fund (UNICEF). (2003a). A year later, children still waiting for leaders to deliver. Press release. Retrieved from http://www.unicef.org

United Nations Children's Fund (UNICEF). (2003b). *The state of the world's children 2003.* New York: Author.

United Nations Development Programme. (2000). Global facts of life. *Human development report 2000.* Retrieved from http://www.undp.org

UN Wire. (2004, June 2). UNICEF report finds number of child soldiers growing. United Nations Foundation. Retrieved from www.unwire.org/UNWire/20040602/unwire/

U.S. Census Bureau. (2004). Income, Poverty and Health Insurance Coverage. Retrieved from www.census.gov/prod/2004

Valliantos, C. (2000, July). Child sexual exploitation exposed. *NASW News,* 10.

van Wormer, K. (1997). *Social welfare: A world view.* Belmont, CA: Wadsworth.

van Wormer, K. (2001). *Counseling female offenders and victims: A strengths-restorative approach.* New York: Springer.

van Wormer, K. (2004). *Confronting oppression and restoring justice: From policy analysis to social action.* Alexandria, VA: Council on Social Work Education.

van Wormer, K., & Berns, L. (2004). The impact of priest sexual abuse: Female survivors' narratives. *Affilia, 19*(1), 53–68.

Viswanathan, N., & Arje, M. (1995). Street children: An international perspective. Paper presented at the International Social Welfare in a Changing World Conference, University of Calgary, Alberta, Canada.

Watkinson, A. M. (2001). Human rights laws: Advocacy tools for a global civil society. *Canadian Social Work Review, 18*(2), 267–286.

Watson, D. (2002, August 14). U.S. welfare "reform" forces more children to separate from their parents. Worldwide Socialist website. Retrieved from http://www.wsws.org

Wharf, B. (1995). Toward a new vision for child welfare in Canada. *Child Welfare, 74*(3), 820–839.

Willis, B. M., & Levy, B. S. (2002). Child prostitution: A global problem. *Lancet, 359,* 1417–1421.

Wulczyn, F., Harden, R., & Goerge, R. (1997). *Foster care dynamics (1983–1994): An update from the multistate foster care data archive.* Chicago: Chjapen Hall Center for Children, University of Chicago.

Zastrow, C. (2004). *Introduction to social work and social welfare* (8th ed.). Belmont, CA: Brooks-Cole.

Never clean the water until you get the pigs out of the creek.

TRADITIONAL IOWA SAYING

Health/Mental Health Care

© Rupert van Wormer

This chapter begins with a look at health conditions in a global context. Following a consideration of such topics as the AIDS pandemic in Africa, and maternal mortality throughout poor regions of the world, we turn to an overview of the U.S. health care system. In this section, as in this chapter, a comparative approach is taken; a comparison between the privatized form of delivery in the United States and universal provisions, as in Europe and Canada, is offered. A boxed reading takes us inside the daily workings of the emergency room. The following discussions on homelessness, physical and mental disabilities, and AIDS, similarly, are highlighted by boxed readings that pull together the personal with the political. Central to this chapter is the concept of harm reduction. This framework, which permeates the global health literature, posits that our focus should be on disease prevention, in terms of both general disease and drug dependency. The chapter closes with a brief look at exemplary health care programs in the United Kingdom, Canada, and Cuba.

Transcending all the health crises touched upon in this chapter is the need for massive investment in primary public health services. A large part of the effort must be directed toward public education and the availability of personnel trained in prevention strategies and early-stage disease care. Consistent with World Health Organization (WHO) philosophy, we can come to realize that global change requires global as well as local solutions.

An Overview of World Health

Headlines from national and international services call our attention to the world's health crises:

- "America's Life Expectancy Rises, but Health Mixed" (D. Brown, 2002, *Washington Post*, p. A02)
- "Afghanistan: UNICEF, U.S. Warn of High Maternal Mortality Rates" (United Nations Foundation, 2002, http://www.unwire.org)
- "HIV Epidemic Restructuring Africa's Population" (L. Brown, 2000)
- "Smoking Leads to Half of TB Deaths in India" (Ross, 2003, *Chicago Sun-Times*, http://www.suntimes.com)
- "Russia's Raging TB Plague" (*World Press Review*, 2001, pp. 11–12)
- "AIDS Crushes a Continent" (Will, 2000, *Newsweek*, p. 64)
- "Drinking, Smoking Blamed for Short Russian Lives" (Boston University, http://www.jointogether.org)
- "AIDS: Forty Million Orphans" (*The Economist*, 2002, p. 41)
- "Malaria Is Alive and Well and Killing More Than 3,000 Children Every Day" (UNICEF, 2003, http://www.unicef.org)
- "Iraqi Cancers, Birth Defects Blamed on U.S. Depleted Uranium" (Johnson, 2002, *Seattle Post–Intelligences*, http://seattlepi.nwsource.com)
- "The Overtreated American" (Brownlee, 2003, *The Atlantic Monthly*, pp. 89–91)

The three deadliest diseases facing today's world are AIDS, tuberculosis, and malaria (which is the leading killer of African children under 5 years old). The sudden invasion of SARS also shook up the world's travel industry and China's health care system for a time. Some of these almost overwhelming crises are related to global interconnectedness by commerce and war, but central to all the problems revealed in the headlines listed previously is the absence of a clear and unadulterated public health focus. Such a focus is the urgent priority of international bodies such as the WHO.

On a global scale, the universal system of health care is rare. Its opposite—specialized and residual care for the rich who can pay and emergency care for the poor—is the standard pattern. Much of the health care offered is curative rather than preventive and geared toward the young rather than the old; much of it is out of reach to the ordinary person. Take a look at vitamin deficiency, for example. According to a report originating from the United Nations Children's Fund (UNICEF), up to 40 percent of children under age 5 in the poor countries of the world have compromised immune systems because of a lack of vitamin A in their diets, while iodine deficiency causes up to 20 million babies a year to be born mentally impaired (International Federation of Social Workers [IFSW], 2004). Simple public health interventions could eradicate both problems. While public attention is generally focused on headliners like the West Nile and Ebola viruses, measles is an entirely preventable disease that claims the lives of nearly a million children every year (Global Health Council, 2002).

The impetus toward privatization and a two-tier system in such unlikely places as China and Chile is at least partially responsible for the widespread loss of life. In an epidemiological study of Latin America, it was determined that many high-income nations with inequitable distributions of income (e.g., Brazil) have lower life expectancies than low-income nations such as Peru (D. Brown, 2002). We could add Costa Rica and Cuba to the list of countries with a success in disease control that is seemingly at variance with economic indices (Escobar, 2002; Saney, 2004).

AIDS is the modern-day plague. It is equivalent in its path of destruction and horror to the catastrophic Black Death of 1348, which wiped out one-third of the population of Europe and spread terror throughout the populace. In 2003, about 3 million people worldwide had died of AIDS, and an estimated 40 million people were living with HIV (Sternberg, 2003). Its impact cannot be exaggerated. The continent of Africa as a whole is home to 90 percent of the world's HIV-infected children. In some countries, such as Zimbabwe and Botswana, one in four adults is infected (Will, 2000). In contrast to most infectious diseases that take their toll on the very old and the very young, AIDS takes its greatest toll among young adults (L. Brown, 2000). Females are infected at an earlier age than males because they have sexual relations with older men who are more likely to be HIV-positive. By 2010, Africa is expected to have 40 million orphans; many will become street children, ripe for recruitment into the ranks of the fighting warlords ("AIDS: Forty Million Orphans," 2002). South Africa's incredibly high incidence of rape may be linked to the fact that so many men have been traumatized through the loss of parenting, the increasing male-to-female ratio, and the widespread belief by males infected with the AIDS virus that sex with a virgin will provide a cure. Accordingly, even infant girls are raped (Beresford, 2003).

The recognition of a need for focusing on women's rights ("girl power") and ending female victimization has been a long time in coming. However, as Landsberg (2001) happily proclaimed, "At last, at long last, the world's powerful leaders seem to have faced up—with shock and profound gravity—to an overwhelming truth: it is the grotesque, worldwide inequality, powerlessness, poverty, and violation of women and girls that is fuelling the rapid-fire spread of the AIDS pandemic. They got it. They know the world has to change" (p. A2). The powerful leaders to whom Landsberg was referring were United Nations (U.N.) spokespersons in attendance at the U.N. Special Session on AIDS. Spokespersons including Secretary-General Annan lamented such practices as forced marriages of young girls to older men, the refusal of infected men to wear condoms, as well as rape, genital mutilation, and sex trafficking. Uganda was praised for its appointment of powerful women to cabinet posts, gender equity educational programming to change attitudes, and universal education for girls.

This brings us to the related subject of maternal mortality. Maternal mortality (the death rate of women from pregnancy and illegal abortions) is arguably the most neglected health problem in the world (United Nations Foundation, 2002). In Afghanistan, almost half of all deaths among women of reproductive age result from pregnancy and childbirth. Throughout the world, some 600,000 women die each year from pregnancy-related causes; practically all these deaths are preventable (WHO/AFRO, 2003). An additional 70,000 lives are lost to unsafe abortion because so few women have access to safe family planning methods or safe abortion ("Figuring It Out," 1999; WHO/AFRO, 2003).

Under the Clinton administration, the United States provided substantial funding to planned parenting efforts for poor nations. In 2003, however, the State Department restored an earlier rule, called the Global Gag rule by opponents, on countries requesting aid. Under this policy, foreign family planning agencies cannot receive U.S. funds if they provide or advocate for abortion services (Fox, 2003). The focus on sex education must be on abstinence outside of marriage. Accordingly, family planning clinics from Romania to Kenya have closed. Opponents deride this policy because of the rise in unwanted pregnancy, illegal abortion, and the spread of AIDS that will ensue from it.

Clearly there can be no sustainability of life without health care policies that are carefully conceived and carried out to avoid unintended consequences. This is as true in the United States as elsewhere, as demonstrated in the next section discussing the state of health care in the United States.

Health Care in the United States

In one sense, the United States has the best medical care in the world. For complicated procedures, the world's rich people often travel to the United States' top hospitals for treatment. The United States spends substantially more per capita on health care than does any other nation. Yet, there are glaring, inexorable problems. In contrast to other industrialized nations in which health care is viewed as having a service orientation, the health care system in the United States has the dual (and often conflicting) objectives of providing a service *and* of making a profit (Zastrow, 2004). Because treatment is more profitable than prevention, preventive medicine is given low priority. Crisis-oriented medicine receives the greater share of research funding, allocation of health care personnel, and building construction. American physicians are the highest paid in the world. Still, their rate of pay has steadily declined, and in any case, it pales alongside the money that hospital CEOs (chief executive officers) get in one year, a figure that may reach into the millions. Major profits are made in private hospitals in affluent sections of large cities, nursing homes, and the drug industry.

A report in *Business Week* puts the country's annual medical bill at a staggering 1.7 trillion dollars (Organization for Economic Cooperation and Development, 2003). Health spending for 2003 rose to a record high at 15 percent of the gross domestic product (GDP) (Toner & Pear, 2003). Exorbitant medication fees are a significant proportion of these medical costs. Employers are balking as health care costs skyrocket. The biggest issue in labor strikes today is the threatened reduction in medical benefits as employers seek to shift some of the burden to workers (Appleby, 2003). Because many small businesses are discontinuing health care coverage, the percentage of uninsured Americans has risen to 15.2 percent ("Number of Americans without Insurance Grows," 2003).

Lobbying efforts in Washington reflect the vested interest of the various parties with vast sums to lose under a government-directed single-payer plan. At the heart of the difficulty is the political clout of the pharmaceutical companies. According to a report by Fairness and Accuracy in Reporting (2003), the pharmaceutical industry gave $21.7 million to Republicans and $7.6 million to Democrats in the 2000 election; the insurance sector contributed a similar amount. In 2002, the drug industry spent a record $91.4 million on lobbying activities (Public Citizen, 2003). Such contributions have had a widely recognized impact on the passage of the 2004 Medicare bill, which protected the drug industry from price controls (Angell, 2004).

Unique to U.S. health care is the claim often made by the pharmaceutical companies that they must be given financial free rein because of the research that they do into cures for disease. In truth, the major part of the research is oriented toward improved marketing of drugs and profit-making (Angell, 2004). Much of the really creative work in inventing new drugs is done at universities and government labs, then licensed to industry. Yet the drug companies are rewarded with exclusive rights and tax breaks as if they were performing a public service. According to a report from *HealthDay* (2004), drug makers are seeking greener pastures in more profitable drugs such as cholesterol-lowering medication and abandoning research into ordinary drugs such as antibiotics. Yet patients are in urgent need of new medications today that fight antibiotic-resistant bacteria.

Federal health care policy is comprised of two major programs: Medicare and Medicaid. The larger of the two programs, Medicare, is a social insurance program paid for by payroll taxes and operated by the federal government to cover all persons over age 65 as well as younger people with a long-term disability such as kidney failure (DiNitto, 2003). As will be discussed in Chapter 10, recent changes in Medicare law have seriously undermined its universal nature by setting different reimbursement levels based on income and in its thrust toward privatized services.

Medicaid, in contrast to Medicare, has always been a public assistance program designed to help the very poor of all ages. Most TANF (Temporary Assistance for Needy Families) and SSI (Supplemental Security Income) recipients receive Medicaid. Medicaid financing is shared between the federal government (which funds approximately 61 percent of the total cost) and the states. Two-thirds of Medicaid expenditures go to the aged and disabled, much of it for nursing home care (Toner & Pear, 2003). Government medical programs have displayed a strong institutional bias; hospitals and nursing homes receive far more money than home health or community services. However, because hospitals (under constraints from third-party payers) are discharging patients long before they are healed or well, home care is now the fastest-growing segment of U.S. health care.

An unintended consequence of the Medicaid reimbursement scheme is that it has the means to limit physician payments while reimbursing hospitals fully. As a net result, many doctors have opted out of Medicaid. Preventive care is not provided, and the poor resort to expensive emergency room use in public or private hospitals. Health care rates have soared as hospitals have shifted costs to third-party payers and to patients who pay cash. In recent times, cost containment strategies have prevented a recoupment of such costs, so private hospitals have "dumped" nonpaying patients into public hospitals, sometimes with tragic results. Today, 45 million U.S. citizens are uninsured; 20 million of these citizens are workers (Connolly & Witte, 2004).

At the same time that Medicaid is being decimated to cut costs at the state level, companies are laying off workers who then lose their health care benefits; some are discontinuing the provision of health care benefits in the first place. The practice of linking health care to employment started during the worker shortage after World War II as a way to compete for workers at a time when wage controls prohibited raising salaries ("Job-Based Health Care: It's Nutso," 2003). Linking health care benefits to employment, however, cuts into corporate revenues, puts workers at the mercy of their employers, and ultimately inflates the prices of American goods on the international market.

Managing Health Care Costs

With health care costs soaring due to new highly expensive technologies, the greater reliance on overpriced medications, and the steady aging of the population, health care reform has become one of the major political issues of the 21st century. Managing health care costs is extremely complex. Much of the expense is devoted to care of chronically ill people who cannot work and the elderly; today, 3 percent of the population consumes 40 percent of health care dollars (Gleckman, 2002). Health care industry profits have dropped considerably in recent years and lag behind the rest of the economy. Hospitals rely on third-party payments to pay bills; emergency treatments for poor, uninsured persons have to be written off. Congress has placed strict limits on Medicare reimbursements; reimbursement is only allowed for changes for each condition (DiNitto, 2003). The one area where price controls have not been imposed is on pharmaceutical products.

In a huge scramble to offer the cheapest prices, hospitals are competing to attract managed care contracts from large insurers and health maintenance organizations (HMOs). The HMOs consist of prepaid medical group practices to which individuals pay monthly fees and receive specific types of health care at no (or only minimal) additional cost (Ambrosino et al., 2001). Although HMOs were designed to make health care services more available to patients, the CEOs of these organizations increase profits by decreasing payouts—thus shortening hospital stays, depriving patients of certain treatments, denying referrals to specialists, and so on. Too-short hospital stays, in the end, lead to multiple readmittances for emergency treatment. Managed care organizations override the recommendations of physicians in many cases. Reduced reimbursements from managed care companies have led many hospitals to eliminate staff jobs, especially those of registered nurses (Jacoby, 2003). Such policies place burdens on already overworked nursing staff and lead to high burnout rates.

Because of the hodgepodge of insurance plans providing individual coverage, administrative costs to health care organizations have spiraled out of control. Accordingly, health care in the United States is drowning in red tape. According to a recent Harvard Medical School study, the United States spends three times what Canada spends on administering its health care system. The bureaucratic cost of treating one U.S. patient averages more than $1,000 per year, compared to $307 per capita in paperwork costs for Canadians ("A Bloated Health-Care System," 2003). The cost of administrative paperwork is 15 percent of health care costs but only 3 percent for U.S. Medicare, which is a single-payer system and much easier to administer (Johnson, 2003).

Each state responds differently to the public's need for affordable health care. Vermont, Maine, Hawaii, and Minnesota are generally considered to have exemplary programs. The Vermont Health Access Plan provides managed care coverage for low-income persons with health insurance (see http://www.dsw.state.vt.us). Hawaii, in fact, is the only state in the United States to provide a right to health care in its state constitution (Hawaii State Government, 2000). Hawaii requires employers to insure most of their workforce, and the state covers the rest. The Minnesota Care program extends insurance to low-income residents; charges are on a sliding-fee basis, and dental care and prescriptions are included (see http://www.dhs.state.mn.us).

Maine's focus is on prevention. The Dirigo Health Plan provides affordable access to health care for self-employed persons and for people who work for small companies. This program, therefore, is immensely helpful to small businesses and hospitals (Walcott, 2003). Prescription medications are affordable due to direct negotiations between the state and pharmaceutical companies. Other states have tried to trim their Medicaid budgets in response to skyrocketing health care costs by launching joint ventures on prescription drugs among states. The federal government, however, has refused to approve the plan ("Roadblocks Frustrate State Efforts to Cut Drug Costs," 2004).

To appreciate the difficulty that individual states have in offering progressive health care programming, we need to recognize the impact of the fiscal crisis that is currently roiling state legislatures. As Toner and Pear (2003) carefully document in a state-by-state account, state officials are being forced to reduce their share of Medicaid payments to nursing homes and other providers—and to eliminate benefits for children, pregnant women, and others in need of medical coverage. All told, millions of low-income Americans face the loss of health insurance or sharp cuts in coverage for prescription drugs under proposals that are rapidly moving through state legislatures around the country. The people who are hit hardest by the Medicaid cutbacks, sadly, are those receiving home and community services (Lieberman, 2003).

People who are living with chronic conditions such as diabetes or depression and who are privately insured are especially vulnerable to problems with paying medical bills. Low-income, privately insured people, in fact, are as likely as their low-income, uninsured counterparts to spend a significant portion of their income on health care. This development likely reflects the impact of increased patient cost-sharing for insured people as well as rising health care costs. These facts are from a new study by the Center for Studying Health System Change, which conducted a household survey of working-age adults (Tu, 2004).

While Americans pay more for their health care than citizens of any other nation, the U.S. health care system does not produce superior outcomes. The absurd inefficiency of a market-driven model (hundreds of different insurance companies, each with its own paperwork and bureaucratic requirements) is obvious to any outside observer. Thirteen countries have lower infant mortality rates while 17 have longer life expectancies than the United States (Ambrosino et al., 2001). Not revealed in these statistics is the perpetual disparity in health care for the rich and for the working and nonworking poor.

Treatment Disparities by Class and Race

The belief that Americans needing medical treatment will be helped regardless of ability to pay is decidedly untrue. According to a national study, more than 18,000 Americans died prematurely in 2000 because of lack of health insurance ("Lack of Insurance Can Be Fatal," 2002). If you are a victim of a traumatic accident, for example, you are 37 percent more likely to die if you enter the hospital without medical coverage. (Many people are not even admitted to the hospital nearest them.) Since larger proportions of minorities are poor, their health is more apt to fall victim to the strain of poverty. In 2002, about one-third of Latinos were uninsured, compared to one-fifth of blacks and one-tenth of whites ("Number of Americans without Insurance Grows," 2003). Although infant mortality rates have improved overall, African American babies are still two and one-half times more likely to die than white babies (Chaudhuri, 2003). It is not only a matter of not being able to afford medical visits and prescription medication, but also a matter of living in roach-infested buildings in areas of high industrial or traffic pollution.

These disparities related to classism and racism are obvious, but what is not so obvious has been revealed in a new medical study by the University of Michigan regarding racism in pain management. African Americans and Latinos are less likely than non-Hispanic whites to receive pain relief even when under a doctor's care. Latinos with broken limbs, for example, are twice as likely to go without pain medication during emergency room visits, and black cancer patients in nursing homes were 64 percent more likely than whites to not get such medication (Malveaux, 2003).

Among American Indians and Alaska Natives, health care lags even further behind than with other groups. Native Americans suffer a poverty rate of 26 percent, twice the national average (Muneta, 2003). Poverty and its associated problems, including alcoholism and lack of access to medical care, contribute to an average life expectancy of around 71 for Native Americans (Manning, 2003). In California, the state with the largest concentration of American Indians, 70 percent of whom live in urban areas, the poverty level is about one in three, and only about half have health insurance ("Urban American Indians Not Getting Needed Health Services," 2002). Despite the presence of federally funded clinics run by tribes both on reservations and in urban areas, American Indians have some of the poorest health indicators in the country; this includes extremely high rates of diabetes and diabetic kidney disease as well as the highest accident rate of all ethnic groups, according to a statement by the president of the Association of American Indian Physicians (Muneta, 2003).

The emergency room is the place where the ranks of the uninsured get the bulk of their Medicaid treatment. Each year nearly 100 million people visit hospital emergency departments across the nation (Fiske, 2003). Because emergency room treatment is not profitable for hospitals, managed care companies refuse to pay for most visits, and many hospitals are closing down their emergency departments. Where such departments still exist, physicians who work there have difficulty getting sick patients admitted into the hospital ("'90s Boom Did Little for the Public Good," 2001). To read about the kind of social services that still are offered at some of the larger and better-funded hospitals (but no longer, sadly, at Graduate Hospital in Philadelphia), read Box 9.1.

Marketing Disease and Treatment

What is happening in the hospital industry is a microcosm of what is happening to the economy as a whole. The market determines the price, and the price determines who gets the business for greater profits. The combination of privatization and competition has led to the development of for-profit medical facilities that can cream off well-insured, high-fee-paying patients. Furthermore, as Hartman (1992) noted, the distribution and character of health care have been altered by the enormously influential presence of third-party payers. The cost of health care is exorbitant, both to the individual and to the nation. The system

9.1 Social Work in the Emergency Room

Mary Boes, ACSW, DSW

For eight years I was a social worker in the emergency room at Graduate Hospital, Philadelphia. In this inner-city setting I worked with hundreds of homeless people. Looking back on this experience now, I am impressed with the discrepancy between the image that one gets on the city sidewalks of the solitary man sleeping on a vent or the "shopping bag lady" and the wide variety of humanity that happened through our hospital doors. Patients with end-stage AIDS, drug abusers, victims of terrible violence—we saw it all.

Whatever brought the homeless to the hospital—the need for "three hots and a cot" or medical ailments associated with living on the streets—their arrival in the emergency room setting marks a rare encounter between those who live outside the social system and representatives of mainstream society, the hospital staff.

Although the basic roles of social work—broker, advocate, clinician—apply in the emergency room, the methods of carrying them out reflect the uniqueness of the atmosphere. To get a picture of what it is like, imagine a theater in the round in which the main characters are rushing to and fro in apparent chaos. The sights: blood, vomit, faces of people in shock. The sounds: shrieks and screams, barking of orders, phones ringing off the wall. The smells: urine, feces, sweat, disinfectants. The impact jars the senses. Add to this a sense of urgency in dealing with situations of life and death.

Now upon this scene, enter the homeless, a population whose numbers are swelling for reasons external to themselves and connected to adjustments in the economy and in the provision of medical and mental health services. All areas of social work are affected, but the inner-city emergency room especially so. To get some indication of the challenges that faced me as an emergency room social worker, let's view my work in terms of the standard social work roles. As a *broker,* I referred patients to detoxification centers, prenatal health crisis centers, homeless shel-

ters, and battered women's shelters. Placement in these facilities was extremely hard to arrange. Detox centers refused to accept patients after 5:00 P.M. or on the weekends. As a social worker in the emergency room on the evening shift, I had to convince drug and alcohol liaisons of insurance companies of the need to provide exceptions to their rigid policies and procedures. With regard to the number of battered women's shelters, there were many more shelters for animals in Philadelphia than for women. In short, due to the lack of available facilities, my job was extremely difficult.

Related to the broker's role was *advocacy.* Interceding on behalf of the patients with the doctors was a crucial aspect of this job. Sometimes this was verbal; at other times, it involved physical management of the patient's appearance. I found that doctors were much more responsive to patients' needs if patients were deloused. Social workers in other fields might find this surprising, but there were times when I took patients into the shower myself to clean them before they saw the doctor. It was rewarding to be able to dress them in fresh clothes that we kept on the premises. This will sound even more strange, but on occasion I found myself taking up collections from doctors and other staff members on behalf of desperate homeless people; I have seen doctors take off their socks right then to give to someone in need.

In my role as *clinician,* I had to make spur-of-the-moment decisions concerning mental illness and alcohol abuse. Relying solely on observation and listening skills, I would inform the attending physician of the need for a psychiatric consultation. One problem with working with the homeless was trying to decide what was cause and what was effect. In other words, to what extent did the disorientation, drinking, depression, and so on precede the homeless state, and to what extent did these traits result from the homeless experience itself?

(continued)

| 9.1 *continued* |

The following cases typify the social worker's role. Frank wandered into the hospital, suffering from the aftereffects of a gunshot wound to the stomach. In my role as a *broker,* I rushed out to meet the fire rescue team and to obtain the necessary information. Then, as was my task, I telephoned the next-of-kin. When Frank's sister answered the phone, I told her Frank had been shot. As was typical, she let out a shriek and called out to others in her house. Frank recovered. On discovering that he had a drug dependency problem, I went to great lengths to get a treatment facility to admit Frank as a patient.

Joe, who suffered from paranoid schizophrenia, was admitted with gangrene; he had not removed his shoes since 1987! "The doctor told me never to take them off," he explained. The attendants and social workers had to wear gas masks because the smell was so overpowering. In the end, however, Joe recovered the use of his feet, and he got a new pair of shoes.

Bruce appeared in the waiting room covered from head to toe with excrement. He could not be bathed because of the severity of his frostbite. After staying two hours overtime to arrange a transfer for him to a shelter, I left him in the waiting room to await transportation. To my horror, I learned the next day that the security guards had thrown him out in the cold and that he froze to death on the streets.

In many ways, the emergency room, especially the inner-city emergency room, captures in microcosm society's failure to provide for its citizens. The sights, sounds, and smells of this country's casualties should cause us to stand up and take note. There is only so much doctors and nurses can do to alleviate the pain and misery often caused by the condition of homelessness—the frostbite in winter, heat exhaustion in summer, the street victimizations, alcohol overdoses to end the pain, and flared-up psychosis caused by stress, not to mention malnutrition. There are only so many places to which the social worker can refer people who have no place to go, and only so much that can be done at the end of the line when the problems emanate from way up ahead. When one social institution breaks down, often another one has to pick up the pieces. So it is today with America's inner-city emergency rooms.

Source: M. Boes, "Emergency Room Encounters with the Homeless," in K. van Wormer, *Social Welfare: A World View* (1997), pp. 444–446. Belmont, CA: Wadsworth. Printed with permission of Mary Boes, University of Northern Iowa.

rewards the use of drugs, as well as unnecessary diagnostic and other preventive measures. Use of life-sustaining, highly advanced technological equipment for people who are terminally ill and in pain or who are brain-dead has raised a number of questions. This sort of treatment may appear to be prolonging death rather than prolonging life. In any case, the amount of money spent on extraordinary interventions reduces the resources available for ordinary forms of care.

In 1994 when health care reform became a real possibility, the biggest, costliest, and most heavily lobbied battle ever to come before Congress ensued. Health care interests donated $25 million to congressional campaigns and poured tens of millions more into mass media advertising (Welch, 1994). Members of Congress on committees working most directly on health care policies received millions in contributions and entertainment in connection with out-of-town speaking engagements. The leading sponsor of these trips was the American Medical Association (AMA). Other top health care contributors of political action committee (PAC) money were major businesses that opposed mandatory employer financing, the United Auto Workers who wanted protection, insurance companies that wanted to maintain control, and the Association of Trial Lawyers who wanted to be able to sue. More recently, in 1998, the AMA spent around $16 million on lobbying efforts. Their concern was different at that time; like that of social workers, their concern was with the need for tighter controls on managed care operations (Morgan, 1999).

Thanks to privatization, health care is big business throughout the world. Many forms of treatment are marketed. The first marketing step is creating a need for the service, as seen in the grosser aspects of cosmetic surgery where there is no need. The cosmetic surgery industry in the United States is a $7.7 billion industry and growing (Glover, 2004). Liposuction to remove fat is the top surgical procedure today. The most popular nonsurgical cosmetic procedure is botox injections to remove wrinkles. Since Naomi Wolf (1991), author of *The Beauty Myth*, alerted the public to the business aspect of cosmetic surgery, the trend toward medical mutilation has exploded, partly due no doubt to the presence of the Internet. Yet, as Wolf stated, "If women suddenly stopped feeling ugly, the fastest-growing medical specialty would be the fastest dying" (p. 234). Throughout Asia, cosmetic surgery is booming as never before; in Taiwan alone, a million procedures were performed in 2001. Asians in Korea, Japan, and China increasingly are asking their surgeons for wider eyes, longer noses, less muscular calves, and fuller breasts (Cullen, 2002). Some of the surgeries have been botched with disastrous consequences, especially those surgeries performed in unlicensed beauty-science centers.

A former editor of the *Journal of the American Medical Association,* Lundberg (2001), is highly critical of the manufacturing of needs and wants that otherwise would not exist by medical marketers. The medical system actively promotes the use of expensive, invasive, and often risky treatments while failing to give comfort to patients. Lundberg's plea is that we capture medicine from commercial interests, perhaps through extending Medicare to all age groups. In his view, the system today pits the interests of doctors, insurers, medical centers, and drug firms against those of sick people.

Nearly 8,000 U.S. physicians recently issued a statement calling for government-financed national health insurance. The focus of the physicians' concern is on HMOs, which have raised Medicare costs by billions; investor-owned hospital chains, which have been rocked by scandal; and drug firms, which have secured the highest profits and lowest taxes of any industry. Their proposal for a universal, single-payer system was published in the *Journal of the American Medical Association* and widely publicized in the press (Sherman, 2003).

There is a huge outcry today concerning rising drug prices. Prices are surging upward by around 17 percent a year. Advertising directly to consumers, a controversial practice banned in nearly all other Western countries, has added to the demand for new drugs (Barry, 2002). More than $2 billion is spent by the drug industry per year on mass media advertising. The success drug companies have enjoyed in protecting high prescription prices and fighting generic versions of their products is reflected in their huge profits, which are five-and-a-half times greater than the median for all industries represented in the Fortune 500 group (Public Citizen, 2003). Drug industry claims that the high drug prices are necessary for research and development are refuted in the use of the money for marketing.

The marketing of products to cure disease, paradoxically, is matched by the marketing of other products of an addictive nature that cause disease in the first place. The assault that marketers make on children is especially worrisome. Children who want to appear cool and grown up, and women who want to stay slim, have been specifically targeted by marketing strategies of a highly sophisticated sort. The success of the tobacco companies in increasing sales through mass marketing campaigns has been phenomenal. The numbers of female smokers skyrocketed with the Virginia Slims brand of cigarette for women. In 1995, a scandal ensued when data indicated a rising market share for Camel cigarettes among youths following a highly controversial cartoon campaign surreptitiously aimed at children (Pierce & Gilpin, 1995). The advertisements were abruptly stopped. Recently, the WHO adopted a sweeping antitobacco treaty that aims to control marketing of tobacco to children worldwide, but especially in the poorest countries. The biggest exporter of cigarettes, Philip Morris, came in for special criticism (Associated Press, 2003).

Physical Disability

Negativism toward those with physical blemishes harks way back to ancient history when imperfect infants were eliminated in one way or another. Much later, "defective persons" were thrown in concentration camps in Nazi Germany for experimentation and extermination. In the present day, people who are handicapped, especially those who are mentally retarded or extremely obese, are the butt of endless jokes and ridicule. In short, people with disabilities still face discrimination, restrictions, and resentment.

Disability is defined by the United Nations as "any restriction or lack (resulting from an impairment) of ability to perform an activity in the manner or within the range considered normal for a human being" (Disabled People's Association, 2003). What this definition fails to take into account, however, is the challenge that comes not from the impairment itself but rather from society's response (discrimination) or nonresponse (lack of accommodation) to this impairment. The meaning of disability, as Hiranandani (2004) suggests, must be understood as a construct related to the prevailing economic organizations, institutions, and political contexts in a particular historical period.

Spurred by the civil rights movement in the 1950s and 1960s, a consciousness of injustice was awakened in people with physical and mental disabilities (Zastrow, 2004). These people and their families began speaking out against and seeking legal action to end job discrimination, limited educational opportunities, and architectural barriers. Because of the body beautiful cult in the United States and the documented preference in hiring for those who are tall, slim, and physically fit, people with disabilities have found it necessary to lobby for protection against job discrimination. In 1973, Congress passed the Vocational

Passed in the 1990s, the Americans with Disabilities Act offers the rights of persons with disabilities to participate in all aspects of society.

Rehabilitation Act, one section of which includes an affirmative action policy wherein employers who receive federal funds must demonstrate efforts to hire people with disabilities. The Education for All Handicapped Children Act, enacted in 1975, mandates that education be open to all children. In other words, children with various mental and physical impairments were to be mainstreamed, as is now the case. In 1990, the Americans with Disabilities Act prohibited discrimination in employment and through limited access to public buildings.

One can expect much progress in disability rights to take place across Europe following the European Union's passage of a comprehensive disability law prohibiting discrimination in housing, education, transportation, and so on ("Europe's First Comprehensive Disability Rights Law Unveiled," 2003). In 1995 in the United Kingdom (U.K.), the Disability Discrimination Act was passed. It provided for employment rights and set minimum standards for accessible public transportation to go into effect by 2004 (U.K. Government, 2003). The U.K. disability movement advocates that the state pay individuals in need of care directly so they can have more control over their choice of care (Dominelli, 2002). The National Health Service in the United Kingdom provides funding so that nurses and/or people in government-funded careers can pay prostitutes for providing sexual services to people with disabilities. In the Netherlands, people with disabilities can be provided with prostitutes paid for directly by the state (Harlow, 1999).

One promising piece of legislation in the United States was the New Freedom Initiative signed into law under the Bush administration in 2001. Under this law, funding is provided by the Department of Health and Human Services for community living, educational programs, affordable housing, and personal assistance services in the home (Dannelke, 2002). Problem areas addressed by these initiatives include the exceptionally high unemployment rate (at 70 percent) of people with disabilities coupled with low annual incomes. Individuals who are working when injury or disease strike often find that business policies are less than accommodating. Most disability policies define illness as total impairment and do not allow for halfway measures such as a reduction in workload. In addition, employers often fear the cost of providing medical insurance, which brings us back to the shortcomings in work-based health benefits.

Due to wars, birth defects, and poor health care, disability is an ongoing problem worldwide. As a result of U.N. leadership, much useful information and statistical data have been collected since the early 1980s. In general, according to Seipel (1994), people with disabilities in the poorest regions of the world are overrepresented in the illiterate and minimal education categories. Moreover, employment opportunities are extremely limited; even in the industrialized nations, people with disabilities are more often directed to welfare systems than to labor markets. Japan, Egypt, and Sweden, however, reserve a certain number of public sector jobs for people with disabilities who are unemployed. These and other countries use shelter workshops to provide rehabilitation and employment for the severely disabled.

Norway provides an example of grassroots activity initiated at the level of the marginalized group itself and ultimately adopted by the government despite a storm of resistance from those who would preserve the status quo. Ingstad and Whyte (1995) described how the situation came about. In 1965, the journalist father of a mentally retarded child took the other parents of disabled children and social workers in institutions to task for the institutions' neglect of disabled children who were kept hidden away. From the first step, the movement kept growing, and an association called Justice for the Handicapped was formed. Today, an umbrella organization represents all forms of disability and is in direct dialogue with the government. The key themes of the new discourse are integration, normalization, and decentralization (community control). All state institutions and special schools recently were closed down. Community and home care have been generously funded.

Cheryl Brown (2002), a social worker who, like practically all social workers, has worked extensively with people disabled by disease and physical problems, lists some of the recurring challenges faced by people with disabilities:

- Dealing with the health care system
- Living with chronic pain
- Dealing with an illness's uncertain path
- Coping with the impact on intimate relationships
- Giving up versus holding onto hope
- Feeling and being alone
- Searching for meaningful work

"Working with these clients," concludes Brown, "is sad at times, but it is also a privilege to enter their world. While they are people with serious illness, they are also special people with intelligence, humor, and perseverance" (p. 7).

Within the disability movement, a paradigm shift is evident. This shift is from a medical diagnostic perspective with a focus on limitations toward a more holistic approach. Even within social work, the predominant discourse on disability has been based on the medical model that defines disability as individual deficit (Hiranandani, 2004). In *Rethinking Disability: Principles for Professional and Social Change,* DePoy and Gilson (2004) have paved the way for social work to recognize people with disabilities under the diversity rubric, to consider what they have to offer the world. Disabled social workers have a great deal to offer through conscious use of self. A social worker with multiple sclerosis interviewed by Stoesen (2003), for example, tells how she uses her illness as an example for the clients in her treatment group.

For a personal narrative provided by a social work educator who teaches part-time and engages in human rights activism and grant writing, read Box 9.2.

Mental Health Care

If managed care has been bad for general health care, it has been even worse for mental health care. Stigma and misunderstanding surround mental illness. A study by the National Association of State Mental Health Program Directors found that states' mental health expenditures declined between 1990 and 1997 (Graham, 1999). Only the most severe cases of mental illness are getting services. Within the context of managed care, the current emphasis on psychopathology sets the stage for illness-centered practice instead of a focus on health and justice (DeWees, 2002).

Mental illness is among the most poorly treated of all diseases. This is true even though about one in five Americans suffers from it at some point, and about 3 to 5 percent of these people are unable to function in any normal way (Brink, 1999). A recent President's New Freedom Commission on Mental Health provided this assessment: "America's mental health delivery system is in shambles" (O'Neill, p. 7). This statement was in reference to the system's incapability of financing and delivering effective treatments as well as the fragmentation of responsibility among agencies. The system's failings have led to unnecessary and costly disability, homelessness, school failure, and incarceration, according to the report.

The presidential commission's report also called for equal insurance coverage (parity) for those with mental illness, that is, the same insurance coverage provided for other forms of illness (Findlay, 2003). Progress in this direction has been stymied as employers have argued that parity for mental disorders would drive up costs considerably (Graham, 1999). Many employers, in fact, have cut costs by limiting mental health benefits as they moved to managed care approaches. Many states, facing an unprecedented budget crisis, have cut mental health services, either through their mental health agencies or Medicaid reimbursement (NASW, 2003c). Vermont, however, has passed a comprehensive

9.2 The Making of a Disability Rights Activist

Jane Nelson, MSW

I became ill in May of 1988 and had already been accepted to graduate school for September of 1988. My diagnosis was rheumatoid arthritis. I decided that even though I had a chronic progressive illness, I might as well go to graduate school because I wanted to get my MSW and get on with my life. After two months of being bedridden, I came to the decision that I would move to the university community and begin my graduate studies.

In graduate school, my first barrier was that I now used a walker instead of walking on my own. The university seemed overwhelming in size, and the rolling hills of the campus intimidated me. When I brought my concerns to the attention of student services, they referred me to the Student Disability Services office. "You have to have a thorough medical evaluation stating that you are 'sick' and therefore qualified for service," the counselor said. The implication was that a chronic progressive illness didn't "cut it," or that I had to "prove" that I was "sick" so that I could be "fixed" in some way in order to be successful in my studies.

But worse things than this were also said. A medical intern took one look at me and said, "The only

thing wrong with you is morbid obesity." I became angry and insisted on seeing the regular clinic physician. But evidently disabled people are not expected to express themselves. The nurse at the rheumatology clinic asked me if I wanted to go to the psychiatric clinic—just because I had asked to speak to another physician. Naturally, I felt demoralized, but I did get the evaluation I needed and became more committed than ever to continue my quest for the MSW.

My coping mechanism was this: I had been educated in the ecological perspective in undergraduate school and decided to approach my new life (as a disabled person) as a "person-in-the-environment." I looked at my strengths for making assessments, and I assessed my environment. I needed to get to school without using all my energy. First, I investigated transportation and found that the university had a paratransit system for students with disabilities. I signed up for the service. I found a teaching assistantship in the same building where the majority of my classes were taught. I obtained medical care to try to cope with the pain and immobility, and went to physical therapy to increase my strength and ability to cope

parity law that includes all mental health diagnoses and addiction problems (National Association of Social Workers [NASW], 2003c).

The problems with mental health care mirror the problems with health care provision in general—the disjointed provision of services and the financial barriers faced by so many people with disabilities. Finding help for children with serious mental health problems is so difficult, in fact, that in 2001 more than 12,700 parents relinquished custody so that their children could enter foster care, as indicated in a new congressional report (Ordoñez, 2003). Foster children are entitled to government-funded mental health care. This expensive solution to the problem is itself a problem, as such families become needlessly separated.

with long days of studying and working. I felt isolated, since I did not have the stamina to socialize after class or work. My social life consisted of talking to students who were studying in the halls and who ate in the same lunchroom where I ate. I did socialize some with students who utilized the Student Disability Services office and had become my peers.

I ended up volunteering in the Student Disability Services office and was able to work with other students who were experiencing the same types of barriers and feelings. This is how I came to membership in the disability rights culture. When I ran into institutional barriers, I knew that other members in the disability community on campus were experiencing similar barriers. For example, one barrier I ran into was: The front of the buildings on the quad had steps, so people with mobility impairments were expected to walk, roll, or crawl around to the back of the building and go into the building through the back door. The elevator that I had to use if I needed to go to a different floor, however, was at the front of the building.

Since my encounters with such barriers took place during the days prior to the Americans with Disabilities Act (ADA) of 1990, accommodations for students with disabilities were not a campus priority. When I started talking with my peers at the Student Disability Services office about this phenomenon of physical barriers, however, we decided to try to join the committee on campus that remodels buildings and approves plans for new buildings to point out how they could make the buildings more accessible to students like us. We were able to join the committee.

I graduated by the time the ADA was passed, but by keeping in touch with the students and workers at the Student Disability Services office, I learned that the students who participated in services from this office were asked to participate in developing the campus audit to be in compliance with the ADA. This, to me, was a victory because the university was being pro-active and embracing this disability model rather than the paternalistic medical or rehabilitation models.

Working as a social worker and being a member of the disability community have helped me to understand policy making better. Being a member of the disability community also has helped me to see where the medical and rehabilitation models come up short. Both are based on the premise that people with disabilities have an orphanlike dependence on able-bodied persons. The disability rights movement has encouraged people to oppose our social devaluation by able-bodied, paternalistic people. I believe the disability community has been and can continue to be successful by developing a strong disability community family and celebrating a proud disability culture. As a social worker, I have learned to focus on the strengths of the people I work for and to embrace an empowerment-based practice.

Source: Printed with permission of Jane Nelson, Hawkeye Community College, Waterloo, Iowa.

The emergency room, ill-equipped as it is, also has become a repository for mental health problems ranging from schoolchildren at risk for violence to adults having psychiatric breakdowns. Under the circumstances, Fiske (2003) calls for more social workers in schools to alleviate the stress on emergency department staffs. As Fiske indicates, social worker services are also vital in hospital emergency departments for making proper split-second assessments and referrals.

Jails and prisons are the mental health institutions of the 21st century. Between 600,000 and 700,000 mentally ill people are jailed annually (O'Reilly, 2003). The Justice Department found that more than a quarter million people with mental illness were behind bars in the year of one study; jails and prisons with security as their first concern can hardly be expected to provide adequate treatment (Shapinsky, 1999). Years of reduced access to mental health care—from the deinstitutionalization of the 1970s to Reagan's omnibus legislation of 1981, which shifted responsibility to the states and therefore to managed care—have contributed to the treatment crisis of today. The original plan to provide adequate public funding for well-integrated community mental health services for the newly deinstitutionalized people never materialized (Suppes & Wells, 2003). Canada experienced a parallel sequence of events with deinstitutionalization after the 1960s and again in the 1980s, also without adequate community health facilities being provided. Then, during the 1990s, the Liberals who were in power in Canada began passing responsibility for housing onto the provinces. Today, staff members at shelters in cities like Toronto are being overwhelmed with the demand for services (Beadnell, 2003).

A promising innovation is the development of mental health courts established or bolstered by grants from the U.S. Department of Justice. Mental health courts are set up to handle misdemeanor offenses committed by persons with severe mental disorders. Each client appearing before such a court must have a case manager involved in conjunction with judicial oversight. The government's goal is to reduce the incarceration rate and recidivism rate among offenders by providing people who are out of touch with reality and/or in need of antipsychotic medication (and perhaps a supervised housing arrangement) with the help they need. Presently, there are 23 mental health courts nationwide. Since social work is the leading profession providing mental health treatment, clinical social workers can be expected to play an active role in the administration and provision of services.

Advances in psychotropic medicine have made it easier in many ways for social workers and other professionals to help clients with mental illness. In recent years such advances, in fact, have been just short of revolutionary. Whereas the previous generation of antipsychotic drugs alleviated some of the symptoms of psychosis, their side effects ranged from jerky body movements to chronic dehydration. The newer drugs are far more user-friendly and safer. Similar groundbreaking developments have taken place with pharmaceutical products to treat mood disorders such as anxiety and depression (Jackson, 2003). Such psychiatric drugs—of which Prozac, Paxil, and Zoloft are the best known examples—manipulate brain neurochemicals to restore a sense of well-being. Such drugs not only curb depression but also pathological cravings for a wide range of addictive substances and activities from cocaine to gambling. The new drugs, which are classified as "selective serotonin reuptake inhibitors" (SSRIs), have been successfully used for obsessive-compulsive disorder and eating disorders as well (van Wormer & Davis, 2003).

The problem in mental health care is the stigma associated with psychiatric illness and the concomitant lack of resources available for holistic care, although cash assistance is provided through the Social Security Disability Insurance (SSDI) program for former workers and through the Supplemental Security Income (SSI) program for persons of no or limited income. Still, the criteria are very stringent, and these programs reach only a small proportion of people in need of help (NASW, 2003c). Many people with mental illness end up on the streets. An in-depth analysis of data from the U.S. Census Bureau found that a majority of the 800,000 or so homeless people have mental illness and/or some other chronic disease such as drug addiction; 39 percent have mental illness alone ("Survey Shows Most Homeless Sick, Mentally Ill," 1999). The survey also found that when such people received the services they needed, such as housing subsidies, health care, substance abuse treatment, and educational training, most could leave shelters for permanent housing.

The Homeless Mentally Ill

Health care and housing can be construed, in short, as two interlocked forms of social welfare. People without shelter are unhealthy people, physically and men-tally—many resort to substance abuse to cope; and unhealthy people, unable to cope in the first instance, often end up without shelter. The right to adequate housing is one of the basic rights enshrined in international law (see Article 25 of the U.N. Universal Declaration of Human Rights in Appendix A of this text). Thiele (2002), drawing on the WHO's Health Principles of Housing, lists three major principles governing the relationship between habitable housing and health: (1) protection against communicable disease; (2) protection against injuries, poisonings, and chronic diseases; and (3) reduction of psychological and social stresses. Just as health and adequate housing are inextricably linked, so also is safe and sanitary housing essential to one's emotional well-being.

The lack of affordable housing is a major factor today in a variety of social problems associated with the poor. Federal policies promoting urban renewal and gentrification have exacerbated the problem. Housing units that were demolished were never replaced. Instead of offering emergency services, many cities, "fed up with the growing hordes of homeless people begging and sleeping on their streets," have begun taking desperate steps to restrict their behavior, or to run them out of town (Sanchez, 2002). The Orlando, Florida, city council voted to jail people lying or sitting on downtown sidewalks, while authorities in New Orleans have removed benches from Jackson Square to keep homeless people from sleep-ing there. Elsewhere, cities have passed laws against giving money to panhandlers.

Transitional housing programs, though few and far between, provide a par-tial answer to homelessness. Such programs seek to empower individuals through teaching them the skills they need for independent living and providing housing for them (Washington, 2002). These programs are funded by grants and serve applicants screened for drugs; the focus is on homeless families. Evaluations such as that provided by Washington of Estival Place in Memphis, Tennessee, have revealed the importance of this offering of social services to for-merly homeless families.

Few supportive housing projects, however, have been designed for homeless people who are not only mentally ill but also at varying stages of chemical dependency. Keep this in mind as you read, in Box 9.3, about a remarkable proj-ect conducted under the auspices of the Downtown Emergency Service Center in Seattle, Washington.

9.3 A Day in the Life of a Mental Health Case Manager

Rupert van Wormer, MSW

It is Monday morning, the busiest day of the week at the Downtown Emergency Service Center (DESC) Mental Health Program. After a half-hour bus ride, I arrive in downtown Seattle—more specifically, in the Pioneer Square district, which is the old part of the downtown area. The agency itself is one block away from Yesler Way, famed for being the original Skid Row. Hundreds of homeless people live in this area today, and the area is reported as having the highest arrest rates in the entire city: Panhandling, public consumption of alcohol, drug dealing, and prostitution are common sights.

The alleyway next to the building that houses the outpatient mental health program is commonly used by people as a place to smoke crack cocaine and inject heroin. As I approach the front entrance to the clinic where I work as a mental health case manager, I see a crowd of about 30 people, mostly our clients, waiting for the door to open at 9:00 A.M. As I unlock the door to let myself in, I am greeted by four or five of my clients simultaneously; some just say hello, while others ask to meet with me immediately. I explain that I will see them after the clinic opens at 9:00. (In this job, it is important to set limits.) I enter the building, locking the door behind me.

I have an interesting and unique caseload. Many of my clients have been dually diagnosed. Several have either schizophrenia with coexisting chemical dependency or major depression with chemical dependency. The schizophrenics are generally prescribed what are called "atypical antipsychotics," which include Clozaril, Risperdall, Seroquel, and Zyprexa. For depression, Paxil, Prozac, Zoloft, Effexor, and Wellbutrin are commonly prescribed. Drugs most commonly misused by my clients include: heroin, crack cocaine, methamphetamines, marijuana, and alcohol. Many of my clients also have physical health concerns as well, including hepatitis C, tuberculosis, HIV/AIDS, and diabetes.

At DESC, we endorse the harm reduction model. We would like to get our clients off drugs, but we will settle for keeping them alive and helping them stay out of trouble. If someone has a bad liver, for example, I might advise him or her to smoke marijuana rather than taking drugs that would hurt the liver. For a man who is breaking antennae off cars to use to smoke crack, I might advise him to buy a glass pipe at a shop.

We run prerecovery treatment groups at the center; sometimes clients are nodding off in the groups from heroin. Still, we'd rather have them come in that condition than lose touch with them. We provide coffee and bagels and plenty of nurturance. The groups are unstructured, with a focus on being open and honest about substance use. When our clients go off to AA or NA meetings or traditional treatment programs, though, they get confused. They are told to get off their antidepressants that the doctors at our clinic have urged them to take. Because of their emotional instability, these clients can't handle such contradictions. Also, they often can't resist the temptation to use when they are off their antidepressants.

I pour myself a cup of coffee and walk back to my cubicle. I check my voicemail, taking notes on the messages that require a response. I typically have anywhere between five and fifteen messages on a Monday morning. Often these messages are from clients or mental health workers reporting an incident, arrest, or hospitalization that occurred after clinic hours. A few minutes after 9:00, the receptionist at the front desk pages me with a list of my clients who have requested to meet with me and are now waiting in the reception area. I try to be as fair as possible; however, clients with emergency situations are always bumped to the top of the list. I usually reserve the first hour or two of each day for this type of client, the "walk-ins." The rest of the day I spend meeting with the more stable clients who have scheduled appointments.

Fourteen of my 28 clients are money management clients, which means that my agency is their representative payee. Their SSI and SSDI (disability) checks are sent to my agency, and we assist these clients with their finances. For most of our payee clients, this means we pay their bills and disperse cash to them between one and five times per week, depending on their level of need. At the end of each month, I sit down with these clients individually and help them plan the next month's budget. One client I work with comes in daily, Monday through Friday, to pick up $10 a day. He also picks up his daily medications at the nurse station during this time.

For many clients, the money management program encourages treatment involvement. For example, a client I'll call Ben lived a life of instability until recently when he became a payee client. Before this change, his SSDI check was sent to his mother, who would then send a money order for the full amount ($688) at the beginning of each month. Ben would be flat broke in less than two weeks, would have nothing to show for the money he had spent, and would still be living at the shelter to get room and board. During this time, Ben had frequent drug binges and took his psychiatric medications for schizophrenia inconsistently. This resulted in frequent psychiatric hospitalizations. While Ben was "decompensated," he would think he was a pedophile and would turn himself in at police stations. But after DESC became his representative payee, stability returned to his life one step at a time. Ben started coming in regularly for medications. I met with him twice a week, during which time I helped him fill out housing applications and encouraged him to continue taking his medications consistently. I also used our time together to discourage him from using alcohol and other drugs. After a few weeks of this, I used role-playing to coach and prepare him for an interview with an apartment manager. He did well at the interview and was able to get "clean and sober" housing that provided daily medication monitoring.

The clients I see first thing in the morning are usually money management clients. Money is a good engagement tool. While I am giving them their money, I have the opportunity to ask them how they are doing. I often ask questions relating to nutrition,

housing, drug use, relationships, personal hygiene, medication compliance, and psychiatric stability. The answers to some of these questions can be observed, so there is no need to ask them. A client who is "decompensated," for example, will often have worse-than-usual hygiene, may be responding to hallucinations, and may seem confused. A few things I always need to monitor for are suicidal ideation, homicidal ideation, and grave disability. Any of these could require immediate psychiatric hospitalization.

By the time 11:45 rolls around, I have met individually with nine clients for money management. Today their sessions ranged from 5 minutes to a half hour. Those clients who need additional time with me are given appointment times later in the week.

The afternoon is spent doing the progress notes for each of the client interactions I had in the morning and answering mail. Today there is a letter from the Social Security Administration telling me that one of my clients is up for "disability review." I fill out the multipage form and drop it in the outgoing mailbox.

Then it is off to the DESC Shelter, home to about 250 people each night, and a place to socialize or rest by day. My visit is to look for a man in his mid-40s, diagnosed with schizophrenia, whom I have not seen for several weeks. This part of the job is referred to as "outreach and engagement." As I walk through the shelter hallway, I am reminded of a 19th-century insane asylum. The place is dirty; there is a foul odor, and dozens of disheveled people line the walls and floors. Some are standing or sitting, while others are stretched out asleep on the linoleum tile floor. Scanning the faces looking for my client, I notice one man talking to himself in "word salad." Then I see my client. He is leaning against a wall, staring blankly. I say hello to him, try to interest him in reconnecting with mental health services, and suggest that we meet later to work on housing applications. We set a time for the meeting, and I return to my office.

Back at the office, I check my voicemail: a few new messages but nothing urgent. It is now 2:15 P.M., and my 2:00 appointment is still not here. I have

(continued)

9.3 *continued*

in my office some possessions that belong to a client who has recently moved into an assisted living facility. Since this person's new residence is only about ten blocks away, I decide now would be a good time to take these things to her. Gathering them up, I put them in a bag and start walking to her residence.

I get about a half block from my building when I notice one of my other clients, Joe, walking toward me. He stops in front of me and says, "Guess what?" Since Joe has a big smile on his face, I expect that his news will be something positive. To my surprise, it is not (a case of inappropriate affect). Joe tells me that he has just swallowed all of his medications and injected a gram of heroin, an obvious suicide attempt or suicidal gesture. I get him to come with me back to the clinic so we can get a "med list" from the nurse. After getting the list, we go to the emergency room and push our way to the front of the line. I explain the situation to the intake nurse and give her the med list. While Joe is getting his stomach pumped, I talk to the hospital social worker and advocate for my client to be admitted onto the inpatient psychiatric unit of the hospital after he is medically cleared. Feeling confident that the appropriate follow-up care will be provided, I leave.

It is now almost 5:00 P.M. A few blocks from the hospital is the assisted living facility that was my original destination this afternoon. Fortunately I remembered to bring this other client's bag with me. I make the delivery and call it a day.

One of the toughest things about my job is the difficulty associated with trying to get clients into in-patient chemical dependency programs. Frequently clients will reach the point when they realize they are in need of inpatient chemical dependency treatment, and they are ready and willing to get the intensive treatment they need. The hard part for me at this moment comes when I have to tell them that I will try to get them on a list somewhere but it may be three months to a year before they will be admitted. This problem stems from the shortage of publicly funded inpatient chemical dependency centers. As a result, the centers that do exist have the option of being selective when it comes to choosing who gets in and who doesn't. Clients with a dual diagnosis of schizophrenia, bipolar mood disorder, or major depression as well as chemical dependency generally have a harder time getting into treatment than people who are not identified as having mental health issues in addition to chemical dependency issues. One client, a daily crack cocaine user, had his moment of clarity nearly six months ago. He completed an application to an appropriate treatment facility, and we are still waiting. Another client from our agency was awaiting an opening at another treatment center, but before she could get the help she needed, she was picked up by the police and later sentenced to three years in prison for providing an undercover agent with crack cocaine.

Source: "A Day in the Life of a Mental Health Case Manager," in K. van Wormer & D. R. Davis, *Addiction Treatment: A Strengths Perspective* (2003), pp. 266–268. Belmont, CA: Brooks/Cole. Reprinted by permission of Rupert van Wormer and Brooks/Cole.

Harm Reduction Policies

In the United States, 7 to 10 million people have at least one mental disorder as well as an alcohol or drug use disorder (Substance Abuse and Mental Health Services Administration [SAMHSA], 2003). Too often people are treated for only one of these twin disorders if they receive any treatment at all.

Traditionally, substance misuse has been treated as a criminal justice rather than as a mental health problem. If there has been treatment, often under court order, the goal of total abstinence has been enforced with a zero tolerance policy: One failed urinalysis test, and a probationer or parolee may have to complete the sentence in prison (van Wormer & Davis, 2003).

Harm reduction, in contrast, is a pragmatic approach to control the risks of substance abuse by teaching safer using practices. Harm reduction is to substance abuse what preventive medicine is to health care. Typical examples are immunization efforts to halt the spread of disease and birth control clinics to prevent unwanted pregnancy. Such public health approaches are widely accepted practices. Other harm reduction initiatives include, at the educational level, Head Start for preschool-aged children and, at the nutritional level, food stamps and the Special Supplemental Food Program for Women, Infants, and Children (WIC).

With regard to people in the throes of chemical addiction, often accompanied by a mental disorder as well, harm reduction strategies have been considered and continue to be considered quite controversial. Harm reduction strategies are based on knowledge from research concerning treatment effectiveness of an approach geared to the client's level of motivation for change. The harm reduction model is commonly contrasted with the traditional, confrontational approach to chemical dependency treatment (van Wormer & Davis, 2003).

Ann Abbott (2003) urges a best practices approach to intervention. Harm reduction, as Abbott indicates, exemplifies the underlying social work value base and our professional commitment to social justice and human rights. Harm reduction and its treatment intervention counterpart, motivational interviewing (a person-centered approach), strive to meet the client where the client is and to take it from there. When mental illness or drug addiction is manifested, social workers want to ensure that clients receive the least restrictive treatment available (NASW, 2003b). The NASW policy recommendation is that services be fully integrated for consumers with dual diagnoses, that mental health treatment be provided in parity with treatment for other types of illness, and that social workers play an active role in advocacy for such parity. As Suppes and Wells (2003) point out, however, the masses of people, especially mentally ill people, without health care insurance in the first place have little to gain by a parity law. It would be of benefit, though, to people who have or whose families have health insurance coverage.

The NASW (2003a) policy statement on alcohol, tobacco, and other drugs makes a strong case that substance use is a public health problem and, therefore, the focus should be on prevention in addition to treatment. The adoption of such a public health policy permits the development of more sensible policies with respect to diseases such as AIDS and tuberculosis. The NASW endorses appropriate harm reduction treatment responses. Although the organization did not single out needle exchange per se, the preferred harm reduction strategy to prevent the contraction of HIV/AIDS is the exchange of dirty needles for clean ones. Although Congress has refused to fund such programs, several major cities have instituted them.

Methadone maintenance is another popular harm reduction program. Under this program, qualified physicians at methadone clinics provide doses of a synthetic replacement drug for heroin to heroin addicts as a way to prevent illicit drug use. Europe, consistent with a philosophy of pragmatism, has established more comprehensive harm reduction programming in the effort to monitor drug use. Age limits on alcohol consumption are far less restrictive than those in the United States as well.

Because of America's punitiveness toward substance abuse and recent cutbacks in treatment options, many people with substance use disorders do not receive the professional help they need. In 2002, over 350,000 people tried but were unable to obtain treatment for their addiction problems, according to a national household survey conducted by the U.S. Department of Health and Human Services (2003).

Harm reduction strategies have special relevance in regard to HIV/AIDS prevention. Social workers play a major role in providing psychological treatment to people living with AIDS. Box 9.4 reveals how one social worker came to grips with the reality of the magnitude of this often fatal disease.

What We Can Learn from Other Countries

There is much to be learned from both negative and positive examples of health care provision in other countries. First, let us look across the Atlantic to Europe. *The European Health Report 2002,* a publication of the United Nations' World Health Organization (WHO; 2002) reveals two basic themes related to health care. The first concerns spending disparities; the second relates to the level of poverty.

According to this report, large disparities in health care spending exist across the European region. Countries in western Europe such as Austria, Belgium, France, Germany, Iceland, and Switzerland spend more than $300 per person annually on medical care. Countries of the former Soviet Union such as Azerbaijan and Moldova, on the other hand, spend about $10 per person. Tuberculosis and HIV/AIDS are growing problems in eastern Europe. Combined with a major alcoholism problem, the average life expectancy in these countries is now only 56 years. Poverty is a problem in most member states of the WHO in that poverty makes access to health systems more difficult; privatization practices have shut the poor out of needed medical services. The inequality between countries is thus paralleled by inequality within countries.

On the positive side, there are many programs from abroad that the WHO speaks of as good practices from which we can learn (Wetzel, 2004). The provision of universal and public health care services were discussed earlier in the chapter. In the area of mental health care, so neglected in the United States, we can learn from the model offered by a large cotton factory in Beijing, China, which accommodates workers who develop mental illness in a special hospital and apartments until they are well enough to return to work. In a number of countries in Europe, as Wetzel further informs us, *social firms* are being developed in which persons with mental illness work side-by-side with nondisabled people and are paid regular wages; supportive services are provided as needed. Italy relies on social cooperatives to provide job opportunities for people with

9.4 **AIDS in the Life of a Social Worker**

Laura Kaplan, LISW, PhD

My first introduction to HIV disease was in 1982. I was having dinner with a friend who was an emergency room (ER) doctor at the local university hospital in our largely rural southern state. Our conversation concerned the increasing number of young men coming to the ER with symptoms related to an unfamiliar disease. He was troubled—young men were dying of an illness that was obviously spreading, but how? Where did it come from? The illness was very new in our part of the country; I did not know that it was becoming quickly known in New York City and San Francisco. There wasn't a name for it, there wasn't a treatment, and there wasn't a cure. It was ten years later when I recalled our conversation and realized that my friend had been speaking about HIV/AIDS.

In 1986, as a social worker, I had a vague awareness of HIV/AIDS. As an alcohol and drug addiction counselor, I was aware that our clients were part of a very high-risk group for HIV infection. Social workers had begun talking about prevention—condoms, clean needles, and sobriety to prevent transmission. But I still had not been personally touched.

Sue, a client with a history of needle drug use, was ill with respiratory flu symptoms and a skin rash. Sue had a checkup at the health department clinic where she returned after a week for laboratory results. She returned to our treatment center shaken. She reported that medical staff met her in the lobby where they told her they did not know what her diagnosis was. They were very apologetic, shaking their heads and looking very sorry. They told her to return in a week if she still felt ill. The medical staff reactions to Sue frightened and confused her (feelings that put recovering addicts at risk of relapse; in fact, Sue left our treatment center within a week of the medical appointment). She wondered why they seemed to feel so sorry for her and why they met her in the lobby instead of in an office to talk with her. I also wondered why they treated her in this way.

I don't know what happened to Sue, but the reaction of the medical staff toward her was fairly common among many professionals and laypersons early in the HIV/AIDS pandemic—pity, fear, a lack of respect for confidentiality or privacy, and helplessness and hopelessness, particularly toward gay men and alcohol and drug users. For example, some people threw dishes in the garbage if they knew or thought a gay man had eaten from them, and some people stopped any physical contact with individuals they thought might be infected. (For some, this was everyone outside of their household, while for others it was only those who were known to be HIV-positive.) Suddenly, the avoiding of hugging, shaking hands, kissing on the cheek, and even using public toilets or borrowing pens from anyone thought to have untrustworthy behaviors became the standard operating procedure for many people. Injecting drug users in addiction treatment programs were approached differently from those addicted to alcohol. They became "untouchables" not only to some treatment professionals but also to some people in twelve-step communities, as well as to family, friends, and other clients.

In the 1980s, people needed information about HIV/AIDS, but it was still so new that few facts from research were available. Out of fear, perhaps, speculation was rampant. Media misinformation fed the fears regularly—today HIV infection was transmitted via mosquitoes, tomorrow it would be spread via toilet seats and doorknobs. The public was frightened and unsure of anything except that testing HIV-positive was a death sentence. Kristen, another client in our addiction recovery program, was hospitalized for an eating disorder. Kristen told us that whenever medical or housekeeping personnel entered her room, they were dressed in full protection gear—masks, gloves, booties, and gowns; and no one stood close to her bed if they didn't have to. She was confused and scared

(continued)

9.4 *continued*

until she realized that a note in her chart and a sign on her door stated "HIV RISK" in large red letters. She did not have an HIV or an AIDS diagnosis, but the staff knew she was a recovering drug addict.

By the late 1980s and early 1990s, the media reported increasing numbers of children who tested positive for HIV and were harassed out of school. One family's home was set on fire and destroyed. The family had two children who carried the HIV infection, and many people in the community opposed their living in the neighborhood and attending the local public schools. By this time, researchers had found that HIV is a blood-borne pathogen, and it was estimated that more than 50 percent of people living with hemophilia were likely infected with HIV via blood transfusions they were given in the years before blood centers tested their supplies (see http://www.HIVpositive.com). Fortunately, through the leadership of people both infected and affected by the loss of loved ones, a powerful grassroots movement brought focus on the need for research, legislation, prevention, and education. Universal precautions, the testing of blood and plasma used for transfusions, laws pertaining to confidentiality, accessible low-cost HIV testing, right to fair treatment, and research in treatment and prevention are just a few of the policies that have resulted from the movement's efforts.

As a social worker, my first officially HIV/AIDS diagnosed client was Matt. I met him in 1990 at the state psychiatric hospital where he was periodically treated for schizoaffective disorder. Since individuals with serious mental illnesses are usually in and out of hospitals for years, I worked with Matt during his admissions for the next four years, until his death from AIDS-related complications. Through all of the struggles living with two significant illnesses, Matt held fiercely to his independence and to his life. He always lived alone; he had attended college and worked for a government agency before becoming disabled. He refused to live anywhere but his own apartment, wanting to direct his own life even when others thought it was unwise. Usually he returned to the state hospital on involuntary admissions. In November 1994, Matt became very ill from infections related to his weakened immune system. He was psychiatrically ready to leave the hospital, but I was very worried about his physical health. Several nurses and the doctor wanted him to stay longer. He wanted to leave and stated he was going to leave— either with our help or against medical advice. I organized a team of social workers from three agencies to coordinate Matt's follow-up services. We found an apartment, furnished it, and helped him move in. It was the week before Thanksgiving; none of us would be working over the holiday, and he

disabilities. Another best practices program is found in Spain where 12 service centers employ more than 800 mentally ill people at a commercial furniture factory; social amenities are provided for them in the community.

Health Care in the United Kingdom

Health care under the British National Health Service (NHS) accounts for about 6 percent of the gross domestic product (GDP), unlike in France and Germany where social insurance contributions are the predominant means of funding

refused to stay in the hospital. He preferred his own place for the holiday no matter how ill he felt. During the next week, our case manager visited and found him unconscious. Matt never regained consciousness in the hospital that week before he died. If he had listened to the psychiatric hospital staff, he would never have been independent again; he would have, at best, moved to another hospital and died there.

In 1999, I traveled to South Africa with a group exploring ways to assist the region in HIV/AIDS prevention education. During a hospital visit, we stopped at a small outpatient clinic set apart from the main facility. Women with babies on their laps, elderly women, and young women and men were seated on folding chairs and wooden benches along the walls of the small waiting room; more people were standing outside. Some played with children while others paced. The director of the clinic, a nurse, gave a brief talk—this was the HIV clinic, but in response to a question, she informed us that many of the patients were unaware of their diagnosis. The clinic staff treated symptoms (most often this was how HIV/AIDS was diagnosed); the patients came for treatment of associated illnesses. She told us there was no point in requiring HIV tests of their patients, as there was insufficient medicine for treatment in this poor area and great risk for people who were identified as testing HIV-positive. This was before changes in laws and social policies helped make medication more accessible (though even today there are still tremendous restrictions on access). People identified as having HIV disease were not just shunned by communities; they were often brutalized and killed, particularly if they were women (in some areas of the world this still occurs). Not only might a patient's life be saved if not identified as having HIV disease, but not knowing meant that people could, perhaps, hold onto their belief in their own independence and safety—not knowing prevented the labels, hate, and violence brought on by HIV-positive status.

Today, in this country, people with HIV disease are no longer committed to a death sentence. My friend Rick is a college business major who has had HIV/AIDS since he was 17 years old. He is now well into his 30s. Rick has survived beyond friends and family members who did not have life-threatening diseases.

We now have all been touched by HIV disease—from friends, lovers, family members, and neighbors in our communities, as well as throughout the United States and the rest of the world. Yet, I am amazed that I continue to meet people who believe that HIV/AIDS does not affect them—people who think that only homosexuals and drug addicts get infected—and who believe that the millions of adults and children living and dying everyday around the world is not their problem. The health and well-being of all people in the world is our problem, which means we all have responsibility. I am reminded of Doctors Without Borders founder Bernard Kouchner's statement, "We already know how to treat AIDS, we know how to cure tuberculosis, we know how to provide sanitation and clean water—all that is lacking is the will to do so."

Source: Printed with permission of Laura E. Kaplan, LISW, PhD, University of Northern Iowa.

service (Dixon, 2003). Health services in the United Kingdom are largely tax-financed. Except for some doctors who are employed in the private sector, most physicians are employed by the government. Family doctors contract for service independently based on the number of patients and services provided. Anyone who watches the *Prime Minister's Questions,* a weekly BBC production in which Members of Parliament pounce on the prime minister with the concerns of their constituents, is familiar with some of the problems of the NHS, mostly caused by underfunding and the mound of paperwork now required of doctors. Under the Labour government, as the prime minister is prone to emphasize, spending has been increased. Koen (2000) sums up the situation: "While the budget constraints were traditionally tight in the NHS, leading to pervasive rationing and queuing as well as diversion towards the private sector, it has been relaxed somewhat with the budgetary boost announced by the Government in March 2000" (p. 2). Spending on mental health, however, has lingered behind spending in other areas of health care.

The Canadian Model

In contrast to the British system, the Canadian system is much more generously financed and makes more use of advanced technology; about 10 percent of the Canadian gross national product (GNP) goes to health care. The prescription benefit coverage, however, is not as complete; most Canadians pay for their prescription drugs, albeit at reduced rates due to cost controls imposed upon pharmaceuticals.

Health and social services are key institutions in Canadian society. Public health care systems, as Canadian practitioners Roy and Montgomery (2003) suggest, are cited as being among the best in the world, "symbols of our national pride" (p. 126). In a television interview, ABC News medical editor Tim Johnson, MD (2003), differentiated the British from the Canadian system: In the United Kingdom, the government finances health care, employs the doctors, and manages the hospitals. This is socialized medicine. In the Canadian system, in contrast, the government only runs the financial part while the delivery system is free. "People can choose whatever doctor or hospital they want to go to," Johnson explained. "So, we have a system like that in this country. It's called Medicare." (See the interview at http://www.abcnews.go.com.) The Canadian medical system is called Medicare as well.

Risks to the exemplary Canadian health care standards are apparent in Ontario and Alberta where ballooning costs and long delays for surgery have created incentives to privatize (B. Brown, 2002). The administration and delivery of health care services are the responsibility of each individual province. Over 95 percent of Canadian hospitals are private, nonprofit entities (Health Canada, 2002). To test the desirability of moving toward a for-profit, investor-owned system, a team of Canadian and American doctors conducted extensive research of the U.S. system, in which 15 percent of the hospitals are for-profit or investor-owned (these are the hospital chains). The findings were startling: Roughly 2,000 people died each year simply because they were treated in such hospitals (Sternberg, 2002). The results were attributed to staff shortages and other cost-cutting measures.

"Private Clinics Strain Health System" (2003)—this editorial headline in the *Toronto Star* is indicative of criticism directed toward any attempts to allow for the establishment of private clinics to offer specialized services. According to the editorial, the risk is that the private clinics will siphon off staff from the public medical system. The basic problem seems to be that the federal share of health spending has fallen by almost three-quarters over the past 20 years ("Health Care in Canada: Theatre of Discontent," 2002). A doctor-nurse shortage is a serious concern. Still, in a first-ever national survey, almost 85 percent of Canadians rated their health services as very good or excellent. The Canadian system may not be perfect, but by most measures, it is the best the world has to offer.

For the first time in a national poll, a majority of the American people (60 percent) said they would prefer a system that provided universal coverage and was not linked to employment; two-thirds said they believe we should be able to import drugs from Canada (Connolly & Deane, 2003).

Cuba: Rural Health Care

Today, the Cuban health system serves as an international model for rural health care. Despite the fact that Cuba is one of the poorest countries in this hemisphere, and despite the fact that advanced technologies (even x-ray machines) are often unavailable, the inhabitants report health indicators that rival those of rich countries, such as the United States. While the average life expectancy is 76 compared to 77 in the United States, Cuba reports an infant mortality rate below the U.S. rate (Saney, 2004). So, how do they do it? The answer is found in their focus on education and preventive care. Primary care doctors are scattered across the countryside, living among the people. The rural health clinics are more like community centers than medical facilities. Health representatives work at the centers and know every family in the area. They make home visits and ensure that children receive all immunizations.

Because they have educated a large number of doctors and can meet their own needs, Cuba has been able to send thousands of physicians abroad to provide free medical care to people in Nicaragua, Honduras, and South Africa ("Cuba Spreads Medical Care as Political Tool," 2001). In the 1980s, the Cuban health care system even became the model for rural programs for Native Americans in California. Numerous Cuban clinics and sanitariums engage in international charity work; for example, according to a Russian news weekly, Cuban facilities successfully treat thousands of cancer patients from Russia and Ukraine every year (Aleksandroy, 2003).

Summary and Conclusion

The quote that begins this chapter reminds us of the need to get the pigs out of the creek first, and then clean the water. In other words, we need to get to the root of the problem, to concentrate our resources on prevention rather than treatment, in the interests of public health. In maternal health terms, the capacity to plan, postpone, or prevent pregnancy is the best guarantee of reproductive health. Harm reduction proponents favor birth control over abortion, and legal abortion over the back-alley variety.

This chapter considered health care policies and programs in international context. Following Midgley's (1995) formulation, we can contrast distorted development, which concentrates services at the higher echelons, with social development that benefits the masses. Countries singled out by Midgley as examples of social development include Austria, Sweden, and Switzerland, all of which have made systematic efforts to promote the development of *all* the people, not only of the few at the expense of the many. Where such extensive health and social services are provided, social problems are minimized accordingly. Outside of Europe, Costa Rica, Cuba, and Taiwan deserve recognition for their successes in fostering both economic and social development. Yet, as Midgley reflects, the problem of distorted development remains widespread.

The universal dilemma is whether the government should play a strong role, part benevolent and part coercive, in ensuring health care and housing for all, or whether nations would do better in focusing on economic investment and technological advancement in the belief that the market forces will ultimately take care of the needs of the people. How this issue is played out is seen in the barter for child prostitutes in Thailand, the global epidemic in maternal mortality, the increasing overpopulation in sub-Saharan Africa, and the unconscionable level of homelessness in the United States. The three deadly diseases that threaten human life and lower the life span across the world are AIDS, tuberculosis (TB), and malaria. Unlike almost any other disease epidemic, AIDS strikes at people in their prime—youths and parents of young children. The spread of HIV/AIDS is fueling a massive tuberculosis crisis, as TB is the most common infection among people living with HIV/AIDS and the leading killer of these people (British Broadcasting Company, 2004). Joint treatments for TB and AIDS are necessary, according to the WHO, to curb the growing death rate, yet such treatment is rarely provided. In sub-Saharan Africa, this scourge has left millions of orphans in its wake.

In the United States, the issue of how to take care of people's needs has been resolved on the side of the market forces of profit-making constituencies who have a strong influence on public policy, the mass media, and maintenance of the status quo. The reduction in the federal government's involvement in housing and health care is being felt, above all, by the most vulnerable populations in society—single women and their children, and people of color. The poor and racial minorities have higher rates of illnesses and shorter life expectancies than others in the popu-

lation undoubtedly related to the inadequacy of preventive care such as nutritional, prenatal, and neonatal programs.

The tug-of-war between prevention and tertiary care is resolved in modern society in favor of tertiary, or after-the-fact, care. This tension is as true in housing as it is in health care. Once people are living on the streets or are terminally ill, all the emergency services in the world cannot undo the damage. Programs that for decades have been the bedrock of what used to be our social welfare infrastructure are being dismantled. People who are already disadvantaged by a myriad of factors bear the most visible cost of the transformation of American social welfare and of American cities through urban renewal and downtown revitalization. What our society fails to grasp is that applying the logic of the market place to human service is fraught with peril.

Compared to the universal programs in other countries discussed in this chapter, the American health care system is generally regarded as a failure, even in terms of the very market economy that influenced its development in the first place. The huge investment in dollars is not providing a good return on the resources invested. The U.S. government provides health care for only about one-fourth of its citizens; another one-sixth have no health insurance at all. The rest are insured on their own at great expense or by their employers, always with the fear that with loss of job or at the company's discretion, these health care benefits will be cut off.

Administrative costs of health care in the United States are staggering, caused in part by the multiplicity of third-party payers. Every insurance company has different forms, regulations, and policies. Despite or because of all the efforts at cost containment, the costs cannot be contained. There is much that can be learned from countries such as Canada with its universal health care under a single-payer system and Cuba with its community prevention approach.

Whether we were looking at mental health care, or medical or substance abuse treatment, one theme that has emerged again and again in these pages is to what extent the various politically generated cost-cutting measures are expensive in the long run. Because of the abandonment of a commitment to provide affordable housing, for example, city streets have become lined with people who are homeless; cutbacks in health care services, including substance abuse treatment, have made for more serious problems later. When people cannot afford medication, similarly, far more expensive remedies may be required. When society fails, social workers often inherit the task of trying to help their clients pick up the pieces.

The four boxed readings included in this chapter introduced us to social work roles in the emergency room, in physical disability advocacy, in helping homeless heroin addicts reduce the harm to themselves, and mental health counseling in the age of AIDS. Because of their work within the system and as advocates for patients in need of medical services, social workers, such as those who contributed their personal narratives for this chapter, are joining policy makers in the call for change. In order for such change to become a reality, some or all of the following steps need to occur:

- Campaign finance reform to reduce the undue influence of special interest groups, including pharmaceutical and insurance companies
- Concentration on efforts for innovative solutions on a state-by-state basis
- An end to the hegemony of the pharmaceutical companies to ensure that the prices of drugs can be closer to their actual production costs
- The conducting of informational campaigns in the media and elsewhere to tout the cost-effectiveness of home health care versus institutional care
- A societal paradigm shift from a cure–treatment model to a harm reduction–prevention model to reduce the spread of disease
- The bolstering of Medicare and expansion of its services through a gradual lowering of age for coverage so that eventually the care for one age group would be the care for all age groups and the health care/mental health care system would be truly universal

Thought Questions

1. What does the metaphor about first getting the pigs out of the creek, and then cleaning the water, have to do with health care?
2. Based on the assortment of headlines presented at the beginning of the chapter, analyze the state of global health.
3. Discuss appropriate public health remedies to the AIDS pandemic.
4. What does the unconscionable high rate of maternal mortality say about women's roles generally?
5. Differentiate Medicaid from Medicare. Discuss the possibility of extending Medicare to all age groups.
6. Relate the ascendancy of the radical right to universal health care.
7. How can the United States be considered to have the best health care in the world in spite of the deficiencies? Why is it so expensive?
8. What is the role of HMOs? Discuss the facts pertaining to various lobbying groups. What are social HMOs?
9. Consider some of the states' cost-saving initiatives.
10. How do race, class, and gender relate to the state of one's health? What do the statistics tell us?
11. Delineate the social worker roles in emergency room care.
12. What is meant by the marketing of disease? Provide examples. What kinds of unsafe

products are marketed to economically poor countries?

13. Account for the political clout of the pharmaceutical companies. What can be done to control them?

14. Recall the history of mental health treatment in the United States, and discuss the meaning of this statement: "Jails and pris-

ons are the mental health institutions of the 21st century."

15. Discuss the concept of harm reduction for various areas of health care.

16. What can we learn from other countries? Compare the British, Canadian, and Cuban health care systems.

References

Abbott, A. (2003, May). Meeting the challenges of substance misuse: Making inroads one step at a time. *Health and Social Work, 28(2), 83–88.*

AIDS: Forty million orphans. (2002, November 30). *The Economist,* 41.

Aleksandroy, A. (2003, September 17). The secrets of Cuban medicine. Reprinted in *The World Press* from *Fakty* (Moscow weekly), p. 39.

Ambrosino, R., Heffernan, J., Shuttlesworth, G., & Ambrosino, G. (2001). *Social work and social welfare: An introduction.* Belmont, CA: Thomson Brooks/Cole.

Angell, M. (2004). *The truth about the drug companies: How they deceive us and what to do about it.* New York: Random House.

Appleby, J. (2003, January 9). Health insurance costs fire up unions. *USA Today,* pp. A1–A2.

Associated Press. (2003, May 22). WHO adopts anti-tobacco pact: U.S. remains undecided about signing. *USA Today,* p. A13. Barry, P. (2002, March). Ads, promotions drive up costs. *AARP Bulletin, 3,* 17.

Beadnell, M. (2003, February 6). Dickensian conditions in Canada: Homeless mother could be jailed for leaving baby at City Hall. *World Socialist Web Site.* Retrieved from http://www.wsws.org

Beresford, D. (2003, June 29). South Africans rape children as cure for AIDS. *The Observer.* Retrieved from http://www.observer.co.uk

A bloated health-care system. (2003, August 26). Editorial. *Des Moines Register,* p. A8.

Brink, S. (1999, December 20). For severe mental illness, a higher profile and new hope. *U.S. News & World Report,* 62–63.

British Broadcasting Company (BBC). (2004, September 21). Call for combined HIV and TB

care. BBC News. Retrieved from http://news.bbc.co.uk

Brown, B. (2002, February 28). Canadian provinces move toward privatizing healthcare. *Christian Science Monitor,* 7.

Brown, C. (2002, December 23). Through the looking glass: The world of disability and disease. *Social Work Today,* 6–7.

Brown, D. (2002, September 23). America's life expectancy rises, but health mixed. Washington Post, p. A02.

Brown, L. (2000, October 31). HIV epidemic restructuring Africa's population. The Worldwatch Institute. Retrieved from http://www.globalpolicy.org

Brownlee, S. (2003, January/February). The overtreated American. *The Atlantic Online.* Retrieved from http://www.theatlantic.com

Canada's health care system at a glance. (2002, November 28). *Health Canada Online.* Retrieved from http://www..hc-sc.gc.ca

Chaudhuri, T. (2003). Country struggling to make Dr. King's dream a reality. Children's Defense Fund. Retrieved from http://www.childrensdefense.org

Connolly, C., & Deane, C. (2003, October 20). Poll finds backing for drug reimports. *Washington Post,* p. A12.

Connolly, C., & Witte, G. (2004, August 27). Poverty rate up third year in a row. *Washington Post,* p. A1.

Co-occurring disorders. (2003, Spring/Summer). *ATTC Networker, 5(1),* 1, 4–5.

Cuba spreads medical care as political tool. (2001, January 1). *USA Today.* Retrieved from http://www.usatoday.com

Cullen, L. T. (2002, August 5). Changing faces. *Time: Asia.* Retrieved from http://www.time.com/time/asia/magazine

Dannelke, L. (2002, December 23). Reforms for people with disabilities: A primer. *Social Work Today,* 10–12.

DePoy, E., & Gilson, S. (2004). *Rethinking disability: Principles for professional and social change.* Belmont, CA: Wadsworth.

DeWees, M. (2002). Contested landscape: The role of critical dialogue for social workers in mental health practice. *Journal of Progressive Human Services, 13*(1), 73–91.

DiNitto, D. (2003). *Social welfare: Politics and public policy* (5th ed.). Boston: Allyn & Bacon.

Disabled People's Association. (2003). The definition of disability. Retrieved from http://www.dpa.org.sp

Dixon, A. (2003, August). Funding health care: Options for Europe. *The World Bank Health Systems Development.* Retrieved from http://www.worldbank.org

Dominelli, L. (2002). *Feminist social work: Theory and practice.* New York: Palgrave.

Drinking, smoking blamed for short Russian lives. (2002, March 28). Boston University. Retrieved from http://www.jointogether.org/home/

Escobar, M. (2002). Costa Rica: World bank to support health sector reform. DevNews Media Center. Retrieved from http://worldbank.org

Europe's first comprehensive disability rights law unveiled. (2003, March 12). European Disability Forum. Retrieved from http://www.dpi.org

Europe: WHO says East facing unprecedented life expectancy decline. (2002, September 18). *UNWire* (United Nations Foundation). Retrieved from http://www.unfoundation.org

Fairness and Accuracy in Reporting. (2003, December 2). Networks don't follow the money in Medicare story. *Fair Action Alert.* Retrieved from http://www.fair.org/activism

Figuring it out. (1999, December). *World Press Review.* Reprinted from *Times of India,* p. 15.

Findlay, S. (2003, October 1). For many in U.S., good health care barely exists. *USA Today,* p. A23.

Fiske, H. (2003, July). Mending minds psychiatric social work in the emergency department. *Social Work Today,* 13–15.

Fox, M. (2003, September 24). U.S. abortion policy hits clinics abroad—study. *Reuters.* Retrieved from http://www.truthout.org

Gleckman, H. (2002, August 26). Welcome to the health-care economy. *Business Week,* 144–148.

Global Health Council. (2002, August 14). Local-global partnerships combat infectious diseases. *News Advisory.* Retrieved from http://www.globalhealth.org

Glover, L. (2004, February 9). In depth: Health care: Cosmetic. *Pittsburgh Business Times.* Retrieved from http://pittsburgh.bizjournals.com/pittsburgh

Graham, J. (1999, December 14). Mental health stigma is target of U.S. report. *Chicago Tribune,* sec. 1, p. 4.

Harlow, J. (1999, May 30). NHS nurses provide prostitutes for sex with disabled patients. *The Sunday Times.* Retrieved from http://www.timesonline.co.uk/section/0,,176,00.html

Hartman, A. (1992). Health care: Privilege or entitlement. *Social Work, 37*(3), 195–196.

Hawaii State Government. (2000, January 1). Constitution of the State of Hawaii. Online at http://www.capitol.hawaii.gov

Health Canada. (2002, November 28). Canada's health care system at a glance. Retrieved from http://www.hc-sc.gc.ca/english/media/releases/2002

Health care in Canada: Theatre of discontent. (2002, October 5). *The Economist,* 33.

Health-Day. (2004, March 13). Health highlights. Drugmakers abandon research into antibiotics. Retrieved from http://www.healthday.com

Hiranandani, V. (2004). Rethinking disability in social work: Interdisciplinary perspectives. In G. May & M. Raske (Eds.), *Ending disability discrimination: Strategies for social workers* (pp. 71–81). Boston: Allyn & Bacon.

Ingstad, B., & Whyte, S. (1995). Public discourses on rehabilitation: From Norway to Botswana. In B. Instad & S. Whyte (Eds.), *Disability and culture* (pp. 174–195). Berkeley: University of California Press.

International Federation of Social Workers (IFSW). (2004, February 23). One third of world hurt by vitamin deficiency, UNICEF says. *IFSW Update,* 5.

Jackson, K. (2003, August). Better living through chemistry: Advances in psychotropic medicine. *Social Work Today,* 10–13.

Jacoby, S. (2003, May). The nursing squeeze. *AARP Bulletin.* Retrieved from http://www.aarp.org

Job-based health care: It's nutso. (2003, July 13). Editorial. *Des Moines Register,* p. OP1.

Johnson, L. (2002, November 12). Iraqi cancers, birth defects blamed on U.S. depleted uranium. *Seattle Post-Intelligencer.* Retrieved from http://seattlepi .nwsource.com

Johnson, T. (2003, October 21). Interview by Peter Jennings, ABC News. Retrieved from http://www .abcnews.go.com

Koen, V. (2000, August 29). Public expenditure reform: The health care sector in the United Kingdom. OECD (Organization for European Cooperation and Development) Economics Department Working Papers. Retrieved from http://www.oecd.org

Lack of insurance can be fatal. (2002, June 4). *Des Moines Register, Iowa Weekly,* p. W28.

Landsberg, M. (2001, July 1). U.N. recognizes women double victims of AIDS. *Toronto Star,* p. A2.

Lieberman, T. (2003, October). Feeling the squeeze. *AARP Bulletin,* 8–10.

Lunday, S. (2001, July 9). Old-fashioned doctoring keeps Cubans healthy. *Los Angeles Times.* Retrieved from http://www.latimes.com/features/ health/la

Lundberg, G. (2001). *Severed trust: Why American medicine hasn't been fixed.* New York: Basic Books.

Malaria is alive and well and killing more than 3,000 children every day. (2003, April 25). UNICEF. http://www.unicef.org

Malveaux, J. (2003, October 3). Racism holds painful legacy. *USA Today,* p. A20.

Manning, A. (2003, August 1). Indians health still lags others'. *USA Today,* p. A4.

Midgley, J. (1995). *Social development.* London: Sage.

Morgan, D. (1999, July 5). Lobbyists get aggressive on health care issue. *Washington Post,* p. A3.

Muneta, B. (2003, July 16). Statement of Ben Muneta, MD, president, Association of American Indian Physicians. The House of Representatives, House Resource Committee. Retrieved from http:// resourcescommittee.house.gov/108cong/full/ 2003jul16/muneta.htm

National Association of Social Workers (NASW). (2003a). Alcohol, tobacco, and other substance abuse. In NASW, *Social work speaks: NASW policy statements 2003–2006* (pp. 20–27). Washington, DC: NASW Press.

National Association of Social Workers (NASW). (2003b). Mental health. In NASW, *Social work speaks: NASW policy statements 2003–2006* (pp. 252–260).

National Association of Social Workers (NASW). (2003c, November). Mental health programs said lacking. *NASW News,* 9.

'90s boom did little for the public good. (2001, August 12). *Waterloo–Cedar Falls Courier,* pp. A1, A9.

Number of Americans without insurance grows. (2003, September 30). *Waterloo–Cedar Falls Courier,* pp. A1, A4.

O'Neill, J. (2003, January). Mental health system said "in shambles." *NASW News,* 7.

Ordoñez, F. (2003, April 28). Custody or care? *Newsweek,* 12.

O'Reilly, B. (2003, April 21). Mental health courts: Assessing offender's basic needs. *Social Work Today,* 22–25.

Organization for Economic Cooperation and Development. (2003, September 23). Making health systems fitter. *OECD Observer.* Retrieved from http://www.oecdobserver.org

Pierce, J., & Gilpin, E. (1995, May). Looking for a market among adolescents. *Scientific American,* 50–51.

Private clinics strain health system. (2003, July 30). *Toronto Star,* p. A20.

Public Citizen. (2003, June 23). Drug industry employs 675 Washington lobbyists. Retrieved from http://www.citizen.org

Roadblocks frustrate state efforts to cut drug costs. (2004, March 1). Today's debate. *USA Today,* p. A14.

Ross, E. (2003, August 15). Smoking leads to half of TB deaths in India. *Chicago Sun-Times.* Retrieved from http://www.suntimes.com

Roy, G., & Montgomery, C. (2003). Practice with immigrants in Quebec. In A. Al-Krenaui & J. Graham (Eds.), *Social work in Canada: Working with diverse ethno-racial minorities* (pp. 122–145). Oxford, England: Oxford University Press.

Russia's raging TB plague. (2001, June). *World Press Review,* 11–12.

Sanchez, R. (2002, October 30). Exasperated cities move to curb or expel the homeless. *Washington Post,* p. A1.

Saney, I. (2004). *Cuba: Revolution in motion.* London: Zed Press.

Seipel, M. (1994). Disability: An emerging global challenge. *International Social Work, 37,* 165–178.

Shapinsky, D. (1999, December 11). Troubling statistics, persistent problems. *ABCNEWS.com.* Retrieved from http://www.abcnews.go.com

Sherman, M. (2003, August 12). 8,000 doctors urge national insurance. *ajc.com (The Atlanta Journal Constitution).* Retrieved from http://www.ajc.com

Sternberg, S. (2002, May 28). Study: For-profit hospital could be more hazardous to your health. *USA Today,* p. D9.

Sternberg, S. (2003, November 26). Global AIDS epidemic: "More infections than ever before." *USA Today,* p. D15.

Stoesen, L. (2003, April). The focus should be on diversity, some say rearranging the perception of disability. *NASW News.* Retrieved from http://www.socialworkers.org

Substance Abuse and Mental Health Services Administration (SAMHSA). (2003, Spring/Summer). Co-occurring disorders. *ATTC Networker, 5*(1), 1, 4.

Suppes, M., & Wells, C. (2003). *The social work experience: An introduction to social work and social welfare* (4th ed.). Boston: McGraw-Hill.

Survey shows most homeless sick, mentally ill. (1999, December 9). *Join Together Online.* Retrieved from http://www.jointogether.org/home/

Theatre of discontent. (2002, October 5). *The Economist,* 33–34.

Thiele, B. (2002, May). The human right to adequate housing: A tool for promoting and protecting individual and community health. *American Journal of Public Health, 92*(5), 712–715.

Toner, R., & Pear, R. (2003, April 28). Cutbacks imperil health coverage for state's poor. *Truthout.* Retrieved from http://www.truthout.org

Tu, H. T. (2004, September). Rising health costs, medical debt and chronic conditions. *Issue Brief No. 88.* Health System Change. Retrieved from http://www.hschange.org

U.K. Government. (2003). The disability discrimination act of 1995. Government documents. Retrieved from http://www.disability.gov.uk

United Nations Foundation. (2002, November 7). Afghanistan: UNICEF, U.S. warn of high maternal mortality rates. *UNWire* (United Nations Foundation). Retrieved from http://www.unwire.org

Urban American Indians not getting needed health services. (2002, April 19). University of California, Irvin New Medical Center. Retrieved from http://www.ucihealth.com

U.S. Department of Health and Human Services. (2003, September 5). 22 million in U.S. suffer from substance dependence or abuse. Retrieved from http://www.dhhs.gov

van Wormer, K., & Davis, D. R. (2003). *Addiction treatment: A strengths perspective.* Belmont, CA: Brooks/Cole.

Walcott, W. (2003, August 3). Dirigo health is a good plan. *SJOnline.* Retrieved from http://www.sunjournal.com

Washington, A. (2002). The homeless need more than just a pillow, they need a pillar: An evaluation of a transitional housing program. *Families in Society, 83*(2), 183–188.

Welch, W. (1994, July 22). Battle of the big bucks: "Historically unprecedented." *USA Today,* p. A5.

Wetzel, J. W. (2004). Mental health lessons from abroad. In M. C. Hokenstad & J. Midgley (Eds.), *Lessons from abroad: Adapting international social welfare innovations* (pp. 93–116). Washington, DC: NASW Press.

Will, G. (2000, January 10). AIDS crushes a continent. *Newsweek,* 64.

WHO adopts anti-tobacco pact; U.S. remains undecided about signing. (2003, May 22). *USA Today,* p. A13.

WHO/AFRO. (2003, September 4). Africa records nearly half of world's 600,000 pregnancy-related deaths. World Health Organization, Africa. Retrieved from http://www.afro.who.int/press

Wolf, N. (1991). *The beauty myth.* New York: William Morrow.

World Health Organization (WHO). (2002). The European health report, 2002. New York: Author.

Zastrow, C. (2004). *Introduction to social work and social welfare: Empowering people* (8th ed.). Belmont, CA: Thomson Brooks/Cole.

That's life boy,
Gettin' and losin',
Losin' and gettin'

GREGORY PECK, *THE YEARLING*, **1946**

As we care for our parents, we teach our children to care for us.

MARY PIPHER, *ANOTHER COUNTRY*, **1999**, P. **10**

Care at the End
of the Life Cycle

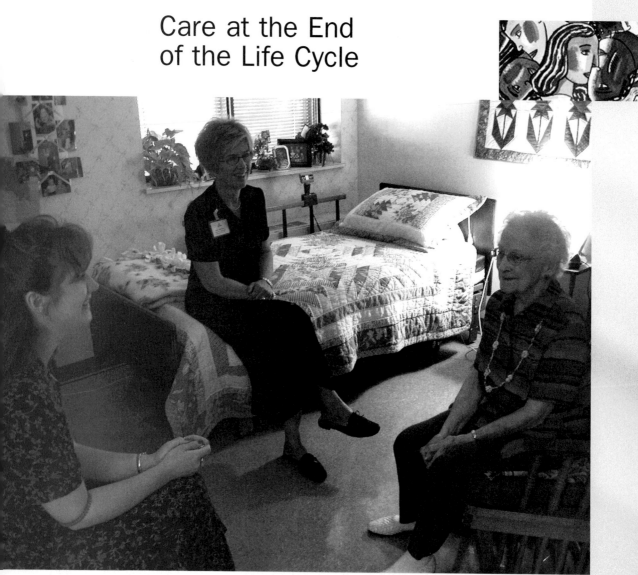

© Rupert van Wormer

At first the message taken from the mounting death toll of France's unprecedented heat wave in the summer of 2003 concerned evidence that fears about global warming were real. But as the numbers continued to climb—estimates shot up from 1,000 to over 14,000 dead—the fears turned away from the weather to the asking of essential questions regarding modern values and the functioning of materialistic and highly individualistic societies such as France (Moisi, 2003). The people who died all had one thing in common: They were very old, very alone, and very vulnerable. The moral crisis that has preoccupied France ever since was exacerbated by the realization that so many of the elderly were abandoned, even during a dangerous heat wave, because their relatives did not want to interrupt their summer vacations at places like the Côte d'Azure and the Swiss mountains. Even worse, after death, some families did not claim the bodies for the same reason and to avoid funeral expenses. Perhaps, also, as French journalist Moisi concluded, the aged were neglected in the hour of their need due to our own denial of the ravages of old age, our desire not "to be confronted with the statistical category to which we will belong one day, that of very old people" (p. 13).

Across the life span, we are all aging, constantly changing over time. Aging occurs from the moment of conception until death. How old a person looks, in fact, is one of the primary characteristics we notice about a person. Sometimes there are age restrictions for certain privileges, as evidenced by such inquiries as "Let me see your ID card" (to buy an alcoholic beverage) or, at the other end of the age spectrum, "Do you qualify for a senior discount?"

Erik Erikson (1963) saw life development as a series of tasks to be mastered at various stages. In the final stage, the challenge is to achieve integrity rather than despair. Retirement, widowhood, and the accumulation of losses can lead to loneliness and depression. Ideally, at the final stage of life, one comes to accept his or her life as having been meaningful and worthwhile. An interviewee in the book *Understanding Older Chicanas* (Facio, 1996) personalizes this acceptance: "I've done what I've had to do . . . but I don't feel useless. It's a different life now. . . . I have the [retirement] center, my friends, my grandchildren, and my garden" (p. 110). Similarly, my mother, a native New Orleanian, views the final stage of her life as "lagniappe," a little something extra, a gift.

Today, 12.4 percent or one of eight Americans are age 65 or over (U.S. Department of Health and Human Services, 2001). Seven percent of women and 4 percent of men are 85 and older (U.S. Census Bureau, 2003). There are now more than ten times as many people aged 65 and older as there were 100 years ago. The population of older people in the population is rising because fewer births are occurring. Because of the shorter life span of men, generally, women will continue to outnumber men in this older age group by a wide margin, with more than twice as many women as men in the over-85 age group. The reason for the bulge in older Americans is the baby boom that took place after World War II when the soldiers returned home. In 2000, an estimated 84 percent of the older population was non-Hispanic white, but this population will be much more diverse in the future, with the Hispanic elderly outnumbering the non-Hispanic black population in the next 20 years ("Older Americans 2000," 2003).

Never before have so many people lived for as long as will members of this postwar cohort. Whereas in 1900 a baby boy could expect to live to age 48, today such a baby can expect to live well into the 70s (Peterson, 1999).

The graying of America, where one in ten Americans will be over age 80 early into the 21st century, is a trend found virtually everywhere in the industrialized world. The graying of the world is bound to change the way we live and the way we view aging. This demographic revolution is both a triumph and a problem—a triumph in terms of longevity, and a problem in terms of medical costs. As our nation's people age, how will we respond to the population shift? How will we handle the health care demands? Who will care for the frail elderly? And what lessons can we learn from other nations concerning attitudes toward aging and care of people who can no longer care for themselves? These are among the questions that will be addressed in this chapter.

The bio-psycho-social-spiritual model provides a ready framework for the study of the aging process. Following an overview of the demographics of aging worldwide, we examine the physiological, psychological, social, and spiritual dimensions of advanced age. The remaining portion of this chapter explores empowering practice approaches to aged clients and ways of confronting ageism in society. That there is much we can learn from other nations, other cultures, is an underlying theme of this discussion.

Concept of Aging Worldwide

The same global economy that is having a negative impact on the most industrialized of nations also is promoting individualism and materialism elsewhere. Increasing materialism has been at the expense of the traditional family values of respect and care for the elderly and familial interdependence. Worldwide, the communications revolution promoting modern and Western commercialism has continued to undermine the traditional foundations of family roles and function. But let us start with a view of aging closer to home.

In the United States and Europe

A self-proclaimed member of the baby boom generation, psychologist Mary Pipher (1999) describes the landscape of old age as "another country." Aging in America, she says, is harder than it needs to be. The distance between parents and their adult children in a highly mobile society is part of the problem. Ignorance about the needs of the older generation due to physical separation is another part. Whereas historically humans of all generations spent time together, people today tend to be grouped by age: 3-year-olds are together; preteens are together; and many retired people live in segregated communities.

During the colonial period, older individuals generally were looked on with respect (Popple & Leighninger, 2002). Older relatives played active roles in the family, on the farm, and in helping with the young. There were social class differences, of course, in who had high esteem. Nevertheless, as Popple and

Leighninger indicate, the elderly continued to be viewed in a positive light and were cared for within families. Attitudes toward old age began to shift by the mid-1800s, and old age began to be equated with ugliness, disease, and uselessness. The shift in attitude was related in part to industrialization and in part to the new philosophy of social Darwinism, which stressed survival of the fittest and efficiency. Rapid advances of science and technology tended to limit the value of elders' knowledge—knowledge that, in any case, could be obtained from books rather than passed down orally (Zastrow, 2004).

Consistent with the economic demands of modern industrialization and urbanization has been the gradual decline in the extended kinship system. Within the families of earlier centuries, parents were rarely without children. Women were often grandmothers before the birth of their last child (Barusch, 2002). Under urbanization, family size became limited; the generation gap increased, and the older generation lost its central function, as Barusch indicates. Of Western countries, the birthrate is the lowest in Spain at only 1.15 children per woman. In Spain, therefore, where sons and daughters are obliged to pay a share of the monthly cost of nursing home or community care for their parents, there will be few siblings in the future to share the expense (Large, 2001). Italy, Czechoslovakia, and Romania are countries with similarly low fertility rates (Longman, 1999). For point of comparison, American women each have about two children on average. Northern Europe has done better than countries southward because of lower unemployment, adequate child care provisions, and strong economic incentives for childbearing. Modern industrialized society is work- and productivity-oriented, with a focus on the future—on progress rather than tradition.

Even among the most familial-oriented groups, the thrust of mainstream values cannot be ignored. In her participant observation study *Understanding Older Chicanas,* Facio (1996) explored the meaning of old age to Mexican American women. During their childhood, grandparents were a vital part of the family:

> Older Chicanas . . . were socialized with certain ideas about old age: that it would bring harmony, status, respect, and solace. However, the reality of their present lives [poverty, family structural changes, differential life expectancies, longevity] calls for the aged to reassess their expectations and thus redefine their old age. Older Chicanas, in particular, must deal with traditions that reinforce a gender hierarchy. (p. 15)

In mainstream America, in contrast, the first retirement programs inadvertently reinforced the idea that the elderly were incapable of useful work (Popple & Leighninger, 2002). By 1910, poorhouses had been transformed into old-age homes. Meanwhile, the numbers of the aged in the population continued to increase. Only after the social turmoil associated with the Great Depression did the idea of Social Security catch on as a means of providing social insurance for workers and their families—insurance against loss of a parent, disabilities, and old age.

The policies of today are linked to the orientations and solutions of yesterday. Two developments from the 18th and 19th centuries are germane to our treatment of the elderly at the present time—a lack of coordination in a federally operated system that developed in an ad hoc fashion, and a tendency to favor the young for their future potential. In European countries, in contrast, operations under one government are less complex and less fraught with power imbalances and irregularities in providing services.

Today, 10 percent of those 65 and over are below the poverty line; the numbers break down to 12.4 percent for women and 7 percent for men (U.S. Census Bureau, 2003). In a materialistic society, the old are devalued because they are poor, and they are poor because they are devalued. In this, as in other matters, the economic and social systems are intertwined. The poverty of older adults clearly reveals the order of priorities in our society. Social Security benefits are well below the official poverty level. While other Western nations divert a substantial portion of their national wealth into old-age supplements, in the United States, getting older generally means getting poorer. Lack of money, lack of adequate transportation, the high cost of health care in spite of Medicare and other programs, the mandatory loss of occupational roles: these all combine to produce a social situation in which, as Pipher (1999) puts it, to be old is to be "phased out" (p. 52).

Much of the literature and the mass media today are decidedly unsympathetic to the needs of the aged. Often older adults' needs are pitted against the needs of the very young who, it is said, lack voting power (unlike the elderly) and are therefore neglected (Cox, 1999). According to most public officials, the demands of the elderly are consuming a disproportionate share of the national budget. Consider this statement from a no less revered source than the Children's Defense Fund (2001): "Child poverty has grown while national efforts to improve economic security have focused on the elderly. If America lifted low-income children out of poverty in the same proportion as we currently lift low-income seniors, three out of four poor children would no longer be poor" (p. 2 of 3). In fact, the elderly who are really elderly, from age 75 on up, suffer hardships that the statistics on poverty do not reveal. (We return to this subject in a later section.)

Following a barrage of press reports, in effect, blaming the needs of the elderly for the current fiscal crisis, resentment by the general public is mounting. Viewed as politically powerful and selfishly pursuing their own interests, the aged are justified in suspecting that they have become the sacrificial lambs of the country's austerity policies. "Why should the young be saddled with high taxes to support retired people?" is a question commonly asked.

Such sentiments plus the influence of special interest groups on politicians have created a climate ripe for a retrenchment of the popular and smooth-functioning Medicare program. As was mentioned in the previous chapter, the new Medicare drug prescription program, passed by Congress under the George Bush administration and under the guise of reform, has been described as more a windfall for the pharmaceutical and insurance companies than a program to protect seniors. The legislation forbids the following: negotiating bulk discounts on drug prices as other nations do, the purchase of supplemental insurance for drugs unacknowledged by Medicare, and importing less expensive drugs from

Canada (Lapham, 2004). The $400 billion legislation (the official estimate for a ten-year period) defrays only some prescription costs and offers huge business incentives to health maintenance organizations (HMOs). This legislation if not overturned, as it well might be, ensures the eventual collapse of the entire Medicare apparatus through a move away from social insurance toward privatization and means testing (Lapham).

Nations Coping with Population Imbalance

The United Nations proclaimed 1999 as the International Year of the Older Person. In so doing, this global organization was providing recognition of concerns and problems related to the aging of the world's populations. Three years later in Madrid, representatives from 160 countries and organizations met at a United Nations (U.N.) conference to address the challenges posed by the soaring elderly growth rate ("U.N. Grapples with World's Booming Elderly Population," 2002). Whether one talks of the "aging of America" or the "graying of Japan," the similarities cross all cultures (Gombos, 1999). Not only is population aging universal, but it also has been unprecedented historically. For the first time in history, people over age 60 will outnumber children 14 and younger in industrialized nations (Longman, 1999).

In the advanced economic regions of the world today, there are roughly three working taxpayers for every nonworking person on a pension (Peterson, 1999). By 2030, this figure probably will be reduced to a scant 1.5. The problem lies not in the large numbers of the elderly, but in the population imbalance resting on too few workers as taxpayers. Higher pension and health care costs are expected to shrink even the most productive economies. Throughout the economically advanced world, total public spending per older person is two to three times as great as public spending per child (Longman, 1999). In Germany, for example, two people now work for every retired worker; the retirement is just over 60 on average, and state pensions, as in France, are extremely generous ("Loosen Up or Lose Out," 2002).

The predictions for Japan, the nation with the highest percentage of the elderly, are especially dire. According to a special supplement to *The Economist* ("Consensus and Contraction," 2002), Japan has been aging faster than any other society in the world; the over-65 age group has more than doubled since 1970. An extremely low birthrate is connected to women's liberation and reluctance to marry in a nation in which the wife-mother traditionally stays home to tutor children and care for her spouse and her spouse's parents. Because of the stigma of illegitimacy, the abortion rate is high. Compounding the problem, the Japanese do not welcome foreigners, much less immigrants, into their homogenous society. An influx of young immigrant workers as exists in the United States and Canada would help correct the age imbalance, though at the risk of overpopulation. Japan also is feeling the effects of the custom of underpaying young workers as part of a seniority system that guarantees job security and much higher salaries for long-time employees.

In China, a nation that has traditionally venerated its elders and emphasized filial duty, the old ways are weakening under the influence of capitalism, world trade, and the one-child-only policy. Generally, the family is expected to take care of any of its members who are old, frail, sick, or disabled. It is an offense, punishable by a fine, to neglect elderly members of the family (Webb, 1992). (Singapore has a similar law.) If there is no family to help, the state will step in. Pensions are provided to ex-government workers (workers at state-owned factories also qualify). Nevertheless, the old security system is now in turmoil (Large, 2001).

While the challenge of caring for progressively larger numbers of vulnerable elderly persons is the same the world over, the way in which this challenge is met varies greatly from country to country. Moisi (2003) observed these differences firsthand at a world conference on globalization and ethics:

> The following question was ultimately asked: Who in each society is in charge of taking care of the weakest and the poorest, a category of which very old people belong? For the Americans, close to Max Weber's point of view in the *Protestant Ethic*, the richest citizens had the most fundamental role to play through charity work. For the Asians, the family links remained essential, the family being conceived in a broader sense than in the West. Finally, for the Europeans, it was the state that should assume that responsibility. (p. 13)

The essence of successful long-term care for the frail elderly is in the kind of health care and social services available in the wider society. Nations with collectivist approaches assume that frailty among the aged is a social problem engendering social solutions. Sweden, Finland, Israel, and France provide services universally and with dignity for those in need of aid. In Sweden and Finland, as in the rest of Scandinavia, pensions and housing allowances are viewed as essential components of elder care. Britain and Canada, in contrast, despite an entitlement approach to health care, place the responsibility on the family to provide long-term care; programs are developed only to fill gaps when emergency care is needed. The promotion of greater privatization in both countries is threatening to create a greater gap between the "haves" and the "have-nots." In the United States, the continued emphasis on individualism and self-reliance fosters a tradition of privately provided support including support by family members.

What is the role of the immediate family in caring for the aged? In all the nations studied, Olson (1994) found that informal care remains in the women's domain. In Israel, where few of the elderly are living alone and with a strong Jewish tradition of honoring one's parents, the family plays a major role in caregiving. In Japan, likewise, more than 60 percent of people aged sixty-five and over and nearly 80 percent of those aged eighty and over live with their adult children. And in China, familism based on the Confucian concept of filial piety promotes cooperation and obligation among the generations. The daughters-in-law provide the actual care; if they work, they often must take a leave of absence from their jobs.

A second aspect of elder care is the degree to which the aged are institutionalized. Many of the countries studied by Olson (1994) have similar institutionalization rates, usually around 5 percent as in the United States, with a high of 7.5 percent in Canada and a low of 2 percent in Japan. In both the United States and Britain, there have been nursing home scandals of abuse, lack of proper hygiene, fire hazards, and other problems. Nursing homes in many of the countries studied, however, provide normal, homelike atmospheres as opposed to medical environments. Due to both economic and humanitarian considerations, there is a thrust toward state funding for home and community-based services. Service apartments in Scandinavia provide a wide range of supportive services for the elderly including prepared meals. Israel, which has provided extensive care for the large influx of elderly immigrants, is shifting to a focus on community-based services including day care. Germany, similarly, offers a variety of services but still fails to meet the needs of all the frail elderly, especially of those who are poor.

Regardless of political economy, the common theme in every country with extended life expectancies is the struggle with varying political, social, economic, and psychological issues associated with caring for growing older populations. Furthermore, the steady increase in the number of mentally impaired older people tends to be a worldwide issue: Currently 5 to 7 percent of the elderly have some form of dementia. Suicide is another problem; actually it is the tragic solution to a host of problems, including loneliness and depression. In the United States, elderly men are more likely to commit suicide than any other age group—eight out of ten of the suicides involve the use of firearms (Talaga, 1999). The U.S. suicide rate for both elderly males and females is double the Canadian rate. In Hungary, which has the highest elder suicide rate in the world, and China, a close second, the sex ratios of elder suicide are more even, according to the World Health Organization (WHO) figures cited by Talaga. In Japan, contrary to the tradition of veneration of elders, suicide among the elderly has become an epidemic; this development is related to the recession and increasing isolation of older family members (Goldsmith, 2003).

Daly (2001), in examining care-related policies in the western European welfare states, found that care is as much a feature of a society's value system as it is of circumstances. The concept of social citizenship in the Scandinavian countries guarantees "cradle to grave" care of dependents. Increasingly, however, emphasis is on care for the young. In continental European countries, in contrast, the notion that care of the elderly should in the first instance be provided by the family prevails. Three countries that have a mixed pattern of care are Ireland, the United Kingdom, and Italy. While public services for children are relatively weak, they have a well-developed network of provision for elderly care. Pressures from economic globalization, however, are undermining pension systems in countries like the United Kingdom, United States, and New Zealand with the thrust toward the privatization of pensions and health care (Walker, 2002).

Shah (1992) traveled across the world to report on care for the aged in nations already dealing with population shifts toward the upper end of the age spectrum. What she found can be summarized briefly. Balking from the high cost of health and social spending, Sweden has seen fit to trim many other programs. In workaholic Japan, retired persons, especially men, have much difficulty with leisure time so the government is organizing activities at neighborhood centers. And India, where care is provided through the extended family, is unprepared for the explosion of old people as it still struggles to feed the young. China's government, meanwhile, is promising support to its citizens in their old age as a means of keeping the birthrate down; resources are lacking, however. Chinese government officials are building retirement homes at a breakneck pace; more than 300 have been built in Beijing alone (Litke, 2001). But most of the elderly Chinese prefer to remain in their own neighborhoods. In a more innovative program to meet their needs, neighborhood residents provide caregiving to their neighbors. Volunteers document their home in a public logbook. Then when the caregivers grow older, they will be entitled to the same amount of care that they have provided. This program is called the "Time Bank" (Litke).

Throughout the world, care of an elderly parent is often regarded by the children as an unwanted burden. The concept of the *sandwich generation* bears out this negativism. This term refers to middle-aged people who are pulled in two directions by the needs of both children and parents (Suppes & Wells, 2003). In their discussion of family strengths, however, Suppes and Wells cited a study commissioned by the American Association of Retired Persons (AARP) that found that 70 percent of the middle-aged caregivers of the "sandwich generation" felt comfortable in their roles rather than burdened by them.

In a thoughtful comparison of two works of literature, Donow (1990) revealed how two cultures—the American and Japanese—approached a similar family crisis involving the need to care for an elderly father or father-in-law. Anderson's play *I Never Sang for My Father* (1968), later made into a movie starring Gene Hackman and Melvyn Douglas, is a deeply moving drama depicting the agony experienced by the children of an 80-year-old autocratic father who descends suddenly upon them. "My responsibility is to my husband and my children," declares the anguished daughter (p. 95). The son, somewhat more sensitively, reveals his pain in these words: "I can't tell you what it does to me as a man . . . to see someone like that . . . a man who was distinguished, remarkable . . . just become a nuisance" (p. 94). In this play, the adult children wrestle with their guilt feelings and issues that they are never able to resolve so much as to endure. The Japanese novel *Kokotsu no Hito (The Twilight Years)* by Ariyoshi (1984/1972) is told from the perspective of Akiko who faces the crisis of caring for her father-in-law, an egocentric and difficult man suffering from dementia. Unlike its American counterpart, in this story the central character, though nearly overwhelmed by the impact of her father-in-law's illness, emerges richer for the experience, as does her father-in-law. Donow concluded, from his comparative study of these culturally distinct but circumstantially similar texts, that both works leave us with some troubling questions about family relations and what role other social institutions ought to play in the care of an elderly parent. Written in the 1970s, the Japanese novel represents traditions that are rapidly giving way as many women seek professional roles.

Campbell (1995) praised Japan for its success in shaping innovative policy and being at the forefront in the establishment of a long-term care insurance system to provide the kinds of services that are now becoming necessary. Japan's moves, as Campbell argued, contrast starkly with those of the United States where the focus seems to be all on cost-saving measures rather than the provision of adequate long-term care. Since Campbell made his observations, however, pension underfunding by Japanese companies has become a recognized problem, and the companies seem bent on restructuring such plans to reduce payment obligations to employees (Jopson, 2003). Increasingly, too, the pattern of fierce loyalty to older members seems to be breaking down.

Overlooked Positives of Population Imbalance

The reader undoubtedly will have noticed, as I did, that the literature on global aging cited earlier is decidedly negative. The information from U.N. reports and academic research alike is replete with dire forebodings of falling productivity rates, low consumption of goods, and a financial burden on our social welfare, health, retirement, and family systems. Yet there are positive aspects to the longevity phenomenon that are almost entirely overlooked. Elderly citizens, for example, provide a vital resource; both collectively and as individuals, their potential contribution to society is enormous. A challenge for NGOs (nongovernmental organizations) advocating for the needs of the elderly is to convince countries, particularly countries struggling to be economically competitive, that most seniors can be viewed not as a liability but as a resource (Weisman, 1999). Their wisdom and experience can be utilized by providing them with opportunities for decision making in their respective communities.

In a positive vein, the U.N. (1999) has developed five principles essential to the situation of older persons. These five principles, which became a blueprint for the International Year of the Older Person, are:

- *Independence,* including the opportunity to work and earn income
- *Participation* in the life of the community
- *Care* in the home and community as needed
- *Self-fulfillment* in the cultural life of the community
- *Dignity* to be preserved regardless of one's economic circumstances

Regarding the need for independence, some sort of mass transportation is essential so that persons who do not drive can get where they need to go without having to depend on others.

Quite apart from (and in contradiction to) the literature on the pending age imbalance, I have drawn up my own list of positives. Keep in mind, in any case, that the dreaded population imbalance that has received such negative media coverage is related to the baby boom population bulge, and therefore this imbalance is strictly temporary. Here is my list of positives:

- A low crime rate in a society in which there are proportionately fewer youths
- A reduced rate of illicit substance abuse and alcoholism in a population skewed toward the elderly end of the spectrum (many hardened drug users and alcoholics never reach old age)
- More jobs available for the young, a crucial factor as technologies continue to replace workers

- A pool of retired persons available for caregiving and volunteer work
- An older generation to provide a sense of connectedness with the cultural past
- An older generation to be a source of love and guidance to the young
- The chance for grown children to return the care that was once given to them

In addition, because resources are not finite, the ultimate decline in the world's population is consistent with the goals of agricultural and environmental sustainability.

Biological Factors in Aging

Shakespeare summed up the physiological changes—ravages—of very old age, a time characterized by losses:

> [The] last scene of all
> That ends this strange eventful history
> Is second childishness, and mere oblivion
> Sans teeth, sans eyes, sans taste,
> sans everything.
>
> —Shakespeare, *As You Like It* (1600), Act II, scene vii

The pace of biological aging differs among individuals, but its course is inevitable over time. The morbid side of growing old—illness, infirmity, and looming death—often is underplayed in the literature. Television ads, on the other hand, in the interests of promoting sales, play up the negatives. Biologists use the word *senescence* to refer to the process of aging for all life forms. The process of aging involves a certain deterioration; health and vitality decrease, and vulnerability increases (Mann, 1995). The process of aging is not uniform, however, but occurs in spurts (Zastrow, 2004).

Aldous Huxley's *Brave New World* (1969/1932) depicted a future that contained death but not aging. Through the miracle of chemistry, the old did not physically age and therefore died as physically young people. In the real world, however, only through death can we stave off the effects of the ravages of time. The inevitability of growing old is accompanied by an obvious physical decline. Four out of five people over age 65 can count on having at least one chronic condition; among the most common are arthritis, hearing impairments, various forms of cardiovascular diseases, and cancer (Dunkle & Norgard, 1995). The exact relationship between chronological age and the decrease in capabilities, however, has yet to satisfactorily be determined.

Many of the health problems faced by elderly persons result from a general decline in the circulatory system (Zastrow, 2004). Reduced blood supply impairs mental sharpness, and other body organs are affected as well. Adjusting to changes in external temperature becomes increasingly difficult. Bones become more brittle; sensory capacities decline as well. Because it affects all of one's dealings with people, hearing impairment is crucial in its consequences. Among characteristics of the aging process is the marked inability to hear clearly in such crowded places as restaurants and theaters or where there is background noise from appliances, air conditioning, television sets, or radios. Hearing aids exaggerate such extraneous noise. Much sound, such as loud music, can become irritating in later life. Other age-related changes—in vision, muscular strength, and reaction time—lead to a sense of vulnerability and fear in strange and unusual surroundings.

Physical limitations coupled with lack of adequate transportation limit older persons in their ability to shop, obtain legal counsel, or get needed medical care. About 30 percent of the elderly people are severely disabled (Popple & Leighninger, 2002). With the rapid increase in the number of people over age 85, Alzheimer's disease and other forms of dementia are much more frequent occurrences than in the past. An estimated 4.5 million Americans are living today with Alzheimer's, a number that is expected to double over the next several decades (Drackley, 2003). Nearly one in five of persons over age 85 is living in a nursing home. Half of all nursing home residents suffer from this disease or a related form of dementia. Because an individual with Alzheimer's disease lives an average of eight years beyond the onset of symptoms, the demands of care can be formidable (Drackley).

Recent years have brought a barrage of media ads touting the wonders of modern medicine, but overmedication and the prescribing of drugs that have been tested on young people but should be avoided by older people can present major problems. Elders under medical care often take as many as 15 or 20 different medications per day (Hogan, 2004). Harmful interactive effects are common; symptoms such as disorientation and lack of concentration may resemble dementia. Moreover, the risk of side effects is maximized for elderly as opposed to younger patients in that their metabolism is less efficient, so the drugs remain in their systems longer. Sometimes people diagnosed with dementia see their functioning restored by simply cutting back on their medication. Consultation with one's local pharmacist is recommended in light of the pharmacist's expertise in chemical interactions (Hogan).

"Every age," notes Grossman (2003), "has its own way of dying. The 19th century had consumption; the 20th century had the heart attack, and the 21st century will be the age of Alzheimer's disease" (p. 65). Medical science is frantically searching for a cure for this dread disease; some medications have recently been developed in hopes of arresting its progress. The newly created Allen Institute for Brain Science in Seattle is a privately funded institute with the goal of mapping every gene's role in the human brain so that medical researchers can find new drugs and treatments for disorders such as Alzheimer's and schizophrenia (Davis, 2003).

Two recent memoirs provide disturbing and unsentimental chronicles of life with a parent in the late stages of Alzheimer's. *The Story of My Father* by Sue Miller (2003) records the mental decline of a once quiet, spiritual man whose mind led him into the darkness of paranoia to the extent that his daughter could only feel relief when his miserable existence was over. In *Death in Slow Motion*, Eleanor Cooney (2003), similarly recalls how she became distraught at her mother's fits of rage and hallucinations. As a caregiver, she resorted to medicating herself with Valium and alcohol.

Cancer is another important target area of medical research. With this disease as well, gene studies are the focal point. Through studies of gene instability (one of the major hallmarks of malignancy) it is hoped that the secrets of how the life span operates its own clock might be uncovered. Curiously, studies of similarities between humans and baker's yeast aim at providing scientists with a new model to test theories (Fred Hutchinson Cancer Research Center, 2003). The quest is to discover the reason for late-life vulnerability to cancer and other age-related diseases. Such research is crucial inasmuch as after reaching late-middle age, men face a 50 percent chance of developing cancer, and women have a 35 percent chance.

As the population ages, we can expect that the increasing medical attention to treatments for the elderly will continue. Consider the plethora of television ads for drugs for arthritis, impotence, depression, and the like. Historically, medical care was instituted to treat the young—to deal with war wounds, industrial accidents, childbirth, and children's diseases. Consequently, as McDaniel and Gee (1993) indicate, the physician-oriented, and cure-based nature of health care is unsuited to the needs of older people who typically have chronic conditions with social dimensions. The use of advanced technologies on the aged who may finish out their lives on a respirator in intensive care results in unnecessary pain for such patients, guilt feelings for family members, and great expense for society. This process further creates a convenient scapegoat—the elderly themselves—for a society facing rising health care costs. This brings us to the psychological aspects of aging.

The Psychology of Aging

Psychological aging is related to biological aging in the way the mind is very closely linked to the body. The psychological dimension refers to changes in personality or ways of processing information accompanying the aging process. Factors of health, idleness, loss of contemporaries, reduced income, and many other social variables shape the psychological reality experienced by older adults. The 2002 Hollywood movie *About Schmidt* poignantly yet humorously takes us on a journey with Warren Schmidt (convincingly played by Jack Nicholson) as he attempts to find meaning in his seemingly meaningless life following his retirement party and the death of his wife. With the vastness of the future no longer before them and the typical emptiness of the present, the past assumes an ever-increasing importance to many elderly persons.

Two of Erikson's (1963) eight stages of life development, the last two, have relevance to late adulthood. These are generativity versus stagnation and ego integrity versus despair, the eighth stage mentioned at the start of this chapter. Generativity, as Robbins, Chatterjee, and Canda (1998) noted, has two faces—charity and *agape* (the Greek word for love). Erikson, as Robbins et al. further suggest, was concerned about greed in modern life and its effect on future generations. The depletion of the Earth's resources is clearly the opposite of generativity. The poem in Box 10.1 by Elise Talmage, age 81, was inspired by the following exchange with an irascible old man: "Why don't you plant some flowers?" Talmage asked. "What's the point?" he replied. "I probably won't live long enough to see them bloom" (personal conversation with van Wormer, May 2003).

The work of the final stage of life, as defined by Erikson (1963), is geared toward the achievement of integrity. In this last scenario, the elderly person wants to feel that his or her life has been meaningful and worthwhile (Popple & Leighninger, 2002). Advanced age is a time of reflection on one's life and on the life choices that one has made at various turning points along the way. Allie Walton (1981), who described herself as "a freelance Quaker do-gooder and peacemaker," and who is no longer with us, once wrote a piece on aging that was widely read in Quaker circles. Here it is in part:

> Long ago, when I was still quite young, I discovered George Bernard Shaw's witty remark—"Youth is such a wonderful thing; it's too bad it is wasted on the young." . . .
> And now—I'm 70, and it's been awhile since I dared to climb a tree, and I take the stairs one at a time. I still chuckle over Shaw's wit, but it seems a dated joke. By now, I realize life is not divided into "youth" and "middle age" and "old age." It all runs together. It is all part of a piece, constantly moving and growing and intertwining. Physical activity is a joy, your grandchildren are a treasure, and work keeps body and soul together, but at 70 I am chuckling over new discoveries. How relaxing to be past the time of constant attention to the many details of family needs. How nice to know it doesn't matter whether or not you are a wall-flower. (p. 8)

This is generativity in a nutshell.

Old-Old Age

In her book *Another Country,* Mary Pipher (1999) skillfully encapsulates the link between the elderly person's biological condition and his or her state of mind. The developmental period of old age, argues Pipher, is about major physical and social disruptions and psychological stresses. Old-old persons (those over age 75) often feel ashamed of what is a natural stage of the life cycle. The greatest challenge of old age is learning to accept vulnerability and to ask for help. The old-old are less sanguine than their young-old counterparts (persons in their 60s or early 70s). As Pipher explains: "They lead lives filled with the loss of friends and family, of habits and pleasures, and of autonomy. One of the cruel ironies of old-old age is that often when people suffer losses, they must search for new homes" (p. 30). Moving away often makes life more difficult through loss of familiar places and lifelong routines.

Despite their forgetfulness, the elderly have a storehouse of memories. The past is often more real than the present. Some of the memories involve buried parts of the past such as war memories that return in later years. Like other victims of trauma, the old-old can become obsessed with deeply disturbing events of the past and be inclined to tell the same story over and over. As Pipher

10.1 But Someone Surely Will

Elise Talmage

Let's rake leaves in little piles
So hurry while the wind is still.
I may not see the springtime grass
But someone surely will.

Let's dig holes for tulip bulbs
And spread on rich black dirt to fill.
I may not be here in the spring
But someone surely will.

Let's plant yellow poplar trees
all along the left-hand hill.
I may not see them really grow
But someone surely will.

I feel very spry today
not ready for the shelf.
I bet I'll fool the hourglass
and see the Spring myself.

Source: Unpublished poem. Printed by permission of Elise Talmage who lives on a farm near Bowling Green, Kentucky.

(1999) astutely observes, this storytelling is not about communication; it is about therapy.

In a cruel twist of fate, people who have survived unimagined horrors earlier in life against all odds and who have refused to dwell on such memories often end up returning in old age to those long-ago horrors. The Baycrest Centre for Geriatric Care in Toronto provides residential services for about 1,000 Holocaust survivors (Ubelacker, 2003). A social worker who works at the care facility describes the phenomenon of dementia-related return to long-repressed memories from the past as "heartbreaking." With the onset of age-related conditions such as Alzheimer's, people can no longer separate the past from the present; short-term memories begin to disintegrate, while earlier memories may remain sharply in focus. The ability to compartmentalize such memories is lost. Passing out food, lineups to board a bus, the sight of security officers' uniforms, arrangements to take a shower—all are triggers that can lead to reactions of hysteria in these Holocaust survivors.

Facing Death

As we live in the present and invest in the future, old age and death are commonly denied. The painful paradox of death in the midst of life is addressed with rare eloquence in Becker's classic, *The Denial of Death* (1973):

We saw that there really was no way to overcome the real dilemma of existence, the one of the mortal animal who at the same time is conscious of his mortality. A person spends years coming into his own, developing his discriminations about the world, broadening and sharpening his appetite, learning to bear the disappointments of life, becoming mature, seasoned—finally a unique creature in nature, standing with some dignity and nobility and transcending the animal condition, no longer a complete reflex, not stamped out of any mold. And then the real tragedy, as André Malraux wrote in *The Human Condition:* that it takes sixty years of incredible suffering and effort to make such an individual, and then he is good only for dying. (p. 268)

When I was working for a brief period at a community home health care and hospice in Washington state, I pondered the remarkable resilience of the staff in dealing with death and dying every day. I began to study the various styles of coping by staff and family alike. By the time I left the hospice, I had drawn up a list of coping devices, all normal reactions to the psychological demands of work with the bereaved and the dying (van Wormer, 1997).

From the literature on death and dying and from my work, I have filtered out five ideologies, all different but all united by the theme of denial—the denial of the reality of death. All are escape mechanisms but, under circumstances in which escape is not necessary, are unhealthy responses. *Blaming the victim,* the first theme, offers a way we can divorce ourselves from our sense of the injustice of death, especially of premature death. This ideology is manifested in blaming patients for lifestyle activities that destroyed their health and also in blaming patients for not following specific medical orders and even for their failure to recover. *Denial of death,* the second defense mechanism, is consistent with the American creed that stresses youth, optimism, and progress. Denying death involves maintaining the patient with expensive and painful medical treatments past the point when trying to get well makes any sense. The healthy side of denial is that people (the patient or friends and relatives) can go on; they can delay coping with cruel realities until they are ready. The remaining three psychological strategies for dealing with death are *escape through medical jargon* (used by nurses where I worked), *escape through social death* (used by some family members who seem to have already buried the dying person), and *escape through redefinition,* which, as the direct opposite of denial, is an overly positive approach (almost a romanticization of the death and dying process).

Fortunately, there are many excellent hospice-connected programs set up to provide quality of life to the terminal patient and to assist the patient at home or in a homelike setting. Pain relief is encouraged to keep the person as comfortable as possible (Zastrow, 2004). Hospice workers, often social workers, also assist families throughout the bereavement process. Knowledge and understanding of the dynamics of dealing with the loss of a patient or loved one is essential to effective social work with individuals who are at the end of their lives.

Assisted Suicide

Increasingly, Americans and some Europeans are seeking ways to exert some measure of control over where and how they die. The topic of euthanasia is highly controversial and is frightening both in society's acceptance and in society's rejection of it. The former opens up the possibility of people being coaxed to die; the latter presents images of horrible pain and indignity of life prolonged artificially by machines.

According to survey data cited by McInnis-Dittrich (2002), two thirds of the public and a majority of physicians in the United States support physician-assisted suicide as a legitimate right in cases of incurable and debilitating disease. The U.S. Supreme Court has ruled that the decision to allow physician-assisted suicide should be decided by the states. Oregon, alone among the states, has legalized this process under strictly controlled conditions. Oregon's Death with Dignity Act allows doctors to prescribe (but not administer) a lethal dosage of drugs at the request of terminally ill patients with less than six months to live (Zastrow, 2004). As of 2002, five years after the Oregon law was passed, there had been only 91 cases of assisted suicide; the system had not been abused as opponents had feared (Register Editorial Board, 2002). The vast majority who chose this route were people in the late stages of cancer under hospice care. At the present time, only in the Netherlands are physicians permitted to give dying patients who qualify a lethal dose of drugs. The advantage of the voluntary euthanasia option for elders is in empowering them to exert some control over the manner of their death and its timing.

The Social Side of Aging

In a youth-oriented, fast-paced industrialized society, the process of aging begins to acquire a negative meaning as we move past early adulthood. The middle-aged and elderly often suffer from internalized ageism, seeing themselves as failing to meet prevailing ideals of beauty and health and therefore as substandard in some way. A sense of worthlessness and depression may result, not from the aging process itself, but from the perception of themselves as embarking on a downward spiral, as being "over the hill." Such a perception may set in as early as the late 20s.

The *social* side of aging refers to the cultural expectations for people at various stages of their lives. Socially constructed definitions are important because they ultimately are translated into public policies. The extent to which the elderly are expected to continue making an active contribution to their families and to society, or conversely, to disengage from responsibility in deference to the younger generation, has profound—and perhaps unsettling—implications for one's social adjustment to growing old.

Race, ethnicity, and social class status are significant determinants of an individual's experience with aging. Minorities, only around 16 percent of the elderly population in 2000, are projected to represent about one fourth of the total population by 2030 (U.S. Department of Health and Human Services, 2001). Membership in an extended family is a primary buffer against the losses associated with advancing age. About twice as many African Americans and Latinos live in extended family situations as do European Americans ("Older Americans 2000," 2003). The group with the smallest percentage of persons living alone is the Asian and Pacific Islander populations. See Box 10.2 to learn of the importance of family ties in Latin American households.

10.2 Latino Family Ties

Lydia Perez Roberts

Not long after I moved out of my parents' house, I began to plan for when my parents would move in with me. Now this was never something we discussed but rather something that was observed. Like the seasons of a year—after a while you just know that this is the way it is and always has been.

My first recollection of this type of living arrangement began with my occasional trips as a 4-year-old to my *abuelita's* (great-grandmother's) shacklike house in the barrio (neighborhood) of the west side. I remember my mother explaining that during the part of the year that Abuelita lived with her daughter (my grandma Olivia), she would spend the weekends living in this little house with a close friend who was her age—who she considered to be family. The other half of the year, Abuelita lived with another daughter in Virginia. I found this versatility in living arrangements to be fascinating, and I remember thinking that Abuelita was a woman of adventure, despite her frailty and being 70-plus years old. She appeared to move with the seasons, and like the seasons, she appeared to determine much of her own destiny. Her dark, long, black hair held up in a tight bun and the masculine cigarettes she puffed on only confirmed my suspicions. I remember thinking that the bun in her hair was for show only, as if her spunky spirit was wrapped up in between the long strands of black hair that she only let down on special occasions, in which small children like me were not allowed to partake. My mother's voice while explaining Abuelita's living arrangement was not laced with pity or shame but rather with normalcy and even a tinge of admiration. And for a long time, this is how I envisioned all elderly women living—carefree and with people who loved them and longed to share in their adventure.

Twenty-four years later, like my *abuelita* before her, my grandma Olivia now lives in her own house with her two daughters and one of her grandchildren. By no means is she considered "dependent" upon them or a "burden." Rather, she is the spunky head-of-the-household who calls the shots and lets few be tricked by her grandmotherly looks. She still cooks the best meals and has the best stories, and the ring of her laughter is heard throughout the house during all of our family gatherings. To have her in your household is an honor because you know you have the spirit of adventure and wisdom to look upon and admire.

And just as Latinos and Latinas throughout the world carry on this tradition with pride and a feeling of connectedness to their ancestors before them, I know that the time will come when my mother will be an addition and blessing to my home. With her dark, long, black hair she will be the spunk in our home, and will give more than she could ever take. She cooks better than I ever could and will always know the best way to cure a cold. And even if the time comes when I have to take on the parent role, my caring for her could never outmatch what she has given through her decades of parenting and grandparenting. Her many years of keeping our household intact and safe and holding our hands as children while we discovered the adventurous spirit within ourselves could never be outweighed or overshadowed by any temporary swapping of caretaking roles. In the end she will always be the guide and I, just the follower. I will only aspire to be so adventurous, wise, and comforting.

And because the seasons continually change, my mother will one day no longer be on earth with her children and grandchildren, but her spirit and the honor she earned from her family and ancestors will live on. I can only hope that one day, when I am worn with years and filled with stories to share, my son Nathan will be able to see the twinkle in my eye and admire my spunky spirit. May my laughter ring across his home and bring warm memories to his heart, and may he always see me as the adventurous woman with the dark, long, black hair.

(continued)

| 10.2 *continued* |

Addendum

In an e-mail communication (October 15, 2003) related to this article, Lydia Roberts discussed how she approached the different attitudes between two of her Latina social work students and their Iowa classmates. By way of explaining to the class how mainstream Anglo-Saxon culture tends to shut problems away, Roberts stated:

> I then gave examples, like the mentally ill who society shuts out, the criminals in jails, the pregnant teens in alternative schools, the runaways in shelters, and the elderly in nursing homes. . . . I explained that in

Mexican culture, to put people away because they are an inconvenience is almost unheard of. . . . I told them how we even joke about it in our family (sending our parents off to nursing homes when they're old). . . . This is kind of how the Dia de los Muertos celebration is too. Mexicans have a fun celebration of the day of the dead because it is their way of honoring the dead but at the same time laughing in the face of death. Not letting it get the best of them.

Source: Printed with permission of Lydia Perez Roberts, MSW.

Extended family ties are strong among many North American Indian groups as well. Most tribes assign to elders meaningful roles as transmitters of traditional culture, values, and education. Among upper-upper-class Anglos, similarly, the elderly occupy a position of honor due to their link to an illustrious and perhaps more prosperous past. Older people with higher incomes report their health as being much better than that of those with lower incomes (Popple & Leighninger, 2002). Nevertheless, regardless of ethnic background or social class, elderly people are faced with the constant concerns of health and loss of functioning, while economic factors provide hardship for most of the very old.

The Elderization of Poverty

"You can be young without money, but you can't be old without it." These words of wisdom were spoken by Maggie in the Tennessee Williams (1954) play *Cat on a Hot Tin Roof* (p. 54). Paralleling the term *feminization of poverty,* which refers to the social and economic structures and processes that have increasingly locked women into poverty (Barker, 2003), I am introducing the term *elderization of poverty*—or alternatively, *povertization of the elderly*—to refer to a trend that goes beyond the census data statistics. This trend relates to the quality of life that awaits a large percentage of the rapidly growing group of older people who can expect to live in poverty, many in abject poverty.

The overall poverty rate for the over-65 age group in 2002 was 10.1 percent, a number that is deceptively low because it lumps together all persons over age 65 and fails to take into account high expenses related to advanced aging—the costs of living alone, buying medication, and hiring help to perform physical tasks that people could previously perform themselves. The median income for all older persons in 2002 was only $13,769 (U.S. Department of Health and Human Services, 2001).

When ethnic and racial characteristics are factored in, the situation becomes ever more dismal. The poverty rate of Latinos over sixty-five is 18.8 percent and that of African Americans 22.3 percent, compared to only 8.9 percent for elderly whites. For older women living alone, nearly one in four lives below the poverty level. The highest rate of poverty (38.3 percent) is experienced by older Hispanic women who live alone or with nonrelatives. This seems to be the case for the following reasons: Much of women's work has been unpaid and thus without retirement benefits (even now the majority of working women are not covered by private pension plans); women will be very likely to take care of their spouses and then be left alone (only 12 percent of women over age 85 live with a spouse compared with 58 percent of men [U.S. Census Bureau, 2003]); and many women will live to advanced age. Thus, women's greatest blessing—longevity—turns into their greatest woe, and the feminization of poverty and the elderization of poverty become one. In the United States, as in most other countries, elderly women have a far higher rate of poverty than do elderly men. Older women's incomes are on average only about 58 percent of the incomes of older men (U.S. Department of Health and Human Services, 2001). In 2002, older women had a poverty rate of 12.4 percent and older men 7 percent (U.S. Census Bureau, 2003).

Just as the major component of caregivers for the elderly is female, so is the major component of this aging population female. From a global perspective, Gombos (1999) draws our attention to the extent of older-woman hardships in such places as: sub-Saharan Africa, where nearly half the adult relatives caring for children orphaned by AIDS are grandmothers; Ethiopia, where the number of destitute elderly women rivals the number of street children; Thailand, where older female workers in the textile industry are displaced by younger, cheaper workers; and France, where teenage gangs target elderly women to rob. Millions of older women live on the margins of their societies; in short, they face daily economic pressures and receive negligible health care and support services. The need for government-supported remedies to alleviate such struggles and living conditions is increasingly obvious.

As is apparent from the statistics presented earlier, we need to make a distinction between two segments of the older population—the young-old (aged 65 to 75) and the old-old (aged 75 and up). Newly retired people, compared to other age groups in the United States, are doing quite well. Their health is good; marriages and relationships boost their income and reduce expenses; and their retirement benefits have not yet been eaten by inflation. After age 75, the numbers of the living are diminished. For those still living, their incomes decline significantly while their expenses climb. The oldest-old (85 years or more) experience a poverty rate twice that of people aged 65 to 75 (Dunkle & Norgard, 1995). The expense of nursing home care can quickly exhaust one's savings. We can conceive, then, of a slowly but surely escalating elderization of poverty. Only those people with vast accumulations of wealth are invulnerable once they pass a certain age.

U.S. Government Programs

Most elderly people rely on Social Security benefits. Much is made of the fact that, due to Social Security and Supplemental Security Income, poverty has been reduced in the overall elderly population to nearly the average for the population as a whole. In fact, however, the Census Bureau applies a different poverty standard to elders (in the belief that they need less income and that they eat less than younger people) than to those below age 65 (Suppes & Wells, 2003).

In light of extremely high health care expenses, especially for medication, the elderly very often have to choose between filling a prescription and buying food. Iowa seniors, for example, pay an average of $1,250 per year in out-of-pocket prescription costs ("Iowa's Aging Population Highlights Need for Prescription Program," 2002). A frail elderly woman, typically, may have to find a way to obtain long-term health care for an ailing spouse when she no longer can physically provide the care herself. But with expenses for institutionalized health care skyrocketing, even the most scrupulous handling of finances over decades of retirement cannot protect a formerly middle-income family from eventual ruination. Housing deteriorates over time, and many of the homes of elderly people require renovation to make them handicap-accessible. About 30 percent of the elderly live in substandard housing; many reside in crime-ridden neighborhoods and are easy prey for thieves and muggers. Tragically, in Chicago during the heat wave of 1995, 529 people died of the heat; the majority were old people who lived alone. Their burglarproof homes prevented adequate ventilation, pushing indoor temperatures to dangerously high levels (*Facts on File,* 1995). When pronouncements are made about how well the elderly are doing in America, it is important to be aware of the stark realities.

The Social Security Act of 1935, discussed in Chapter 3, is the cornerstone of legislation for older people. Never intended to be the main source of income for the elderly, but rather as a supplement to assets, the Social Security system has become the sole support for many individuals (Zastrow, 2004). About 90 percent of seniors receive Social Security benefits; the more they paid into this program in their working years, the more they receive. Married persons can receive benefits based on their spouse's contributions. Unlike most private pension plans, Social Security is indexed to inflation. In the 1960s, before a reorganization of government programs, one-third of all elderly had incomes below the poverty line. Due to improvements in the standard of living and in Social Security and pension benefits, the poverty rate was cut in half between 1966 and 1974 (Dunkle & Norgard, 1995). Social Security is considered an entitlement program in that recipients have a legal right to its benefits. Supplemental Security Income (SSI) was initiated in 1972 as an extra supplement for very-low-income elderly and disabled persons (Suppes & Wells, 2003). Food stamps are another entitlement program available to poor older adults.

To pay for such programs, four out of five American workers pay more in payroll taxes than they do in income taxes (Reich, 2003). This tax is regressive in that the poor pay more. This tax is paid only up to a threshold of $87,000 except for the small Medicare portion. So the very rich, as Reich indicates, pay only a fraction of what others do percentagewise. In the years ahead, when Social

Security no longer generates a surplus due to the aging baby boomers, the solution is obvious—to eliminate the threshold.

Medicare and Medicaid were signed into law by President Johnson in the 1960s. Medicare provides health care to people 65 and over and to persons who are disabled, but typically it does not cover long-term care. Medicaid, a means-tested program, provides health care to poor and older Americans as well as long-term care to individuals of all ages. The greatest single outlay of Medicaid funds goes to the elderly for nursing home care (Karger & Stoesz, 2002).

The Medicaid program provides aid not only to the eligible poor but also to middle-class nursing home residents who have been forced to exhaust their savings in paying the nearly prohibitive nursing home fees. Many of the expenses of institutionalized care could be avoided if home health care provisions were sufficient. Current health care reform proposals have curbed spending by shifting more of the responsibility to the financing of Medicaid over to the states. One thing is certain: In the short run, as federal funding is cut, seniors will have few options and will be forced to turn to emergency rooms for much of their care (Vesely, 2003). Access to choices such as assisted living facilities is restricted to those with independent resources.

We can predict with some certainty that the cohort known as the baby boom generation, or "baby boomers," who did so much to change the meaning of education, marriage, and the family will not stand idly by when it comes to public policies pertaining to the elderly. The political clout of people over age 65 likely will grow as their numbers double in the years ahead (Torres-Gil & Puccinelli, 1995). But in the meantime, services for the elderly are under great strain. As the government relinquishes control over all forms of health care, private providers are rapidly moving in to claim the territory.

An additional government-funded program that is more promise than reality is the array of human and social services for the elderly offered under the rubric of the Older Americans Act. Enacted in 1965, with the ambitious goal of ensuring the well-being of the elderly, this federal program provides funding to the states for community programs and informational services for those over age 60.

Nursing Home Care

By way of introduction to some of the jarring facts concerning present-day nursing home care, let us trek back to the world of Jane Addams. Following her visit to the elderly women confined in the Cook County Infirmary, Addams (1910) commented:

> To take away from an old woman whose life has been spent in household cares all the foolish little belongings to which her affections cling and to which her very fingers have become accustomed, is to take away her last incentive to activity, almost to life itself. To give an old woman only a chair and a bed, to leave her no cupboard in which her treasures may be stowed, not only that she may take them out when she desires occupation, but that her mind may dwell upon them in moments of reverie, is to reduce living almost beyond the limit of human endurance. (p. 156)

Similarly, today a forced move from home to a nursing facility can be traumatic. Surprisingly, even elderly prison inmates can find this transition severely disturbing. This fact was illustrated in the popular 1994 Hollywood film *The Shawshank Redemption,* in which Morgan Freeman's character loses his place in the world upon his release. The movie echoed a theme in the 1979 satirical movie *Going in Style.* In that film, George Burns played one of three elderly men who decided to rob a bank. "What have we got to lose?" asks Burns. In prison, during the grand finale, the unrepenting hero remarks that his life on the outside was a prison anyway. Actually his life could have been much worse; he could have ended up in a nursing home.

Although only around 5 percent of the elderly are currently in a nursing home, nearly one in three people aged 85 and over will find their way to one of them eventually. Created as an alternative to expensive hospital care, nursing homes, for the most part, are supported by the federal government through Medicaid and Medicare (Zastrow, 2004). A billion-dollar industry, nursing homes now contain more patient beds than do hospitals. These institutions, moreover, have become the repositories for mentally ill elderly people, released prisoners, and even some formerly homeless people. It is very hard to discharge homeless people, as they have no other place to go (Fiske, 2002). As hospitals close or drastically shorten the length of stays as part of government-enforced cost containment measures, nursing homes are picking up the slack.

Turnover rates of professional staff in nursing homes are quite high due to poor working conditions and better options for nurses and social workers elsewhere. At small facilities, social workers tend to feel isolated from others of their profession and devoid of peer support (e.g., in their role as client advocate). Fiske (2003a) lists several other factors related to social worker burnout in this field—relatively low salaries, excessive paperwork requirements, continual government cutbacks, and increasingly large workloads. At larger facilities, however, programs may be more diversified, and a team of social workers is available for personal and professional support. Nursing home practice does have one key advantage over acute-care hospital practice—long-term involvement with the patient and his or her family, which brings its own special reward. While federal inspectors focus on medical protocol, it is often the relationship element that is more essential to patient well-being. Social workers hold family meetings and intercede with staff members in situations of difficulty. The social workers interviewed by Fiske urged schools of social work to offer courses in gerontology due to the increasing need for social workers in this expanding field.

Personal care facilities range enormously in price, quality, size, and services offered. For self-paying patients, the costs average thousands of dollars per month. In the nation's 17,000 nursing homes, about two-thirds of which are for-profit, severe cuts in Medicare spending have taken their toll (Sherrid, 2002). Because Medicaid payments are actually below the cost of nursing home care, the Medicare reimbursements are vital to keep the nursing homes financially solvent.

A danger of nursing home care is the potential abuse of residents by staff members. One third of nursing homes in the United States have been cited by state

Western Home Community, Cedar Falls, Iowa. This staff member at this exemplary nursing home is also the resident's daughter.

inspectors as being abusive to residents ("Some Golden Years," 2001). Zastrow (2004) describes scandals related to patients found lying in their own feces or urine, being overly sedated, or fed unappetizing food high in carbohydrates; poor sanitation standards; and serious safety hazards. Recently, due to the absence of sprinkling equipment, eight residents died in a fire at a nursing home in Nashville, Tennessee, and dozens of others required hospital care (Reeves, 2003).

According to an article in *Business Week Online* (Weber, 2001), substandard care has become the shocking norm in far too many nursing homes. Federal reimbursement levels have fallen, and some of the biggest for-profit companies have filed for bankruptcy. Due to understaffing, other facilities are quickly going backward toward the chronic maltreatment of the 1960s. One helpful initiative from the federal government is the publishing of inspection reports of all 17,000 nursing homes (see http://www.medicare.gov). Measurements are provided on such matters as the percentages of patients with bedsores, pain, and weight loss (Sherrid, 2002).

Conditions of nursing homes in Ontario, Canada, compare unfavorably to those in other Canadian provinces and in many U.S. states such as Florida. Criticism is mounting in the Canadian press, especially since a provincial auditor found that 68 Ontario nursing homes were decrepit and that contagious disease outbreaks were not uncommon (McKay, 2003). Recommended reforms are to provide mandatory nursing care standards for registered nursing care, to increase funding, and to institute mandatory unannounced inspections.

Complaints about nursing homes are coming from the United Kingdom as well, many in regard to inappropriate medication being administered to patients (e.g., excessive use of tranquilizers and laxatives). In British nursing homes, typically, only one nurse is on call. During the 1990s, long-stay National Health Service (NHS) hospital beds were available; now the choice for the frail elderly often is premature discharge from the hospital to home or receiving inadequate care in a nursing home (Boseley, 2003). Local authorities provide funding at differential rates, and some "care homes" have been closed and their residents evicted when the reimbursement rates were too low. Two elderly residents, one aged 102, died as a result of such closings ("A Matter of Life and Death," 2003).

Community Care Options

Much more can be done to help families keep their elderly and disabled members at home, such as providing tax breaks for informal caretakers or, better yet, paying them for their care. Homemaker services, visiting nurse services, meals-on-wheels, adult foster care, day care, and group home care are among the offerings that can prevent the need for nursing home care. An innovative program in Wisconsin offers a host of alternative services such as homemaker services, home-delivered meals, adult foster care, and group home care. The program is cost-effective and preferred by clients over institutionalized care (Zastrow, 2004). It is only for the indigent, however; social workers and nurses assess patients for eligibility.

Adult foster care programs offer care in private homes at about half the cost of nursing home care. The program in Arkansas is for elderly veterans and in Oregon for nonveterans. When private resources are exhausted, Medicaid pitches in ("Adult Foster Care—'Best Kept Secret,'" 2003). Among financially secure seniors, assisted living facilities provide arrangements that are in between institutional and in-home care. Social workers who work in such facilities describe them as stressing independence with a focus on residents' strengths (Russek, 2003). Help is provided with cooking and showering, as needed, while congregate meals provide socializing opportunities. Various levels of care are offered as medical needs demand it. A major drawback is that social workers who are trained to offer counseling geared toward clients' psychosocial needs sometimes find themselves pushed by these privately owned companies into playing marketing roles instead.

Services to help older adults remain in their homes are vital—services such as homemaker care, help with bathing and dressing, and visits by home health aides to change bandages and give injections. Unfortunately, Medicare and Medicaid reimbursement for such services is problematic due to complicated eligibility requirements; active medical care of a serious nature is required (Suppes & Wells, 2003). For effective care of the frail elderly, a continuum of care is needed; this must include a health care component as part of the funded package.

Some communities offer social health maintenance organization (HMO) initiatives for the frail elderly, many of whom would be otherwise institutionalized. Social HMOs offer social services that are Medicare-funded on an experimental basis; the purpose is to prevent hospitalization. Tremendous cost savings accrue to Medicare with such arrangements due to the focus on prevention rather than treatment (Suppes & Wells, 2003). A private U.S. company, EverCare, is crossing the ocean to serve as a model for the British NHS. EverCare focuses on patients aged 85 and over who have had at least two hospital admissions over the past year to identify long-term problems. The British interest in U.S. health care coincides with the introduction of new reforms to sharpen up market-style incentives, according to *The Guardian* (Lewis, 2003).

The best and most imaginative program that has come to my attention is found in Denmark. According to a cover story in the British social work news magazine *Community Care,* Denmark has the highest proportion of home care services for elders in the world ("We've Seen the Future," 1999). Care of the elderly in Denmark, as in Sweden, is considered a state responsibility. Whereas Sweden is cutting down on hours provided in services for the young-old to focus on those most in need, Denmark provides generous provisions to persons over the retirement age of 67. Offerings include recreational centers, cafeterias, sheltered living with alarm systems, and home help services as needed. Institutional care is being largely phased out.

Elder Abuse

Home, however, is not always the best place for the aged. Elder or parent abuse occurs most often when the parents live with their children or are dependent on them. Tensions can mount. Under the category of elder abuse, Suppes and Wells (2003) include physical mistreatment, emotional abuse, material or financial abuse, violation of rights, and life-threatening neglect. Although exact statistics are not available due to the strong reluctance of elderly family members to report their children or spouses for abuse, it is generally estimated that 3 to 6 percent of older adults suffer some form of abuse or neglect (Brownell, 2002). What we know from sources such as the National Center for Elder Abuse is this: Women, especially over age 80, are most likely to be abused or neglected; the alleged abuser is often a family member such as the spouse; and most mistreatment occurs in the home (Thompson, 2003). In 2001, according to the same source, Iowa logged 888 complaints, and Florida 41,542 complaints. In both states reporting is mandatory, but in Florida such reporting is required of every person, not just of professionals. For help in cases of elder domestic violence, programs such as the Older Abused Women's Program in Milwaukee can provide much-needed support (Wilke & Vinton, 2003).

The most poignant portrait of emotional mistreatment that I have come across is presented in *The Trip to Bountiful* by playwright Horton Foote (1953). In the play, the elderly Mrs. Watts, who is constantly badgered and taunted by her daughter-in-law Jessie Mae, is highly opinionated yet delightfully headstrong. The main sources of contention between the women are the older woman's hymn-singing and the whereabouts of her Social Security check. In a climatic scene, Mrs. Watts slips away to visit her hometown of Bountiful, Texas, for one last look. While on the Greyhound bus, she tells her life story to a young fellow traveler. Geraldine Page brilliantly brought the character of Mrs. Watts to life in the film version for which she won an Academy Award.

Social workers are the best equipped to address elder abuse because as professionals they work with families in so many different capacities and in a variety of agency settings. Brownell (2002) offers a social work assessment protocol. Information obtained in this format is pertinent to the intervention strategy. For example, abuse perpetuated by a spouse in the secondary stage of Alzheimer's disease would suggest a different strategy than abuse inflicted by a substance-abusing grandchild. By remaining alert to the possibility of abuse, social workers, as Brownell suggests, can improve the safety and well-being of the clients they serve.

How about situations in which the elderly person is or was the abuser? I am referring to a reversal of elder abuse, to the configuration in which family members are providing care for elderly persons who abused them, usually in their childhoods. Fiske (2003b) addresses this rarely addressed, but not unheard of, problem. When an incest survivor faces the prospect of having to care for his or her offender, complex emotions, understandably, are aroused. Other family members, such as a stepmother, are often unaware of the survivor's state of mind. The survivor who refuses to care for the now frail victimizer is often misunderstood. Jane Smiley's (1991) Pulitzer prize–winning novel, *A Thousand Acres,* brought to the screen in 1997 with memorable performances by Michelle Pfeiffer and Jessica Lange, fictionalizes such a situation. A modernized version of Shakespeare's *King Lear,* the story is told from the neglectful daughter's standpoint. In both renditions, the elderly father is treated mercilessly by two of his daughters. But in the modern version, as we learn through flashbacks, the reason for the rejection lies in dark secrets from their past.

Ageism

At the societal level, our concern is with elder abuse of a different sort. A society that equates beauty with youth, denies aging and death, and lacks valued rituals for passages through all the stages of life is a society that practices ageism. *Ageism* refers to discrimination against older people and stereotyping about people on the basis of their ages (Barker, 2003). Examples of ageism are: devaluing older workers because they are regarded as slow and having skills that are outmoded; using the word *old* in an intolerant and pejorative way; avoiding dining in restaurants frequented by seniors; using the word *burden* in reference to care for the old but not to care for the young; derogatory mass media portrayals of old persons such as comedy routines making fun of aging bodies; having upper age limits for car rentals as in parts of Europe and North Africa; and politically attacking social welfare programs that make life tolerable for the older population (prevalent in the United States and Canada). If you visit a nursing home, note the tone of voice sometimes used by staff, a condescending tone that

I was astonished to find this example of ageism at a branch of my bank in Waterloo, Iowa. See if you can find the 3 or 4 instances of ageism in this life-size stuffed doll.

is usually reserved for use with small children. This is an example of how ageism permeates U.S. culture in ways that are not always noticed.

When it comes to health care, sometimes ageism can be life-threatening. A recent study by the RAND corporation, in which researchers examined the medical records of more than 350 frail seniors treated by physicians at two managed care organizations, revealed that the seniors got the correct medical care only half the time, and even less often for age-related illnesses (Fackelmann, 2003). For a comprehensive view of ageism, both in its causes and consequences, see *Ageism: Stereotyping and Prejudice Against Older Persons* (Nelson, 2002).

To the extent that our culture venerates the old, respect is reserved for the old who seem young, for those who do not look or act their age. In my personal observation, ageism is particularly pronounced in the conversations of people in their late middle years, about the time they perceive signs of aging in themselves. Such ageism often takes the form of self-deprecating remarks such as, "This dates me," "I'm showing my age," "He's been around the block a few times," or "She's over the hill." Students often belittle older professors by referring to them as "a relic from the sixties" or "an old [this or that]." Recently at a conference on gerontology, a participant in self-introductions said, "I certainly hope I don't seem to be a member of the group we came to discuss."

Several years ago, at the 50th birthday party of our dean, the entire event took the form of gallows humor related to the aging process. Each present the dean received was a joke, and each was more tasteless than the last. Such "over the hill" birthday parties, which have become a sort of tradition in our society, are a way of using humor to cope with our fears about aging. Pipher (1999) says that such jokes reflect our anxieties about aging in a youth-oriented culture. Checking out the birthday cards at her local drugstore, Pipher found the following examples:

> "Have you picked out your bench at the mall yet?" There are jokes about hearing loss, incontinence, and losing sexual abilities and interest. There are cards on saggy behinds, gray hair, and wrinkles, and cards about preferring chocolate or sleep to sex. "You know you're getting old when someone asks if you're getting enough and you think about sleep." (p. 40)

In short, instead of celebrating age, we seek to escape by one means or another, whether through games of denial, self-deprecating humor, or cosmetic cover-ups. Cosmetic surgery to hide the signs of age is a booming industry.

Internalized ageism is inevitable in an atmosphere of such negativism. No wonder so many elderly people come to devalue themselves as worthless, useless, ugly, and inferior to the young. They remember well how they felt about old people "way back when." Paradoxically, the category of the elderly is one of the few minority groups we both are prejudiced against and also end up joining.

Avenues to Empowerment

Recognition of the importance of autonomy and patient participation in community-based long-term care and other social service agencies has increased over the past two decades (Cox, 1999). Social workers, using a strengths perspective, can help older clients and their families draw on their own resources in gaining access to the desired services to maintain an optimum level of self-sufficiency. Empowering social work, first and foremost, is centered on the relationship. Even after the essential services have been provided, a lot of work is yet to be done to sustain the individual in the new living circumstances. The challenge of strengths-based case management with elderly clients is to resolve or at least reduce the interpersonal conflicts within the personal support networks that inevitably arise (Fast & Chapin, 2002). For isolated individuals, the practitioner can help them to reestablish their ties to the community and neighborhood. The strengths model, as Fast and Chapin indicate, advocates employing natural helpers and resources whenever possible. Relevant questions to ask elderly clients to this end are:

- Who is important to you in your life?
- What has worked well for you in the past?
- What makes life worth living for you?

Whether they encounter elderly clients in nursing homes, home health care programs, mental health centers, substance abuse treatment centers, or hospitals, social workers need to use an integrated, holistic approach to address the kinds of multifaceted problems that older people confront. Instead of leading the client to view old age as a period of decline from youth, following Betty Friedan's (1993) *Fountain of Age,* social workers can work from a strengths perspective, helping older clients forge creative adaptations to the challenges of later life. Many older women, for example, form "families of choice" that may consist of friends and neighbors. However they accomplish it, older people need to be productive, to feel that they continue to make a contribution to society and to other people's lives. Some elderly persons are resuming work roles on a part-time basis; others are engaging in volunteer activities through organizations such as the Retired Senior Volunteer Program (RSVP). The RSVP places volunteers in places such as hospitals, schools, and libraries.

Spirituality

Attending to the spiritual realm of human life is central to a strengths perspective. In the lives of elders, the roles of both organized religious institutions and private spiritual activity can assume major importance. For many, a spiritual self is a critical component in defining the meaning of one's life and one's relationship with a Higher Power.

The postmodern emphasis of the social work profession on spirituality is particularly relevant to social work practice with elders (McInnis-Dittrich, 2002). For Hispanic and African American elders, religious beliefs and practices are second only to families as the major source of emotional support. McInnis-Dittrich draws our attention to the aesthetic and social functions of religion to older African Americans—the enlivening music, the energizing sermons, the deep sense of communal worship, and the catharsis of emotional expression.

Canda (2002), in his personal life review and collection of narratives about people coping with chronic illness, documented the empowering attributes of spirituality, a major component in resilience. Spiritual beliefs, he found, "provided resources for managing suffering, persevering in health care, appreciating life and loved ones, and looking into and beyond the nitty-gritty physicality of mortality" (p. 76). Through his research and personal growth, Canda became appreciative of spiritual styles and language very different from his own as he recognized themes of commonality in transcending the self and personal limitations to grasp a higher meaning and interconnectedness.

Advocacy and Political Empowerment

Advocacy is an important aspect of gerontological social work—advocacy for clients in need of accessible social services, and advocacy for the special needs of elderly clients whose interests and limitations by virtue of age are apt to be ignored in diverse agency settings. In a social climate of federal budget cuts and increasing competition among various interest groups for scarce resources coupled with societal ageism, social action is a must.

The elderly, in fact, as Zastrow (2004) points out, are one of the most politically organized and influential groups in the United States. One action-oriented group, the Gray Panthers, seeks to end ageism and to effect social change through getting the elderly to vote as a bloc on behalf of their special interests. The activism of the Gray Panthers, an organization founded in 1970 and inspired by the civil rights era to fight discrimination against the aged, has done much to refute the negative image of the elderly. Such social activism was instrumental in promoting enforcement of the Age Discrimination in Employment Act in 1967. This act provides some protection against blatant age bias in the workplace, but cannot protect people from discrimination in its subtler forms. The Gray Panthers are also credited with banning mandatory retirement laws, which has made a difference for many workers. High voting rates among the elderly give this group considerable clout.

One of the most powerful political organizations in the United States is AARP, formerly the American Association of Retired Persons (the name was changed to simply the acronym because almost half the membership are not, in fact, retired.). Membership is open to anyone over 50; for a minimum fee, members receive subscriptions to *AARP: The Magazine* and *The AARP Bulletin* as well as discounts on goods and services (especially hotel fees). "To serve, not to be served" is the motto (see http://www.aarp.org). Recently, AARP has come under a wealth of criticism due to its support of Medicare privatization; AARP has vested interests in health insurance activities from which it receives about half of its revenue (Dreyfuss, 2004). Tens of thousands of members to date have now resigned in outrage over the law and AARP's role in its passage.

Continued or renewed militancy by the elderly and their allies will go a long way to confront ageism and its manifestations. Perhaps advocacy for such exemplary programs as the following will some day bring about favorable results:

- Pay to family members for caregiving (available in northern Europe and Nova Scotia, Canada)
- State hiring of retired persons to clean for and care for the frail elderly in their own homes (available in a few areas of the United States and Norway)
- Passage of a long-term care act providing the right to nursing care for all older people in need of such care (as legislated in Israel)
- Extensive home help services, day care centers, and communally owned old people's homes (as offered in Finland)
- Guaranteed pensions whether one was a wage earner or not, and service apartments for semi-independent living (as in Sweden)
- Subsidized medication

Summary and Conclusion

This chapter completes Part II of the text. This section of the book addressed social welfare needs across the life span, from childhood through old age. Taking these four chapters as a whole, one theme that emerges is demographic: Mass aging coupled with a huge drop in the birthrates is a phenomenon worldwide. A major challenge in the Global North and large parts of the Global South thus becomes: Who will care for the frail elderly?

Given the demographic realities, social workers, whatever the professional setting of their encounters, must be knowledgeable about the biological changes that accompany aging and the concomitant psychological, social, and spiritual dimensions. This chapter was designed to summarize such knowledge organized from a life span perspective. Accordingly, attention was devoted to some of the most prominent physiological changes that take place at the end of the life cycle, and the psychological means of coping with changes in bodily functioning and with the inevitability of ultimate debilitation and death.

The social side of aging constituted most of the space in this chapter, starting with the concept of *elderization of poverty,* a term introduced to depict a reality that transcends the statistics. This recognition of economic factors in aging was a major theme of this chapter. The reality is that those who are born poor are apt to die poor. This fact is true within the United States and cross-culturally. Children at risk for poverty, ill health, and maltreatment enter the world with a tremendous vulnerability both educationally and socially. Lack of access to the essential preventive health care, nutrition, and housing compounds any existing problems and may lead to loss of health or homelessness. Phrased succinctly, the infantilization of poverty breeds the elderization of poverty.

A second aspect of the social side of aging is gender. The stress on gender in this chapter relates to the fact that those persons who survive to the oldest and poorest age groups are overwhelmingly female. In the lives and economic well-being of aging women, we see the interaction of ageism, sexism, and racism. And classism, as discussed earlier, is a key component as well. The conditions of poverty in old age, although related to gender, transcend gender when class enters the picture. Men over age 85 and especially men of color are apt to be poor. With so many men suffering loss of job security and generous pensions, the postretirement years may be expected to bring extreme hardship to some. The high suicide rate for elderly men is a statistic that requires no comment. Inflated medical expenses, including nursing home care, affect both genders in need of professional care due to advanced age.

The plight of elderly people who finish their lives in overcrowded, understaffed nursing homes is often the plight of those who have outlived their health, their husbands or wives, and their siblings. These people face exhausting their savings as well. Under a means-tested welfare system such as exists in the United States, the very poor sometimes fare better than the working and middle classes. In any case, the increasing subordination of social policy to economic policy is taking a heavy toll on programs affecting the elderly.

The retrenchment of federal funding for housing, health care, and financial aid pits the interests of children against the interests of seniors. What is needed is not an array of piecemeal policies providing benefits to one group at the expense of another but a unified agenda ensuring economic security, health care, and adequate housing across the life span. A government's investment in its children is, in a real sense, an investment in their old age. Such an investment may even determine whether or not an individual reaches old age.

Ethnic and racial diversity are further variables in the sociology of aging. In parts of American society and of the world, the older generation continues to function in multigenerational contexts until the time of death. Elsewhere, in the context of chronic underfunding of government services for elders and the increasing unavailability of women to play caretaking roles, a decline in the quality of care for older people is inevitable. Consider what happened during the 2003 record-breaking heat wave in France, the story that began this chapter. The horrendous death toll of the very old, left alone while their relatives vacationed, brings into sharp relief the world's desperate need to provide preventive care and somehow maintain the interconnectedness of the generations. Only when all ages are integrated into the mainstream of life can our culture maintain its communal and spiritual health.

From the literature on aging, policy recommendations as reviewed in this chapter are the assurance of minimal income levels to protect the many who are without adequate pensions, the provision of universal health care covering prescription drugs, effective housing and transportation assistance, comprehensive homemaker and home health care programs, and the availability of homelike nursing homes for persons in need of round-the-clock assistance. The best prevention of the *elderization of poverty,* in short, is a social welfare system guaranteeing the right to health, housing, and quality of life across the life span. In this way, the child who learns to trust (as in Erikson's first stage) can achieve integrity (as in Erikson's final stage). In the wise words of Erikson (1963), "Children will not fear life if their elders have integrity enough not to fear death" (p. 269).

Thought Questions

1. What does it mean to describe old age as "another country?"
2. What is the image of old age in the United States? How has old age been viewed historically?
3. Explain how aid to one group—children—is played off against another group—the elderly.
4. Discuss demographic changes across the world pertaining to the elderly.
5. Describe the service apartments in Scandinavia and the types of services they provide.
6. What is the Japanese experience of aging? How is the situation in sub-Saharan Africa unique?
7. Relate the movie and play *I Never Sang for My Father* to U.S. society's values.
8. Discuss the contributions of older people to society from a strengths perspective. Relate to the poem introduced in this chapter, "But Someone Surely Will."
9. Relate Erik Erikson's last two stages of the life span to aging.
10. Distinguish between the young-old and the old-old in terms of health care needs.
11. Describe each of the five escape mechanisms used by people to cope with death.
12. There is controversy concerning whether many of the elderly in the United States can be considered poor. Take a stand on this issue and present the facts.
13. Discuss the benefits offered under the Social Security Act of 1935, Medicaid, Medicare, and the Older Americans Act.
14. Describe how the average citizen finances nursing home care.
15. Discuss the need for safety regulations for nursing home care.
16. Discuss some options that are alternatives to nursing home care. How is Denmark handling care for older people?
17. What are the facts concerning elder abuse? Contrast domestic and institutional elder abuse.
18. How can ageism be confronted? What has social activism achieved to date?
19. Discuss the pros and cons of assisted suicide for the terminally ill.
20. Discuss advocacy and political organizing as avenues of empowerment.

References

Addams, J. (1910). *Twenty years at Hull House.* New York: Macmillan.

Adult foster care—"best kept secret." (2003, May 5). *Caregivers USA News.* Retrieved from http://www.thoushalthonor.org

Anderson, R. (1980/1968). I never sang for my father. In R. Lyell (Ed.), *Middle age, old age: Short stories, poems, plays and essays on aging* (pp. 55–110). New York: Harcourt Brace Jovanovich.

Ariyoshi, S. (1984/1972). *The twilight years.* (M. Thahara, Trans.). London: Peter Owen.

Barker, R. (2003). *The social work dictionary* (5th ed.). Washington, DC: NASW Press.

Barush, A. (2002). *Foundations of social policy: Social justice, public programs, and the social work profession.* Itasca, IL: Peacock.

Becker, E. (1973). *The denial of death.* New York: Free Press.

Boseley, S. (2003, March 14). Elderly getting inadequate care homes, says report. *The Guardian.* Retrieved from http://www.guardian.co.uk

Brownell, P. (2002). Elder abuse. In A. Roberts & G. Greene (Eds.), *Social workers' desk reference* (pp. 723–727). New York: Oxford University Press.

Campbell, J. (1995, August). Is there a Japanese-style welfare state? *Social Science Japan, 4,* 22.

Canda, E. R. (2002). The significance of spirituality for resilient response to chronic illness: A qualitative study of adults with cystic fibrosis. In D. Saleebey (Ed.), *The strengths perspective in social work practice* (pp. 63–79). Boston: Allyn & Bacon.

Children's Defense Fund. (2001, December). Facts and FAQs. Retrieved from http://www.childrensdefense.org

Consensus and contraction. (2002, April 20). *The Economist* (Supplement), 8–10.

Cooney, E. (2003). *Death in slow motion: A memoir of a daughter, her mother and beast called Alzheimer's.* New York: HarperCollins.

Cox, E. (1999). Never too old: Empowerment—The concept and practice in work with the frail elderly. In W. Shera & L. M. Wells (Eds.), *Empowerment practice in social work* (pp. 178–195). Toronto: Canadian Scholar's Press.

Daly, M. (2001). Care policies in Western Europe. In M. Daly (Ed.), *Care work: The quest for security* (pp. 33–55). Geneva: International Labour Office.

Davis, R. (2003, September 16). Billionaire provides $100 M to help map brain genes: Treating Alzheimer's disease a primary goal. *USA Today,* p. 3A.

Donow, H. (1990). Two approaches to the care of an elder parent: A study of Robert Anderson's *I never sang for my father* and Sawako Aryoshi's *Kokotsu no hito. Gerontologist, 30*(4), 486–490.

Drackley, J. (2003, September 7). A generation at risk. *Waterloo–Cedar Falls Courier,* pp. A1, A6.

Dreyfuss, B. T. (2004, June 7). The seduction: The shocking story of how AARP backed the Medicare bill. *The American Prospect.* Retrieved from http://www.truthout.org/docs

Dunkle, R., & Norgard, T. (1995). Aging overview. In *The encyclopedia of social work* (19th ed., pp. 142–152). Washington, DC: NASW Press.

Erikson, E. (1963). *Childhood and society.* New York: W. W. Norton.

Facio, E. (1996). *Understanding older Chicanas.* Thousand Oaks, CA: Sage.

Fackelmann, K. (2003, November 3). Health system fails seniors half the time. *USA Today.* Retrieved from http://www.usatoday.com

Facts on File. (1995). Heat wave kills 100s: Chicago hit hard. *World News Digest, 55*(2852), 540–541.

Fast, B., & Chapin, R. (2002). The strengths model with older adults: Critical practice components. In D. Saleebey (Ed.), *The strengths perspective in social work practice* (pp. 143–162). Boston: Allyn & Bacon.

Fiske, H. (2002, September 16). Nursing home social work. *Social Work Today,* 10–12.

Fiske, H. (2003a, January 13). Nursing home social workers speak out. *Social Work Today,* 8–11.

Fiske, H. (2003b, April 7). Sexual abuse survivors: Caring for aging abusers. *Social Work Today,* 6–9.

Foote, H. (1954). *The trip to bountiful.* New York: Dramatists Play Service.

Fred Hutchinson Cancer Research Center. (2003, September 25). New findings in yeast may reveal why growing older is the greatest carcinogen in humans. Retrieved from http://www.fhcrc.org

Friedan, B. (1993). *Fountain of age.* New York: Simon & Schuster.

Goldsmith, R. (2003, March 19). Suicide "epidemic" among Japan's elderly. BBC Radio 4's Crossing Continents. Retrieved from http://www.bbc.co.uk

Gombos, A. (1999, February 3). Focus on world's older women. *Christian Science Monitor,* p. 9.

Grossman, L. (2003, March 24). Laughter and forgetting. *Time,* 65.

Hogan, B. (2004, September). The pharmacist who says no to drugs. *AARP Bulletin.* Retrieved from http://www.aarp.org/bulletin/prescription

Huxley, A. (1969/1932). *Brave new world.* New York: Harper & Row.

Iowa's aging population highlights need for prescription program. (2002, December 18). *Waterloo–Cedar Falls Courier,* p. 7.

Jopson, B. (2003, September 9). Study warns on Japan's pension deficit. *Financial Times.* Retrieved from goobalaging.org

Karger, H., & Stoesz, D. (2002). *Social welfare policy: A pluralist approach* (4th ed.). Boston: Allyn & Bacon.

Lapham, L. H. (2004, February). Notebook: Bad medicine. *Harper's Magazine,* 9–11.

Large, M.-J. (2001). Care of the elderly throughout the world. *Stride Magazine.* Online at http://www.stridemagazine.com

Lewis, R. (2003, October 1). The American way. *The Guardian.* Retrieved from http://society.guardian.co.uk

Litke, M. (2001, January 2001). Care for elderly today, be paid back tomorrow. *ABCNEWS.com.* Retrieved from http://www.abcnews.go.com

Longman, P. (1999, March 1). How global aging will challenge the world's economic well-being. *U.S. News and World Report,* 38–39.

Loosen up or lose out. (2002). *The Economist* (Supplement), 10–13.

Mann, J. (1995). Ageing and social work. In W. Johnson (Ed.), *The social services: An introduction* (pp. 223–239). Itasca, IL: Peacock.

A matter of life and death. (2003, August 7). *Community Care.* Retrieved from http://www.communitycare.co.uk

McDaniel, S., & Gee, E. (1993). Social policies regarding caregiving to elders: Canadian contradictions. In S. Bass & R. Morris (Eds.), *International per-

spectives on state and family support for the elderly* (pp. 57–52).

McInnis-Dittrich, K. (2002). *Social work with elders: A biopsychosocial approach to assessment and intervention.* Boston: Allyn & Bacon.

McKay, P. (2003, April 26). Cut-rate care. *The Ottawa Citizen.* Retrieved from http://www.canada.com

Miller, S. (2003). *The story of my father.* New York: Knopf.

Moisi, D. (2003, November). The elderly: Our "South." *Les Echoes.* Reprinted in *World Press Review,* 12–13.

Nelson, T. (Ed.). (2002). *Ageism: Stereotyping and prejudice against older persons.* Cambridge, MA: MIT Press.

Older Americans 2000. (2003). *Population: Older Americans 2000: Key indicators of well-being.* Federal Interagency on Aging. Retrieved from http://www.agingstats.gov

Olson, L. (1994). Introduction. In L. Olson (Ed.), *The graying of the world: Who will care for the elderly?* (pp. 1–23). New York: Haworth Press.

Peterson, P. (1999). *Gray dawn: How the coming age wave will transform America—and the world.* New York: Crown.

Pipher, M. (1999). *Another country: Navigating the emotional terrain of our elders.* New York: Riverhead Books.

Popple, P., & Leighninger, L. (2002). *Social work, social welfare, and American society* (5th ed.). Boston: Allyn & Bacon.

Reeves, S. (2003, September 27). Nursing home owner warned about insurance. *The Washington Post.* Retrieved from http://www.washingtonpost.com

Register Editorial Board. (2002, August 31). The Oregon option: Iowa should consider that state's experience with assisted death. *Des Moines Register.* Retrieved from http://www.dmregister.com

Reich, R. (2003, February). A better way to spur the economy. *AARP Bulletin,* 14.

Robbins, S., Chatterjee, P., & Canda, E. (1998). *Contemporary behavior theory: A critical perspective for social work.* Boston: Allyn & Bacon.

Russek, A. (2003, August). Assisted living facilities on the rise and clearly needed. *Social Work Today,* 17–19.

Shah, R. (1992, August 2). Aging around the world. *St. Petersburg Times,* p. A1.

Sherrid, P. (2002, May 27). Nursing homes to Congress: We really need Medicare. *U.S. News & World Report*, 36–38.

Smiley, J. (1991). *A thousand acres.* New York: Knopf.

Smith, D. (2003, April). *The older population in the United States: March 2002.* Washington, DC: U.S. Census Bureau.

Some golden years. (2001, August 13). *U.S. News & World Report*, 8.

Suppes, M., & Wells, C. (2003). *The social work experience: An introduction to social work and social welfare* (4th ed.). Boston: McGraw-Hill.

Talaga, T. (1999, August 20). Suicides among elderly men epidemic: MDs. *The Toronto Star.* Retrieved from http://www.thestar.com

Thompson, K. (2003, March 28). Abuse of elderly women on the rise. *Women's Enews.* Retrieved from http://www.womensenews.org

Torres-Gil, F., & Puccinelli, M. (1995). Ageing: Public policy issues and trends. In *The encyclopedia of social work* (19th ed., pp. 159–164). Washington, DC: NASW Press.

Ubelacker, S. (2003, September 27). Holocaust survivors face old horrors as Alzheimer's returns them to the past. *Lifewise FM.* Retrieved from http://www.canoe.ca/LifewiseFamilyRetired

U.N. grapples with world's booming elderly population. (2002, April 7). *Waterloo–Cedar Falls Courier*, 7.

United Nations (U.N.). (1999). *Principles for the older person.* Retrieved from http://www.un.org/esa/socdev

U.S. Census Bureau. (2003). The older population in the United States: March 2002. Washington, DC: U.S. Government Printing Office.

U.S. Department of Health and Human Services. (2001). *A profile of older Americans.* Washington, DC: Department of Health and Human Services, Administration on Aging.

van Wormer, K. (1997). *Social welfare: A world view.* Belmont, CA: Wadsworth.

Vesely, R. (2003, March 21). Elderly women will bear the brunt of Medicaid cuts. *Women's Enews.* Retrieved from http://www.womensenews.org

Walker, A. (2002, October 11–12). The impact of globalisation on ageing policies. Paper presented at International Conference on Social Welfare, Seoul National University, Seoul, Korea.

Walton, A. (1981, Spring). Youth is such a wonderful thing . . . *The Friendly Woman, 5*(2), 8.

Webb, S. (1992). Child checkers. *Social Work Today, 23*(17), 20.

Weber, J. (2001, May 7). Commentary: Nursing home care: Code blue. *Business Week Online.* Retrieved from http://www.businessweek.com

Weisman, C. (1999, June 12). Ageing is not a disease: The United Nations international year for older persons. In N.-T. Tan & I. Dodds (2002), *Social work around the world, II.* Berne, Switzerland: IFSW Press.

We've seen the future. (1999, October 28). *Community Care*, 20–23.

Wilke, D., & Vinton, L. (2003, Spring/Summer). Domestic violence and aging: Teaching about their intersection. *Journal of Social Work Education, 39*(2), 225–235.

Williams, T. (1954). Cat on a hot tin roof. In *The theatre of Tennessee Williams* (vol. III). New York: New Directions.

Zastrow, C. (2004). *Introduction to social work and social welfare: Empowering people* (8th ed.). Belmont, CA: Brooks/Cole.

Putting It All Together

Don't get discouraged. Hope is like a road in the country. In places where there never was a road before, when many people walk the same path, a road comes into existence.

ROMANIAN SAYING, CONTRIBUTED BY STELA SLAPAC, MSW

Figuratively speaking, the world has grown smaller. New technologies and economic changes in one nation have become the new technologies and economic changes in all nations. The imperatives of the global market (the production of ever-cheaper products) have taken precedence over the needs of the people and created similar social problems everywhere. Fortunately, some of the same developments that unite the corporate world, the information technologies, can serve to arouse the public awareness of some of the worst features of globalization—the environmental despoliation, worker exploitation, and cutbacks in welfare protections. The anti–world trade movement, for example, has captured much media attention, but other equally important developments are taking shape as well: Women of the world are convening and uniting in ways never before imagined, as are the world's indigenous populations; gays, lesbians, and bisexuals; environmentalists; and children's rights advocates. Highly respected nongovernmental organizations (NGOs) such as Amnesty International, Human Rights Watch, Save the Children, and The World Watch Institute provide documentation of human rights violations for the world bodies including the United Nations; such facts, which are readily accessible through press releases and the Web sites of the respective organizations, bolster human rights campaigns.

To see "The U.S. in Global Perspective," the mission of this text, is to understand the structural nature of personal problems at home and abroad. Global developments such as those we have examined throughout the pages of this volume have profound implications for the needs of a nation's people and for the social workers who strive to help people get those needs met. An international perspective is invaluable in revealing not just problems, but also solutions to problems that have been tried elsewhere and found to be successful or unsuccessful. So many places in the world are facing the same issues as those we face in America—the need to rethink the boundaries for social care between the family and the state, reckoning with the rapid aging of the population, and bearing responsibility toward marginalized groups including refugees; racial, ethnic, and sexual minorities; and indigenous populations. We all more or less face the same universal paradox, namely, the paradox of how to achieve a balance between people's welfare entitlements and the conflicting demands of the global market. Because of its relevance to every population and age group studied in this book, the paradox of social welfare in the global economy can be considered the central theme of this book.

The fact that each nation wrestles with the same problems is not to say, however, that cultural differences are not important. In the face of mass unemployment, for example, one country may enforce policies that require the few to work harder and lay off the rest, while another country may strive to spread the work around by reducing the workweek. To understand the essence of these cultural differences not only from Canada and European countries but also from further afield, this *Introduction to Social Welfare and Social Work* text adopted a comparative approach. Only within such a comparative context can we view the uniqueness of America's ambivalent approach to the social welfare state. More specifically, the key American values that I filtered from the literature were: work, equal opportunity, mobility, competition, individualism, independence, primacy of the nuclear family, and, arguably the most transcendent, moralism. These value dimensions, each of which was explored in depth in Chapter 2, provided the backdrop for the following chapter entitled "Emergence of Social Work." That social work was grounded in altruistic principles and that the profession has continued to transmit such ideals are key arguments of the historical overview provided in Chapter 3.

The quest for what I have termed our *social work imagination* reaches back to the world of our inheritance, to our foremothers—Addams, Konopka, and Reynolds—and forward to a burgeoning new age of ecological awareness. By ecological awareness, I mean a sense of the synthesis, connectedness of things— for example, the future to the past, the parts to the whole, the biological to the social, the inner self to the outer environment, the personal to the political, and the local to the global. Our future as a profession depends on our grasping the essence of this awareness, this almost spiritual sense of beingness and relatedness.

Social work is at once personal and political, aiming interventions at both the individuals within the system and the system itself. Against the tyranny of economic constraints, the social work imagination takes us into the realm of deeper questions such as: How can we end violence—do we start with the family or society, or both? How do we promote the central social work values of self-determination, human rights, and social equity when human resources are drained to finance a war economy? How do we fight oppression in an oppressive world? Only through addressing these issues can we recapture some of the psychic and creative energies that have gone into making the field of social work what it is today.

In Chapter 4, under the rubric of "Economic Oppression," global and local poverty were major concerns. Due to famine, war, disease, and overpopulation, the number of people living in abject poverty has increased in urban and rural areas everywhere. In rich and not-so-rich countries alike, pressures from global competition bring an effect to bear on the world of work. A discussion of the impact on work of the new technologies constituted the focal point of Chapter 4.

Chapter 5 moved us into the social realm, into an examination of the correlates of oppression—classism, racism, sexism, heterosexism, and so on. Pivotal to fighting oppression in these areas is the adoption of a human rights perspective. Social workers outside the United States have already adopted such a perspective, having moved beyond the social justice concept into the arena of international law. A human rights discourse for social work readily navigates between global and local realms and can provide a lens for creative practice that links both elements in an empowering way (Ife, 2001). Social welfare issues and human rights are inextricably linked. People cannot enjoy a sense of security and well-being if their rights are systematically violated by the very state representatives from whom they would seek protection. Nor can they enjoy the benefits of human rights such as exists in a democracy if their social welfare needs for such things as food, shelter, and clothing are not met. As structural protections weaken today against the throes of the global market, a human rights framework is of increasing relevance.

From a human rights perspective, Chapter 6 revealed the need for state structural protections for marginalized peoples, among them, women, indigenous populations of the world, victims of hate crimes and "ethnic cleansing," convicts, and sexual minorities. From what would otherwise be grim accounts of the persecution of the world's peoples, hope shines forth in the international mobilization against such practices, a mobilization aided by the global communications network. Hope is found also in the establishment of the newly formed International Criminal Court, which was set up under the auspices of the United Nations (U.N.) to enforce the human rights standards as embodied in international law.

The principles of social and economic justice as enunciated in the U.N. Universal Declaration of Human Rights (see Appendix A) closely parallel the values practiced by the founding mothers of social work since the earliest days and those more recently spelled out in the National Association of Social Workers (NASW) *Code of Ethics*. The relevance of the principle of restorative justice to social work is one of the lessons we can learn from Canadian and New Zealand social workers, as discussed in Chapter 6; the restorative concept promotes healing where wrongdoing has occurred and can function as an antidote to human rights violations. In its many forms (e.g., victim-offender reconciliation and family group conferencing), restorative justice is a major instrument of peacemaking. Reconciliation at the individual level has, as its counterpart, reparations at the community level. This concept merges with a human rights focus and links to other critical concepts in social work, such as belief in the basic goodness of humankind, in self-determination, and in cultural and personal empowerment.

The topics covered in the second half (Part II) of this book are the more conventional social work topics. For organizational purposes, I chose to use a life span approach, with the chapters advancing chronologically from childhood through old age. Uniquely, in social welfare literature, I began this section of the book with a chapter on the dynamics of human behavior. Consistent with social work's bio-psycho-social-spiritual perspective, the seventh chapter provided an overview of these multiple aspects of human existence. Central to Chapter 7 and a focal point of this book was the discussion of environmental sustainability. The case was made for a politics of sustainability for the health of the planet and the people who live there.

Moving the policy issues (at the macro level in Chapter 7) to a middle-range level, Chapters 8 through 10 focused on policies pertaining to child welfare, health care, and elder care, respectively. Although some of the illustrations that infuse these chapters are uplifting, much of the material makes for harrowing reading—for instance, the brutalization of children throughout the world; the cruel paradox of homelessness in the midst of plenty; the appalling lack of universal health care; and the prevalence of elder abuse in institutions and in the home. From a policy standpoint, a comparative analysis was provided. A major purpose of this policy analysis was to show how a particular country's treatment of its most vulnerable citizens is consistent with the cultural ethos peculiar to that country. A second purpose inherent in this comparative approach was to reveal a range of possible solutions from other countries to common problems—solutions that otherwise might not be considered or might be considered as being unfeasible.

In reflecting back across the spectrum of the last three chapters, as well as those that went before, one fundamental theme emerges: The inequities and maltreatment practiced against the first and most formative age group, the young, are carried forward into all later periods of development. Children brought up in poor and unhealthy environments are likely to suffer in their schooling and work histories and, if they reach old age, to live in a situation of extreme economic dependency on others. Children who are physically or psychologically abused, similarly, are unlikely to reach their full potential in later life. Simply put, societies that are good to their elders also tend to be societies that are good places in which to grow up.

Comment on the Writing of This Book

International insights informed all the major divisions of this text. The scope of the book—social welfare worldwide—was daunting. And, as always, in writing on the various topics of social welfare, keeping abreast of the constant political changes was a major challenge. Relative to the United States, all through the writing of this book, the expanding military budget and reductions in the tax base were beginning to wreak havoc at the state and local levels. State college tuitions were soaring while funding for social welfare programs—including public education, departments of human services and child care services, and nursing home/home health care—were being dismantled. During the same time period, there was a palpable shift in the American mainstream media from a glowing, almost gloating, reporting of the "attack on Iraq" to the taking of a more well-rounded approach. Interestingly, Canadian, European, and especially British journalism seemed more concerned with journalistic integrity and had assumed a more critical stance all along.

There is no question that in the writing of this book, I was influenced consciously or otherwise by the barrage of information about the war on Iraq and its ugly aftermath. So pervasive was this influence, in fact, that whether the subject matter was government spending or personal trauma, war images were apt to intrude upon the content. Probably for this reason I found myself choosing to open Chapter 4 (on poverty) with a quote by President Eisenhower on the true impact of military spending and in Chapter 7 (on human behavior) to include the poem "Closure," which recorded the emotional anguish of a son perpetually grieving for his father who was killed in an earlier war but which resonates today.

In addition to the breadth of the material, a second major challenge in shaping a textbook of this sort pertains to the nature of the subject matter itself—controversial, emotionally laden, and, at times, jarring to the senses. Consider a few examples of the kind of material dealt with: loyal workers tossed to the winds as profitable companies downsize; women throughout the world dying in childbirth and illegal abortion due to lack of proper medical care; genital mutilation of young females; girls starving as their brothers thrive; small boys recruited as soldiers and deliberately brutalized; executions, hate crimes, and atrocities of war. The challenge was to be objective but not dispassionate. For verification of facts that seemed somewhat astonishing or even possibly exaggerated, I drew upon multiple sources from across the political spectrum, relying heavily on *The Economist* and *Business Week* for economic developments, and on the U.N. and NGOs such as Amnesty International for statistics and analysis of the data. News reports from around the world and from sources such as *The World Press* and *The Christian Science Monitor* were helpful in offering firsthand accounts from reporters stationed across the globe. Social work literature furnished a holistic, social justice perspective that helped place seemingly disparate facts in theoretical context to reveal, for example, the interplay of institutional forces of social exclusion such as sexism, ageism, classism, and racism.

During the first decade of the 21st century, challenges to human ecology, social justice, and world peace abound. The harmful consequences of economic globalization, consequences that are felt by families around the world, even in the rich nations, confront the limits of our social work imagination. Global causes call for global solutions. As citizens of the world, our mission is to promote peace and justice through working to eradicate racism, poverty, sexism, injustice, and other forms of oppression worldwide. At the professional level, our call is to educate ourselves and others not just as citizens of our individual countries but as citizens of the world, and to promote the internationalization of social work for active leadership in this still new century—a century that promises to be at once dangerously and excitingly global.

References

Ife, J. (2001). *Human rights and social work: Towards rights-based practice.* Cambridge, England: Cambridge University Press.

Slapac, S. (2002, March 28). Domestic violence in Romania. Presentation at the University of Northern Iowa, Cedar Falls.

United Nations Universal Declaration of Human Rights

Adopted and proclaimed by General Assembly resolution 217A (III) of 10 December 1948

On December 10, 1948, the General Assembly of the United Nations adopted and proclaimed the Universal Declaration of Human Rights, the full text of which appears in the following pages. Following this historic act, the Assembly called upon all member countries to publicize the text of the Declaration and "to cause it to be disseminated, displayed, read and expounded principally in schools and other educational institutions, without distinction based on the political status of countries or territories."

Preamble

Whereas recognition of the inherent dignity and of the equal and inalienable rights of all members of the human family is the foundation of freedom, justice and peace in the world,

Whereas disregard and contempt for human rights have resulted in barbarous acts which have outraged the conscience of mankind, and the advent of a world in which human beings shall enjoy freedom of speech and belief and freedom from fear and want has been proclaimed as the highest aspiration of the common people,

Whereas it is essential, if man is not to be compelled to have recourse, as a last resort, to rebellion against tyranny and oppression, that human rights should be protected by the rule of law,

Whereas it is essential to promote the development of friendly relations between nations,

Whereas the peoples of the United Nations have in the Charter reaffirmed their faith in fundamental human rights, in the dignity and worth of the human person and in the equal rights of men and women and have determined to promote social progress and better standards of life in larger freedom,

Source: United Nations, Resolution 217A (III). Passed by General Assembly, December 1948. Reprinted by permission of the United Nations Publications.

Whereas Member States have pledged themselves to achieve, in co-operation with the United Nations, the promotion of universal respect for and observance of human rights and fundamental freedoms,

Whereas a common understanding of these rights and freedoms is of the greatest importance for the full realization of this pledge,

Now, Therefore, THE GENERAL ASSEMBLY proclaims THIS UNIVERSAL DECLARATION OF HUMAN RIGHTS as a common standard of achievement for all peoples and all nations, to the end that every individual and every organ of society, keeping this Declaration constantly in mind, shall strive by teaching and education to promote respect for these rights and freedoms and by progressive measures, national and international, to secure their universal and effective recognition and observance, both among the peoples of Member States themselves and among the peoples of territories under their jurisdiction.

Article 1
All human beings are born free and equal in dignity and rights. They are endowed with reason and conscience and should act towards one another in a spirit of brotherhood.

Article 2
Everyone is entitled to all the rights and freedoms set forth in this Declaration, without distinction of any kind, such as race, colour, sex, language, religion, political or other opinion, national or social origin, property, birth or other status. Furthermore, no distinction shall be made on the basis of the political, jurisdictional or international status of the country or territory to which a person belongs, whether it be independent, trust, non-self-governing or under any other limitation of sovereignty.

Article 3
Everyone has the right to life, liberty and security of person.

Article 4
No one shall be held in slavery or servitude; slavery and the slave trade shall be prohibited in all their forms.

Article 5
No one shall be subjected to torture or to cruel, inhuman or degrading treatment or punishment.

Article 6
Everyone has the right to recognition everywhere as a person before the law.

Article 7

All are equal before the law and are entitled without any discrimination to equal protection of the law. All are entitled to equal protection against any discrimination in violation of this Declaration and against any incitement to such discrimination.

Article 8

Everyone has the right to an effective remedy by the competent national tribunals for acts violating the fundamental rights granted him by the constitution or by law.

Article 9

No one shall be subjected to arbitrary arrest, detention or exile.

Article 10

Everyone is entitled in full equality to a fair and public hearing by an independent and impartial tribunal, in the determination of his rights and obligations and of any criminal charge against him.

Article 11

(1) Everyone charged with a penal offence has the right to be presumed innocent until proved guilty according to law in a public trial at which he has had all the guarantees necessary for his defence.

(2) No one shall be held guilty of any penal offence on account of any act or omission which did not constitute a penal offence, under national or international law, at the time when it was committed. Nor shall a heavier penalty be imposed than the one that was applicable at the time the penal offence was committed.

Article 12

No one shall be subjected to arbitrary interference with his privacy, family, home or correspondence, nor to attacks upon his honour and reputation. Everyone has the right to the protection of the law against such interference or attacks.

Article 13

(1) Everyone has the right to freedom of movement and residence within the borders of each state.

(2) Everyone has the right to leave any country, including his own, and to return to his country.

Article 14

(1) Everyone has the right to seek and to enjoy in other countries asylum from persecution.

(2) This right may not be invoked in the case of prosecutions genuinely arising from non-political crimes or from acts contrary to the purposes and principles of the United Nations.

Article 15

(1) Everyone has the right to a nationality.
(2) No one shall be arbitrarily deprived of his nationality nor denied the right to change his nationality.

Article 16

(1) Men and women of full age, without any limitation due to race, nationality or religion, have the right to marry and to found a family. They are entitled to equal rights as to marriage, during marriage and at its dissolution.
(2) Marriage shall be entered into only with the free and full consent of the intending spouses.
(3) The family is the natural and fundamental group unit of society and is entitled to protection by society and the State.

Article 17

(1) Everyone has the right to own property alone as well as in association with others.
(2) No one shall be arbitrarily deprived of his property.

Article 18

Everyone has the right to freedom of thought, conscience and religion; this right includes freedom to change his religion or belief, and freedom, either alone or in community with others and in public or private, to manifest his religion or belief in teaching, practice, worship and observance.

Article 19

Everyone has the right to freedom of opinion and expression; this right includes freedom to hold opinions without interference and to seek, receive and impart information and ideas through any media and regardless of frontiers.

Article 20

(1) Everyone has the right to freedom of peaceful assembly and association.
(2) No one may be compelled to belong to an association.

Article 21

(1) Everyone has the right to take part in the government of his country, directly or through freely chosen representatives.
(2) Everyone has the right of equal access to public service in his country.

(3) The will of the people shall be the basis of the authority of government; this will shall be expressed in periodic and genuine elections which shall be by universal and equal suffrage and shall be held by secret vote or by equivalent free voting procedures.

Article 22

Everyone, as a member of society, has the right to social security and is entitled to realization, through national effort and international co-operation and in accordance with the organization and resources of each State, of the economic, social and cultural rights indispensable for his dignity and the free development of his personality.

Article 23

(1) Everyone has the right to work, to free choice of employment, to just and favourable conditions of work and to protection against unemployment.
(2) Everyone, without any discrimination, has the right to equal pay for equal work.
(3) Everyone who works has the right to just and favourable remuneration ensuring for himself and his family an existence worthy of human dignity, and supplemented, if necessary, by other means of social protection.
(4) Everyone has the right to form and to join trade unions for the protection of his interests.

Article 24

Everyone has the right to rest and leisure, including reasonable limitation of working hours and periodic holidays with pay.

Article 25

(1) Everyone has the right to a standard of living adequate for the health and well-being of himself and of his family, including food, clothing, housing and medical care and necessary social services, and the right to security in the event of unemployment, sickness, disability, widowhood, old age or other lack of livelihood in circumstances beyond his control.
(2) Motherhood and childhood are entitled to special care and assistance. All children, whether born in or out of wedlock, shall enjoy the same social protection.

Article 26

(1) Everyone has the right to education. Education shall be free, at least in the elementary and fundamental stages. Elementary education shall be compulsory. Technical and professional education shall be made generally available and higher education shall be equally accessible to all on the basis of merit.
(2) Education shall be directed to the full development of the human personality and to the strengthening of respect for human rights and fundamental

freedoms. It shall promote understanding, tolerance and friendship among all nations, racial or religious groups, and shall further the activities of the United Nations for the maintenance of peace.

(3) Parents have a prior right to choose the kind of education that shall be given to their children.

Article 27

(1) Everyone has the right freely to participate in the cultural life of the community, to enjoy the arts and to share in scientific advancement and its benefits.

(2) Everyone has the right to the protection of the moral and material interests resulting from any scientific, literary or artistic production of which he is the author.

Article 28

Everyone is entitled to a social and international order in which the rights and freedoms set forth in this Declaration can be fully realized.

Article 29

(1) Everyone has duties to the community in which alone the free and full development of his personality is possible.

(2) In the exercise of his rights and freedoms, everyone shall be subject only to such limitations as are determined by law solely for the purpose of securing due recognition and respect for the rights and freedoms of others and of meeting the just requirements of morality, public order and the general welfare in a democratic society.

(3) These rights and freedoms may in no case be exercised contrary to the purposes and principles of the United Nations.

Article 30

Nothing in this Declaration may be interpreted as implying for any State, group or person any right to engage in any activity or to perform any act aimed at the destruction of any of the rights and freedoms set forth herein.

NASW* Code of Ethics

*Approved by the 1996 NASW Delegate Assembly and revised by the
1999 NASW Delegate Assembly*

Preamble

The primary mission of the social work profession is to enhance human well-being and help meet the basic human needs of all people, with particular attention to the needs and empowerment of people who are vulnerable, oppressed, and living in poverty. A historic and defining feature of social work is the profession's focus on individual well-being in a social context and the well-being of society. Fundamental to social work is attention to the environmental forces that create, contribute to, and address problems in living.

Social workers promote social justice and social change with and on behalf of clients. "Clients" is used inclusively to refer to individuals, families, groups, organizations, and communities. Social workers are sensitive to cultural and ethnic diversity and strive to end discrimination, oppression, poverty, and other forms of social injustice. These activities may be in the form of direct practice, community organizing, supervision, consultation, administration, advocacy, social and political action, policy development and implementation, education, and research and evaluation. Social workers seek to enhance the capacity of people to address their own needs. Social workers also seek to promote the responsiveness of organizations, communities, and other social institutions to individuals' needs and social problems.

The mission of the social work profession is rooted in a set of core values. These core values, embraced by social workers throughout the profession's history, are the foundation of social work's unique purpose and perspective:

- Service
- Social justice
- Dignity and worth of the person
- Importance of human relationships
- Integrity
- Competence

This constellation of core values reflects what is unique to the social work profession. Core values, and the principles that flow from them, must be balanced within the context and complexity of the human experience.

---

*National Association of Social Workers

Source: National Association of Social Workers, Washington DC. Reprinted with permission of NASW.

Purpose of the NASW Code of Ethics

Professional ethics are at the core of social work. The profession has an obligation to articulate its basic values, ethical principles, and ethical standards. The *NASW Code of Ethics* sets forth these values, principles, and standards to guide social workers' conduct. The *Code* is relevant to all social workers and social work students, regardless of their professional functions, the settings in which they work, or the populations they serve.

The *NASW Code of Ethics* serves six purposes:

1. The *Code* identifies core values on which social work's mission is based.
2. The *Code* summarizes broad ethical principles that reflect the profession's core values and establishes a set of specific ethical standards that should be used to guide social work practice.
3. The *Code* is designed to help social workers identify relevant considerations when professional obligations conflict or ethical uncertainties arise.
4. The *Code* provides ethical standards to which the general public can hold the social work profession accountable.
5. The *Code* socializes practitioners new to the field to social work's mission, values, ethical principles, and ethical standards.
6. The *Code* articulates standards that the social work profession itself can use to assess whether social workers have engaged in unethical conduct. NASW has formal procedures to adjudicate ethics complaints filed against its members.*

The *Code* offers a set of values, principles, and standards to guide decision making and conduct when ethical issues arise. It does not provide a set of rules that prescribe how social workers should act in all situations. Specific applications of the *Code* must take into account the context in which it is being considered and the possibility of conflicts among the *Code's* values, principles, and standards. Ethical responsibilities flow from all human relationships, from the personal and familial to the social and professional.

Further, the *NASW Code of Ethics* does not specify which values, principles, and standards are most important and ought to outweigh others in instances when they conflict. Reasonable differences of opinion can and do exist among social workers with respect to the ways in which values, ethical principles, and ethical standards should be rank ordered when they conflict. Ethical decision making in a given situation must apply the informed judgment of the individual social worker and should also consider how the issues would be judged in a peer review process where the ethical standards of the profession would be applied.

Ethical decision making is a process. There are many instances in social work where simple answers are not available to resolve complex ethical issues. Social workers should take into consideration all the values, principles, and

---

NASW Procedures for the Adjudication of Grievances can be found at http://www.naswdc.org.

standards in this *Code* that are relevant to any situation in which ethical judgment is warranted. Social workers' decisions and actions should be consistent with the spirit as well as the letter of this *Code.*

In addition to this *Code,* there are many other sources of information about ethical thinking that may be useful. Social workers should consider ethical theory and principles generally, social work theory and research, laws, regulations, agency policies, and other relevant codes of ethics, recognizing that among codes of ethics social workers should consider the *NASW Code of Ethics* as their primary source. Social workers also should be aware of the impact on ethical decision making of their clients' and their own personal values and cultural and religious beliefs and practices. They should be aware of any conflicts between personal and professional values and deal with them responsibly. For additional guidance social workers should consult the relevant literature on professional ethics and ethical decision making and seek appropriate consultation when faced with ethical dilemmas. This may involve consultation with an agency-based or social work organization's ethics committee, a regulatory body, knowledgeable colleagues, supervisors, or legal counsel.

Instances may arise when social workers' ethical obligations conflict with agency policies or relevant laws or regulations. When such conflicts occur, social workers must make a responsible effort to resolve the conflict in a manner that is consistent with the values, principles, and standards expressed in this *Code.* If a reasonable resolution of the conflict does not appear possible, social workers should seek proper consultation before making a decision.

The *NASW Code of Ethics* is to be used by NASW and by individuals, agencies, organizations, and bodies (such as licensing and regulatory boards, professional liability insurance providers, courts of law, agency boards of directors, government agencies, and other professional groups) that choose to adopt it or use it as a frame of reference. Violation of standards in this *Code* does not automatically imply legal liability or violation of the law. Such determination can only be made in the context of legal and judicial proceedings. Alleged violations of the *Code* would be subject to a peer review process. Such processes are generally separate from legal or administrative procedures and insulated from legal review or proceedings to allow the profession to counsel and discipline its own members.

A code of ethics cannot guarantee ethical behavior. Moreover, a code of ethics cannot resolve all ethical issues or disputes or capture the richness and complexity involved in striving to make responsible choices within a moral community. Rather, a code of ethics sets forth values, ethical principles, and ethical standards to which professionals aspire and by which their actions can be judged. Social workers' ethical behavior should result from their personal commitment to engage in ethical practice. The *NASW Code of Ethics* reflects the commitment of all social workers to uphold the profession's values and to act ethically. Principles and standards must be applied by individuals of good character who discern moral questions and, in good faith, seek to make reliable ethical judgments.

Ethical Principles

The following broad ethical principles are based on social work's core values of service, social justice, dignity and worth of the person, importance of human relationships, integrity, and competence. These principles set forth ideals to which all social workers should aspire.

Value: *Service*

Ethical Principle: *Social workers' primary goal is to help people in need and to address social problems.*

Social workers elevate service to others above self-interest. Social workers draw on their knowledge, values, and skills to help people in need and to address social problems. Social workers are encouraged to volunteer some portion of their professional skills with no expectation of significant financial return (pro bono service).

Value: *Social Justice*

Ethical Principle: *Social workers challenge social injustice.*

Social workers pursue social change, particularly with and on behalf of vulnerable and oppressed individuals and groups of people. Social workers' social change efforts are focused primarily on issues of poverty, unemployment, discrimination, and other forms of social injustice. These activities seek to promote sensitivity to and knowledge about oppression and cultural and ethnic diversity. Social workers strive to ensure access to needed information, services, and resources; equality of opportunity; and meaningful participation in decision making for all people.

Value: *Dignity and Worth of the Person*

Ethical Principle: *Social workers respect the inherent dignity and worth of the person.*

Social workers treat each person in a caring and respectful fashion, mindful of individual differences and cultural and ethnic diversity. Social workers promote clients' socially responsible self-determination. Social workers seek to enhance clients' capacity and opportunity to change and to address their own needs. Social workers are cognizant of their dual responsibility to clients and to the broader society. They seek to resolve conflicts between clients' interests and the broader society's interests in a socially responsible manner consistent with the values, ethical principles, and ethical standards of the profession.

Value: *Importance of Human Relationships*

Ethical Principle: *Social workers recognize the central importance of human relationships.*

Social workers understand that relationships between and among people are an important vehicle for change. Social workers engage people as partners in the helping process. Social workers seek to strengthen relationships among people in a purposeful effort to promote, restore, maintain, and enhance the well-being of individuals, families, social groups, organizations, and communities.

Value: *Integrity*
Ethical Principle: *Social workers behave in a trustworthy manner.*
Social workers are continually aware of the profession's mission, values, ethical principles, and ethical standards and practice in a manner consistent with them. Social workers act honestly and responsibly and promote ethical practices on the part of the organizations with which they are affiliated.

Value: *Competence*
Ethical Principle: *Social workers practice within their areas of competence and develop and enhance their professional expertise.*
Social workers continually strive to increase their professional knowledge and skills and to apply them in practice. Social workers should aspire to contribute to the knowledge base of the profession.

Ethical Standards

The following ethical standards are relevant to the professional activities of all social workers. These standards concern (1) social workers' ethical responsibilities to clients, (2) social workers' ethical responsibilities to colleagues, (3) social workers' ethical responsibilities in practice settings, (4) social workers' ethical responsibilities as professionals, (5) social workers' ethical responsibilities to the social work profession, and (6) social workers' ethical responsibilities to the broader society.

Some of the standards that follow are enforceable guidelines for professional conduct, and some are aspirational. The extent to which each standard is enforceable is a matter of professional judgment to be exercised by those responsible for reviewing alleged violations of ethical standards.

1. Social Workers' Ethical Responsibilities to Clients

1.01 Commitment to Clients
Social workers' primary responsibility is to promote the well-being of clients. In general, clients' interests are primary. However, social workers' responsibility to the larger society or specific legal obligations may on limited occasions supersede the loyalty owed clients, and clients should be so advised. (Examples include when a social worker is required by law to report that a client has abused a child or has threatened to harm self or others.)

1.02 Self-Determination
Social workers respect and promote the right of clients to self-determination and assist clients in their efforts to identify and clarify their goals. Social workers may limit clients' right to self-determination when, in the social workers' professional judgment, clients' actions or potential actions pose a serious, foreseeable, and imminent risk to themselves or others.

1.03 Informed Consent

(a) Social workers should provide services to clients only in the context of a professional relationship based, when appropriate, on valid informed consent. Social workers should use clear and understandable language to inform clients of the purpose of the services, risks related to the services, limits to services because of the requirements of a third-party payer, relevant costs, reasonable alternatives, clients' right to refuse or withdraw consent, and the time frame covered by the consent. Social workers should provide clients with an opportunity to ask questions.

(b) In instances when clients are not literate or have difficulty understanding the primary language used in the practice setting, social workers should take steps to ensure clients' comprehension. This may include providing clients with a detailed verbal explanation or arranging for a qualified interpreter or translator whenever possible.

(c) In instances when clients lack the capacity to provide informed consent, social workers should protect clients' interests by seeking permission from an appropriate third party, informing clients consistent with the clients' level of understanding. In such instances social workers should seek to ensure that the third party acts in a manner consistent with clients' wishes and interests. Social workers should take reasonable steps to enhance such clients' ability to give informed consent.

(d) In instances when clients are receiving services involuntarily, social workers should provide information about the nature and extent of services and about the extent of clients' right to refuse service.

(e) Social workers who provide services via electronic media (such as computer, telephone, radio, and television) should inform recipients of the limitations and risks associated with such services.

(f) Social workers should obtain clients' informed consent before audiotaping or videotaping clients or permitting observation of services to clients by a third party.

1.04 Competence

(a) Social workers should provide services and represent themselves as competent only within the boundaries of their education, training, license, certification, consultation received, supervised experience, or other relevant professional experience.

(b) Social workers should provide services in substantive areas or use intervention techniques or approaches that are new to them only after engaging in appropriate study, training, consultation, and supervision from people who are competent in those interventions or techniques.

(c) When generally recognized standards do not exist with respect to an emerging area of practice, social workers should exercise careful judgment and take responsible steps (including appropriate education, research, training, consultation, and supervision) to ensure the competence of their work and to protect clients from harm.

1.05 Cultural Competence and Social Diversity

(a) Social workers should understand culture and its function in human behavior and society, recognizing the strengths that exist in all cultures.

(b) Social workers should have a knowledge base of their clients' cultures and be able to demonstrate competence in the provision of services that are sensitive to clients' cultures and to differences among people and cultural groups.

(c) Social workers should obtain education about and seek to understand the nature of social diversity and oppression with respect to race, ethnicity, national origin, color, sex, sexual orientation, age, marital status, political belief, religion, and mental or physical disability.

1.06 Conflicts of Interest

(a) Social workers should be alert to and avoid conflicts of interest that interfere with the exercise of professional discretion and impartial judgment. Social workers should inform clients when a real or potential conflict of interest arises and take reasonable steps to resolve the issue in a manner that makes the clients' interests primary and protects clients' interests to the greatest extent possible. In some cases, protecting clients' interests may require termination of the professional relationship with proper referral of the client.

(b) Social workers should not take unfair advantage of any professional relationship or exploit others to further their personal, religious, political, or business interests.

(c) Social workers should not engage in dual or multiple relationships with clients or former clients in which there is a risk of exploitation or potential harm to the client. In instances when dual or multiple relationships are unavoidable, social workers should take steps to protect clients and are responsible for setting clear, appropriate, and culturally sensitive boundaries. (Dual or multiple relationships occur when social workers relate to clients in more than one relationship, whether professional, social, or business. Dual or multiple relationships can occur simultaneously or consecutively.)

(d) When social workers provide services to two or more people who have a relationship with each other (for example, couples, family members), social workers should clarify with all parties which individuals will be considered clients and the nature of social workers' professional obligations to the various individuals who are receiving services. Social workers who anticipate a conflict of interest among the individuals receiving services or who anticipate having to perform in potentially conflicting roles (for example, when a social worker is asked to testify in a child custody dispute or divorce proceedings involving clients) should clarify their role with the parties involved and take appropriate action to minimize any conflict of interest.

1.07 Privacy and Confidentiality

(a) Social workers should respect clients' right to privacy. Social workers should not solicit private information from clients unless it is essential to providing services or conducting social work evaluation or research. Once private information is shared, standards of confidentiality apply.

(b) Social workers may disclose confidential information when appropriate with valid consent from a client or a person legally authorized to consent on behalf of a client.

(c) Social workers should protect the confidentiality of all information obtained in the course of professional service, except for compelling professional reasons. The general expectation that social workers will keep information confidential does not apply when disclosure is necessary to prevent serious, foreseeable, and imminent harm to a client or other identifiable person. In all instances, social workers should disclose the least amount of confidential information necessary to achieve the desired purpose; only information that is directly relevant to the purpose for which the disclosure is made should be revealed.

(d) Social workers should inform clients, to the extent possible, about the disclosure of confidential information and the potential consequences, when feasible before the disclosure is made. This applies whether social workers disclose confidential information on the basis of a legal requirement or client consent.

(e) Social workers should discuss with clients and other interested parties the nature of confidentiality and limitations of clients' right to confidentiality. Social workers should review with clients circumstances where confidential information may be requested and where disclosure of confidential information may be legally required. This discussion should occur as soon as possible in the social worker–client relationship and as needed throughout the course of the relationship.

(f) When social workers provide counseling services to families, couples, or groups, social workers should seek agreement among the parties involved concerning each individual's right to confidentiality and obligation to preserve the confidentiality of information shared by others. Social workers should inform participants in family, couples, or group counseling that social workers cannot guarantee that all participants will honor such agreements.

(g) Social workers should inform clients involved in family, couples, marital, or group counseling of the social worker's, employer's, and agency's policy concerning the social worker's disclosure of confidential information among the parties involved in the counseling.

(h) Social workers should not disclose confidential information to third-party payers unless clients have authorized such disclosure.

(i) Social workers should not discuss confidential information in any setting unless privacy can be ensured. Social workers should not discuss confidential information in public or semipublic areas such as hallways, waiting rooms, elevators, and restaurants.

(j) Social workers should protect the confidentiality of clients during legal proceedings to the extent permitted by law. When a court of law or other legally authorized body orders social workers to disclose confidential or privileged information without a client's consent and such disclosure could cause harm to the client, social workers should request that the court withdraw the order or limit the order as narrowly as possible or maintain the records under seal, unavailable for public inspection.

(k) Social workers should protect the confidentiality of clients when responding to requests from members of the media.

(l) Social workers should protect the confidentiality of clients' written and electronic records and other sensitive information. Social workers should take reasonable steps to ensure that clients' records are stored in a secure location and that clients' records are not available to others who are not authorized to have access.

(m) Social workers should take precautions to ensure and maintain the confidentiality of information transmitted to other parties through the use of computers, electronic mail, facsimile machines, telephones and telephone answering machines, and other electronic or computer technology. Disclosure of identifying information should be avoided whenever possible.

(n) Social workers should transfer or dispose of clients' records in a manner that protects clients' confidentiality and is consistent with state statutes governing records and social work licensure.

(o) Social workers should take reasonable precautions to protect client confidentiality in the event of the social worker's termination of practice, incapacitation, or death.

(p) Social workers should not disclose identifying information when discussing clients for teaching or training purposes unless the client has consented to disclosure of confidential information.

(q) Social workers should not disclose identifying information when discussing clients with consultants unless the client has consented to disclosure of confidential information or there is a compelling need for such disclosure.

(r) Social workers should protect the confidentiality of deceased clients consistent with the preceding standards.

1.08 Access to Records

(a) Social workers should provide clients with reasonable access to records concerning the clients. Social workers who are concerned that clients' access to their records could cause serious misunderstanding or harm to the client should provide assistance in interpreting the records and consultation with the client regarding the records. Social workers should limit clients' access to their records, or portions of their records, only in exceptional circumstances when there is compelling evidence that such access would cause serious harm to the client. Both clients' requests and the rationale for withholding some or all of the record should be documented in clients' files.

(b) When providing clients with access to their records, social workers should take steps to protect the confidentiality of other individuals identified or discussed in such records.

1.09 Sexual Relationships

(a) Social workers should under no circumstances engage in sexual activities or sexual contact with current clients, whether such contact is consensual or forced.

(b) Social workers should not engage in sexual activities or sexual contact with clients' relatives or other individuals with whom clients maintain a close personal relationship when there is a risk of exploitation or potential harm to the client. Sexual activity or sexual contact with clients' relatives or other individuals with whom clients maintain a personal relationship has the potential to be harmful to the client and may make it difficult for the social worker and client to maintain appropriate professional boundaries. Social workers—not their clients, their clients' relatives, or other individuals with whom the client maintains a personal relationship—assume the full burden for setting clear, appropriate, and culturally sensitive boundaries.

(c) Social workers should not engage in sexual activities or sexual contact with former clients because of the potential for harm to the client. If social workers engage in conduct contrary to this prohibition or claim that an exception to this prohibition is warranted because of extraordinary circumstances, it is social workers—not their clients—who assume the full burden of demonstrating that the former client has not been exploited, coerced, or manipulated, intentionally or unintentionally.

(d) Social workers should not provide clinical services to individuals with whom they have had a prior sexual relationship. Providing clinical services to a former sexual partner has the potential to be harmful to the individual and is likely to make it difficult for the social worker and individual to maintain appropriate professional boundaries.

1.10 Physical Contact

Social workers should not engage in physical contact with clients when there is a possibility of psychological harm to the client as a result of the contact (such as cradling or caressing clients). Social workers who engage in appropriate physical contact with clients are responsible for setting clear, appropriate, and culturally sensitive boundaries that govern such physical contact.

1.11 Sexual Harassment

Social workers should not sexually harass clients. Sexual harassment includes sexual advances, sexual solicitation, requests for sexual favors, and other verbal or physical conduct of a sexual nature.

1.12 Derogatory Language

Social workers should not use derogatory language in their written or verbal communications to or about clients. Social workers should use accurate and respectful language in all communications to and about clients.

1.13 Payment for Services

(a) When setting fees, social workers should ensure that the fees are fair, reasonable, and commensurate with the services performed. Consideration should be given to clients' ability to pay.

(b) Social workers should avoid accepting goods or services from clients as payment for professional services. Bartering arrangements, particularly involving services, create the potential for conflicts of interest, exploitation, and inappropriate boundaries in social workers' relationships with clients. Social workers should explore and may participate in bartering only in very limited circumstances when it can be demonstrated that such arrangements are an accepted practice among professionals in the local community, considered to be essential for the provision of services, negotiated without coercion, and entered into at the client's initiative and with the client's informed consent. Social workers who accept goods or services from clients as payment for professional services assume the full burden of demonstrating that this arrangement will not be detrimental to the client or the professional relationship.

(c) Social workers should not solicit a private fee or other remuneration for providing services to clients who are entitled to such available services through the social workers' employer or agency.

1.14 Clients Who Lack Decision-Making Capacity

When social workers act on behalf of clients who lack the capacity to make informed decisions, social workers should take reasonable steps to safeguard the interests and rights of those clients.

1.15 Interruption of Services

Social workers should make reasonable efforts to ensure continuity of services in the event that services are interrupted by factors such as unavailability, relocation, illness, disability, or death.

1.16 Termination of Services

(a) Social workers should terminate services to clients and professional relationships with them when such services and relationships are no longer required or no longer serve the clients' needs or interests.

(b) Social workers should take reasonable steps to avoid abandoning clients who are still in need of services. Social workers should withdraw services

precipitously only under unusual circumstances, giving careful consideration to all factors in the situation and taking care to minimize possible
adverse effects. Social workers should assist in making appropriate
arrangements for continuation of services when necessary.

(c) Social workers in fee-for-service settings may terminate services to clients
who are not paying an overdue balance if the financial contractual
arrangements have been made clear to the client, if the client does not
pose an imminent danger to self or others, and if the clinical and other
consequences of the current nonpayment have been addressed and discussed with the client.

(d) Social workers should not terminate services to pursue a social, financial,
or sexual relationship with a client.

(e) Social workers who anticipate the termination or interruption of services
to clients should notify clients promptly and seek the transfer, referral, or
continuation of services in relation to the clients' needs and preferences.

(f) Social workers who are leaving an employment setting should inform
clients of appropriate options for the continuation of services and of the
benefits and risks of the options.

2. Social Workers' Ethical Responsibilities to Colleagues

2.01 Respect

(a) Social workers should treat colleagues with respect and should represent
accurately and fairly the qualifications, views, and obligations of colleagues.

(b) Social workers should avoid unwarranted negative criticism of colleagues
in communications with clients or with other professionals. Unwarranted
negative criticism may include demeaning comments that refer to colleagues' level of competence or to individuals' attributes such as race, ethnicity, national origin, color, sex, sexual orientation, age, marital status,
political belief, religion, and mental or physical disability.

(c) Social workers should cooperate with social work colleagues and with colleagues of other professions when such cooperation serves the well-being
of clients.

2.02 Confidentiality

Social workers should respect confidential information shared by colleagues in
the course of their professional relationships and transactions. Social workers
should ensure that such colleagues understand social workers' obligation to
respect confidentiality and any exceptions related to it.

2.03 Interdisciplinary Collaboration

(a) Social workers who are members of an interdisciplinary team should participate in and contribute to decisions that affect the well-being of clients
by drawing on the perspectives, values, and experiences of the social work

profession. Professional and ethical obligations of the interdisciplinary team as a whole and of its individual members should be clearly established.

(b) Social workers for whom a team decision raises ethical concerns should attempt to resolve the disagreement through appropriate channels. If the disagreement cannot be resolved, social workers should pursue other avenues to address their concerns consistent with client well-being.

2.04 Disputes Involving Colleagues

(a) Social workers should not take advantage of a dispute between a colleague and an employer to obtain a position or otherwise advance the social workers' own interests.

(b) Social workers should not exploit clients in disputes with colleagues or engage clients in any inappropriate discussion of conflicts between social workers and their colleagues.

2.05 Consultation

(a) Social workers should seek the advice and counsel of colleagues whenever such consultation is in the best interests of clients.

(b) Social workers should keep themselves informed about colleagues' areas of expertise and competencies. Social workers should seek consultation only from colleagues who have demonstrated knowledge, expertise, and competence related to the subject of the consultation.

(c) When consulting with colleagues about clients, social workers should disclose the least amount of information necessary to achieve the purposes of the consultation.

2.06 Referral for Services

(a) Social workers should refer clients to other professionals when the other professionals' specialized knowledge or expertise is needed to serve clients fully or when social workers believe that they are not being effective or making reasonable progress with clients and that additional service is required.

(b) Social workers who refer clients to other professionals should take appropriate steps to facilitate an orderly transfer of responsibility. Social workers who refer clients to other professionals should disclose, with clients' consent, all pertinent information to the new service providers.

(c) Social workers are prohibited from giving or receiving payment for a referral when no professional service is provided by the referring social worker.

2.07 Sexual Relationships

(a) Social workers who function as supervisors or educators should not engage in sexual activities or contact with supervisees, students, trainees, or other colleagues over whom they exercise professional authority.

void engaging in sexual relationships with col-
ential for a conflict of interest. Social workers
n, or anticipate becoming involved in, a sexual rela-
ue have a duty to transfer professional responsibili-
avoid a conflict of interest.

exually harass supervisees, students, trainees, or col-
includes sexual advances, sexual solicitation, requests
r verbal or physical conduct of a sexual nature.

leagues
ve direct knowledge of a social work colleague's
e to personal problems, psychosocial distress, sub-
stance abuse, or mental health difficulties and that interferes with practice
effectiveness should consult with that colleague when feasible and assist
the colleague in taking remedial action.

(b) Social workers who believe that a social work colleague's impairment
interferes with practice effectiveness and that the colleague has not taken
adequate steps to address the impairment should take action through
appropriate channels established by employers, agencies, NASW, licensing
and regulatory bodies, and other professional organizations.

2.10 Incompetence of Colleagues

(a) Social workers who have direct knowledge of a social work colleague's
incompetence should consult with that colleague when feasible and assist
the colleague in taking remedial action.

(b) Social workers who believe that a social work colleague is incompetent
and has not taken adequate steps to address the incompetence should
take action through appropriate channels established by employers, agencies, NASW, licensing and regulatory bodies, and other professional
organizations.

2.11 Unethical Conduct of Colleagues

(a) Social workers should take adequate measures to discourage, prevent,
expose, and correct the unethical conduct of colleagues.

(b) Social workers should be knowledgeable about established policies and
procedures for handling concerns about colleagues' unethical behavior.
Social workers should be familiar with national, state, and local procedures
for handling ethics complaints. These include policies and procedures created by NASW, licensing and regulatory bodies, employers, agencies, and
other professional organizations.

(c) Social workers who believe that a colleague has acted unethically should
seek resolution by discussing their concerns with the colleague when feasible and when such discussion is likely to be productive.

(d) When necessary, social workers who believe that a colleague has acted unethically should take action through appropriate formal channels (such as contacting a state licensing board or regulatory body, a NASW committee on inquiry, or other professional ethics committees).

(e) Social workers should defend and assist colleagues who are unjustly charged with unethical conduct.

3. Social Workers' Ethical Responsibilities in Practice Settings

3.01 Supervision and Consultation

(a) Social workers who provide supervision or consultation should have the necessary knowledge and skill to supervise or consult appropriately and should do so only within their areas of knowledge and competence.

(b) Social workers who provide supervision or consultation are responsible for setting clear, appropriate, and culturally sensitive boundaries.

(c) Social workers should not engage in any dual or multiple relationships with supervisees in which there is a risk of exploitation of or potential harm to the supervisee.

(d) Social workers who provide supervision should evaluate supervisees' performance in a manner that is fair and respectful.

3.02 Education and Training

(a) Social workers who function as educators, field instructors for students, or trainers should provide instruction only within their areas of knowledge and competence and should provide instruction based on the most current information and knowledge available in the profession.

(b) Social workers who function as educators or field instructors for students should evaluate students' performance in a manner that is fair and respectful.

(c) Social workers who function as educators or field instructors for students should take reasonable steps to ensure that clients are routinely informed when services are being provided by students.

(d) Social workers who function as educators or field instructors for students should not engage in any dual or multiple relationships with students in which there is a risk of exploitation or potential harm to the student. Social work educators and field instructors are responsible for setting clear, appropriate, and culturally sensitive boundaries.

3.03 Performance Evaluation

Social workers who have responsibility for evaluating the performance of others should fulfill such responsibility in a fair and considerate manner and on the basis of clearly stated criteria.

3.04 Client Records

(a) Social workers should take reasonable steps to ensure that documentation in records is accurate and reflects the services provided.

(b) Social workers should include sufficient and timely documentation in records to facilitate the delivery of services and to ensure continuity of services provided to clients in the future.

(c) Social workers' documentation should protect clients' privacy to the extent that is possible and appropriate and should include only information that is directly relevant to the delivery of services.

(d) Social workers should store records following the termination of services to ensure reasonable future access. Records should be maintained for the number of years required by state statutes or relevant contracts.

3.05 Billing

Social workers should establish and maintain billing practices that accurately reflect the nature and extent of services provided and that identify who provided the service in the practice setting.

3.06 Client Transfer

(a) When an individual who is receiving services from another agency or colleague contacts a social worker for services, the social worker should carefully consider the client's needs before agreeing to provide services. To minimize possible confusion and conflict, social workers should discuss with potential clients the nature of the clients' current relationship with other service providers and the implications, including possible benefits or risks, of entering into a relationship with a new service provider.

(b) If a new client has been served by another agency or colleague, social workers should discuss with the client whether consultation with the previous service provider is in the client's best interest.

3.07 Administration

(a) Social work administrators should advocate within and outside their agencies for adequate resources to meet clients' needs.

(b) Social workers should advocate for resource allocation procedures that are open and fair. When not all clients' needs can be met, an allocation procedure should be developed that is nondiscriminatory and based on appropriate and consistently applied principles.

(c) Social workers who are administrators should take reasonable steps to ensure that adequate agency or organizational resources are available to provide appropriate staff supervision.

(d) Social work administrators should take reasonable steps to ensure that the working environment for which they are responsible is consistent with and encourages compliance with the NASW Code of Ethics. Social work administrators should take reasonable steps to eliminate any conditions in their organizations that violate, interfere with, or discourage compliance with the Code.

3.08 Continuing Education and Staff Development

Social work administrators and supervisors should take reasonable steps to provide or arrange for continuing education and staff development for all staff for whom they are responsible. Continuing education and staff development should address current knowledge and emerging developments related to social work practice and ethics.

3.09 Commitments to Employers

(a) Social workers generally should adhere to commitments made to employers and employing organizations.

(b) Social workers should work to improve employing agencies' policies and procedures and the efficiency and effectiveness of their services.

(c) Social workers should take reasonable steps to ensure that employers are aware of social workers' ethical obligations as set forth in the NASW Code of Ethics and of the implications of those obligations for social work practice.

(d) Social workers should not allow an employing organization's policies, procedures, regulations, or administrative orders to interfere with their ethical practice of social work. Social workers should take reasonable steps to ensure that their employing organizations' practices are consistent with the NASW Code of Ethics.

(e) Social workers should act to prevent and eliminate discrimination in the employing organization's work assignments and in its employment policies and practices.

(f) Social workers should accept employment or arrange student field placements only in organizations that exercise fair personnel practices.

(g) Social workers should be diligent stewards of the resources of their employing organizations, wisely conserving funds where appropriate and never misappropriating funds or using them for unintended purposes.

3.10 Labor-Management Disputes

(a) Social workers may engage in organized action, including the formation of and participation in labor unions, to improve services to clients and working conditions.

(b) The actions of social workers who are involved in labor-management disputes, job actions, or labor strikes should be guided by the profession's values, ethical principles, and ethical standards. Reasonable differences of opinion exist among social workers concerning their primary obligation as professionals during an actual or threatened labor strike or job action. Social workers should carefully examine relevant issues and their possible impact on clients before deciding on a course of action.

4. Social Workers' Ethical Responsibilities as Professionals

4.01 Competence

(a) Social workers should accept responsibility or employment only on the basis of existing competence or the intention to acquire the necessary competence.

(b) Social workers should strive to become and remain proficient in professional practice and the performance of professional functions. Social workers should critically examine and keep current with emerging knowledge relevant to social work. Social workers should routinely review the professional literature and participate in continuing education relevant to social work practice and social work ethics.

(c) Social workers should base practice on recognized knowledge, including empirically based knowledge, relevant to social work and social work ethics.

4.02 Discrimination

Social workers should not practice, condone, facilitate, or collaborate with any form of discrimination on the basis of race, ethnicity, national origin, color, sex, sexual orientation, age, marital status, political belief, religion, or mental or physical disability.

4.03 Private Conduct

Social workers should not permit their private conduct to interfere with their ability to fulfill their professional responsibilities.

4.04 Dishonesty, Fraud, and Deception

Social workers should not participate in, condone, or be associated with dishonesty, fraud, or deception.

4.05 Impairment

(a) Social workers should not allow their own personal problems, psychosocial distress, legal problems, substance abuse, or mental health difficulties to interfere with their professional judgment and performance or to jeopardize the best interests of people for whom they have a professional responsibility.

(b) Social workers whose personal problems, psychosocial distress, legal problems, substance abuse, or mental health difficulties interfere with their professional judgment and performance should immediately seek consultation and take appropriate remedial action by seeking professional help, making adjustments in workload, terminating practice, or taking any other steps necessary to protect clients and others.

4.06 Misrepresentation

(a) Social workers should make clear distinctions between statements made and actions engaged in as a private individual and as a representative of the social work profession, a professional social work organization, or the social worker's employing agency.

(b) Social workers who speak on behalf of professional social work organizations should accurately represent the official and authorized positions of the organizations.

(c) Social workers should ensure that their representations to clients, agencies, and the public of professional qualifications, credentials, education, competence, affiliations, services provided, or results to be achieved are accurate. Social workers should claim only those relevant professional credentials they actually possess and take steps to correct any inaccuracies or misrepresentations of their credentials by others.

4.07 Solicitations

(a) Social workers should not engage in uninvited solicitation of potential clients who, because of their circumstances, are vulnerable to undue influence, manipulation, or coercion.

(b) Social workers should not engage in solicitation of testimonial endorsements (including solicitation of consent to use a client's prior statement as a testimonial endorsement) from current clients or from other people who, because of their particular circumstances, are vulnerable to undue influence.

4.08 Acknowledging Credit

(a) Social workers should take responsibility and credit, including authorship credit, only for work they have actually performed and to which they have contributed.

(b) Social workers should honestly acknowledge the work of and the contributions made by others.

5. Social Workers' Ethical Responsibilities to the Social Work Profession

5.01 Integrity of the Profession

(a) Social workers should work toward the maintenance and promotion of high standards of practice.

(b) Social workers should uphold and advance the values, ethics, knowledge, and mission of the profession. Social workers should protect, enhance, and improve the integrity of the profession through appropriate study and research, active discussion, and responsible criticism of the profession.

(c) Social workers should contribute time and professional expertise to activities that promote respect for the value, integrity, and competence of the social work profession. These activities may include teaching, research, consultation, service, legislative testimony, presentations in the community, and participation in their professional organizations.

(d) Social workers should contribute to the knowledge base of social work and share with colleagues their knowledge related to practice, research, and ethics. Social workers should seek to contribute to the profession's literature and to share their knowledge at professional meetings and conferences.

(e) Social workers should act to prevent the unauthorized and unqualified practice of social work.

5.02 Evaluation and Research

(a) Social workers should monitor and evaluate policies, the implementation of programs, and practice interventions.

(b) Social workers should promote and facilitate evaluation and research to contribute to the development of knowledge.

(c) Social workers should critically examine and keep current with emerging knowledge relevant to social work and fully use evaluation and research evidence in their professional practice.

(d) Social workers engaged in evaluation or research should carefully consider possible consequences and should follow guidelines developed for the protection of evaluation and research participants. Appropriate institutional review boards should be consulted.

(e) Social workers engaged in evaluation or research should obtain voluntary and written informed consent from participants, when appropriate, without any implied or actual deprivation or penalty for refusal to participate; without undue inducement to participate; and with due regard for participants' well-being, privacy, and dignity. Informed consent should include information about the nature, extent, and duration of the participation requested and disclosure of the risks and benefits of participation in the research.

(f) When evaluation or research participants are incapable of giving informed consent, social workers should provide an appropriate explanation to the participants, obtain the participants' assent to the extent they are able, and obtain written consent from an appropriate proxy.

(g) Social workers should never design or conduct evaluation or research that does not use consent procedures, such as certain forms of naturalistic observation and archival research, unless rigorous and responsible review of the research has found it to be justified because of its prospective scientific, educational, or applied value and unless equally effective alternative procedures that do not involve waiver of consent are not feasible.

(h) Social workers should inform participants of their right to withdraw from evaluation and research at any time without penalty.

(i) Social workers should take appropriate steps to ensure that participants in evaluation and research have access to appropriate supportive services.

(j) Social workers engaged in evaluation or research should protect participants from unwarranted physical or mental distress, harm, danger, or deprivation.

(k) Social workers engaged in the evaluation of services should discuss collected information only for professional purposes and only with people professionally concerned with this information.

(l) Social workers engaged in evaluation or research should ensure the anonymity or confidentiality of participants and of the data obtained from them. Social workers should inform participants of any limits of confidentiality, the measures that will be taken to ensure confidentiality, and when any records containing research data will be destroyed.

(m) Social workers who report evaluation and research results should protect participants' confidentiality by omitting identifying information unless proper consent has been obtained authorizing disclosure.

(n) Social workers should report evaluation and research findings accurately. They should not fabricate or falsify results and should take steps to correct any errors later found in published data using standard publication methods.

(o) Social workers engaged in evaluation or research should be alert to and avoid conflicts of interest and dual relationships with participants, should inform participants when a real or potential conflict of interest arises, and should take steps to resolve the issue in a manner that makes participants' interests primary.

(p) Social workers should educate themselves, their students, and their colleagues about responsible research practices.

6. Social Workers' Ethical Responsibilities to the Broader Society

6.01 Social Welfare
Social workers should promote the general welfare of society, from local to global levels, and the development of people, their communities, and their environments. Social workers should advocate for living conditions conducive to the fulfillment of basic human needs and should promote social, economic, political, and cultural values and institutions that are compatible with the realization of social justice.

6.02 Public Participation
Social workers should facilitate informed participation by the public in shaping social policies and institutions.

6.03 Public Emergencies
Social workers should provide appropriate professional services in public emergencies to the greatest extent possible.

6.04 Social and Political Action

(a) Social workers should engage in social and political action that seeks to ensure that all people have equal access to the resources, employment, services, and opportunities they require to meet their basic human needs and to develop fully. Social workers should be aware of the impact of the political arena on practice and should advocate for changes in policy and legislation to improve social conditions in order to meet basic human needs and promote social justice.

(b) Social workers should act to expand choice and opportunity for all people, with special regard for vulnerable, disadvantaged, oppressed, and exploited people and groups.

(c) Social workers should promote conditions that encourage respect for cultural and social diversity within the United States and globally. Social workers should promote policies and practices that demonstrate respect for difference, support the expansion of cultural knowledge and resources, advocate for programs and institutions that demonstrate cultural competence, and promote policies that safeguard the rights of and confirm equity and social justice for all people.

(d) Social workers should act to prevent and eliminate domination of, exploitation of, and discrimination against any person, group, or class on the basis of race, ethnicity, national origin, color, sex, sexual orientation, age, marital status, political belief, religion, or mental or physical disability.

IFSW–IASSW
Code of Ethics*

Adopted by the IFSW General Meeting, Adelaide, Austalia, October 2004.

Introduction

This document was adopted at the IFSW and IASSW General Meetings in Adelaide, Australia, October 2004, and replaces the Ethical Principles and Standards adopted in Sri Lanka in 1994. The document is designed to be shorter than the 1994 version, and remains largely at the level of general principles. It is not the role of IFSW to prescribe more detailed rules of conduct for social workers in the many different countries in membership of IFSW. Rather, it is expected that member organizations will develop their own ethical guidance and codes with reference to this document, along with their own procedures for disciplining those who violate the ethical guidance and mechanisms for promoting education, debate and discussion on ethical issues in social work.

Ethics in Social Work, Statement of Principles

1. Preface

Ethical awareness is a fundamental part of the professional practice of social workers. Their ability and commitment to act ethically is an essential aspect of the quality of the service offered to those who use social work services.

The purpose of IASSW and IFSW's work on ethics is to promote ethical debate and reflection in the member organisations, among the providers of social work in member countries, as well as in the schools of social work and among social work students. Some ethical challenges and problems facing social workers are specific to particular countries; others are common. By staying at the level of general principles, the joint IASSW and IFSW statement aims to encourage social workers across the world to reflect on the challenges and dilemmas that face them and make ethically informed decisions about how to act in each particular case. Some of these problem areas include:

- The conflicting interests that impact upon social workers' loyalties
- Social workers' roles as both helpers and controllers

---

*International Federation of Social Workers (IFSW); International Association of Schools of Social Work (IASSW)

Source: Used by permission of IFSW.

- The conflicts between the duty of social workers to protect the interests of the people with whom they work and societal demands for efficiency and utility.
- Limited social resources

This document takes as its starting point the definition of social work adopted separately by the IFSW and IASSW at their respective General Meeting in Montreal, Canada in July 2000 and then agreed as a joint one in Copenhagen in May 2001 (section 2). This definition stresses principles of human rights and social justice. The next section (3) makes reference to the various declarations and conventions on human rights that are relevant to social work, followed by a statement of general ethical principles under the two broad headings of human rights and dignity and social justice (section 4). The final section introduces some basic guidance on ethical conduct in social work, which it is expected will be elaborated further by the various codes of ethics, ethical guidance and guidelines provided by the member organisations of IFSW and IASSW.

2. Definition of Social Work

The social work profession promotes social change, problem solving in human relationships and the empowerment and liberation of people to enhance well-being. Utilising theories of human behaviour and social systems, social work intervenes at the points where people interact with their environments. Principles of human rights and social justice are fundamental to social work.

3. International Conventions

International human rights declarations and conventions form common standards of achievement, and recognise rights that are accepted by the global community. Documents particularly relevant to social work practice and action are:

- *Universal Declaration of Human Rights*
- *The International Covenant on Civil and Political Rights*
- *The International Covenant on Economic Social and Cultural Rights*
- *The Convention on the Elimination of All Forms of Racial Discrimination*
- *The Convention on the Elimination of All Forms of Discrimination against Women*
- *The Convention on the Rights of the Child*
- *Indigenous and Tribal Peoples Convention (ILO convention 169)*

4. Principles

4.1. Human Rights and Human Dignity
Social work is based on respect for the inherent worth and dignity of all people, and the rights that follow from this. Social workers should uphold and defend

each person's physical, psychological, emotional and spiritual integrity and well-being. This means:

1. Respecting the right to self-determination—Social workers should respect and promote people's right to make their own choices and decisions, irrespective of their values and life choices, provided this does not threaten the rights and legitimate interests of others.
2. Promoting the right to participation—Social workers should promote the full involvement and participation of people using their services in ways that enable them to be empowered in all aspects of decisions and actions affecting their lives.
3. Treating each person as a whole—Social workers should be concerned with the whole person, within the family, community and societal and natural environments, and should seek to recognise all aspects of a person's life.
4. Identifying and developing strengths—Social workers should focus on the strengths of all individuals, groups and communities and thus promote their empowerment.

4.2. Social Justice

Social workers have a responsibility to promote social justice, in relation to society generally, and in relation to the people with whom they work. This means:

1. Challenging negative discrimination—Social workers have a responsibility to challenge negative discrimination on the basis of characteristics such as ability, age, culture, gender or sex, marital status, socio-economic status, political opinions, skin colour, racial or other physical characteristics, sexual orientation, or spiritual beliefs.
2. Recognising diversity—Social workers should recognise and respect the ethnic and cultural diversity of societies in which they practice, taking account of individual, family, group and community differences.
3. Distributing resources equitably—Social workers should ensure that resources at their disposal are distributed fairly, according to need.
4. Challenging unjust policies and practices—Social workers have a duty to bring to the attention of their employers, policy makers, politicians and the general public situations where resources are inadequate or where distribution of resources, policies and practices are oppressive, unfair or harmful.
5. Working in solidarity—Social workers have an obligation to challenge social conditions that contribute to social exclusion, stigmatisation or subjugation, and to work towards an inclusive society.

5. Professional Conduct

It is the responsibility of the national organisations in membership of IFSW and IASSW to develop and regularly update their own codes of ethics or ethical guidelines, to be consistent with the IFSW statement. It is also the national organisation's responsibility to inform social workers and schools of social work about these codes or guidelines.

Social workers should act in accordance with the ethical code or guidelines current in their country. These will generally include more detailed guidance in ethical practice specific to the national context. The following general guidelines on professional conduct apply:

1. Social workers are expected to develop and maintain the required skills and competence to do their job.
2. Social workers should not allow their skills to be used for inhumane purposes, such as torture or terrorism.
3. Social workers should act with integrity. This includes not abusing the relationship of trust with the people using their services, recognising the boundaries between personal and professional life, and not abusing their position for personal benefit or gain.
4. Social workers should act in relation to the people using their services with compassion, empathy and care.
5. Social workers should not subordinate the needs or interests of people who use their services to their own needs or interests.
6. Social workers have a duty to take necessary steps to care for themselves professionally and personally in the workplace and in society, in order to ensure that they are able to provide appropriate services.
7. Social workers should maintain confidentiality regarding information about people who use their services. Exceptions to this may only be justified on the basis of a greater ethical requirement (such as the preservation of life).
8. Social workers need to acknowledge that they are accountable for their actions to the users of their services, the people they work with, their colleagues, their employers, the professional association and to the law, and that these accountabilities may conflict.
9. Social workers should be willing to collaborate with the schools of social work in order to support social work students to get practical training of good quality and up to date practical knowledge
10 Social workers should foster and engage in ethical debate with their colleagues and employers and take responsibility for making ethically informed decisions.
11. Social workers should be prepared to state the reasons for their decisions based on ethical considerations, and be accountable for their choices and actions.
12. Social workers should work to create conditions in employing agencies and in their countries where the principles of this statement and those of their own national code (if applicable) are discussed, evaluated and upheld.

Outline for Anti-Oppressive Policy Analysis

I. Description of the Social Condition/Problem
   A. What is the social condition that is oppressive?
   B. What are the facts (from official and unofficial reports) concerning the social condition?
      1. What does documentation through review of the literature show?
      2. What do we know from agency records, surveys, and interviews with key experts?
      3. What forecasts have been made for future problems and expenses related to the problem?
   C. To what extent is the social condition perceived as a social problem?
      1. How is the problem defined at the various levels of society?
         a. What value biases are implicit?
         b. To what source(s) is the problem attributed?
      2. For whom is the situation in question a problem?

II. Historical Analysis
   A. What were the relevant social conditions like in the past?
   B. How did the social condition (e.g., child beating) come to be defined as a problem?
      1. How was the problem later defined in terms of changing social values?
      2. How was the problem dealt with?
   C. Which influential groups were involved in supporting and opposing proposed remedies? Are the groups the same today?
   D. What are the precedents for the ideas and values being used to correct the situation?
   E. To what extent were the approaches to the problem effective or ineffective?
   F. How did the manifest goals differ from the unstated or latent goals of potential solutions?
   G. Comment on the lessons of history relevant to the present issue.

III. Policy Formulation Overview
   A. What are the goals (manifest and latent) of your proposed policy?
   B. What can we learn from people's (clients') narratives about the need to strengthen resources?

C. What are the pros and cons of various ways of dealing with the problem?
   1. How does each of these competing policies meet the criteria of self-determination, empowerment, adequacy, feasibility, and efficiency?
   2. How is your proposal superior to other remedies?
D. To what extent can public opinion be mobilized in support of your proposed policy?
E. In general what do the research findings tell us about the problem?
F. What are anticipated barriers to policy change?

IV. The Global Context
   A. What can we learn about alternative policies or approaches to meet the same need?
   B. Discuss differences in funding sources and levels of support.
   C. How is your proposed policy integrated within the cultural values of one or more other countries?
   D. Could we advocate a similar policy for the United States given U.S. traditional values?
   E. Relate the policy under consideration to the relevant section of the U.N. Universal Declaration of Human Rights.

V. Economic Analysis
   A. How much will the proposed initiative cost?
      1. How does this expense compare with present or other proposed offerings?
      2. How will the proposed program be funded?
   B. What will be the projected cost savings (the benefits) to the state, county, or agency?
   C. Which groups benefit financially from the social problem (e.g., landlords from housing shortages)?
   D. Discuss the initiative in terms of its bearing on economic oppression.
   E. If the initiative entails an economic benefit, is the benefit means-tested?

VI. Political Analysis
   A. Who are the major players involved in the policy innovation or policy to be changed (politicians, professionals, populations at risk)?
   B. Who are the major stakeholders who have vested interests in making/resisting the proposed change?
      1. Assess the extent of opponents' political backing, clout, and media access.
      2. Assess the extent of supporters' political backing, clout, and media access.
   C. What is the political context within which the policy initiative has been conceived? Is political/racial/gender oppression an issue of public concern?

D. What are the major political arguments used by opponents against the proposal? Draw on research data to refute or acknowledge the truth of these arguments.

E. How are the NASW *Code of Ethics* standards and the NASW policy statements (see *Social Work Speaks*) relevant to the policy?

F. Describe any lobbying efforts, if any, and any relevant legislative bills introduced.

G. Which profession (lawyers, psychologists, etc.) controls the territory? How does this affect the policy's acceptability?

H. Gauge the likelihood of having the policy implemented and anticipate possible unintended (positive and negative) consequences of the initiative's enactment.

Relevant Internet Sites

The Global Economy

http://www.nationmaster.com	Comparative World Statistics
http://www.cifinternational.com	Council of International Fellowship
http://www.globalissues.org	Global Issues That Affect Everyone
http://www.ied.info/about.html	Institute for Economic Democracy
http://www.ifg.org	International Forum on Globalization
http://www.newint.org	New Internationalist (a communications cooperative)
http://www.50years.org	U.S. Network for Global Economic Justice

Professional Links

http://www.bpd-l@listserv.iupui.edu	Baccalaureate Program Directors
http://www.cswe.org	Council on Social Work Education
http://www.lib.gcal.ac.uk/heatherbank	Heatherbank Museum of Social Work, Glasgow, Scotland
http://www.uic.edu/jaddams/college	Information on Hull House Museum
http://www.iassw.soton.ac.uk	International Association of Schools of Social Work
http://www.ifsw.org/	International Federation of Social Workers
http://www.naswdc.org	National Association of Social Workers
http://www.pantucek.com/swlinks_gb.html	Social Work Gateway
http://www.undp.org	United Nations Development Programme
http://www.sc.edu/swan	University of South Carolina (multiple links)
http://www.nyu.edu/socialwork/www.rsw	World Wide Web Resources for Social Workers

Government Resources

http://canada.gc.ca	Canadian Government Main Site
http://www.cdc.gov	Centers for Disease Control
http://www.nida.nih.gov	National Institute of Drug Abuse
http://www.nih.gov	National Institute of Health
http://www.nimh.nih.gov	National Institute of Mental Health
http://www.nmai.si.edu	National Museum of the American Indian
http://www.census.gov	U.S. Bureau of the Census
http://www.ojp.usdoj.gov/bjs	U.S. Bureau of Justice Statistics
http://www.os.dhhs.gov	U.S. Department of Health and Human Services
http://www.house.gov	U.S. House of Representatives
http://www.senate.gov	U.S. Senate

Social Action Policy

http://www.aarp.org	American Association of Retired Persons
http://2ssw.che.umn/edu/rjp	Center for Restorative Justice Peacemaking
http://www.cwla.org	Child Welfare League
http://www.dpi.org	Disabled Peoples' Association
http://www.greenbike.org	The Green Bike Tour of Renewable Energy
http://www.statepolicy.org	Influencing State Policy
http://www.MoratoriumCampaign.org	Moratorium Campaign against the Death Penalty
http://www.moveon.org	Move On, Grassroots Politics
http://www.restorativejustice.org/uk	Restorative Justice Consortium
http://www.restorativejustice.org	Restorative Justice Resources (articles)
http://socialwelfareactionalliance.org	Social Welfare Action Alliance
http://www.warresisters.org	War Resisters League
http://www.who.org	World Health Organization

Human Rights

http://www.ability.org.uk	Ability, Disabilities Advocacy
http://www.atforum.com	Addiction Treatment Forum
http://www.amnesty.org	Amnesty International (type in specific country's name)
http://www.childrensdefense.org	Children's Defense Fund
http://www.datalounge.com	The Data Lounge: Lesbian/Gay
http://www.disabilityinfo.gov	Disability Information
http://www.dpi.org	Disabled Person's International
http://www.drugpolicy.org	Drug Policy Alliance Action Center
http://www.glsen.org	Gay, Lesbian, and Straight Education Network
http://www.hrw.org	Human Rights Watch
http://www.kwru.org	Kensington Welfare Rights Union
http://www.minoityrights.org	Minority Rights Group International
http://www.nami.org	National Alliance for the Mentally Ill
http://www.ngltf.org	National Gay and Lesbian Internet Task Force
http://now.org	National Organization for Women
http://www.pflag.org	Parents, Families, and Friends of Lesbians and Gays
http://www.unsystem.org	United Nations System of Organization
http://www.whrnet.org	Women's Human Rights

Index

TO THE OWNER OF THIS BOOK:

I hope that you have found *Introduction to Social Welfare and Social Work: The U.S. in Global Perspective* useful. So that this book can be improved in a future edition, would you take the time to complete this sheet and return it? Thank you.

School and address:_____

Department:_____

Instructor's name:_____

1. What I like most about this book is:_____

_____

_____

2. What I like least about this book is:_____

_____

_____

3. My general reaction to this book is:_____

_____

_____

4. The name of the course in which I used this book is:_____

_____

5. Were all of the chapters of the book assigned for you to read?_____

   If not, which ones weren't?_____

6. In the space below, or on a separate sheet of paper, please write specific suggestions for improving this book and anything else you'd care to share about your experience in using this book.

_____

_____

_____

THOMSON

BROOKS/COLE

BUSINESS REPLY MAIL
FIRST-CLASS MAIL   PERMIT NO. 102   MONTEREY CA

POSTAGE WILL BE PAID BY ADDRESSEE

Attn: Lisa Gebo, Social Work

BrooksCole/Thomson Learning
60 Garden Ct Ste 205
Monterey CA 93940-9967

OPTIONAL:

Your name:_____ Date: _____

May we quote you, either in promotion for *Introduction to Social Welfare and Social Work: The U.S. in Global Perspective,* or in future publishing ventures?

Yes: _____   No: _____

Sincerely yours,

Katherine van Wormer